the Unofficial Guide® to

Central Italy
Florence, Rome, Tuscany, & Umbria

2nd Edition

the Unofficial Guide® to Central Italy

Florence, Rome, Tuscany, & Umbria

2nd Edition

Melanie Mize Renzulli

WILEY

Please note that prices fluctuate in the course of time, and travel information changes under the impact of many factors that influence the travel industry. We therefore suggest that you write or call ahead for confirmation when making your travel plans. Every effort has been made to ensure the accuracy of information throughout this book, and the contents of this publication are believed correct at the time of printing. Nevertheless, the publishers cannot accept responsibility for errors or omissions or for changes in details given in this guide or for the consequences of any reliance on the information provided by the same. Assessments of attractions and so forth are based upon the author's own experience, and therefore, descriptions given in this guide necessarily contain an element of subjective opinion, which may not reflect the publisher's opinion or dictate a reader's own experience on another occasion. Readers are invited to write the publisher with ideas, comments, and suggestions for future editions.

Published by:

John Wiley & Sons, Inc.

111 River Street

Hoboken, NJ 07030

Produced by Menasha Ridge Press
Cover design by Michael J. Freeland
Interior design by Michele Laseau

For information on our other products and services or to obtain technical support please contact our Customer Care Department within the U.S. at (800) 762-2974, outside the U.S. at (317) 572-3993 or fax (317) 572-4002.

John Wiley & Sons, Inc. also publishes its books in a variety of electronic formats. Some content that appears in print may not be available in electronic formats.

ISBN 0-7645-4992-8

Manufactured in the United States of America

5 4 3 2 1

Contents

Part Five   **Dining in Central Italy   137**

List of Maps

Acknowledgments

The author is grateful to the tourist offices of Rome, Florence, Tuscany, Umbria, and the Marches for their assistance, and a special "thank you" goes to Antonia Imperoli of the Italian Government Tourist Board in New York. Many thanks also to Anthony, Heidi, Judy (for help in Florence and Siena), Frank and Nancy, Dante and Lucy, and all others who motivated and inspired me along the way.

—*Melanie Mize Renzulli*

About the Author

Never a coffee drinker until she lived in Rome, **Melanie Mize Renzulli** is now a cappuccino connoisseur and a fan of black truffles, Bernini, and Italian pop. She is the author of *Frommer's Irreverent Guide to Rome,* a contributor to *The Unofficial Guide to the Southeast with Kids,* and has written shopping, dining, and travel articles for *Bell'Italia,* AOL Digital Cities, the *Washington Post,* and Epicurious.com. She currently lives with her husband Anthony in Washington, DC.

Introduction

Welcome to Central Italy

Auguri! (Congratulations!) You're on your way to Central Italy, a region that has captivated the hearts, the souls, and, indeed, the stomachs of travelers for more than two millennia. Occupying the zone between the shin and the meaty calf of the boot-shaped peninsula, Central Italy encompasses the cultural and historic cities of Florence and Rome, former Etruscan villages, medieval hill towns, regal Renaissance hamlets, and tranquil, seaside communities.

Central Italy is at once completely familiar. Who hasn't read about or seen photos of landmarks such as the Colosseum or the Leaning Tower of Pisa? Without a doubt, many first-time tourists come to see what all the fuss is about, to see monuments that have existed only in their imaginations. And, more often than not, Central Italy exceeds most travelers' wildest dreams. Hills are blonder, vineyards more fragrant, ivy-draped cobbled streets more romantic. In the countryside, medieval castles and ancient aqueducts appear from out of nowhere, while in city centers, church domes and renowned monuments loom larger than expected.

Of course, it's not just the landmarks that have brought tourists back time and time again, ensuring Italy a top-five place among the most-visited countries, and Rome and Florence among the most-visited cities, in the world. A trip to Central Italy is all about finding yourself. It's a time to unplug the television, ignore the daily news, stop checking your e-mail, and drop out of life for just a little while. Go ahead—enjoy a nice glass of wine with lunch. No one will bat an eyelash. Better yet, if you can spare the time, take a nap in the middle of the day. You're on vacation, after all.

Being a tourist in Central Italy is easy. All you need is an active curiosity, a strong eye for detail, and a high threshold for beauty. It helps to have an understanding wallet, even though you should know that some of the most satisfying activities, such as people-watching in the *piazze* and admiring a sunset, are all free. Also, make sure you have a flexible stomach—and, perhaps, a forgiving pair of pants—so that you can take pleasure in every bite of tiramisu or every sip of vino.

Granted, despite the region's mesmerizing beauty, there will be times when you'll want to pull your hair out. In other words, you'll need to be prepared for anything. Italy's transportation workers are notorious for calling strikes in the middle of tourist season, halting trains and planes at the drop of a hat. Other headaches include endless lines at museums, maddening traffic (both vehicle and pedestrian), surly taxi drivers, over-booked hotels, and just about anything else likely to spoil your vacation if you don't take it in stride. A sense of humor is essential. And, some-times, so is a backup plan.

That's where the *Unofficial Guides* come in. We'll show you how to enjoy Italy at any speed you like, whether you're here for a family vacation, trav-eling with friends, or on a business trip. This nook of the world is undeni-ably romantic, and a perfect destination for two. But we'll also show you how to make the most of your trip if you're traveling alone (though, who is going to share that lunchtime bottle of Chianti with you?). In sum, we'll help you plan your itinerary—and work out any kinks—so you will feel comfortable while discovering what centuries of travelers have deemed the most magical region on earth. *Buon divertimento!*

About This Guide

Most travel guides about Central Italy follow the usual tracks of the typ-ical tourist, automatically sending readers to the well-known sights with-out any information about how to see them painlessly, recommending restaurants and hotels indiscriminately, and failing to recognize the limits of human endurance in sight-seeing. Furthermore, most guides focus on Florence or Rome, giving short shrift to the small villages in Tuscany or Latium, and often ignoring the medieval hillside communities in Umbria or the untouched, bucolic burgs in the Marches. This guide is different: We know that every traveler has his or her opinion on what a vacation in Italy should be, and we understand that some prefer idyllic landscapes to urban streetscapes. Unless you are an exchange student—or embarking on a new life abroad—you won't be able to explore a majority of the expanse that makes up Central Italy. Therefore, you must make some tough decisions. Are you looking for an up-tempo, cosmopolitan vaca-tion where world-class restaurants, museums, and nightlife are at your disposal? Or would you prefer to unwind in the country and thumb your nose at a schedule? We'll show what is possible, no matter if you have a week or a month to spend.

As the typical trip to Central Italy lasts approximately two weeks, and includes stops in Florence, Rome, or both, we've made sure that we cover all the bases, with information on which museums and archaeological sites are visit-worthy and which are a waste of time. We'll give you the straight dope on tourist traps, and whenever possible we'll tell you how to book tickets ahead of time so that you can minimize your wait and budget your time. There will be instances when we have to include a restaurant or a hotel because of its historic significance; but if the place is all style and no substance, we tell you so.

An integral part of touring around Central Italy is discovering quaint, out-of-the-way haunts. Of course, some places ain't so quaint—especially during high season when hordes of day-trippers take over. In many places, the crowds are inevitable. Our aim is to tell you which towns merit a spot on the itinerary (despite the crowds) and which are best to skip. We'll also make suggestions of where to *really* get off the beaten path. After all, the sun is just as welcoming in Latium, Umbria, and the Marches as it is in Tuscany.

No doubt about it: Italy in general, and its central regions in particular, ooze history. Every city corridor, *piazza*, valley, and hill has a tale to tell, making it difficult for us to edit out the trivial. Tuscany, Latium, Umbria, and the Marches are made up of hundreds of towns filled with thousands of attractions. In this *Unofficial Guide*, we've tried to sort them into first-rate and special interest categories, giving space to only the best. As with all of our books, we have tried to anticipate the special needs of older people, families with young children, families with teenagers, solo travelers, people with different levels of physical ability, and those who have a particular passion for art, architecture, literature, sports, shopping, dining, and so on. We can help you customize your trip to accommodate both your personal interests and the amount of time you have to spend. Additionally, at the beginning of each chapter we've outlined our favorites for you. We hope that our choices serve as a guide for planning your itinerary; but we also hope that you will venture out on your own and discover what you like best. We know that some of you don't wish to do it all yourselves, so we've also listed a number of good commercial and customized tour companies in Part Two, Planning Your Visit to Central Italy.

While many of you may not consider exercise an essential part of your vacation, we realize that there may come a time when you've piled just too many spoonfuls of *parmigiano* onto your pasta or overdosed on gelato. Not to mention, you may feel sluggish after a long flight. So we have included a list of opportunities for exercise and getting outdoors. Physical activities, such as biking through the countryside, will keep you fit enough to lug all of your new purchases home—plus you'll have a rosy glow in all your vacation photos.

Please remember that prices and admission hours change constantly; we have listed the most up-to-date information available, but it never hurts to double-check (opening times in particular; if prices of attractions change, it is generally not by much). Also remember that this is one of the busiest tourist areas in the world, so make your reservations early and reconfirm at least once.

How Come "Unofficial"?

Readers care about authors' opinions. The authors, after all, are supposed to know what they are talking about. This, coupled with the fact that the traveler wants quick answers (as opposed to endless alternatives), dictates that travel authors should be explicit, prescriptive, and above all, direct. The authors of the *Unofficial Guide* try to do just that. We spell out alternatives and recommend specific courses of action. We simplify complicated destinations and attractions to allow the traveler to feel in control in the most unfamiliar environments. The objective of *Unofficial Guide* authors is not to give the most information or all of the information but to offer the most accessible, useful information. Of course, in a region like Central Italy, there are many hotels, restaurants, and attractions that are so closely woven into the fabric of the area that to omit them from our guide because we can't recommend them would be a disservice to our readers. We have included all the famous haunts, giving our opinion and experience of them, in the hopes that you will approach (or avoid) these institutions armed with the necessary intelligence.

An *Unofficial Guide* is a critical reference work; we focus on a travel destination that appears to be especially complex. Our authors and researchers are completely independent from the attractions, restaurants, and hotels we describe. *The Unofficial Guide to Central Italy: Florence, Rome, Tuscany, & Umbria* is designed for individuals and families traveling for fun as well as for business, and it will be especially helpful to those hopping "across the pond" for the first time. The guide is directed at value-conscious, consumer-oriented adults who seek a cost-effective but not Spartan travel style.

SPECIAL FEATURES

- Vital information about traveling abroad
- Friendly introductions to Central Italy's big cities and small villages
- "Best of" listings giving our well-qualified opinions on everything from cappuccino to Roman ruins
- Listings that are keyed to your interests, so you can pick and choose
- Advice to sight-seers on how to avoid the worst crowds; advice to business travelers on how to avoid traffic and excessive costs

- Recommendations for lesser-known sights that are off the well-beaten tourist path, but no less worthwhile
- Detailed maps to make it easy to find places you want to visit and avoid places you don't
- A hotel section that helps you narrow down your choices rapidly, according to your needs and preferences
- A table of contents and detailed index to help you find things quickly
- Insider advice on best times of day (or night) to go places

WHAT YOU WON'T GET

- Long, useless lists where everything looks the same
- Information that gets you to your destination at the worst possible time
- Information without advice on how to use it

How This Guide Was Researched and Written

In preparing this work, we took nothing for granted. Each hotel, restaurant, shop, and attraction was visited by trained observers who conducted detailed evaluations and rated each according to formal criteria. Team members conducted interviews with tourists of all ages to determine what they enjoyed most and least during their visit to Central Italy.

Though our observers are independent and impartial, they are otherwise "ordinary" travelers. Like you, they visited Florence, Rome, and towns in Central Italy as tourists or as business travelers, noting their satisfaction or dissatisfaction.

The primary difference between the average tourist and the trained evaluator is the evaluator's skills in organization, preparation, and observation. A trained evaluator is responsible for more than just observing and cataloging. Observer teams use detailed checklists to analyze hotel rooms, restaurants, nightclubs, and attractions. Finally, evaluator ratings and observations are integrated with tourist reactions and the opinions of patrons for a comprehensive quality profile of each feature and service.

In compiling this guide, we recognize that a tourist's age, background, and interests will strongly influence his or her taste in Central Italy's wide array of attractions and will account for a preference for one sight or museum over another. Our sole objective is to provide the reader with sufficient description, critical evaluation, and pertinent data to make knowledgeable decisions according to individual tastes.

Letters, Comments, and Questions from Readers

We expect to learn from our mistakes, as well as from the input of our readers, and to improve with each new book and edition. Many of those who use the *Unofficial Guides* write to us asking questions, making comments, or sharing their own discoveries and lessons learned in Central Italy. We appreciate all such input, both positive and critical, and encourage our readers to continue writing. Readers' comments and observations will be frequently incorporated in revised editions of the *Unofficial Guide* and will contribute immeasurably to its improvement.

How to Write the Author

Melanie Mize Renzulli
The Unofficial Guide to Central Italy
P.O. Box 43673
Birmingham, AL 35243
unofficialguides@menasharidge.com

When you write, be sure to put your return address on your letter as well as on the envelope—sometimes envelopes and letters get separated. Remember, our work takes us out of the office for long periods of time, so forgive us if our response is delayed.

How This Guide Is Organized:
By Subject and by Geographic Area

We have organized this guide in the order in which you will need it. Thus, Part One, Understanding Central Italy, gives a quick tutorial on the Italian language and explains how numbers and prices are handled. Part Two, Planning Your Visit to Central Italy, provides an in-depth discussion of the preparations you should make before leaving home, including when to go and what to pack. In Part Three, we give you advice on Arriving, Getting Oriented, and Departing, taking you through your first and last days—the two most stressful days of any trip. Also in this section, we provide you with all the general information you'll need to know in order to send a letter, make a phone call, take public transportation, etc. Part Four deals with Hotels, and explains in detail the types of hotels, inns, and lodging alternatives available in Central Italy. Here, we have organized information about all of the recommended accommodations in Central Italy so that you have all of the lodging info, complete with rankings, rates, amenities, and descriptions at your fingertips. Part Five introduces you to the fine art of cuisine in Central Italy, and there we also point the way to several of the region's best restaurants.

Beginning with Part Six, we discuss in depth the four regions that comprise Central Italy, and we describe what they have to offer in terms of sight-seeing, shopping, and entertainment:

Florence and the Best of Tuscany

Tuscany is one of the most talked-about destinations in the world, and there's good reason. Florence is an art mecca and Renaissance gem with

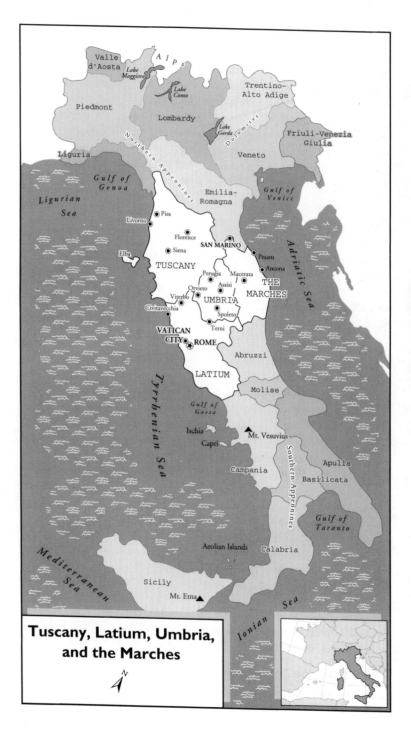

Tuscany, Latium, Umbria, and the Marches

the Uffizi Gallery and the imposing Duomo at its core. Though the city is compact, it is packed to the gills with stuff to see, making it the obvious home base for first-time tourists and seasoned Italophiles. Siena, Florence's perennial rival, is also laden with glorious churches, a delightful, medieval square (the Campo), and grandiose *palazzi*. And, let's not forget Pisa, the famous, if touristy, small-town home of an architecture project gone awry in the Leaning Tower. Stretching from the Tyrhennian Sea to the heart of Central Italy, Tuscany is made up of heart-stopping vistas, both urban and rural. We've outlined tons of Tuscan towns such as the tony seaside haunt Forte dei Marmi, historic San Gimignano, artful Cortona, and the vineyard villages in the Chianti region.

Rome and the Best of Latium

Rome is, well, Rome. No one needs to tell you that the amount of stuff to see in Rome is overwhelming; the Colosseum, the Sistine Chapel, the Pantheon, the Trevi Fountain, and countless churches and museums merit a lifetime of exploration. In fact, the "Eternal City" and its treasures greatly overshadow the rest of Latium. However, there is much to discover beyond Italy's capital, including the ancient ruins of nearby Tivoli and Ostia Antica, Etruscan relics in Viterbo and Tarquinia, lovely beaches, and traditional hilltop villages.

The Best of Umbria

Known as the "Green Heart of Italy," Umbria is the only landlocked Italian region. Modest, like its native son St. Francis of Assisi, Umbria offers all of the beauty and charm of the hill towns in Tuscany—but typically without the busloads of tourists. Assisi and Orvieto, notable for their spectacular cathedrals and delicious white wines, remain huge draws, especially for tourists coming from Florence or Rome during high season. But many leisure travelers have yet to discover this region, largely untouched by urbanization. Perugia, the regional capital, is a handsome walled city, home to the Umbria Jazz Festival as well as the Eurochocolate Festival. Spoleto, in southern Umbria, is also lively, with a world-renowned music festival in June and July. A journey to Gubbio or Todi is a step back in time to the Middle Ages.

The Best of the Marches

Nestled between the Apennine mountains and the Adriatic, the Marches region rarely appears on a traveler's itinerary—a fact that makes a trip here all the more worthwhile. Ancona, the most populous city, serves as one of Italy's largest ports, with commercial and ferry service to the east, namely to Greece and Turkey. There's also Pésaro, a summer resort town, and Urbino, native home of Raphael and the jewel of the region. The Marches has less to offer in terms of quantity than its well-known neighbors, so expect to encounter unspoiled vistas and few English speakers. One of the smallest independent countries on earth—the republic of San Marino, just north of the border of the Marches—is worth a day trip if only to score some unusual stamps and coins.

On Being a "Tourist"

Although we've tried to avoid referring to our readers as "tourists," we do use the term throughout the book. There is no shame in being a tourist. A tourist is simply a person who travels for pleasure, and we assume that that's what you are. In fact, the best way to visit Central Italy is as a tourist. The negative images the word conjures up stem from the early days of mass-group travel, when Europe became accessible to Americans and cultural sensitivity was often less considered. Hence, the term "ugly American tourist." If you follow our advice, you won't be confused with one of them.

FAST FACTS ABOUT CENTRAL ITALY

Capital of Italy   Rome. The Republic of Italy (the official name) consists of 20 regions.

Population of Italy   57,634,300 (2000 estimated figures)

Chief of State   Italy is governed by a president, who is elected by an electoral college and 58 regional representatives, and a prime minister, who is chosen by the president and approved by Parliament. The president is elected for a seven-year term.

Religion   Overwhelmingly Catholic, with established Jewish and Protestant communities and a growing Muslim community.

Store Hours   Most shops are open Monday–Saturday, 9 a.m.–1 p.m. and from 3:30–7:30 p.m., sometimes until 8 p.m. during summer months. Stores are usually closed on Sundays, but may open Sunday afternoon in bigger cities and/or tourist areas.

Banking Hours   Most banks are open only on weekdays (Monday–Friday) from 8:30 a.m.–1:30 p.m. and from 3:30–4:30 p.m.

Time   Central Italy is on GMT +1.

Electric Current   Italian appliances run on 220 volts. You will need an adapter for appliances that run on 110 volts, the standard for American electrical appliances such as hair dryers, electric razors, etc.

Official Language   Italian, though English is spoken in larger hotels and also in stores and restaurants in larger cities.

Currency   On January 1, 2002, the euro became the official currency of Italy and 11 other countries in the European Union.

Size of Country   116,280 square miles, roughly twice the size of the state of Florida

PUBLIC HOLIDAYS IN ITALY

January 1   New Year's Day

March/April   Good Friday, Easter Monday

April 25   Liberation Day *(Anniversario della Liberazione)*

May 1   Labor Day *(Festa del Lavoro)*

August 15   Assumption of the Virgin Mary *(Ferragosto)*

November 1   All Saints' Day *(Ognissanti)*

December 8   Day of the Immaculate Conception *(Immacolata Concezione)*

December 25   Christmas Day *(Natale)*

December 26   St. Stephen's Day

Understanding Central Italy

A Brief History of the Region

If you're a history buff, you've come to the right place. When you travel to central Italy, you become a time traveler. Where else can you explore the mansion of Nero, pray in the same chapels as Michelangelo and Amerigo Vespucci, or drink pure water from aqueducts built more than a millennium ago? There'll be a little bit of history in everything you do while touring through Rome, Florence, or Assisi. Forget your concept of *old*. Heck, even the Trevi Fountain is considered a relatively new artwork in Rome, a city that marks its official birthday as April 21, 753 B.C.

Keep in mind that understanding one region of central Italy does not mean that you'll understand the other. Sure, they all speak the same language—or some dialect thereof—and all cook their pasta *al dente,* but knowing the Tuscan countryside will not necessarily prepare you for the frenzy of Florence or the lazier pace of Urbino in the Marches. Every *città* tells a story. Every region also has its own tale to tell.

We have provided for you a very brief outline of the history of central Italy. Following that is an abridged timeline. To learn more about specific cities and regions, see the beginning of each chapter.

Early History:
The Etruscans and Other Peoples of Central Italy

Forebears of the Romans, the Etruscans developed one of the earliest civilizations in Italy, having settled in central Italy possibly as early as the 12th century B.C. Although the Etruscans left behind many remnants of their society, including an alphabet, town planning expertise, and elaborate, frescoed tombs, their origins have remained a mystery to most anthropologists and historians. Some theorize that the pre-Roman tribe migrated to Italy from central Asia; others claim that the Etruscans are, in fact, indigenous to the peninsula. Either way, we are certain that Greek influence in art, commerce, and politics from early Hellenic settlements in southern Italy fanned upward toward Etruscan villages. The "Etruscan belt," as it is sometimes called, stretched from Florence south to Rome and east to Umbria, with strongholds in Volterra, Arezzo, and Cortona in Tuscany; in Perugia and Orvieto in Umbria; and in Cerveteri, Tarquinia, and Veio near Rome. Thousands of artifacts, including black clay vases *(buccheri)*, coins, jewelry, tools, and weapons, all featured in museums throughout central Italy, attest to the productiveness of the Etruscan society, as well as to its domination on the peninsula.

It is important to note that several other tribes were also present in central Italy during the time of the Etruscans. The Umbrii, of which we have little record, lived in what is today northern Umbria. For the most part, the Umbrii kept to themselves, until their land and culture were absorbed by the Romans. Meanwhile, in the Marches, the rabble-rousing Piceni held their ground between the Apennine and the Adriatic until they succumbed to the powerful Romans in the first half of the second century B.C.

The Roman Republic and the Roots of Empire

The beginning of Rome's domination over Italy, and eventually over most of the known world, began shortly after the defeat of the tyrannical Tarquinius Superbus (534–510 B.C.), the last of a short line of Etruscan rulers. From the ashes of the Etruscan kingdom rose the Roman republic, the first government to succeed in unifying the peninsula. Initially, the patrician class (aristocracy) held all of the power and wealth in the republic, electing two *consuls,* who served jointly for a one-year term, and *quaestors,* early bureaucrats. Meanwhile, the *plebeians,* or middle and lower classes, who accepted the largest burden of debt but had no say in government, felt the need to rise up against the ruling patricians. Eventually, the plebes organized themselves, effectively creating a separate state with their own laws and tribunes. Knowing that they could not ignore the masses, the aristocracy finally caved in, thereby ceding a share of power to the plebeians. By 287 B.C., the plebeians enjoyed the right to make laws and vote on consuls and quaestors. This type of power-sharing, no doubt mimicked by future governments within and outside Italy, lasted until roughly 50 B.C., with the rise of Julius Caesar.

In addition to creating one of the first democratic political systems, the Roman republic succeeded in expanding and unifying the Roman domain. Unlike the Etruscans, whose Etruscan League consisted of mostly autonomous city-states, the Romans conquered cities and then incorporated them into the empire, offering them economic and defensive privileges. Those cities that didn't cooperate came under Roman control through resettlement programs. Eventually, the Romans defeated the

Carthaginians in Sicily and northern Africa (during the Punic Wars), and wrested control of northern Italy and southern France from the Gauls.

The Caesars

The beginning of the Roman empire can be attributed to one man: Julius Caesar. In 59 B.C., consul-hopeful Julius Caesar made an alliance with Crassus and Pompey, thereby creating the First Triumvirate. The bond was sealed when Pompey married Caesar's daughter, Julia. However, with the sudden death of Julia and the increased ego of Caesar after a notable victory in Gaul, Caesar sought total control of the growing empire. By 47 B.C., Crassus was dead, Pompey had fled to Egypt, and Julius ruled by default. Caesar had his tenure as emperor of the Roman empire extended to ten years, and in 44 B.C., he declared himself dictator for life. Caesar's thirst for power no doubt alienated many within the Senate, and he was famously betrayed and murdered on the Ides of March in that same year.

Caesar's death caused a power struggle. At first, Mark Antony took control of Rome. Then, Caesar's heir apparent and great-nephew Octavian came to claim what had been willed to him. A Second Triumvirate was formed with Mark Antony, Octavian, and Lepidus, an army commander. Soon, the empire was divided and ruled by Octavian in the west and Mark Antony in the east. But, like his great-uncle, Octavian had bigger plans. After discovering that Mark Antony had been cheating on his wife, Octavian's sister, Octavian dispatched his general Marcus Agrippa to defeat the smug Antony. Both Antony and his lover, Cleopatra, committed suicide less than a year later.

However, hoping to avoid Julius Caesar's fate, Octavian made sure that he didn't appear power hungry. In 27 B.C., he surrendered his powers to the Senate, and they promptly gave them back. Octavian, now called Augustus (Your Eminence), also emphasized artistic endeavors, commissioning the Pantheon and the Ara Pacis. In the end, Caesar Augustus ruled for 40 years.

From Empire to Christianity

Following Octavian, Rome was ruled by a motley succession of emperors, some noteworthy, some notorious. Taciturn Tiberius reformed government but lived most of his rule in seclusion on the coast of Latium and in Capri. Caligula, the ruler best known for having made his horse a consul, followed. The crazy Caligula only managed to squeeze in four years before his own guard assassinated him. Nero, the man who built a lavish estate over Rome's ashes, wasn't far behind. After Nero committed suicide, Rome fell into the hands of the Flavian dynasty, which saw the reigns of Vespasian, Titus, and Domitian and the inauguration of the Colosseum. Following years of infighting and political and religious persecutions brought on by the Flavians, Rome saw great political stability under the rule of the "Five Good Emperors." Nerva, Trajan, Hadrian, Antoninus Pius, and Marcus Aurelius ruled from A.D. 96 to 180. Sadly, this stable and prosperous time came to a close as Marcus Aurelius's corrupt son Commodus took power.

In the meantime, the cult of Christianity had been gaining ground among plebeians, soldiers, and a large swath of citizens throughout the empire. Sts. Peter and Paul were murdered for their beliefs; Emperors Nero and Titus, to name just two, had thousands of other Christians slaughtered for laughs. Emperor Decius (renamed Trajunus), who ruled from A.D. 248 to 251, instituted the first systematic persecution of Christians. Tyrants Septimius Severus, Diocletian, and Caracalla did nothing to change the anti-Christian laws, resulting in the torture of hundreds of thousands. It was not until the reign of Constantine (from 306 to 312) that Christianity was proclaimed the official religion of the empire and that the persecutions against Christians ceased. His conversion, which was the result of having seen a vision of the cross bearing the inscription *in hoc signo vinces* (in this sign you will be victorious), was to forever change the church and the empire. In 312, Constantine moved the imperial capital to Byzantium, later Constantinople (today's Istanbul), thus dividing the Roman empire—and loyalties—for hundreds of years.

Medieval Times

The late fifth to the late 14th centuries constituted the end of an omnipotent Roman kingdom and signaled the rise of geographical and political divisions among Italians. During this time, Italy lost the hegemony that it had acquired as an empire, not to be seen again until the *Risorgimento* (see below), as a powerful papacy emerged and foreign factions invaded. The rifts that resulted from the split of the Roman empire into East and West spilled over into medieval times, pitting the Guelphs (pro-papacy) against the Ghibellines (pro–Holy Roman emperor). From Tuscany to the Marches, citizens took sides. But the divisions had little to do with faith and more to do with city pride or local wealth. In cities like San Gimignano (Tuscany) or Áscoli-Piceno (the Marches), loyalties often stood with the patrician family who could build the tallest watchtower. Likewise, allegiance shifted as new houses came to power. The Church in Rome was especially threatened during these tumultuous times and eventually moved for a time to Avignon, France. Further infighting subdivided the papacy when the king of France did not recognize the Italian pope and elected one of his own. The "Great Schism" lasted for 68 years, between 1378 to 1417, and ended with the reign of Pope Martin V and the return to Rome. This solidified the power of the papacy and made for conditions that gradually gave way to the golden years of the Renaissance.

The Renaissance

It was a time of scientific invention, artistic improvement, rigorous religiosity, and tremendous wealth for those in the upper class. The Renaissance (rebirth) saw a revival in classical interests, from Greek philosophy to Roman sculpture, and basically saw Italy (and the rest of Europe) transition into modern times. Humanism helped shape the mindset of Renaissance Italy. The "Renaissance man" was one who studied many subjects, such as art, politics, mathematics, and philosophy, to foster a greater knowledge of the world as a whole. However, the driving force behind much of the ingenuity between the 14th and 16th centuries was largely religious, inspiring future masters such as Michelangelo, Raphael, and Leonardo da Vinci to create colorful frescoes, pious portraits, and monumental sculptures based on poignant moments in biblical history. Of course, that was only half of it. Patrician families and guilds were getting richer by the day thanks to expanded trade routes and fortified affiliations. Bankers (like the Medici in Florence), textile merchants, and other members of the elite were an integral part of the patronage system in Florence, Rome, and throughout Italy, commissioning chapels, artworks, and entire buildings in their names. By pacifying the church elders and donating much of their wealth to the Church, these wealthy citizens hoped to ensure themselves a seat in heaven.

The Sack of Rome and the Counter-Reformation

The 16th century was an especially tumultuous time, marked by political, cultural, and religious upheaval. In 1513, Pope Leo X (Giuliano de' Medici) ascended to the papacy and continued the construction of St. Peter's Basilica. In order to finance this massive project, Leo sold indulgences, or, in effect, forgave the sins of those who added to the Church coffers. This fraudulent use of power incensed a young German friar named Martin Luther, who, with his 95 Theses, would spark the religious revolution in 1517 known as the Reformation. Clearly threatened by Luther's theses (such as "every believer is a priest before God"), the pope had Luther excommunicated, and the Holy Roman Emperor, Charles V, also spoke out against the heretic. Yet, Luther's influence grew in Germany and began to spread throughout the continent.

Meanwhile, Charles V, a Hapsburg emperor with control of Spain, the Netherlands, the Kingdom of Naples, and Sicily, among other territories, sought to expand his empire. In 1527, he targeted Rome, which was ruled at the time by Clement VII, another Medici pope. With his band of underpaid mercenaries, Charles V sacked the Eternal City and held the pope captive for months. Subsequently, the Medici clan was also expelled from Tuscany for three years. The Sack of Rome and the Medici ouster are widely considered to signal the end of the Renaissance.

A TIMELINE OF ITALIAN HISTORY

B.C.

753	Romulus and Remus found Rome (according to legend)
700–510	Etruscans rule the peninsula
509–50	Republican Rome
312	Via Appia and Rome's first aqueduct, the Aqua Appia, built; more than 6,000 slaves are crucified on the Via Appia for participating in Spartacus's slave revolt
60	Triumvirate of Pompey, Crassus, and Caesar
59	Florentia (Florence) founded as a town for retired Roman soldiers
49–44	Julius Caesar, dictator of Rome
20	Military colony of Saena (Siena) founded

A.D.

64	Fire of Rome during Nero's rule destroys city
67	Sts. Peter and Paul executed for practicing Christianity
72	Work on Colosseum begun under rule of Vespasian
80	Colosseum inaugurated by Titus
128	Rebuilding of Pantheon completed under Hadrian
270	Aurelian Wall begun
284	Roman empire divided into East and West
312	Constantine wins control of the Roman empire after victory at the Milvian Bridge
313	Constantine grants freedom of worship to Christians
320	Construction of the first St. Peter's Basilica
380	Christianity declared the official religion of the empire by Theodosius
410	Rome sacked by Alaric and the Goths
455	Rome sacked by the Vandals
475	Western Roman empire falls; Byzantium becomes seat of empire
590–604	Papacy strengthened under rule of Pope Gregory I (known as Gregory the Great)
773–774	Charlemagne conquers Italy
800	Charlemagne becomes first Holy Roman emperor and is crowned in St. Peter's
1076	Matilda becomes countess of Tuscany
1082	Florence goes to war against Siena
1181–1226	Life of St. Francis
1296	Construction of Florence's Duomo begun
1300	First Holy Year proclaimed by Pope Boniface VIII
1302	Dante Alighieri begins writing *The Divine Comedy*

1309	Pope Clement V moves the papacy to Avignon, France
1378–1417	The Great Schism of the papacy in Avignon
1417	Pope Martin V ends the Great Schism
1434–1743	The Medici family rules Florence
1436	Brunelleschi completes Florence's Duomo
1444	Sandro Botticelli born
1475	Michelangelo Buonarroti born
1483	Raffaello Sanzio (a.k.a., Raphael) born
1506	Pope Julius II orders construction to begin on the new St. Peter's
1507	Michelangelo begins painting the ceiling of the Sistine Chapel
1527	Sack of Rome by Charles V and the symbolic end of the Renaissance era
1537–1541	Michelangelo paints *The Last Judgment* in the Sistine Chapel
1633	Galileo excommunicated because of his astronomical observations
1796	Napoleon begins his first campaign in Italy
1799	Napoleon expelled from Italy by Austrians and Russians
1800–1801	Napoleon retakes Italy
1807	Garibaldi born
1848	Nationalist uprising in Rome causes pope to flee
1849	Pope is restored to power by French troops
1861	Vittorio Emanuele II king of Italy; first elections and Parliament in a unified Italy
1870	Rome becomes capital of unified Italy
1900	King Umberto I assassinated
1911	Vittorio Emanuele Monument is completed in Rome
1915	Italy enters World War I
1922	Fascists march on Rome; Benito Mussolini becomes prime minister
1929	Lateran Treaty creates the Vatican City
1940	Italy enters World War II as an Axis power
1943	Fall of the fascists
1944	Allied troops liberate Rome from the Nazis
1946	Italy established as a republic
1960	Olympic Games held in Rome
1962	Vatican II brings about church reforms
1966	Floods in Florence
1978	Karol Wojtya of Poland elected Pope John Paul II
1993	Terrorist explosion damages part of the Uffizi Gallery
2000	Italy celebrates the Jubilee

In response to Luther's theses and the Reformation came the Counter-Reformation in the second half of the 16th century. Under Pope Paul III, the Church consolidated power in Rome and quashed dissent. Paul instituted the Roman Inquisition, officially recognized the Jesuits, and appointed commissions to report abuses in the Papal States. In the century to follow, numerous groups, including scientists, Jews, Protestants, and artists, were persecuted, including Galileo in Florence and Giordano Bruno in Rome. However, those who were able to conform to the Church's heightened piety were rewarded. The Baroque movement in art, of which Gianlorenzo Bernini and Francesco Borromini are especially notable, followed in line with the Counter-Reformation by portraying in sculpture and painting themes like religious ecstasy and the supernatural.

Il Risorgimento

From the late 16th to the 19th century, a succession of rulers from Spain, France, and other kingdoms governed various parts of Italy. Even Napoleon's troops held stakes in Rome, Tuscany, and the Marches at the end of the 18th century. The Risorgimento (or reawakening) was a highly romanticized political movement that sought to unite the many city-states and principalities in Italy into one nation, linked not only by geography but also by government. Europe, especially Austria, Russia, Prussia, and Great Britain (the four major powers of the time), was wholly against the reformation of Italy as a state, as evidenced by the Congress of Vienna in 1814–1815, but the citizens of the peninsula were hopeful of a republic. One such citizen was Giuseppe Mazzini, widely considered the father of the Italian nation, who helped initiate public interest in Italian unification through his literature. In 1848, the Risorgimento began to sprout legs, as minor revolts shook the balance of power from southern Italy up through Austria. But the movement couldn't fully gain ground until it enlisted the help of a king, Vittorio Emanuele II, a statesman, Camillo Cavour, and a revolutionary, Giuseppe Garibaldi. By 1870, the actions of these main players, including Mazzini, and the will of the people, had resulted in the creation of what we know today as the modern Italian state.

Fascism and World War II

No sooner had Italy earned freedom as an independent and unified state than it fell under the leadership of a tyrant. After fighting in World War I, Italy fell under mismanagement, and the government was fundamentally weak. These conditions, however, were favorable for fascist leader Benito Mussolini. In 1922, the former elementary school teacher–turned-despot became prime minister of Italy. While he espoused the ideals that Garibaldi and his followers had—that is, the vision of a united Italy—Mussolini took the dream a step further, hoping to regain the dominance that Rome had during the days of empire. Mussolini sought to extend the line of imperial Rome by reconquering Europe. He even created a physical link between himself and the emperors of yore by bull-dozing through the Roman Forum and creating a wide boulevard, Via dei Fori Imperiali, that led from the Colosseum to his headquarters in Piazza Venezia.

By the outbreak of World War II, Mussolini saw an ally in world domination in Hitler and plunged his country into war in 1940. All in all, Mussolini and fascism were junior partners to Hitler and Nazism. By 1943 the Germans occupied Rome and installed Mussolini as a puppet dictator in northern Italy. Subsequently, Allied forces were able to take advantage of the situation and launched a massive bombing campaign on the region. Many of Italy's city centers are still scarred by the devastation.

Modern History

Although more than 50 coalitions have governed postwar Italy, the state has remained relatively stable. Industrial innovation, fueled by American aid, cheap labor, and a demand for exports, helped usher in Italy's "economic miracle" between 1959 and 1962. And companies that gained ground during this time, including Olivetti, Fiat, and others, have continued to contribute to the nation's bottom line. By 1987, in fact, Italy experienced the "Sorpasso," which meant that its gross domestic product surpassed that of Great Britain, making it a major contender on the economic stage of Europe and the world. Italy's involvement with the European Union has also been a factor in the country's success.

The Language: Italiano

You probably already know a number of Italian words, thanks to years of Italian-American innovation in the media, music, and culinary corners. Dino Crocetti (a.k.a. Dean Martin), taught us *amore* (love). Francis Ford Coppola introduced us to *la famiglia* (the family). Today many American kitchens are stocked with pasta, *prosciutto* (ham), *formaggio* (cheese), and *vino* (wine).

The language of music, art, and love, *la lingua italiana* (the Italian language) moves with the rhythm of Italian life and, in turn, has many regional variations. In Rome, for instance, syllables are slurred and swallowed as the Roman dialect has adapted to the city's fast-paced lifestyle. In Tuscany, you'll hear a clearer, unadulterated version of Italian; both Florence and Siena, rivals since the Middle Ages, claim to speak the purest form of the language. Meanwhile, people of Umbria and the Marches switch gears between accentless Italian and a hodge-podge of dialects, having been influenced linguistically by their regional neighbors.

Indeed, the Italian way of life is neatly tied up with the *lingua italiana,* but that doesn't mean that you won't be able to get by with English. Over the past several decades, as tourism has engulfed the peninsula, many Italians have bet the farm on learning English. Hoteliers, restaurateurs, taxi drivers, shopkeepers, and even that little old *nonna* crossing the street are sure to know an English phrase or two. On the other hand, if you really want to endear yourself to the Italians you meet, try practicing some vocabulary before you go. It could mean the difference between being a regular tourist and a world traveler.

Getting Linguistically Equipped

If you took French or Spanish in high school (and we bet that you did), then Italian may look quite familiar to you. As the original Romance language, Italian stemmed from Latin and has many root words and pronunciations in common with its linguistic cousins. Consider the Italian phrase *per favore* (please); it looks and sounds similar to the Spanish *por favor. Città* (chee-TAH) in Italian become *cité* in French, and *city* in English. There are numerous examples of Italian words that you'll be able to understand on sight or from context.

As far as pronunciation goes, Italian is fairly straightforward in that all syllables are pronounced and almost all words end in a vowel (thus perpetuating the musicality of the language). Emphasis in a word is usually on the second to the last syllable, unless otherwise noted with an accent mark. Below (and throughout the text) we have laid out a beginner's Italian course for you, complete with a pronunciation guide. The uppercase letters indicate the accented syllable.

Pronto? (PRAWN-toh?) Ready? *Andiamo!* (ahn-dee-AM-oh!) Let's go!

Survival Italian

For the most part, the Italians you encounter will speak fast but clearly. You'll have to tell them to slow down *(per favore, parla più lentamente).* You may also want to initiate conversation with the phrase *parla inglese?* (Do you speak English?). If you're lucky, the answer will be *sì!* (yes!). If the answer is no, then you may need to try out some Italian. Remember, too, that the Italians also speak with their hands—quite useful if you're asking for directions.

Saying Hello and Goodbye

Buon giorno, signora/signore
   (bwon JOR-no, seen-YORE-ah/seen-YORE-ay)

Buona sera, signora/signore
   (BWON-ah SAIR-ah, seen-YORE-ah/seen-YORE-ay)

Arrivederci, signora/signore
   (ah-REEV-eh-DAIR-chee, seen-YORE-ah/seen-YORE-ay)

A more casual way to say hello is *'giorno* or *'sera,* depending on the time of day. The ubiquitous *ciao,* like the Hawaiian *aloha,* can be used for both a greeting and a salutation.

Questions

Quanto costa . . . ? (KWAHN-toh KOST-a . . . ?)
How much does (this item) cost?

Dov'è . . . (DOHV-ay . . .)   Where is . . . ?

Quando . . . ? (KWAHN-doh)   When . . . ?

Time and Days of the Week

Un minuto   One minute

Un'ora   One hour

Mezz'ora (METTS-OHR-ah)   Half hour

Un giorno   One day

Una settimana (sett-ee-MAHN-ah)   One week

Un'anno   One year

Lunedì (loon-eh-DEE)   Monday

Martedì (mart-eh-DEE)   Tuesday

Mercoledì (mare-cole-eh-DEE)   Wednesday

Giovedì (jove-eh-DEE)   Thursday

Venerdì (ven-err-DEE)   Friday

Sabato (sab-a-TOH)   Saturday

Domenica (doh-MEN-ee-kah)   Sunday

Numbers

Uno (OON-oh)   1

Due (DOO-ay)   2

Tre (TRAY)   3

Quattro (KWAT-roh)   4

Cinque (CHEEN-kway)   5

Sei (SAY)   6

Sette (SET-tay)   7

Otto (OHT-oh)   8

Nove (NOH-vay)   9

Dieci (dee-AY-chee)   10

Undici (OON-dee-chee)   11

Dodici (DOH-dee-chee)   12

Tredici (TRAY-dee-chee)   13

Quattordici (kwat-TOR-dee-chee)   14

Quindici (KWEEN-dee-chee)   15

Sedici (SAY-dee-chee)   16

Diciassette (DEE-cha-SET-tay)   17

Diciotto (DEECH-oh-toh)   18

Diciannove (DEECH-ah-NOH-vay)   19

Ventì (vayn-TEE)   20

Trenta (TRAYN-tah)   30

Quaranta (kwahr-AHN-tah)   40

Cinquanta (cheen-KWAHN-tah)   50

Sessanta (says-SAHN-tah)   60

Settanta (set-TAWNT-tah)   70

Ottanta (oh-TAHN-tah)   80

Novanta (noh-VAHN-tah)   90

Cento (CHAYN-toh)   100

Mille (MEEL-ay)   1,000

Milione (meel-YOHN-ay)   1,000,000

Numbers and Prices: The Euro

Make sure you double-check prices before booking a hotel or making other purchases. (As we went to press, the dollar had plunged below the euro in currency trading, running at about $1.27 to €1.) For the most current information on the euro, consult the European Union's website at **europa.eu.int/euro.** If you need further conversion help and up-to-date rates, try **oanda.com,** which has a handy "Cheat Sheet for Travelers" that you can print and carry with you. Remember: Italians—indeed, most Europeans—use the comma where Americans would traditionally use the decimal point. Thus, $50.50 would be written $50,50 in Italy. Conversely, large numbers are separated by decimal points rather than by commas.

FURTHER READING ABOUT CENTRAL ITALY

History and Culture

- Barker, Graeme and Tom Rasmussen, *The Etruscans*
- Barzini, Luigi, *The Italians*
- Burckhardt, Jacob, *The Civilization of the Renaissance in Italy*
- D'Epiro, Peter and Mary Desmond Pinkowish, *Sprezzatura: 50 Ways Italian Genius Shaped the World*
- Ginsbourg, Paul, *A History of Contemporary Italy*
- Von Goethe, Johann Wolfgang, *Italian Journey*
- Hibbert, Christopher, *Rome: Biography of a City*. See also *The House of Medici: Its Rise and Fall*
- James, Henry, *Italian Hours*
- Lamb, Richard, *War in Italy 1943–1945: A Brutal History*
- Lawrence, D. H., *Etruscan Places*
- Masini, Giancarlo and Iacopo Gori, *How Florence Invented America: Vespucci, Verrazzano, and Mazzei and Their Contribution to the Conception of the New World*
- Origo, Iris, *The Merchant of Prato*
- Ridley, Jasper, *Garibaldi*
- Smith, Dennis Mack, *Mazzini*
- Suetonius, Gaius, *The Twelve Caesars*

Religion, Food, and the Arts

- Bruschini, Enrico, *In the Footsteps of Popes: A Spirited Guide to the Treasures of the Vatican*
- Hutchinson, Robert J., *When in Rome: A Journal of Life in the Vatican City*
- King, Ross, *Brunelleschi's Dome: How a Renaissance Genius Reinvented Architecture* and *Michelangelo and the Pope's Ceiling*
- McCarthy, Mary, *The Stones of Florence*
- Root, Waverley, *The Food of Italy*
- Vasari, Giorgio, *Lives of the Artists*

Literature

- Alighieri, Dante, *The Divine Comedy* (particularly the *Inferno*)
- Castiglione, Conte Baldassare, *The Courtier*
- Forster, E. M., *A Room with a View*
- Machiavelli, Niccolò, *The Prince*
- Shakespeare, William, *Julius Caesar*
- Sobel, Dava, *Galileo's Daughter*
- Virgil, *The Aeneid*
- Vreeland, Susan, *The Passion of Artemisia*

Part Two

Planning Your Visit to Central Italy

How Far in Advance Should You Plan?

There are many advantages to planning your trip as far in advance as possible. We say that because we think that you are more likely to land better rates for hotels and airfare if you start planning at least three or four months prior to your trip, especially if you wish to travel during high season. What's more, allowing yourself enough time before your trip will give you opportunities to read up on destinations or sites that interest you or to map out your budget. However, much can also be said for the traveler who doesn't mind packing up his suitcase at the drop of a hat—or a fare. In today's highly competitive travel market, the chance of coming across round-trip tickets for under $600 isn't unheard of.

When to Go

For the most part, there is no bad time to visit Central Italy, so you should take into account personal considerations such as budget, mood, and interests. Seasoned travelers who wish to linger longer in galleries, take in top-notch theater productions, or spend a lot of time in restaurants and cafés will do well to travel during the cooler months. Of course, the weather can be dreary in midwinter—even in a Mediterranean country—but there'll be fewer tourists to get in your way and more true Italian moments to savor. First-timers may want to visit Italy in spring or early fall, to enjoy warm days, cool nights, and all the joys that come with these pleasant seasons. However, be warned: Central Italy can feel like one enormous theme park during high season. Be sure to pack your patience.

Pricing

Italy's high season lasts the entire summer, all the way from June through mid-September. Conversely, the low season—when you are bound to find the best deals and the dreariest weather—is quite short, lasting from

November through mid-December and from New Year's until the end of March. In our opinion, the "shoulder season," which lasts from April through May and mid-September through October is the best time to travel: The crowds have thinned, and, as a result, airlines and hotels are more apt to offer discounts.

Again, if your plans include many hours inside museums, churches, or generally indoors, you can save *molto* by traveling in the off-season, or picking a week or two during the shoulder season. If you must travel during high season, don't worry. You can find good deals for travel during the high season if you know where to look. We'll show you how below.

Weather

The weather in Central Italy is mostly mild year-round. Even in February, temperatures often reach into the mid-60s to low 70s—a wake-up call for anyone whose bulky sweaters are bringing on the blues. Spring-time sees more gorgeous weather and lively Easter celebrations. May to mid-July is the typical high season, and for good reason. Marvelous Mediterranean breezes, sidewalk café dining, and midnight strolls are all components of a summer vacation in Central Italy. Pleasant autumn temperatures and harvest festivals (of grapes, olives, and truffles, for instance) have made September and October busy months. And, with Christmas fairs, papal addresses, and glittery street decorations, the months of December and January are fun, if a bit frosty.

By now, you have probably heard that all the cities of Italy become ghost towns in August, when citizens take leave of their bustling burgs in favor of the beach or the mountains. In fact, many restaurants, shops, and small inns do shut their doors from mid-August (Ferragosto) until the beginning of September. But most major museums and galleries are open throughout August (though perhaps on an abbreviated schedule), and you can certainly find vacancies in major hotels. Perhaps the worst aspect of traveling during August is the heat, especially the oppressive, urban jungle kind of heat you find in Rome and Florence in the dead of summer. Yes, some places will have air-conditioning to help you cope. But don't always count on that cute country farmhouse to have AC. Be aware, too, that some lower-budget hotels charge extra for an arctic blast. Frankly, the Italians aren't married to their air conditioners the way Americans are.

Weather can be a deterrent during the month of November, too. Each November, like clockwork, the heavens open up, the wind blows stronger, and the sky is a perpetual shade of dark gray. Central Italy is generally dark, damp, dreadful, and, not surprisingly, void of visitors during this time. Most of the tourists that cloud the landscape the rest of year have gone into hibernation come November. So, if you're the type who cringes at the thought of long museum queues—and you can brave a few raindrops—then a November vacation may be for you.

AVERAGE TEMPERATURES

	Florence		Rome	
	low	high	low	high
January	3°C (37°F)	11°C (52°F)	5°C (41°F)	14°C (57°F)
February	4°C (39°F)	13°C (55°F)	5°C (42°F)	14°C (58°F)
March	6°C (43°F)	16°C (60°F)	7°C (45°F)	16°C (61°F)
April	9°C (47°F)	20°C (67°F)	9°C (49°F)	18°C (65°F)
May	12°C (54°F)	24°C (76°F)	13°C (56°F)	23°C (73°F)
June	16°C (60°F)	28°C (83°F)	17°C (63°F)	26°C (79°F)
July	18°C (64°F)	32°C (89°F)	20°C (68°F)	29°C (85°F)
August	18°C (64°F)	31°C (88°F)	20°C (69°F)	29°C (85°F)
September	15°C (59°F)	27°C (81°F)	18°C (64°F)	27°C(81°F)
October	11°C (52°F)	22°C (71°F)	14°C (58°F)	23°C (73°F)
November	7°C (45°F)	16°C (60°F)	9°C (48°F)	18°C (64°F)
December	4°C (39°F)	9°C (52°F)	7°C (44°F)	15°C (59°F)

AVERAGE RAINFALL

	Florence	Rome
January	75 mm (2.8")	75 mm (2.9")
February	75 mm (2.8")	70 mm (2.7")
March	70 mm (2.7")	65 mm (2.5")
April	70 mm (2.7")	55 mm (2.2")
May	70 mm (2.7")	45 mm (1.7")
June	55 mm (2.1")	30 mm (1")
July	35 mm (1.2")	15 mm (0.5")
August	50 mm (1.9")	30 mm (1")
September	75 mm (3")	<5 mm (<0.1")
October	100 mm (3.9")	95 mm (3.8")
November	110 mm (4.2")	105 mm (4.1")
December	85 mm (3.3")	95 mm (3.7")

Airfare Deals and Package Tours

Start with Your Local Travel Agent

If you already know of a good travel agent, give him or her a call. Provide your agent with a range of dates during which you wish to travel, if you prefer to fly a certain airline, how much you are planning to spend, etc. Also, if you're willing, let your travel agent know if you would consider flying into alternative cities. One Italophile we talked with said that on a recent trip to Italy, she told her travel agent that she was willing to fly into Florence's smaller Peretola airport, rather than into Rome's Fiumicino. Her agent found her a flight to Florence that was $200 less than one to Rome.

A high-quality travel agent should be flexible enough to work within your budget and time constraints. However, we should point out that not all travel agents are equal. Agents that do a higher volume of business can often get you a better deal, simply because they have well-established relationships with airlines, tour companies, and the like. You can also do yourself a service by asking your agent if her recommendations are from first-hand experience. The best-case scenario is that your agent will have visited the places that she is recommending, and will be able to tell you with certainty if a hotel is in the bad neighborhood or if a town is easy to navigate. Don't worry if you feel like you're prying—almost all people like to talk about trips they have taken. Travel agents are no exception. And, nine times out of ten, their enthusiasm for a particular bed-and-breakfast or destination will result in a pleasurable vacation for you.

All in all, you should let your agent do the legwork so you can concentrate on planning the fun parts.

Check the Travel Section of Your Local Newspaper

Use your local paper as a *guide*—but not as an authority—for information on package tours. Deals featured in the paper are often snapped up before you even have a chance to inquire about them. Check out which tour operators are offering deals, then call and ask if they are still offering the deal in the paper, or if they have similar, upcoming deals. Be sure to ask about blackout dates and other restrictions before proceeding.

Surf the Web

One of the only sectors to have turned a small profit in these start-up/shut-down times is the travel sector, specifically online airfare sites. You've probably even searched some of the more popular ones like **expedia.com** and **travelocity.com** on your own.

The reason these sites have managed to stay afloat is because more and more travelers want to be their own travel agents. Think about it: You have access to thousands of flights and a dizzying array of fares. You can choose between window seat or aisle and regular meal or kosher. Airfare sites basically give you the power to plan your vacation in the matter of a few clicks, and all without speaking to a single person.

Alas, there's the caveat! While airfare sites do make travel more convenient, they are as good as gone when you have a problem. Most sites only offer nonrefundable tickets. Plus, travelers who book online generally have a harder time finding another flight when they get bumped.

One word of advice: If you do book online, request a paper ticket. Some sites will send you a hard copy upon request, while, in other cases, you will need to contact the airline on which you are flying to secure a paper ticket. Especially in light of the tragic events of September 11,

2001, it is essential that you travel with a paper ticket, or at least a printed confirmation of your electronic reservation, for security purposes.

The airlines' own travel sites are also good when it comes to browsing cheap fares (see listing of airline websites below). You can also have airfare deals e-mailed to you from sites like **Last Minute Travel (www.last minute.com), 11th Hour Vacations (www.11thhourvacations.com), BestFares (www.bestfares.com), Orbitz (www.orbitz.com), Cheap Tickets (www.cheaptickets.com),** or **Travel Zoo (www.travelzoo.com).**

As for package deals, one of the first places you should look is on the Web, as many tour operators only maintain an Internet presence (i.e., they don't advertise their deals in the local paper). For example, a quick search at **away.com**, a website that maintains an extensive database of active and cultural vacations, turned up a two-week language study package in Florence for $560 per person, not including airfare, but inclusive of all lodging and some meals. That's already less than $40 per night for a hotel room. A number of airlines also offer package deals these days, allowing you to order up airfare, accommodations, rental cars, and guided tours in a matter of clicks. During another Web search, we turned up a two-week "Fly-Drive" package deal for two from American Airlines Vacations. The package, from Los Angeles to Rome, included air, hotel, and car for a total of $1,576. Meanwhile, Alitalia had a four-day, three-night weekend deal from New York or Boston to Rome, including airfare, hotel, transfers, and sightseeing tour for $779 per person.

Contact the Airlines Directly

Unless you plan on cashing in your frequent flier miles for a ticket, you needn't waste time on hold with the airlines. In most cases, you'll be able to find a cheaper fare online or through your travel agent. However, if you don't mind holding the line for an intolerable amount of time—*and* if you're persistent—you may be able to land a reasonable fare.

As is the case when contacting travel agents, make sure you ask a lot of questions. Inquire whether the fare is cheaper if you leave on a Tuesday rather than a Monday. Ask about student or senior discounts, or whether the airline is offering any specials. Also, be mindful of the numerous airline partnerships that are out there. For instance, Northwest Airlines and KLM, American Airlines and British Airways, and Continental Airlines and Lufthansa share many major routes; so if the agent at one airline is being fussy with you, try its partner. True, there may not be much of a cost difference, but one airline may be more helpful than another.

Another trick, says Peter Greenberg, best-selling author of *The Travel Detective,* is to avoid telling the airline *when* you want to fly from Chicago to Rome, but rather to ask the agent what the lowest published fare is for a flight from Chicago to Rome. If the agent refuses to tell you the cheapest fare, hang up and call again until you find an agent who will assist you.

If you prefer to dig around for deals on your own without the help of an airline representative, consider the Web your best friend. All of the major airlines have websites these days, with detailed info on flights, schedules, and discounts. While we find the practice highly discriminatory, some airlines even post Web-only specials on their sites. The easiest way to catch wind of these online deals is to sign up for e-mail alerts from the airlines.

AIRLINE CONTACT INFORMATION FROM NORTH AMERICA

Airline	Phone	Web
Air Canada	(800) 776-3000 (U.S.) (800) 268-7240 (Canada)	www.aircanada.com
Air France	(800) 237-2747	www.airfrance.com
Alitalia	(800) 223-5730	www.alitalia.com
American Airlines	(800) 433-7300	www.aa.com
British Airways	(800) 247-9297	www.british-airways.com
Continental	(800) 525-0280	www.continental.com
Delta	(800) 221-1212	www.delta.com
Icelandair	(800) 223-5500	www.icelandair.com
KLM	(800) 374-7747	www.klm.com
Lufthansa	(800) 645-3880	www.lufthansa.com
Northwest Airlines	(800) 225-2525	www.nwa.com
Qantas Airways	(800) 227-4500	www.qantas.com
SAS	(800) 221-2350	www.scandinavian.net
TWA	(800) 221-2000	www.twa.com
United Airlines	(800) 241-6522	www.ual.com
USAirways	(800) 428-4322	www.usairways.com
Virgin Atlantic	(800) 862-8621	www.fly.virgin.com

Suggested Tour Operators

Given Italy's popularity among international destinations, just about every tour operator offers some kind of package trip to Florence or Rome. Even the sheer number of package tours to Tuscany alone overwhelms us! On that note, we knew that you would need a little help in weeding out the mediocre from the magnificent.

No doubt you have seen the television commercials of Mario Perillo and son, Steve, touting the glories of a package tour to Italy. **Perillo Tours,** operating since 1945, is, in fact, the best known and one of the best informed of the numerous package tour operators to Italy. Currently, Perillo Tours has ten tours during high season and six off-season tours. Perillo Tours is a good choice for any first-time visitor to Italy, families, seniors, or travelers who enjoy getting to know others within a large group. One drawback with Perillo, however, is that the company does not accept credit-card payments, claiming that this practice keeps prices low.

Perillo Tours   577 Chestnut Ridge Road; Woodcliff Lake, NJ 07677; (800) 431-1515, (201) 307-1234; fax (201) 307-1808; perillo@perillotours.com

If you're more of the independent type, but still prefer to have someone else do all the legwork as far as your trip is concerned, then you may want to contact **Caravella Italia,** a smaller tour operator with branches in the U.S. and Italy. Caravella's tours are smaller, with no more than 12 travelers in each tour group, and are often unique. For instance, in 2001, Caravella arranged a "Jewish Heritage Tour of Italy," an itinerary that proves Caravella's passion for revealing the many sides of the peninsula. What's more, Caravella can customize a tour for you, your family, and friends.

Caravella Italia   112 Walnut Street; Philadelphia, PA 19103; (888) 665-2112, (215) 665-1233; info@caravella.com

Other quality tour operators to Italy include:

Alternative Travel Group   ATG Oxford; 69-71 Banbury Road; OX2 6PJ Oxford; U.K.; (+44) 01 865 315 678, fax (+44) 01 865 315 697. This is one of the few tour operators we found that offered trips focusing on the Marches region (e.g., "Paths to Urbino").

Ciclismo Classico   30 Marathon Street; Arlington, MA 02474; (800) 866-7314, (781) 646-3377, fax (781) 641-1512. Biking adventures through the Tuscan countryside—a great way to work off all those carbs!

Grand Circle Travel   (800) 955-1034; **www.gct.com.** Specialists in travel for the over-50 set.

The International Kitchen   (800) 945-8606, (312) 726-4525, fax (312) 803-1593; info@intl-kitchen.com, **www.theinternationalkitchen.com.** Culinary tours to Tuscany, Umbria, and other Italian destinations.

ITALY PACKAGE TOURS ON THE WEB

www.aavacations.com	www.great-travels.com
www.abercrombiekent.com	www.maupintour.com
www.away.com	www.perillotours.com
www.backroads.com	www.theinternationalkitchen.com
www.butterfieldandrobinson.com	www.tourcrafters.com
www.caravella.com	www.trafalgartours.com
www.ciclismoclassico.com	www.tuscanway.com
www.gct.com	www.unitedvacations.com

Italian Government Tourist Office (ENIT)

Although each region outlined in this book has its own tourism office (see individual chapters for details), the Italian Government Tourist Office, or **ENIT** (Ente Nazionale Italiano per il Turismo), can provide you with most of the essential information you will need. We requested general information on Florence and Rome, and received an envelope stuffed with fascinating brochures and booklets with information covering where to explore Etruscan ruins and where to find Raphael frescoes. While you can find the organization on the web—at **www.enit.it/uk**, or, in North America, at **www.italiantourism.com**—you may want to contact one of its many international branches directly.

In the United States

Chicago
500 North Michigan Avenue
Chicago, IL 60611
(312) 644-0996
fax (312) 644-3019
enitch@italiantourism.com

Los Angeles
12400 Wilshire Boulevard, Suite 550
Los Angeles, CA 90025
(310) 820-2977
fax (310) 820-6357
enitla@earthlink.net

New York
630 Fifth Avenue, Suite 1565
New York, NY 10111
(212) 245-4822
fax (212) 586-9249
enitny@italiantourism.com

In Canada
17 Bloor Street East, Suite 907
M4W 3R8 Toronto, Ontario
(416) 925-4882
fax (416) 925-4799
enit.canada@on.aibn.com

In the United Kingdom
1 Princess Street
W1R 9AY London
(44) 20 7355 1557
fax (44) 20 7493 6695
enitlond@globalnet.co.uk

In Australia
Level 36-44 Market Street
NSW 2000 Sydney
(612) 92 621 666
fax (612) 92 621 677
lenitour@ihug.com.au

Italian Chambers of Commerce Abroad

If you're heading to Italy for commercial or professional reasons, you may want to contact an Italian Chamber of Commerce for answers to questions pertaining to your business.

In the United States
Camera di Commercio Italo-Americana,
  Chicago
30 South Michigan Avenue, Suite 504
Chicago, IL 60603
(312) 553-9137; fax (312) 553-9142

Camera di Commercio Italo-Americana
  Houston
4605 Post Oak Place Drive, Suite 226
Houston, TX 77027
(713) 626-9303; fax (713) 626-9309

Camera di Commercio Italo-Americana, West
10350 Santa Monica Blvd., Ste. 210
Los Angeles, CA 90025
(310) 557-3017; fax (310) 557-1217

Camera di Commercio Italo-Americana,
  Southeast
One S.E. 15th Road, Suite 150
Miami, FL 33129
(305) 577-9868; fax (305) 577-3956

Camera di Commercio Italo-Americana,
  New York
730 Fifth Avenue, Suite 600
New York, NY 10019
(212) 459-0044; fax (212) 459-0090

Camera di Commercio Italo-Americana,
  Mid-Atlantic Chapter
200 South Broad Street, Suite 700
Philadelphia, PA 19102
(215) 790-3778; fax (215) 790-3600

Italian Chambers of Commerce Abroad *(continued)*

In Australia

*Camera di Commercio e Industria
    Italiana in Australia*
262A Carrington Street
SA 5000 Adelaide
(618) 82 324 022
(618) 82 324 033

*Camera di Commercio e Industria
    Italiana, Queensland*
120, Main Street Kangaroo Point
QLD 4069 Brisbane
(617) 33 922 499
fax (617) 33 921 022

*Camera di Commercio e Industria
    Italiana, Melbourne*
Level 5, 499 St. Kilda Road
VIC 3004 Melbourne
(613) 98 665 433
fax (613) 98 677 337

*Camera di Commercio e Industria
    Italiana, Perth*
235 Fitzgerald Street
WA 6000 Perth
(618) 92 276 005
fax (618) 92 275 718

Camera di Commercio Italiana, Sydney
26/44 Market Street
NSW 2000 Sydney
(612) 92 625 744
fax (612) 92 625 745

In Canada

Camera di Commercio Italiana in Canada
550, rue Sherbrooke Ouest
Bureau 680
H3A 1B9 Montréal, Québec
(514) 844-4249; fax (514) 844-4875

Camera di Commercio Italiana, Toronto
901 Lawrence Avenue West, Suite 306
M6A 1C3 Toronto, Ontario
(416) 789-7169; fax (416) 789-7160

*Camera di Commercio Italiana,
    British Columbia*
206-850 West Hastings Street
V6C 1E1 Vancouver, B.C.
(604) 682-1410; fax (604) 682-2997

Camera di Commercio Italiana, Manitoba
1055 Wilkes Avenue, Unit 113
R3P 2L7 Winnipeg, Manitoba
(204) 487-6323; fax (204) 487-0164

In the United Kingdom

Camera di Commercio e Industria Italiana
1 Princess Street
W1R 8AY London
(44) 20 7495 8191
fax (44) 20 7495 8194

What to Pack

We know, we know—the urge is to take your entire wardrobe. You fear that if you don't take it, you'll need it. Resist the temptation. Too many travelers—even seasoned ones—make the mistake of packing too much. We feel that a lot of today's overpacking stems from the fact that many now travel with convenient roller bags, which allow for heavier loads. Keep in mind that if you will be moving around a bit once you arrive in Italy, the over-packed roller bag will become your worst enemy, especially when you're stuck hoisting it in and out of trains. When we have packed our suitcases to bulging, we like to remind ourselves that "the lesser packed, the more to bring back!" Repeating that mantra makes us feel much better about leaving behind our entire CD collection and photos of Aunt Selma.

All joking aside, there are a number of useful items you may want to take with you on your trip. Small binoculars have always come in handy for us during our adventures in Italy. You can use them to examine the ceilings of the Sistine Chapel more closely, as well as to survey the hills of Tuscany from atop Siena's slender Mangia Tower. If you're spending a lot of time in wine country, pack a wine key (but only in your checked luggage—see below). You may want to bring along a calculator to figure out all those euro conversions. Bring an adapter if you are toting an electric shaver, hair dryer, or laptop computer. All of Italy is wired to 220 volts (as opposed to North America's 110 volts), so you will need the proper, round-prong adapter if you're bringing items that run on 110 volts. (Keep in mind, however, that most hotel bathrooms will have hair dryers.) You can find an adapter for Italy at most Radio Shacks. **Travel Arts** also has all sorts of adapters and converters. Contact them at (800) 203-3422 or online at **www.travel-arts.com**. Other valuable travel tools include a compass, an alarm clock, a money belt, film, sunglasses and/or a hat, and sunscreen. Also, make sure that you bring along a photocopy of your passport, keeping it at all times in a place separate from your passport.

Travel Security Restrictions

Airport security these days is extremely tight, so those who choose to travel should be mindful of what they pack and where they pack it. The Federal Aviation Administration (FAA) has imposed tough carry-on restrictions, allowing only one carry-on bag plus one handbag, such as a purse or briefcase. Carry-on bags must be airline regulation size (13 inches by 21 inches by 9 inches) or less and weigh approximately 40 pounds or less. If you must bring the following items, pack them only in your *checked luggage:*

- Any type of knife or cutlery, including steel nail files or clippers, plastic knives, etc.
- Razor blades
- Tradesmen's tools, such as hammers, screwdrivers, wrenches, etc.
- Darts
- Scissors
- Hypodermic needles (unless you carry a written note from your doctor explaining your medical need)
- Knitting needles
- Most sporting equipment, including baseball bats, golf clubs, all racquets, pool cues, etc.
- Guitar strings
- Umbrellas
- Corkscrews
- Swiss army knives, manicure sets, or similar utility tools or kits

Electronic tickets are also a bit tricky these days. If you have booked an airline ticket over the Internet, make sure to bring along a printed copy of your confirmation. Otherwise, try your best to secure a paper ticket before traveling.

It's anybody's guess how long such particular restrictions will last, or if new restrictions will be imposed. Please use your common sense, and check with your airline and/or your travel agent before you leave. Also, contact your local airport before your departure to find out how many hours ahead of your flight you should arrive.

Passport and Visas

Citizens of the United States, Canada, Britain, and other European Union countries who will be traveling in Italy for three months or less do not need a visa. All you need is a valid passport, the expiration date of which should not fall shorter than three months after the date of your expected return. Smart travelers will carry a photocopy of their passport in a separate place in case their real passport is lost or stolen.

Italian Consular Offices

Italian consulates abroad can issue you visas for work or study and address many other administrative and legal questions prior to your trip.

In the United States

Boston
Italian Consulate General
100 Boylston Street, Suite 900
Boston, MA 02116
(617) 542-0483; fax (617) 542-3998
www.italianconsulateboston.org

Chicago
Italian Consulate General
500 North Michigan Avenue, Ste. 1850
Chicago, IL 60611
(312) 467-1550; fax (312) 467-1335
www.italconschicago.org

Detroit
Italian Consulate
Buhl Building
535 Griswold, Suite 1840
Detroit, MI 48226
(313) 963-8560; fax (313) 963-8180
www.italconsdetroit.org

Houston
Italian Consulate General
1300 Post Oak Boulevard, Suite 660
Houston, TX 77056
(713) 850-7520; fax (713) 850-9113
www.italconshouston.org

Los Angeles
Italian Consulate General
12400 Wilshire Boulevard, Suite 300
Los Angeles, CA 90025
(310) 820-0622; fax (310) 820-0727
www.conlang.com

Miami
Italian Consulate General
1200 Brickell Avenue, 7th Floor
Miami, FL 33131
(305) 374-6322; (305) 374-7945
www.italconsmiami.com

New York
Italian Consulate General
690 Park Avenue
New York, NY 10021
(212) 737-9100; fax (212) 249-4945
www.italconsulnyc.org

Newark
Italian Vice Consulate
744 Broad Street, Suite 2800
Newark, NJ 07102
(973) 643-1448; fax (973) 643-3043
www.reference.it/vcnewark

Philadelphia
Italian Consulate General
1026 Public Ledger Building
100 South Sixth Street
Philadelphia, PA 19106-3470
(215) 592-7329; fax (215) 592-9808
www.italconphila.org

San Francisco
Italian Consulate General
2590 Webster Street
San Francisco, CA 94115
(415) 292-9210; fax (415) 931-7205
www.italcons-sf.org

Italian Consular Offices *(continued)*

In the United States *(continued)*

Washington, DC
Italian Embassy-Consular Section
3000 Whitehaven Street, N.W.
Washington, DC 20008
(202) 612-4405
fax (202) 518-2142
www.italyemb.org

In Canada

Edmonton
Italian Consulate
1900 Royal Trust Tower
Edmonton Centre
T5J 2Z2 Edmonton, Alberta
(780) 423-5153
fax (780) 423-5176

Montréal
Italian Consulate General
3489 Drummond Street
H3G 1X6 Montréal, Québec
(514) 849-8351
fax (514) 499-9471
www.italconsul.montreal.qc.ca

Toronto
Italian Consulate General
136 Beverley Street
M5T 1Y5 Toronto, Ontario
(416) 977-1566
fax (416) 977-1119
www.toronto.italconsulate.org

Vancouver
Italian Consulate General
Standard Building
1100-510 West Hastings Street
V6B 1L8 Vancouver, British Columbia
(604) 684-7288
fax (604) 685-4263

In the United Kingdom

London
Italian Consulate General
38 Eaton Place
SW1X 8AN London
(44) 20 7235 9371
fax (44) 20 7823 1609

Manchester
Italian Consulate General
Rodwell Tower
111 Piccadilly Street
M1 2HY Manchester
(44) 161 236 9024
fax (44) 161 236 5574

In Australia

Melbourne
Italian Consulate General
509 St. Kilda Road
VIC 3004 Melbourne
(03) 98 675 744
fax (03) 98 663 932

Sydney
Italian Consulate General
The Gateway, Level 45
1 Macquarie Place
NSW 2000 Sydney
(02) 93 927 900
fax (02) 92 524 830

In New Zealand

Wellington
Italian Embassy-Consular Section
34-38 Grant Road
P.O. Box 463
Thorndon, Wellington
(644) 47 353 39
fax (644) 47 272 55

How to Dress

Because much of Italian life is spent outside the home—in *piazze,* cafés, and strolling from one shop to another—emphasis on dress is key. Most Italians, especially those that live in major urban areas like Florence and

Rome, tend to dress up for all occasions, sporting the latest styles and colors. Italy is known the world over for its leather, suede, and silk apparel, and the appeal of these fabrics is not lost on the ever-stylish Italians. People here even wear jeans with a sense of flair, complementing them with trendy shoes, a bold belt, or a suit jacket.

So, where does this leave you, the tourist, who prefers baggy jeans to slacks and comfortable sneakers to loafers? When going out, always err on the side of dressing up. Men should bring at least one dress shirt and tie if planning to dine at an upscale restaurant. Women can get away with wearing a casual dress, a skirt-and-blouse ensemble, or sensible trousers. If your night involves a tour of the club circuit, keep in mind that jeans are a faux pas, unless you're going to a pub, and sneakers are best left in the hotel room (if not in your closet back home). If you're in doubt, choose something simple in black.

Not only must you worry about your nighttime garb, but also what you wear while sight-seeing. Churches throughout Italy impose a strict dress code for visitors. The guards at St. Peter's Basilica will turn you away if you're wearing shorts or a sleeveless shirt. Women should not wear short skirts if their daily schedule involves a visit inside a church. Long skirts or skirts that hit several inches below the knee are best for basilica browsing. These rules may be difficult to adhere to on days when the mercury soars. But, if you want to ensure that your plans go ahead as scheduled, heed this advice—and bring along a light cardigan. On the other hand, if you plan to while away the day throwing coins into the Trevi Fountain or trekking through Roman ruins, wear whatever keeps you comfortable.

As for winter dressing, think layers. An Italian will layer a jacket on top of a sweater on top of a dress shirt, then pull it all together with a cozy wool scarf and stylish leather gloves. Bringing a assortment of shirts and sweaters of variable weights will ensure that you don't melt while inside a hot department store, or that you won't get caught unprepared during an early burst of springtime.

A Word on Tourist Garb

White sneakers, baseball caps, and fanny packs are all dead giveaways that you are a tourist, making you unwittingly a target for pickpockets, rogue taxi drivers, and other schemers. Of course, we want you to feel as comfortable as possible while traveling in Italy—and, often, having our favorite clothes on-hand makes us feel at ease, too—but there are ways to enjoy yourself while blending in.

Consider packing a pair of good walking shoes, like leather loafers or cushy sandals, instead of your worn-out pair of gym shoes. Pack two pairs of shoes—one for touring and one for hitting the town. When packing, we often pick out our shoes *first,* then plan our suitcase wardrobe around them.

As for day bags, we find that the less conspicuous, the better. Go for zippered tote bags in neutral shades that are large enough to accommodate a camera, film, this guidebook, an umbrella, a water bottle, and any other necessity you will need throughout the day. Don't forget to bring along your money belt—otherwise, find a secure place (perhaps a zippered side pocket) for your wallet. And never, ever leave your bag unzipped or unattended. Be sure to leave your valuable jewelry at home, as there is no sense in drawing undue attention to yourself.

If you're having trouble leaving your Dallas Cowboys sweatshirt or your cut-off shorts at home, then think of your vacation to Italy as your chance to become European for a short while. If there's anywhere that you should wear your classier duds, it's here. Once you get your trip photos back, you'll see what we mean.

Part Three

Arriving, Getting Oriented, and Departing

Arriving and Departing

The only days that you really need to be on your toes are the days you arrive and depart from your destination. Be aware, be on time—but don't be stressed. Below, we have provided detailed information about getting to and from the airport, riding the train, renting a car, changing money, and so on, which should help curb—or, hopefully, eliminate—any anxious feelings you may have about the travel process.

Beating Jet Lag

Central European Time (CET), Italy's time zone, is six hours ahead of Eastern Standard Time (EST) and nine hours ahead of Pacific Standard Time (PST). The majority of flights from North America depart in the early evening, arriving in Italy between the hours of 8 a.m. and noon. Of course, even if your watch indicates that it's midmorning when you arrive, your body clock will still think it's the middle of the night. Here are a few tips to help you cope with what is perhaps the worst aspect of international travel:

- Try to exercise the day of your flight. Good circulation and fatigued muscles will make it easier to fall asleep during the flight.

- Opt for water or juice instead of caffeinated soda or alcohol. Dehydration exacerbates the grogginess that accompanies jet lag.

- Take melatonin. Many travelers swear by this herbal sleep aid. Of course, consult your physician before using this product.

- Avoid taking a nap when you arrive at your destination. Instead, take a stroll or do some lazy sight-seeing. Chances are, once you're out and about and stretching your legs, you will likely forget just how tired you are. If you must take a nap, make it a short one.

- Turn in early on your first night, but not too early. A long night's sleep at the beginning of your trip should get you on track for the rest of your vacation.

Airports in Central Italy

The largest and most modern airport in Central Italy is Rome's Leonardo da Vinci airport, more often called **Fiumicino** (airport code: FCO). Fiumicino handles the most volume, and is the most popular "airport-of-call" for travelers visiting Florence, Rome, and points south. Travelers heading to Florence and other parts of Tuscany may also want to consider **Pisa International Airport** (airport code: PSA). Named after Galileo Galilei, Pisa's airport is ideal for its central location. It also has a convenient train connection to Florence. Other, smaller airports in Central Italy are **Ciampino** (in Rome), **Peretola** (in Florence), **San Egidio** (in Perugia), and **Falconara** (in Ancona).

Leonardo da Vinci Airport (Fiumicino)

Served by Alitalia, American Airlines, British Airways, Continental, Delta, Lufthansa, Qantas, and many others, Rome's Fiumicino is the Italian hub of most major airlines. The airport is divided into three terminals—A, B, and C—and has undergone a long period of renovation, giving way to more gates, better signage, and improved services. Long- and short-term parking lots, available via Terminals A and B, have also been expanded.

Terminals B and C handle both international arrivals and departures, while Terminal A is for domestic arrivals and departures (though B also services some domestic flights). Most likely, you will arrive at Terminal C, where you can claim your luggage. After you pick up your bags, you'll go through Customs for passport checks and luggage searches. Then you'll proceed to the covered walkway that leads to the train station, or outdoors to ground transportation. The Arrivals halls in Terminal C also contains a 24-hour left luggage office, a post office, a lost luggage desk (06 656 349 56), and several currency exchange offices. Terminal B offers similar services in its Arrivals hall. Both terminals are well connected to ground transportation.

Traveling to Rome from Fiumicino

Chances are, if you've flown into Rome's Fiumicino airport, you've arrived at your final destination, or, at the least, you are planning to stay a few days in Rome before heading off to the next stop on your itinerary. Now you must make the crucial decision: Will you take a taxi, train, or bus to your hotel?

If you do not have a lot of luggage, your best bet is to take the train. From Fiumicino, there is both a local and an express train into Rome. Another option is to take one of the COTRAL buses that stops near the International Arrivals hall. (Night buses are also available. But chances are, if you took a direct flight here, you'll arrive very early in the morning.) If you're pressed for time, your luggage is unwieldy, and you've got money to burn, take a cab. A taxi from the airport to the center of Rome should cost approximately €40–€45. This includes the standard airport-to-city rate plus the cost of handling two pieces of luggage. Unfortunately, predicting a cab fare in Rome is not as exact a science as in New York City.

Train Service and the "Leonardo Express"   Your fastest and most reliable transportation option to the city is the train. Both an escalator and elevator in Terminal C connect to a walkway that leads directly to the station.

When you arrive in the covered train terminal, you will see a board listing train arrivals *(arrivi)* and departures *(partenze)*. Trains run every 15 to 30 minutes from 5:57 a.m.–11:27 p.m. each day, so you won't have to wait too long to make your connection. You can buy train tickets from machines, the ticket office, the Alitalia desk, the airport *tabacchi,* or from the small kiosk near the entrance to the train terminal.

The local train to Tiburtina (a small depot in Rome, see more under "Arriving and Departing by Train") departs the airport every 15 minutes during the day, and every 30 minutes from 9:27 p.m.–11:27 p.m., making stops at Termini Station (Rome's main train depot) as well as at Trastevere, Ostiense (near Metro stop Piramide), Tuscolana, and, finally, Tiburtina. The ride lasts approximately 30–45 minutes, and costs €4.50.

For €8.80, you can take the "Leonardo Express" train, which travels every 30 minutes nonstop to Termini Station. Even though it doesn't make any stops along the way, the express train doesn't save you much time, taking about 30 minutes to reach its destination. However, we feel that the train merits an extra €4 simply because the ride is smooth and the double-decker cars are usually immaculate.

Make sure to validate *(convalida)* your ticket by stamping it in one of the yellow boxes located at the head of the platform before boarding the train.

Taxis   Rogue taxi drivers like to hang out at Rome's airports and train stations to prey on unsuspecting tourists. Such men—and they are always men—will approach you whispering "taxi," or may even surprise you with a little bit of English. These normal-looking chaps seem like bona fide cabbies, until they drop you off at your hotel and demand an exorbitant amount of money for a merely decent ride.

Taxi jockeys are a big problem in Italy, bilking numerous tourists out of cash. When you get to Fiumicino, ignore anyone who asks you if you need a cab and proceed to the taxi ranks. There, you will see authorized yellow or white taxicabs, usually from the company Radio Taxi, waiting for your fare. Ask first what the price will be (this should be done every time you take a cab). The driver will quote you a fare, not inclusive of luggage surcharges. Fares to the city center range from €31–€34, plus a €8 airport surcharge and the luggage surcharge.

Bus Service between Rome and Fiumicino Consider taking the bus between the airport and your destination as a last resort. Train service is quicker, cleaner, and much more dependable. However, if you find yourself stuck in the airport after 10:30 p.m. or need to get to the airport before 5 a.m., there is a night bus that runs between Fiumicino and Tiburtina train station. From Fiumicino, buses leave at 1:15 a.m., 2:15 a.m., 3:30 p.m., and 5 p.m. From Tiburtina, buses leave at 12:30 p.m., 1:15 a.m., 2:30 a.m., and 3:45 a.m. You can purchase tickets (approximately €3.50) from an automatic vendor in either station. Keep in mind that both Tiburtina and Fiumicino can be quite unsavory places to be during the wee hours, so we don't recommend this service. However, given that the wait time between buses is more than an hour, you'll probably feel like giving in and springing for a taxi anyhow.

Car Rental Before you go, you can reserve a car from either Avis or Hertz. Both companies have rental offices at Fiumicino and throughout Rome.

Avis (phone (800) 230-4898 U.S., (800) 272-5871 Canada; **www. avis.com**) has two locations in the city: at Via Sardegna (near the Villa Borghese; 06 428 247 28) and at Termini Station (06 481 4373). Avis's office at Fiumicino Airport (06 650 115 31) is open daily from 7 a.m. to midnight.

Hertz (phone (800) 654-3131 U.S., (800) 263-0600 Canada, **www. hertz.com**) has multiple locations in Rome. The most convenient are at the Villa Borghese (Via del Galoppatoio, 33; 06 321 6831), Vatican City (Via Gregorio VII, 207; 06 393 788 08), Termini Station (06 474 0389), and Fiumicino (06 650 115 53). If you're staying at the Cavalieri Hilton Hotel, you can pick up or drop off your rental car at the Hertz location there (06 353 437 58).

Other car rental companies in the area include **Maggiore Budget** (Fiumicino Airport; 06 650 106 78), **Thrifty** (Fiumicino Airport; 06 652 9134), and **Europcar** (Fiumicino Airport; 06 650 108 79).

Ciampino Airport

It is highly unlikely that you will be flying into Rome's Ciampino Airport. The Eternal City's second airport, Ciampino handles only a low volume of European flights, budget airlines, charter flights, and military craft. For more information about Ciampino airport, call 06 794 941.

Galileo Galilei Airport (Pisa International)

Pisa International Airport, served by Alitalia, British Airways, Lufthansa, Air France, and a handful of smaller carriers, is, according to its website, "growing." Judging by that statement, it means that airlines flying into here are offering more competitive fares. If you plan to base your entire trip in Tuscany, then you may want to fly into Pisa International. The airport is about 20 minutes from downtown Pisa and connected by rail to Florence, an hour-and-a-half train ride away. For more information, phone 050 500 707, or look up **www.pisa-airport.com**.

Lost Luggage

Call Pisa International's Baggage Assistance office at 050 849 400 should your bags end up missing or damaged.

Travel To and From Pisa International Airport

As the largest international airport in Tuscany, Pisa International has long been the best option for travelers visiting Pisa, Florence, Siena, and the surrounding towns. As a result, you'll find numerous transportation options from the airport to wherever you are going.

Train   Direct train service to Florence's Santa Maria Novella train station is available from Pisa's airport. Trains run between the two stops about once an hour between 10:30 a.m. and 5:45 p.m. The train service is a boon to travelers, but it was designed more for commuters between Pisa and Florence. (This explains the irregular train schedule after 6 p.m.) Tickets cost €4.50, and you can purchase them on the platform.

When departing from Florence, if you're flying Alitalia, you can even check your bags at the Alitalia desk located on the platform in Santa Maria Novella.

Amerigo Vespucci Airport (Peretola)

The airport in Florence, also known as Peretola, has only recently begun accepting international flights, which explains why the airport is so small. Only two terminals—one for arrivals and one for departures— make up the Florence airport, and they include, simply, a lost luggage desk, two baggage carousels, one coffee bar, and one exchange desk (in the Departures hall). If you arrive or depart from Peretola, you can take the convenient Volainbus (literally, "Fly by Bus") service, operated jointly by the ATAF and SITA bus lines, which takes about 20 minutes from the terminal to Santa Maria Novella train station. Tickets can be purchased on board the bus and cost €4. Meanwhile, taxi ranks are right outside the Arrivals hall. Most cab drivers are well-informed about flight arrivals, so you shouldn't have to wait long should you choose to taxi in. Cab rides between the airport and the city center last about 20 minutes and cost approximately €16, with an extra surcharge for luggage. For more information, phone 055 373 498, or look up **www.aeroporto.firenze.it**.

Umbria International Airport (San Egidio)

The airport at Perugia, known as Aeroporto Internazionale dell'Umbria, or, by its shorter name, San Egidio, handles a very low volume of domestic routes to and from Milan's Malpensa Airport and international flights. You may opt to fly into San Egidio if your itinerary consists mostly of destinations in Umbria and the Marches.

Buses run from San Egidio to Perugia's main square, Piazza Italia, and to its main train station, four times daily, at 10:50 a.m., 2:10 p.m., 5:45 p.m., and 9:30 p.m. A one-way bus ticket costs €2.50. Bus connections are meant to coincide with flight arrivals, but this isn't always the case, given circumstances such as flight delays. If this happens to you, proceed to the bank of taxis waiting outside the Arrivals hall. Cab fare should not cost more than €35, including luggage handling and tip.

You can also rent a car at San Egidio, as **Avis** (075 692 9346), **Budget** (075 500 7499), **Hertz** (075 500 2439), and **Europcar** (075 573 1704) have desks at the airport. If you choose this mode of transportation, consider booking before you leave to save time. For more information about San Egidio airport, call 075 592 141.

Changing Money at the Airport

If you weren't able to secure some euros before your trip, you will probably need to change money at the airport so that you can take a cab, bus, or train to your hotel. Unfortunately, airport exchange offices often charge higher commission fees and have poorer rates than what you'd find at an exchange office in town.

If you are carrying a large amount of cash (which we don't recommend), exchange just a portion of it at the airport exchange desk, and save the rest for later when you can scout out better rates. Better yet, look to see if there is an ATM in the vicinity of the exchange office. Often, there is. ATMs usually offer the best exchange rates, but check with your bank before you leave to see what they charge for withdrawing cash from foreign ATMs. If the fee per transaction is unusually large, you will want to take out a larger amount of money at one time. Remember that if you choose to take a taxi into town, you should have at least €50 to €70 on hand for cab fare and the inevitable surcharges.

Departing

Ideally, you'll just want to reverse your steps from your arrival. Make sure that you arrive at the airport at least two hours before your flight is scheduled to leave. Murphy's Law suggests that you'll get stuck behind a large tour group when you're the most pressed for time. Also note that these days it takes considerably longer to go through security checkpoints, as baggage is sometimes checked two or three times. Nonstop flights from Europe to North America generally leave late in the morning, between 10 a.m. and noon. If you must first make a connection at another European destination before flying home, be prepared to arrive at the airport at the break of dawn.

Confirming Your Flight: Reaching the Airlines

Don't be surprised if you call up Alitalia in the middle of the day and get no answer. Even airline desks tend to keep typical Italian business hours, meaning that they close an hour or two for lunch. This is incredibly frustrating, especially for Americans who expect companies within the service sector to remain on-call 24/7. To ease anxiety, try to call your airline during business hours a day or two before your flight. If you must call around lunchtime, give it a shot. Someone may answer the phone after hearing it ring a dozen times.

Fiumicino Information	06 659 51
Ciampino Information	06 794 941
Pisa International Information	050 500 707
Peretola Information	055 373 498
San Egidio Information	075 592 141

AIRLINE CONTACT INFORMATION IN ITALY

Airline	Phone	Web
Air Canada	06 655 7117	www.aircanada.com
Air France	06 487 9155	www.airfrance.com
Alitalia	800 551 350 (toll free)	www.alitalia.com
American Airlines	02 679 144 00	www.aa.com
British Airways	848 825 125 (toll free)	www.british-airways.com
Continental	06 489 005 37	www.continental.com
Delta	167 864 114 (toll free)	www.delta.com
KLM	800 800 193 (toll free)	www.klm.com
Lufthansa	06 46 601	www.lufthansa.com
SAS	06 420 136 19	www.scandinavian.net
TWA	02 748 664 01	www.twa.com
United Airlines	02 482 9800	www.ual.com

Getting to the Airport on Time

Now that airport security is increasingly vigilant, you will want to make sure that you arrive at the airport at least two hours before your flight. To be on the safe side, make it three. You never know what type of line you might encounter at the ticket desk, and you may want to allow yourself some time to browse through the duty-free shops before you begin your long, restless trip back home.

If you're staying in the center of Florence, allow yourself one hour to get to the airport, no matter if you're taking the taxi or bus. If you're staying in Florence and your plane leaves from Pisa International, plan for an even longer commute of up to two-and-a-half hours from door to door. You may even want to stay in Pisa the night before your flight to make things easier. If you're staying in Rome, give yourself between 45 minutes and an hour-and-a-half to get to either Fiumicino or Ciampino. For any other destination not served by an airport, use common sense and ask the concierge or front desk.

If you have rented a car, inquire with the rental agency to determine their policy on returning the car. Perhaps you can return the car the night before at a location that is more convenient to your hotel. Some rental agencies, like Hertz, will even let you drop off the car at an alternate location within the same city with little or no charge. If you've made it this far, you know that driving in Italy is nerve-wracking; there's no need to add to your stress level if you don't have to.

Claiming Your VAT Refund on Purchases

You can't avoid paying sales tax in Italy, as an Imposta di Valore Aggiunto (IVA) tax is included in the cost of most everything. However, if you live outside the European Union community, you can claim a value-added tax refund on some purchases upon leaving Italy. Look for stores that display the "Global Refund/Tax Free Shopping" sign. Then, if you spend approximately €155 or more in the same store on the same day, you qualify for a "tax free check." You must fill out a special form and have it stamped at the store where you make your purchases. When leaving Italy, present the form, the receipt from your purchase, and the item(s) purchased to Customs (Dogane). You can then proceed to the **Global Refund** desk, where you can apply for your refund. In most cases, you can get your refund on the spot, either in cash or credited to a bank account or credit card. You can also choose to have the refund payment mailed to you at a later date. Further information about VAT refunds is available from the **Directorate of Customs Services** at 06 502 420 51 (in Italy). The European Union also has information about value-added tax laws on its website at **www.eurunion.org**. Global Refund, the most recognized refund company in Europe, has information about the VAT refund on its website at **www.globalrefund.com**.

Arriving and Departing by Train

Maybe you have concocted a dream vacation in Europe, one in which you fly into Paris and wind your way via rail through the French countryside and the Swiss Alps into northern Italy and further on toward the Umbrian hill town of Spello. You're in luck. Most Italians rely on the train to get them from Point A to Point B—and even to points X, Y, and Z. So you can bet that almost any town you choose will have a train depot, however small. Look for more detailed information on train stations, including Florence's Santa Maria Novella Station and Rome's Termini Station, in the chapters on Tuscany, Latium, Umbria, and the Marches.

Train Reservations and Tickets

At first glance, it may seem daunting to step up to the ticket window and ask for two round-trip tickets. But, don't worry. The ticket agent has seen your type before. And, in many cases, his English will be good enough for you to carry out your purchase without a hitch.

If you're traveling to a tiny dot on the map, we suggest that you consult a ticket agent to make sure that you get on the right train. However, if you're a savvy traveler—and hate wasting even a second by standing in line—you can now buy tickets from a ticket kiosk, featured at many of the larger train stations. Termini Station has a whole bank of kiosks at its Piazza Repubblica entrance, for instance, and a there are a few cached away near the information office at the far end of Santa Maria Novella Station. Buying a ticket from a kiosk can't be easier—as long it's in working order. Just waltz up to the machine, touch the British/American flag on the screen (indicating instructions in English), and begin the process. You can pay with either cash or credit card by choosing the particular option when the time comes to pay. Don't be surprised if an Italian asks you for help—you'll look like you know what you're doing.

Kiosks also allow you to check schedules for travel between any station within the national rail system, called the Ferrovie dello Stato, or "FS" (eff-ay ess-ay), for short. If the kiosks are out of order, or if too many savvy travelers are waiting to use them, you can use the low-tech way of finding information on arrivals and departures. Look for signs marked "Arrivi" (arrivals) and "Partenze" (departures)—usually located in the most highly trafficked area of the station.

If you'd like to check schedules *before* you leave home, you can click on **www.trenitalia.com**, the official website of Italy's national rail system. Note that when you plug in the dates of your journey, you should type the day first, then the month.

Lockers and Left Luggage

For starters, don't confuse the terms "left luggage" and "lost luggage." Left-luggage desks at airports and train stations are designed for travelers who want to stash their bags during a long layover or short day trip. Rome's Termini Station has a left-luggage service, located at the top of Platforms 1 and 22. The office is open daily from 5:15 a.m. until 2 a.m. Meanwhile, Santa Maria Novella's left-luggage office, located near Track 16, is open daily from 4:15 a.m. until 1:30 a.m. Both stations charge approximately €2.60 per bag for up to 12 hours, payable up front. Be sure to keep your receipt in a safe place, so that you can present it to the left luggage staff when you retrieve your bags. As for lockers, many airports and train stations are phasing them out, fearing they are a security risk. We've always been a bit skeptical about using lockers on our travels.

If you must dump your bags for a while, keep in mind that most hotels will store your luggage for a few hours after you check out for no charge.

Lost and Found

The FS (national rail company) runs a general lost-and-found *(oggetti rinvenuti)* office. Call 06 473 066 82 if you have lost anything of value.

Eurail Passes

The Eurail pass has long been the backpacker's passport to Europe. Allowing train travelers to zoom quickly and (almost) effortlessly between 17 European countries, the pass is a smart idea if you plan to "country-hop," or if you wish to travel extensively throughout Italy. Eurail passes can be purchased in increments of 8, 15, 21, or 30 days from your travel agent, or from **www.raileurope.com**.

If you are limiting your vacation to the areas covered in this book (Tuscany, Latium, Umbria, and the Marches), a Eurail pass is not advised. Travel on Italy's regular train system is incredibly cheap, and the distance between most destinations is negligible. If you do choose to purchase any type of Eurail pass, note that a pass does not ensure a reservation aboard a train. You must pay a supplement to reserve a seat, and this can be done either at your departing station's ticket window or aboard the train.

Is It Worthwhile to Go First Class?

Many first-time train travelers in Italy will mistakenly purchase first-class rail tickets, thinking that the difference between first class and second class is as wide as the one between first and coach classes on a jetliner. What we have found is that the first-class cars are generally cleaner and quieter. But they sure ain't swank.

If you're traveling a short distance, you should opt for second class. In fact, many short-haul trains don't even offer you the choice of first class. Of course, if you're traveling longer distances, it's your call whether you want first- or second-class tickets. The majority of Italians, from businessmen to servicemen to grandmothers, ride second class, providing you with incredible people-watching opportunities and, inevitably, more colorful tales to tell upon your arrival back home.

Arriving and Departing by Car

Get ready for a wild ride! Whether you're streaking down the *autostrada* (Italy's answer to the autobahn), or navigating your way through claustrophobic, cobbled streets, your driving experience in Italy will be one you'll want to put on paper—or banish from your memory completely. New York taxi drivers seem tame compared to average Italian drivers who regularly run lights, speed up at pedestrian crosswalks, blast their horns, and burn rubber at the first sight of open road. Italian friends have told this author that traffic laws are merely "traffic suggestions" when it comes to driving; this is hardly an exaggeration.

Rules of the Road

If you possess a driving license from the United States or Canada, you are allowed to drive in Italy. However, the law requires that you also carry with you a translation of your license. You can obtain this from the **Automobile Club Italiano** (ACI) in Rome (Via Marsala, 8; 00185 Rome; phone 06 499 81, fax 06 499 824 69) or from an ACI office in any province. If this proves too much of a hassle, you're better off getting an International Driving License. AAA offices in North America can issue you an international license for a small fee. International Driving Licenses are valid for one year.

Gas

Rather expensive in Italy and the rest of Europe, a liter of gas *(benzina)* costs roughly the same as a gallon of gas back home. Gas is heavily taxed in Europe, on the one hand to encourage more people to use public transportation, and on the other, to alleviate air pollution. A number of cars still run on diesel *(gasolio)* fuel. However, all rental cars run on unleaded *(senza piombo)*. Service stations on the *autostrada* are required to be open 24 hours a day, while city service stations observe business hours (7:30 a.m.–12:30 p.m., and 3–7 p.m.).

Traffic

Traffic in city centers is atrocious, and should be deterrent enough from driving, should your plans include only Florence and/or Rome. Many city centers, including the narrow medieval streets of Siena, are completely closed to all traffic except taxis and cars picking up or dropping off passengers at hotels. Additionally, many streets in Florence are open to traffic only during certain hours of the day, usually before 8 a.m. and after 6 p.m. Choose public transportation if you're staying in town. It's the most reliable and least stressful way to get from here to there.

Conversely, if you will be spending the majority of your time in the countryside, you needn't worry too much about traffic. The winding, open road is a reality in Chianti and many other provinces. You can get more information about the motorways in Italy by logging on to **www.autostrade.it,** which has details about service stations, construction work, and a map of general routes.

Understanding Those First Signs and Getting Directions

It's bad enough getting lost, but getting lost in a foreign country where few speak your language can be scary. So, try to equip yourself with a few useful Italian words and phrases before you embark on your adventure. Face it—you'll need to ask for directions at some point. (Note that bolded syllables signify stress.)

Scusi, dove sono i servizi? [**Scoo**-zee, **doh**-vay **so**-no ee sair-**veetz**-ee?] Excuse me, where is the restroom?

Scusi, dove posso trovare un taxi? [**Scoo**-zee, **doh**-vay **pohs**-so tro-**vahr**-ay **oon** taxi?] Excuse me, where can I find a taxi?

Scusi, dove posso noleggiare una macchina? [**Scoo**-zee, **doh**-vay **pohs**-so no-ledge-**jah**-ray **oon**-a **mack**-ee-na?] Excuse me, where can I rent a car?

Scusi, dove posso comprare una carta telefonica? [**Scoo**-zee, **doh**-vay **pohs**-so com-**prahr**-ay **oon**-a **kart**-ah tay-lay-**fone**-ee-ka?] Excuse me, where can I buy a phone card?

Scusi, dove posso trovare un bancomat? [**Scoo**-zee, **doh**-vay **pohs**-so tro-**vahr**-ay **oon bahnc**-o-mat?] Excuse me, where can I find an ATM?

Destra [**des**-trah] Right

Sinistra [see-**nee**-stra] Left

Avanti [ah-**vahn**-tee] forward, straight ahead

Per favore [**pair** fah-**vohr**-ay] please

Grazie [**grahts**-ee-ay] Thank you

Prego [**pray**-go] You're welcome

Talking Transportation

Need some help with your Italian vocabulary? The words and phrases below will help you navigate the world of transportation, Italian style:

Autobus [**ow**-toe-boos] Bus

Pullman Coach

Taxi Taxi

Treno [**train**-o] Train

Tram Tram

Stazione [**stahts**-ee-yo-nay] Station

Biglietto/i [bill-**yet**-o/ee] Ticket/s

Solo andata [**so**-lo ahn-**dah**-tah] One way

Andata e ritorno [ahn-**dah**-tah ay ree-**torn**-o] Round trip

Fermata [**fair**-mah-tah] Stop

Prossima fermata [**pros**-seem-ah **fair**-mah-tah] Next stop

Capolinea [**kap**-o-**leen**-ya] Starting point, or, literally, head of the line

Binario [bee-**nahr**-ee-o] Train platform

Entrata [en-**traht**-ah] Entrance

Uscita [oo-**sheet**-ah] Exit

Scende la prossima? [**shin**-day **la pros**-seem-ah] Are you getting off at the next stop? (A frequent question heard on Rome's packed Metro trains and buses. If you're not getting off, then you should give way to those who are.)

Telephone, E-mail, and Postal Services

That First Phone Call

Calling home from Italy shouldn't be a chore, but it is often an obstacle for travelers straight out of the gate. Right away, the dial tone sounds a bit funny—a low, dull tone, rather than the usual treble hum. Then, you have to take into account country codes, area codes, phone cards, calling cards, operators, and a whole host of other things to confuse you.

A Prominent Word on Calling Italy

If you're like us, you are terribly annoyed by guidebooks that forget to give you dialing instructions both to and from Italy. So, that said, if you wish to **call from North America to Italy,** dial 011 39, then the number. Remember that "39" is the country code for Italy. When placing a **call from Italy to North America,** dial 001, then the area code and number. For example, if you are calling Rome's Fiumicino Airport from your home in Denver, dial 011 39 06 659 51. From within Rome, dial 06 659 51. Rome's area code is 06, while Florence's area code is 055. When placing **domestic calls within Italy,** you must dial the area code. Another thing you may find a bit confusing about the phone numbers in Italy is that they tend to have no rhyme or reason whatsoever. You may find that some places, like taxi companies, for instance, have only a four-digit phone number, while others have a six- or seven-digit number. It seems that whenever Telecom Italia exhausts its list of four-digit numbers, it moves on to five-digit numbers, and so on. Note that toll-free numbers (*numeri verdi*) usually begin with 800. To reach directory assistance, dial 12 (limited English).

Wait until you get to your hotel or a friend's residence before making your first call. You'll feel more relaxed and you'll be able to place your call in peace and quiet. Most hotel phones require that you dial "0" or "9" before you dial out. Don't forget to consider the time difference before you call your loved ones. They may be thrilled that you made it to Italy—but they might not want to hear about it at 4 a.m.!

Come Prepared

If you plan to use the calling card issued by your domestic telephone company while you are in Italy, call the company beforehand to inquire about international phone plans. Many offer one-country calling plans that can save you a chunk of change, as long as the international calls made are only between your home country and the country you have chosen for the plan. For instance, Sally from Cincinnati signs up for the "Italy plan," which charges her only $0.25 per minute to call to and from

Italy, as opposed to the regular $1 per minute (connection fees not included). Such a plan works the other way, too, making it cheaper in the days prior to your trip as you call to reconfirm your reservations with hotels, museums, and restaurants.

Almost every telephone company offers some sort of global plan these days, and most do charge a small fee (usually around $3 per month) for this service. You can sign up for the plan a month before you leave and cancel it upon return. Sure, this may create a hassle for you and some extra paperwork for the phone company, but it's your money.

Now that you've got your plan in place and calling card in hand, you're ready to go. Once in Italy, use the following toll-free numbers to connect to your phone company:

AT&T	172 1011
MCI	172 1022
Sprint	172 1877

You will reach a recording that will elicit Touch Tone responses. In some cases, you may reach the company's international operator. Inquire with AT&T, Sprint, or MCI whether they charge an additional fee for operator assistance.

Using Italian Telephones

Even though Florentine-born Antonio Meucci was the real inventor of the telephone (Alexander Graham Bell stole the idea and was wealthy enough to afford the patent registration fee), using public telephones in Italy is not a joy. Pay phones are almost always located on the loudest, busiest street or in the most crowded bar, and they are often out of order, sometimes literally ripped out of their sockets.

Once you find a phone that works, you will need to have in your possession a phone card. Very few if any pay phones in Italy still take coins. A *carta telefonica* is available at *tabacchi* (tobacconists) and newsstands, and come in increments of €1, €2.50, €5, and €8. Rates vary depending on where you call, the minimum being about €0.10 per minute for city-to-city calls. Using a phone card to phone the States is pretty useless, because the card often expires before you have a chance to say *ciao*. We recommend instead that you use a phone card and your calling card in tandem, using the former to dial up the local access number of your phone company. This method allows you to make calls on the go.

Be wary of stickers that promise "Cheap International Long Distance Rates Using Your Credit Card." These ads, which are often posted inside telephone booths, are deceptive, as they are perhaps the most expensive calling plans around.

Dialing from City to City

You must always use the area code in Italy, even if calling from place to place within the same city. Area codes start with "0" and are followed by one or two numbers. For example, Rome's area code is 06, Florence's is 055, and so on. Area codes for cell phones are usually four digits.

Using E-mail and the Internet

While many travelers would rather get away from the Horoscope-a-Day mailings and spam lists, others depend on the Internet in general and e-mail in particular to be their lifeline while abroad. Now, if you're really on vacation, you probably should avoid logging on (it's time to unplug, remember?). But, if you're a business traveler or a student, you need e-mail access to be cheap, readily available, and easy to use.

Internet cafés are "virtually" everywhere in Italy now; but it's still not all that simple to log on to your e-mail account from your hotel. Not only can it be difficult dialing out from your hotel room (see "That First Phone Call," above), but we also find that it's hard to find Internet service providers (ISPs) that maintain Italian access numbers. Recently, we stayed on hold with MSN for 20 minutes, only to find out that the only way that we could log on to our MSN account from Italy was to use the access number we usually dial.

"Don't you realize how expensive that is?" we asked.

"That's all we can tell you," the operator said.

None of this made sense, considering that MSN has quite a strong presence in Italy with its **msn.it** website. Nevertheless, if you have an account with MSN, you're better off using MSN web-based mail (Hotmail, **www.hotmail.com**) while abroad—at least you can access it at net cafés. Many other websites also offer free web-accessible e-mail, such as Yahoo! (**www.yahoo.com**).

If privacy is a big concern, you definitely will want to be able to read your e-mail in the safety of your hotel room or office. Luckily, there are a few ISPs that allow you to dial up their access numbers in Italy, though all levy expensive surcharges for this service. Keep in mind that your monthly Internet usage fee will not cover the costs of calls from your hotel.

If You Use AOL Local Dial-up ($6/hour surcharge)
Florence	055 501 5540	Pisa	050 503 694
Rome	06 651 985 04		

If You Use Compuserve ($3/hour surcharge)
Rome   06 830 209 82

If You Use Earthlink ($0.15/minute surcharge)
Ancona	071 246-0900	Florence	055 520-0900
Perugia	075 652-0900	Rome	06 8 302-0900
Siena	057 769-0900		

Pre-paid Internet Access

A new service, introduced by start-up **MaGlobe** in early 2001, allows travelers to pre-pay for Internet access before they travel, thus avoiding some of the high costs of dial-up. MaGlobe allows you to download its dial-up software and buy blocks of Internet time over its website at **www.maglobe.com.** The company's Traveler Plus card costs $29.99 and is good for up to six hours of net time abroad (and approximately 30 hours stateside). Larger increments of time are also available. Note that MaGlobe's service does not cover phone costs from your hotel. But, in the long run, it sure beats haggling with your ISP when you get home.

Internet Cafés

Internet cafés are big business in Italy, catering to tourists looking for a cheap way to communicate with friends and family back home and to the majority of Italians who do not have home, work, or school access to the Internet. Some of the bigger cafés are the NetGate (**www. thenetgate.it**), Internet Train (**www.internettrain.it**), and Easy Everything (**www.easyeverything.com**).

Using the Poste Italiane

Notoriously slow and inefficient, the **Poste Italiane,** or Italian Postal Service, will make you long for the just-adequate postal services back home. If you send a letter or postcard, don't be surprised if you make it home well before it does. Postcards and letters up to 20 grams in weight sent from Italy to the United States or Canada cost approximately €0.77. If Rome is on your itinerary, you may want to wait until you get there to send your cards. The Poste Vaticane, run by the Vatican City, is actually very competent. Perhaps they get a bit more help from the postal gods.

Buying Stamps

You can buy stamps *(francobolli* [frank-o-**bowl**-ee]*)* at authorized tobacconists *(tabacchi* [ta-**bahk**-ee]*)* or at the post office. *Tabacchi* shops are plentiful—look for a big, white **T** on a black or a blue background—so, if one shop has run out of stamps for the week, you can always try the next one on the block. Enterprising *tabacchi* in tourist areas will often sell postcards, too, so you can kill two birds with one stone. If you're mailing a bulky envelope or package, head to the post office to get the item weighed. Hold off on buying stamps if your itinerary includes a visit to the Vatican or to the Republic of San Marino. Both of the small states sell their own stamps, adding both value and conversational interest to the postcards you send home.

Money Matters

Estimating Your Budget

Use the following information as a rough indicator for the basics *per person,* noting that there are great variations in the costs of accommodations, dining out, shopping, and entertainment. These estimates are based on *two people traveling for a week.* Airfare is not included.

Airport transfers	$35–$70
Hotel room	$75 (based on a two-star property, per person, per night)
Meals	$25 (lunch and dinner, moderately-priced restaurants, per person, per day)
Museum passes	$15–$30
Miscellaneous	$50
TOTAL	**$250**

Understanding the Euro

The euro became the new, official currency of Italy and 11 other member states of the European Union on January 1, 2002. Euro notes are available in denominations of 5, 10, 20, 50, 100, 200, and 500 euros. Euro coins are available in denominations of 1, 2, 5, 10, 20, and 50 cents, and also in 1- and 2-euro denominations. All euro notes and coins display national symbols from each of the participating states. Italy's symbols include, for example, the Colosseum, Leonardo da Vinci's *Anatomy of Man,* and Botticelli's Venus from his masterpiece *The Birth of Venus.* The official abbreviation for the euro is EUR. The symbol for the euro is "€".

Changing Money

Thinking in Euros

Travelers can thank their lucky stars that they no longer have to drop a few zeros and divide by two to figure out the lira-to-dollar ratio. Since its debut on paper, the euro has been roughly equivalent to the dollar, give or take a few cents. Double-check the exchange rates before you travel (**www.oanda.com**) so you know if you're coming out ahead or short-changing yourself.

ATMs

You already know how to use them. ATMs are the most convenient way to change money, simply because you needn't trade cash for cash at all. Just insert your bank card, select the amount of cash you need (for conversions from euros to dollars, see Part One, Understanding Central Italy). Rates are almost always lower at ATMs than anywhere else.

Hotels

If you have no other options, then change your money at the hotel. But, be warned. Hotel exchange rates tend to be the highest rates around, and you'll also get killed on the commission. Hotel exchange offices in out-of-the-way places know they have a captive market.

Change Bureaus

It's not the best idea to bring a wad of cash with you in the first place. But, if you do, then the change bureau isn't the worst place to trade for euros. Change bureaus are very common in the centers of Rome and Florence, and they offer competitive rates and low commissions. Change bureaus can also handle traveler's checks and bankcard transactions. Not surprisingly, change bureaus can be attractive hangouts for schemers and pickpockets. Find a well-lit change bureau in a pedestrian zone and keep your surroundings in check. Also, be wary of people standing nearby who offer you a better rate than the exchange bureau. These types prey on naive tourists who can't differentiate euros from rubels. You could end up with counterfeit money and a fine, if the cops catch you.

American Express Travel Offices

AMEX card members can use the travel office to buy or exchange traveler's checks, wire money, or replace lost or stolen cards. Additionally, the AMEX Travel Office in Florence allows cardholders to send or receive e-mail using a special AMEX e-mail account.

American Express Travel Services, Florence
Via Dante Alighieri, 22r
50122 Florence
055 509 81
fax 055 509 82 81
amexfirenze@cdc.it

American Express Foreign Exchange Service, Rome
Largo Caduti di El Alamein, 9
00173 Rome
06 722 80 308
fax 06 722 2753

Banking in Italy

Several hundred independent banks, savings and loans, and financial institutions cloud the banking landscape of Italy. The banking profession was practically invented here by the Romans, and, in fact, Monte dei Paschi, founded in 1472 in Siena, is the oldest bank in the world. In fact, it sometimes feels that Italy's banks are still living in the past: Long queues, short hours, and inescapable paperwork are still the hallmarks of banking here.

Dear traveler, you're in luck! Unless you are staying in Italy for a long period of time, and need to open an account, you probably won't need to deal with bank tellers at all. Automatic cash machines are everywhere—especially in the big cities—begging for you to make a withdrawal. However, we've found that it pays (literally) to use ATMs at some of the bigger banks. Their financial affiliations tend to be more extensive (i.e., they have relations with Visa, MasterCard, and the Plus Network), and they are more apt to replenish their money supply on a regular basis. Below, a listing of banks to look for in Central Italy:

Tuscany
Monte dei Paschi di Siena
Cassa di Risparmio di Firenze
Cassa di Risparmio di Pisa

Latium
Banca di Roma
Banca Popolare dell'Etruria e del
   Lazio

Umbria
Banca dell'Umbria
Cassa di Risparmio di Perugia

The Marches
Banca delle Marche
Banca Popolare di Ancona
Cassa di Risparmio di Áscoli
   Piceno

Getting in the Bank Door

So, you need to go to the bank to exchange money, get a cash advance, or wire money. The problem is, just how do you get in? Italy's bank security is much more stringent than that in other countries, a response to one too many armed robberies and other crimes. Thus, customers are now required to enter *one at a time* in order to allow the bank security guard to monitor each patron's movement.

First, before you even attempt to step inside, take note of the lockers just outside the main bank door. If you're carrying a large pack, security will require that you place your bag in one of the (free) lockers, taking only the locker key and your wallet with you into the bank. Next, you will encounter a set of cylindrical glass doors—much like something you'd see in Star Trek. Press the green button and wait for the door to open. Once the door is fully open, step inside. (Don't worry—you won't be sucked into a chute somewhere.) Once inside, the doors will close behind you, then the second set of doors will open. You're inside! Too bad the bank service isn't as rigidly efficient. To get out, retrace your steps. And don't forget to retrieve your bag from the locker.

Getting Money Wired

If you need money sent to you or you need to send money to someone else, you can depend on **Western Union** (**www.westernunion.com**) to do the job. With outlets at many exchange offices and most post offices in Italy, Western Union can transfer money to just about anywhere. The way it works is that someone back home contacts Western Union and wires a specific amount of dollars to you. That person will then need to phone you to give you the transaction code. Once you have the code, you can go anywhere you see a Western Union sign and say that you would like to pick up a wire transfer. Give them the code, show them your passport, and they will give you the equivalent amount of money in euros. The whole process takes about 20 minutes. If your wallet has been stolen, your credit card company may offer to send you a cash advance using this service. In the end, this is costly—but, it's better than not having any money at all.

Using Credit Cards

For those of us who dream of a paperless society, it is surprising to see that there are restaurants, shops, and other merchants in Italy that still don't accept credit cards. Credit cards are much more widely accepted in Italy now than they were, say, ten years ago. No doubt, this stems from the fact that so many of us plastic lovers who vacation in Italy spend even more when we can use our AMEX, Visa, and MasterCard. (Not to mention, we like the protection it gives us should we dispute a charge.)

But, as strange as it may sound, there are still first-class eateries right in the middle of tourist-laden Florence that don't take plastic. Double-check the front door of a shop or the menu of a restaurant to make sure that they take credit cards, should that be the type of currency you wish to deal in. If you're still not sure, ask the maître d' before sitting down to dinner. Don't forget, however, that sometimes the most authentic restaurants are the ones that don't take credit cards.

As for accommodations, there are very few hotels that don't take credit cards, though quite a number of family-run inns and bed-and-breakfasts only accept cash. Before you reserve, ask.

Note that we have listed at the end of this chapter the customer-service phone numbers in Italy for American Express, MasterCard, and Visa.

Traveler's Checks

Most large hotels and upscale restaurants accept traveler's checks, preferably in euros. If you use traveler's checks in dollar denominations, the dollar amount will usually be converted into euros before change is made. Many exchange offices will let you exchange traveler's checks for euros, but most will accept only American Express Traveler's Cheques.

Tipping

Most restaurant menus will tell you if service is included. Almost always a *pane e coperto* charge—a supplement that covers the table at which you are sitting and the basket of bread upon it—is tacked onto dining checks, usually approximately €2 per person. In fact, for the most part, tips are included in the price of most services. But, as Americans are pre-programmed to tip, Italians have come to expect a little extra change for a job well done (or adequately done). Here is a general guideline to tipping in Italy:

Waitstaff and bartenders   Round up to the nearest euro for meal tabs, and tip at least €1 for each drink you purchase from a bartender.

Taxis   Round up the fare. If you received particularly good service or advice, throw in extra.

Porters   €1 per bag.

Room service/housekeeping   €2–€5 per day.

Concierge   Not necessary to tip, unless they are extremely helpful with bookings or advice.

Hairdressers   15–20% of the service.

Tour guides   Whatever you can spare, preferably €5 minimum. Many tour guides are students who work solely on commission.

Things the Locals Already Know

Getting an English-language Newspaper

The *International Herald Tribune, USA Today,* and British newspapers such as the *Independent* and the *Guardian,* are widely available. Business-minded travelers should look for the *Wall Street Journal Europe* and the *Financial Times.* Also, some newsstands, especially those in larger cities, may carry magazines like *Time* or *Newsweek.* It doesn't hurt to ask.

Keep in mind that you're not the only tourist craving news about home, so visit the newsstand early in the morning to ensure that you get the periodical of your choice.

Everything You Need Is at the Tabacchi Bar

From stamps *(francobolli),* to cigarettes *(sigarette),* to your morning cappuccino, the tobacconist *(tabacchi)* is Italy's answer to the convenience store. You can find *tabacchi* on almost every block in major cities, and you'll find at least one or two in smaller villages. We like to call them "T Stores" because a square sign containing a large, white T on a black or blue background distinguishes them from regular bars. A list of things that you can buy at the *tabacchi*:

Cigarettes, cigars, and lighters

Stamps (though supplies don't last very long)

Bus tickets

Domestic and international phone cards

Gum and candy

Postcards

Cappuccino, espresso, and light snacks

Public Toilets

In general, public toilets in Italy are horrendous; but if you've gotta go, you've gotta go. Most public toilets *(servizi)* are located near high-traffic (and usually high-tourist) areas, and charge at least €0.50 for the privilege. Some toilets even have the nerve to charge only women. (Apparently, the men are lower maintenance.)

Even if you must pay to use the toilet, remember that the payment has no bearing on service or hygiene. Most public toilets are often severely untidy and usually lack toilet paper and/or paper towels. So, we always like to warn people to arm themselves with tissues or napkins before heading out for the day—just in case.

If you can't bear the thought of paying to relieve yourself, you may want to try asking a bar if you can use its restroom. If you ask nicely enough, you may be able to get in for free.

Health

Tap Water

In Italy, the water out of the tap is cool, clean, and 100% safe—a direct result of the ingenious Roman aqueduct system. Most Italians prefer to drink bottled water, but you needn't hesitate to get water from the faucet. Additionally, in many cities, and especially in Rome, you'll find little fountains *(fontanelle* or *nasoni)* where you can fill up a bottle of water, should you run out.

Pharmacies

Just about everything you could need, from condoms to toothbrushes to prescription drugs, is available at the pharmacy. Over-the-counter medications are few and far between in Italy, and general drugstores are almost unheard of. Because the *farmacia* (farm-a-**chee**-ah) is so vital to daily Italian life, hours of operation are convenient, usually from 8:30 a.m.–12:30 p.m. and 3–7 p.m. In larger cities, such as Florence and Rome, you'll find 24-hour pharmacies. Nighttime service is provided on a shift basis, whereby all of the pharmacies in town take turns working nights. All pharmacies are required to post their hours outside of the shop and to post the address and phone of the nearest 24-hour pharmacy. You will also be able to find a listing of 24-hour pharmacies in the local newspaper.

Prescription Medication

Bring enough prescription medications for your entire trip with you, and pack them in your carry-on. It helps to carry a copy of your prescription with you, and you may also want to ask your doctor or pharmacist what the generic name for your prescription is. Generic brands of common drugs are widely used in Italy, and, for that matter, throughout Europe, because the governments of European companies aren't as obliged to the powerful pharmaceutical lobbies. Because this is the case, some prescriptions may be cheaper than they are back home (and you may want to try to get an extra bottle or two while overseas).

Glasses and Contact Lenses

Look for an *ottica* (optical shop) if you need to buy solution for your contact lenses *(lenti a contatto)* or if you need your glasses repaired. A *foto ottica* sells prescription lenses and glasses, as well as film and photo accessories.

Travelers with Disabilities

Two service organizations, **CO.IN.** (Consorzio Cooperative Integrate) and **A.N.T.H.A.I.** (Associazione Nazionale Tutela Handicappati ed Invalidi), provide information and assistance to disabled travelers, and they have been working closely with officials in Rome to bring disabled access up to snuff. Sadly, the country still lags far behind the United States and Canada in terms of making all of its streets, libraries, government buildings, churches, hotels, museums, and monuments accessible. Since 1993, CO.IN. has published a quarterly called *Turismo per Tutti,* written in both Italian and English. If you're going to Rome, you can also request a copy of *Roma Accessibile.* Both publications are available by mail, but you will have to pay for postage. Otherwise, check with the tourist office when you arrive; they should have copies on hand (though they often don't).

Another handy service offered by CO.IN. is a disabled traveler hotline called *Vacanze Serene* (worry-free holidays). English-language operators are available from 9 a.m.–5 p.m., Monday–Friday, to answer questions on the accessibility of monuments, hotels, restaurants, theaters, parks, and other venues throughout Italy. Call 06 232 692 31 for details.

CO.IN.	A.N.T.H.A.I.
Via Enrico Giglioli, 54	Corso Vittorio Emanuele, 154
00186 Rome	00186 Rome
06 712 901 79	06 682 191 68
fax 06 712 901 40	fax 06 688 926 84
www.coinsociale.it	www.anthai.org

Hotels Equipped for Travelers with Disabilities

The sad fact is that many hotels are not equipped for handicapped visitors. Sure, the hotel will claim to have an elevator, but occasionally you have to climb or descend stairs to get to that elevator—and often it's too small to fit a standard-size wheelchair. See a list of hotels equipped for disabled access in Part Four, Hotels in Central Italy.

Using Public Transport if You're Disabled

We do not recommend that you use public transportation if you are wheelchair-bound; however there are services in place to assist you should you need to board a bus, train, or taxi. The Italian travel agency

CIT Tours (phone (800) 248-8687, **www.cit-tours.com**), now with offices in North America, can arrange for ramps and assistance at rail stations if you book train tickets through them. You can also request a special brochure from the Italian Government Tourist Office called *Services for Disabled People.* This pamphlet, published by the national rail service (FS), is updated regularly.

Restaurants and Disabled Access

Outdoor dining and ground-floor restaurants are plentiful, but many do not have wheelchair-accessible restrooms and/or the restrooms are found at the top or bottom of a flight of stairs.

Monuments and Disabled Access

Italy is coming around to equipping its monuments with ramps, elevators, and other vital equipment for wheelchair-bound visitors. For instance, the Colosseum was recently retrofitted with an elevator, allowing disabled persons unprecedented access to the ancient stadium's upper floors. On the other hand, there are many equally stunning and ancient monuments throughout Italy that can't be renovated to accommodate handicapped persons—or else the funds are not available for such work. If you have questions about accessibility for certain buildings, landmarks, and museums, contact CO.IN.'s *Vacanze Serene* line.

CO.IN. 06 712 901 79, fax 06 712 901 40

Vacanze Serene 06 232 692 31

Safety and Security

Violent crime is not common, but pickpockets, vandalism, and car theft are major epidemics in Italy. You will see signs in train stations, in airports, and on buses warning "Attenzione i borseggiatori!" (Beware of pickpockets!) Petty thieves have come up with tons of schemes to scam unknowing tourists. Most of the time, pickpockets travel in pairs—one distracts you (with flowers, fake jewelry, tourist trinkets, etc.) while the other pinches your wallet. Purse snatchers usually work alone, typically preying on unwatched backpacks and shopping bags in train stations and at outdoor cafés. Sadly, many thieves are poor immigrants or *roma* (gypsy) children, who have grown up learning the tricks of the trade. The bottom line: Don't let potential thieves think that you have something they want. Avoid wearing flashy jewelry while on vacation, and try not to be obvious if you are carrying a lot of cash. Wearing a concealed money belt around your waist is always a good precaution. If you are feeling especially vulnerable, you may want to register with your country's consulate upon arrival in Italy to make a record of your whereabouts.

Emergency Numbers

Police (Polizia) 113   **Carabinieri** 112
Fire (Vigili del Fuoco) 115   **Medical Emergencies** 118
Highway Rescue
   (Soccorso Stradale) 116

If You're a Victim of Theft ...

Nothing could be worse than being robbed or mugged during your vacation. Sadly, anyone can be a victim of theft, no matter what precautions he or she takes. If you lose your wallet, call your bank and/or credit card company *immediately* to notify them of your loss (numbers listed below). If your passport comes up missing, or if you are a victim of a more serious crime, contact your embassy or consulate for help (listings below):

AMEX   06 722 82

MasterCard   800 870 866 (toll-free from Italy)

Visa   800 819 014

United States Embassy and Consulate
Via V. Veneto, 119/A
00187 Rome
06 467 41
fax 06 467 422 17
www.usis.it

United States Consulate General in Florence
Lungarno Amerigo Vespucci, 38
50123 Florence
055 239 8276, 055 217 605
fax 055 284 088
www.usembassy.it/florence

Canadian Embassy
Via Zara, 30
00198 Rome
06 445 981
fax 06 445 989 12
www.canada.it

British Embassy
Via XX Settembre, 80a
00187 Rome
06 422 026 00
fax 06 422 023 34
www.britain.it

British Consulate in Florence
Lungarno Corsini 2
50123 Florence
055 284 133
fax 055 219 112

Irish Embassy
Piazza di Campitelli, 3
00186 Rome
06 697 9121
fax 06 679 2354

Australian Embassy
Via Alessandria, 215
00198 Rome
06 852 721
www.australian-embassy.it

Australian Consulate
Corso Trieste, 25C
00198 Rome
06 852 721
fax 06 852 72300

New Zealand Embassy
Via Zara, 28
00198 Rome
06 440 2928
fax 06 440 2984

PLACES OF WORSHIP IN CENTRAL ITALY

Below is a list of Catholic churches in Italy where mass is celebrated in English. We have also provided a short list of non-Catholic places of worship, including synagogues and mosques.

Catholic Churches

In Florence
Santa Maria del Fiore (Duomo)
Piazza del Duomo

Church of the Hospital of San
  Giovanni di Dio
Borgo Ognissanti, 16

In Rome
Santa Susanna (the national church
  of the United States)
Via XX Settembre, 14

SS. Martiri Canadesi (the national
  church of Canada)
Via G. B. de Rossi, 46

San Silvestro in Capite (the
  national church of England)
Piazza San Silvestro, 1

Sant'Isidoro (the national church of
  Ireland)
Via degli Artisti, 41

Non-Catholic Churches

In Florence
St. James American Episcopal
Via B. Rucellai, 9

Church of England
Via Maggio, 16

In Rome
Anglican Church of All Saints
Via del Babuino, 153

Baptist
Piazza San Lorenzo in Lucina, 35

Church of Christ
Viale Jonio, 286

International Protestant
Via Chiovenda, 57

Methodist
Via Firenze, 38

Synagogues

Ancona
Via Fanti, 2

Florence
Via Farini, 4

Pisa
Via Palestro, 24

Rome
Via Lungotevere Cenci

Mosques

Centro Islamico Culturale Delle
  Marche
V. Maggini Alessandro, 274

Ancona
Centro Culturale Islamico
  Piazza degli Scarlatti, 1/r

Florence
Centro Culturale Islamico
  Via delle Belle Donne, 16

Pisa
Centro Islamico Culturale d'Italia
Viale della Moschea

Rome
Centro Islamico Culturale
Piazza Scala Bartolomeo, 13

Part Four

Hotels in Central Italy

The Hotel Scene

Italy's hospitality industry, which fuels more than two-thirds of the country's economy, has come up with hundreds of ways to help you part with your money. If you roam around Rome and amble through Florence, you'll see block after block of hotels, boutique hotels, *pensioni*, bed-and-breakfasts, *residenze*, hostels, and a range of accommodations from no-stars to five-star. Elsewhere in Central Italy are farmhouse inns, villas for rent, and rooms to let. Translated, that means that no matter if you're in the middle of Florence or the middle of nowhere, you are bound to find lodging.

The hitch? Most of Italy's 38,000 hotels and inns are privately owned, each with their own style, character, facilities, and amenities. For example, many of the hotels you'll find in the bigger cities in Central Italy are located in historic buildings, so rooms and bathrooms tend to be smaller.

The choices of modern accommodations have grown exponentially in the past several years. Hundreds of lodgings were updated prior to the 2000 Jubilee to accommodate millions of pilgrims. Today in Italy's cities, it isn't uncommon to find dazzling modern architecture and furnishings behind centuries-old façades. Furthermore, cosmopolitan hotels have tried to stay with the times by such adding amenities as satellite TV and Internet access. The Jubilee anticipation also ushered in a host of new business and convention hotels near airports and big-name factories. Truth be told, these recent additions to the hotel scene are not so pleasing to the eye. But, like 'em or not, we recognize that these newcomers are a boon to travelers averse to change.

Luckily, old traditions die hard here. Italy in general, and Central Italy in particular, is still the place where you can find a hotel that enables you to escape everyday monotony. In the foothills of the Apennines and the countryside of the Marches, for example, there hasn't been as much incentive to provide state-of-the-art amenities like TV or Internet access.

Instead, you'll have to make do with technicolor landscapes, chirping birds, and quiet conversations over dinner.

We are unable to outline all of the spectacular hotels and inns that Central Italy has to offer, but we do provide you with many suggestions to help you plan a unique stay. Following is a detailed list of what to look for in lodging, including price, amenities, services, and location. Furthermore, we have also weeded through hundreds of suggestions from readers and avid travelers and have come up with a list of our favorite hotels in Central Italy's most frequented areas. Though we know that hotel preferences are highly subjective, we feel that you are sure to get a good night's sleep if you take our advice. Enjoy your stay!

Understanding Your Options

Location

Where you hang your hat is important, but it's not the only consideration. One of the most common questions we hear from travelers to Central Italy is, "Will I be able to stay within spitting distance of the Colosseum or in the shadow of the Leaning Tower?" Well, yes, sometimes—but it will cost you. There are some hotels that make a killing because of their location, charging tourists an exorbitant amount for a room with—or without—a view. Truth be told, these same hotels may indeed have rooms with a view of a famous landmark, but they also have dozens of rooms that look out over a courtyard or a side street. If it's a view you want, then ask before you book to make sure you get the right accommodations. On the other hand, if you want a quiet room in a hotel that's not far from the star attractions, then you might want to ask for a back room. You didn't travel all this way only to enjoy the view from your hotel window, did you?

If you only want to hang out in Florence or Rome, then look for a hotel that is in or not far from the city center. These two major tourist towns have so many hotels, inns, residences, and hostels within their city limits that you are bound to find a wide range of accommodations—from affordable to upscale—within walking distance of restaurants, shops, and museums. The biggest bonus is that you can stay up longer, gazing at floodlit monuments and sampling the local color, without having to scurry back to a lonely, suburban hotel at too early an hour.

Central Italy is so big and its diversions so great that many travelers opt to rent a car. If you plan to drive while on vacation, then you may not want to stay in a city center at all. As we mentioned in Part Three, Arriving, Getting Oriented, and Departing, many cities have closed their streets to most traffic, opting to preserve roads and buildings from pollution and general wear and tear. If you are determined to have a car and drive it, too, it can be done. Just be forewarned that parking lots and garages in the city are few and far between, and they charge around $25 per night.

Types of Lodging

Small versus Large

Small and large hotels are not created equal. But that doesn't mean that small is subpar and big is better. Both types of lodging have their advantages and disadvantages.

We find that a lot of first-time travelers to Italy prefer to stay in large and/or chain hotels. Big hotels offer spacious rooms and, for the most part, lots of amenities, whereas smaller hotels tend to have cramped quarters (by American standards) and fewer perks. More rooms at a large hotel also means that there's more flexibility in terms of price. Check online or call the hotel directly and ask if they have any special discounts for children, senior citizens, or large groups, if those types of things apply to your trip. If it's low season and the hotel has a surfeit of vacant rooms, you might strike gold with a luxury room at a reduced price. Finally, at most large hotels, you'll find a 24-hour staff, and you'll be able to come and go as you like. On the other hand, small, family-run inns may impose a curfew or may not be able to call a cab for you at 3 a.m.

Indeed, big hotels have many advantages. But we have found throughout our travels that small hotels are usually the way to go. You can remain virtually anonymous at a large hotel, but you're rarely treated as just another cog in the tourist wheel if you stay in a smaller hotel. Many small hotels have been family-run for generations. When you stay in one of these inns, it's almost as if you are staying in another person's home. If you're open-minded and eager to get to know another culture, the staff at smaller hotels can be your best reference for finding out where to dine or where the nearest flea market is. Another advantage to a small hotel? The price. Modest furnishings are the norm at small or family-run inns. So what the hotel saves going with plain décor is often translated into lower rates for you.

Chains versus Independents

North American chain hotels like Marriott, Holiday Inn, and Hilton have made inroads in Central Italy, and they offer the standard amenities you'd expect back home—shower, TV, safe, and so on. These brand names typically are rated as at least three stars (according to the Italian government's official star rating system; see explanation below) and tend to be slightly pricier than their counterparts back home. But if you're the type who doesn't like surprises, you may prefer to stick with a name you know. It's up to you. Conversely, independently owned lodging can vary from block to block in style, size, clientele, management, and prices, though they are almost always charming. Independent hotels outnumber chain hotels by about 10 to 1 and range from five-star swanky to simple one- and two-stars (formerly known as *pensioni*). Like a box of chocolates, you never know what you're going to get with an independent hotel, which is exactly why we prefer them. After all, traveling is all about discovering something new. Later on, we profile a number of independent hotels and very few chain hotels. If you'd like more information on chain hotels in Italy, call their toll-free numbers in North America or visit their websites. That contact information is below.

- **Best Western**   (800) 528-1234   www.bestwestern.com
- **Hilton**   (800) 445-8667   www.hilton.com
- **Six Continents Hotels**   www.sixcontinentshotels.com
  (including Crowne Plaza (800) 227-6963
  and Holiday Inn)   (800) 465-4329
- **Starwood Hotels**   (888) 625-5144   www.starwood.com
  (including Sheraton and Westin)

Italian and European Hotel Chains

Italian hotel chains are thin on the ground, at least compared to their North American counterparts, but they are catching up. The **Jolly Hotels** chain manages or franchises about 41 medium- to large-size hotels throughout the country; **Notturno Italiano** boasts approximately 75 boutique-style hotels. Smaller Italian chains include **Bettoja** and **Leonardi,** which have several hotels in Florence and Rome. Both the French-owned **Accor,** which owns the **Novotel** and **Mercure** names, and Dutch-owned **Golden Tulip** have a number of hotels in Italy and a good reputation. Italy's **Charming Hotels** chain is a collection of independent luxury hotels. Phone numbers below are Italian numbers unless otherwise noted. More information is available on the hotels' websites.

- **Accor**   (800) 221-4542 (U.S.)   www.accor-hotels.itweb
- **Bettoja**   06 485 951 (Italy)   www.travel.it/roma/bettoja
- **Charming Hotels**   800 515 253 (Italy)   www.charminghotels.it
- **Golden Tulip**   02 860 227 (Italy)   www.goldentulip.com
- **Jolly Hotels**   800 017 713 (Italy) or   www.jollyhotels.it
  (800) 221-2626 (North America)
- **Leonardi**   06 868 00116 (Italy)   www.leonardihotels.com
- **Notturno Italiano**   06 474 2606 (Italy)   www.notturno.it

Italian Star-rating System

In Italy, hotels are rated on a scale of one to five stars, with five stars being the best. Provincial tourist boards are responsible for the awarding of stars, so criteria tends to vary from city to city and region to region on what constitutes a one-star hotel or what sets a two-star apart from a three-star. When it comes to five-star accommodations, however, there is no gray area: Luxury is luxury, no matter where you are.

Quite a number of hotels in Italy lack any stars at all. But that does not mean that the accommodations are cheap. Bed-and-breakfast inns—which are just now starting to come of age in this country—monastic quarters, and country farmhouses all fall under the one- or no-star classification, frankly because a system has yet to be developed to grade the amenities and facilities that these lodgings provide. Just as you shouldn't judge a book by its cover, don't judge a hotel in Italy by its number of stars. There really are some gems hiding behind low numbers.

For further help in deciphering the stars, get in touch with the regional or provincial tourist boards. Contact information is listed at the beginning of each region's section.

WEBSITES FOR LODGING IN CENTRAL ITALY

Hotel Listings	Villa and Apartment Rental
www.italyhotels.it	www.barclayweb.com
www.enit.it/uk/alberghi.asp	www.homebase-abroad.com
www.venere.it	www.italianvillas.com
www.hotelsearch.it	www.theparkercompany.com
www.italyguide.com	www.villasitalia.com
www.le-marche.com	**Additional Lodging Options**
www.turismo.toscana.it	www.federcampeggio.it
www.romaturismo.com	www.touringclub.it
www.umbria2000.it	www.ostellionline.org

Specialized and Unusual Accommodations

Because hospitality has been such big business in Italy for hundreds of years, there are several lodging options here that you wouldn't find anywhere else.

Convents and Monasteries

Monastic is fantastic when accommodations are un-convent-ional. To handle the hundreds of thousands of pilgrims that trek through Italy and to get a small piece of the multimillion-dollar tourist industry, many monasteries, convents, and church-owned inns have opened their doors to tourists. As expected, religious lodging is sober, with few amenities, and most nun-run facilities impose an 11 p.m. curfew. If you can deal with that, then you'll find dirt-cheap (but immaculate) accommodations, sometimes within minutes of major attractions or in an inspiring, idyllic setting. In fact, rates can start as low as €15 per night. Monastic lodging is not for everyone, of course, but it's worth a try—especially if you arrive at your destination without reservations *(senza prenotazioni)*. Below, we have listed a few religious lodging options for Rome and Florence, as well as for the major pilgrimage towns of Assisi (Umbria) and Loreto (Marches). *A final note:* Church-owned *pensioni* do not accept credit cards.

Florence
Pensionato Pio X   Via dei Serragli, 106; 50125, phone 055 225 044

Rome
Casa di Santa Francesca Romana   Via dei Vascellari, 61; 00153, phone 06 581 2125, fax 06 583 5797

Nostra Signora di Lourdes   Via Sistina, 113; 00187, phone 06 474 5324. 10:30 p.m. curfew. Women and married couples allowed.

Assisi
Cittadella Ospitalità   Via Ancajani, 3; 06081 Assisi; phone 075 813 231, fax 075 812 445

Loreto
Sacra Famiglia di Nazareth   Via Maccari, 7; 60025; phone 071 970 181, fax 071 750 4604

Agriturismo: Farm Holidays

A very popular holiday trend among Italians and a growing one among North American travelers, the farm holiday, called *agriturismo,* allows vacationers a chance to relax in a more natural setting. The simple yet comfortable cottage accommodations are usually very affordable. If you're lucky, you may be able to spend lazy days picking tomatoes or stomping on bunches of grapes. Tuscany, Italy's primary agricultural region, leads the pack with hundreds of farm-holiday options. Umbria is second, and the regions of Latium and the Marches are gaining.

We have included a few agricultural accommodations in our profiles. For more information, contact one of the following organizations—they can help you weed through a database of farmhouses to find the perfect choice for you. Keep in mind that many farm lodgings require a minimum stay of three days to up to two weeks, and that many *agriturismo* farms are closed to visitors from November through March.

Agriturist   Corso Vittorio Emanuele II, 101; 00186 Rome; phone 06 685 2342, fax 06 685 2424

Terranostra   Via XXIV Maggio, 43; 00187 Rome; phone 06 468 2370

Turismo Verde   Via Mariano Fortuny, 20; 00196 Rome; phone 06 361 1051, fax 06 360 00294

Villas and Furnished Apartments

How would you like to stay in a restored villa in the Umbrian country-side or live in your own apartment overlooking the rooftops of Florence? Thanks to a number of villa and apartment rental agencies, you can. If you're traveling with your family or a similarly large group, or if you are escaping to Central Italy for several weeks, you may want to consider renting accommodations where you can cook your own meals and set your own itinerary. Pricing for apartment and villa rentals can vary greatly depending on location and season, costing you anywhere from $600 to $2,000 per week. Yes, in some instances, you can save money by renting a villa. A number of companies in both the United States and Italy can help you find accommodations that fit your schedule and budget. Some good ones are listed below.

Barclay International Group rents out furnished apartments in Florence and Rome and manages a number of villas in Tuscany, Latium, Umbria, and the Marches, starting from approximately $650 per week; 3 School Street; Glen Cove, NY 11542; (516) 759-5100, (800) 845-6636, fax (516) 609-0000; **www.barclayweb.com.**

Homebase Abroad has private-home rental in Rome, Florence, Tuscany, and Umbria, ranging from $2,000 to $35,000 per week; 29 Mary's Lane; Scituate, MA 02066; (781) 545-5112, fax (781) 545-1808; **www.homebase-abroad.com.**

Italian Villas offers many villa rentals in Tuscany and also has properties in Latium and Umbria, all starting at $600 per week; 8 Knight Street, Suite 205; Norwalk, CT 06851; (203) 855-8161, (800) 700-9549, fax (203) 855-0506; **www.italianvillas.com.**

Italian Vacation Villas is run by a husband-and-wife team who specialize in quality home and villa rentals in Tuscany (particularly in Chianti) and Umbria that sleep up to 14 people and range from $1,200 to $9,600 week; P.O. Box 9586; Washington, DC 20016; (202) 333-6247, fax (202) 333-6625; **www.villasitalia.com.**

The Parker Company has cottage, castle, and farmhouse rentals for every region in Italy, ranging from $500 to $15,000 per week; Seaport Landing 152; Lynn, MA 01902; (781) 596-8282, (800) 280-2811; **www.theparkercompany.com.**

Camping

Central Italy has no shortage of campgrounds. In fact, there are even camping sites just outside of Florence and Rome. The **Touring Club Italiano** publishes a book called *Campeggi in Italia,* which details, in Italian, all of the more than 1,700 campsites in the country. You can also get a free map and campsite listings from the **Federazione Italiana del Campeggio e del Caravanning** (Federcampeggio). The Italian Government Tourist Board can usually provide you with a copy, or you can send away for it directly. Federcampeggio's website is also a valuable tool for finding information on campgrounds in Central Italy. For more information, contact one of these organizations:

Touring Club Italiano   Corso Italia, 10; 20122 Milan; phone 02 85 261, fax 02 852 6362; **www.touringclub.it**

Federcampeggio   Via Vittorio Emanuele, 11, 50041 Calenzano, Florence; phone 055 882 391, fax 055 882 5918, **www.federcampeggio.it.**

Noteworthy Campsites near Florence and Rome

Camping Panoramico Fiesole   Via Peramonda, 1; 50014 Fiesole; phone 055 599 069, fax 055 59 186, **www.campingtoscana.it.** Open year-round.

Camping Flaminio Village   Via Flaminia Nuova, 821; 00189 Rome; phone 06 333 1431, fax 06 333 0653, **www.villageflaminio.com.** Open year-round.

Hostels in Central Italy

Temporary and long-term student housing is available in many areas in Central Italy, especially in university towns like Pisa and Perugia. For as little as €15 per night, you can stay in safe, clean quarters, sometimes near the center of town. Hostels *(ostelli)* do not accept credit cards, and most have an 11 p.m. or midnight curfew.

Below is a list of a few hostels in Florence and Rome. If you'd like more information about hostels, you can order the free pamphlet "Guide for Foreign Students" from the Italian Ministry of Education, Viale Trastevere, 00153 Rome. The **Italian Youth Hostels Association** (Associazione Italiana Alberghi per la Gioventù, Via Cavour, 44; 00186 Rome; phone 06 487 1152; **www.ostellionline.org**) can help with booking a room anywhere in the country. If you're heading to Rome, you can contact the student association **Enjoy Rome** (Via Varese, 39; 00187 Rome; phone 06 445 1843), whose English-speaking staff offers many services, including room-booking assistance.

Ostello Archi Rossi   Via Faenza, 94r; 00182 Florence; phone 055 290 804, fax 055 230 2601

Ostello della Gioventù Foro Italico   Via delle Olimpiadi, 61; 00194 Rome; phone 06 323 6267, fax 06 324 2613

Hotels for Business Travelers

The number of business hotels in Central Italy is constantly growing. As we've seen over the last several years, business travelers have registered demands for more high-tech meeting rooms, on-site business centers, in-room data ports, and access to phone and fax machines. Rome is by far the best equipped to deal with business travelers. Central Italy's commercial and governmental hub, Rome has many business-oriented hotels (mostly in the suburbs near EUR), as well as a number of four- and five-star hotels inside the city proper that can handle the everyday needs of the business traveler. Elsewhere in Central Italy, business hotels have cropped up where they are needed, mostly near convention centers and airports (see profiles). Because business travelers often want to stay near the airport, we have outlined a few convenient hotels in the following section. Keep in mind that business hotels charge higher rack rates during conference season, usually from September through November and March through May. Most business hotels are convenient options only if your company is paying.

HOTELS AT THE AIRPORTS

Galileo Galilei Airport (Pisa/Florence)
Pisa Migliarino   (62 rooms) Via Aurelia Km. 342; Migliarino Pisano, 56010; phone 050 800 8100, fax 050 803 315; holidayinn.pisa@alliancealberghi.com

Peretola Airport (Florence)
Novotel Firenze Nord Aeroporto   (180 rooms) Via Tevere, 23; 50019 Florence; phone 055 308 338, fax 055 308 336; novotel.firenze@accor_hotels.it

Fiumicino/Leonardo da Vinci Airport (Rome)
Hilton Rome Airport   (517 rooms) Via Arturo Ferrarin, 2; 00050 Rome Fiumicino; phone 06 65258, (800) 445-8667 U.S. and Canada; **www.hilton.com**. As close as you can get—this hotel is connected via an overpass to the airport.
Sheraton Hotel Roma   (650 rooms) Viale del Pattinaggio; 00144 Rome; phone 06 54531, fax 06 594 0689; **www.sheraton.com/roma**

San Egidio Airport (Perugia)
Park Hotel   (140 rooms) Via A. Volta, 1; 06087 Perugia; phone 075 599 0444, fax 075 599 0455; parkhotel@perugiaonline.com

Ancona Falconara
Jolly Hotel Ancona   (89 rooms) Rupi di Via XXIX Settembre, 14; 60122 Ancona; phone 071 201 171, fax 071 206 823

Hotels for Disabled Travelers

As discussed in Part Three, Arriving, Getting Oriented, and Departing, finding a hotel with adequate access for the disabled is not as easy in Italy as it is in North America. Two organizations, **CO.IN.** (Consorzio Cooperative Integrate; Via Enrico Giglioli, 54; 00186 Rome; phone 06 712 901 79, fax 06 712 901 40; **www.coinsociale.it**) and **A.N.T.H.A.I.** (Associazione Nazionale Tutela Handicappati ed Invalidi; Corso Vittorio Emanuele, 154; 00186 Rome; phone 06 682 191 68, fax 06 688 926 84), provide information and assistance to disabled travelers.

We have also noticed that most North American chain hotels are a better bet for disabled travelers because their facilities are usually built to comply with stricter American and Canadian safety and disability standards. In Italy, facilities for the disabled must have entrances at street level, must provide a lift, and must be equipped with doors of at least 75 centimeters (29.5 inches) in width. But don't expect to find complete accessibility. For instance, hotels that claim to have disabled access are not obliged to install safety bars in bathrooms and showers. Most hotels will only offer one or two rooms with full accessibility and bathrooms.

Following is a list of a few of our favorite hotels that provide access for the disabled. For more information, contact CO.IN. or A.N.T.H.A.I., who constantly update their lists of lodging for the disabled.

Florence

Corona d'Italia   (5 rooms with adapted bathrooms) Via Nazionale, 14; 50123 Florence; phone 055 261 501, fax 055 288 639;   **www.hotel coronaditalia.com**

Hotel Kraft   (5 rooms with adapted bathrooms) Via Solferino, 2; 50100 Florence; phone 055 284 273, fax 055 239 8237; **www.kraft hotel.it**

Il Guelfo Bianco   (2 rooms with adapted bathrooms) Via Cavour, 57r; 50129 Florence; phone 055 288 330, fax 055 295 203; **www.ilguelfo bianco.it**

Pisa

Grand Hotel Duomo   (3 rooms with adapted bathrooms, disabled services) Via Santa Maria, 94; 56100 Pisa; phone 050 561 894, fax 050 560 418; **www.grandhotelduomo.it**

Siena

Academy Hotel   (All 136 rooms are accessible, with adapted bathrooms) Via Lombardi, 41; 53100 Siena; phone 0577 5755, fax 0577 332 409; **www.academyhotel.it**

Rome

Fontanella Borghese   (2 rooms with adapted bathrooms) Largo Fontanella Borghese, 84; 00186 Rome; phone 06 688 09504, fax 06 686 1295; **www.fontanellaborghese.com**

Marriott Grand Hotel Flora   (4 rooms with adapted bathrooms) Via Veneto, 191; 00187 Rome; phone 06 489 929, fax 06 482 0359; **www.marriott.com**

Plaza   (8 rooms with adapted bathrooms) Via del Corso, 126; 00187 Rome; phone 06 699 211 11, fax 06 699 415 75; **www.hotelplaza rome.com**

Perugia
Hotel La Rosetta   (2 rooms with adapted bathrooms) Piazza Italia, 19; 06100 Perugia; phone 075 572 0841, fax 075 572 0841

Urbino
Albergo San Domenico   (2 rooms with adapted bathrooms) Piazza Rinascimento, 3; 61029 Urbino; phone 0722 2626, fax 0722 2727

The Italian Hotel Room

It is difficult to pinpoint a prototypical hotel room, as accommodations come in a broad spectrum of shapes, sizes, comfort, and décor. But there are a few things that are common among all hotels. First, keep in mind that Europeans number the floors of a building differently. If you want to stay on the first floor (read: ground floor), make sure that you ask for the *piano terra*. The first floor is the floor above the ground floor, what we would call the second floor. When you check into your hotel, have your passport handy. All hotels in Italy are required by law to have a record of your stay.

As for the differences from room to room, there are many. For example, walking into an Italian bathroom is like entering a science lab. There are buttons on walls, pedals on the floor, and equipment that you may never have seen before. In most affordable hotels, you are given the option of staying in a room with a bathtub *(vasca)* or a shower *(doccia)*—not both. Rooms with bathtubs tend to cost slightly more, because more space is required. Another fixture you are sure to see in your hotel bathroom is a bidet, an oh-so-European bathroom fixture that was designed to clean a person's private parts in the days when baths were not an everyday luxury. Bidets are typically equipped for both hot and cold water, so you can use them to your advantage. For instance, the shin-level sink is handy for soaking feet after a long day of touring and rinsing out socks and undies.

Heating and air-conditioning are also not a given when it comes to accommodations. Climatization is a sore subject among Italian hoteliers and invading American tourists. On the one hand, the Italian hotel-keeper doesn't feel that a guest needs to walk around comfortably in shorts in his hotel room in the dead of winter, while American visitors often can't comprehend why the air-conditioning is turned off at night in the thick of July. At many small hotels and *pensioni,* air-conditioning and heat are a luxury, only to be turned on at the most crucial times: mornings, from 7 to 11 a.m., and evenings, from 4 to 9 p.m. Some hotels will even—gasp!—charge guests a fee for using the air or heat. Many hotels in Florence and Rome have done away with this little annoyance, but that's not always the case with lodging in small towns and the countryside.

Finally, when in Italy, know that paying through the nose for lodging does not guarantee that breakfast is included. Actually, we've found that the more expensive a hotel is, the more likely it is that you'll have to pay extra for breakfast. This should drive us crazy, but it rarely does. Why? Well, if you're staying in the center of town, you'll usually find a cheap, delicious breakfast just around the corner from your hotel. No pancakes, scrambled eggs, or French toast here, of course—but what you will find are croissants *(cornetti)* filled with hazelnut spread, custard, or jam, and piping-hot espresso and cappuccino, all for around $1.50. If your hotel doesn't serve breakfast, or charges an exorbitant amount for it, consider getting your morning eats on the outside. You may just save yourself around $15 per day.

Central Italy Hotels Rated and Ranked

Following this section are detailed profiles of the best hotels in Central Italy. The profiles are organized by region—Florence, the rest of Tuscany, Rome, the rest of Latium, Umbria, and finally the Marches and the Republic of San Marino. Each section begins with a convenient table that lets you see at a glance how the profiled properties stack up. Florence and Rome hotels are listed alphabetically; for regions, profiles are listed by province, then by city, and then alphabetically by name.

Our Star System and Price Ranges

Our system of awarding stars is based on overall quality of the hotel and has not been influenced by the stars assigned officially by the Italian Board of Tourism.

★★★★★   Superior Rooms, very high class, deluxe   €400–€550

Tasteful and luxurious. Be prepared to feel like royalty. Insist on it. Hotels in this category are generally not profiled in this guide, but are listed under the section "Cream of the Crop."

★★★★   Extremely nice rooms, high class   €150–€400

What you'd expect at a luxury chain hotel, but with added touches of European elegance. We've profiled a number of these that offer the best value for the high price. For your information only, we include one- and two-star descriptions, although we recommend the three-, four-, and five-star hotels we highlight.

★★★   Very comfortable rooms   €100–€250

What you'd expect at a midrange chain hotel, but with more style and charm. We focus on numerous hotels in this category.

★★   Adequate rooms   €70–€100

Clean, comfortable, and functional without any frills, but in some cases, a surprising amount of character and overall quality. The less interesting two-stars are not mentioned here.

★   Super budget, rooms of basic comfort   Under €70

Simple rooms with or without toilets or showers in rooms. Often less central, but not necessarily. Safe and clean, though. The ones provided here represent good value.

Overall Ratings

We have distinguished properties according to relative quality, tasteful-ness, state of repair, cleanliness, and size of standard rooms, grouping them into classifications denoted by stars. Overall star ratings in this guide do not correspond to ratings awarded by the tourist boards or other travel critics. Overall ratings are presented to show the difference we perceive between one property and another. They are assigned with-out regard to location, or whether a property has restaurants, recreational facilities, entertainment, or other extras.

★★★★★	Superior	Tasteful and luxurious by any standard
★★★★	Extremely Nice	Above average in appointments and design; very comfortable
★★★	Nice	Average, but quite comfortable
★★	Adequate	Plain, but meets all essential needs
★	Budget	Spartan, not aesthetically pleasing, but clean

Quality Ratings

In addition to overall ratings (which delineate broad categories), we also employ quality ratings. They apply to room quality only and describe the property's standard accommodations. In addition to standard accommo-dations, many hotels offer luxury rooms and special suites that are not rated in this guide. Our rating scale is one to five stars, with five stars as the best possible rating and one star as the worst.

Value Ratings

We also provide a value rating to give you some sense of the quality of a room in relation to its cost. As before, the ratings are based on the qual-ity of the room for the money and do not take into account location, services, or amenities. Our scale is as follows:

★★★★★	An exceptional bargain
★★★★	A good deal
★★★	Fairly priced (you get exactly what you pay for)
★★	Somewhat overpriced
★	Significantly overpriced

Prices in Profiled Listings

Cost estimates are based on the hotel's published rack rates for standard rooms for two people with full bathroom (usually a shower, not a tub). Hotels in Italy generally list different rack rates for high season and low season, and rates are often charged based on the number of people stay-ing in the room and not just per room. Note that some hotels have des-ignated "single" rooms that are often smaller than the standard. A general price range appears at the top of each profile, with more detailed infor-mation listed under "Pricing."

Cream of the Crop

If you want to stay in the best accommodations money can buy, browse the quick list below. Rooms at these premier hotels run between €440 and €1,320 ($400 and $1,200 U.S.) per night.

Florence

Excelsior (146 rooms, 22 suites) Piazza Ognissanti, 3; 50123 Florence; phone 055 2715, fax 055 10278; **www.starwood.com.** Il Cestello restaurant.

Grand Hotel (90 rooms, 17 suites) Piazza Ognissanti, 1; 50123 Florence; phone 055 288 781, fax 055 217 400; **www.starwood.com.** InCanto restaurant.

Grand Hotel Villa Medici (89 rooms, 14 suites) Via il Prato, 42; 50123 Florence; phone 055 238 1331, fax 055 238 1346; **www.sinahotels. com.** Lorenzo de' Medici restaurant.

Helvetia & Bristol (37 rooms, 12 suites) Via dei Pescioni, 2; 50123 Florence; phone 055 287 814, fax 055 288 353; **www.charming hotels.it.** The Bristol restaurant.

Hotel Villa San Michele (77 rooms) Via Doccia, 4; 50014 Fiesole; phone 055 59451, fax 055 567 8250; **www.villasanmichele.orient-express.com.** Cenacolo restaurant; Loggia *al fresco* restaurant.

Savoy (98 rooms, 9 suites) Piazza della Repubblica, 7; 50123 Florence; phone 055 27351, fax 055 273 588; **www.rfhotels.com.** L'Incontro restaurant.

Rome

Cavalieri Hilton (375 rooms) Via Cadlolo, 101; 00136 Rome; phone 06 35091, fax 06 350 92241; **www.cavalieri-hilton.it.** La Pergola restaurant.

Hassler Villa Medici (100 rooms) Piazza Trinità dei Monti, 6; 00187 Rome; phone 06 699 340, fax 06 678 9991; **www.hotelhassler roma.com.** Hassler Rooftop Restaurant.

Hotel de Russie (129 rooms) Via del Babuino, 9; 00187 Rome; phone 06 328 881, fax 06 328 88888; **www.hotelderussie.it.** Hotel de Russie Garden Restaurant.

Majestic (95 rooms) Via Veneto, 50; 00187 Rome; phone 06 421 441, fax 06 488 0984; **www.hotelmajesticroma.com.** La Veranda restaurant.

St. Regis Grand (170 rooms) Via Vittorio Emanuele Orlando, 3; 00185 Rome; phone 06 470 91, fax 06 474 7307; **www.stregis.com/ grandrome.** Vivendo restaurant.

Westin Excelsior (327 rooms) Via Veneto, 125; 00187 Rome; phone 06 470 81, fax 06 482 6205; **www.westin.com/excelsiorroma.** La Cupola restaurant.

Hotel Profiles—Florence

	THE BEST HOTELS IN FLORENCE			
Hotel	Overall Rating	Quality Rating	Value Rating	Price
Hotel Botticelli	★★★★★	★★★★★	★★★★★	€80–€180
Hotel Lungarno	★★★★★	★★★★★	★	€200–€450
Fenice Palace	★★★★	★★★★★	★★★★	€155–€215
Residenza dei Pucci	★★★★	★★★★	★★★★★	€90–€145
Hotel Consigli	★★★★	★★★★	★★★★★	€150–€180
Hotel Morandi alla Crocetta	★★★★	★★★★	★★★★★	€115–€200
Hotel Calzaiuoli	★★★★	★★★★	★★★★	€85–€245
Hotel Berchielli	★★★★	★★★★	★★★	€230–€320
B&B dei Mori	★★★★	★★★	★★★★★	€80–€140
Hotel Il Guelfo Bianco	★★★★	★★★	★★★★★	€120–€220
Hotel Porta Rossa	★★★★	★★★	★★★★	€100–€240
Sofitel Firenze	★★★★	★★★	★	€300–€350
Hotel Brunelleschi	★★★½	★★★★★	★★	€215–€300
Il Porcellino	★★★½	★★★½	★★★★★	€50–€95
Hotel Sanremo	★★★	★★★	★★★★★	€83–€191
Hotel Palazzo Vecchio	★★★	★★★	★★★★	€75–€120
Grand Hotel Cavour	★★★	★★★	★★★★	€100–€225
Hotel Croce di Malta	★★★	★★★	★★	€130–€370

B&B dei Mori   €80–€140

OVERALL ★★★★ | QUALITY ★★★ | VALUE ★★★★★ | SANTA CROCE

Via Dante Alighieri, 12; 50122 Florence; phone/fax 055 211 438; www.bnb.it/deimori/dmrh.htm

As a bed-and-breakfast should be, the dei Mori is a no-frills kind of place. Three guest rooms of six share a bathroom down the hall, there are no televisions in the rooms, and, during the summer, the air-conditioning is shut down overnight to cut costs. But these simple facts don't tell the whole story. The bed-and-breakfast's managers, Daniele and Franco, will help you with your luggage or suggestions for sight-seeing at a moment's notice. Décor is well placed and tasteful, giving the inn a homey feel. Oh, did we mention the location? The dei Mori is in the heart of it all, about halfway between the Piazza della Signoria and the Piazza del Duomo. The bed-and-breakfast is open year-round and requires a minimum stay of two nights.

SETTING & FACILITIES

Location South of the Duomo, near the Bargello. **Quietness Rating** B. **Dining** Breakfast included in rates.

ACCOMMODATIONS

Rooms 6. **All** Phone. **Bathrooms** Shower or shared bathroom down the hall, no hair dryer. Three rooms have sinks. **Comfort & Décor** The Persian rugs, antique cabinets, and pieces of art here are what you'd find in many a Florentine household. Rooms are modest and a bit small, but some retain original ceiling frescoes and wood-beam details.

RATES, RESERVATIONS, & RESTRICTIONS

Pricing Singles €80–€90, doubles €90–€140. Discounts can be arranged for long stays. **Credit Cards** AMEX, MC, V. **Check-In/Out** 2 p.m./noon. **Elevator** No. **English Spoken** Yes.

Fenice Palace   €155–€215

OVERALL ★★★★ | QUALITY ★★★★★ | VALUE ★★★★ | SAN GIOVANNI

*Via Martelli, 10; 50123 Florence; phone 055 289 942, fax 055 210 087;
www.hotelfenicepalace.it*

The newly renovated Fenice Palace is one of the most exclusive hotels in town. Across the street from the Medici-Riccardi palace and a stone's throw from the attractions in the city center, the former 17th-century mansion has some of the most thoughtful décor we've seen, including cushy couches in the lobby and fabulously firm beds in the guest rooms.

SETTING & FACILITIES

Location A few blocks from the Duomo. **Quietness Rating** B. **Dining** Breakfast included in rates; bar serves light snacks. **Services** Room-service breakfast available.

ACCOMMODATIONS

Rooms 72. **All** Phone, minibar, soundproof windows, satellite TV. **Bathrooms** Shower or bathtub, hair dryer. **Comfort & Décor** The rooms and common areas are hyper-styled, as if out of an interior design catalog. Carpets are lush, drapes are elegant, and each room has its own bold look. Fresh flowers and houseplants create an intimate and homey setting.

RATES, RESERVATIONS, & RESTRICTIONS

Pricing Singles €155, doubles €215. **Credit Cards** AMEX, MC, V. **Check-In/Out** 2 p.m./noon. **Elevator** Yes. **English Spoken** Yes.

Grand Hotel Cavour   €100–€225

OVERALL ★★★ | QUALITY ★★★ | VALUE ★★★★ | SAN GIOVANNI

*Via del Proconsolo, 3; 50121 Florence; phone 055 282 461, fax 055 218 955;
www.hotelcavour.com*

A three-star property that calls itself "grand" better have something to show for it, and the Grand Hotel Cavour doesn't disappoint. The lobby is lavish, with marble statues, ornate lamps, a polychrome marble floor, and antique rugs. In the rooms you'll find handmade furniture and enough space to stretch your limbs. You certainly can't beat the location (just steps from the Casa di Dante and the Bargello), and the rooftop terrace has one of the better views of Florence's signature structures. But the central location has its drawbacks—the din from outside will be your morning wake-up call.

SETTING & FACILITIES

Location Near the Bargello. **Quietness Rating** C. **Dining** Buffet breakfast included in rates; Ristorante Beatrice, an independent restaurant on the premises, offers discounted meals for hotel guests. **Amenities** Parking nearby, meeting facilities, Internet access. **Services** Room service.

ACCOMMODATIONS

Rooms 92. **All** Double-glazed windows, phones, satellite TV. **Bathrooms** Shower or bathtub; one room on each floor is equipped for disabled guests, hair dryer. **Comfort & Décor** Rooms are carpeted but otherwise frugally decorated. Bathrooms tend to be cramped, except for those in the rooms designated for disabled guests.

RATES, RESERVATIONS, & RESTRICTIONS

Pricing Singles €101–€117, doubles €140–€180, triple, €215–€225. **Credit Cards** MC, V. **Check-In/Out** 2 p.m./noon. **Elevator** Yes. **English Spoken** Yes.

Hotel Berchielli €230–€320

OVERALL ★★★★ | QUALITY ★★★★ | VALUE ★★★ | SAN GIOVANNI

Lungarno Acciauoli, 14; 50123 Florence; phone 055 218 636, fax 055 264 061; www.berchielli.it

Situated on the banks of the Arno, between the Vecchio and Santa Trinità bridges, the Berchielli delivers on location, ambience, and, well, location. Walk out the door and you're seconds away from shopping on Via Tornabuoni. In the summer, you can take your breakfast on the rooftop terrace, where there's a fantastic view of the cupola of the Duomo and the city's rooftops. Rooms on the back are the quietest but lack the river view.

SETTING & FACILITIES

Location Between the Ponte Vecchio and Ponte Santa Trinità. **Quietness Rating** B. **Dining** Breakfast included in the rates; the bar also serves light snacks. **Amenities** Roof garden, parking nearby, Internet access, meeting facilities. **Services** Baby-sitting, room service.

ACCOMMODATIONS

Rooms 72, 4 suites. **All** Phone, minibar, satellite TV, in-room safe. **Bathrooms** Shower or bathtub, hair dryer. **Comfort & Décor** Rooms tend to be small but are very comfortable and sumptuously decorated.

RATES, RESERVATIONS, & RESTRICTIONS

Pricing Singles €230, doubles €320. **Credit Cards** AMEX, DC, V. **Check-In/Out** 2 p.m./noon. **Elevator** Yes. **English Spoken** Yes.

Hotel Botticelli €80–€180

OVERALL ★★★★★ | QUALITY ★★★★★ | VALUE ★★★★★ | SAN GIOVANNI

Via Taddea, 8; 50123 Florence; phone 055 290 905, fax 055 294 322;
www.panoramahotelsitaly.com

Named after one of the city's most acclaimed artists, the Botticelli hotel is as lovely as its namesake's paintings. This 16th-century building was once the home of a wealthy Florentine family, and you can still see some of its original architectural elements on the gorgeous vaulted ceiling in the lobby and in the guest rooms. There is a porch decorated with flower-boxes on the third floor—a great place to write postcards or unwind from a day of sight-seeing. The price is right for the location (a few paces from the Mercato Centrale and the San Lorenzo outdoor market) and you won't find a friendlier staff anywhere.

SETTING & FACILITIES

Location San Lorenzo. **Quietness Rating** A. **Dining** Breakfast included in rates. **Amenities** Parking nearby, common area with TV. **Services** Baby-sitting, room service.

ACCOMMODATIONS

Rooms 34. **All** Phone, minibar, satellite TV, in-room safe. **Bathrooms** Shower or bath-tub, hair dryer. **Comfort & Décor** Rooms are extremely comfortable, though a little small, and are decorated in muted shades of pink, green, and beige. Antique furnishings mix with the modern to create a very put-together look—more like home than a hotel.

RATES, RESERVATIONS, & RESTRICTIONS

Pricing Singles €80–€115, doubles €120–€180. **Credit Cards** MC, V. **Check-In/Out** 2 p.m./noon. **Elevator** Yes. **English Spoken** Yes.

Hotel Brunelleschi €215–€300

OVERALL ★★★½ | QUALITY ★★★★★ | VALUE ★★ | SAN GIOVANNI

Piazza Santa Elisabetta, 3; 50122 Florence; phone 055 27370, fax 055 219 653;
www.hotelbrunelleschi.it

Rather than rushing out to the city's tourist attractions, you can stay at the historic Brunelleschi, which is set in the ruins of a Byzantine tower, a deconsecrated church, and a few medieval houses. A small museum inside the hotel explains all of the architectural features and details its renovation. As for the rooms, they are modern (disappointingly so, given the hotel's history) and uninspiring, except for two suites, which feature whirlpools. Some rooms on the upper floor are blessed with a view of the Duomo. The Brunelleschi's concierge is ever-helpful and can get you reservations for primo restaurants and even museum and theater tickets.

SETTING & FACILITIES

Location Near the Duomo. **Quietness Rating** A–. **Dining** Breakfast included in rates; restaurant. **Amenities** Parking nearby, Internet access. **Services** Shuttle service to train station, room service, baby-sitting, on-site car rental, laundry.

ACCOMMODATIONS

Rooms 89 rooms, 7 suites. **All** Phone, minibar, satellite TV, in-room safe, soundproof windows. **Bathrooms** Bathtub and shower, hair dryer. **Comfort & Décor** Rooms and bathrooms are definitely spacious, and the closets are deep enough for a longer stay. Tile floors, frumpy drapes, and mismatched rugs and bedding are inconsistent with the hotel's rates.

RATES, RESERVATIONS, & RESTRICTIONS

Pricing Singles €217, doubles €295. **Credit Cards** AMEX, MC, V. **Check-In/Out** 2 p.m./noon. **Elevator** Yes. **English Spoken** Yes.

Hotel Calzaiuoli   €85–€245

OVERALL ★★★★ | QUALITY ★★★★ | VALUE ★★★★ | SAN GIOVANNI

Via Calzaiuoli, 6; 50123 Florence; phone 055 212 456, fax 055 268 310; www.calzaiuoli.it

The Calzaiuoli is situated on one of the main strolling and shopping drags in Florence and is approximately halfway between the Duomo and the Uffizi Gallery—so it's not surprising that the hotel is almost always booked solid. The digs are noteworthy, too. Follow the grand *pietra serena* staircase (or take the elevator) to the cozy rooms. The ones in the front afford views of the carnival-like atmosphere down below, and the rooms in the back offer glimpses of the Duomo and/or the Renaissance rooftops. Book months in advance, if possible.

SETTING & FACILITIES

Location Near the Duomo. **Quietness Rating** Front rooms, B; back rooms, A. **Dining** Breakfast included in rates; bar serves light snacks. **Amenities** Parking nearby, Internet access, pets allowed. **Services** Laundry, room service available for breakfast.

ACCOMMODATIONS

Rooms 45. **All** Phone, minibar, soundproof windows, satellite TV, in-room safe. **Bathrooms** Shower or bathtub, hair dryer. **Comfort & Décor** Rooms range from Spartan to frilly but are generally spacious. All are carpeted and feature a sitting area and/or desk. Larger rooms are decorated with antique etchings and paintings.

RATES, RESERVATIONS, & RESTRICTIONS

Pricing Singles €85–€177, doubles €88–€245. **Credit Cards** AMEX, DC, V. **Check-In/Out** 2 p.m./noon. **Elevator** Yes. **English Spoken** Yes.

Hotel Consigli   €150–€180

OVERALL ★★★★ | QUALITY ★★★★ | VALUE ★★★★★ | SANTA MARIA NOVELLA

Lungarno A. Vespucci, 50; 50123 Florence; phone 055 214 172, fax 055 219 367; www.hotelconsigli.com

We're not quite sure why the Hotel Consigli usually falls under the radar of most hotel reviewers, but we're glad of it. This pristine inn due west of the historic center occupies the former palace of Russian Prince Demidoff and still features vaulted ceilings, complete with frescoes, herringbone hardwood floors, and antique clocks, cabinets, and chandeliers. The breakfast room is especially pretty, and the buffet breakfast is filling. From the rooftop terrace you can enjoy panoramic views of the city, the Arno, and the surrounding hills.

SETTING & FACILITIES

Location West of Piazza Ognissanti. **Quietness Rating** A. **Dining** Breakfast included in rates; bar serves light snacks. **Amenities** Parking nearby, Internet access. **Services** Baby-sitting, room service available for breakfast.

ACCOMMODATIONS

Rooms 14 rooms, 2 suites. **All** Phone, satellite TV, soundproof windows, in-room safe. **Bathrooms** Shower or bathtub, hair dryer. **Comfort & Décor** The refined rooms are decorated in shades of saffron and peach with tastefully patterned wallpaper and 19th-century furnishings. Some rooms have a fireplace. Lighting is dim.

RATES, RESERVATIONS, & RESTRICTIONS

Pricing Doubles €150, triples €180. **Credit Cards** AMEX, MC, V. **Check-In/Out** 2 p.m./noon. **Elevator** Yes. **English Spoken** Some.

Hotel Croce di Malta €130–€370

OVERALL ★★★ | QUALITY ★★★ | VALUE ★★ | SANTA MARIA NOVELLA

Via della Scala, 7; 50123 Florence; phone 055 218 351, fax 055 287 121; www.crocedimalta.it

The Croce di Malta is on a busy side street near the train station, but once inside, the hotel is an oasis. There's a shady patch of green out back, complete with a trickling fountain and swimming pool. Inside, the cozy sitting room looks a bit weathered in its 1970s-era oranges and browns, but it is airy, with a nice view of the garden. In the common areas, architectural features and fixtures are bold and masculine—the same is true of the hotel's meeting rooms. But the guest rooms tend to be more feminine, with antique dressers, dainty wall sconce lighting, and flower-print rugs.

SETTING & FACILITIES

Location Santa Maria Novella. **Quietness Rating** Back rooms, A, front rooms, B. **Dining** Restaurant on the premises; breakfast, €13. **Amenities** Private garden, swimming pool, garage nearby, pets allowed. **Services** Conference facilities, laundry.

ACCOMMODATIONS

Rooms 98, plus 15 rooms with lounge areas. **All** Phone, minibar, satellite TV, soundproof windows. **Bathrooms** Shower or bathtub, hair dryer. **Comfort & Décor** The hotel is geared for business types and therefore has corresponding amenities, including an on-site, Florentine-style restaurant and piano bar. Guest-room beds tend to be firm, and each room has work space. Some rooms have balconies.

RATES, RESERVATIONS, & RESTRICTIONS

Pricing Singles €130–€230 , doubles €180–€300, doubles with lounge €270–€370. **Credit Cards** AMEX, MC, V. **Check-In/Out** 2 p.m./noon. **Elevator** Yes. **English Spoken** Yes.

Hotel Il Guelfo Bianco   €120–€220

OVERALL ★★★★ | QUALITY ★★★ | VALUE ★★★★★ | SAN GIOVANNI

Via Cavour, 29; 50129 Florence; phone 055 288 330, fax 055 295 203; www.ilguelfobianco.it

This smallish inn, located in a Renaissance palazzo, combines tastefully classic rooms with modern conveniences. The hotel is divided into two sections, the main part and the "Cristallo," an annex that opened in the mid-1990s. In some rooms in the latter, you'll find original wood-beam-and-terra-cotta brick ceilings or 17th-century frescoes, whereas in the rooms of the former, you'll find convincing reproductions of antique fixtures. For spectacular views, try to reserve room 42, with a drop-dead glimpse of the cupola of the Duomo. If it's peace you want, room 11 looks out over the hotel's courtyard. Breakfast is served in a quaint Art Deco room or, during warmer months, in the garden out back. Two rooms on the ground level are fully adapted for disabled travelers.

SETTING & FACILITIES

Location San Lorenzo. **Quietness Rating** A. **Dining**. Breakfast included in price. **Amenities** Parking nearby, bar on the premises.

ACCOMMODATIONS

Rooms 43 rooms. **All** Phone, satellite TV, minibar. **Bathrooms** Shower or bathtub, hair dryer. **Comfort & Décor** Contemporary art and futon furniture contrast nicely with wood beamed ceilings and arched doorways. All rooms in the hotel are similar; all those in the Cristallo are different. Each guest room is nicely decorated with soft colors and ample lighting. Triple-glazed windows successfully block out the noise from Via Cavour.

RATES, RESERVATIONS, & RESTRICTIONS

Pricing Singles €120, doubles €220. **Credit Cards** AMEX, MC, V. **Check-In/Out** 2 p.m./noon. **Elevator** Yes. **English Spoken** Yes.

Hotel Lungarno   €200–€450

OVERALL ★★★★★ | QUALITY ★★★★★ | VALUE ★ | OLTRARNO

Borgo San Jacopo; 50125 Florence; phone 055 272 61, reservations 055 272 64000, fax 055 268 437, fax reservations 055 272 64444; www.lungarnohotels.com

One of the best-situated hotels in Florence, the Hotel Lungarno is owned by the Ferragamo family (of footwear fame) and resides on the tony Borgo San Jacopo, with postcard views across the Arno of the Duomo, the Palazzo Vecchio, and the Ponte Vecchio. Some rooms have balconies overlooking the river; other rooms are conversation pieces in themselves, having been built into the ancient walls of the hotel.

SETTING & FACILITIES

Location Oltrarno. **Quietness Rating** A. **Dining** Breakfast included in rates. **Amenities** Parking garage nearby, meeting facilities. **Services** Laundry, shuttle service to the train station, room service.

ACCOMMODATIONS

Rooms 68 rooms, 12 suites. **All** Phone, minibar, satellite TV, fax and modem line. **Bathrooms** Shower or bathtub, hair dryer. **Comfort & Décor** Recently renovated, rooms are striking, with canopy beds and antique furniture.

RATES, RESERVATIONS, & RESTRICTIONS

Pricing Singles €210, doubles €450. **Credit Cards** AMEX, MC, V. **Check-In/Out** 2 p.m./noon. **Elevator** Yes. **English Spoken** Yes.

Hotel Morandi alla Crocetta €115–€200

OVERALL ★★★★ | QUALITY ★★★★ | VALUE ★★★★★ | SAN GIOVANNI

Via Laura, 50; 50121 Florence; phone 055 234 4747; fax 055 248 0954; www.hotelmorandi.it

Book early at this hotel, a renovated 16th-century convent, and you may get to stay in the former chapel, which still has its original wall frescoes. Elsewhere in the 10-room hotel, you'll find other religious relics, preserved woodwork, and Victorian antiques hand-picked by the expatriate Briton proprietor Katherine Doyle Antuono. Her son Paolo runs the hotel now, paying careful attention to maintenance and customer service.

SETTING & FACILITIES

Location East of San Lorenzo, near the Museo Archeologico. **Quietness Rating** A+. **Dining** Breakfast, €11. **Amenities** Parking nearby, pets allowed. **Services** Babysitting, room service available for breakfast, staff can arrange private tours.

ACCOMMODATIONS

Rooms 10. **All** Phone, satellite TV, in-room safe. **Bathrooms** Shower or bathtub, hair dryer. **Comfort & Décor** Like staying in your Italian grandmother's home, the Morandi Hotel has a cozy sitting room, fluffy beds, and Persian rugs. Tones of ochre, saffron, peach, and burgundy create a warm, inviting atmosphere. Fresh flowers also add a nice touch.

RATES, RESERVATIONS, & RESTRICTIONS

Pricing Singles €118, doubles €200. **Credit Cards** AMEX, DC, MC, V. **Check-In/Out** 2 p.m./noon. **Elevator** Yes. **English Spoken** Yes.

Hotel Palazzo Vecchio €75–€120

OVERALL ★★★ | QUALITY ★★★ | VALUE ★★★★ | SANTA MARIA NOVELLA

Via Cennini, 4; 50123 Florence; phone 055 212 182 or 055 238 1209, fax 055 216 445; www.hotelpalazzovecchio.it

One block from Santa Maria Novella train station and the Congress Center (and nowhere near the actual Palazzo Vecchio), this hotel is an inexpensive option, especially for business travelers. If you're driving rather than taking the train, then you can park in the hotel's private parking lot.

SETTING & FACILITIES

Location Santa Maria Novella. **Quietness Rating** B–. **Dining** Breakfast included in rates. **Amenities** Garden, parking on site.

ACCOMMODATIONS

Rooms 25, 5 of which are singles. **All** Phone, satellite TV. **Bathrooms** Shower or bathtub, hair dryer. **Comfort & Décor** Recent renovations resulted in more spacious bedrooms with new bed linens and window treatments.

RATES, RESERVATIONS, & RESTRICTIONS

Pricing Singles €78, doubles €119. **Credit Cards** MC, V. **Check-In/Out** 2 p.m./noon. **Elevator** Yes. **English Spoken** Some.

Hotel Porta Rossa   €100–€240

OVERALL ★★★★ | QUALITY ★★★ | VALUE ★★★★ | SAN GIOVANNI

Via Porta Rossa, 19, 50123; phone 055 287 551, fax 055 282 179

The oldest hotel in Florence (built in 1386) has hosted guests such as Stendhal and D. H. Lawrence. Porta Rossa shows its age, with heavy doors, lead-framed windows, and sexagenarian porters. At times, it seems more stodgy than snug. But the lobby, decorated with a patterned marble floor, stained-glass ceiling, high archways, and leather lounge chairs, is regal. The location is a just a stroll away from the Piazza della Signoria, and if you book a room in the hotel's medieval tower, you'll enjoy sweeping views of the Palazzo Vecchio.

SETTING & FACILITIES

Location Due south of Piazza della Repubblica. **Quietness Rating** B. **Dining** Breakfast included in rates. **Amenities** Internet access, meeting room, bar.

ACCOMMODATIONS

Rooms 2 singles and 6 doubles without baths; 8 singles and 63 doubles with baths. **All** Phone, satellite TV. **Bathrooms** Shower or bathtub available in most rooms. **Comfort & Décor** Because the hotel is so old, many of the amenities had to be retrofitted. Elevators are small, and showers are even smaller. Accommodations are rather Spartan but clean, and some rooms are enormous.

RATES, RESERVATIONS, AND RESTRICTIONS

Pricing Singles €109–€124, doubles €140–€166, triples/quads, €208–€240. **Credit Cards** AMEX, MC, V. **Check-In/Out** 2 p.m./noon. **Elevator** Yes. **English Spoken** Yes.

Hotel Sanremo   €83–€191

OVERALL ★★★ | QUALITY ★★★ | VALUE ★★★★★ | OLTRARNO

Lungarno Serristori, 13; 50125 Florence; phone 055 234 2823, fax 055 234 2269;
vo.dada.it/hotelsanremo-fi

The Sanremo is located just across the river from Santa Croce in a quiet
residential neighborhood on the Arno. Rooms are clean and pretty, if a
bit frumpy. But what the Sanremo lacks in décor, it makes up for in the
view. About half of the 20 rooms have riverfront views with the Duomo
in the background, and the back rooms look over a quiet, shady street.
Staying here allows you to begin and end your day with a peaceful stroll
along the Arno, which is, of course, one of the simple pleasures of visiting Florence. Book early.

SETTING & FACILITIES

Location In the shadow of Piazzale Michelangelo. **Quietness Rating** A. **Dining** Small
breakfast area. **Amenities** Parking, some rooms are equipped for Internet access.

ACCOMMODATIONS

Rooms 20. **All** Private baths, satellite TV, phone, safe. **Bathrooms** Shower or bath,
hair dryer. **Comfort & Décor** The furnishings here are done in a "rustic Tuscan" style,
and no two rooms are alike. Some accommodations were a bit dowdy. The cool, tiled
floors provide a shock first thing in the morning.

RATES, RESERVATIONS, & RESTRICTIONS

Pricing Singles €83–€108, doubles €109–€139, triples/quads, €134–€191. **Credit
Cards** AMEX, MC, V. **Check-In/Out** 2 p.m./noon. **Elevator** No. **English Spoken**
Some.

Il Porcellino   €50–€95

OVERALL ★★★½ | QUALITY ★★★½ | VALUE ★★★★★ | SAN GIOVANNI

Piazza del Mercato Nuovo, 4; 50123 Florence; phone 055 282 686, fax 055 218 572;
www.hotelporcellino.it

Right above the Mercato Nuovo, the Porcellino (named after the market's famous boar statue) is a well-kept and very friendly guesthouse on
the third floor of a renovated 19th-century building. All of the inn's six
rooms are very bright, with huge windows that open up to the sights and
sounds of the market (amusing the first day, but it can get loud). Furthermore, the Porcellino opened only a few years back, meaning that all
the furniture is new, and the bedding is far from broken in. This is an
ideal choice for first-time visitors to Florence, budget travelers, and
returnees, so book early and often. The guesthouse is closed during the
entire month of August.

SETTING & FACILITIES

Location Mercato Nuovo. **Quietness Rating** B–. **Dining** No. **Amenities** Private
bath, satellite television, telephone.

ACCOMMODATIONS

Rooms 2 singles, 4 doubles. **All** Private bathrooms, satellite TV, phone. **Bathrooms** Shower only; one double has a tub. **Comfort & Décor** These are great accommodations for allergy sufferers—terra cotta floors are immaculate, and the presence of few rugs means there's less dust. Rooms are bigger than what you'll find at other hotels and are decorated discretely with antique headboards, hand-painted furniture, and a few choice pieces of art.

RATES, RESERVATIONS, & RESTRICTIONS

Pricing Singles €52–€68, doubles €72–€93. **Credit Cards** AMEX, DC, MC, V. **Check-In/Out** Between 8:30 a.m. and 6 p.m./before 10:30 a.m. **Elevator** No. **English Spoken** Yes.

Residenza dei Pucci   €90–€145

OVERALL ★★★★ | QUALITY ★★★★ | VALUE ★★★★★ | SAN GIOVANNI

Via dei Pucci, 9; 50122 Florence; phone 055 281 886, fax 055 264 314;
residenzapucci.interfree.it

You'll be hard-pressed to find another such well-appointed, inexpensive inn so close to the Duomo. The design-savvy pair Alessandra and Cristina have completely redone eight rooms in this 19th-century building with firm beds (some four-poster), marble-top tables, and a smattering of modern art. Although Residenza dei Pucci boasts few in-room amenities (just a TV and private bathroom), it is becoming a hit with frequent travelers to Florence who just need a place to unwind.

SETTING & FACILITIES

Location Near the Duomo. **Quietness Rating** B. **Dining** Light breakfast included in the rates. **Amenities** Parking nearby.

ACCOMMODATIONS

Rooms 8. **All** Private bathrooms, TV. **Bathrooms** Shower or bath. **Comfort & Décor** All rooms are unique and are color-coordinated from floor to ceiling with chintz fabrics in bold prints and stripes. Rooms aren't flooded with light, but the dimness adds to the ambience.

RATES, RESERVATIONS & RESTRICTIONS

Pricing Double for single use, €90–€130, doubles €105–€145. **Credit Cards** AMEX, MC, V. **Check-In/Out** 2 p.m./noon. **Elevator** No. **English Spoken** Yes.

Sofitel Firenze   €300–€350

OVERALL ★★★★ | QUALITY ★★★ | VALUE ★ | SAN GIOVANNI

Via de' Cerretani, 10; 50129 Florence; phone 055 238 1301, fax 055 238 1312;
www.sofitel.com

Our one wish for the Sofitel would be that it would "update" its look with period furnishings and a more Florentine ambience. Currently, this hotel, situated in a converted 17th-century palace a few blocks from the Duomo and San Lorenzo, has about as much character as a convention hotel. Despite its aesthetic shortcomings, the Sofitel does its best to keep you comfortable. Service is polite and diligent. Il Patio, the hotel's restaurant, is good in a pinch, with authentic, reasonably priced Tuscan fare. Meanwhile, wall-to-wall carpeting and separate sitting areas in each of the guest rooms make it easy to spread out and settle in.

SETTING & FACILITIES

Location Near the Duomo. **Quietness Rating** A. **Dining** Breakfast included in rates; restaurant and bar on premises. **Amenities** Internet access, parking nearby, pets allowed. **Services** Baby-sitting, laundry service, room service, secretarial services, shuttle to the airport.

ACCOMMODATIONS

Rooms 77 doubles, 6 singles. **All** Phone, satellite TV, soundproof windows, in-room safe, radio, minibar, data port connections. **Bathrooms** Shower or bathtub. **Comfort & Décor** Disappointingly, the décor in the Sofitel contrasts greatly with the 17th-century palace that the hotel occupies. Nevertheless, rooms are clean and spacious.

RATES, RESERVATIONS, & RESTRICTIONS

Pricing Singles €305, doubles €330. **Credit Cards** AMEX, MC, V. **Check-In/Out** 2 p.m./11 a.m. **Elevator** Yes. **English Spoken** Yes.

Hotel Profiles—The Rest of Tuscany

THE BEST HOTELS IN THE REST OF TUSCANY				
Hotel	Overall Rating	Quality Rating	Value Rating	Price
The Province of Florence				
Galluzzo				
Relais Certosa	★★★	★★★	★★	€160–€330
Chianti				
Castello Vicchiomaggio	★★★★	★★★★	★★★	€200–€300
Villa Le Barone	★★★	★★★★	★★★	€210–€260
The Province of Siena				
Siena				
Academy Hotel	★★★	★★★	★★★	€90–€250
Hotel Antica Torre	★★★	★★★	★★★	€85–€105
Hotel Chiusarelli	★★	★★★	★★★★	€70–€100
Hotel Duomo	★★★	★★★	★★★	€120–€180
Pensione Palazzo Ravizza	★★★★	★★★★	★★★	€105–€390
The Province of Arezzo				
Arezzo				
Hotel Continentale	★★★	★★★	★★★	€60–€165

	Overall	Quality	Value	
Hotel	**Rating**	**Rating**	**Rating**	**Price**
THE BEST HOTELS IN THE REST OF TUSCANY *(continued)*				
The Province of Arezzo (continued)				
Cortona				
Il Falconiere	★★★★★	★★★★★	★★	€240–€500
The Province of Lucca				
Lucca				
Hotel La Luna	★★★	★★★	★★★★	€90–€200
Villa La Principessa	★★★★★	★★★★★	★★★★★	€155–€275
Riviera Versilia				
Hotel President	★★★★	★★★★	★★★	€120–€315
Goya	★★★	★★★	★★★	€140–€415
The Province of Pisa				
Pisa				
Royal Victoria Hotel	★★★★	★★★	★★★★	€55–€185
Hotel Francesco	★★★	★★★	★★★	€72–€106
Hotel Roseto	★★	★★	★★★★	€52–€124

The Province of Florence

Galluzzo

Relais Certosa   €160–€330

OVERALL ★★★ | QUALITY ★★ | VALUE ★★ | LOCALITÀ GALLUZZO

Via Colle Ramole, 2; Florence 50124; phone 055 204 7171, fax 055 268 575;
www.bettojahotels.it

Ideal for drivers just passing through to Siena, the Relais Certosa sits in a valley beneath an immense 14th-century Carthusian monastery, which houses some unfinished works by Pontormo. By all accounts, this is a business hotel—most rooms look alike, and decorations are bland. But some rooms do open up onto sunny terraces with lounge chairs. Room 511 is especially nice and airy. The Relais is a bit of a haul from the center of Florence, but that might just be the thing for travelers who prefer to avoid tourist traps. ATAF bus service to Florence and SITA bus service to Siena are available just outside the hotel grounds.

SETTING & FACILITIES

Location South of the city center, in Galluzzo. **Quietness Rating** A+. **Dining** Breakfast included in rates; restaurant available for lunch and dinner. **Amenities** Parking, above-ground swimming pool, surrounded by a forest, restaurant on the premises. **Services** Shuttle service to Florence's center can be reserved through the concierge.

ACCOMMODATIONS

Rooms 70. **All** Satellite TV, phone, private bath, safe. **Bathrooms** Shower or bath, hair dryer. **Comfort & Décor** Rooms are small, and accoutrements, such as linens and drapes, show signs of wear. Conversely, the bathrooms are huge.

RATES, RESERVATIONS, & RESTRICTIONS

Pricing Doubles €160–€240, triples/suites, €260–€330. **Credit Cards** AMEX, MC, V. **Check-In/Out** 2 p.m./noon. **Elevator** Yes, but you must climb a flight of stairs to reach it. **English Spoken** Yes.

Chianti

Castello Vicchiomaggio   €200–€300

OVERALL ★★★★ | QUALITY ★★★★ | VALUE ★★★ | GREVE IN CHIANTI (CHIANTI FIORENTINA)

Via Vicchiomaggio, 4; 50022 Greve in Chianti; phone 055 854 079, fax 055 853 911; www.vicchiomaggio.it

Set in a medieval castle among the vineyards, the Castello Vicchiomaggio claims to have hosted Caterina Medici back in the day. You can stay in the Caterina de' Medici suite, or any of the other 11 suites, all of which are decorated in a graceful but grandmotherly style. Vicchiomaggio's restaurant is one of the finest in Tuscany (see Part Five, Dining in Central Italy). When you're not indoors, you can survey the grounds or sign up for a tour of the wine cellars.

SETTING & FACILITIES

Location In the Chanti hills. **Quietness Rating** A. **Dining** The restaurant on the premises serves traditional Tuscan fare. **Amenities** Free parking, restaurant.

ACCOMMODATIONS

Rooms 12. **All** Phone, satellite TV. **Bathrooms** Shower, hair dryer. **Comfort & Décor** Rooms are large and stately, with high ceilings and tiled floors. These are old quarters, so it can get drafty. Bathrooms are retrofitted and a bit cramped.

RATES, RESERVATIONS, & RESTRICTIONS

Pricing Suites, €200–€300, two-night minimum stay. **Credit Cards** MC, V. **Check-In/Out** 3 p.m./noon. **Elevator** No. **English Spoken** Yes.

Villa Le Barone   €210–€260

OVERALL ★★★ | QUALITY ★★★★ | VALUE ★★★ | PANZANO IN CHIANTI (CHIANTI FIORENTINA)

Via San Leolino, 19; 50020 Panzano in Chianti; phone 055 852 621, fax 055 852 277; www.villalebarone.it

The famous della Robbia family, who produced Luca and Andrea of tile-making fame, has owned this Chiantishire residence since the 16th century. All of the guest rooms are in different buildings on the estate. The manor house room is particularly pretty. An on-site restaurant, which caters only to hotel guests, is located in the former stables. Open April through November.

SETTING & FACILITIES

Location In the Chianti hills. **Quietness Rating** A. **Dining** Breakfast and dinner included in rates. **Amenities** Free parking, swimming pool, tennis courts.

ACCOMMODATIONS

Rooms 30. **All** Phone. **Bathrooms** Shower or bathtub, hair dryer. **Comfort & Décor** Guest rooms vary in size and décor, but tend to be intimate. Furnishings are far from fancy, but they are attractive, conveying the feel of a hunting lodge or country home.

RATES, RESERVATIONS & RESTRICTIONS

Pricing €210–€260. **Credit Cards** AMEX, MC, V. **Check-In/Out** 3 p.m./noon. **Elevator** No. **English Spoken** Some.

The Province of Siena

Siena

Academy Hotel	€90–€250

OVERALL ★★★ | QUALITY ★★★ | VALUE ★★★ | SIENA

Via Lombardi, 41; 53100 Siena; phone 0577 5755, fax 0577 332 409; www.academyhotel.it

An oddly modern hotel, given the medieval setting of Siena, but ideal for travelers passing through. Right off the highway, the hotel has its own parking lot. It is also fully equipped to deal with disabled travelers. There are roll-in showers and very wide halls and doorways. Business travelers will also find the Academy convenient, as it has a few large meetings rooms, and guest rooms have phones with modem jacks. A bus stop across the street will take you into town. Bus tickets can be purchased from the hotel's front desk.

SETTING & FACILITIES

Location On the outskirts of Siena. **Quietness Rating** A. **Dining** Buffet breakfast included in rates. **Amenities** Private parking.

ACCOMMODATIONS

Rooms 136. **All** Phone, satellite TV, minibar. **Bathrooms** Shower, hair dryer. **Comfort & Décor** Spartan, uninteresting décor is typical of a suburban hotel, and it's typical here, too. Rooms have wide picture windows, which, sadly, offer no inspirational views. Bathrooms are spacious and adapted for wheelchairs. Tile floors keep the entire room cool, but there are ample blankets in the closets.

RATES, RESERVATIONS, & RESTRICTIONS

Pricing Doubles €90–€155, triples/suites, €155–€250. **Credit Cards** AMEX, MC, V. **Check-In/Out** 2 p.m./noon. **Elevator** Yes. **English Spoken** Yes.

Hotel Antica Torre   €85–€105

OVERALL ★★★ | QUALITY ★★★ | VALUE ★★★ | SIENA

Via Fieravecchia, 7; 53100 Siena; phone/fax 0577 222 255.

The old tower has two rooms per floor, each flanking a dramatic, twisting stone staircase. Located about ten minutes from Piazza del Campo, the architecturally interesting hotel is a hit with many tourists, so don't arrive without reservations.

SETTING & FACILITIES

Location In the southeast corner of town. **Quietness Rating** A. **Dining** Breakfast included in rates (but it's small). **Amenities** Safe available at front desk.

ACCOMMODATIONS

Rooms 8. **All** Phone, TV. **Bathrooms** Showers; hair dryer available at front desk. **Comfort & Décor** When was the last time you tried to make a 16th-century watchtower comfortable? The family that owns the Antica Torre has taken great care in choosing tasteful and delicate furnishings for the rooms. Every room is different and cozy.

RATES, RESERVATIONS, & RESTRICTIONS

Pricing €85–€105. **Credit Cards** MC, V. **Check-In/Out** 2 p.m./noon. **Elevator** No. **English Spoken** Yes.

Hotel Chiusarelli   €70–€100

OVERALL ★★ | QUALITY ★★★ | VALUE ★★★★ | SIENA

Viale Curtatone, 15; 53100 Siena; phone 0577 280 562, fax 0577 271 177

Located in a pretty, ochre-washed villa on the edge of town, the Chiusarelli is just a short bus ride away from the city center (the bus stop is next to the hotel). The façade shows signs of neglect, especially the crumbling balconies, but the rooms were revamped in 2000. There's a small garden in the back.

SETTING & FACILITIES

Location Outside the city gates. **Quietness Rating** B. **Dining** Hotel Chiusarelli serves classic Tuscan cuisine. **Amenities** Meeting room, parking nearby.

ACCOMMODATIONS

Rooms 49. **All** Phone, satellite TV, in-room safe, minibar. **Bathrooms** Shower or bathtub, hair dryer. **Comfort & Décor** Recent renovations have improved the hotel's furnishings and fixtures, but the décor is still quite spartan. Plenty of room to stretch out.

RATES, RESERVATIONS, & RESTRICTIONS

Pricing €70–€100. **Credit Cards** MC, V. **Check-In/Out** 2 p.m./noon. **Elevator** No. **English Spoken** Yes.

Hotel Duomo €120–€180

OVERALL ★★★ | QUALITY ★★★ | VALUE ★★★ | SIENA

Via Stalloreggi, 38; 53100 Siena; phone 0577 289 088, fax 0577 43 043;
www.hotelduomo.it

Located in a 17th-century palace, the Hotel Duomo is a modest three-star property in the historical center. On the upper floors, you can enjoy views over Siena's medieval rooftops. Breakfast is served on the ground floor of the building, under original stone vaults.

SETTING & FACILITIES

Location A few blocks from the Duomo. **Quietness Rating** A. **Dining** Breakfast included in rates. **Amenities** Free parking.

ACCOMMODATIONS

Rooms 23. **All** Phone, satellite TV. **Bathrooms** Shower or bathtub, hair dryer. **Comfort & Décor** Rooms are rather plain but were recently outfitted with new linens.

RATES, RESERVATIONS, & RESTRICTIONS

Pricing Doubles €120–€180. **Credit Cards** MC, V. **Check-In/Out** 2 p.m./noon. **Elevator** No. **English Spoken** Yes.

Pensione Palazzo Ravizza €105–€390

OVERALL ★★★★ | QUALITY ★★★★ | VALUE ★★★ | SIENA

Via Pian dei Mantellini, 34; 53100 Siena; phone 0577 280 462, fax 0577 221 597;
www.palazzoravizza.it

Set in a Renaissance-era palazzo within the city walls, the Palazzo Ravizza is a gorgeous gem of a hotel. A hotel since the 1920s, the Ravizza was renovated in 2000, and special care was given to the restoration of its vaulted ceilings and original tiled floors. The hotel has a pretty courtyard with bistro tables, where you can dine for breakfast of dinner. Room 12 has a fantastic view of the Tuscan *campagna*.

SETTING & FACILITIES

Location On the corner of town, southwest of the Piazza del Campo. **Quietness Rating** A. **Dining** Breakfast included in rates, full and half-board available. **Amenities** Free parking, Internet access. **Services** Room service, laundry service, twice-daily maid service.

ACCOMMODATIONS

Rooms 31 doubles, 4 suites. **All** Phone, satellite TV, in-room safe, minibar. **Bathrooms** Shower or bathtub, hair dryer; suites have hot tubs. **Comfort & Décor** Though they vary in size and style, the guest rooms are luxurious by any standard. All have their original terra cotta or parquet floors, and some are decorated with four-poster beds.

RATES, RESERVATIONS, & RESTRICTIONS

Pricing Doubles €105–€200, suites €225–€390. **Credit Cards** MC, V. **Check-In/Out** 3 p.m./11 a.m. **Elevator** No. **English Spoken** Yes.

The Province of Arezzo

Arezzo

Hotel Continentale   €60–€165

OVERALL ★★★ | QUALITY ★★★ | VALUE ★★★ | AREZZO

Piazza Guido Monaco, 7; 52100 Arezzo; phone 0575 20 251, fax 0575 350 485;
www.hotelcontinentale.com

Traveling with a group to see the frescoes in San Francesco? The Hotel Continentale is ideal for groups of 20 or more, and it has a conference room that accommodates up to 300. Other travelers will enjoy the hotel's prime position near the train station and the church, as well as the roof deck, which affords views over the spires and gables.

SETTING & FACILITIES

Location Near the church of San Francesco. **Quietness Rating** A. **Dining** Buffet breakfast, €8. **Amenities** Meeting room, roof garden.

ACCOMMODATIONS

Rooms 73. **All** Phone, satellite TV, minibar. **Bathrooms** Shower or bathtub, hair dryer. **Comfort & Décor** Room décor is old-fashioned and quite frumpy.

RATES, RESERVATIONS, & RESTRICTIONS

Pricing Singles €60–€70, doubles €75–€100, triples/quads €130–€165. **Credit Cards** MC, V. **Check-In/Out** 2 p.m./noon. **Elevator** Yes. **English Spoken** Yes.

Cortona

Il Falconiere   €240–€500

OVERALL ★★★★★ | QUALITY ★★★★★ | VALUE ★★ | CORTONA

Localitá San Martino, 370; 52044 Cortona; phone 0575 612 679, fax 0575 612 927;
www.ilfalconiere.com.

Live out your sunny Tuscan fantasies at Il Falconiere, one of the premier country villas in Tuscany. The former home of poet Antonio Guadagnoli, the vision of the 17th-century building set among lone cypresses, rosemary hedges, and all manner of flowering bushes will surely make your heart sing. Young Riccardo Baracchi is the patriarch of the villa estate, and he and his wife Silvia, the genius in the Falconiere's restaurant, have taken great care to balance hotel luxury with homey comfort. The sights of Cortona, Arezzo, and Perugia are not far away from here. But, why would you want to leave when romance and relaxation are so close at hand?

SETTING & FACILITIES

Location Approximately two miles north of Cortona **Quietness Rating** A+. **Dining** Breakfast included with rates; Il Falconiere restaurant is one of the best in Tuscany. **Amenities** Swimming pool, garden terrace, free parking, Internet access. Winery, wildlife refuge, and horseback riding on premises. Cooking-class packages are available.

ACCOMMODATIONS

Rooms 19. **All** Phone, satellite TV, minibar, in-room safe. **Bathrooms** All are private with showers, some have whirlpools; hair dryer. **Comfort & Décor** Rooms are outfitted sumptuously with antiques, heirloom linens, and oriental rugs. Surrounded by gardens, vineyards, and Tuscan pines, the Falconiere estate is big enough that you're likely to feel as if you're the only guest.

RATES, RESERVATIONS & RESTRICTIONS

Pricing Doubles €240–€300, suites €400–€500. **Credit Cards** AMEX, MC, V. **Check-In/Out** 2 p.m./11 a.m. **Elevator** Yes. **English Spoken** Yes.

The Province of Lucca

Lucca

Hotel La Luna   €90–€200

OVERALL ★★★ | QUALITY ★★★ | VALUE ★★★★ | LUCCA

Via Fillungo-Corte Compagnoni, 12; 55100 Lucca; phone 0583 493 634, fax 0583 490 021; www.hotellaluna.com

A small hotel within the ramparts of Lucca, La Luna is ideal for a relaxing stay. Two fully renewed 17th-century *palazzi* make up the hotel, and between them sits a tranquil courtyard. Even if you don't get a room that faces the courtyard, the only noises you're likely to hear are church carillons and bicycle bells. The suites have sitting rooms and fireplaces.

SETTING & FACILITIES

Location Lucca city center. **Quietness Rating** A. **Dining** Breakfast included in price. **Amenities** Private garage, meeting facilities, 24-hour bar.

ACCOMMODATIONS

Rooms 30. **All** Private bathroom, satellite TV. **Bathrooms** Bathtub with shower nozzle. **Comfort & Décor** Furnishings are sumptuous, given the room rates. Hand-painted headboards, gilded furniture, and mirrors provide an elegant touch.

RATES, RESERVATIONS, & RESTRICTIONS

Pricing Doubles €90, suites (2) €120–€200. **Credit Cards** AMEX, DC, MC, V. **Check-In/Out** 2 p.m./noon. **Elevator** No. **English Spoken** Yes.

Villa La Principessa   €155–€275

OVERALL ★★★★★ | QUALITY ★★★★★ | VALUE ★★★★★ | LUCCA

S.S. del Brennero (Via Nuova per Pisa), 1616; 55050 Lucca, phone 0583 370 037, fax 0583 379 136; www.lunet.it/aziende/villaprincipessa/welcome.html

Its not uncommon for guests of Villa la Principessa to feel like pampered kings and queens during their stay. Set among acres of the Tuscan *campagna* in a renovated 14th-century villa, the Principessa is one of the loveliest hotels in all of Italy. Converted into a hotel in 1973, the property boasts many modern comforts, not the least of which are its pool and massage services, yet it still maintains the architectural and design integrity intended when it was built by the duke of Lucca. Although it is conveniently located to Lucca and the mountainous Garfagnana valley and is less than a 30-minute drive away from Florence, Villa la Principessa is often a destination in itself. We highly recommend it for honeymooners, nature lovers, and pleasure seekers.

SETTING & FACILITIES

Location In the countryside below Lucca. **Quietness Rating** A. **Dining** Restaurant and bar are on the premises, half board is available for approximately €40 per person per night. **Amenities** Parking on site, swimming pool, tennis courts, nonsmoking rooms, meeting rooms. **Services** Ticket booking services, car rental desk, massage, room service, laundry service.

ACCOMMODATIONS

Rooms 40. **All** Satellite TV, radio, in-room safe, phone, minibar. **Bathrooms** Shower and bath, hair dryer. **Comfort & Décor** From the chandeliers on the ceiling to the polychrome marble floors, every inch of Villa La Principessa oozes opulence.

RATES, RESERVATIONS, & RESTRICTIONS

Pricing Singles €155, doubles €244, triples/suites €275. **Credit Cards** AMEX, MC, V. **Check-In/Out** 2 p.m./noon. **Elevator** Yes. **English Spoken** Yes.

Riviera Versilia

Goya	€140–€415

OVERALL ★★★ | QUALITY ★★★ | VALUE ★★★ | FORTE DEI MARMI

Via Carducci, 59; 55042 Forte dei Marmi; phone 0584 787 221, fax 0584 787 269; www.hotelgoya.it

Close to shopping and the beach, Hotel Goya offers simple, comfortable accommodations in the upper-crust town of Forte dei Marmi. If you want to see how the other half lives but not pay through the nose for it, book early. If you do, you may be able to score a room with a balcony, which will afford you incredible views of the Apuane Alps and the shore. Prices for the suites at Hotel Goya are significantly higher but not worth the extra expense.

SETTING & FACILITIES

Location Blocks from the oceanfront. **Quietness Rating** B. **Dining** Breakfast included in rates, restaurant on the premises. **Amenities** Parking, bike rental, garden, hot tub, conference room.

ACCOMMODATIONS

Rooms 47. **All** Satellite TV, in-room safe. **Bathrooms** Shower, hair dryer; two suites have whirlpool baths. **Comfort & Décor** Like most of the hotels on the Versilian Coast, the Goya is done in an Art Deco/Liberty style. Public rooms here are much nicer than the bedrooms, which are kept clean but free of any interesting décor.

RATES, RESERVATIONS & RESTRICTIONS

Pricing Singles €140–€170, doubles €150–€200, suites €260–€415. **Credit Cards** AMEX, MC, V. **Check-In/Out** 2 p.m./noon. **Elevator** Yes. **English Spoken** Yes.

Hotel President   €120–€315

OVERALL ★★★★ | QUALITY ★★★★ | VALUE ★★★ | VIAREGGIO

Viale Carducci, 5; 55049 Viareggio; phone 0584 962 712, fax 0584 963 658;
www.hotelpresident.it

The refined guest rooms and stellar location of the Hotel President have made it a year-round favorite with carnivalgoers and beachcombers. Rooms here are huge; most feature balconies and lounge areas, which are perfect places to unwind after a long day of windsurfing and sunbathing. The shaded rooftop restaurant and bar is ideal for an afternoon snack. When you're done, take the glass elevator down to the lobby, which opens up onto to the bustling Viareggio promenade.

SETTING & FACILITIES

Location On the boardwalk. **Quietness Rating** B. **Dining** Buffet breakfast included in rates; restaurant and bar on the premises. **Amenities** Car-rental desk, parking, meeting rooms. **Services** Ticketing desk, beach umbrella sales, room service.

ACCOMMODATIONS

Rooms 37. **All** Satellite TV, phone, in-room safe, minibar. **Bathrooms** Shower or bath, hair dryer. **Comfort & Décor** The décor in the public areas is smart, done in bold shades that recall the sunset. All of the bedrooms were recently refurbished and feature firm, new beds and reupholstered couches and chairs in the sitting rooms.

RATES, RESERVATIONS, & RESTRICTIONS

Pricing Doubles €120–€200, suites €220–€315. **Credit Cards** AMEX, MC, V. **Check-In/Out** 2 p.m./noon. **Elevator** Yes. **English Spoken** Yes.

The Province of Pisa

Pisa

Hotel Francesco   €72–€106

OVERALL ★★★ | QUALITY ★★★ | VALUE ★★★ | PISA

Via Santa Maria, 129; 56100 Pisa; phone 050 554 109, fax 050 556 145;
www.hotelfrancesco.com

If you're looking for no-frills lodging near the Leaning Tower, you'll like the Francesco, located on a side street near the Botanical Gardens. The rooms are very simple and decorated with contemporary wood furnishings. One room is fully equipped for travelers with disabilities. The hotel restaurant is cute, with vaulted ceilings and a checkerboard floor, and it serves a selection of pizzas and traditional Tuscan entrées. Francesco's roof garden is its best feature; it offers a view of the tower above the treetops.

SETTING & FACILITIES

Location Near the Botanical Gardens. **Quietness Rating** A. **Dining** Breakfast included in rates; restaurant on premises. **Amenities** Meetings rooms, parking nearby. **Services** Shuttle to the airport, bike and scooter rental.

ACCOMMODATIONS

Rooms 13, 1 adapted for disabled guests. **All** Phone, TV, minibar. **Bathrooms** Shower or bath, hair dryer. **Comfort & Décor** The décor is a bit frumpy and cold, but big picture windows that let in the fresh air of the Orto Botanico make up for it.

RATES, RESERVATIONS, & RESTRICTIONS

Pricing Singles €72–€88, doubles €78–€106. **Credit Cards** AMEX, DC, V. **Check-In/Out** 2 p.m./noon. **Elevator** Yes. **English Spoken** Yes.

Hotel Roseto €52–€124

OVERALL ★★ | QUALITY ★★ | VALUE ★★★★ | PISA

Via P. Mascagni, 24; 56100 Pisa; phone 050 42596, fax 050 42087

A funky mishmash of colors and styles, the Hotel Roseto isn't all that pleasing to the eye, but it's very kind to your wallet. The fact that this two-star property is located near the train station means that there's always a steady stream of visitors. But luckily, the Roseto doesn't suffer from an overabundance of American tourists (which is the case at most hotels in Pisa). There's a pretty garden out back where, during warmer months, you can enjoy breakfast. The rest of the year, *prima colazione* is served in the breakfast room—one of the better-looking parts of the hotel, where you'll find cathedral ceilings and large antique mirrors.

SETTING & FACILITIES

Location Near the train station. **Quietness Rating** B. **Dining** Breakfast included in rates.

ACCOMMODATIONS

Rooms 22. **All** Satellite TV, phone, minibar. **Bathrooms** Shower or bath, hair dryer. **Comfort & Décor** The color scheme here is a ghastly combination of purple, mustard, and teal. But, once you're asleep, you won't notice. Some beds are on the thin side.

RATES, RESERVATIONS, & RESTRICTIONS

Pricing Singles €52, doubles €74, triples €102, quads €124. **Credit Cards** MC, V. **Check-In/Out** 2 p.m./noon. **Elevator** No. **English Spoken** Some.

Royal Victoria Hotel €55–€185

OVERALL ★★★★ | QUALITY ★★★ | VALUE ★★★★ | PISA

Lungarno Pacinotti, 12; 56100 Pisa; phone 050 940 111, fax 050 940 180; www.royalvictoria.it

It's no coincidence that the Royal Victoria maintains a sort-of Old World charm. Managed by the Piegaja family since the 1830s, the hotel is the result of early renovations to a 10th-century tower and several medieval buildings. This isn't the fanciest hotel in town; nevertheless, tourists have been coming here for years for the outstanding customer service. The concierge is helpful with sight-seeing information and restaurant suggestions. As for the rooms, many are huge and have wide windows overlooking the Arno. If you don't get a room with view, rent a bike from the front desk and take a ride along the river.

SETTING & FACILITIES

Location Along the Arno, within walking distance from the Leaning Tower. **Quietness Rating** B. **Dining** Breakfast included in rates; bar serves light snacks. **Amenities** Safe at front desk, meeting facilities, on-site garage. **Services** Laundry, bike rental, currency exchange desk, room service.

ACCOMMODATIONS

Rooms 34. **All** Phone, satellite TV. **Bathrooms** Shower or bathtub, hair dryer. You can save money by staying in a room without a bathroom. **Comfort & Décor** The décor is also old-fashioned, with trompe-l'oeil paintings on the walls, thin beds, and Victorian lamps and furnishings. Rooms are huge, bathrooms less so.

RATES, RESERVATIONS, & RESTRICTIONS

Pricing Singles without bath, €57; single with bath, €87; doubles without bath, €68; doubles with bath, €102; suites, €111–€183. **Credit Cards** AMEX, DC, MC, V. **Check-In/Out** 2 p.m./noon. **Elevator** Yes. **English Spoken** Yes.

Hotel Profiles—Rome

	Overall Rating	Quality Rating	Value Rating	Price
THE BEST HOTELS IN ROME				
Hotel				
Ripa All Suites Hotel	★★★★★	★★★★★	★	€211–€516
Hotel Raphaël	★★★★★	★★★★★	★	€230–€620
Regina Hotel Baglioni	★★★★★	★★★★★	★	€300–€490
Hotel Villa San Pio	★★★★	★★★★	★★★★	€50–€200
Hotel Fori Imperiali Cavalieri	★★★★	★★★★	★★★★	€85–€215
Hotel Locarno	★★★★	★★★★	★★★★	€90–€200
Hotel Cardinal	★★★★	★★★★	★★★★	€100–€200
Hotel Portoghesi	★★★★	★★★★	★★★★★	€115–€170
Hotel Fontanella Borghese	★★★★	★★★★	★★★	€115–€320
Hotel Residence Palazzo al Velabro	★★★★	★★★★	★★★★	€150–€270
Albergo del Sole al Pantheon	★★★★	★★★★	★★★	€210–€300
Daniel's Hotel	★★★★	★★★★	★★	€245–€475
Hotel Valadier	★★★★	★★★★	★★	€100–€350

	THE BEST HOTELS IN ROME *(continued)*			
Hotel	Overall Rating	Quality Rating	Value Rating	Price
Grand Hotel Minerva	★★★★	★★★★	★★	€310–€510
Hotel Amalia	★★★★	★★★	★★★★	€95–€305
Hotel Santa Maria	★★★★	★★★	★★★	€124–€260
Hotel Scalinata di Spagna	★★★★	★★★	★★	€195–€310
Edera Hotel	★★★	★★★	★★★★★	€90–€210
Spring House	★★★	★★★	★★★★	€55–€210
Hotel Teatro di Pompeo	★★★	★★★	★★★★	€90–€180
Hotel Due Torri	★★★	★★★	★★★★	€110–€230
Hotel Le Cappellette di San Luigi	★★★	★★★	★★★★	€125–€300
Hotel Duca D'Alba	★★★	★★★	★★★	€80–€255
Hotel Columbus	★★★	★★★	★★★	€124–€295
Delta Colosseo	★★★	★★★	★★★	€125–€270
Hotel Quirinale	★★★	★★★	★★	€220–€300
Hotel des Artistes	★★	★★★	★★★★★	€109–€250
Hotel Oceania	★★	★★★	★★★★★	€52–€135
Hotel Navona	★★	★★	★★★★★	€60–€115
Albergo Abruzzi	★	★	★★★★★	€60–€80

Albergo Abruzzi   €60–€80

OVERALL ★ | QUALITY ★ | VALUE ★★★★★ | CENTRO STORICO

Piazza della Rotonda, 69; 00186 Rome; phone 06 679 2021

What the Albergo Abruzzi doesn't have—private bathrooms, sumptuous furnishings, breakfast, a website—it makes up for in price and location. Located right on Piazza della Rotonda, spitting distance from the Pantheon, the Abruzzi is cheap and clean, with rates starting at €60 (cash only). Rooms on the front come with views of the ancient temple and the "atmospheric" noise of the clinking cafés below. Rooms on the back are quieter but lack the view, of course.

SETTING & FACILITIES

Location By the Pantheon. **Nearest Metro** Spagna (Line A) and Cavour (Line B); more easily reached by bus. **Quietness Rating** B. **Dining** No. **Amenities** Safe at front desk.

ACCOMMODATIONS

Rooms 27. **Bathrooms** Shared. **Comfort & Décor** The uninspiring décor comes in a variety of neutral colors, probably to decrease the appearance of wear and tear.

RATES, RESERVATIONS, & RESTRICTIONS

Pricing Singles €60, doubles €80. **Credit Cards** Not accepted. **Check-In/Out** 2 p.m./noon. **Elevator** No. **English Spoken** Yes.

Albergo del Sole al Pantheon   €130–€300

OVERALL ★★★★ | QUALITY ★★★★ | VALUE ★★★ | CENTRO STORICO

Piazza della Rotonda, 63; 00186 Rome; phone 06 678 0441, fax 06 699 40689; www.hotelsolealpantheon.com

A charming hotel that has hosted the likes of Jean Paul Sartre, Simone de Beauvoir, and *Cavalleria Rusticana* composer Pietro Mascagni, the Albergo del Sole has been accommodating travelers since the 15th century. Ten of the hotel's rooms have postcard views of the Pantheon, and you'll feel that you're so close that you can practically toss a ball into the building's open oculus. Albergo del Sole has been lovingly refurbished, from the terra cotta tile floor to the wood beam ceiling. Some rooms have hand-painted tiles and furnishings. In warmer months, breakfast is served in the outdoor garden in back.

SETTING & FACILITIES

Location By the Pantheon. **Nearest Metro** Spagna (Line A) and Cavour (Line B); more easily reached by bus. **Quietness Rating** A (triple-glazed windows). **Dining** Breakfast included in rates; bar serves light snacks. **Services** Laundry, room-service, free newspaper in the morning.

ACCOMMODATIONS

Rooms 25. **All** Phone, satellite TV, radio, minibar, in-room safe. **Bathrooms** Most have whirlpool baths, all have hair dryers. **Comfort & Décor** Walnut wood bed frames, seductive arched doorways, and a calming, pastel color scheme make for a very romantic atmosphere.

RATES, RESERVATIONS, & RESTRICTIONS

Pricing Singles €130–€210, doubles €210–€280, suites €280–€300. **Credit Cards** MC, V. **Check-In/Out** 2 p.m./noon. **Elevator** Yes. **English Spoken** Yes.

Daniel's Hotel   €245–€475

OVERALL ★★★★ | QUALITY ★★★★ | VALUE ★★ | TRIDENTE

Via Frattina, 107; 00187 Rome; phone 06 693 80203, fax 06 693 80194; www.danielshotel.it

No, you haven't died and gone to Michelangelo's marble workshop in the sky. But the stark marble entrance and lobby will make you do a double-take. Tucked away on the chic Via Frattina around the corner from name-brand shopping on Via Condotti, this four-star property is small but incredibly elegant . . . and one of the newest hotels in town. A bit of creative engineering went into wedging the Daniel's into a preexisting space, so rooms are quite tiny and somewhat dark. However, the rooftop garden has some great views of St. Peter's and the Victor Emanuele Monument. Besides—when you're smack dab in the heart of the city, you needn't spend much time in your hotel room.

SETTING & FACILITIES

Location Near Via Condotti and the Spanish Steps. **Nearest Metro** Spagna (Line A). **Quietness Rating** A. **Dining** Breakfast included. **Amenities** Rooftop terrace.

ACCOMMODATIONS

Rooms 14. **All** Phone, satellite TV, minibar, in-room safe, soundproof windows, radio. **Bathrooms** Bathtub and shower with whirlpool, hair dryer. **Comfort & Décor** Room décor can be disappointing, given the marvelous lobby, but rooms are equipped for comfort with big beds, wall-to-wall carpet, and separate sitting areas. Some suites, of which there are five, have reproduction Louis XVI furniture and colorful ceiling frescoes (also faux). Bathrooms are cramped, but the whirlpool bathtubs make up for it.

RATES, RESERVATIONS & RESTRICTIONS

Pricing Doubles €245–€330, suites €295–€475. **Credit Cards** MC, V. **Check-In/Out** 2 p.m./noon. **Elevator** Yes, but you must climb a few stairs to get to the lobby. **English Spoken** Yes.

Delta Colosseo   €125–€270

OVERALL ★★★ | QUALITY ★★★ | VALUE ★★★ | ANCIENT CITY

Via Labicana, 144; 00184 Rome; phone 06 770 021, fax 06 700 5781;
www.accor-hotels.it

This large, modern hotel looks like a Club Med from the outside, with large palm trees at the entrance. Echoing that theme is the crystal blue rooftop pool, from which you can gaze at the massive Colosseum. The Delta Colosseo's location, just a couple blocks from the ancient amphitheater, and its pool—a godsend in the summer—are the highlights. Rooms are sparse, with warehouse-direct furniture and typical amenities, and the marble lobby is cold and unwelcoming. Get a room on back, and you'll enjoy views of the Colle Oppio park. Rooms on front face the racetrackish Via Labicana. Parking is available in the hotel's private garage for a fee.

SETTING & FACILITIES

Location Near the Colosseum. **Nearest Metro** Manzoni (Line A). **Quietness Rating** B. **Dining** Breakfast included in rates; bar serves cocktails and light snacks. **Amenities** Swimming pool, parking garage.

ACCOMMODATIONS

Rooms 160. **All** Phone, satellite TV, pay-per-view, minibar, in-room safe. **Bathrooms** Bath and shower, hair dryer. **Comfort & Décor** Rooms are unexciting but huge, and bedding and drapes show no visible signs of wear and tear.

RATES, RESERVATIONS, & RESTRICTIONS

Pricing Singles €125–€200, doubles €150–€270. **Credit Cards** AMEX, MC, V. **Check-In/Out** 2 p.m./noon. **Elevator** Yes. **English Spoken** Yes.

Edera Hotel   €90–€210

OVERALL ★★★ | QUALITY ★★★ | VALUE ★★★★★ | ESQUILINO

Via Angelo Poliziano, 75; 00184 Rome; phone 06 868 00116, fax 06 868 00124

Its location near the Colle Oppio park makes the Edera Hotel a quiet getaway from the chaos of Rome. Still, its proximity to such attractions as the Colosseum, Santa Maria Maggiore Church, and the Domus Aurea make this a perfect base for tourists. The Edera has a lovely sitting room full of potted plants, and there's a small garden where guests can relax and write postcards.

SETTING & FACILITIES

Location Near the Colosseum and Domus Aurea. **Nearest Metro** Vittorio Emanuele (Line A). **Quietness Rating** A. **Dining** Buffet breakfast included in rates. **Amenities** On-site bar, private parking, garden.

ACCOMMODATIONS

Rooms 37. **All** Phone, satellite TV, radio, minibar. **Bathrooms** Shower, hair dryer. **Comfort & Décor** The hotel is tucked away in a residential neighborhood, and décor reflects a very familial, Italian country look. Accommodations are simple, but rooms are well lit and carpeted. Furniture is of thick, unvarnished oak.

RATES, RESERVATIONS, & RESTRICTIONS

Pricing Singles €90–€110, doubles €135–€160, triples €190–€210. **Credit Cards** AMEX, MC, V. **Check-In/Out** 2 p.m./noon. **Elevator** Yes. **English Spoken** Yes.

Grand Hotel Minerva   €310–€510

OVERALL ★★★★ | QUALITY ★★★★ | VALUE ★★ | CENTRO STORICO

Piazza della Minerva, 69; 00186 Rome; phone 06 695 201, fax 06 679 4165

Situated in a 17th-century palace that was renovated in 1990 by Paolo Portoghesi, the Grand Hotel Minerva is one of the finest luxury hotels in the Centro Storico. Only recently separated from its parent company, Holiday Inn Crowne Plaza, the Grand still boasts a helpful staff and tons of services. From its rooftop terrace, you can admire the hotel's enviable location behind the Pantheon and adjacent to the pretty Gothic church of Santa Maria Sopra Minerva. Some rooms look out on the traffic-free piazza, and others have views of the inner courtyard.

SETTING & FACILITIES

Location Near the Pantheon. **Nearest Metro** Spagna (Line A) and Cavour (Line B); more easily reached by bus. **Quietness Rating** A. **Dining** Buffet breakfast, €26. **Amenities** Internet access, parking nearby, business center, meeting rooms. **Services** Laundry service, room service, airport shuttle, beauty salon/barber, ticket desk, currency exchange desk.

ACCOMMODATIONS

Rooms 134. **All** Phone, satellite TV, in-room safe, minibar, coffee pot. **Bathrooms** Shower and bathtub, hair dryer. **Comfort & Décor** Rooms have ultra-modern fixtures, but the renovations left the original wood beamed ceilings. Bathrooms are spacious.

RATES, RESERVATIONS, & RESTRICTIONS

Pricing Doubles and suites, €310–€510. **Credit Cards** AMEX, DC, MC, V. **Check-In/Out** 2 p.m./noon. **Elevator** Yes. **English Spoken** Yes.

Hotel Amalia   *€95–€305*

OVERALL ★★★★ | QUALITY ★★★ | VALUE ★★★★ | VATICAN AREA

Via Germanico, 66; 00192 Rome; phone 06 397 23356, fax 06 397 23365; www.hotelamalia.com

Well-situated a couple blocks from the Vatican and right next to the Ottaviano metro stop, this bright coral-colored hotel is easy to find. Completely refurbished in 2001, the Amalia now has superior sound-proof windows, new furniture and fixtures, and high-speed Internet access available in all of the guest rooms. The moderately priced hotel has two types of rooms, classic and superior, all of which sport allergy-friendly marble floors. As for the staff, who are on call around-the-clock, we found them to be just as cheerful as the hotel's colorful façade.

SETTING & FACILITIES

Location Near the Vatican. **Nearest Metro** Ottaviano (Line A). **Quietness Rating** A. **Dining** Breakfast included in rates. **Amenities** Parking nearby, Internet access, non-smoking. **Services** Laundry, airport transfer.

ACCOMMODATIONS

Rooms 30. **All** Phone, satellite TV, minibar, Internet access, in-room safe. **Bathrooms** Bathtub with shower attachment, hair dryer. **Comfort & Décor** Rooms have been retooled for proper insulation, and windows are noise- and pollution-proof. All rooms have fine wood furnishings, matching bedding and drapes, and ample bathrooms.

RATES, RESERVATIONS, & RESTRICTIONS

Pricing Singles €95–€130, doubles €150–€210, triples/quads/suites €190–€305. **Credit Cards** AMEX, DC, MC, V. **Check-In/Out** 2 p.m./noon. **Elevator** Yes. **English Spoken** Yes.

Hotel Le Cappellette di San Luigi   *€125–€300*

OVERALL ★★★ | QUALITY ★★★ | VALUE ★★★★ | ESQUILINO

Via Liberiana, 21; 00185 Rome; phone 06 489 30318, fax 06 481 4837; www.hotellecappellette.com.

Opened in mid-2001, this former papal residence is now one of the city's only completely nonsmoking hotels. During the refurbishment, the building's stucco walls and marble floors were left intact, and the tiny, 18th-century chapel, from which the hotel derives its name, retained its original sunburst altar. Rooms are intimate (read: on the small side), but most look out onto the tranquil cobblestone courtyard. Other rooms have views of Santa Maria Maggiore church.

SETTING & FACILITIES

Location Next to Santa Maria Maggiore. **Nearest Metro** Termini (Line A, Line B). **Quietness Rating** A. **Dining** Breakfast included in rates; bar serves cocktails and light snacks. **Amenities** Private parking, two courtyards, nonsmoking.

ACCOMMODATIONS

Rooms 40. **All** Phone, satellite TV, minibar, soundproof windows. **Bathrooms** Shower or bathtub. **Comfort & Décor** Whitewashed rooms have hardwood floors, antique reproduction furniture, and thick, comfortable bedding in rich hues.

RATES, RESERVATIONS, & RESTRICTIONS

Pricing Singles €125–€155, doubles €170–€215, triples €225–€300. **Credit Cards** MC, V. **Check-In/Out** 2 p.m./noon. **Elevator** Yes. **English Spoken** Yes.

Hotel Cardinal   €100–€200

OVERALL ★★★★ | QUALITY ★★★★ | VALUE ★★★★ | CENTRO STORICO

Via Giulia, 62; 00186 Rome; phone 06 688 02719, fax 06 612 373.

Bramante, architect of St. Peter's Basilica, designed the Palazzo dei Tribunali, which today is the sumptuously decorated, four-star Hotel Cardinal. Located on the Via Giulia, an ivy-draped, Renaissance-era street, the hotel is minutes from authentic restaurants, antiques shops, and lively wine bars. Many of the Cardinal's guests return year after year because of the hotel's splendid location, attentive service, and refined atmosphere. Book months in advance, if possible.

SETTING & FACILITIES

Location Near Campo dei' Fiori. **Nearest Metro** Not close to Metro; use tram or bus. **Quietness Rating** A. **Dining** Breakfast included in rates; restaurant serves typical Roman fare. **Amenities** Garden patio.

ACCOMMODATIONS

Rooms 73. **All** Phone, TV, minibar. **Bathrooms** Shower or bathtub, hair dryer. **Comfort & Décor** The hotel's lobby is a gilded affair, with huge antique mirrors, crystal chandeliers, cherrywood furniture, and plenty of cardinal-red touches. Rooms are more functional, with relatively plain décor, but feature high ceilings and some antique pieces. Guest rooms are quite huge and feature desks and a sitting room.

RATES, RESERVATIONS, & RESTRICTIONS

Pricing Singles €103–€120, doubles €130–€200. **Credit Cards** MC, V. **Check-In/Out** 2 p.m./noon. **Elevator** No. **English Spoken** Yes.

Hotel Columbus   €124–€295

OVERALL ★★★ | QUALITY ★★★ | VALUE ★★★ | VATICAN AREA

Via della Conciliazione, 33; 00193 Rome; phone 06 686 5435, fax 06 686 4874; www.hotelcolumbus.net

The big, bold lobby is enough to scare first-time visitors away. Once a former monastery, the Hotel Columbus still retains a very self-righteous air, which has filtered down to its polite but aloof staff. Nevertheless, this is a pretty hotel, with big rooms and original baroque fixtures. You're sure to be on time to your audience with the pope if you stay here.

SETTING & FACILITIES

Location Down the road from St. Peter's Basilica. **Nearest Metro** Ottaviano (Line A). **Quietness Rating** B. **Dining** Breakfast included in rates. **Amenities** Meeting rooms, parking available. **Services** Laundry service, baby-sitting, car rental desk.

ACCOMMODATIONS

Rooms 92. **All** Phone, satellite TV, minibar. **Bathrooms** Shower or bathtub, hair dryer. **Comfort & Décor** Rooms are very eye-catching and well equipped with modern comforts. Rooms facing the street have great views of the Vatican; others look out over the well-kept garden.

RATES, RESERVATIONS, & RESTRICTIONS

Pricing Singles €124–€190, doubles €190–€295. **Credit Cards** MC, V. **Check-In/Out** 2 p.m./noon. **Elevator** Yes. **English Spoken** Yes.

Hotel des Artistes   €109–€250

OVERALL ★★ | QUALITY ★★★ | VALUE ★★★★★ | ESQUILINO

Via Villafranca, 20; 00185 Rome; phone 06 445 4365, fax 06 446 2368; www.hoteldesartistes.com

Rome on a shoestring doesn't have to look cheap. A boon to backpackers who want quality digs, the Hotel des Artistes is conveniently located near the train station. Other travelers will appreciate the young hotel's laid-back but helpful staff that is ever willing to assist you with calling a cab or making a restaurant reservation. Other attractive features of the hotel include its rooftop deck, which becomes an impromptu socializing spot in the summer. Some of the rooms of the Hotel des Artistes are equipped with private bathrooms, but if you want to save cash, you can opt for a room with a shared bath or bed down in the hotel's adjacent hostel, where rooms start as low as €35. All rooms in both properties are nonsmoking.

SETTING & FACILITIES

Location A few blocks from Termini Station. **Nearest Metro** Termini (Line A and B) and Castro Pretorio (Line B). **Quietness Rating** B. **Dining** 24-hour bar on the premises. **Amenities** Parking nearby, Internet access available, TV room.

ACCOMMODATIONS

Rooms 32. **All** Phone. **Bathrooms** Some rooms have private baths; others share bathrooms on the hall. **Comfort & Décor** The funky Hotel des Artistes is designed with bohemians in mind and features Oriental rugs, velvet drapes, and unique art in all of the guest rooms. All rooms are nonsmoking and are kept extremely tidy.

RATES, RESERVATIONS, & RESTRICTIONS

Pricing Doubles €109–€185, triples €139–€250. **Credit Cards** AMEX, DC, MC, V. **Check-In/Out** 2 p.m./noon. **Elevator** Yes. **English Spoken** Yes.

Hotel Duca D'Alba   €80–€255

OVERALL ★★★ | QUALITY ★★★ | VALUE ★★★ | ANCIENT CITY

Via Leonina, 14; 00184 Rome; phone 06 484 471, fax 06 488 4840;
www.hotelducadalba.com

Its location alone makes the Duca d'Alba a good option for touring
Rome. The hotel is approximately equidistant from the grand church of
Santa Maria Maggiore and the Colosseum. Additionally, it is located
down the block from the Cavour metro station, which makes it easy to
tour the rest of the city. The Duca d'Alba was refurbished in 1994, and
yet its rooms already seem quite dated. Nevertheless, the public areas are
inviting. There's a small bar that's open for early evening cocktails.

SETTING & FACILITIES

Location Colosseum/Forum. **Nearest Metro** Cavour (Line B). **Quietness Rating**
B. **Dining** Breakfast included in rates. **Amenities** Parking nearby.

ACCOMMODATIONS

Rooms 24. **All** Phone, satellite TV, minibar, in-room safe. **Bathrooms** Shower or bath,
hair dryer. **Comfort & Décor** Not particularly elegant, the rooms of the Duca D'Alba
are frumpy at best. Curtains and rugs show signs of wear. Beds are comfortable but
small.

RATES, RESERVATIONS, & RESTRICTIONS

Pricing Singles €80–€200, doubles €98–€255. **Credit Cards** AMEX, DC, MC, V.
Check-In/Out 2 p.m./noon. **Elevator** Yes. **English Spoken** Yes.

Hotel Due Torri   €110–€230

OVERALL ★★★ | QUALITY ★★★ | VALUE ★★★★ | CENTRO STORICO

Vicolo del Leonetto, 23, 00186; phone 06 687 6983, fax 06 686 5442;
www.hotelduetorriroma.com

Hidden on a medieval side street near Piazza Navona, the Due Torri
occupies a 16th-century building that once housed visiting cardinals and
bishops. The marble lobby is the loveliest room in the hotel and is set
apart with Oriental rugs, walnut credenzas, bronze statuettes, and big
potted plants.

SETTING & FACILITIES

Location Piazza Navona. **Nearest Metro** Spagna (Line A) and Cavour (Line B); more
easily reached by bus. **Quietness Rating** A. **Dining** Breakfast included in rates.
Amenities Central air-conditioning, paid parking nearby. **Services** Concierge assistance with ticket bookings.

ACCOMMODATIONS

Rooms 26, including 7 singles, 15 doubles, and 4 apartments. **All** Phones, satellite TV,
radio, in-room safe. **Bathrooms** Shower or bath, hair dryer. **Comfort & Décor**
Antique furnishings done in cardinal-issue red and gold give the rooms a regal look.
Rooms are well decorated and comfortable.

RATES, RESERVATIONS, & RESTRICTIONS

Pricing Singles €110–€160, doubles €170–€230. **Credit Cards** AMEX, DC, MC, V.
Check-In/Out 2 p.m./noon. **Elevator** Yes. **English Spoken** Yes.

Hotel Fontanella Borghese   €115–€320

OVERALL ★★★★ | QUALITY ★★★★ | VALUE ★★★ | CENTRO STORICO

Largo Fontanella Borghese, 84; 00186 Rome; phone 06 688 09504,
fax 06 686 1295; www.fontanellaborghese.com

Sister hotel to the Hotel Due Torri, the Fontanella Borghese is a graceful
three-star property near the chic shopping avenues of the Via del Corso
and Via Condotti. Once owned by the noble Borghese family, the rooms
of the hotel look out over the Borghese palace courtyard or the busy
street below.

SETTING & FACILITIES

Location Off Via del Corso. **Nearest Metro** Spagna (Line A); more easily reached by
bus. **Quietness Rating** A. **Dining** Breakfast included in rates. **Amenities** Parking
garage nearby.

ACCOMMODATIONS

Rooms 24. **All** Phone, satellite TV, radio, minibar. **Bathrooms** Shower or bathtub, hair
dryer. **Comfort & Décor** Spacious rooms are rather plain but are filled with light.

RATES, RESERVATIONS, & RESTRICTIONS

Pricing Singles €115–€170, doubles €185–€320. **Credit Cards** MC, V. **Check-
In/Out** 2 p.m./noon. **Elevator** Yes. **English Spoken** Yes.

Hotel Fori Imperiali Cavalieri   €85–€215

OVERALL ★★★★ | QUALITY ★★★★ | VALUE ★★★★ | ANCIENT CITY

Via Frangipane, 34; 00184 Rome; phone 06 679 6246, fax 06 679 7203;
www.cavalieri.it/hotel

One of the finest three-stars in the area, the Fori Imperiali Cavalieri does
not have views over the Forum, but it is only a short walk from the ruins.
The hotel makes up for its panoramic shortcomings with brightly decorated rooms and an excellent staff. The lobby, with its royal blue and gold
stripes and solids, has a French provincial look, which is a welcome
departure from typical hotel design. Breakfast here is ample.

SETTING & FACILITIES

Location Near the Forum. **Nearest Metro** Cavour (Line B). **Quietness Rating** A.
Dining Breakfast included in rates. **Amenities** Parking garage nearby.

ACCOMMODATIONS

Rooms 24. **All** Phone, satellite TV, in-room safe, minibar. **Bathrooms** Shower and bathtub, hair dryer. **Comfort & Décor** Rooms are sufficiently accommodating and feature
parquet floors and new furnishings. Décor is in muted shades of rose and neutrals.

RATES, RESERVATIONS, & RESTRICTIONS

Pricing Singles €85–€130, doubles €140–€215. **Credit Cards** MC, V. **Check-In/Out** 2 p.m./noon. **Elevator** Yes. **English Spoken** Yes.

Hotel Locarno   €90–€200

OVERALL ★★★★ | QUALITY ★★★★ | VALUE ★★★★ | CENTRO STORICO

Via della Penna, 22; 00186 Rome; phone 06 361 0841, fax 06 321 5249; www.hotellocarno.com

A leftover from the Art Deco age, the Hotel Locarno is a delight of wrought-iron fixtures, Tiffany lamps, and Lalique-inspired furnishings. The hotel was refurbished just prior to the Jubilee year, which meant a re-oiling of its fabulous period elevator and a polish to its pristine lobby. You can borrow a bike from the front desk for a scoot around town, but the ride is much more harrowing now than it was back when the hotel opened in 1925.

SETTING & FACILITIES

Location Close to Piazza del Popolo and Via del Corso. **Nearest Metro** Flaminio (Line A). **Quietness Rating** A. **Dining** Buffet breakfast, €13. **Amenities** Garage nearby.

ACCOMMODATIONS

Rooms 48. **All** Phone, satellite TV, in-room safe, minibar. **Bathrooms** Shower and bathtub, hair dryer. **Comfort & Décor** Most rooms in the Locarno are huge and feature full-sized, colorfully tiled bathrooms.

RATES, RESERVATIONS, & RESTRICTIONS

Pricing Singles €90–€120, doubles €160–€200. **Credit Cards** MC, V. **Check-In/Out** 2 p.m./noon. **Elevator** Yes. **English Spoken** Yes.

Hotel Navona   €60–€115

OVERALL ★★ | QUALITY ★★ | VALUE ★★★★★ | CENTRO STORICO

Via dei Sediari, 8; 00186 Rome; phone 06 686 4203, fax 06 688 03802; www.hotelnavona.com

It's not much to look at, but the Hotel Navona will provide you with a historical stay near all of the action. Emperor Agrippa's baths were located here, and you can see evidence of this on the ground floor. Upstairs, both John Keats and Percy Bysshe Shelley spent the night. The Hotel Navona is a fantastic bargain, and we recommend it for independent travelers.

SETTING & FACILITIES

Location Near Piazza Navona. **Nearest Metro** Spagna (Line A); more easily reached by bus. **Quietness Rating** B. **Dining** Breakfast, €5.

ACCOMMODATIONS

Rooms 30. **All** Phone. **Bathrooms** Showers, hair dryer on request. Some rooms must share a bathroom. **Comfort & Décor** The furnishings here have seen better days, but they'll do for the price. This isn't the best place to stay in the summer, as there is an extra charge for air conditioning (€15 per day).

RATES, RESERVATIONS, & RESTRICTIONS

Pricing Singles €60–€85, doubles with shared bath €75–€95, doubles with private bath €90–€115. **Credit Cards** Not accepted. **Check-In/Out** 2 p.m./10 a.m. **Elevator** No. **English Spoken** Yes.

Hotel Portoghesi   €115–€170

OVERALL ★★★★ | QUALITY ★★★★ | VALUE ★★★★★ | CENTRO STORICO

Via dei Portoghesi, 1; 00186 Rome; phone 06 686 4231, fax 06 687 6976; www.hotelportoghesiroma.com.

Situated on the quiet, ivy-draped Via Portoghesi and named after Rome's Portuguese parish nearby, this inn is well positioned near Piazza Navona and just over the bridge from Castel Sant'Angelo. Owned by the Sagnotti family for more than 150 years, Hotel Portoghesi is an intimate getaway. Rooms are sparse but spacious.

SETTING & FACILITIES

Location Piazza Navona. **Quietness Rating** A. **Dining** Breakfast included in rates. **Amenities** Roof garden.

ACCOMMODATIONS

Rooms 27. **All** Telephone, satellite television, minibar. **Bathrooms** Shower or bath. **Comfort & Décor** Most rooms in the hotel are blandly decorated.

RATES, RESERVATIONS, & RESTRICTIONS

Pricing Singles €115–€130, doubles €160–€170. **Credit Cards** MC, V. **Check-In/Out** 2 p.m./noon. **Elevator** Yes. **English Spoken** Yes.

Hotel Quirinale   €220–€300

OVERALL ★★★ | QUALITY ★★★ | VALUE ★★ | QUIRINALE

Via Nazionale, 7; 00184 Rome; phone 06 47 07, fax 06 482 0099; www.hotelquirinale.it

For all intents and purposes, the Quirinale is a business hotel, conveniently located to governmental offices on Via Nazionale and the train station. But the hotel has become sort of a cult favorite among music lovers, as it features a private entrance to the Teatro dell'Opera. Beyond the traffic-clogged street of Via Nazionale, the hotel is an oasis, with triple-glazed windows and a lovely leafy courtyard. In the summer, breakfast is served outdoors.

SETTING & FACILITIES

Location Near the Teatro dell'Opera. **Nearest Metro** Repubblica (Line A). **Quietness Rating** B. **Dining** Breakfast included in rates. **Amenities** Parking, private entrance to Teatro dell'Opera, Internet access. **Services** Room service, laundry service, ticket desk for Teatro dell'Opera.

ACCOMMODATIONS

Rooms 200. **All** Phone, satellite TV, in-room safe, minibar. **Bathrooms** Shower and bathtub, hair dryer. **Comfort & Décor** Recently refurbished rooms drip with gilded antiques and reproduction Louis XV furniture. Ceilings are high, and rooms are airy.

RATES, RESERVATIONS, & RESTRICTIONS

Pricing Singles €220–€230, doubles €260–€300. **Credit Cards** MC, V. **Check-In/Out** 2 p.m./noon. **Elevator** Yes. **English Spoken** Yes.

Hotel Raphaël   €230–€620

OVERALL ★★★★★ | QUALITY ★★★★★ | VALUE ★ | CENTRO STORICO

Largo Febo, 2; 00186 Rome; phone 06 682 831, fax 06 687 8993;
www.raphaelhotel.com

Eclectic elegance is one way to describe the Raphaël, a romantic four-star property in the heart of the Centro Storico. The façade of the hotel is draped with ivy; inside you'll find a variety of antiques, including a collection of ceramics designed by Pablo Picasso. Guest rooms are put together with the same kind of style and impeccable attention to detail. This is one hotel that exceeds its star rating.

SETTING & FACILITIES

Location Near Piazza Navona. **Nearest Metro** Spagna (Line A); more easily reached by bus. **Quietness Rating** A. **Dining** Buffet breakfast, €20; Raphaël's restaurant serves French haute cuisine. **Amenities** Parking nearby, rooftop garden, fitness center, sauna, meeting rooms. **Services** Room service, laundry service, baby-sitting, car service can be arranged.

ACCOMMODATIONS

Rooms 70. **All** Phone, satellite TV, in-room safe, minibar. **Bathrooms** Shower and bathtub, hair dryer. **Comfort & Décor** Guest rooms were recently refurbished with the finest marbles and moldings. The premium bed and bath linens are like new.

RATES, RESERVATIONS, & RESTRICTIONS

Pricing Singles €230–€270, doubles €350–€620. **Credit Cards** AMEX, DC, MC, V. **Check-In/Out** 2 p.m./noon. **Elevator** Yes. **English Spoken** Yes.

Hotel Residence Palazzo al Velabro   €150–€270

OVERALL ★★★★ | QUALITY ★★★★ | VALUE ★★★★ | ANCIENT CITY

Via del Velabro, 16; 00186 Rome; phone 06 679 2758, fax 06 679 3790

If you're staying in Rome for longer than a week, you may want to consider settling into a flat in the Palazzo al Velabro. Located in a 16th-century building, the hotel overlooks the ruins of the Palatine hill and is close to the attractions of ancient Rome. Independent travelers can take pleasure in cooking up their own meals in the suites' kitchenettes. The hotel provides daily maid service and a 24-hour reception desk. There is a three-night minimum stay.

SETTING & FACILITIES

Location Near the Forum and Palatine. **Nearest Metro** Circo Massimo (Line B). **Quietness Rating** A. **Dining** Breakfast included in rates, rooms have kitchenettes. **Amenities** Parking garage nearby, laundry facilities. **Services** Baby-sitting, airport transfers.

ACCOMMODATIONS

Rooms 34 apartments. **All** Phone, satellite TV, radio, kitchenette. **Bathrooms** Shower and bathtub, hair dryer. **Comfort & Décor** The spacious apartments are appointed with soft lighting and modern wood furnishings.

RATES, RESERVATIONS, & RESTRICTIONS

Pricing Studio suites, €150–€185, double suites €240–€270. **Credit Cards** AMEX, MC, V. **Check-In/Out** 2 p.m./noon. **Elevator** Yes. **English Spoken** Yes.

Hotel Santa Maria   €124–€260

OVERALL ★★★★ | QUALITY ★★★ | VALUE ★★★ | TRASTEVERE

Vicolo del Piede, 2; 00153 Rome; phone 06 589 4626, fax 06 589 4815; www.htlsantamaria.com

Located in a completely renovated 15th-century cloister, the Hotel Santa Maria is a recent (2000) and welcome addition to the Rome hotel scene. To get to the hotel you must weave through a maze of medieval streets just a few blocks from the Piazza Santa Maria in Trastevere and enter through a gate. Inside, you'll find a quiet courtyard, private parking, a helpful staff, and adorably decorated rooms. The hotel is in an artistic, residential neighborhood, just a step away from bakeries, pizzerias, and crafts shops, but you can expect to hear the hum of *motorini* and frolicking students on occasion. The Santa Maria comes highly recommended to those who are looking for accommodations off the beaten track.

SETTING & FACILITIES

Location Trastevere. **Nearest Metro** Not close to the Metro; more easily reached by bus or tram. **Quietness Rating** A. **Dining** Breakfast included in rates; bar serves light snacks. **Amenities** Parking nearby, airport transfers can be arranged. **Services** Can arrange shuttle service, guided tours.

ACCOMMODATIONS

Rooms 12. **All** Telephone, satellite television, minibar. **Bathrooms** Shower and bathtub, hair dryer. **Comfort & Décor** Guest rooms are small, but one must remember that these were once cloister cells. Bright, floral patterns were used here, and they create an inviting atmosphere in the bedrooms. Terra cotta floors keep the room cool during the summer, but can be a drawback in cooler months.

RATES, RESERVATIONS, & RESTRICTIONS

Pricing Singles €124–€155, doubles €145–€207, triples/quads €155–€260. **Credit Cards** AMEX, MC, V. **Check-In/Out** 2 p.m./noon. **Elevator** No. **English Spoken** Yes.

Hotel Scalinata di Spagna   €195–€310

OVERALL ★★★★ | QUALITY ★★★ | VALUE ★★ | TRIDENTE/SPAGNA

Piazza Trinità dei Monti, 17; 00187 Rome; phone 06 679 3006, fax 06 699 40598;
www.hotelscalinata.com

Only the Scalinata di Spagna and the Hassler Hotel (see "Cream of the
Crop," above) have views over the Spanish Steps—and you'll have to ante
up to see them. Only two rooms have private terraces that allow you to
peer over the goings-on of the crowded Spanish Steps. Those without a
balcony can enjoy the panorama of the Rome skyline from the roof deck.
The Scalinata di Spagna is popular with just about everyone, so book as
soon as possible.

SETTING & FACILITIES

Location At the top of the Spanish Steps. **Nearest Metro** Spagna (Line A). **Quietness Rating** A–. **Dining** Breakfast is included in the rates. **Amenities** Parking available nearby.

ACCOMMODATIONS

Rooms 16. **All** Phone, satellite TV, in-room safe, minibar. **Bathrooms** Shower or bathtub, hair dryer. **Comfort & Décor** Like the chic streets that surround it, the hotel is
stylish. Rooms are barely big enough to turn around in but are well appointed with
modern furniture and matching wallpaper and drapes.

RATES, RESERVATIONS, & RESTRICTIONS

Pricing Doubles €195–€310. **Credit Cards** MC, V. **Check-In/Out** 2 p.m./noon. **Elevator** No. **English Spoken** Yes.

Hotel Teatro di Pompeo   €90–€180

OVERALL ★★★ | QUALITY ★★★ | VALUE ★★★★ | CENTRO STORICO

Largo del Pallaro, 8; 00186 Rome; phone 06 683 00170, fax 06 688 05531

Every so often you come across a hotel that just blows you away. The Teatro
di Pompeo is choice because of its history—it occupies part of a building
that was part of the first-century B.C. Theater of Pompey. You can admire
these old ruins every day at breakfast. As the hotel is small, fairly inexpensive, and well located, make sure to book months in advance.

SETTING & FACILITIES

Location Close to Campo de' Fiori. **Nearest Metro** Spagna (Line A); more easily
reached by bus or tram. **Quietness Rating** A–. **Dining** Breakfast included in rates.
Amenities Small business center, baby-sitting.

ACCOMMODATIONS

Rooms 12. **All** Phone, TV, minibar. **Bathrooms** Shower or bath. **Comfort & Décor**
The 12 rooms are simply appointed, with hardly a decoration on the walls. Wood-beam
ceilings give the place a rustic feel—unusual here in the heart of the city.

RATES, RESERVATIONS, & RESTRICTIONS

Pricing Singles/doubles €90–€180. **Credit Cards** AMEX, MC, V. **Check-In/Out** 2 p.m./11 a.m. **Elevator** Yes. **English Spoken** Yes.

Hotel Valadier   €100–€350

OVERALL ★★★★ | QUALITY ★★★★ | VALUE ★★ | CENTRO STORICO

Via della Fontanella, 15; 00186 Rome; phone 06 361 1998, fax 06 320 1558; www.hotelvaladier.com

That this hotel was a convent and then a brothel before it was transformed into tourist accommodations should shed some light on Valadier's peculiar décor. We like to think of this place as a well-positioned love nest, where lovers retreat after a day of shopping on the Via Condotti. The central focus of each room seems to be the bed (note the mirrors on the ceiling), and the hotel provides enough amenities that it's not necessary to wander far. Have dinner on the rooftop or have cocktails in the piano bar and enjoy.

SETTING & FACILITIES

Location Near the Spanish Steps. **Nearest Metro** Spagna (Line A). **Quietness Rating** A. **Dining** Breakfast included in rates; restaurant and wine bar on the premises. **Amenities** Meeting room, restaurant, parking garage nearby.

ACCOMMODATIONS

Rooms 60 **All** Phone, satellite TV, minibar, in-room safe. **Bathrooms** Shower or bathtub, hair dryer. **Comfort & Décor** Walls are have walnut-finish paneling and mirrors are affixed to the ceiling. Rooms are truly intimate.

RATES, RESERVATIONS, & RESTRICTIONS

Pricing Singles €103–€240, doubles €150–€350. **Credit Cards** MC, V. **Check-In/Out** 2 p.m./noon. **Elevator** Yes. **English Spoken** Yes.

Hotel Villa San Pio   €50–€200

OVERALL ★★★★ | QUALITY ★★★★ | VALUE ★★★★ | AVENTINO

Via Santa Melania, 19; 00153 Rome; phone 06 578 3214, fax 06 574 1112; www.aventinohotels.com

A charming hotel in a residential neighborhood on the Aventine hill, the Villa San Pio is for discerning travelers who favor service over location. The staff here is extremely helpful from the time you drop your bags off in the glass lobby to your last day, when you need to arrange to get to the airport. Another plus here is the buffet breakfast, which is accompanied on most mornings with lovely piano music and impromptu arias. The Villa San Pio is convenient to the Circus Maximus and the municipal rose garden, as well as to its sister hotels the Sant'Anselmo and the Aventino.

SETTING & FACILITIES

Location On the Aventine hill. **Nearest Metro** Piramide or Circo Massimo (Line B). **Quietness Rating** A. **Dining** Breakfast included in rates. **Amenities** On-street parking, Internet access in rooms. **Services** Shuttle service to airport, laundry service.

ACCOMMODATIONS

Rooms 84. **All** Phone, satellite TV, in-room safe, minibar. **Bathrooms** Shower and bathtub, hair dryer; some bathrooms have whirlpools. **Comfort & Décor** Rooms are big with balconies, firm beds, and luxurious bathrooms. Closets are stocked with extra pillows and blankets for chilly nights.

RATES, RESERVATIONS, & RESTRICTIONS

Pricing Singles €50–€120, doubles €80–€200. **Credit Cards** AMEX, MC, V. **Check-In/Out** 2 p.m./noon. **Elevator** Yes. **English Spoken** Yes.

Regina Hotel Baglioni   €300–€490

OVERALL ★★★★★ | QUALITY ★★★★★ | VALUE ★ | VIA VENETO

Via Veneto, 72; 00187 Rome; phone 06 421 1111, fax 06 420 12130; www.baglionihotels.com

For those who don't mind paying to go on a gilt trip, the Regina Hotel Baglioni offers the best in lavish furnishings and discreet service. The hotel gets its name from the fact that it was once the abode of Queen *(Regina)* Margherita, and it has stayed true to form with dazzling marble statuettes, antique mirrors and frames, and sumptuous decorations. The lobby's spiral staircase is an original.

SETTING & FACILITIES

Location On the Via Veneto. **Nearest Metro** Barberini (Line A). **Quietness Rating** A. **Dining** Breakfast, €26. **Amenities** Parking nearby.

ACCOMMODATIONS

Rooms 129. **All** Phone, satellite TV, in-room safe, minibar. **Bathrooms** Shower and bathtub, hair dryer. **Comfort & Décor** The Baglioni caters to its mostly celebrity clientele with the finest in modern comforts. Look for the bathrobe in the closet and mints on your pillow.

RATES, RESERVATIONS, & RESTRICTIONS

Pricing Singles €300–€350, doubles €420–€490. **Credit Cards** AMEX, MC, V. **Check-In/Out** 2 p.m./noon. **Elevator** Yes. **English Spoken** Yes.

Ripa All Suites Hotel   €211–€516

OVERALL ★★★★★ | QUALITY ★★★★★ | VALUE ★ | TRASTEVERE

Via Luigi Gianniti, 21; 00153 Rome; phone 06 58611, fax 06 581 4550; www.ripahotel.com

Few hotels in Rome are trendier. The Ripa All Suites Hotel has an on-site café, where, in the evenings you can groove with the locals to DJ-spun tracks or forego pasta for bites of sushi. For some, the location of the hotel in the bohemian neighborhood of Trastevere is ideal; for others, it's too far from the main sites. Nevertheless, most people choose the Ripa All Suites (managed by the Golden Tulip company) for its highly conceptual, modern design. Think lots of light, clean-lined furniture and minimalist décor.

SETTING & FACILITIES

Location Deep in the heart of Rome's left bank. **Nearest Metro** Not close to a Metro; more easily reached by bus or tram. **Quietness Rating** B. **Dining** Breakfast included in price; RipArte Café sells sushi and fusion Italian cuisine. **Amenities** Parking, fitness center, meeting facilities, on-site bar and nightclub. **Services** Laundry, dry cleaning, baby-sitting.

ACCOMMODATIONS

Rooms 170. **All** Phone, satellite TV, in-room safe, sitting area, minibar. **Bathrooms** Bathtub and shower. **Comfort & Décor** The Ripa All Suites definitely stands out, looking more like an installation at the Museum of Modern Art than a hotel in old Rome. The Asian-inspired furnishings may strike some as cold and uncomfortable. On the contrary, beds are fluffy and carpet is plush. The minimalist furnishings mean there's plenty of space to move around in.

RATES, RESERVATIONS, & RESTRICTIONS

Pricing Singles suites €211–€232, double suites €258–€360, superior suites €413–€516. **Credit Cards** AMEX, MC, V. **Check-In/Out** 2 p.m./noon. **Elevator** Yes. **English Spoken** Yes.

SPRING HOUSE   €55–€210

OVERALL ★★★ | QUALITY ★★★ | VALUE ★★★★ | VATICAN AREA

Via Mocenigo, 7, 00192; phone 06 397 20948, fax 06 397 21047; www.hotelspringhouse.com

Excellently located a few blocks from the Vatican Museums, you can beat the morning queues with a stay at Spring House. The rooms and public areas here are meticulously well kept and feature all-new furnishings and fixtures. You'll find few bargain hotels of this caliber anywhere in the city.

SETTING & FACILITIES

Location Walking distance to the Vatican Museums. **Nearest Metro** Ottaviano (Line A). **Quietness Rating** A. **Dining** Breakfast included in rates. **Amenities** Meeting room, parking garage.

ACCOMMODATIONS

Rooms 35. **All** Phone, satellite TV, minibar, radio, data port, in-room safe. **Bathrooms** Shower and bath, hair dryer. **Comfort & Décor** The charming rooms have understated décor, parquet floors, and large picture windows. Most rooms have separate sitting areas.

RATES, RESERVATIONS, & RESTRICTIONS

Pricing Singles €55–€180, doubles €60–€210. **Credit Cards** MC, V. **Check-In/Out** 3 p.m./11 a.m. **Elevator** Yes. **English Spoken** Yes.

Hotel Profiles—The Rest of Latium

	Overall	Quality	Value	
THE BEST HOTELS IN THE REST OF LATIUM				
Hotel	Rating	Rating	Rating	Price
The Province of Viterbo				
Viterbo				
B&B Dei Papi	★★★★	★★★★	★★★	€70–€120
Tuscia Hotel	★★½	★★	★★★	€66–€100
The Province of Latina				
Riviera D'Ulisse				
Hotel Grazia	★★★½	★★★★	★★★	€47–€91

The Province of Viterbo

Viterbo

B&B Dei Papi   €70–€120

OVERALL ★★★★ | QUALITY ★★★★ | VALUE ★★★ | VITERBO

Via del Ginnasio, 8; 01100 Viterbo; phone 0761 309 039; www.bbdeipapi.it

With only three rooms to let, B&B Dei Papi has carved out an exclusive and charming niche among Viterbo's lodging choices. Located in the patrimonial palace of the Tignosi family, one of Viterbo's two most important clans during the 14th century, this ivy-covered bed-and-breakfast is steps from the Quartiere San Pellegrino, city-center attractions, shops, and markets. In keeping with their historical pedigree, the three apartments are utterly stately, with antique and gilded accents. Dei Papi also offers a bevy of surprises uncommon for most one-stars, including discounts to the curative baths outside of Viterbo and assistance in planning sight-seeing itineraries.

SETTING & FACILITIES

Location Viterbo's medieval Centro Storico. **Quietness Rating** A. **Dining** Breakfast included in rates. **Amenities** On-site art gallery, discounts to local spas.

ACCOMMODATIONS

Rooms 3. **All** Private bath. **Bathrooms** Showers and bathtub, hair dryer. **Comfort & Décor** Shades of peach, pink, and blue-green recall the marble pallette of Tuscan gothic cathedrals. Skylights, over-sized fireplaces, and plenty of mirrors add to the spaciousness of the suites, while the smattering of modern art makes the bed-and-breakfast feel less like a museum and more like a private home.

RATES, RESERVATIONS, & RESTRICTIONS

Pricing €70—€120, depending on season. Three-day minimum stay. **Credit Cards** MC, V. **Check-In/Out** 2 p.m./11 a.m. **Elevator** No. **English Spoken** Some.

Tuscia Hotel   €66–€100

OVERALL ★★½ | QUALITY ★★ | VALUE ★★★ | VITERBO

Via Cairoli, 41; 01100 Viterbo; phone 0761 344 400, fax 0761 345 976; www.tusciahotel.com

This no-frills hotel in the heart of a city that doesn't see too many tourists is a rather inexpensive base from which to explore the narrow streets of Viterbo's San Pellegrino Quarter or beyond to the Etruscan heartland. When compared to similarly sized rooms in the Rome, the Tuscia is competitive, boasting big, soft beds, breakfast nooks, and, sometimes, balconies. We also found that the staff were less jaded than their Roman and Florentine counterparts, ever eager to direct us to their favorite haunts around town.

SETTING & FACILITIES

Location Near the heart of the medieval quarter. **Quietness Rating** B. **Dining** Breakfast included in rates. **Amenities** Meeting room, lounge, paid parking in hotel garage.

ACCOMMODATIONS

Rooms 37, 3 suites. **All** Telephone, satellite television, minibar. **Bathrooms** Shower, hair dryer. **Comfort & Décor** The lobby and public spaces were designed with business in mind, thus furnishings are utilitarian. Rooms are sizable, but there is a charge for air-conditioning (about €7 per day), and it must be reserved in advance. Consider a stay in fall or spring.

RATES, RESERVATIONS & RESTRICTIONS

Pricing Doubles €66–€88, suites €87–€100. **Credit Cards** AMEX, DC, MC, V **Check-In/Out** 3 p.m./noon **Elevator** Yes. **English Spoken** Limited.

The Province of Latina

Riviera D'Ulisse

Hotel Grazia   €47–€91

OVERALL ★★★½ | QUALITY ★★★★ | VALUE ★★★ | SPERLONGA

Via M.A. Colonna, 8; 04029 Sperlonga; phone 0771 548 223, fax 0771 549 533; www.hotelgrazia.com

With stunning views of the Tyrrhenian and quick access to the strand, Hotel Grazia offers affordable lodging on the seaside. A favorite gathering place for free climbers, who come to Sperlonga to scale the steep, limestone cliffs, the hotel easily accommodates groups with proper notice, and will also offer discounts.

SETTING & FACILITIES

Location Steps from the Tyrrhenian Sea. **Quietness Rating** A+. **Dining** Breakfast included in some rates; half- and full-board options available; restaurant and bar on premises. **Amenities** Free parking, private beach with towel and umbrella service for guests.

ACCOMMODATIONS

Rooms 18. **All** Phone, satellite TV, in-room safe, minibar. **Bathrooms** Shower and bathtub, hair dryer. **Comfort & Décor** Rooms here may be a bit smaller than standard, but they are kept immaculately clean and free of beach sand.

RATES, RESERVATIONS, & RESTRICTIONS

Pricing Singles €47–€75, doubles €60–€91. **Credit Cards** MC, V. **Check-In/Out** noon/9:30 a.m. **Elevator** Yes. **English Spoken** Yes.

Hotel Profiles—Umbria

THE BEST HOTELS IN UMBRIA				
Hotel	Overall Rating	Quality Rating	Value Rating	Price
The Province of Perugia				
Perugia				
Etruscan Chocohotel	★★★	★★★	★★★★	€60–€105
La Rosetta	★★★★★	★★★★	★★★★	€75–€160
Locanda della Posta	★★★★★	★★★★★	★★★	€85–€200
Assisi				
Albergo Dei Priori	★★★★	★★★★	★★★	€70–€210
Hotel Subasio	★★★★★	★★★★★	★★★	€150–€250
Hotel Umbra	★★★★	★★★★	★★★★	€90–€115
Gubbio				
Castello Cortevecchio	★★★	★★	★★★★	€70–€300
Park Hotel ai Cappuccini	★★★★★	★★★★★	★★★	€150–€310
Spoleto				
Albergo Gattopone	★★★	★★★	★★★	€90–€130
Colle Lignani	★★★	★★★	★★★★★	€60–€90
The Province of Terni				
Orvieto				
Villa Ciconia	★★★	★★★	★★★	€125–€150
Virgilio	★★★	★★★	★★★	€80–€120

The Province of Perugia

Perugia

Etruscan Chocohotel   €60–€105

OVERALL ★★★ | QUALITY ★★★ | VALUE ★★★★ | PERUGIA

Via Campo di Marte, 134; 06100 Perugia; phone 075 583 7314, fax 075 583 7314;
www.chocohotel.it

"A business hotel with flair" is how the Etruscan Chocohotel describes itself, drawing on Umbria's Etruscan roots and Perugia's chocolate heritage for inspiration. Closer to Perugia's main train station and convenient to the *autostrada,* the Chocohotel is in the rather uninteresting section of lower Perugia and devoid of those idyllic, Umbrian hill town views. But the hotel sets itself apart with chocolate. In the lobby is a chocolate shop with all manner of dark and milk chocolate bars in various shapes and sizes. The on-site restaurant bases its menu around chocolate, too, churning out such delicious dishes as gnocchi with chocolate and truffles. Here's the kicker—each guest receives a bar of chocolate on check-in. The affable Alberto Guarducci oversees the operations of this hotel, and other members of the Guarducci family manage the theme hotel Gio' Arte e Vini, an art-and-wine hotel across town. A third hotel dedicated to jazz is in the works.

SETTING & FACILITIES

Location Via Campo di Marte, 134 (lower Perugia). **Quietness Rating** B. **Dining** Buffet breakfast included in rates; the restaurant often serves prix-fixe meals for approximately €30. **Amenities** Parking, meeting facilities, swimming pool.

ACCOMMODATIONS

Rooms 94. **All** Phone, satellite TV, in-room safe. **Bathrooms** Shower and bathtub, hair dryer. **Comfort & Décor** Rooms are modern, with functional desks, data ports, large windows, and spacious bathrooms. Walls are painted with various Etruscan motifs and patterns, and much of the artwork is vintage chocolate advertisements.

RATES, RESERVATIONS, & RESTRICTIONS

Pricing Singles €50–€100, doubles €60–€105. **Credit Cards** MC, V. **Check-In/Out** 2 p.m./noon. **Elevator** Yes. **English Spoken** Yes.

La Rosetta   €75–€160

OVERALL ★★★★★ | QUALITY ★★★★ | VALUE ★★★★ | PERUGIA

Piazza Italia, 19; 06100 Perugia; phone and fax 075 572 0841

Located in a tranquil, ivy-draped cove off of Piazza Italia, La Rosetta is one of the premier hotels in Umbria. You are steps away from the sweeping views of the Rocca Paolina and at an ideal starting point for strolls down Main Street.

SETTING & FACILITIES

Location In Perugia's main square. **Quietness Rating** A. **Dining** Breakfast included; cocktail bar on the premises. **Amenities** Parking garage, meeting room, TV room.

ACCOMMODATIONS

Rooms 94. **All** Phone, satellite TV, minibar. **Bathrooms** Shower and bathtub, hair dryer. **Comfort & Décor** High frescoed ceilings, dramatic chandeliers, and sumptuous Rococo furniture make staying in one of La Rosetta's rooms an unforgettable experience. All 94 rooms are unique and their sizes palatial.

RATES, RESERVATIONS, & RESTRICTIONS

Pricing Singles €75–€95, doubles €115–€160. **Credit Cards** MC, V. **Check-In/Out** 2 p.m./noon. **Elevator** Yes. **English Spoken** Yes.

Locanda della Posta   €85–€200

OVERALL ★★★★★ | QUALITY ★★★★★ | VALUE ★★★ | PERUGIA

Corso Vannucci, 97; 06100 Perugia; phone 075 572 8925, fax 075 573 2562

Perugia's first hotel has hosted the likes of Goethe and Hans Christian Andersen and is the only hotel that faces onto the Corso Vannucci. The Locanda has maintained much of its 18th-century good looks, including its high, vaulted ceilings and ornate exterior. Rooms have been refurbished with modern amenities, and many have balconies that hang over the main pedestrian thoroughfare.

SETTING & FACILITIES

Location On Perugia's main drag. **Quietness Rating** A. **Dining** Breakfast included in rates. **Amenities** Safe available at front desk, parking garage.

ACCOMMODATIONS

Rooms 39. **All** Phone, satellite TV, minibar. **Bathrooms** Shower and bathtub, hair dryer. **Comfort & Décor** Guest rooms are spacious to the point of being intimidating. Leather furniture and reproduced frescoes make bedrooms look like boardrooms.

RATES, RESERVATIONS, & RESTRICTIONS

Pricing Singles €85–€130, doubles €160–€200. **Credit Cards** MC, V. **Check-In/Out** 2 p.m./noon. **Elevator** No. **English Spoken** Yes.

Assisi

Albergo Dei Priori   €70–€210

OVERALL ★★★★ | QUALITY ★★★★ | VALUE ★★★ | ASSISI

Corso Mazzini, 15; 06081 Assisi; phone 075 812 237, fax 075 816 804

In a 16th-century palazzo around the bend from St. Francis Cathedral, the Albergo dei Priori does a booming business with pilgrims and small tour groups. It's moderately priced, given its location, but rooms with views will cost you. Closed December through February.

SETTING & FACILITIES

Location Near the Basilica. **Quietness Rating** A. **Dining** Breakfast included in rates. **Amenities** Meeting room, bar, disabled facilities. **Services** Baby-sitting.

ACCOMMODATIONS

Rooms 34. **All** Phone, satellite TV, minibar. **Bathrooms** Shower or bathtub, hair dryer. **Comfort & Décor** The hotel has a refined atmosphere but handles such a high volume of tourists that its furnishings are a bit worn. Rooms are small and tidy.

RATES, RESERVATIONS, & RESTRICTIONS

Pricing Singles €70–€90, doubles €90–€170, suites €120–€210. **Credit Cards** AMEX, MC, V. **Check-In/Out** 2 p.m./noon. **Elevator** Yes. **English Spoken** Yes.

Hotel Subasio   €150–€250

OVERALL ★★★★★ | QUALITY ★★★★★ | VALUE ★★★ | ASSISI

Via Frate Elia, 2; 06081 Assisi; phone 075 812 206, fax 075 816 691

This hotel is as close as you can get without actually staying in the basilica. Hotel Subasio has a colonnaded walkway that connects it to the church, a godsend on rainy days (of which Assisi has quite a few). Italian and international celebrities have been spotted in the hotel's restaurant, and, as such, haughty Italian families like to stay here when they're passing through. Some rooms have terraces that afford views of the basilica and the Umbrian *campagna*.

SETTING & FACILITIES

Location Faces St. Francis Basilica. **Quietness Rating** A at night, B during the day. **Dining** Breakfast included in rates, Ristorante Subasio is renowned for its formal Umbrian cuisine. **Amenities** On-site restaurant and bar.

ACCOMMODATIONS

Rooms 66. **All** Phone, satellite TV, minibar, in-room safe. **Bathrooms** Shower and bathtub, hair dryer. **Comfort & Décor** As Assisi's fanciest hotel, you can expect the best in modern comforts at the Subasio. Décor is unfortunately dowdy and formal.

RATES, RESERVATIONS, & RESTRICTIONS

Pricing Doubles €150–€170, deluxe suites €180–€250. **Credit Cards** MC, V. **Check-In/Out** 2 p.m./noon. **Elevator** Yes. **English Spoken** Yes.

Hotel Umbra   €90–€115

OVERALL ★★★★ | QUALITY ★★★★ | VALUE ★★★★ | ASSISI

Via degli Archi, 6; 06081 Assisi; phone 075 812 240, fax 075 81365

In town, but far enough away from the hordes by the basilica, the Umbra is a pretty hotel with quite a few surprises. The garden is magnificent and contains a jumble of tropical and hanging plants. Rooms are also very charming; some even feature patios that overhang the stunning backdrop of the Umbrian hills. Rooms with a view (for instance, #34) are more expensive, but worth it. The hotel is closed from January through March.

SETTING & FACILITIES

Location In Piazza del Comune. **Quietness Rating** A. **Dining** Breakfast included in rates, Ristorante Umbra serves quality Umbrian fare. **Amenities** On-site restaurant.

ACCOMMODATIONS

Rooms 26. **All** Phone, satellite TV, in-room safe. **Bathrooms** Shower or bathtub, hair dryer. **Comfort & Décor** Your stylish aunt could have personally picked out the doilies and antiques that decorate the rooms. Accommodations are conservative but stylish.

RATES, RESERVATIONS, & RESTRICTIONS

Pricing Doubles €90–€115. **Credit Cards** AMEX, MC, V. **Check-In/Out** 2 p.m./noon. **Elevator** No. **English Spoken** Yes.

Gubbio

Castello Cortevecchio   €70–€300

OVERALL ★★★ | QUALITY ★★ | VALUE ★★★★ | GUBBIO

Località Nogna; 06020 Gubbio; phone 075 924 1017, fax 075 924 1079

The castle and manor that now form the Castello Cortevecchio date from medieval times. Today, this is a relatively modern farmhouse inn, where olive oil, honey, and liqueurs are produced. Castello Cortevecchio is surrounded by a lush nature preserve—ideal for strolls and mountain biking.

SETTING & FACILITIES

Location In the Eugubine hills. **Quietness Rating** A. **Dining** Half-board, €50 supplement; full-board, €70 supplement; there's a barbecue available for guest use. **Amenities** Free parking, swimming pool.

ACCOMMODATIONS

Rooms 11 one-room apartments, 5 two-room apartments. **All** Phone, kitchenette. **Bathrooms** Shower and bathtub, hair dryer on request. **Comfort & Décor** Rooms are sparse, done in a rustic style. Decorations include antiques and personal effects collected by the owners.

RATES, RESERVATIONS, & RESTRICTIONS

Pricing One-room apartments, €70–€100, two-room apartments, €150–€300. **Credit Cards** MC, V. **Check-In/Out** 2 p.m./noon. **Elevator** No. **English Spoken** Some.

Park Hotel al Cappuccini   €150–€310

OVERALL ★★★★★ | QUALITY ★★★★★ | VALUE ★★★ | GUBBIO

Via Tifernate; 06024 Gubbio; phone 075 9234, fax 075 922 0323.

Splashing out in Gubbio is as easy as staying at the Park Hotel, easily the area's most luxurious digs. Located in a 17th-century Capuchin monastery just outside of town, the Park Hotel is surprisingly equipped with some of the most modern facilities, including a fitness center and a sauna. The grounds here are surrounded by olive groves and a pretty garden, where you can unwind with a cocktail and watch the sun set.

SETTING & FACILITIES

Location Two miles out of town. **Quietness Rating** A. **Dining** Breakfast included in rates; the Park Hotel Ristorante is among the best in Umbria and uses the freshest ingredients. **Amenities** Meeting room, indoor swimming pool, fitness center, free parking, **Services** Room service, laundry service.

ACCOMMODATIONS

Rooms 32. **All** Phone, satellite TV, minibar, radio, in-room safe. **Bathrooms** Shower and bathtub, hair dryer. **Comfort & Décor** All public areas and bedrooms are swank, furnished with leather chairs, delicate drapes, and Oriental rugs.

RATES, RESERVATIONS, & RESTRICTIONS

Pricing Doubles €150–€310. **Credit Cards** AMEX, MC, V. **Check-In/Out** 2 p.m./noon. **Elevator** No. **English Spoken** Yes.

Spoleto

Albergo Gattopone	€90–€130

OVERALL ★★★ | QUALITY ★★★ | VALUE ★★★ | SPOLETO

Via del Ponte, 6; 06049 Spoleto; phone 0743 36147

An enviable view of the gorge and the Torri del Ponte is the only decoration that this modest hotel needs. The Gattopone is popular with musicians and music lovers, so book early if you want to stay here during the Festival dei Due Mondi.

SETTING & FACILITIES

Location Near the Torri del Ponte. **Quietness Rating** A. **Dining** Breakfast included in rates. **Amenities** Meeting rooms, parking.

ACCOMMODATIONS

Rooms 16. **All** Phone, satellite TV, minibar. **Bathrooms** Shower or bathtub, hair dryer. **Comfort & Décor** Tasteful furnishings can be found in the public areas and in the guest rooms. The older rooms have reproduction antiques, whereas the newer ones are outfitted with understated, modern fixtures.

RATES, RESERVATIONS, & RESTRICTIONS

Pricing €90–€130. **Credit Cards** MC, V. **Check-In/Out** 2 p.m./noon. **Elevator** No. **English Spoken** Yes.

Colle Lignani	€60–€90

OVERALL ★★★ | QUALITY ★★★ | VALUE ★★★★★ | SPOLETO

Via dei Pini, 21; 06049 Spoleto; phone 0743 49676, fax 0743 229 961;
www.collelignani.com

This farmhouse inn is worth a mention for its desirable position on a hill overlooking the Valle Umbra. If you're here during the summer, you can take a dip in the pool. In the winter, sample the fresh-pressed olive oil and wine, which are made on the premises.

SETTING & FACILITIES

Location On the edge of town. **Quietness Rating** A. **Dining** None. **Amenities** Free parking, swimming pool, horseback riding, tennis.

ACCOMMODATIONS

Rooms 9. **All** Phone, kitchenettes, terrace. **Bathrooms** Shower and bathroom, hair dryer. **Comfort & Décor** Not surprisingly, the rooms here are spacious and simple, with tile floors, farmhouse tables, and wood-beamed ceilings. Some rooms have fireplaces. There is also plenty of open space surrounding the inn if you want to stretch your legs and get some fresh air.

RATES, RESERVATIONS, & RESTRICTIONS

Pricing Doubles €60–€70, apartments €75–€90. **Credit Cards** MC, V. **Check-In/Out** 2 p.m./noon. **Elevator** No. **English Spoken** Some.

The Province of Terni

Orvieto

Villa Ciconia	€125–€150

OVERALL ★★★ | QUALITY ★★★ | VALUE ★★★ | ORVIETO

Via dei Tigli, 69; 05018 Orvieto; phone 0763 305 582, fax 0763 302 077; www.hotelvillaciconia.com

This three-floor manor in the suburb of Ciconia is a pretty setting for a country hotel. Climb the long staircase (there is no elevator), and you'll find spacious and extremely quiet rooms, where you're sure to get a good night's sleep. Ristorante Ciconia is one of the best in the area and serves honest Umbrian cuisine and local wines. When it's time to visit Orvieto, you can catch the bus several blocks down the road.

SETTING & FACILITIES

Location In the valley below town. **Quietness Rating** A. **Dining** Breakfast is included in rates; the restaurant on the premises serves rustic Umbrian fare, including numerous truffle dishes. **Amenities** Free parking.

ACCOMMODATIONS

Rooms 12. **All** Phone, satellite TV, minibar, in-room safe. **Bathrooms** Shower or bathtub, hair dryer. **Comfort & Décor** Tall doors lead into plain and comfortable rooms. Windows in the spacious rooms open up onto views of the Umbrian countryside.

RATES, RESERVATIONS, & RESTRICTIONS

Pricing €125–€150. **Credit Cards** AMEX, MC, V. **Check-In/Out** 2 p.m./noon. **Elevator** No. **English Spoken** Yes.

Virgilio	€80–€120

OVERALL ★★★ | QUALITY ★★★ | VALUE ★★★ | ORVIETO

Piazza del Duomo, 5/6; 05018 Orvieto; phone 0763 41882, fax 0763 343 797

A fantastic location facing the Duomo is the Virgilio's best asset. When the day trippers have gone home, you can peer out at the pedestrian-free Piazza del Duomo and enjoy the splendor of the Gothic cathedral in silence.

SETTING & FACILITIES

Location By the Duomo. **Quietness Rating** A. **Dining** Breakfast included in rates. **Amenities** On-site bar.

ACCOMMODATIONS

Rooms 13. **All** Phone, satellite TV, minibar, in-room safe. **Bathrooms** Shower or bathtub, hair dryer. **Comfort & Décor** With such stunning views of the cathedral (on the front), who needs much else? The rooms are a bit cramped and modestly furnished.

RATES, RESERVATIONS, & RESTRICTIONS

Pricing €80–€120. **Credit Cards** MC, V. **Check-In/Out** 2 p.m./noon. **Elevator** No. **English Spoken** Yes.

Hotel Profiles—The Marches and the Republic of San Marino

THE BEST HOTELS IN THE MARCHES AND THE REPUBLIC OF SAN MARINO

Hotel	Overall Rating	Quality Rating	Value Rating	Price
The Province of Pésaro-Urbino				
Urbino				
Nenè	★★★½	★★★	★★★★★	€37–€73
San Domenico	★★★★	★★★	★★★★	€70–€210
The Republic of San Marino				
Hotel Villa Giardi	★★★½	★★★	★★★★	€60–€130
The Province of Ancona				
Ancona				
Grand Hotel Palace	★★★★	★★★★	★★★	€115–€180
Hotel Passetto	★★★½	★★★★	★★★	€115–€215
Loreto				
Hotel Villa Tetlameya	★★★★	★★★★	★★★★	€70–€150
Riviera Conero				
Fortino Napoleonico	★★★★	★★★★	★★★	€100–€215

Hotel	Overall Rating	Quality Rating	Value Rating	Price
THE BEST HOTELS IN THE MARCHES AND THE REPUBLIC OF SAN MARINO *(continued)*				
The Province of Macerata				
Macerata				
Claudiani	★★★	★★★	★★★	€65–€165
Agriturismo Floriani	★★★½	★★★	★★★★	€52–€92
The Province of Áscoli-Piceno				
Áscoli-Piceno				
Gioli	★★★★	★★★★	★★★★★	€65–€100
Hotel Palazzo Guiderocchi	★★★½	★★★★	★★½	€85–€250

The Province of Pésaro-Urbino

Urbino

Nenè   €37–€73

OVERALL ★★★½ | QUALITY ★★★ | VALUE ★★★★★ | URBINO

Strada Rossa Crocicchia; 61029 Urbino; phone 0722 2996, fax 0722 350 161; www.neneurbino.com

If you want to escape to the Marches countryside, then the economical Hotel Nenè is a good choice. Situated in a farmhouse deep in the Montefeltro hills, Nenè is ideal for families or couples who need to get away from it all. One of the best reasons to stop here is for dinner at Ristorante Nenè, which serves up serious traditional food. When you're ready to act like a tourist again, the treasures of Urbino are only minutes away (accessible from a bus near the hotel).

SETTING & FACILITIES

Location In the countryside outside of Urbino. **Quietness Rating** A+. **Dining** A restaurant serving rustic Marchigian specialties is located on the premises. Full- and half-board rates available. **Amenities** Acres of woodland, free parking.

ACCOMMODATIONS

Rooms 6. **All** Phone, satellite TV, ironing board, minibar. **Bathrooms** Shared. **Comfort & Décor** Nenè's rooms are very plain but have windows that open wide onto the countryside. Cold terra cotta floors are invigorating during the summer but make the room kind of drafty in cooler months.

RATES, RESERVATIONS, & RESTRICTIONS

Pricing Singles €37–€47, doubles €47–€60, triples €60–€73. **Credit Cards** Not accepted. **Check-In/Out** 3 p.m./noon. **Elevator** No. **English Spoken** Some.

San Domenico   €70–€210

OVERALL ★★★★ | QUALITY ★★★ | VALUE ★★★★ | URBINO

Piazza Rinascimento, 3; 61029 Urbino; phone 0722 2626, fax 0722 2727

The nondescript entrance to Hotel San Domenico belies the riches inside. Once a monastery, the centrally located hotel has been gorgeously refurbished with all the amenities. A long portico decorated with Ducal chandeliers leads from the pretty but unpretentious main rooms toward the airy breakfast room, which comes complete with a baby grand piano. You can also enjoy the sound of the piano in the late afternoon while you watch the sunset over the courtyard. Two rooms on the ground floor are adapted for travelers with disabilities. The owners of San Domenico also own local hotels Residenza dei Duchi and Hotel Bonconte.

SETTING & FACILITIES

Location Down the street from the Palazzo Ducale. **Quietness Rating** A. **Dining** Breakfast, €8–€16. **Amenities** Parking nearby. **Services** Room service, laundry service, access to swimming pool and fitness facilities at affiliated hotels in Urbino and Pésaro.

ACCOMMODATIONS

Rooms 151, plus 10 suites. **All** Phone, satellite TV, in-room safe. **Bathrooms** Shower or bathtub, hair dryer. **Comfort & Décor** Guest rooms are uncluttered and decorated in muted shades of gold and peach. All have handsome views over the courtyard.

RATES, RESERVATIONS, & RESTRICTIONS

Pricing Singles €70–€95, doubles €95–€170, suites €145–€210. **Credit Cards** MC, V. **Check-In/Out** 2 p.m./noon. **Elevator** Yes. **English Spoken** Little.

The Republic of San Marino

Hotel Villa Giardi   €60–€130

OVERALL ★★★½ | QUALITY ★★★ | VALUE ★★★★ | SAN MARINO

Via Palmede Ferri, 22; 47890 San Marino; phone 0549 991 074, fax 0549 992 285

An Alpine setting on an Appenine ridge, this small, chalet-style hotel is a cozy perch from which to enjoy the views of the Marches and the assets of San Marino. A short walk from the sprawling Parco Naturale and the Centro Storico, and a short drive to Urbino and the beach, Villa Giardi is one of the more tranquil and well-positioned options in the area. Discounts are given for stays of at least one week—an especially affordable incentive for families or groups of three or four.

SETTING & FACILITIES

Location High on a hill overlooking the Marches countryside. **Quietness Rating** A+.

Dining Buffet breakfast included. **Amenities** Private garden, free parking in hotel garage, fax, Internet access; most rooms have balconies.

ACCOMMODATIONS

Rooms 8. **All** Phone, satellite TV, minibar, in-room safe. **Bathrooms** Shower and bathtub, hair dryer. **Comfort & Décor** Recently updated, the rooms are as inviting as a relative's guest bedroom, with gauzy curtains, colorful linens, and cherry wardrobes and desks. The cool mountain breeze is a free amenity to be relished in the summer months.

RATES, RESERVATIONS & RESTRICTIONS

Pricing Doubles €60–€96, triples/quads €72–€130. **Credit Cards** AMEX, DC, MC, V. **Check-In/Out** 3 p.m./11 a.m. **Elevator** No. **English Spoken** Yes.

The Province of Ancona

Ancona

Grand Hotel Palace	€115–€180

OVERALL ★★★★ | QUALITY ★★★★ | VALUE ★★★ | ANCONA

Lungomare Vanvitelli, 24; 60020 Ancona; phone 071 201 813, fax 071 207 4832

The Palace is a lavish four-star property on the port, with spectacular views of the Arch of Trajan and the Adriatic coast. You can watch the sun rise and set from the roof garden or settle in with cocktails by the fireplace in the swank lobby. The breakfast room has a fantastic view of the cruise ships and freightliners below, and watching them call each morning makes for an interesting spectator sport.

SETTING & FACILITIES

Location In the port of Ancona. **Quietness Rating** B. **Dining** Buffet breakfast included in rates. **Amenities** Meeting rooms, paid parking nearby.

ACCOMMODATIONS

Rooms 41. **All** Phone, satellite TV, in-room safe, minibar. **Bathrooms** Shower and bathtub, hair dryer. **Comfort & Décor** The rooms of this renovated 17th-century manor are decked out with crystal chandeliers, walnut desks, and fine art prints. There's more than enough space here.

RATES, RESERVATIONS, & RESTRICTIONS

Pricing Doubles €115–€180. **Credit Cards** MC, V. **Check-In/Out** 2 p.m./noon. **Elevator** Yes. **English Spoken** Yes.

Hotel Passetto	€115–€215

OVERALL ★★★½ | QUALITY ★★★★ | VALUE ★★★ | ANCONA

Via Thaon de Revel, 1; 60010 Ancona; phone 071 31307, fax 071 32856

A modern façade that sticks out of the Conero pines like a white hair, the Passetto is the sleekest business hotel we've seen. Fully equipped with meeting rooms and respective equipment, the hotel also boasts a swimming pool and a sun room, and it's within walking distance of an elevator that leads down the rock face to the sea. The ever-helpful staff can direct you towards tennis and golf facilities nearby. Additional excursion ideas are available from the Ancona tourist office, conveniently located a few doors down from the hotel.

SETTING & FACILITIES

Location In a residential neighborhood overlooking the Adriatic. **Quietness Rating** A. **Dining** Breakfast included in rates. Lunch and dinner available at Ristorante Passetto. **Amenities** Meeting rooms, business center, free parking, outdoor swimming pool (open only in summer).

ACCOMMODATIONS

Rooms 42 **All** Phone, satellite TV, in-room safe, minibar. **Bathrooms** All bathrooms equipped with whirlpools and hair dryers. **Comfort & Décor** Passetto has rooms that you will want to live in. Canopy beds, persian rugs, neutral furniture, and understated art and lighting create a sophisticated, adult atmosphere.

RATES, RESERVATIONS, & RESTRICTIONS

Pricing Singles €115–€175, doubles €140–€215. **Credit Cards** AMEX, DC, MC, V. **Check-In/Out** 3 p.m./noon. **Elevator** Yes, but must walk up small flight of stairs to reach it. **English Spoken** Yes.

Loreto

Hotel Villa Tetlameya   €70–€150

OVERALL ★★★★ | QUALITY ★★★★ | VALUE ★★★★ | LORETO

Via Villa Costantina, 187; 60025 Loreto; phone 071 978 863, fax 071 976 639

The site of one of the Loreto area's best restaurants—Zi' Nene—the Hotel Villa Tetlameya is a restructured 19th-century mansion located due east of the city center. Such an elite address is hardly appropriate for a pilgrim's stay, but the rather moderate room rates should alleviate any guilt.

SETTING & FACILITIES

Location Between Loreto and the sea. **Quietness Rating** A+. **Dining** Breakfast, €5; supplements for lunch/dinner, €19 per person per night. **Amenities** Free parking, meeting rooms, private park, baby-sitting.

ACCOMMODATIONS

Rooms 8. **All** Phone, satellite TV, in-room safe, mini bar. **Bathrooms** Shower and bathtub, hair dryer. **Comfort & Décor** Opulence abounds from the villa's parquet floors to its cathedral ceilings. Beautiful cherrywood furnishings, hand-painted door and fixtures, and suffused lighting make up for the small bedding.

RATES, RESERVATIONS, & RESTRICTIONS

Pricing Singles €70–€87, doubles €105–€150. **Credit Cards** MC, V. **Check-In/Out** 2 p.m./10 a.m. **Elevator** Yes. **English Spoken** Some.

Riviera Conero

Fortino Napoleonico	€100–€215

OVERALL ★★★★ | QUALITY ★★★★ | VALUE ★★★ | PORTONOVO

Via Poggio, 166; 60020 Portonovo; phone 071 801 450, fax 071 801 454; www.hotelfortino.it

Built by Napoleon's Italian viceroy in the early 19th century, this two-tiered beach fortress has been transformed into a first-class hotel. Part of the hotel operates as a bed-and-breakfast, and the rest is a full-service inn. Access to the Adriatic is right out the door, and the hotel runs a shuttle to the airport and the Ancona harbor.

SETTING & FACILITIES

Location On the Conero Riviera. **Quietness Rating** A. **Dining** On-site restaurant specializes in seafood. **Amenities** Beach access, parking, restaurant.

ACCOMMODATIONS

Rooms 30. **All** Phone, satellite TV, balconies. **Bathrooms** Shower and bathtub, hair dryer. **Comfort & Décor** Unusual for a beachside hotel, the rooms here feature beautiful antiques and elegant furnishings. Beds are hidden behind sumptuous drapes.

RATES, RESERVATIONS, & RESTRICTIONS

Pricing Singles €100–€160, doubles €135–€190, suites €150–€215. **Credit Cards** MC, V. **Check-In/Out** 2 p.m./noon. **Elevator** No. **English Spoken** Some.

The Province of Macerata

Macerata

Agriturismo Floriani	€52–€92

OVERALL ★★★½ | QUALITY ★★★ | VALUE ★★★★ | MACERATA

Contrada Montanello, 3; 62100 Macerata; phone 0733 492 267; www.florianicompagnoni.it

Getting away from it all is easy at this *agriturismo* set in the hills about one mile north of Macerata. Owned by the Floriani family, whose ancestors helped to build Malta, the estate consists of two weathered farmhouses, a tavern, and stables, where the family archives are kept. Apartment #3 is especially spacious, with enough room for two couples or a family of four to stretch out. Personal touches like antique wardrobes, charming, floral-print bed linens, and small, framed prints of the Italian countryside (found within each room and apartment) provide a very comfortable and familial home-away-from-home.

SETTING & FACILITIES

Location In the green hills outside Macerata. **Quietness Rating** A+. **Dining** Breakfast €5.50–€7 per person, depending on season. Restaurant on premises. **Amenities** Free parking, private park, vineyards.

ACCOMMODATIONS

Rooms 4 rooms, 3 apartments. **All** Phone, satellite TV, in-room safe. Apartments have kitchenettes. **Bathrooms** Private shower, hair dryer. **Comfort & Décor** Rooms are cozy, but perhaps a bit dark. Towel- and sheet-changing service is available upon request; otherwise, every four days during stay.

RATES, RESERVATIONS, & RESTRICTIONS

Pricing Doubles €52–€72, apartment €56–€92. Reservations require deposit of 30% of room rate. Stays of at least one week in August. **Credit Cards** AMEX, MC, V. **Check-In/Out Elevator** No. **English Spoken** Yes.

Claudiani   €65–€165

OVERALL ★★★ | QUALITY ★★★ | VALUE ★★★ | MACERATA

Via Ulissi, 8; 62100 Macerata; phone 0733 261 400, fax 0733 261 380; www.hotelclaudiani.it

The newest hotel in Macerata is set inside the original walls of a 17th-century palace. The interior, however, is completely up to date, with modern conference facilities, contemporary marble floors, and all-new leather furniture in the lobby. Macerata's main sights are reachable on foot in only a few minutes.

SETTING & FACILITIES

Location In the center. **Quietness Rating** A. **Dining** Breakfast included in rates. **Amenities** Meeting rooms, paid parking on premises, €8–€12.

ACCOMMODATIONS

Rooms 40. **All** Phone, satellite TV, radio, minibar. **Bathrooms** Shower or bathtub, hair dryer. **Comfort & Décor** Room décor is modern, but rather provincial, lacking much in the way of style. Beds are firm, and the wall-to-wall carpet is new.

RATES, RESERVATIONS, & RESTRICTIONS

Pricing Singles €65–€85, doubles €80–€120, suites €120–€165. **Credit Cards** MC, V. **Check-In/Out** 2 p.m./noon. **Elevator** Yes. **English Spoken** Some.

The Province of Áscoli-Piceno

Áscoli-Piceno

Gioli   €65–€100

OVERALL ★★★★ | QUALITY ★★★★ | VALUE ★★★★★ | ÁSCOLI-PICENO

Viale de' Gasperi, 14; 63100 Áscoli-Piceno; phone and fax 0736 255 550

Located near Piazza Arringo and the Duomo, the Gioli is a pretty four-star property with modern décor. The lobby is intimate, with a small bar and a TV room. Gioli's biggest asset is its parking garage, one of the few in the city.

SETTING & FACILITIES

Location In the city center. **Quietness Rating** A. **Dining** Breakfast included in rates. **Amenities** Parking garage, 24-hour room service.

ACCOMMODATIONS

Rooms 56. **All** Phone, satellite TV, minibar. **Bathrooms** Shower or bathtub, hair dryer. **Comfort & Décor** Rooms are rather small but are furnished with modern travelers in mind. Beds are firm, closets are ample, and each room has a small desk and vanity.

RATES, RESERVATIONS, & RESTRICTIONS

Pricing Singles €65, doubles €100. **Credit Cards** MC, V. **Check-In/Out** 2 p.m./noon. **Elevator** Yes. **English Spoken** Some.

Hotel Palazzo Guiderocchi   €85–€250

OVERALL ★★★½ | QUALITY ★★★★ | VALUE ★★½ | ÁSCOLI-PICENO

Via Cesare Battisti, 3; 63100 Áscoli-Piceno; phone 0736 244 011, fax 0736 243 441; www.palazzoguiderocchi.com

Located in a converted 17th-century palace that once housed the offices of the pope's tax collectors, Palazzo Guiderocchi has recently undergone a million-dollar transformation, resulting in the preservation of its Corinthian columns, vaulted ceilings, gilded mouldings, and floral frescoes. When not admiring the beautiful interior, look out your window to enjoy dramatic views of the Piazza Bonfine, notable for its churches, cafés, and ionic temple ruins.

SETTING & FACILITIES

Location Among the towers of Áscoli-Piceno. **Quietness Rating** A. **Dining** Breakfast included in rates; restaurant on premises. **Amenities** 24-hour reception, laundry service, Internet point, meeting room.

ACCOMMODATIONS

Rooms 24. **All** Phone, satellite TV, in-room safe. **Bathrooms** Shower and bathtub, hair dryer. **Comfort & Décor** Only the most luxurious fabrics and drapery in the boldest hues have been used in the guest rooms. Many beds have canopies and down comforters. Reception staff is helpful and discreet.

RATES, RESERVATIONS, & RESTRICTIONS

Pricing Singles €85–€130, doubles €150–€210, suites €190–€250. **Credit Cards** AMEX, DC, MC, V. **Check-In/Out** 2 p.m./11 a.m. **Elevator** Yes. **English Spoken** Some.

Part Five

Dining in Central Italy

Buon Appetito!

The highlight for most travelers to Italy, be they first-timers or old pros, is a chance to chow down on the country's many culinary delights. Indeed, many tourists come to Italy not to shop or to cruise museums but to eat. And why not? Among Americans, Italian food is consistently rated as the favorite cuisine. Just wait until you try to real thing.

Italians are concerned with two factors when it comes to eating: freshness and pleasure. When the first tomatoes of the season beckon at the market with their juicy, red plumpness, or when mushrooms and truffles have their autumnal debut in risottos, Italians are there with forks and knives ready. Appetites here wax and wane with the seasons, and it seems that everyone is in tune to what's ripe. This inherited knowledge of what to eat and when enables Italians to enjoy a fruit or vegetable at its peak, which leads to ultimate gastronomic bliss at dinner.

While you are in this mecca of Mediterranean eats, you may have a hankering for an old standard, like spaghetti and meat sauce or a simple slice of cheese pizza. Give in to your cravings! But, also try to do as the Romans do and indulge in the succulent produce of summer, the complex, earthy flavors of fall, and the cornucopia of flavors that you may encounter in Italy. Memories of those unique meals with last a lifetime.

When to Eat

Breakfast, *prima colazione,* or simply *colazione,* is very small (a roll and coffee, if anything at all), and is typically consumed before 9 a.m. There's nothing unusual there. However, you'd be hard pressed to find an Italian drinking a milky cappuccino after 11 a.m. It's just not done. Lunch, *pranzo,* has been traditionally the largest meal of the day, which is why many boutiques and markets close at noon for a couple of hours. Years ago, most Italians went home at this time to enjoy lunch with the family and then take a nap *(siesta)*. Such a luxury is on the decline these days. Now you'll find that many restaurants are swamped between 1 and 2 p.m. Early-bird Americans will be upset to learn that dinner, *cena,* in Italy is rarely eaten before 8 p.m.; most Italians make restaurant reservations for 8:30 or 9 p.m. Of course, in larger cities you should be able to find restaurants serving dinner at 6 p.m., though be warned—most restaurants open that early cater to tourists and, therefore, are rarely recommended.

You should also be aware that almost every restaurant you encounter will have a rest day, or *giorno del riposo.* These are usually taken on a Sunday or Monday night, though you might find an odd restaurant that closes on a Wednesday or a Saturday. To avoid disappointment, take note of the *riposo* day, posted outside every restaurant, or inquire when you make your reservations.

Types of Eateries in Italy

Ristoranti

The most formal of Italy's dining establishments, *ristoranti* typically have discrete service, fancy-schmancy décor, and overpriced menus. You'll want to wear your cuff links and pearls here, and set aside at least two hours to savor a full-course meal.

Osterie/Hostarie

Less formal than a *ristorante,* an *osteria* (sometimes spelled *hostaria*) is, in the traditional sense, a family-owned restaurant with less expensive but fine fare. You needn't dress too formally to dine at an *osteria.* However, take note that many up-market restaurants have capitalized on the name "osteria" to lure in diners with promises of economical, rustic fare.

Trattorie

A *trattoria* is very much like an *osteria,* in that it is commonly a family-run eatery with inexpensive food. *Trattorie,* with their hand-scribbled menus and amiable service, are even more relaxed than osteria.

Tavole Calde

The *tavola calda,* or literally, "hot table," is akin to American self-serve cafeterias, but the selections are generally much better. Catering to the business set, *tavole calde* offer hot entrées like roasted chicken and potatoes *(polla arrosto con patate),* pastas, salads, and sides of vegetables *(contorni)* at very affordable prices. Dishes are premade, so they are often heated up in the microwave when you order them. But they are ideal for a quick bite. Another note: Unlike with *caffès,* where there is a sharp price difference between bar orders and table service, a *tavola calda* has no table service, and thus no extra charge for sitting at a table.

Pizzerie

In Italy, pizza is served in two ways. People on the go opt for *pizza a(l) taglio,* or pizza by the slice. At this kind of stand-up *pizzeria,* you choose which and how much pizza you want, and the *pizzaiolo* will cut it for you on the spot. In most instances, the slice is weighed (a regular-size slice costs approximately €1) and wrapped in paper to keep your fingers and clothes clean while you eat. If you want your pizza to be heated *(caldo)* before you chow down, ask the *pizzaiolo/a,* and he or she will pop the slice into the oven for you at no charge. You may also see *pizza al taglio* referred to as *pizza alla romana,* for it was the busybody Romans who invented this convenient way to enjoy the pie. Other items you can buy in the *pizza al taglio* shop are calzone, *suppli* (balls of rice and mozzarella cheese breaded and fried), and, in the Marches, *olive ascolane* (olives stuffed with meat, anchovies, or cheese, then breaded and fried).

Head to a typical, sit-down *pizzeria* for a longer, more casual lunch or dinner. Here, you'll find even more varieties of pizza for vegetable or meat lovers, as well as salads and light appetizers. You can easily share a pizza at a traditional *pizzeria*—pies measure about 10 inches diameter—but this practice is frowned on. Prices range from €7 to €10 per pie.

Wine Bars (Enoteche)

Linguists and wine aficionados should recognize that the words *enoteca* (wine store/bar) and *oenology* (science of viticulture) derive from the same Greek origin. The *enoteca* (plural, *enoteche*) is the oasis for anyone who wants to sample a variety of wines at relatively inexpensive prices. During the day, most *enoteche* are in the business of selling bottles of wine, though they also serve wines by the glass along with light plates of cheese or antipasto to those who wish to settle down in between shopping excursions or touring. By night, in some towns, the *enoteca* becomes the spot for a drink before dining or dancing. In some cases, the *enoteca* is *the* nighttime destination. Below is a list of some of our favorite *enoteche* in Florence and Rome.

Florence

Enoteca de' Giraldi   Via de' Giraldi, 4 (Santa Croce); phone 055 216 518; **www.vinaio.com**

Cantinetta Antinori   Piazza Antinori, 3 (Santa Maria Novella); phone 055 292 234; **www.antinori.it**

Pitti Gola e Cantina   Piazza Pitti, 16 (Oltrarno); phone 055 212 704

Rome
Angolo Divino   Via dei Balestrari, 12 (Centro Storico); phone 06 686 4413

Enoteca al Parlamento   Via dei Prefetti, 15 (Centro Storico); phone 06 687 3446

Enoteca Antica di Via della Croce   Via della Croce, 76b (Spanish Steps); phone 06 679 0896

Vineria   Campo de' Fiori, 15 (Centro Storico); phone 06 688 03 268

Slow Food
An organization that developed in response to the globalization of fast food, the Slow Food Movement states in its manifesto that it exists to "protect the right to taste." The organization puts a premium on restaurants that cook the old-fashioned way (i.e., "slowly"), using fresh ingredients and time-tested techniques. Equally important to Slow Food is the ability of the consumer to savor a gourmet meal without feeling rushed.

Approximately 60,000 restaurants and wine makers from around the world—and at least 30,000 in Italy—have been designated as Slow Food establishments, and more members are waiting in the wings. Most restaurants that become Slow Food members make this fact known by posting the group's snail decal on a door or window. Other Slow Food restaurants prefer to stay incognito, so as to maintain a savvy, gourmand clientele.

Before taking your culinary journey through Italy, consider checking out Slow Food's website, where you can find a comprehensive listing of restaurants, wineries, and groceries that do things the slow way. You can also write or call Slow Food's representatives in the United States (phone (212) 965-5640), in Canada (phone (866) 266-6661) or in the United Kingdom (phone 0800 917 1232).

Slow Food   Via Mendicità Istruita 14; 12042 Bra (Cuneo); phone 0172 419 611, fax 0172 421 293; **www.slowfood.it**

The Dining Experience: Before and after You Sit Down

Making a Reservation
Many family-run *trattorie* do not accept reservations, preferring to work on a first-come, first-serve basis. Most eateries in Italy, except for the really haughty ones, used to prefer this method, but reservations are now *de rigueur* among Italians, who often have to compete with hordes of visitors from abroad. For tourists, the *prenotazione* (pray-no-TATS-yo-nay) may often be the only way to score a table at a reputable establishment. That's easier said than done.

Your best bet for making a reservation as a non–Italian-speaking trav-eler is to investigate whether the restaurant has a fax machine. Many hot spots, such as Enoteca Pinchiorri in Florence, which is often booked months in advance, allow diners to reserve a table via fax. But you will still need to call to confirm your reservation—right after you make it, and some weeks prior to your trip. If you're already in the country (better yet, if you're already in town), stop by the restaurant during lunch hours and inquire about reservations. Making a reservation with someone face to face is much simpler, and, who knows, you may get a seat due to a late cancellation by another party. Finally, if you must rely on the telephone to book a table, remember this important phrase: *"Parla inglese?"* Chances are, the maitre d'hôtel will know exactly why you are calling and will take it from there.

Dressing for Dinner

Use common sense when dressing for dinner in Italy. As we've mentioned before, Italians tend to dress up more than Anglos, so it's always best to err on the more formal side. Besides, what's wrong with looking your best while dining out? On the other hand, if your suitcase is full of jeans, you may want to eat at a *pizzeria* or a more casual *trattoria.*

Pane e Coperto

This "bread and cover" charge can be the source of much anguish for for-eign diners if they don't know what it is. At most eateries, be they *ris-toranti* or *trattorie,* an extra charge is automatically tacked onto the check, no matter if the diners eat bread or not. The *pane e coperto* is a service charge per person, starting at about €2 per person and/or roughly 5–10% of the check. What's more, the supplemental charge usually does not take into account the charge for service, which sometimes is an oblig-atory 15%. Of course, it would make sense for restaurants to factor this bread and cover cost into the price of meals—but you're in Italy, and they do things differently here. To avoid a surprise, glance at the menu (it often lists the charge at the bottom of the page) or inquire about the *pane e coperto* before you sit down for dinner.

Nonsmoking Sections

Although there is a law that requires every restaurant in Italy to provide a nonsmoking section, it is hardly ever enforced. Italian smokers outnum-ber nonsmokers three to one, so when a restaurant does provide for a nonsmoking section, the area is usually small and tucked off to the side away from the main dining room.

In some tiny diners, you may even find that the nonsmoking section abuts the smoking section, which can be a real kick in the face if you have reserved a nonsmoking table. If you want to avoid secondhand smoke during your meal, our advice is to try to secure an outdoor table, where the effects of smoke are less exaggerated. If you're visiting during the cooler months, try dining out before 8:30 p.m—smokers seem to prefer to eat later.

Reading the Menu

Many restaurants near tourist attractions will have menus either translated into English or an English-speaking server who will help you navigate your dining options. Far off the tourist track, you're on your own. If you're unsure of the difference between *anatra* and *ananas,* look to our following list of common food items:

Fruits and vegetables

Albicocca	apricot
Ananas	pineapple
Arancia	orange
Carciofo	artichoke
Fagioli	beans
Fragola	strawberry
Frutta	fruit
Funghi	mushrooms
Limona	lemon
Mela	apple
Melanzana	eggplant
Noci	nuts (typically hazelnuts)
Patata	potato
Peperoni	peppers
Pera	pear
Pesca	peach
Pomodoro	tomato
Pompelmo	grapefruit
Tartufo	truffle
Uva	grape

Meat, fish, and dairy

Acciughe	anchovies
Agnello	lamb
Anatra	duck
Bistecca	steak
Calamari	squid
Carne	meat
Cinghiale	wild boar
Coniglio (or *lepre*)	rabbit
Formaggio	cheese

Meat, fish, and dairy *(continued)*

Gamberi	shrimp
Latte	milk
Manzo	beef
Pesce	fish
Pollo	chicken
Porchetta	pork
Prosciutto	ham
Salsiccia	sausage
Uovo	egg
Vongole	clams

Breads and grains

Cornetto	croissant
Dolci	sweets
Pane	bread
Panino	sandwich
Torta	cake

Beverages

Birra	beer
Caffè	coffee
Spremuta	(fresh squeezed) juice
Succo	juice
Tè	tea
Vino	wine

Miscellaneous

Cioccolato	chocolate
Dolci	sweets
Pepe	pepper
Sale	salt
Zucchero	sugar

Ordering Wine

Chances are, unless you're a wine connoisseur, your waiter or waitress will be more knowledgeable than you are about what wine to drink with your meal. *Vino* is about as common as water in Central Italy, which means that most natives have an inborn sense of what red or white goes with which dish. Don't be timid—just ask.

On the other hand, if you wish to go it alone, your best bet for choosing a wine with your meal is to know which vintages are indigenous to the town or region that you are visiting. In Italy, cuisine and viticulture have matured in tandem, which means that, for example, if you order up a plate of pasta with truffles while in Umbria, then you'd probably do well to choose the Orvieto Classico *vino bianco* as an accompaniment. Likewise, a *bistecca alla fiorentina* in Tuscany calls for a bold red, or perhaps an expensive nip of Brunello di Montalcino.

In 1963, the Italian government enacted a set of regulatory laws that were intended to help guarantee a vintage's quality and ensure its provenance. Today, the three classifications for Italian wine are **DOCG** (Denominazione di Origine Controllata e Garantita), wine of the utmost quality (very few vintages have been awarded this label); **DOC** (Denominazione di Origine Controllata), wine of very good quality; and, since 1992, **IGT** (Indicazione Geographica Tipica), good to very good wine that has yet to prove itself as a DOC. Most restaurants will list on the menu whether a wine is a DOC, DOCG, or IGT vintage, though it's unlikely that you'll find the latter at fine dining establishments.

The regions of Central Italy, most especially Tuscany, produce some of the best *vini* that Italy has to offer. Some vintages to remember:

Tuscany
Brunello di Montalcino, Chianti, Chianti Classico, Vino Nobile di Montepulciano; Vernaccia di San Gimignano

Latium
Colli Albani, Est!Est!Est!, Frascati

Umbria
Sagrantino di Montefalco; Orvieto Classico

The Marches
Rosso Conero; Verdicchio dei Castelli di Jesi, Verdicchio di Matelica

Paying the Bill

When you ask for the bill *(il conto)* in a restaurant in Italy, don't be surprised if you have to wait a short while. The tab is usually tallied after you ask, rather than throughout the meal. Because waiters here don't work for extra tips, they are rarely in a rush to turn their tables. (Some restaurants will automatically add about a 10% gratuity to the bill. Those that do will usually state this fact on the menu or on the bill itself.)

Most restaurants have wised up to the fact that tourists prefer to pay with credit cards, so you shouldn't have any problem paying with your Visa or MasterCard. Some eateries take American Express, as well. Restaurants usually indicate if they accept credit cards on their doors or menus. On the other hand, quite a few *osterie* and *trattorie* operate on a cash-only system. You'll encounter only a handful of these old-school restaurants in the tourist hubs of Florence and Rome. But be aware that paying for your meal with cash is still common practice in small, out-of-the-way towns.

A tip of at least a couple euros (rounded up to the nearest even amount) is expected of foreign tourists. If you choose to pay by credit card, try to pay your tip in cash. Otherwise, it is unlikely that the house will share the gratuity with your waiter.

Settling a Dispute

If you have a problem with your meal, notify your waiter immediately. Otherwise, you might not have two legs to stand on when the check comes. One of the most common dilemmas that a foreign diner encounters in Italy is that what he orders is not always what he gets. For example, if you order *spaghetti al ragu,* you'll get long pasta with a meat sauce, not just a plain, red sauce. This could be a potential disaster for vegetarians. Other modifiers you may want to watch out for are *piccante* (spicy), *noce* or *nocciola* if you're allergic *(allergico)* to nuts, or *crudo* if you're not particularly fond of undercooked meat or fish. The point is that many problems can be solved before you even begin your meal.

On the other hand, dear tourist, it's not always your fault. Even Italian chefs make mistakes sometimes, and it's your right to point out a problem after you take your first bite. Notify your server if your food is too cold *(freddo),* burned *(bruciato),* undercooked *(poco cotto),* stale *(vecchio),* or spoiled *(avariato).* A fly *(mosca)* in your soup is cause for alarm. If you get a wine that is corked, tell the waiter, *"Questo vino sa di tappo!"*

Our Favorite Restaurants in Central Italy

Following this section are detailed profiles of the best *ristoranti, pizzerie,* and *trattorie* to be found in in Central Italy. The profiles are organized by region—Florence, the rest of Tuscany, Rome, the rest of Latium, Umbria, and finally the Marches and the Republic of San Marino. First, we provide an overview of the cuisines of the four main regions. Next is a convenient table that lets you see at a glance how the profiled properties in that city or region stack up. Florence and Rome restaurants are listed alphabetically; for regions, profiles are listed by province, then by city, and then alphabetically by name. Each profile features an easily scanned heading that allows you to check out the restaurant's name, cuisine, overall rating, cost, quality rating, and value rating.

Cuisine This is actually less straightforward than it sounds. A couple of years ago, for example, "pan-Asian" restaurants in the United States were typically serving what was then generally described as "fusion" food—Asian ingredients with European techniques, or vice versa. Since then, there has been a pan-Asian explosion, but nearly all specialize in what would be street food back home: noodles, skewers, dumplings, and soups. Once-general categories have become subdivided—French into bistro fare and even Provençal; "new continental" into regional American and "eclectic"—and others have broadened and fused: Middle Eastern and Provençal into Mediterranean, Spanish, and South American into nuevo Latino, and so on. In these cases, we generally use the broader terms (i.e., "Italian"), but sometimes added a parenthetical phrase to give a clearer idea of the fare. Again, though, experimentation and fusion are ever more common, so don't hold the chefs to too strict a style. Conversely, we avoid creating hybrid cuisine categories except as a last resort.

Overall Rating The overall star rating encompasses the entire dining experience, including style, service, and ambience in addition to the taste, presentation, and quality of the food. Five stars is the highest rating possible and connotes the best of everything. Four-star restaurants are exceptional, and three-star restaurants are well above average. Two-star restaurants are good. One star is used to indicate an average restaurant that demonstrates an unusual capability in some area of specialization—for example, an otherwise unmemorable place that has great barbecue chicken.

Cost To the right of the overall star rating is an expense description that provides a comparative sense of how much a complete meal will cost. A complete meal for our purposes consists of a main course with vegetable or side dish and choice of soup or salad. Appetizers, desserts, drinks, and tips are excluded.

Inexpensive	€15 and less per person
Moderate	€16–€30 per person
Expensive	Over €30 per person

Quality Rating The food quality is rated on a scale of one to five stars, five being the best rating attainable. The quality rating is based expressly on the taste, freshness of ingredients, preparation, presentation, and creativity of food served. There is no consideration of price. If you are a person who wants the best food available and cost is not an issue, you need look no further than the quality ratings.

Value Rating If, on the other hand, you are looking for both quality and value, then you should check the value rating, expressed as stars.

★★★★★	Exceptional value, a real bargain
★★★★	Good value
★★★	Fair value, you get exactly what you pay for
★★	Somewhat overpriced
★	Significantly overpriced

Pricing Here we supply an average price per person to eat a full meal at the profiled restaurant. We'll also tell you if the restaurant offers prix-fixe menus (or only offers prix-fixe menus), and how much they cost.

Payment   We've listed the type of payment accepted at each restaurant using the following code: AMEX equals American Express, CB equals Carte Blanche, D equals Discover, DC equals Diners Club, MC stands for MasterCard, and V is for Visa. For the most part, restaurants in Italy that do take credit cards only accept the big names—MasterCard, Visa, and American Express. In the case a restaurant does not accept any credit cards, we have indicated this with the phrase "cash only."

The Cuisine of Tuscany

Although Tuscany (Toscana) is one of the most popular regions in Italy, its cuisine is not as well known. Much of the *cucina Toscana* is centered around age-old peasant recipes that call for simple ingredients, like beans *(fagioli)*, bread, seasonal vegetables, and locally available meats, like wild boar *(cinghiale)*, duck *(anatra)*, and rabbit *(lepre)*.

Traditional first-course dishes you'll find in *trattorie* all over Tuscany are the twice-cooked, or "reboiled" *ribollita*, a soup of stale bread, cabbage, beans, and other ingredients, and *pappa al pomodoro*, a mush of tomatoes and bread. Though simple, both dishes have depth of flavor, are delicious, and need to be sampled at least once. Variations exist from town to town.

Despite having a cuisine rife with vegetable-based dishes, Tuscans are meat eaters. The *bistecca alla fiorentina*, one of the most characteristic *secondi* on Tuscan menus, is the closest thing Italians have to a Texas-size steak. (However, mad-cow disease scares have made this dish less than popular over the past couple of years.) Wild boar is extremely common in Tuscany (and, actually, throughout Central Italy) to the point that many restaurants, cafés, and butchers will display a hairy, snouty boar's head above the front door or a mantel. You'll likely find *cinghiale* mixed with tomato sauces for pasta or dressed up as salami on an *antipasto* plate. Duck, rabbit, and animal innards, especially tripe *(trippa)*, sometimes appear as featured menu items at even the most elegant of restaurants. You can expect that most meats will come roasted *(arrosto)* or grilled *(alla griglia)*.

From appetizers to dessert, there are many provincial variations on Tuscan cuisine. Florence is renowned for its *bistecca*, and, throughout the world, anything *alla fiorentina* indicates that spinach plays a big role in the recipe. Along the coast, *cacciucco*, a five-fish stew, is a staple, and nowhere more so than in Livorno. Meanwhile, the Sienese sweet tooth has contributed *pan forte*, a sophisticated kind of fruit cake, to Tuscany's dessert menu.

Below you'll find our picks for the best dining options in Florence and Tuscany. For convenience, Florence restaurants are listed by quality and then by neighborhood, followed by their respective restaurant profiles sorted alphabetically.

Restaurant Profiles—Florence

THE BEST RESTAURANTS IN FLORENCE						
Restaurant	**Cuisine**	**Overall**	**Price**	**Quality**	**Value**	**Neighborhood**
Osteria de' Benci	Italian	★★★★★	Inexp/ Mod	★★★★★	★★★★★	Santa Croce
La Congrega	Tuscan	★★★★½	Mod	★★★★★	★★★★	San Giovanni
Enoteca Pinchiorri	French/ Tuscan	★★★★½	Exp	★★★★★	★	Santa Croce
Garga	Contemporary Tuscan	★★★★	Mod/ Exp	★★★★★	★★★	Santa Maria Novella
Beccofino	Contemporary Tuscan	★★★★	Exp	★★★★★	★★	Oltrarno
Il Pizzaiuolo	Pizzeria	★★★★	Inexp	★★★★	★★★★★	Santa Croce
Acqua al 2	Italian	★★★★	Mod	★★★★	★★★	Santa Croce
Osteria Santo Spirito	Italian	★★★★	Inexp/ Mod	★★★½	★★★	Oltrarno Spirito
Trattoria La Casalinga	Traditional Tuscan	★★★★	Inexp	★★★	★★★★★	Oltrarno
Trattoria Za-Za	Tuscan	★★★½	Mod	★★★½	★★★½	San Giovanni
Baccus	Pizzeria	★★★½	Mod	★★★	★★	Santa Maria Novella
Il Latini	Tuscan/ Italian	★★★	Mod	★★★	★★★	Santa Maria Novella

Acqua al 2 (Due)   ★★★★

ITALIAN | INEXPENSIVE/MODERATE | QUALITY ★★★★ | VALUE ★★★ | SANTA CROCE

Via della Vigna Vecchia, 40r; phone 055 284 170, fax 055 230 2696

Customers Well-to-do students, yuppies, Chelsea Clinton. **Reservations** Highly recommended. **When to Go** Early evening or on a weeknight. **Pricing** €16–€25. **Payment** V, MC, AMEX. **English Spoken** Yes. **Bar** None. **Wine Selection** Up to 30 wine choices, mostly Tuscan varieties. **Dress** Casual chic. **Disabled Access** None.

Hours Daily, 7:30 p.m.–1 a.m.; closed Monday, 1 week in August

Setting & Atmosphere Though the name may seem to imply that it is for couples, Acqua al 2 is usually full to the brim with gossiping locals and out-of-towners. As it does a brisk business, the service is sometimes rushed. But despite the frenzy, everyone seems to be having a grand old time.

House Specialties Sample platters of pasta, cheeses, or meats.

Summary & Comments Since 1978, when Acqua al 2 opened on the corner of Via dell'Acqua, down the street from the Duomo, foodies have flocked here for the *assaggio*

dei primi, which is a tasting of five of the restaurant's pastas or risottos. This innovative way to dine eventually led to other *assaggi* (for salads and cheeses), and a second location in San Diego, California.

Baccus   ★★★½

PIZZERIA | MODERATE | QUALITY ★★★ | VALUE ★★ | SANTA MARIA NOVELLA

Via Borgo Ognissanti 45r; phone 055 283 714

Customers 30-somethings, tourists. **Reservations** Recommended for dinner. **When to Go** Lunch **Pricing** €12–€25. **Payment** AMEX, MC, V. **English Spoken** Some. **Bar** None. **Wine Selection** At least five varieties of reds and whites by the glass; ample selection of moderately priced Tuscan vintages. **Dress** Casual chic, no jeans or sneakers. **Disabled Access** Yes.

Hours Tuesday–Sunday, 11 a.m.–3 p.m., 7 p.m.–midnight; closed Monday

Setting & Atmosphere In the warmer months, the most coveted tables at Baccus are the cramped two or three that face the *motorino*-filled street. Inside, the restaurant is lofty and accommodating for power lunches.

Summary & Comments Though Baccus does do pizza best, it is far from a typical *pizzeria.* The smiling if distant waitstaff are ever ready to recommend seasonal pastas and big, fresh salads. Check the menu board before grabbing a table because, curiously, the *pizzeria* sometimes dabbles in seafood and fresh fish. Daily specials have included *spaghetti con gamberoni* (prawns) and whole trout simmered with olives and capers.

Beccofino   ★★★★

CONTEMPORARY TUSCAN | EXPENSIVE | QUALITY ★★★★ | VALUE ★★ |
SANTO SPIRITO/OLTRARNO

Piazza degli Scarlatti; phone 055 290 076

Customers Hip locals and tourists looking to splash out. **Reservations** Recommended. **When to Go** Try it for lunch or on a weekday evening (Monday or Tuesday) to avoid long waits. **Pricing** Lunch €20, dinner €30–€40. **Payment** V, MC, AMEX. **English Spoken** Yes. **Bar** Yes. **Wine Selection** More than 500 bottles; at least 50 wines by the glass. **Dress** Casual chic. **Disabled Access** Yes.

Hours Daily, 12:30–3 p.m., 7–11:30 p.m.; wine bar: daily, 12:30–3:30 p.m., 7 p.m.–midnight

Setting & Atmosphere The restaurant and wine bar have that warm, modern look you'd find in New York or London. Lighting is soft, placemats are black leather, and a few unusual pieces of art adorn the walls. The rather calm setting lends credence to the fact that a mosque and an art gallery once occupied this space.

House Specialties Fresh seafood; Tuscan recipes with a twist.

Summary & Comments This much-anticipated second project by Scottish expat David Gardner opened in 1999 and has garnered quite a following of Florentines and tourists. Chef Francesco Berardinelli prepares Tuscan cuisine in innovative ways, including ravioli stuffed with cod, risotto with squab ragu, or *bistecca alla fiorentina* grilled with oranges. An additional wine bar, separated by a large slab of a counter, serves first course, pastas, and desserts and is your best bet for a lighter, quicker, and less expensive meal. All of the buzz surrounding Beccofino is true, making it almost impossible to get a table on the weekends.

Enoteca Pinchiorri ★★★★½

FRENCH/TUSCAN | EXPENSIVE | QUALITY ★★★★★ | VALUE ★ | SANTA CROCE

Via Ghibellina, 87; phone 055 24 2777, fax 055 244 983; www.pinchiorri.it

Customers Aristocratic offspring and wealthy tourists. **Reservations** Required. **When to Go** When you hit the lottery. **Pricing** €80–€130. **Payment** V, MC, AMEX. **English Spoken** Yes. **Bar** Yes. **Wine Selection** The cellar boasts more than 80,000 bottles! **Dress** Formal. **Disabled Access** Yes.

Hours Lunch: Tuesday, Thursday–Saturday, 12:30–2 p.m.; dinner: Tuesday–Saturday, 7:30–10 p.m.; closed Sunday, Monday, Tuesday lunch

Setting & Atmosphere Housed on the first floor of the 16th-century Palazzo Ciofi-Iacometti, Enoteca Pinchiorri has no time for casual diners. Here, you'll dine on the finest china, drink wine from glasses of Austrian crystal, and use Frette napkins to wipe your mouth. Service is serious and stuffy.

House Specialties Braised rabbit in rosemary, duck foie gras, cheese course. Enoteca Pinchiorri also offers several tasting menus.

Summary & Comments Enoteca Pinchiorri, is, in many ways, a tourist trap. For years, it has been considered one of the best restaurants in Italy, and its two Michelin stars have earned it a spot on every fashionable foodie and rich American's itinerary. Indeed, the nouveau Tuscan and French cuisine is delicious. But staying true to the *alta cucina* formula usually means that portions are even smaller than usual. The best bet is to order up a tasting menu *(menù di degustazione)*, which pairs each course with the appropriate wine. On the other hand, when you can choose from almost any vintage ever made in Italy, what's the point in eating?

Garga ★★★★

CONTEMPORARY TUSCAN | MODERATE/EXPENSIVE | QUALITY ★★★★★ | VALUE ★★★ | SANTA MARIA NOVELLA

Via del Moro, 48r; phone 055 211 396; garga@fol.it

Customers Well-heeled Florentines, culinary adventurers. **Reservations** Recommended. **When to Go** At the height of the evening rush—it's theater to watch. **Pricing** €10–€22. **Payment** V, MC, AMEX. **English Spoken** Yes. **Bar** Yes. **Wine Selection** Tuscan reds and whites, starting from €8–€10 per bottle. **Dress** Low-key evening wear. **Disabled Access** Yes.

Hours Tuesday–Saturday, noon–3 p.m., 7:30–11 p.m., Sunday, 7–11 p.m.; closed Sunday lunch, Monday

Setting & Atmosphere The rich hues of Garga's purple, crimson, and emerald walls echo the cuisine's complex flavors, as well as act as a backdrop for the drama of the kitchen and dining room. Opera blares, pots clank, and young waiters hurry to deliver your dish so that you can fully enjoy its wafting aroma.

House Specialties Homemade pasta tossed with sprigs of fresh herbs.

Summary & Comments Florentine Giuliano Gargani and Canadian Sharon Oddson are the husband-and-wife team that keep the engines of this beloved *trattoria* well-lubricated with lots of extra virgin olive oil and heaps of creativity. Locals flock to Garga to sample the nouveau Tuscan cuisine, which is invariably an infusion of fresh pastas, meats, and cheeses with unexpected herbs and spices. The tortellini with orange and mint is only one example of the restaurant's interesting *primi*. During the week, Sharon runs a cooking school from the Garga kitchen. Four-hour courses cost €155.

Il Pizzaiuolo ★★★★

PIZZERIA | INEXPENSIVE | QUALITY ★★★★ | VALUE ★★★★★ | SANTA CROCE

Via de' Macci, 113r; phone 055 241 171

Customers Locals, homesick Neopolitans. **Reservations** Recommended. **When to Go** Early evening. **Pricing** €6–€15. **Payment** Cash only. **English Spoken** Little. **Bar** Yes. **Wine Selection** House wines by the glass, carafe, and half-carafe. **Dress** Casual. **Disabled Access** Yes.

Hours Monday– Saturday, 12:30–3:30 p.m., 7:30 p.m.–1 a.m.; closed Sunday, August

Setting & Atmosphere Photographs of Mt. Vesuvius, lively conversation, and a tavern atmosphere take you back to old Napoli. When the *pizzeria* is packed—and it often is—diners are paired together at long tables, making for an interesting, communal arrangement.

House Specialties There are more than 20 varieties of pizza.

Summary & Comments Il Pizzaiuolo is about the only place in town where you can get an authentic, Naples-style pizza pie, piled high with *muzzarella* (as the Neopolitans call it) and other typical toppings. On the menu are *pizza caprese, pizza napolitana,* and *pizza quattro stagione,* among others. There are also plenty of pastas and antipasti to choose from. *Spaghetti a'Vesuviana* is an especially spicy number.

La Congrega ★★★★★

TUSCAN | MODERATE | QUALITY ★★★★★ | VALUE ★★★★ | SAN GIOVANNI

Via Panicale, 43r; phone 055 264 5027, fax 055 264 8578

Customers 30- to 40-something set and a smattering of expats. **Reservations** Recommended. **When to Go** Before 8:30 p.m. **Pricing** €18–€22. **Payment** V, MC. **English Spoken** Yes. **Bar** Yes. **Wine Selection** A rotating selection of 10–15 wines; house wines by the glass. **Dress** Casual chic. **Disabled Access** Yes, on the lower level.

Hours Monday–Saturday, 8 p.m.–11 p.m.; closed Sunday, August

Setting & Atmosphere The warm, wooden, vaulted-ceiling restaurant is like entering into a cozy Tuscan farmhouse. The dining room is decidedly congenial, with views of the open kitchen, and there is a quieter loft area upstairs appropriate for private parties and couples.

House Specialties Medieval Tuscan cuisine; the gnocchi is outrageous.

Summary & Comments La Congrega bills itself as an *osteria del tempio perso,* or an eatery from days gone by. The fireplace in the lower dining room and the antique mirrors and wagon wheels decorating the walls do give it a rustic feel. Additionally, some of the Tuscan fare is culled from recipes from the Middle Ages. Few restaurants in the city give you a chance to try *ginestrata,* a sort of egg soup, or a salad of cabbage and tripe. For those with a modern palate, La Congrega offers plenty of vegetarian options, including handmade pastas and grilled vegetables. Though the cuisine may be somewhat old school, the chef has an eye for detail and flavor, for example, serving broccoli and tomato gnocchi in a bowl made of hardened, oven-baked Parmesan cheese. Presentation is key.

Il Latini ★★★

TUSCAN/ITALIAN | MODERATE | QUALITY ★★★ | VALUE ★★★ |

SANTA MARIA NOVELLA

Via dei Palchetti, 6r; phone 055 210 916; www.illatini.com

Customers More tourists than locals. **Reservations** Not accepted after 8 p.m.; reserve well in advance for large groups. **When to Go** Lunch. **Pricing** €25–€30. **Payment** V, MC, AMEX, DC. **English Spoken** Yes. **Bar** No. **Wine Selection** Minimal; offers some home-made wines. **Dress** Casual **Disabled Access** Yes.

Hours Lunch: Tuesday–Sunday, 12:30–2:30 p.m.; dinner: Tuesday–Sunday, 7:30–10:30 p.m.; closed Monday, last week in July, first week in August

Setting & Atmosphere Inside is an Italian version of a *biergarten,* where diners, who may or may not know each other, crowd next to one another on benches. Decorations are of the trite variety, including red-and-white checkered tablecloths and bottles of Chianti in basket casks. Dining here is very communal—perhaps to pack in as many as possible—but you'll more than likely be sitting next to other English-speaking tourists anyway.

House Specialties Large portions of Tuscan treats like *ribollita* and *bistecca.*

Summary & Comments Try to arrive at Il Latini with a reservation, or else you'll be stuck waiting in line for a table. Just about every guidebook written in the past ten years has mentioned this laid-back *trattoria,* and there's good reason. Dishes here are hearty and authentic, and the English-speaking waiters are ever-helpful with recommendations for a well-balanced Tuscan meal. Unlike some eateries in Florence that tend to be stuffy and antitourist, Il Latini is far from intimidating—ideal if you're traveling alone. What's more, if you're scheduled to take a night train, the *trattoria* is only blocks away from the Santa Maria Novella station.

Osteria de' Benci ★★★★★

TUSCAN/ITALIAN | INEXPENSIVE/MODERATE | QUALITY ★★★★★ | VALUE ★★★★★ |
SANTA CROCE

Via de' Benci, 13r; phone 055 234 4923

Customers Families, large groups. **Reservations** Strongly recommended. **When to Go** Weeknights. **Pricing** €12–€20. **Payment** V, MC. **English Spoken** Little. **Bar** No. **Wine Selection** Chianti in carafes and half-carafes. **Dress** Anything from casual to business wear. **Disabled Access** Yes.

Hours Monday–Saturday, 1–2:45 p.m., 8–11 p.m.; closed Sunday

Setting & Atmosphere The din of clinking, clanking, and chatter provides the background to this modest neighborhood *osteria.* Service is friendly and efficient.

House Specialties *Bistecca alla fiorentina,* fresh pasta.

Summary & Comments If you don't make a reservation for this little eatery, then be prepared to wait. Even Florentines, who have had prior opportunities to gorge themselves on the Osteria's hearty fare, are willing to stand in line for a spell. The menu changes almost daily but always has local specialties like *bistecca alla fiorentina* and *ribollita,* and Italian standards, like spaghetti bolognese, on the menu. All meals are served with flair on colorful ceramic plates; it's no wonder that diners keep coming back.

Osteria Santo Spirito ★★★★

ITALIAN | INEXPENSIVE/MODERATE | QUALITY ★★★½ | VALUE ★★★ |
SANTO SPIRITO/OLTRARNO

Piazza Santo Spirito, 16r; phone 055 238 2383

Customers Art students, neighborhood folks, a few tourists. **Reservations** Recommended. **When to Go** Go at lunch to watch the goings-on of the flea market. **Pricing**

€15–€26. **Payment** V, MC. **English Spoken** Yes. **Bar** Yes. **Wine Selection** Approximately a dozen varieties of reds and whites by the glass or bottle. **Dress** Casual. **Disabled Access** Yes.

Hours Daily, 12:30–2:30 p.m., 7:30–11:30 p.m.

Setting & Atmosphere This trendy *trattoria* is renowned for its brightly painted walls and modern décor. Multicolored dishes also pack a kaleidoscopic punch, making dining here fun. The outdoor dining area looks out onto one of the most pleasant *piazze* in all of Florence, which is a real treat in the summer.

House Specialties Big salads, fresh pastas, seafood.

Summary & Comments It's no surprise that Italian celebs like to pop in here when they pass through Florence. Osteria Santo Spirito is routinely packed with the see-and-be scene, who like to dish the dirt over diet-friendly salads and bites of Tyrrhenian seafood. Also popular with nibblers are the restaurant's cheese boards, which are a fine accompaniment with the selection of Tuscan wines. At night, patrons can unwind on the terrace with a plate of pasta. The spinach and ricotta gnocchi are particularly delicious.

Trattoria La Casalinga ★★★★

TRADITIONAL TUSCAN | INEXPENSIVE | QUALITY ★★★ | VALUE ★★★★★ |
SANTO SPIRITO/OLTRARNO

Via dei Michelozzi, 9r; phone 055 218 624, fax 055 267 9143

Customers Students, young couples, and a smattering of tourists. **Reservations** Advised, but not necessary. **When to Go** Early evening. **Pricing** €10–€14. **Payment** V, MC. **English Spoken** Very little. **Bar** No. **Wine Selection** A few house wines by the bottle, or quarter-, half-, or full carafes. **Dress** Casual. **Disabled Access** No, but only one step up into one-floor restaurant.

Hours Monday–Saturday, noon–2:30 p.m., 7–10 p.m.; closed Sunday, three weeks in August

Setting & Atmosphere This is the rustic kind of diner that most first-timers to Italy are looking for. Once past the first small room, the interior resembles a large banquet hall, where rowdy student sing-alongs and birthday parties aren't uncommon. The waiters here are friendlier than most.

House Specialties Tuscan standards like *ribollita* and *pappa al pomodoro.*

Summary & Comments *Casalinga* means housewife in Italian, and this *trattoria* serves the kind of fare that you'd find in your *nonna's* kitchen. First courses, like *gnocchi al ragu,* are simple; second courses are hearty; and goodies like figs, porcini mushrooms, or melon are often incorporated in recipes (and scribbled onto the menu) once they're in season. Even if you don't speak a lick of Italian, you can probably find something that you like. Yes, you can even order lasagna.

Trattoria Za-Za ★★★½

TUSCAN | MODERATE | QUALITY ★★★½ | VALUE ★★★½ | SAN GIOVANNI

Piazza del Mercato Centrale, 6r; phone 055 215 411

Customers Young locals. **Reservations** Not necessary. **When to Go** For lunch, or early or late for dinner. **Pricing** €12–€18. **Payment** V, MC. **English Spoken** Some. **Bar** No. **Wine Selection** At least 20 wines by the glass or bottle. **Dress** Casual. **Disabled Access** Yes, but restroom is downstairs.

Hours Monday–Saturday, 11:30 a.m.–11 p.m.; closed Sunday

Setting & Atmosphere Za-Za has a sizable dining room decorated with posters of Italian celebrities. Its two floors and large outdoor dining section, overlooking a square full of passersby, are generally packed with locals and tourists from spring until the end of October.

House Specialties Soups and *crostone* (large pieces of Tuscan bread topped with vegetables or spreads).

Summary & Comments What's not to like about a restaurant where the staff treats you like a regular? Trattoria Za-Za is named after the sound a bee makes, and you'll notice right away that your young server buzzes with friendliness and will help tired tourists and locals alike. Some of the best foods to try at this fairly traditional *trattoria* are the soups, like *ribollita* and *passata di fagioli,* and *crostone* slathered with chicken liver pâté. You can also depend on there always being a few good prix-fixe specials consisting of a first course, second course, and dessert. The wine selection here is slightly disappointing, with very few reds. Luckily, no one minds if you want to sit for a spell sipping wine and grazing. The pace is ideal for the post–sight-seeing blues.

Restaurant Profiles—The Rest of Tuscany

THE BEST RESTAURANTS IN THE REST OF TUSCANY					
Restaurant	**Cuisine**	**Overall**	**Price**	**Quality**	**Value**
The Province Of Florence					
Chianti Fiorentina					
Castello Vicchiomaggio	Tuscan	★★★★	Exp	★★★★★	★★★
The Province of Siena					
Siena					
Al Mangia	Tuscan/Italian	★★★	Mod	★★★	★★★
Osteria Le Logge	Tuscan	★★★★	Mod	★★★★	★★★★
La Sosta Di Violante	Contemporary Tuscan	★★★★★	Mod	★★★★★	★★★★
Chianti Senese					
Badia A Coltibuono	Tuscan	★★★★	Exp	★★★★★	★★★★
The Province of Arezzo					
Arezzo					
Il Saraceno	Tuscan/ Aretine	★★★★	Inexp/ Mod	★★★	★★★★★
Le Logge Vasari	Tuscan/Aretine	★★★★	Exp	★★★★★	★★★½
Le Tastevin	Creative Tuscan	★★★★	Mod/ Exp	★★★★★	★★★
Cortona					
Il Falconiere	Italian	★★★★★	Very Exp	★★★★★	★★★

Restaurant	Cuisine	Overall	Price	Quality	Value
THE BEST RESTAURANTS IN THE REST OF TUSCANY *(continued)*					
The Province of Lucca					
Lucca					
All'Olivo	Seafood	★★★½	Exp	★★★★★	★★½
Buca Di Sant'Antonio	Tuscan/ Lucchese	★★★	Mod/ Exp	★★★★	★★★★
Trattoria Gigi	Italian	★★★★★	Inexp	★★★★★	★★★★★
The Province of Pisa					
Pisa					
Antica Trattoria da Bruno	Pisan/ Italian	★★★★	Inexp/ Mod	★★★★	★★★★
La Nuova Pizzeria del Borgo	Pizzeria	★★★	Inexp	★★★	★★★★★
Osteria La Grotta	Pisan/Enoteca	★★★★	Inexp/ Mod	★★★★	★★★★

The Province of Florence
Chianti Fiorentina

Castello Vicchiomaggio　★★★★

HEARTY TUSCAN | EXPENSIVE | QUALITY ★★★★★ | VALUE ★★★ | GREVE IN CHIANTI

Via Vicchiomaggio, 4; phone 055 854 079; www.vicchiomaggio.it

Customers Tour groups, hotel patrons. **Reservations** Required. **When to Go** Friday or Saturday evening. **Pricing** €30–€55. **Payment** V, MC, AMEX. **English Spoken** Yes. **Bar** Yes. **Wine Selection** The restaurant serves its own vintages, including award-winning reds Ripa delle More and Chianti Riserva La Prima. **Dress** Casual chic. **Disabled Access** No.

Hours Tuesday–Sunday, 7–11 p.m.; closed Monday

Setting & Atmosphere The 11th-century castle in which this restaurant and hotel is housed boasts Caterina Medici as a former guest. The great hall here, complete with white, vaulted ceilings and enormous fireplaces, has been converted into an elegant and timeless dining room. The varying clientele determine whether the atmosphere is somber or spirited.

House Specialties Beef *stracotto,* marinated in at least three liters of wine.

Summary & Comments If you're not staying at the inn here (see profile in Part Four, Hotels in Central Italy), then you may have trouble finding this restaurant tucked away on a dark road in the heart of Chianti. For the last several years, Castello Vicchiomaggio's chef, Francesco Lagi, formerly a sous-chef at Florence's esteemed Enoteca Pinchiorri, has been given creative license and full culinary control of the cooking arm of this award-winning vineyard. The menu he has produced is strictly Tuscan and makes use of the bounty of the surrounding hills. Appetizers, entrées, and desserts here are so delectable that you don't know whether to savor them or gobble them up at once.

The Province of Siena

Siena

Al Mangia ★★★

TUSCAN/ITALIAN | MODERATE | QUALITY ★★★ | VALUE ★★★ | SIENA

Piazza del Campo, 42; phone 0577 281 121

Customers Day trippers. **Reservations** Not necessary. **When to Go** Early evening. **Pricing** €25–€40. **Payment** V, MC. **English Spoken** Yes. **Bar** Yes. **Wine Selection** Vast selection of local Chianti wines by the glass or carafe. **Dress** Casual chic. **Disabled Access** Yes.

Hours Daily, noon–10 p.m.; closed Wednesday during low season.

Setting & Atmosphere The restaurant's most prized outdoor tables look out onto the imposing, medieval buildings of the Piazza del Campo. Inside, the original brick archways set a charming scene.

House Specialties Traditional Tuscan dishes, especially steaks and ribs.

Summary & Comments Most of the touristy *trattorie* that line the Piazza del Campo aren't worth the cost of their red-checkered tablecloths. Al Mangia caters to locals as well as tourists but refuses to act like an overpriced trap. Italians stop by here for the restaurant's honest interpretations of Tuscan-style ribs *(costate)*—basically *bistecca* but cut differently—and entrées of lamb, veal, rabbit, and fowl. The authentic, flavorful food is not as much of a draw for visitors, who are content with being able to eat in the shadow of the Torre del Mangia.

Osteria Le Logge ★★★★

TUSCAN | MODERATE | QUALITY ★★★★ | VALUE ★★★★ | SIENA

Via del Porrione, 33; phone 0577 48 013

Customers Tourists at lunch, locals at night. **Reservations** Recommended. **When to Go** Weeknights. **Pricing** €15–€32. **Payment** AMEX, MC, V. **English Spoken** Some. **Bar** No. **Wine Selection** House reds and whites available by the glass or carafe. **Dress** Casual. **Disabled Access** Yes.

Hours Monday–Saturday, noon–3:30 p.m., 7:30–10 p.m.; closed Sunday, two weeks in November

Setting & Atmosphere White-clothed tables are snug against one another in both the main dining room downstairs and the additional room upstairs. Strong wood accents, antique clocks, and retro prints make this *trattoria* feel like a homey tea den.

House Specialties Menu changes daily.

Summary & Comments Being right off the Piazza del Campo, this old-school *trattoria* gets a healthy share of tourists. But that shouldn't put you off. The menu here is authentic, with hearty *primi* like *risotto alle verdure* and cheese and spinach gnocchi. Beef and lamb figure prominently on the daily menu, but Le Logge also likes to experiment with fish and seafood. To satisfy the Sienese sweet tooth, the dessert menu is appropriately ample.

La Sosta di Violante ★★★★★

CONTEMPORARY TUSCAN | MODERATE | QUALITY ★★★★★ | VALUE ★★★★ | SIENA

Via di Pantaneto, 115; phone 0577 43 774

Customers Students, young and old trendsetters. **Reservations** Recommended; you can make them online. **When to Go** Before 8 p.m. if you have no reservation. **Pricing** €16–€24. **Payment** V, MC. **English Spoken** Some. **Bar** No. **Wine Selection** Ample selection of local reds, like Chianti and Montepulciano, some whites; by the bottle only. **Dress** Casual. **Disabled Access** Yes.

Hours Tuesday–Sunday, 7.–11 p.m.; closed Monday

Setting & Atmosphere The dining room is simple, with a handful of two-top tables and a few larger ones tucked into the corners. On crowded nights, you may find yourself involved in conversation with other tables, given the intimacy of the place and the playful ambience. A small courtyard seats larger groups, and there are a handful of tables outside the entrance when the weather is warm.

House Specialties Carpaccio of salami and zucchini, *ravioli "alla violante."*

Summary & Comments It takes a small stroll off the Campo in Siena to get to this lively new restaurant, but we guarantee you'll be so happy that you passed up all of those eateries on the tourist drag. Here in the shell *(nicchio)* contrada, five young friends and a congenial staff have developed the type of place where you can bring your kids and your parents, vegetarian and carnivorous friends, and culinary novices and food snobs. The chef tweaks ancient recipes with new flavors (try ravioli with radicchio, or beef with red pepper and basil), and makes sure that each plate is a colorful work of art. La Sosta di Violante opened in August 2001, but it's already a hit with the locals. Get there before other tourists discover it.

Chianti Senese

Badia a Coltibuono ★★★★★

TUSCAN | EXPENSIVE | QUALITY ★★★★★ | VALUE ★★★★ | GAIOLE IN CHIANTI

Badia a Coltibuono; phone 0577 74481, fax 0577 74 9235; www.coltibuono.com

Customers Serious gourmands, cooking-school students. **Reservations** Required. **When to Go** In the fall, when the *vino novello* and fresh-pressed olive oil have arrived. **Pricing** €40–€70, tasting menu available for €49. **Payment** V, MC. **English Spoken** Yes. **Bar** Yes. **Wine Selection** Badia vintages and the finest wines from throughout Italy. **Dress** Relaxed elegance. **Disabled Access** No.

Hours Tuesday–Sunday, noon–2:30 p.m., 7–10 p.m.; closed November–March, closed Monday

Setting & Atmosphere The restaurant is set in a restored 11th-century monastery deep in the Chianti valley. Outdoor tables enjoy the shade of the grapevines and trellises and the live sounds of jazz bands and string quartets during the summer. Service is friendly and attentive.

House Specialties Risotto with white beans and braised pork; the house-pressed olive oil.

Summary & Comments Badia al Coltibuono didn't have to work too hard to become one of Italy's best-known restaurants. The pedigrees sported by owners Roberto Stucchi-Prinetti and Lorenza de' Medici ensured that. But that didn't stop the owners from creating a cuisine that is both innovative and undeniably Tuscan. The menu, which changes seasonally, spotlights rustic grains and nuts (like spelt), locally grown Chiana beef, and delights from the garden, including ripe tomatoes, meaty olives, rosemary, basil, and other herbs. The tasting menu is the best value, featuring four courses complimented with the vineyard's own whites and reds.

The Province of Arezzo

Arezzo

Il Saraceno ★★★★

TUSCAN/ARETINE | INEXPENSIVE/MODERATE | QUALITY ★★★ | VALUE ★★★★★ | AREZZO

Via Mazzini, 6; phone 0575 27644

Customers Close friends, gourmets. **Reservations** Not necessary. **When to Go** Lunch. **Pricing** €12–€30. **Payment** AMEX, MC, VISA. **English Spoken** Yes. **Bar** Yes. **Wine Selection** Dozens of reds and whites available by the bottle or half-carafe. Over 20 selections in the "reserve" cellar. **Dress** Casual. **Disabled Access** Yes.

Hours Thursday–Tuesday, noon–3 p.m., 7–11 p.m.; closed Wednesday, July

Setting & Atmosphere Warm and inviting, Il Saraceno is furnished with small, intimate tables which can be put together to accommodate bigger groups. The perimeter of the restaurant is decorated with family mementos and photos from the Giostro. Tantalizing spreads of the day's specials are kept within eyesight of the entrance, making it hard to pass this place up.

House Specialties Roasted meats; Aretine-style *ribollita;* pizza

Summary & Comments An Arezzo institution near the Piazza Grande, the family-owned Il Saraceno puts a friendly face on Arezzo and its local fare. Owned and operated by the ebullient Dragoni family, the *trattoria* straddles the fence between peasant and gourmet fare. Rustic food here consists of lots of game, including Valdichiana beef, rabbit, and wild boar. But, the chef has also filled the menu with enough pasta, pizzas, and soups that any picky eater should be satisfied. Let the waiter order for you, and you will likely be served an assortment from their prix-fixe menus, which range from €20–€30 per person. Particularly inspirational are the ravioli with truffles, the *ribollita aretina,* and the pork loin stuffed with duck.

Le Logge Vasari ★★★★

TUSCAN/ARETINE | EXPENSIVE | QUALITY ★★★★★ | VALUE ★★★½ | AREZZO

Via Vasari, 15 (Piazza Grande); phone 0575 295 894

Customers Locals and tourists. **Reservations** Recommended. **When to Go** Lunch or early evening. **Pricing** €20–€40. **Payment** AMEX, MC, V. **English Spoken** Some. **Bar** Yes. **Wine Selection** House reds and whites available by the glass or carafe; an abbreviated selection of premium vintages. **Dress** Refined, but not formal. **Disabled Access** No.

Hours Daily, noon–3 p.m., 8–11 p.m.; closed Tuesday

Setting & Atmosphere Romance lives under this restaurant's vaulted ceiling, where you'll also find candelabra lighting, fine crystal stemware, and vases of fragrant flowers. From the terrace are lovely views of the Piazza Grande.

House Specialties Handmade pasta; Chianina steak.

Summary & Comments A cozy cove off the main square, Le Logge Vasari is under the arcade of the sumptuously decorated Casa Vasari. Similar to the ochre-hued dining room, the dishes here are sparse but beautiful. *Primi* include innovations with fresh pasta, such as a ravioli of red rapini and Umbrian truffles, while *secondi* are typically plates of beef and pork dressed up with roasted vegetables and dashes of fresh herbs. Meals here are meant to last hours, not minutes, so leave room for a cheese or dessert course.

Le Tastevin ★★★★

CREATIVE TUSCAN | MODERATE/EXPENSIVE | QUALITY ★★★★★ | VALUE ★★★ | AREZZO

Via de' Cenci, 9; phone 0575 28 304

Customers Italian celebrities, locals. **Reservations** Recommended. **When to Go** Weeknights. **Pricing** €15–€32. **Payment** V, MC, AMEX. **English Spoken** Some. **Bar** Yes. **Wine Selection** More than 100 Italian vintages. **Dress** Casual chic. **Disabled Access** Yes.

Hours Monday–Saturday, noon–3 p.m., 7–11 p.m.; closed Sunday

Setting & Atmosphere The large dining room is split into two sections. One section is refined, with dark walnut fixtures, exposed wood-beam ceilings, and delicate chandeliers. The second section is decorated in a quirky style, cluttered with old Hollywood and Cinecittà promotional black-and-whites. During the warmer months, guests can dine outdoors or stick around until late when the restaurant becomes a piano bar.

House Specialties Tuna carpaccio, penne Tastevin.

Summary & Comments Arezzo native actor/director Roberto Benigni, whose skills lie in the ability to make light of serious moments and vice versa, has been known to dine at this centrally located restaurant on occasion. Meanwhile, Le Tastevin is a restaurant that can't decide whether it wants to be a funky, French-style bistro or an elegant Tuscan *trattoria*. No matter what role the restaurant is playing, it always serves meals that are as pleasing to the eye as they are to the stomach. Try the house dish, penne Tastevin, a steaming pasta bowl drizzled with a cream of black truffles and sprinkled with herbs and cheese.

Cortona

Il Falconiere ★★★★★

ITALIAN | VERY EXPENSIVE | QUALITY ★★★★★ | VALUE ★★★ | CORTONA

Località San Marino, 370; phone 0575 612 616; falconiere@relaischateaux.com

Customers The jet set, foodies. **Reservations** Required. **When to Go** Lunch, to enjoy views over the Tuscan countryside. **Pricing** €50–€75. **Payment** V, MC, AMEX. **English Spoken** Yes. **Bar** Yes. **Wine Selection** The sommelier develops a new wine menu each season. **Dress** Formal **Disabled Access** No.

Hours Daily, 12:30–3:30 p.m., 8.–11 p.m.; closed November, Mondays from December to March

Setting & Atmosphere Il Falconiere is, perhaps, the most fancy farmhouse restaurant in Italy. Only the best linens, china, and crystal are used in the dining room, and the waiters here are hushed and meticulous. Fresh flowers, artisan pottery, and lilting classical music complement the scene.

House Specialties Seasonal vegetables dishes, Val di Chiana beef.

Summary & Comments Lauded by Frances Mayes, Il Falconiere is the house restaurant of an inn located in a 17th-century villa once owned by Italian poet Antonio Guadagnoli. Definitely best saved for splurging (entrées start around $25), this restaurant is out of a Tuscan dream. Lunch on the veranda affords views of the rolling landscapes of both Tuscany and Umbria, dotted with cypress, silvery olives trees, and patches of rosemary. By night, you can indulge in Italian *alta cucina,* with hand-rolled rigatini dressed in fresh tomato and fava beans, thin strips of beef carpaccio with capers, and some of the most esteemed vintages in Italy.

The Province of Lucca
Lucca

All'Olivo   ★★★½

SEAFOOD | EXPENSIVE | QUALITY ★★★★★ | VALUE ★★½ | LUCCA

Piazza San Quirico, 1; phone 0583 496 264

Customers Businessmen, anniversary celebrants. **Reservations** Recommended. **When to Go** When you're splashing out. **Pricing** €40–€50. **Payment** AMEX, MC, V. **English Spoken** Limited. **Bar** Yes. **Wine Selection** French and Italian vintages, many premium, by the glass or bottle. **Dress** Business attire. **Disabled Access** Yes.

Hours 12:15–3 p.m., 7:30–11 p.m.; closed Wednesday; mid-January–February

Setting & Atmosphere The restaurant's shaded terrace is its biggest asset, while a neutral pallette in the dining room allows the food to be the centerpiece. Sepia-print portraits and copper pots add the proper amount of rustic elegance.

House Specialties Grilled seafood, Lucchese specialties.

Summary & Comments Locals consider All'Olivo one of the finest restaurants in town and celebrate special occasions here by ordering grilled scampi, lobster, and spaghetti laden with sea scallops, calamari, clams, and mussels. Though seafood is the establishment's strong suit, fancy meat dishes, including Chateaubriand and ossobucco, are given proper attention by both the chef and the clientele. All'Olivo's brief Lucchese menu, including farro soup, is done well, but can be had elsewhere for less.

Buca di Sant'Antonio   ★★★

TUSCAN/LUCCHESE | MOD/EXPENSIVE | QUALITY ★★★★ | VALUE ★★★★ | LUCCA

Via della Cervia, 3; phone 0583 55881

Customers Locals. **Reservations** Recommended. **When to Go** Early evening. **Pricing** €17–€30. **Payment** V, MC, AMEX. **English Spoken** Some. **Bar** Yes. **Wine Selection** Italian wines, especially Tuscan vintages, by the glass or bottle. **Dress** Business attire. **Disabled Access** Yes.

Hours Tuesday–Saturday, 12:30–3 p.m., 7–11 p.m.; Sunday, 12:30–3:30 p.m.; closed Sunday dinner, Monday, last three weeks of July

Setting & Atmosphere Located in an 18th-century tavern that was once a staging post for horses, the restaurant maintains a rustic elegance with farmhouse décor.

House Specialties Farro (spelt, a type of cereal grain) soup.

Summary & Comments One of Lucca's oldest restaurants, Buca di Sant'Antonio (or St. Anthony's Inn) began serving townspeople and traveling Tuscans back in 1782. Puccini supped here, as did Ezra Pound. As for the menu, it reads much the way it did from the beginning, with emphasis on traditional Lucca-style cooking. Some of the rural recipes include farro soup *alla garfagnana,* spit-roasted kid goat with turnips, and stuffed rabbit with a soufflé of green beans and codfish. Buca's chef, Giuliano Pacini, has taken liberties with the old recipes, mixing old flavors with a new combination of herbs, and this has helped keep the restaurant in the culinary spotlight. If you go, save room for dessert—the apple tart is the perfect ending to a country meal.

Trattoria Gigi ★★★★★

ITALIAN | INEXPENSIVE | QUALITY ★★★★★ | VALUE ★★★★★ | LUCCA

Piazza del Carmine, 7, Lucca; phone 0583 467 266

Customers Neighbors, tourists, local soccer stars. **Reservations** Advised for evenings and weekends. **When to Go** Lunch or early evening, Monday–Thursday. **Pricing** €15–€20. **Payment** Visa, MC. **English Spoken** Limited. **Bar** No. **Wine Selection** Lucchese reds and whites available by glass or carafe. **Dress** Casual. **Disabled Access** Yes.

Hours Daily, noon–3 p.m., 7:30–11 p.m.; closed Sunday

Setting & Atmosphere The overly friendly staff will win you over first. Then, prepare to be amused by the colorful assortment of wooden chairs, checkered tablecloths, and local artwork.

House Specialties Pastas, hearty entrées.

Summary & Comments Snootiness is not something you'll want to equip yourself with if you're dining at Gigi's. Possessing the warm atmosphere that all *trattorie* should have, the eatery, located by the market at Piazza del Carmine, is ideal for families or boisterous groups of friends. The kitchen cooks up Italian comfort foods, including fried chicken (rabbit, too), *baccalà*, and lasagna. Appetizers, desserts, and vegetable dishes depend largely on what's available at the market—at least you know it's fresh. Though it's been in operation since the 1950s, Gigi was recently updated with new furnishings and owners. Italian soccer player Michele Tambellini now has a stake in the local favorite, lending this retro dive a a new swagger.

The Province of Pisa

Pisa

Antica Trattoria da Bruno ★★★★

PISAN/ITALIAN | INEXPENSIVE/MODERATE | QUALITY ★★★★ | VALUE ★★★★ | PISA

Via Luigi Bianchi, 12 (Porta a Lucca); phone 050 560 818

Customers Tourists by day, Italians by night. **Reservations** Recommended for evening. **When to Go** Late afternoon, early evening. **Pricing** €13–€22. **Payment** AMEX, DC, MC, V. **English Spoken** Yes. **Bar** Yes. **Wine Selection** Tuscan vintages available by the glass or bottle. **Dress** Casual. **Disabled Access** Yes.

Hours Daily, noon–3 p.m., 7–10:30 p.m.; closed Monday lunch, Tuesday

Setting & Atmosphere Wood-slat ceilings, low lighting, and long banks of tables lend a communal setting and a typical *trattoria* feel.

House Specialties Grilled fish, plus salt cod and eel.

Summary & Comments Pisani tend to shy away from Da Bruno around lunchtime. At just a few blocks from the Leaning Tower, the restaurant can become a mob scene of day-tripping tourists. However, out-of-towners who opt to stay the night can enjoy a meal among locals at one of Pisa's most beloved institutions. As Pisan fare is not well known outside of this city, it is worth it to try the few specialties, including the entrée of salt cod with leeks or the appetizer of grilled eels, which purportedly are plucked from the Arno. If you're feeling less adventurous, sample the trat's fine *pasta e ceci* (pasta with garbanzo beans) or *ribollita alla pisana*.

La Nuova Pizzeria del Borgo   ★★★

PIZZERIA/TRADITIONAL ITALIAN | INEXP | QUALITY ★★★ | VALUE ★★★★★ | PISA

Vicolo dei Tinti, 15; phone 050 580 322

Customers Lost tourists, students, business types. **Reservations** No. **When to Go** Lunch. **Pricing** €10–€15. **Payment** V, MC. **English Spoken** No. **Bar** No. **Wine Selection** House reds and whites by the glass or carafe. **Dress** Casual. **Disabled Access** Yes.

Hours Monday–Saturday, 11 a.m.–11 p.m.; closed Sunday

Setting & Atmosphere Located on a small alley in central Pisa, this part spit-and-sawdust *pizzeria*, part respectable *trattoria* doesn't look like much from the outside. When the weather permits, most customers dine outside under the raggedy awning. There are many tables inside for cooler months and rainy days.

House Specialties Pizza and simple pasta dishes.

Summary & Comments A healthy mix of Italians and budget-minded travelers attest to this restaurant's hearty dishes and bargain prices. The *gnocchi al ragu* is particularly delicious, and you can't go wrong with a *pizza margherita* and a mug of beer. Service is spotty.

Osteria la Grotta   ★★★★

PISAN/ENOTECA | INEXP/MODERATE | QUALITY ★★★★ | VALUE ★★★★ | PISA

Via San Francesco, 103, Pisa; phone 050 578 105

Customers Local wine lovers. **Reservations** Strongly recommended. **When to Go** Early evening for a table, later for atmosphere. **Pricing** €12–€30. **Payment** Cash only. **English Spoken** Limited. **Bar** Yes. **Wine Selection** Hundreds of Italian vintages; daily specials by the glass. **Dress** Casual. **Disabled Access** Yes.

Hours Daily, 7:30–11:30 p.m.; closed Sunday, August

Setting & Atmosphere Friends meet here to clink glasses, smoke, and chat up the opposite sex—a fun place if you're into people-watching as a spectator sport.

House Specialties *Antipasta*, grilled meats, dessert.

Summary & Comments Housed in vaulted cellar and hemmed in with stone to resemble a grotto, Osteria La Grotta is a delightful wine bar with an exceptional kitchen. Little plates of meats, cheeses, olives, and other *antipasto* stand-bys are a specialty, but there are plenty of entrées to choose from, too. The pasta menu, though abbreviated, will please any palate, while carnivores can indulge in tortellini with meat ragu, occasional offal offerings, and mixed grill of meats barbecued *alla maremmano* (from Tuscany's wild Maremma countryside). When you're done, linger for *dolci* and a nip of *vin santo*, else join the crowd for a glass of wine.

The Cuisine of Latium

Rome's overwhelming influence in Latium has strongly affected the region's culture, history, and cuisine. *La Cucina Laziale* is much less refined in comparison to the food in Tuscany, taking its cue from pastoral origins and offal recipes. Poor, hapless slaughterhouse workers who had to make do with the fifth quarter *(quinto quarto)* of slaughtered beasts, or the parts of the animal that the wealthy didn't want, are responsible for developing the region's most beloved carnivorous dishes. If you're visiting Rome, you will definitely see items like brains *(cervetello)*, oxtail soup *(coda alla vaccinara)*, and a number of dishes made with lamb *(pecorino)*, including *pecorino romano* cheese. *Rigatoni alla pajata*, made with the intestines of an unweaned calf, is a delicacy to some, but something to steer clear of if you're the least bit squeamish. Less intimidating specialties from Latium include: *bucatini*, a long, tubular pasta; *alla matriciana*, pasta in a tomato/wild boar/onion sauce; *saltimbocca*, made with prosciutto and veal; and spaghetti *alla carbonara*, an egg and bacon (in this case, cured wild boar bacon) pasta, a dish familiar to many travelers. A nod should also be given to Rome's Jewish community, which has created some of the most memorable dishes in the region, including *carciofi alla giudea* (golden fried artichokes), *fiori di zucca* (zucchini flowers stuffed with anchovies and cheese, then battered and fried), and *filetti di baccalà* (salted codfish).

Diners watching their salt intake should know that Romans are heavy-handed with salt. In olden days, when salt equaled wealth, the more salt a dish was flavored with, the richer a person was deemed to be. For better or for worse, the tradition stuck. If you don't want too much salt on your meal, ask for little salt *(poco sale)* or no salt *(niente sale)*. And order up plenty of water.

In Rome, be on the lookout for the "Sapore di Roma" (Taste of Rome) if you're traveling in late fall. Many restaurants throughout the city participate in this month-long event, allowing diners to enjoy gourmet, prix-fixe meals at reasonable prices.

Below you'll find our picks for the best dining options in Rome and Latium. For convenience, Rome restaurants are listed by quality and then by neighborhood, followed by their respective restaurant profiles sorted alphabetically.

Restaurant Profiles—Rome

THE BEST RESTAURANTS IN ROME						
Name	Cuisine	Overall	Price	Quality	Value	Neighborhood
Cul de Sac	Enoteca & appetizers	★★★★★	Inexp	★★★★★	★★★★★	Centro Storico
La Campana	Roman	★★★★★	Mod/ Exp	★★★★★	★★★★★	Centro Storico
Asinocotto	Contemporary Italian	★★★★★	Mod	★★★★★	★★★	Trastevere

THE BEST RESTAURANTS IN ROME *(continued)*

Name	Cuisine	Overall	Price	Quality	Value	Neighborhood
Osteria dell 'Ingegno	Italian/ Mediterranean	★★★★★	Mod/ Exp	★★★★★	★★★	Centro Storico
San Teodoro	Roman/ Italian	★★★★½	Mod/ Exp	★★★★★	★★★★	Ancient City
'Gusto	Pizza/ Italian/ International	★★★★½	Inexp/ Mod	★★★★	★★★★	Tridente
Ripa 12	Fish/ Seafood	★★★★	Mod/ Exp	★★★★★	★★★	Trastevere
Quinzi e Gabrielli	Fish/ Seafood	★★★★	Exp	★★★★★	★★	Centro Storico
Dar Poeta	Pizza	★★★★	Inexp	★★★★	★★★★★	Trastevere
Al 16 del Portico d'Ottavia	Roman/ Jewish	★★★★	Mod	★★★★	★★★★	Centro Storico
Montevecchio	Italian/ Roman	★★★★	Exp	★★★★	★★★	Vatican Area
Camponeschi	Seafood	★★★★	Very Exp	★★★★	★★	Centro Storico
Sora Lella	Italian	★★★½	Mod	★★★★	★★	Centro Storico
Maccheroni	Italian	★★★½	Mod	★★★	★★	Centro Storico
Margutta Vegetariano	Vegetarian	★★★	Mod/ Exp	★★★★★	★★	Tridente
Checchino dal 1887	Roman/ Offal	★★★	Very Exp	★★★★	★	Aventino
Da Augusto	Italian	★★★	Inexp	★★★	★★★★★	Trastevere
Miscellanea	Italian	★★★	Inexp	★★★	★★★★★	Centro Storico
Settimio al Pellegrino	Italian	★★★	Mod	★★★	★★★★	Centro Storico
Capranica	Italian	★★½	Inexp/ Mod	★★½	★★★	Centro Storico

Al 16 del Portico d'Ottavia   ★★★★

ROMAN/JEWISH | MODERATE | QUALITY ★★★★ | VALUE ★★★★ | CAMPO DE' FIORI

Via del Portico d'Ottavia, 16; phone 06 687 4722; bus 23, 44, 56, 60, 65, 75, 170, 710, 774, 780

Customers Neighborhood folks. **Reservations** Recommended on the weekends. **When to Go** Lunch, weeknights. **Pricing** €12–€21. **Payment** V, MC, AMEX. **English Spoken** Some. **Bar** None. **Wine Selection** More whites than reds; the house white is bottled down the road in the Castelli Romani. **Dress** Business casual. **Disabled Access** Yes.

Hours Wednesday–Monday, 12:30–3 p.m., 7:30–11 p.m.; closed Tuesday

Setting & Atmosphere This *trattoria's* soft lighting and no-frills décor allow the flavorful Jewish dishes to take center stage. Outdoor dining comes with views of the crumbling Octavian Gate.

House Specialties Jewish dishes and homemade pastas.

Summary & Comments One of the cornerstone's of Rome's Jewish Ghetto neighborhood, 16 *(seidici* [SAY-dee-chee]) serves up traditional Roman fare *alla giudea.* The emphasis here is on lean cuts of beef, ample portions of fish (such as *baccalà* and terrines of fish roe), and vegetables fresh from the market. As for pasta, the signature dish is the pennette al 16, a very unkosher combination of sausage, tomatoes, and eggplant.

Asinocotto ★★★★★

CONTEMPORARY ITALIAN/MEDITERRANEAN | MODERATE | QUALITY ★★★★★ | VALUE ★★★ | TRASTEVERE

Via dei Vascellari, 48; phone 06 589 8985; bus 23, 97

Customers Artsy types, adventurous gourmands, and Rome's gay contingent. **Reservations** Required. **When to Go** Thursday and Friday are lively. **Pricing** €20–€30. **Payment** V, MC, AMEX. **English Spoken** Yes. **Bar** Yes. **Wine Selection** Premium Italian and French wines ranging from €10 to €65 per bottle. Some vintages are available by the glass. **Dress** Casual chic. **Disabled Access** Yes.

Hours Tuesday–Sunday, 8 p.m.–midnight; closed Monday, January

Setting & Atmosphere Gay-owned and -operated Asinocotto attracts a vivacious crowd of liberals, gays, young couples, and gourmands. Service is swift and congenial.

House Specialties Mediterranean plates pretty enough to be in a museum.

Summary & Comments This is one of the best places in Rome to sample modern, creative fare and mingle with the locals. Giuliano Brenna, proprietor and chef of the restaurant whose name translates to "cooked ass (donkey)," takes inspiration from classic Italian and Mediterranean ingredients, especially fish, fresh vegetables, and citrus fruits, and mixes them in new ways. Some of the mouth-watering dishes include salmon medallions with spinach and herbs, gnocchi with sweet peppers and mint sauce, and a salad of orange-marinated sea bass. Brenna is always experimenting with what's available at the market, making a visit here a must if you're in Rome.

Capranica ★★½

ITALIAN | INEXP/MODERATE | QUALITY ★★½ | VALUE ★★★ | CENTRO STORICO

Piazza Capranica, 99; phone 06 699 40992; bus 56, 60, 85, 116, 492

Customers Parliamentarians, tourists. **Reservations** Not necessary. **When to Go** Lunch or early evening. **Pricing** €10–€22. **Payment** V, MC, AMEX. **English Spoken** Yes. **Bar** Yes. **Wine Selection** Hundreds of bottles of reds and whites from throughout Italy. **Dress** Your choice—business suits and weekend wear mingle here. **Disabled Access** Yes.

Hours Monday–Saturday, 12:30–3:30 p.m., 7–10 p.m.; closed Sunday

Setting & Atmosphere Inside Enoteca Capranica, the floral upholstery, dark wood moldings, and checkerboard floor clash, resulting in a very frumpy look. Outdoor tables, set under a canopy of vines, are more inviting and are usually packed with tourists. Service can be brusque.

House Specialties Meat, risotto dishes, pizza at lunch.

Summary & Comments Parliamentarians come to Enoteca Capranica at lunch or after work to pow-wow, but tourists will find that this centrally located restaurant is just as good as any for daytime munchies. Pizza and pasta portions here are ample and reasonably priced, and the large wine selection makes this a good stop-and-sip point between landmarks.

Camponeschi ★★★★

SEAFOOD | VERY EXPENSIVE | QUALITY ★★★★ | VALUE ★★ | CAMPO DE' FIORI

Piazza Farnese, 50; phone 06 687 4297, fax 06 686 5244; bus 46, 62, 64

Customers Rome's power brokers, older couples. **Reservations** Required. **When to Go** Avoid Friday, when the place is full to bursting. **Pricing** €35–€60. **Payment** V, MC, AMEX. **English Spoken** Yes. **Bar** None. **Wine Selection** Italian and French vintages, and its own house wine. **Dress** Formal. **Disabled Access** Yes.

Hours Monday–Saturday, 8–11 p.m. (after 11 p.m. with reservations); closed Sunday

Setting & Atmosphere If you eavesdrop here, you're likely to hear heated political debates and hushed conversations about financial plans. Business types love the formality of Camponeschi's *Godfather*-worthy dining room. Even so, couples flock here for extravagant dinners under candlelight. Outdoor seating faces the wide Piazza Farnese and the French embassy.

House Specialties Fish and seafood, especially mussels and clams.

Summary & Comments A Roman institution, Camponeschi has long been synonymous with fish and seafood. Here in one of the most sumptuously decorated restaurants in all of Rome, you can savor appetizers of lobster and black truffles, and main courses of venison and blueberries, or oysters stuffed with lump crab and rosemary. Over the past several years, Camponeschi has increasingly added thick cuts of game and beef to its menu, perhaps to satisfy its masculine clientele's hearty appetites.

Checchino dal 1887 ★★★

ROMAN OFFAL CUISINE | VERY EXPENSIVE | QUALITY ★★★★ | VALUE ★ | AVENTINO

Via di Monte Testaccio, 30; phone 06 574 6318; Metro Piramide (Line B)

Customers Meat lovers. **Reservations** Required. **When to Go** Weeknights. **Pricing** €45–€70. **Payment** V, MC, AMEX. **English Spoken** Some. **Bar** Yes. **Wine Selection** An exhaustive selection of bold reds and some whites. **Dress** Business attire. **Disabled Access** Yes.

Hours Tuesday–Saturday, 7:30–11 p.m.; closed Sunday, Monday, August, Christmas week

Setting & Atmosphere The humble yet elegant surroundings go well with the plebeian food. Walls display old farmhouse tools.

House Specialties Innards, entrails, and thick cuts of meat.

Summary & Comments Only in Rome would one want to dine across from an old slaughterhouse. But Checchino's location is more than appropriate, for it has earned its stripes by cooking the offal cuisine that the old abbatoir workers made famous. In operation since 1887, the restaurant serves traditional favorites like *rigatoni alla pajata* and oxtail stew, plus many other meals sure to make a vegetarian faint. The prices here seem very steep, especially given what the key ingredients are, but Checchino is the place to go if you want the very best in *quinto quarto* cooking.

Cul de Sac ★★★★★

ENOTECA AND APPETIZERS | INEXPENSIVE | QUALITY ★★★★★ | VALUE ★★★★★ |
PIAZZA NAVONA

Piazza Pasquino, 73; phone 06 688 01094; bus 46, 62, 64, 70, 81, 87, 186, 492

Customers Hip locals and tourists. **Reservations** Advised. **When to Go** Early or late evening. **Pricing** €8–€12. **Payment** V, MC. **English Spoken** Some. **Bar** None. **Wine Selection** More than 200 bottles and more than 30 varieties by the glass. **Dress** Casual. **Disabled Access** Yes.

Hours Tuesday–Sunday, noon–3:30 p.m., 7 p.m.–midnight; Monday, 7–11 p.m.; closed Monday lunch

Setting & Atmosphere Cul de Sac's interior space is exhaustive, with booths lining the side walls and wine bottle stacked high on shelves above. The *enoteca's* ten or so outdoor tables, which are highly coveted, look out on the quaint Piazza Pasquino.

House Specialties Outstanding appetizers.

Summary & Comments You can never have a bad meal at Cul de Sac—unless you've left your tastebuds at home. Specializing in wine and savory appetizers, with a few entrées thrown in for good measure, this vibrant neighborhood joint is always packed and consistently rated as one of the best places in Rome to get a bite. The puréed onion soup served with a wedge of crusty bread will always hit the spot on a cool November night, and the escargot (*lumache,* in Italian) swim in a sea of garlic, pesto, and olive oil. Additionally, there's almost always a cheese sampler if you just want a little nibble in between sips of wine. The knowledgeable waiters are more than happy to give you a glass-by-glass tour of Italy.

Da Augusto ★★★

ITALIAN | INEXPENSIVE | QUALITY ★★★ | VALUE ★★★★★ | TRASTEVERE

Piazza de' Renzi, 15; phone 06 580 3978; bus 23, 97; tram 8

Customers Locals, young couples, families, few tourists. **Reservations** No. **When to Go** Anytime. **Pricing** €8–€16. **Payment** Cash only. **English Spoken** Some. **Bar** None. **Wine Selection** House reds and whites. **Dress** Casual. **Disabled Access** Yes.

Hours Monday–Friday, 12:30–3:30 p.m., 7:30–11 p.m.; Saturday, 12:30–3 p.m.; closed Saturday dinner, Sunday

Setting & Atmosphere A traditional *trattoria* in every sense of the word. Here, the management, chef, and waiters are all members of Augusto's family. Customers can also feel the love—the three inside dining rooms are cramped, and outdoor seating consists of communal picnic tables. Lunches here are mellow.

House Specialties *Cacio e pepe, bucatini alla matriciana.*

Summary & Comments Tucked away in an alley in Trastevere, Augusto's is off the main tourist track. Neighborhood folks who want food like Mom used to make at decent prices come here in droves. Specials at this rough-and-ready *trattoria* change every day, and you should take note of them (on the board next to the door) before grabbing a table. Traditional Laziale pastas, such as *bucatini alla matriciana,* are always on the menu, as are Hungry Man–size portions of roasted chicken with peppers and veal chops.

Dar Poeta ★★★★

PIZZA | INEXPENSIVE | QUALITY ★★★★ | VALUE ★★★★★ | TRASTEVERE

Vicolo del Bologna, 45; phone 06 588 0516 Bus 23, 65

Customers Students, young couples, party groups. **Reservations** Recommended. **When to Go** Weeknights. **Pricing** €10–€15. **Payment** V, MC, AMEX. **English Spoken** Some. **Bar** None. **Wine Selection** House reds and whites, and up to 10 varieties by the bottle or glass. **Dress** Casual. **Disabled Access** Yes.

Hours Daily, 7:30–11 p.m.; closed Monday

Setting & Atmosphere Dominating Dar Poeta are large tables that accommodate the after-work pizza crowds. Intimate tables are made less so, as they are inevitably in full view of the frenzy around the wood-burning pizza oven. Waiters and customers seem happy to be here.

House Specialties Pizza.

Summary & Comments Dar Poeta is appropriately named after the people's poet Giacchino Belli, who would have applauded the *pizzeria's* laid-back everyman mentality. Waiters here cavort with the clientele, and, in return, the patrons sometimes serenade the waiters. People come here to nosh on some of the city's best pizza, of which there are at least 15 choices. Folks stick around to enjoy the atmosphere, which is not unlike a local pub at happy hour.

'Gusto ★★★★½

PIZZA, ITALIAN, AND INTERNATIONAL CUISINE | INEXP/MOD | QUALITY ★★★★ | VALUE ★★★★ | TRIDENTE

Piazza Augusto Imperatore, 9; phone 06 322 6273; bus 90, 119, 913

Customers Couples, work colleagues, families, tourists. **Reservations** Recommended on weekends. **When to Go** Tuesday–Thursday. **Pricing** Pizzeria: €12–€20; restaurant: €22–€32. **Payment** V, MC, AMEX. **English Spoken** Yes. **Bar** Yes. **Wine Selection** A rotating, edited selection of Italian reds and whites by the glass or bottle; there's also a separate wine bar on the premises. **Dress** Casual chic. **Disabled Access** Yes, though restrooms are in the basement, accessible only via stairs.

Hours Sunday, Tuesday–Thursday, 12:45.–3 p.m., 7:45–midnight; Friday and Saturday, 12:45–3 p.m., 8 p.m.–2 a.m.; closed Monday

Setting & Atmosphere 'Gusto looks slick and trendy but not intimidating, and it has the professionalism and efficiency you'd expect at restaurants in New York, Toronto, or San Francisco. Young male and female students outfitted in 'Gusto T-shirts make up the waitstaff, a sight that is somewhat uncommon in a country populated with sixtysomething waiters in bow ties and cummerbunds.

House Specialties Bubbling pizzas, *fritto misto.*

Summary & Comments 'Gusto has something for everyone. The lower half of the restaurant is a *pizzeria*, where you can order up thick-crust pies, fried appetizers, and several entrées. As you go upstairs to 'Gusto's restaurant, the prices and the cuisine elevate. Here, you are likely to find Italian standbys next to stir-fry.

La Campana ★★★★★

ROMAN | MODERATE/EXPENSIVE | QUALITY ★★★★★ | VALUE ★★★★★ | PIAZZA NAVONA

Vicolo della Campana, 18; phone 06 686 7820; bus 70, 87, 119, 186

Customers Old-money Romans, politicians, tourists. **Reservations** Recommended. **When to Go** Weeknights. **Pricing** €22–€36. **Payment** V, MC, AMEX. **English Spoken** Some. **Bar** None. **Wine Selection** Premium Castelli Romani vintages by the bottle, a few by the glass. **Dress** Business attire. **Disabled Access** Yes.

Hours Tuesday–Sunday, 12:30–3 p.m., 7:30–11:30 p.m.; closed Monday

Setting & Atmosphere There's a very sober and conservative air about La Campana. The clientele don three-piece Armani suits, and the bow-tie-and-cummerbund waiters are cordial and appropriately attentive.

House Specialties *Bucatini alla matriciana* and *coda all vaccinara.*

Summary & Comments This *trattoria* has been around long enough (since 1528 by some estimates, perhaps even since 1450) to have been able to serve Goethe when he took a spin through the capital city. For several centuries, La Campana has dished out traditional Roman fare, like osso buco, *bucatini alla matriciana,* and *quinto quarto* standards. But despite having had a mention in Goethe's *Roman Elegies,* the *trattoria* hasn't become the overpriced tourist trap that one would expect.

Maccheroni ★★★½

ITALIAN | MODERATE | QUALITY ★★★ | VALUE ★★ | CENTRO STORICO

Via delle Coppelle, 44; phone 06 683 07895; bus 64, 70, 75, 116

Customers Fine young things. **Reservations** Recommended for later in the week and on weekends. **When to Go** Lunch, Monday–Thursday nights. **Pricing** €18–€32. **Payment** V, MC, AMEX. **English Spoken** Yes. **Bar** Yes. **Wine Selection** A variety of reds and whites line the walls and are part of the design aesthetic here. **Dress** As trendy as you want to be. **Disabled Access** None.

Hours Monday–Saturday, 1–3 p.m., 8 p.m.–midnight; closed Sunday

Setting & Atmosphere The décor is understated, but the all-star clientele is not.

House Specialties *Maccheroni* (the generic name for pasta) with all manner of sauces.

Summary & Comments Bono, Martin Scorsese, and Cameron Diaz have all paid Maccheroni a visit while on jaunts in the Eternal City. Truth be told, we're not sure why this restaurant draws so many celebrities, other than the fact that it is tucked away on a quiet street near the lovely Piazza Navona. The food here is very basic, with an emphasis on typical *primi* such as *cacio e pepe, penne all'arrabiata, carbonara,* and *bucatini alla matriciana.*

Margutta Vegetariano ★★★

INTERNATIONAL VEGETARIAN | MODERATE/EXPENSIVE | QUALITY ★★★★★ |
VALUE ★★ | TRIDENTE

Via Margutta, 118; phone 06 326 50577; Metro Spagna (Line A)

Customers Gucci models and natural women. **Reservations** Recommended. **When to Go** Lunch or Sunday brunch. **Pricing** €20–€28. **Payment** V, MC, AMEX. **English Spoken** Yes. **Bar** None. **Wine Selection** Only a few wines by the glass. **Dress** Trendy duds. **Disabled Access** Yes.

Hours Daily, 12:30–3:30 p.m., 7:30 p.m.–midnight

Setting & Atmosphere Modern art mingles with Far East motifs and giant potted plants. The regular clientele are cool and sophisticated.

House Specialties Unique salads, vegetable soufflés.

Summary & Comments This ain't no hippie hangout. Instead, Margutta has established itself as the premier vegetarian restaurant in Rome, convincing even die-hard carnivores to give it a try. The colorful dinners of homemade pasta, organic veggies, and ample spices are memorable, and the portions are generous. At lunch, you can order up a prix-fixe meal (which includes appetizer, entrée, and dessert) for about €12; on Sundays, Margutta's brunch is the best thing going. The vegetarian restaurant's two other locations—Le Cornacchie at Piazza Rondanini (near the Pantheon) and Al Leoncino at Via del Leoncino (near the Ara Pacis)—are more low-key but equally appetizing.

Miscellanea ★★★

ITALIAN | INEXPENSIVE | QUALITY ★★★ | VALUE ★★★★★ | CENTRO STORICO

Via delle Paste, 110a; phone 06 679 3235; bus 64, 70, 75, 116

Customers Working stiffs by day, foreign students by night. **Reservations** Not necessary. **When to Go** Lunch. **Pricing** €8–€12. **Payment** V, MC. **English Spoken** No. **Bar** Yes. **Wine Selection** A few house reds and whites by the glass or carafe. **Dress** Business casual. **Disabled Access** Yes.

Hours Monday–Saturday, noon–3:30 p.m., 7 p.m.–1 a.m.; Sunday, 7 p.m.–midnight

Setting & Atmosphere This is a raucous student pub by night, so the décor here is random, with lots of soccer pennants and photos. Lunchtime meals are prepared and eaten in a jiffy.

House Specialties Gnocchi, *penne all'arrabiata*, big salads.

Summary & Comments While tourists near the Pantheon are making do with fast food or overpriced tourist eats, workers from the neighborhood are getting big, steaming bowls of pasta at this hole in the wall. Here, you can pop in for a quick, no-frills lunch for about the price of a Big Mac meal. Specials change daily.

Montevecchio ★★★★

ITALIAN/ROMAN | EXPENSIVE | QUALITY ★★★★ | VALUE ★★★ | VATICAN AREA

Piazza Montevecchio, 22a; phone 06 686 1319; Metro Ottaviano (Line A)

Customers Locals. **Reservations** Recommended. **When to Go** Weeknights. **Pricing** €22–€30. **Payment** V, MC. **English Spoken** Yes. **Bar** No. **Wine Selection** Dozens of Italian vintages by the bottle, a few by the glass. **Dress** Prim and proper. **Disabled Access** None.

Hours Wednesday–Sunday, 7:30 p.m.–midnight; closed Monday, Tuesday, three weeks in August, two weeks in December

Setting & Atmosphere Long drapes and high ceilings define the boundaries of this classy, family-run restaurant, located in a building where Raphael and Bramante once had studios. The scene is conservative but convivial.

House Specialties Diet-destroying entrées.

Summary & Comments A restaurant of refinement in the very building where Raphael once worked, Montevecchio is the type of restaurant that only does about two seatings per night, so as to allow the customers time to enjoy a pleasurable evening out. Dishes to linger over here include the strudel of porcini mushrooms, gnocchi with cinghiale ragu, seafood lasagna, and roast suckling pig.

Osteria dell'Ingegno ★★★★★

ITALIAN/MEDITERRANEAN | MOD/EXPENSIVE | QUALITY ★★★★★ | VALUE ★★ | CENTRO STORICO

Piazza di Pietra, 45; phone 06 678 0662; bus 64, 70, 75, 116

Customers Young lovers, gourmands. **Reservations** Recommended. **When to Go** Lunch, weeknights before 9 p.m. **Pricing** €15–€35. **Payment** V, MC. **English Spoken** Some. **Bar** Yes. **Wine Selection** At least 10 reds and whites by the glass or bottle. **Dress** Casual chic. **Disabled Access** Yes.

Hours Monday–Saturday, 12:30–3:30 p.m., 8 p.m.–midnight; closed Sunday, two weeks in August

Setting & Atmosphere The vibrant, modern décor looks like it could have been Picasso's dining room. Besides the cute interior, the restaurant faces the ancient ruins of Hadrian's temple, which is gorgeously floodlit by night.

House Specialties Organic ingredients, fresh fish, and lots of choices for vegetarians.

Summary & Comments Had Leonardo da Vinci been a chef, he may have developed the sort of innovative cuisine that the Osteria dell'Ingegno has come to be known for. Using only the freshest (read: seasonal) ingredients, the Osteria has gained a reputation for its fusion-style plates, including Chiana beef with spicy mustard salsa, polenta with Gorgonzola cream, and tortilla soup.

Quinzi e Gabrielli   ★★★★

FISH/SEAFOOD | EXPENSIVE | QUALITY ★★★★★ | VALUE ★★ | CENTRO STORICO

Via delle Coppelle, 6; phone 06 687 9389; bus 64, 70, 75, 116

Customers Seafood fans, well-to-do Romans, tourists. **Reservations** Required. **When to Go** Tuesday or Wednesday (less packed). **Pricing** €30–€55. **Payment** V, MC, AMEX. **English Spoken** Yes. **Bar** Yes. **Wine Selection** Italian and French reds and whites, many of the latter of French provenance. **Dress** Suit and tie. **Disabled Access** Yes.

Hours Monday–Saturday, 8 p.m.–midnight; closed Sunday

Setting & Atmosphere Known for its thoughtful and diligent service, Quinzi e Gabrieli is located in a 15th-century *palazzo* on a quiet street near Piazza Navona. The interior is done in shades of cream and ivory, which offset the colorful bounty of the sea, on display in the front window. There's a small terrace for summer dining.

House Specialties Spaghetti with lumps of lobster, squid, and octopus.

Summary & Comments Fulfill your omega-3 requirement with a stop at Quinzi e Gabrielli, Rome's most exclusive and sophisticated fish and seafood restaurant. The menu here is strictly from the sea, and it varies daily depending on what was caught. Whatever is on the menu—sardines, lobster, turbot, mussels, octopus—you can get a look at it before you order. In fact, the catch of the day, prominently displayed at the entrance, is a ritual part of the restaurant's décor.

Ripa 12   ★★★★

FISH/SEAFOOD | MOD/EXPENSIVE | QUALITY ★★★★★ | VALUE ★★★ | TRASTEVERE

Via San Francesco a Ripa, 12; phone 06 580 9093; bus 23, 97; tram 8

Customers Trastevere locals, young couples. **Reservations** Recommended. **When to Go** Weeknights. **Pricing** €18–€30. **Payment** V, MC. **English Spoken** Some. **Bar** None. **Wine Selection** Several Castelli Romani whites by the glass and bottle. **Dress** Casual chic. **Disabled Access** None.

Hours Monday–Saturday, 8–11:30 p.m.; closed Sunday, August

Setting & Atmosphere A friendly, *trattoria*-style atmosphere tucked away on a medieval street in Trastevere.

House Specialties Sea bass and tuna carpacci (slices of raw fish).

Summary & Comments When Romans want to go out for seafood and not break the bank, they head to this small neighborhood restaurant. Casual meals involve *antipasti* of fresh, thinly sliced slabs of the day's catch, often tuna and sea bass, and *primi* of spaghetti con *vongole* (clams) and homemade tagliatelle prepared with *seppia* (black squid ink). Entrée portions are generous and feature such items as whole grilled fish done Calabrian style and infused with hints of citrus.

San Teodoro ★★★★½

ROMAN/ITALIAN | MODERATE/EXPENSIVE | QUALITY ★★★★★ | VALUE ★★★★ | ANCIENT CITY

Via dei Fienili, 49/51; phone 06 678 0933; Metro Colosseum

Customers Romans, lucky tourists. **Reservations** Highly recommended. **When to Go** Warm summer nights. **Pricing** €25–€36. **Payment** V, MC, AMEX. **English Spoken** Yes. **Bar** None. **Wine Selection** An exhaustive list of Italian red and white vintages by the glass or bottle. **Dress** Casual chic. **Disabled Access** Yes.

Hours Monday–Saturday, 1–3 p.m., 7:30–11:30 p.m.; closed Sunday

Setting & Atmosphere With its vaulted brick ceilings, twinkling chandeliers, and pencil sketches of local monuments, the restaurant possesses an Old World elegance—and an excellent location at the back of the Roman Forum. Dining outdoors with a view of the ancient ruins is a magical experience.

House Specialties Traditional handmade pasta, fish, 100% all-natural ingredients (no additives or preservatives).

Summary & Comments This gem of a restaurant is mere steps away from the ruins of the Forum and the Palatine, which are dramatically floodlit by night. San Teodoro's cuisine is mostly Roman, but there are a few seafood dishes thrown in for good measure. One favorite is a fish stew consisting of tomatoes and zucchini flowers accented with thyme. Heartier fare includes saltimbocca, *coda all vaccinara,* and, occasionally, *trippa alla romana.*

Settimio al Pellegrino ★★★

ROMAN/ITALIAN | MODERATE | QUALITY ★★★ | VALUE ★★★★ | CENTRO STORICO

Via del Pellegrino, 117; phone 06 688 01978; bus 64, 492

Customers Local workers, friends of the management, tourists. **Reservations** Strongly recommended. **When to Go** Lunch. **Pricing** €12–€21. **Payment** Cash only. **English Spoken** Yes. **Bar** None. **Wine Selection** House reds and whites by the glass or carafe. **Dress** Casual. **Disabled Access** None.

Hours Monday–Saturday, 1–3 p.m., 7:30–11 p.m.; closed Sunday

Setting & Atmosphere: A friendly, casually run hangout, where customers are treated like family.

House Specialties Fresh vegetables bought each day at the nearby Campo de' Fiori market.

Summary & Comments This small *osteria* a couple paces from Campo de' Fiori is the real deal, with Mom and Pop owners and an authentic, Roman menu. The food choices change daily according to what's fresh and available at the market. Must-try items include the *rigatoni al sugo,* a basic, tasty pasta with tomato and meat sauce; *carciofi alla romana,* breaded and friend artichokes; and *pollo alla diavola,* chicken with peppers.

Sora Lella ★★★½

TRADITIONAL ROMAN | MODERATE | QUALITY ★★★★ | VALUE ★★ |
CENTRO STORICO

Via Ponte Quattro Capi, 16 (Isola Tiberina); phone 06 686 1601; bus 23, 44, 56, 60, 65, 75, 170, 710, 774, 780

Customers Italian tourists, Romans. **Reservations** Recommended for lunch and dinner. **When to Go** Lunch, Monday–Thursday night. **Pricing** €28–€40. **Payment** V, MC, AMEX. **English Spoken** Some. **Bar** Yes. **Wine Selection** Approximately a dozen varieties each of red and white vintages. **Dress** Comfortably formal. **Disabled Access** None.

Hours Monday–Saturday, 1–2:30 p.m., 8–11 p.m.; closed Sunday, August

Setting & Atmosphere Sora Lella has the unique distinction of being the only restaurant on Rome's Tiber Island (Isola Tiberina). But despite the unusual location, this eatery has the inviting look and feel of a grandmother's dining room. Service is affable.

House Specialties Stick-to-your-ribs Roman fare.

Summary & Comments Elena "Lella" Fabrizi, lovingly known to Italians as "Sora Lella" (Sister Lella), was a Roman actress who made her living being typecast as the wise, plump, and affectionate *nonna* in film and television. True to form, the recipes at this restaurant, opened in her honor by her son in 1993, get back to basics with traditional Roman home cooking. There are the usual *quinto quarto* selections, like *rigatoni alla pajata,* as well as a particularly good *pasta alla matriciana,* done with potato gnocchi rather than bucatini. The ricotta pie is the perfect end to a feast.

Restaurant Profiles—The Rest of Latium

THE BEST RESTAURANTS IN THE REST OF LATIUM					
Name	**Cuisine**	**Overall**	**Price**	**Quality**	**Value**
The Province of Rome					
Castelli Romani					
Antico Ristorante Pagnanelli 1882	Italian	★★★★	Exp	★★★★	★★
The Province of Viterbo					
Viterbo					
Il Richiastro	Italian	★★★	Mod	★★★★	★★
Ristorante La Zaffera	Laziale/Italian	★★★★½	Mod/Exp	★★★★★	★★★

The Province of Rome
Castelli Romani

Antico Ristorante Pagnanelli dal 1882 ★★★★

ITALIAN | EXPENSIVE | QUALITY ★★★★ | VALUE ★★ | CASTEL GANDOLFO

Via A. Gramsci, 4; phone 06 936 0004

Customers Day-tripping Romans. **Reservations** Required. **When to Go** Lunch **Pricing** €30–€50. **Payment** V, MC, AMEX. **English Spoken** Some. **Bar** Yes. **Wine Selection** The restaurant's cellar holds at least 1,000 bottles of premium Italian reds and whites. **Dress** Comfortably formal. **Disabled Access** Yes, one floor of the three-floor restaurant is accessible.

Hours Wednesday–Monday, 1:30–3 p.m., 7:30–10 p.m.; closed Tuesday

Setting & Atmosphere Set in the town that is the pope's summer home, this old restaurant is a conservative eatery with a stunning lakeside view. Service is genteel.

House Specialties Smoked freshwater fish, desserts.

Summary & Comments Located next door to the pope's summer residence and overlooking Lake Albano, this restaurant is the perfect ending—or beginning—to a visit to the Castelli Romani. In the summer, when Pagnanelli does most of its business, the choices of fresh fish, big salads, and small plates of *antipasto* will overwhelm you. For dessert, the restaurant's signature *torta ai fichi* (fig cake) is a unique and delectable finale.

The Province of Viterbo
Viterbo

Il Richiastro   ★★★

ITALIAN | MODERATE | QUALITY ★★★★ | VALUE ★★ | VITERBO

Via della Marrocca, 16; phone 0761 228 009

Customers Locals. **Reservations** Required. **When to Go** The dining room is especially lively at lunch on Sunday. **Pricing** €18–€26. **Payment** Cash only. **English Spoken** Some. **Bar** None. **Wine Selection** Italian reds and whites by the bottle, reasonably priced. **Dress** Comfortably formal. **Disabled Access** None.

Hours Thursday–Sunday, noon–3 p.m., 8–11 p.m.; closed Sunday night, Monday–Wednesday, August 1–7, 31

Setting & Atmosphere: A refined atmosphere in a converted *palazzo*. The restaurant's small, hidden garden is a treat for outdoor dining.

House Specialties Medieval Latium recipes.

Summary & Comments Located in the heart of historical Viterbo, Il Richiastro recreates the farmer fare of days gone by, relying heavily on an archive of medieval recipes. Some of the interesting food you'll find here is garbanzo bean and chestnut soup *(zuppa di ceci e castagne)*, fennel and mushroom salad, and medallions of pork dressed with a sauce of prunes. Carnivores can eat well here, as there are always plenty of roasted meats, including duck, chicken, and rabbit, on the menu.

Ristorante la Zaffera   ★★★★½

LAZIALE/ITALIAN | MOD/EXPENSIVE | QUALITY ★★★★★ | VALUE ★★★ | VITERBO

Piazza San Carluccio, 7; phone 0761 342 714, fax 0761 322 210

Customers Anniversary celebrants, well-to-do locals. **Reservations** Highly recommended. **When to Go** Midday; weekday evenings. **Pricing** €21–€32. **Payment** MC, V. **English Spoken** No. **Bar** No. **Wine Selection** Italian and foreign vintages by the bottle, a few by the glass. **Dress** Business attire. **Disabled Access** Yes.

Hours Daily, 12:30–3:30 p.m., 6–10 p.m.; closed Sunday night, Monday

Setting & Atmosphere Set inside a cloister, the hushed but pleasant La Zaffera inspires you to be on your best behavior. Service is courteous and efficient.

House Specialties Roasted pork and game, fresh pasta.

Summary & Comments Many restaurants in Italy offer you the chance to eat in the shadow of lovely churches, but how many let you eat in the sanctuary itself? Built inside the 15th-century monastery of San Bernardino, La Zaffera is quite possibly one of the best restaurants in northern Latium, both in terms of atmosphere and edibles. Expect to find many staples of the *cucina Laziale* and other filling fare, including fresh tagliatelle with *cinghiale,* hearty lentil soups, and herb-crusted suckling pig. Defer to one of the chef's tasting menus and you'll have ample time to admire the cloister between courses.

The Cuisine of Umbria

Umbria is landlocked and somewhat rural, so much of its cuisine is based on grains, like *farro* (spelt), pork (again, *cinghiale*), and poultry (especially pheasant and squab). Umbria has long been known as the origin of some of the most tangy, sublime olive oils in the world, which are drizzled on soups, salads, and crusty *bruschette.* More recently, foreign visitors are discovering Umbria's other earthy gem, the black truffle *(tartufo nero),* which is found in abundance around Norcia and its environs. Norcia is also famous in Italy for its pork—so much so, in fact, that pork butcher shops throughout the peninsula are referred to as *Norcinerie. Salsiccia di cinghiale* (wild boar sausages), prosciutto, and suckling pig are just a few of the pork products that put Norcia on the map.

Pasta and chocolate, two of the most important words in a sybarite's dictionary, are also associated with Umbria. Both pasta maker Buitoni and confectioner Perugina are based in Perugia, the regional capital, and their brands can be found throughout Italy.

Restaurant Profiles—Umbria

THE BEST RESTAURANTS IN UMBRIA					
Name	Cuisine	Overall	Price	Quality	Value
The Province of Perugia					
Perugia					
Aladino	Mediterranean/ Sardinian	★★★★	Mod	★★★★	★★★★
Antica Trattoria San Lorenzo	Umbrian	★★★★	Exp	★★★★★	★★★
Caffe Sandri	Cafe/Pastries	★★★★★	Inexp	★★★★★	★★★★★
Assisi					
La Fortezza	Umbrian	★★★★★	Inexp	★★★★★	★★★★★
Ristorante Umbra San Francesco		★★★	Mod/Exp	★★★½	★
Gubbio					
La Fornace di Mastro Giorgio	Umbrian/Tuscan	★★★	Mod/Exp	★★★★	★★½

Name	Cuisine	Overall	Price	Quality	Value
THE BEST RESTAURANTS IN UMBRIA *(continued)*					
Gubbio (continued)					
Taverna del Lupo	Umbrian	★★★★½	Mod	★★★★★	★★★★
Spoleto					
Pecchiarda	Umbrian	★★★★	Inexp	★★★	★★★★★
Il Tartufo	Creative Umbrian	★★★★	Mod/Exp	★★★★★	★★★
The Province of Terni					
Orvieto					
I Sette Consoli	Umbrian	★★★★	Mod/Exp	★★★★★	★★★
L'Asino D'Oro	Umbrian	★★★★★	Inexp/Mod	★★★★★	★★★★★

The Province of Perugia

Perugia

Aladino   ★★★★

MEDITERRANEAN/SARDININAN | MODERATE | QUALITY ★★★★ | VALUE ★★★★ |
PERUGIA

Via delle Prome, 11; phone 075 572 0938

Customers Older students, couples, locals. **Reservations** No. **When to Go** Early or late. **Pricing** €18–€25. **Payment** V, MC. **English Spoken** Some. **Bar** Yes. **Wine Selection** Almost every type of Umbrian vintage; also many Tuscan varieties. **Dress** Casual chic. **Disabled Access** None.

Hours Sunday, Tuesday–Thursday, 8:30–11 p.m.; Friday and Saturday, 8:30 p.m.–1 a.m.; closed Monday, two weeks in mid-August

Setting & Atmosphere Aladino has a Mediterranean feel to go with its island-inspired dishes. Deruta-ware and other pieces of art create a cheerful environment.

House Specialties Roasted meats, durum wheat pastas, sweet desserts.

Summary & Comments In a city that reminds you with every step of the somber Middle Ages, this unusual, Sardinian-inspired space is a refreshing change. The magical meals include roasted boar and goat, a bread-based *primo* called *zuppa sarda*, and the occasional bit of fish (usually tuna, imported from the sea) and Trasimene eel.

Antica Trattoria San Lorenzo   ★★★★

CONTEMPORARY UMBRIAN | EXPENSIVE | QUALITY ★★★★★ | VALUE ★★★ | PERUGIA

Piazza Danti, 19/A; phone 075 572 1956

Customers Wealthy Perugians. **Reservations** Recommended. **When to Go** Weeknights. **Pricing** €35–€50. **Payment** V, MC. **English Spoken** Some. **Bar** Yes. **Wine Selection** The sommelier pairs haute cuisine dishes with Umbria's DOCG wines; by the bottle only. **Dress** Business attire. **Disabled Access** Yes.

Hours Tuesday–Sunday, 12:30–3 p.m., 7:30–10 p.m.; closed Monday

Setting & Atmosphere Only the name has a rustic feel. This *trattoria* is refined and modern with soft lighting and fine china. Friendly, attentive waiters liven up the ambience.

House Specialties Unique pastas.

Summary & Comments Opened only in early 2001, the "antica" is a bit of a misnomer. However, the *trattoria* does serve an interesting menu of Umbrian fare, including *mezzalune* (half moons) stuffed with duck and gnocchi with pecorino cheese and local truffles. If you're a chocolate lover, order up the Baci (chocolate and hazelnut) soufflé, a decadent homage to Perugia's most famous confection.

Caffè Sandri ★★★★★

CAFÉ AND PASTRIES | INEXPENSIVE | QUALITY ★★★★★ | VALUE ★★★★★ | PERUGIA

Corso Vannucci, 32; phone 075 572 4112

Customers Perugians of all stripes. **Reservations** Not accepted. **When to Go** Mornings. **Pricing** €2–€5. **Payment** Cash only. **English Spoken** Little. **Bar** Yes. **Wine Selection** None. **Dress** None. **Disabled Access** Yes.

Hours Daily, 8 a.m.–noon, 3–7 p.m.

Setting & Atmosphere A café in the traditional sense, with small bistro tables and a long bar.

House Specialties Cappuccino and brioche.

Summary & Comments You haven't been to Perugia unless you've been to Caffè Sandri, which occupies a prominent spot on the Corso Vannucci. Delectable pastries are the draw here, and locals stop by throughout the day for morsels of *torta di mela* (apple cake) and chocolate and hazelnut concoctions inspired by the star bon-bon of the local Perugina chocolate factory. Moreover, Sandri's frothy and sweet cappuccino is (in our opinion) the best in all of Italy.

Assisi

La Fortezza ★★★★★

UMBRIAN | INEXPENSIVE | QUALITY ★★★★★ | VALUE ★★★★★ | ASSISI

Piazza del Comune; phone 075 812 418

Customers Hotel guests, locals. **Reservations** Recommended. **When to Go** As often as possible. **Pricing** €12–€20. **Payment** MC, V. **English Spoken** Some. **Bar** No. **Wine Selection** Excellent selection of Umbrian wine at respectable prices. **Dress** Casually elegant. **Disabled Access** No.

Hours Daily, 7:30–9:30 p.m.; closed Thursday, February, July

Setting & Atmosphere Recently renovated, the vaulted ceilings and plastered walls have been shored up, linens have been updated, and climatization has been improved. The modest dining room and simple lighting will satisfy sophisticates and romantics.

House Specialties Truffles, game, and fresh pasta.

Summary & Comments Practically hidden away from all but insiders, La Fortezza is a hotel restaurant that even the locals can love. Through an unassuming stone entrance you'll find an unpretentious gourmet haven presided over by the Chiocchetti family since 1960. Umbrian specialities run the gamut from truffle-oil-drizzled crostini to *porchettini umbri ar girarosto,* a pork loin slathered with local olive oil, rosemary, and fennel. Prices for all dishes at La Fortezza are very reasonable, but if you can't make a decision, order up a tasting menu—€22 per person is worth it for some of the best cuisine Umbria has to offer.

Ristorante San Francesco   ★★★

UMBRIAN | MODERATE/EXPENSIVE | QUALITY ★★★½ | VALUE ★ | ASSISI

Via San Francesco, 52; phone 075 812 329, fax 075 815 201

Customers Tourists, tourists, tourists. **Reservations** Recommended. **When to Go** Weeknights. **Pricing** €25–€38. **Payment** V, MC. **English Spoken** Yes. **Bar** None. **Wine Selection** Lungarotti reds and Orvieto Classico mingle with various Italian vintages; a half-dozen wines by the glass. **Dress** Church dress. **Disabled Access** Yes.

Hours Thursday–Tuesday, noon–3 p.m., 7:30–10:30 p.m.; closed Wednesday, first two weeks in July

Setting & Atmosphere Diners flock here for the restaurant's jaw-dropping panorama of the Basilica.

House Specialties Sunday-dinner roasts, including goose, suckling pig, and lamb.

Summary & Comments Don't let the very touristy name and location deter you. The blandly named San Francesco faces the Basilica di San Francesco and features some delicious Umbrian specialties, such as *umbricelli* with black truffles. Entrée portions tend to be ample. Though the food is good and sometimes creative, prices are sometimes higher than they should be—St. Francis would not approve.

Gubbio

La Fornace di Mastro Giorgio   ★★★

UMBRIAN/TUSCAN | MODERATE/EXPENSIVE | QUALITY ★★★★ | VALUE ★★½| GUBBIO

Via Mastro Giorgio, 2; phone 075 922 1836

Customers Locals. **Reservations** Advised. **When to Go** The setting is especially awesome at dinner. **Pricing** €20–€35. **Payment** AMEX, MC, V. **English Spoken** Yes. **Bar** Yes. **Wine Selection** Wine cellar has more than 500 labels. **Dress** Business attire. **Disabled Access** No.

Hours Daily, 2:30–3 p.m., 7:30–11 p.m.; closed Tuesday, Wednesday lunch, January

Setting & Atmosphere As austere as Gubbio itself, La Fornace is ensconced in a dim, 14th-century alcove sure to impress history buffs and depress *al fresco* aficionados. Service is, at times, slow, but always friendly.

House Specialties Light salads, porcini dishes, roasted duck and pork.

Summary & Comments Former site of a 14th-century ceramics works made famous by designer Mastro Giorgio, this hilltop restaurant is about as close as you can get to the stony heart of this medieval city. Run by the Rosati—the hospitality moguls of Gubbio—this first-class restaurant handles Tuscan and Umbrian dishes with enough artistic flair to justify the location. Light fare includes gnocchi with fava beans and pecorino cheese or salads made of arugula and wild fennel. Heartier portions of *umbricelli* with sausage and porcini mushrooms or roasted duck with oranges will warm you when the wind begins whipping Mount Ingino.

Taverna del Lupo   ★★★★½

UMBRIAN | MODERATE | QUALITY ★★★★★ | VALUE ★★★★ | GUBBIO

Via Ansidei, 21; phone 075 927 1269

Customers Locals. **Reservations** Required. **When to Go** Weeknights. **Pricing** €20–€28. **Payment** V, MC. **English Spoken** Yes. **Bar** None. **Wine Selection** A thoughtful and extensive list of Umbrian and Tuscan reds and whites. **Dress** Comfortably formal. **Disabled Access** No.

Hours Tuesday–Sunday, 1–3 p.m., 8–11 p.m.; closed Monday

Setting & Atmosphere Perhaps Gubbio's best restaurant, this is a white-linen napkin kind of place, where tableside service is an art.

House Specialties Medieval Umbrian cooking, truffles.

Summary & Comments What will strike you first about the menu at Taverna del Lupo is the unfathomable selection of dishes whose main ingredient (or flavor) is the truffle. Among the selections are a *terrina di caciotta fusa al tartufo* (caciotta cheese terrine infused with truffles) and *medaglione di filetto con fonduta di formaggi tartufata* (beef medallions drizzled with a cheese/truffle sauce). Other regional specialties worth sampling are *salsiccia di cinghiale* (wild boar sausage) and Umbrian-style lasagna cooked with prosciutto and—you guessed it—thin shavings of black truffles.

Spoleto

Pecchiarda ★★★★

UMBRIAN | INEXPENSIVE | QUALITY ★★★ | VALUE ★★★★★ | SPOLETO

Vicolo San Giovanni, 1; phone 0743 221 009

Customers Spoletini, families and young couples. **Reservations** Recommended. **When to Go** When the touristy restaurants fill up during Festival dei Due Mondi. **Pricing** €12–€20. **Payment** V, MC. **English Spoken** Some. **Bar** None. **Wine Selection** An edited list of Umbrian *vini rossi* and *bianchi*. **Dress** Casual. **Disabled Access** None.

Hours Daily, 1–3 p.m., 7:30–10 p.m.; closed Thursday in winter

Setting & Atmosphere The informal dining room surrounds a glassed-in garden. Waiters dole out advice on the best thing in the kitchen.

House Specialties Thick soups, lamb, truffle dishes.

Summary & Comments When the going gets tough (we mean, when the tourist hordes arrive), then the tough Spoletini head to Pecchiarda, an inexpensive neighborhood joint that cooks up classic Umbrian fare. In the summer, during the big music festival, you probably won't be too interested in the diner's best dishes, which include a soup of chicory and spelt and an equally heavy *gnocchi di ricotta*. However, the menu changes with the season, so, in the summer, you'll find a delicious assortment of *antipasto* and light pastas.

Il Tartufo ★★★★

CREATIVE UMBRIAN | MODERATE/EXPENSIVE | QUALITY ★★★★★ | VALUE ★★★ | SPOLETO

Piazza Garibaldi, 24; phone 0743 40236

Customers *Funghi* fans. **Reservations** Highly recommended. **When to Go** As often as possible. **Pricing** €25–€35. **Payment** AMEX, DC, MC, V. **English Spoken** Yes. **Bar** Yes. **Wine Selection** Premium Umbrian vintages. **Dress** Casually elegant. **Disabled Access** Yes.

Hours Daily, noon–3 p.m., 8–11p.m.; closed Sunday night, Monday, January, July.

Setting & Atmosphere Hardly the dark den you'd expect, Il Tartufo is outfitted in breezy linens and simple flower arrangements, and has a amicable waitstaff to match. A foundation from a Roman villa forms part of the dining room floor, lending the eatery a credible cachet.

House Specialties Mushroom dishes, from appetizers to entrées

Summary & Comments Those lacking a taste for black truffles and porcini usually emerge from Il Tartufo with a new appreciation for one of Umbria's most prized products. Dishes such as a polenta terrine with hazelnuts and fresh truffle shavings (when in season), roasted lamb in a porcini cream sauce, and *crostini* topped with substantial helpings of mushroom *caponata* seasoned with onions and herbs will give even the the the most skeptical the chance to explore the complex flavors of these earthy fruits. As for those who've made a pilgrimage to the Truffle Trail? This is heaven, of course.

The Province of Terni
Orvieto

I Sette Consoli ★★★★

UMBRIAN | MODERATE/EXPENSIVE | QUALITY ★★★★★ | VALUE ★★★ | ORVIETO

Piazza Sant'Angelo, 11A; phone 0763 343 911

Customers Well-to-do Orvietani, tourists. **Reservations** Recommended. **When to Go** Sunday and Monday nights are mellow. **Pricing** €28–€40. **Payment** V, MC. **English Spoken** Yes. **Bar** None. **Wine Selection** Tuscan and Umbria reds and whites by the bottle or glass. **Dress** Comfortably formal. **Disabled Access** None.

Hours Thursday–Tuesday, 8–11 p.m.; closed Wednesday

Setting & Atmosphere Set on a quiet *piazza* a stone's throw from the Duomo, this restaurant is tiny—some say intimate—with only enough tables for a handful of guests.

House Specialties Pork, truffles, a cheese course.

Summary & Comments For such a small restaurant, it's surprising that Sette Consoli is able to turn out such a variety of interesting and flavorful dishes. One typical Umbrian entrée that the restaurant does well is *maiale al finocchio*, or pork with fennel. Other goodies are a *spaghetti alla chitarra con ragu di coniglio* (guitar-shaped pasta with hare ragu) and *tagliatelle al vino rosso* (pasta in red wine sauce). A good value is the tasting menu, which includes three courses with three types of wine for approximately €30.

L'Asino d'Oro ★★★★★

UMBRIAN | INEXPENSIVE/MODERATE | QUALITY ★★★★★ | VALUE ★★★★★ | ORVIETO

Vicolo del Popolo, 9; phone 0763 344 406

Customers Locals. **Reservations** Recommended for evening. **When to Go** Lunch. **Pricing** €12–€20. **Payment** Cash only. **English Spoken** Some. **Bar** Yes. **Wine Selection** Many reds and whites from Tuscany and Umbria. **Dress** Casual. **Disabled Access** Yes.

Hours Daily, 11:30 a.m.–midnight; closed Monday, November, February

Setting & Atmosphere Our experience here has always been relaxing and fuss-free, whether we're joining friends for dinner in the small cantina, or simply enjoying a glass wine at one of the outdoor tables.

House Specialties Fresh salads, *antipasto* plates.

Summary & Comments The mark of a good restaurant can often be discovered in the way that it treats its vegetables. Luckily, Chef Lucio Sforza of the convivial L'Asino D'Oro is as obsessed with the quality of his produce, pastas, and meats as he is with the creativity of his craft. We found salads of wild greens drizzled with lemon-tinged olive oil, simple plates of grilled asparagus and zucchini, and interesting combinations, such as creamy *pancotto* with tomatoes and white bean and fennel soup, the perfect, fresh pick-me-up after a long day of touring.

The Cuisine of the Marches and the Republic of San Marino

The Marches is the crossroads for the sea, the valley, and the mountains, so you'll find a wide variety of dishes based on the ingredients from these environments. Perhaps the most famous specialty of the Cucina Marchigiana is *brodetto,* a fish stew made with anywhere from 8 to 13 different types of fish (depending on where it is made), including mullet, skate, sole, and cod. *Brodetto* should be made with fish only, and any restaurant that "cuts" its stew with seafood should be avoided. *Vincisgrassi,* a lasagna of chicken livers, cream, and truffles, is a hearty staple in the region's interior. Meanwhile, the popular hors d'ouevres *olive ascolane,* or olives stuffed with meat then breaded and fried, was first conceived in the ancient town of Áscoli-Piceno. In sum, you'll find a unique, blend of complex tastes and combinations in the Marches that is sure to surprise you.

Restaurant Profiles—The Marches and the Republic of San Marino

THE BEST RESTAURANTS IN THE MARCHES AND THE REPUBLIC OF SAN MARINO					
Name	Cuisine	Overall	Price	Quality	Value
The Province of Pésaro-Urbino					
Urbino					
L'Angolo Divino	Marchigiana/ Italian	★★★½	Mod/Exp	★★★½	★★★★
Vecchia Urbino	Marchigiana	★★★★	Mod	★★★★★	★★★
The Republic of San Marino					
La Fratta	Italian/ Sammarinese	★★★★	Mod/Exp	★★★★	★★★★
Righi La Taverna	Italian/ Sammarinese	★★★½	Inexp/ Mod	★★★	★★★★
The Province of Ancona					
Ancona					
La Moretta	Seafood	★★★½	Mod	★★★★	★★★
Teatro Strabacco	Anconetana/ Marchigiana	★★★★	Mod	★★★★	★★★★

THE BEST RESTAURANTS IN THE MARCHES AND THE REPUBLIC OF SAN MARINO (continued)

Name	Cuisine	Overall	Price	Quality	Value
The Province of Ancona (continued)					
Senigallia					
La Madonnina Del Pescatore	Seafood	★★★★★	Mod/Exp	★★★★★	★★
The Province of Macerata					
Macerata					
Da Secondo	Marchigiana	★★★	Exp	★★★★	★★
Osteria Dei Fiori	Marchiagiana/ Italian	★★★★	Mod	★★★★	★★★
The Province of Áscoli-Piceno					
Áscoli-Piceno					
Gallo D'Oro	Marchigiana	★★★★½	Mod	★★★★★	★★★★
La Locandiera	Marchigiana	★★★	Mod/Exp	★★★	★★★

The Province of Pésaro-Urbino
Urbino

L'Angolo Divino   ★★★½

MARCHIGIANA/ITALIAN | MODERATE/EXPENSIVE | QUALITY ★★★½ | VALUE ★★★★ |
URBINO

Via Sant'Andrea, 12; phone 0722 327 559

Customers Locals. **Reservations** Recommended. **When to Go** Anytime. **Pricing** €15–€25. **Payment** MC, V. **English Spoken** No. **Bar** No. **Wine Selection** Many Italian vintages by the glass or bottle. **Dress** Casually elegant. **Disabled Access** Yes.

Hours Daily, 12:15–3:30 p.m., 7:15–10:30 p.m.; closed Sunday night, Monday lunch

Setting & Atmosphere Antique and intimate.

House Specialties Fresh pasta, game, offal.

Summary & Comments You may need a translator for this traditional *trattoria's* menu. A number of the Marchigiana and Italian *primi* and *secondi,* such as tagliolini with lamb *(taiulin sa l'agnel sfugit),* are listed in dialect. Otherwise, the elegant eatery offers a wide variety of pastas, including Chitarrine del Duca—the house's tasty homage to Urbino's Renaissance patron—and *antipasto* plates of local mushrooms and *salumi.* Entrées are a bit more adventurous and consist of ample helpings of lamb, rabbit, duck, and offal, of which the pork livers with onions and herbs is exemplary.

Vecchia Urbino   ★★★★

MARCHIGIANA | MODERATE | QUALITY ★★★★★ | VALUE ★★★ | URBINO

Via dei Vasari, 3/5; phone 0722 4447

Customers Carnivores, truffle lovers, locals. **Reservations** Recommended. **When to Go** Wednesday–Friday nights; winter. **Pricing** €16–€22. **Payment** V, MC. **English Spoken** Yes. **Bar** None. **Wine Selection** An exhaustive list of Italian and foreign reds and whites by the bottle. **Dress** Casual chic. **Disabled Access** Yes.

Hours Wednesday–Monday, 12:30–3 p.m., 8–11 p.m.; closed Tuesday

Setting & Atmosphere You can feel the history of the town when you sit in the rustic-style dining room. The restaurant is located in a 16th-century *palazzo* and has an original wood-beam ceiling. The chandeliers are fashioned in the shape of the "ducal star," the symbol of Renaissance Urbino. Service is warm and attentive.

House Specialties Truffles, *vincisgrassi*.

Summary & Comments As the name implies, Vecchia Urbino prides itself on serving the traditional specialties of Urbino and the Marches region. Winter is high season here, when the local truffles are baked into ravioli and used as a complement to heavier entrées of veal, lamb, and rabbit. *Vincisgrassi,* a fattening Marchigiana lasagna made with a sauce of chicken giblets, pork, veal, and *béchamel,* is one of the restaurant's signature dishes.

The Republic of San Marino

La Fratta   ★★★★

ITALIAN/SAMMARINESE | MODERATE/EXPENSIVE | QUALITY ★★★★ |
VALUE ★★★★ | SAN MARINO

Salita alla Rocca, 14; phone 0549 991 594

Customers Gourmands, tourists. **Reservations** Recommended. **When to Go** Evenings. **Pricing** €21–€30. **Payment** MC, V. **English Spoken** Some. **Bar** Yes. **Wine Selection** The Sammarinese vintages are a treat; Italian reds and whites also available. **Dress** Business casual. **Disabled Access** Yes.

Hours Daily, noon–3 p.m., 7–10:30 p.m.

Setting & Atmosphere One of the larger dining rooms in the country, La Fratta bustles with friendly, attentive waiters. Décor is elegant but unpretentious.

House Specialties *Piadina* (Emilia-Romagna-style focaccia), fish specials.

Summary & Comments Considered the country's best, La Fratta attracts foodies from San Marino, the Marches, and beyond. Though it is situated near the base of La Rocca o Guaita, the restaurant steers away from strictly rustic fare, offering surprises like Norwegian-style salmon, red mullet with pomegranate, and frogs' legs. San Marino's wine industry is understandably small, but you'll find most vintages here, including Brugneto and Biancale. Cap off your unusual meal with Aquavit, a sort of grappa.

Righi la Taverna   ★★★½

ITALIAN/SAMMARINESE | INEXPENSIVE/MODERATE | QUALITY ★★★ | VALUE ★★★★ |
SAN MARINO

Piazza Libertà; phone 0549 991 196

Customers Natives, tourists. **Reservations** Not necessary. **When to Go** Lunch. **Pricing** €10–€22. **Payment** MC, V. **English Spoken** Yes. **Bar** Yes. **Wine Selection** House selections of mostly Italian vintages by the glass or carafe. **Dress** Business casual in the restaurant, tourist casual for the ground level. **Disabled Access** Yes.

Hours Daily, noon–3:30 p.m., 7–11 p.m.; closed Monday

Setting & Atmosphere Like most San Marino restaurants, Righi has a pervasive medieval feel, but it delivers with a castle-like interior and a view of courtly Piazza Libertà.

House Specialties Wood-oven pizza, fresh pastas.

Summary & Comments Righi La Taverna serves up a proper amount of the Middle Ages with its moderately priced fare. For lunch, we prefer the bar and *tavola calda*— Righi Bistrot—on the ground level, where you can pick up pizza or panini. Native to these parts, and done well here, is the *passatelli*, a hearty, carbonara-style pasta that even vegetarians will adore. The earthy *cucina Marchigiana* also makes an appearance in truffle-dusted casseroles and roasted meats.

The Province of Ancona
Ancona

La Moretta ★★★½

SEAFOOD | MODERATE | QUALITY ★★★★ | VALUE ★★★ | ANCONA

Piazza Plebiscito, 52; phone 071 202 317

Customers Tourists, seamen, couples. **Reservations** Recommended. **When to Go** Lunch or early evening. **Pricing** €14–€30. **Payment** AMEX, MC, V. **English Spoken** Yes. **Bar** Yes. **Wine Selection** About 500 vintages overall, including many regional reds and whites. **Dress** Business attire. **Disabled Access** Yes.

Hours Daily, 12:15–2:45 p.m., 7:45–10:45 p.m.; closed Sunday

Setting & Atmosphere The dark, wood-paneled restaurant could use an update, so try for a table on the patio overlooking the square. Service is courteous and discreet.

House Specialties Marchigiana-style seafood soups

Summary & Comments Feeding the people of the port of Ancona since 1897, the Moretta is a typical *trattoria* with a seafaring theme. Fish dishes rule, from *brodetto* and *stoccafisso anconetana* (Ancona-style fish soups) and Ligurian *ciotola* to *spaghetti alle vongole* and tagliatelle with oysters. Stick to seafood—earthy dishes are mediocre—and pair your meal with a local Verdicchio.

Teatro Strabacco ★★★★

ANCONETANA/MARCHIGIANA | MODERATE | QUALITY ★★★★ | VALUE ★★★★ |
ANCONA

Via Guglielmo Oberdan, 2; phone 071 56748 Fax 071 54213

Customers Late-night theater, jazz fans, locals. **Reservations** Recommended. **When to Go** Early for a table, late for atmosphere. **Pricing** €18–€25. **Payment** AMEX, DC, MC, V. **English Spoken** Some. **Bar** Yes. **Wine Selection** Hundreds of Italian vintages. **Dress** Business casual. **Disabled Access** Yes.

Hours Daily, 12:15–3:15 p.m., 7:15 p.m.–3 a.m.; closed Monday

Setting & Atmosphere Contemporary murals by local artists give depth to this otherwise rustic-style *osteria*. Service is professional, yet laid back. The dining room's din amps up as the evening rolls on.

House Specialties Local meat and fish, *stoccafisso*.

Summary & Comments   Cool and sophisticated Teatro Strabacco takes the guess-work out of their menu by offering up to ten tasting menus, including wine and dessert. Each of the prix-fixe meals consists of at least one dish native to Ancona and/or the Marches, be it a *brodetto di pesce all'anconetana,* a *vincisgrassi,* or a glass of the local Rosso Conero wine. Many of the tasting menus, such as the *Spiaggia della Salute* and the *Cena dello Stoccafisso,* feature several specialties from the Adriatic, but there are also dinners for meat lovers *(Menu del Poggio)* and vegetarians *(Menu di Ghettarello).* Teatro's kitchen stays open until midnight, while the adjacent *enoteca* hops until 3 a.m.

Senigallia

La Madonnina del Pescatore   ★★★★★

SEAFOOD | MODERATE/EXPENSIVE | QUALITY ★★★★★ | VALUE ★★ | SENIGALLIA

*Lungomare Italia, 11; Marzocca di Senigallia (about 10 miles north of Ancona);
phone 071 698 267; www.madonninadelpescatore.it*

Customers Anconatani, seafood lovers. **Reservations** Strongly recommended.
When to Go Summer days and weeknights (very busy on the weekends). **Pricing**
€38–€50. **Payment** V, MC, AMEX. **English Spoken** Some. **Bar** Yes. **Wine Selection**
Mild-flavored red and white wines from the Marches region, especially labels from small
vintners, are featured on the menu. **Dress** Artfully casual. **Disabled Access** None.

Hours Sunday–Saturday, noon–3 p.m., 8–11 p.m.; closed Monday

Setting & Atmosphere The chef's wife, Mariella Cedroni, keeps an immaculate din-ing room, which is accented with antiques, modern art, and super-slick furnishings. Large windows open up to a lovely view of the sea, and an outdoor patio provides the perfect setting for a casual sushi lunch.

House Specialties An *assaggi* (taste) of eight seafood *antipasti.*

Summary & Comments Having a head chef who was once a naval officer is reason enough to believe that this restaurant doesn't mess around when it comes to serving fresh fish and seafood. Even the name, La Madonnina del Pescatore, which means the "little Madonna of the fisherman," is evidence that the ingredients here are pure and heavenly. The restaurant's patron saint, Chef Moreno Cedroni, is a star chef in Italy, known for his innovative ways with tuna, mussels, shrimp, and octopus. Indeed, his clever creations have earned him comparisons to Thomas Keller, culinary genius of Napa Valley's much-lauded French Laundry.

The Province of Macerata

Macerata

Da Secondo   ★★★

MARCHIGIANA | EXPENSIVE | QUALITY ★★★★ | VALUE ★★ | MACERATA

Via Pescheria Vecchia, 57; phone 0733 260 912

Customers Opera stars, music-loving locals. **Reservations** Highly recommended.
When to Go Weekday evenings. **Pricing** €30–€45. **Payment** All major credit cards.
English Spoken Limited. **Bar** Yes. **Wine Selection** Small list of premium Italian vin-tages. **Dress** Business attire. **Disabled Access** Yes.

Hours Daily, 7–11 p.m.; closed Monday, end of August

Setting & Atmosphere Da Secondo prides itself on premium, fit-for-a-diva service.
House Specialties *Vincisgrassi.*

Summary & Comments The closest Macerata gets to a celebrity hang-out is the well-loved local Da Secondo. Around the time of the opera festival, classical music stars can be seen in this centrally-located eatery digging into plates of *gnocchi al ragu, quaglie al cognac* (quails simmered in cognac), and spit-roasted pork. What makes us come back for the *secondo* time, however, is the *vincisgrassi* and the *ciauscolo,* a soft, savory salami that is slathered on the crustiest fresh bread.

Osteria dei Fiori   ★★★★

MARCHIGIANA/ITALIAN | MODERATE | QUALITY ★★★★ | VALUE ★★★ | MACERATA

Via L. Rossi, 61; phone 0733 260 142

Customers Locals, Italian tourists. **Reservations** Not necessary. **When to Go** Lunch, weeknights. **Pricing** €18–€26. **Payment** V, MC. **English Spoken** Some. **Bar** None. **Wine Selection** A thoughtful selection of regional wines. **Dress** Casual chic. **Disabled Access** Yes.

Hours Monday–Saturday, noon–3 p.m., 8–11 p.m.; closed Sunday

Setting & Atmosphere The intimate little restaurant is located a stone's throw from the Sferisterio. Furnishings are modest and service discreet.

House Specialties An ample selection of seasonal vegetables for *contorni.*

Summary & Comments Honestly priced Osteria dei Fiori is a favorite of locals and tourists looking for creative yet traditional home cooking. The menu here changes with the season and is heavy with fresh fruits, vegetables, and local mushrooms. Recommended dishes are the pasta *maltagliati* (misshaped pasta) with a vegetable ragu.

The Province of Áscoli-Piceno
Áscoli-Piceno

Gallo d'Oro   ★★★★½

MARCHIGIANA | MODERATE | QUALITY ★★★★★ | VALUE ★★★★ | ÁSCOLI-PICENO

Corso Vittorio Emanuele, 13; phone 0736 253 520

Customers Ascolani. **Reservations** Strongly recommended. **When to Go** Lunch, Wednesday–Friday nights. **Pricing** €18–€24. **Payment** V, MC. **English Spoken** Some. **Bar** None. **Wine Selection** A broad selection of Italian and foreign wines. **Dress** Comfortably formal to casual chic. **Disabled Access** Yes.

Hours Daily, 12:30–3:30 p.m., 7:30–11 p.m.; closed Sunday

Setting & Atmosphere Tarcisio Mazziti, current owner and son of the restaurant's founder, maintains the restaurant's elegant reputation with attention to handsome lighting (candles), delicate table settings, and exquisite service.

House Specialties *Fritto misto,* Marches-style game and fowl.

Summary & Comments Its central location and award-winning menu have made Gallo d'Oro *the* place in Áscoli-Piceno to celebrate anniversaries and other special occasions. Since 1960, the restaurant has been serving up typical Picenian dishes; its *fritto misto,* made with *olive ascolane,* lamb cutlets, veal brains, zucchini, and cremini mushrooms, is often cited as one of the highlights. On Wednesday and Friday, freshly caught Adriatic fish is on the menu.

La Locandiera   ★★★

MARCHIGIANA | MODERATE/EXPENSIVE | QUALITY ★★★ | VALUE ★★★ |
ÁSCOLI-PICENO

Via Carlo Goldoni, 2; phone 0736 262 509

Customers Locals, German tourists. **Reservations** Recommended. **When to Go**
Anytime. **Pricing** €16–€30. **Payment** DC, V. **English Spoken** Some. **Bar** Yes. **Wine
Selection** Italian wines by the glass or carafe. **Dress** Casual. **Disabled Access** Yes.

Hours Daily, noon–3 p.m., 7–11 p.m.; closed Sunday night, Monday, August

Setting & Atmosphere This is a friendly neighborhood restaurant, where tourists
are made to feel like locals. Decorations are minimal, save for copper pots and framed
pictures of friends and landmarks.

House Specialties Ample servings of seafood and meats.

Summary & Comments Boasting fare fit for a peasant or a king, La Locandiera has
delicious dishes for every budget. There are plenty of small, reasonably priced plates
that satisfy, including *farro* soup with shrimp or *orzo* with porcini. A tasting menu for
meat (€15) or fish (€25) will reap rewards such as *spezzatino d'agnello con patate* (lamb
and potato stew), fried and grilled seafood, and *lumache alla marchigiana* (snails cooked
in an essence of fennel).

Part Six

Florence and
the Best of Tuscany

A Brief History of Florence

To know Florence (Firenze) is to know Tuscany, for the history of this midsize town on the Arno River has altered and shaped the course of life for much of the region, and, for that matter, much of Italy. At the beginning of the 13th century, we see the dawn of Florence, from a backwater, landlocked village to a growing, independent *comune.* The conflict between the Guelphs (pro-papacy) and the Ghibellines (pro–Holy Roman Empire), a war that lasted two centuries and saw a large swath of the peninsula divided, was sparked in Florence with the assassination of a merchant. As in the rest of Tuscany, loyalties in Florence for the two factions went back and forth, until the Guelphs finally got control of the city. The Guelphic symbol, the lily *fleur-de-lis,* is the symbol of Florence to this day. Of course, the skirmishes didn't stop there. Florentines found something else to argue about and split again into the "blacks" and the "whites." Eventually, the blacks ousted the whites, sending none other than native son Dante Alighieri to live in exile.

By then, Florence was getting rich. The city's woolen cloth merchants, whose guild name was the *Calimala,* made a fortune with a special red dye and overpriced imported cloth. It was through their supervision that the dome of Santa Maria del Fiore—Florence's massive, signature **Duomo**—was built. Meanwhile, Giovanni di Bicci, banker to the pope and the first of the Medici clan, went to work spawning a dynasty.

The Medici, whose name is synonymous with Florence and Tuscany, were the first family from the late 14th century until the mid-18th century. Though not royalty, the Medici used their mettle and their money to build up armies, construct lavish palaces, secure positions as bishops, and commission significant art projects. Were it not for funding from the Medici, Florence's most famous art, such as the *Birth of Venus* by Botticelli (in the **Uffizi**) and the *David* by Michelangelo (in the **Accademia**),

CALENDAR OF EVENTS IN FLORENCE AND TUSCANY

February

Carnevale, Viareggio   Held during the ten days before Ash Wednesday, Viareggio's Carnival is considered second only to the one held each year in Venice.

March

Settimana dei Beni Culturali (Cultural Week)   One week in March or April. During cultural week, all state-owned museums and archaeological sites are open free of charge. For more information, phone 055 23885.

Explosion of the Cart (Scoppio del Carro), Florence   Florentines head to the Piazza del Duomo each Easter Sunday at noon to watch the explosion of a cart full of fireworks. The tradition dates back to the early Middle Ages. If the explosion goes off without a hitch, it is considered a good omen for the city.

April

Mostra Mercato Internazionale dell'Artigianato, Fortezza da Basso, Florence   Last two weeks of April. You can find all manner of fabrics (including silk), glassware, pottery, and crafts at this international arts and crafts fair, just outside Florence's city gates.

Sagra Musicale Lucchese, Lucca   Until early July, sacred music is featured in Lucca's numerous churches.

May

Cantine Aperte, throughout Tuscany   Last Sunday in May. Many private wineries throughout the region hold wine tastings, with flights of their premium vintages going for next to nothing. For info, call 0577 738 312.

would probably never have been realized. The ubiquitous patronage of the Medici encouraged other noble families to contribute their wealth to art, thereby leaving a legacy of rich frescoes, sumptuous sculptures, bold architecture, and gallery after gallery of art.

The period between the 14th and 16th centuries saw Florence as the birthplace of many great Italian thinkers, including artists such as Michelangelo, Sandro Botticelli, Fra Filippo Lippi, Masaccio, Paolo Uccello, and Brunelleschi, to name only a few. As detailed in Giorgio Vasari's *Lives of the Artists,* the paths of many of these Renaissance men crossed. Dante Alighieri, the great poet who penned the *Divine Comedy (Divina Commedia)* was, born and baptized in Florence. Furthermore,

May (continued)

Musical May (Maggio Musicale Fiorentino), Florence   The city's most celebrated arts festival now lasts until the first few weeks of June and highlights classical music, theater, dance, and the performing arts. More info, call 055 211 158, or visit **www.maggiofiorentino.com.**

June

Calcio in Costume, Florence   Late June/early July. This soccer tournament with a twist sees teams of 27 men from Florence's four ancient neighborhoods—Santa Maria Novella, Santa Croce, Santo Spirito, and San Giovanni—compete in medieval dress, usually in a dirt-filled Piazza Santa Croce. Raging testosterone and local rivalries rule the day.

Festa di San Giovanni, Florence   June 24. The Florentines celebrate their patron saint's day with parades, festivals, and a nighttime fireworks display in Piazzale Michelangelo.

Game of the Bridge (Gioco del Ponte), Pisa   Held on the last Sunday of the month. More info, visit the Pisa Tourism Board's website at **www.comune.pisa.it.**

Saracen Joust (Giostra del Saracino), Arezzo   Second-to-last Sunday of the month. An event since the 13th century, the joust is a reenactment of the medieval contest that took place between Arezzo's four quarters *(quartieri).* Lots of colorful, medieval finery, parades, and food. Also held the first Sunday in September. More info, call 0575 377 678, or visit **www.giostradelsaracino.arezzo.it** (in Italian only).

the philosopher Niccolò Machiavelli, author of *The Prince,* crafted theories that still influence political thinking. Probably never again will there be such a concentration of great minds in one city.

After the Medici dynasty came to a halt and the Renaissance petered out, Florence's physical and spiritual development slowed to a snail's pace. The city enjoyed a brief time in the late 19th century as the capital of Italy when Rome was resisting unification. But other moments of glory were beyond Florence's reach.

The leftovers from the Renaissance had already made Florence a tourist center by the beginning of the 20th century. But that fact did not spare the city from German attacks during World War II. All of the

CALENDAR OF EVENTS IN FLORENCE AND TUSCANY

July

Il Palio, Siena   July 2. The famous bareback horse race is held every July 2 and August 16 in the Piazza del Campo.

Puccini Opera Festival, Torre del Lago Puccini (near Lucca)   July/ August. Puccini's greatest works are performed by his lakeside villa.

Pistoia Blues Festival, Pistoia   Mid-July. One of Italy's best blues festivals also dabbles in jazz, funk, and rock 'n' roll. Past performers have included B. B. King, Frank Zappa, and Wilson Pickett. For information, call 0573 358 195, or visit **www.pistoiablues.com.**

La Giostra dell'Orso, Pistoia   July 25. This jousting tournament "of the bear" is a friendly medieval contest that pits Pistoia's four quarters against one another. The bear is featured on Pistoia's coat of arms.

August

Tuscan Sun Festival, Cortona   Second week in August. Celebrates the "art of living well" with musical performances, wine tours, art lectures, and culinary seminars. More info, visit **www.tuscansunfestival.com.**

Festa della Bistecca, Cortona   August 15. A carnivore's fantasy, celebrating the steak.

bridges, except for the Ponte Vecchio, which Hitler apparently admired, were destroyed, as a means of beating back the Allied advance. Later, in 1966, another tragedy on the Arno—this time, a natural one—resulted in the flooding of many of Florence's buildings and irreparable damage to countless masterpieces. In 1993, tragedy struck Florence again, this time in the form of a bomb, set off by the Mafia near the Uffizi Gallery. Five people were killed, and the museum suffered structural damage.

Florence Tourist Board

The tourism offices for the city of Florence and the province of Florence are located in town. Both have detailed information on touring Florence, and should offer info on the region of Tuscany as a whole. The city tourist office also offers a special phone service called **Firenze SOS Turista.** From Monday through Saturday, 10 a.m.–1 p.m., 3–6 p.m., tourists can call 055 276 0382 for emergency assistance. The bilingual operators can act as mediators to settle disputes with hoteliers, or can help should you need to contact the police.

(continued)

August (continued)

Il Palio, Siena   August 16.

Il Baccanale, Montepulciano   Penultimate Saturday of the month. Featuring the local wine, *vino nobile,* food, music, and more.

September

Saracen Joust (Giostra del Saracino), Arezzo   First Sunday of the month (see above).

Crossbow Contest with Gubbio, Sansepolcro   Second Sunday of the month.

November

Florence Marathon (Maratona di Firenze), Florence   Late November/Early December. For more information, call 055 572 885, or visit **www.firenzemarathon.it.**

December

Festa del Santo Stefano/unveiling of the Holy Girdle, Prato   December 25–26.

City of Florence Tourist Office   Via A. Manzoni, 16; 50121 Florence; 055 23320, fax 055 2346286; **www.firenzeturismo.it**

Province of Florence Tourist Office   Via Cavour, 1r (near San Lorenzo); 50120 Florence; 055 290 832; **www.provincia.firenze.it**

Tuscany Regional Tourist Board   Via A. Manzoni, 16; 50121 Florence; 055 23320, fax 055 23462; **www.turismo.toscana.it**

Understanding Florence

Florence is a tightly knit tapestry of medieval churches, Renaissance *palazzi,* and criss-crossing cobblestone streets bisected by a wide watery ribbon called the Arno River. The concentration of Florence's treasures, including the magnificent **Duomo,** the **Palazzo Vecchio,** the **Accademia,** and the **Uffizi Gallery,** lie within a broad semicircle that stretches from **Lungarno Vespucci** in the west to the church of **San Marco** in the north and back down to the river just east of **Santa Croce.**

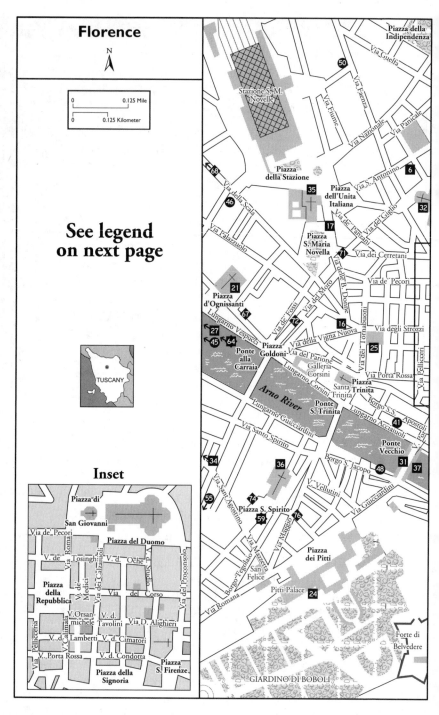

Florence

N

| 0 | 0.125 Mile |
| 0 | 0.125 Kilometer |

See legend
on next page

TUSCANY

Inset

Piazza di
San Giovanni

Via de' Pecori

Piazza del Duomo

Via de' Tosinghi   V. d. Oche

V. dei Medici   Via dei Calzaiuoli   Via del Corso

Piazza
della
Repubblica

V. Orsan-michele   V. d. Tavolini   Via D. Alighieri

V. d. Lamberti   V. d. Cimatori

V. Porta Rossa   V. d. Condotta

Piazza della
Signoria

Piazza
S. Firenze

Piazza della
Indipendenza

Via Guelfa

Via Faenza

Via Fiume

Via Nazionale

Via Panicale

Stazione S. M.
Novella

Piazza
della Stazione

Piazza
dell'Unita
Italiana

Piazza S. Antonino

Via S. Antonino

Via de' Panzani

Via del Giglio

Via della Scala

Via Palazzuolo

Piazza
S. Maria
Novella

Via dei Cerretani

Via de' Pecori

Via delle B. Donne

Piazza
d'Ognissanti

Via de' Rossi

Via del Moro

Via della Vigna Nuova

Via dei Tornabuoni

Via degli Strozzi

Via del Parione

Lungarno Vespucci

Piazza
Goldoni

Ponte
alla
Carraia

Galleria
Corsini

Lungarno Corsini

Via Porta Rossa

Via Pelliceria

Piazza
Santa Trinita

Piazza
Trinita

Borgo S.S. Apostoli

Arno River

Ponte
S. Trinita

Lungarno Acciaiuoli

Lungarno Guicciardini

Via Santo Spirito

Ponte
Vecchio

Via Santo Spirito

Borgo S. Jacopo

Via Sant' Agostino

V. Vellutini

Piazza S. Spirito

Via Maggio

Via Guicciardini

Piazza
dei Pitti

Borgo Tegolaio

San
Felice

Via Mazzetta

Via Romana

Pitti Palace

Forte di
Belvedere

GIARDINO DI BOBOLI

50

68

46

35

6

32

17

71

21

61

72

16

25

27

45   64

41

34

36

55

74

59

76

24

48   31   37

192

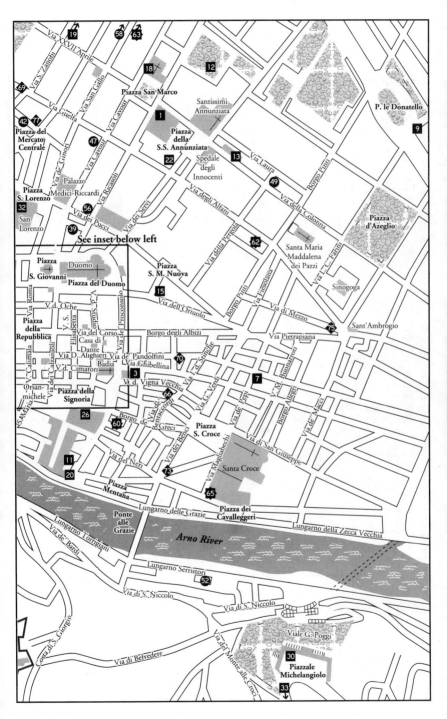

Florence Map Legend

ATTRACTIONS

1. Accademia (The Academy)
2. Badia Fiorentina
3. Bargello
4. Battistero (Baptistry)
5. Campanile (Bell Tower)
6. Cappelle Medicee (Medici Chapels)
7. Casa Buonarroti
8. Casa di Dante
9. Cimitero degli Inglesi (English Cemetery)
10. Duomo (Santa Maria del Fiore)
11. Galleria degli Uffizi (Uffizi Gallery)
12. Giardino dei Semplici
13. Museo Archeologica (Archaeological Museum)
14. Museo dell'Opera del Duomo
15. Museo di Firenze Com'era
16. Museo Mario Marini
17. Museo Salvatore Ferragamo
18. Museo di San Marco
19. Museo Stibbert
20. Museo di Storia della Scienza
21. Ognissanti
22. Opificio delle Pietre Dure
23. Orsanmichele
24. Palazzo Pitti and Giardino Boboli

25. Palazzo Strozzi
26. Palazzo Vecchio
27. Parco delle Cascine
28. Piazza della Republica
29. Piazza della Signoria
30. Piazzale Michelangelo
31. Ponte Vecchio
32. San Lorenzo
33. San Miniato al Monte
34. Santa Maria del Carmine
35. Santa Maria Novella
36. Santo Spirito
37. Vasari Corridor

HOTELS

38. B&B dei Mori
39. Fenice Palace
40. Grand Hotel Cavour
41. Hotel Berchielli
42. Hotel Botticelli
43. Hotel Brunelleschi
44. Hotel Calzaiuoli
45. Hotel Consigli
46. Hotel Croce di Malta
47. Hotel Il Guelfo Bianco
48. Hotel Lungarno
49. Hotel Morandi alla Crocetta
50. Hotel Palazzo Vecchio
51. Hotel Porta Rossa
52. Hotel Sanremo
53. Hotel Savoy

54. Il Porcellino
55. Relais Certosa
56. Residenza dei Pucci
57. Sofitel Firenze
58. Villa San Michele

NIGHTLIFE

59. Cabiria
60. Club Blob
61. JJ Cathedral Pub
62. Jazz Club
63. Tenax
64. Universale
65. The William

RESTAURANTS

66. Acqua al 2
67. Baccus
68. Beccofino
69. La Congrega
70. Enoteca Pinchiorri
71. Garga
72. Il Latini
73. Osteria de' Benci
74. Osteria Santo Spirito
75. Il Pizzaiuolo
76. Trattoria La Casalinga
77. Trattoria Za-Za

Only after Cosimo I (Medici) made it popular to live on the "other side of the river" did the Oltrarno area gain prominence. The attractions here, such as the **Pitti Palace** and the **Brancacci Chapel,** are few but outstanding and occupy a narrower crescent of land. The Oltrarno boundaries scoop down from Lungarno Soderini (an area known as San Frediano), to the Pitti Palace, and back around to the southern (left) bank of the Arno at **Ponte San Niccolo.**

Although Florence offers tourists the opportunity to gorge themselves on art and culture, the city is quite small. First-time tourists should have no trouble navigating the streets to the main sights (use the Duomo as your guide), and return visitors will find plenty of small museums, parks, and churches to keep them wanting more.

Touring Florence's Neighborhoods

As discussed, Florence is fairly compact, being made up of four traditional neighborhoods named after four landmark churches and/or church squares. From west to east, the districts are Santa Maria Novella, San Giovanni, Santa Croce, and across the river and to the south of all three is Santo Spirito/Oltrarno. Below, we have outlined each of the neighborhoods, starting first with San Giovanni, the heart of the city.

Now that you have that straightened out, it's time to throw you for a loop. Just to confuse you, dear tourists, Florence has a dual address system, whereby businesses and residences are numbered using a different sequence. A red number indicates a restaurant, club, or office, and a blue or black number indicates a residence. Adding to the mayhem is that an "r" after an address indicates that it is a business, and not a residence (*r* is for *rosso* [red], not *residence,* by the way). It pays to know this before you start your sight-seeing, otherwise you may walk up and down the same street for hours, looking for the wrong number.

San Giovanni (The Duomo and Environs)

Many of Florence's major attractions, including the **Duomo,** the **Campanile,** the **Baptistry,** the **Accademia,** and the **Medici Chapels,** are located in the city center. Traditionally, this central slice of the city is called San Giovanni after the Baptistry, which was dedicated to St. John the Baptist in the 11th century. The San Giovanni district starts with the area around the Duomo and extends north to the subneighborhoods of San Lorenzo and San Marco, which extend from the churches of the same name. Also located in this area is the **San Lorenzo flea market,** which is a magnet for tourists looking for good deals and pickpockets out for an easy steal, so watch out. San Lorenzo was the parish church of the Medici family, and they claimed this area as their own, building a handsome mansion in the neighborhood (**Palazzo Medici Riccardi**) and funding an enormous chapel to hold their tombs (**Medici Chapels**). The **Giardino dei Semplici,** a lush botanical garden now owned by the University of Florence, was also a Medici contribution. If your holiday in Florence lasts one day or one week, you'll never be too far from here. If you get lost, look to the Duomo's enormous cupola as a reference point.

Santa Croce and East of the Duomo

The **Palazzo Vecchio,** the **Uffizi Gallery,** and the **Ponte Vecchio,** though just a few blocks from the Duomo, are traditionally a part of the Santa Croce neighborhood. Traveling east from the Duomo neighborhood, you'll pass down the main streets here—Via Ghibellina, Via della Vigna Vecchia, and Via de' Neri—which filter down to the church of **Santa Croce,** the church that gives the district its name. Within the church you'll find the tombs of Michelangelo and Machiavelli, among others. On the way to the church, you can pay a visit to the **Bargello.** The northern edge of the Santa Croce quarter features lesser-known points of interest, including the **Museo di Firenze Com'era,** the **Synagogue,** and a leafy park in Piazza Massimo d'Azeglio. If you walk further east from the Uffizi Gallery and the bustling streets around Santa Croce's southwestern edge, you'll find fewer crowds and an easygoing atmosphere.

Santa Maria Novella and West of the Duomo

West of Via de' Tornabuoni, Florence's ritziest shopping avenue, you'll find the Santa Maria Novella neighborhood, which is defined by its thick traffic, business hotels, and a warren of streets lined with *trattorie* and discount clothing stores. If you're arriving by train, you must pass through this neighborhood, because the train station is located here. City buses and coaches are also a heavy presence. But despite the necessary evils of transit and tourism, the city west of the Duomo has one of the loveliest churches in the city in **Santa Maria Novella.** Closer to the Arno, the neighborhood redeems itself with a handful of historic sites, including the church of **Ognissanti** and the noble palaces of the **Corsini** and **Rucellai** families.

Santo Spirito/Oltrarno

The Oltrarno, the section of the city "beyond the Arno," has two personalities. Dominating the district is the **Palazzo Pitti** and the **Boboli Gardens,** the compound from which the Medici ruled Tuscany for 300 years. Nearby, in the Borgo San Jacopo along the Arno between the **Ponte Vecchio** and the **Ponte Santa Trinità,** is a stretch of upmarket hotels, overpriced boutiques, and five-star restaurants. Before the Medici moved into the neighborhood, the area on the south side of the Arno was home to Florence's artisans, laborers, and working-class families. Santo Spirito, the section of the Oltrarno that represents the neighborhood's other personality, is still filled with family-run workshops, modest old apartment blocks, and an interesting cross-section of artisans, students, antiques dealers, and musicians. The modest church of **Santa Maria del Carmine**—home of the **Brancacci Chapel,** which houses some of the most important Renaissance frescoes anywhere—lies in the western half of the Santo Spirito neighborhood.

Public Transportation

You may not need to use public transportation at all while you're in Florence, because the city is compact, and its main attractions are not far from one another. Although Florence is a walking city, you'll want to arm yourself with the basics so you have a backup when your feet start to ache. Take our word for it!

The Florence bus system, run by **ATAF** (Azienda Trasporti Area Fiorentina), covers an area of more than 200 miles, including the town of Fiesole and the immediate Florentine suburbs. The ATAF website, in Italian and English, details useful information routes and schedules. You can also pick up a free map of the ATAF system at the tourist office.

Overland bus service is available from Florence to points throughout Tuscany on **SITA** or **Lazzi Bus Lines.** Both of these companies have websites in Italian and English, and both arrive and depart near the Santa Maria Novella train station. More information about bus and train service is listed in the Tuscany section.

ATAF	800 424 500 (toll-free in Italy)	www.ataf.net
SITA	055 294 955	www.sita-on-line.it
Lazzi Bus Lines	055 363 041	www.lazzi.it

Buying and Using Tickets for Public Transportation

Have a ticket *(biglietto)* in hand before boarding a bus in Florence. You can buy one at tobacconists *(tabacchi)*, some newspaper stands, and from the kiosk outside of Santa Maria train station on Via Valfonda.

A single-use ticket costs €1 and is valid for one hour on any bus. You can also purchase a daily ticket (Biglietto Integrate Giornaliero, or BIG) for €4, or a weekly ticket (Carta Integrate Settimanale, or CIS) for €12. ATAF, Florence's bus authority, also issues a three-day ticket bus pass for €7.20, which we found to be extremely useful and economical.

Remember: you must validate *(convalidare)* your ticket on entry to the bus. For more information, see Part Three, Arriving, Getting Oriented, and Departing.

Buses

Your only public transportation option in Florence is the bus system. Run by ATAF (see above), local bus service is fairly dependable during the week, with a full schedule of in-town and suburban buses. The buses coming in from the Florentine suburbs can get quite full during the morning and afternoon rush hours. By contrast, in-town buses are less crowded; many city dwellers walk or hop on their Vespa. Buses run from approximately 5:30 a.m. until 9 p.m. at 10- to 30-minute intervals. Night buses (routes 67, 68, and 71) run from 9 p.m. to 1 a.m. Only the 70 is a true night bus *(autobus notturne)*, running from 12:30 until 6 a.m., making a circular loop between Santa Maria Novella Station and the Campo di Marte stadium. Night bus tickets cost twice as much (€2) as regular tickets, but you can buy a ticket on board if you have the right change. On the weekends, buses run less frequently.

Some of Florence's buses are fully equipped for disabled travelers, including routes 3, 7, 12, 13, 23, 30, 31, and 36. Look for gray or green buses. These buses have electric wheelchair platforms at the rear; it helps to bring a friend along for assistance. Route D is also fully equipped for wheelchair access.

If you decide to take the bus in Florence, it pays to know some of the most useful routes. Smaller and more energy-efficient electric buses A, B, C, and D travel through Florence proper:

Route A   Santa Maria Novella Station, Via Tornabuoni, Duomo, Orsanmichele, Santa Croce

Route B   Lungarno, Palazzo Vecchio, Uffizi Gallery

Route C   Piazza San Marco to Piazza Santa Croce

Route D   Santa Maria Novella Station, Oltrarno, Piazza del Carmine, Piazza Santo Spirito, Pitti Palace; Bus #7: Santa Maria Novella Station, Piazza San Marco, Fiesole; Buses #12 and #13: Santa Maria Novella to Piazzale Michelangelo

Taxis

There are a few taxi ranks in Florence, and they are indicated by a blue sign with "taxi" written in white letters. Piazza della Repubblica, Piazza del Duomo, Piazza San Marco, Piazza Santa Croce, Piazza Santa Maria Novella, and Piazza della Stazione all have taxi ranks; the latter two almost always will have cabs waiting. In case you can't find a taxi at the ranks, you will have to call or have your hotel concierge call. Remember that in Italy, your fare begins the moment that you *call* the taxi.

Florence Radio Taxi   055 4390, 055 4798, or 055 4242

Driving and Parking in Florence

Driving just a short distance around Florence will really test your sanity. Most streets in the city center are one-way or are pedestrian zones, making traffic a bear. In general, all cars, save for taxis, are prohibited from driving in town from the hours of 9 a.m. to 6 p.m. As a driver of a rental car, you are allowed to drive only if you are picking up or dropping off someone at your hotel. If Florence is the first stop on your trip, take our advice and wait until the day you leave to get your car. It will save you money and headaches. Information on renting a car in Florence can be found in Part Three, Arriving, Getting Oriented, and Departing.

If Florence is a stop between destinations, then you'll need to find parking. First, ask you hotel if it has parking or knows of a nearby parking garage. Many hotels have agreements with parking garages. Parking space is hard to come by in Florence, and some tourists make the mistake of parking in residential lots. To be on the safe side, park your ride in one of the municipal garages. Underground parking garages are located at the Santa Maria Novella train station and at Piazza della Libertà (the convergence of Viale Lavagnini and Viale Matteotti), due northeast from the church of San Marco.

Sight-seeing and Tours in Florence

Planning Visits of Three, Five, and Seven Days

The average stay for most travelers to Florence is less than a week and, more typically, three to five days. Undoubtedly, the sights in Florence could keep a visitor busy for years. But because Italy is chock full of so many things to see and do, Florence is often just a stop on a whirlwind Italian tour.

In the early 19th century, the French writer Stendhal spent a considerable amount of time sight-seeing in Florence and was so taken aback by the city's vast store of art that he came down with an affliction now widely known as Stendhalismo. This overexposure to art to the point of mental and physical exhaustion can get you, too, if you don't pace yourself. Bring your gait down to a relaxing stroll and don't let the buzzing crowds around you determine your itinerary. Take it easy, letting all five of your senses survey the charms of this central Italian mecca of art and culture.

You're not going to see everything, of course, but you should try to make it to these must-see attractions. These sites are profiled in detail later in this chapter.

Accademia   See Michelangelo's *David* and *Quattro Prigioni.* 15 to 30 minutes.

Baptistry   Examine the "Gates of Paradise." Pay to see the baptistry font and mosaics. 15 to 30 minutes.

Bargello   The place for Renaissance sculpture. 1 hour.

Boboli Gardens   Take a breather or take a hike. 1 hour.

Brancacci Chapel (Santa Maria del Carmine)   Get up close then step back and enjoy the rich colors of the newly cleaned chapel. 15 minutes.

Campanile   Climb to the top. 30 minutes to 1 hour.

Duomo   Step inside and gaze at the awesome dome. 15 to 30 minutes. Or, hike to the top. 1 hour.

Medici Chapels   Florence's first family is entombed here in grand fashion. 30 minutes.

Museo di San Marco   Fra Angelico's cloister frescoes are honestly moving. 1 hour.

Palazzo Pitti   Browse the Medici apartments, the Palatine Gallery, and the courtyard. 1 hour.

Palazzo Vecchio   Stare up at the building's belltower, then go inside for a glimpse of the elaborately decorated city hall. 1 hour.

Piazza della Signoria   The only sculpture gallery in Florence where you can enjoy warm breezes and a gelato. 15 minutes or more.

Ponte Vecchio   Walk across, browse the jewelry stalls, enjoy views of the river, and mind your wallet. 15 minutes.

Santa Croce   Pay your respects to Michelangelo, Galileo, and Dante, among others. 30 minutes.

Santa Maria Novella   Admire the candy-colored façade. Check out the ornate chapels. 30 minutes.

Uffizi Gallery   Don't miss the Giottos, Botticellis, and Da Vincis. Make a reservation for a small fee (call 055 264 406). Minimum 2 to 3 hours.

Vasari Corridor   Call ahead for a guided tour along Florence's most perfect perch, phone 055 294 883. 30 minutes.

Touring Florence in Three Days

Day 1

Head to the **Duomo, Baptistry,** and **Campanile** first, allowing yourself to get in step with the pace of city center Florence. Walk through Via Calzaiuoli and the shopping streets that radiate from the Duomo. Visit the Piazza della Signoria and the **Palazzo Vecchio.** Check out the **Ponte Vecchio.**

Day 2

Spend all morning at the **Uffizi.** Stretch your legs with a walk to **Santa Croce,** then back along the Arno. Bask in the afternoon sun at the **Boboli Gardens.** Then, get another dose of art at the **Brancacci Chapel.** Dine in Santo Spirito.

Day 3

Start with a morning tour of the cloisters of **San Marco.** Then gorge yourself on Michelangelo at the **Medici Chapels** and the **Accademia.** Shop in the San Lorenzo and grab a bite at the Mercato Centrale. Go to Piazzale Michelangelo or **San Miniato al Monte** for an unforgettable view of the Florentine cityscape.

Touring Florence in Five Days

Follow the first three days above, then:

Day 4

Take a day trip to **Fiesole** (no. 7 bus from Santa Maria Novella or Piazza San Marco, see profile under "Side Trips from Florence") and compare the view to the one seen the night before. Take the bus back down to the city and depart at **Santa Maria Novella.** Tour the church. Do some window shopping on Via de' Tornabuoni. Spend a night out on the town.

Day 5

Take a tour of the **Vasari Corridor** (entrance at the **Palazzo Vecchio**). Afterward, visit the museums of the Pitti Palace. Lunch in the Oltrarno and antiques shopping in **Santo Spirito.** Stroll along the Arno.

Touring Florence in Seven Days

Follow the three- and five-day itineraries above, then:

Day 6

Tour the **Bargello,** see the churches of **Badia Fiorentina** and **Orsan-michele,** have fun bargain shopping at the **Mercato Nuovo.** Grab dinner and drinks in the Centro.

Day 7

Morning walk to **Cascine Park,** with a stop at **Ognissanti.** Return to your favorite spots to say *"arrivederci."*

City Tours

If time is of the essence, you may want to spring for a guided tour of the city. Such a tour will take you around to the most popular sites—the Uffizi, the Accademia, and so on. Then, you will inevitably board a bus, which will whisk you off to Piazzale Michelangelo, where you can enjoy a sweeping view of the city below.

A few companies in the city offer a variety of standard tours of the city, depending on your interests. The **Association of Tuscan Guides** can arrange walking or bus tours of Florence and the Tuscan countryside. The **Cultural Association of Guides** offers a half-day strolling tour of Florence's major monuments and museums and a full-day walking/coach tour.

The **Florence tourist office** (Via A. Manzoni, 16; 50121 Florence; 055 23320, fax 055 2346286; **www.firenzeturismo.it**) has its own walking tour called the "Piazze di Firenze" (the Squares of Florence), which is a walking lesson of the city's architecture and cultural development. To learn more about Florence's rich artistic heritage, book a tour with **Walking Tours of Florence.** You can choose from standard tours or customize your own.

If you're the type who prefers not to shuffle around from street to street, you can stretch your legs with a bike tour of the city and beyond. **Florence by Bike** has a day-long bike tour past the gates of Florence to the Chianti countryside. Meanwhile, **I Bike Italy** has a more challenging tour to the hills of Fiesole. They also offer a two-day bike tour to Siena.

Association of Tuscan Guides 055 264 5217 www.florencetouristguides.com
Cultural Association of Guides 055 787 7744 www.firenze-guide.com

Florence by Bike	055 488 992	www.florencebybike.com
I Bike Italy	055 234 2371	www.ibikeitaly.com
Walking Tours of Florence	055 264 5033	www.artviva.com

Suggested Walking Itineraries for Florence

Tour 1: A Walk around Florence's City Center

Duration 1 hour

Difficulty Easy

After touring the **Duomo, Campanile,** and **Baptistry,** begin your walk at Piazza San Giovanni (the piazza between the Baptistry and the Duomo) and head south down Via dei Calzaiuoli, Florence's main drag. Browse the wares in the shoe stores, check out the high-end boutiques, or grab a gelato. On the right, you'll pass by **Orsanmichele,** a grain market turned Gothic church. Continue on Via dei Calzaiuoli, and you will come to the vast, open-air sculpture gallery that is the Piazza della Signoria. Spend some time here standing in the shadow of the great **Palazzo Vecchio** and browsing statues by Donatello, Giambologna, and Cellini. The tour goes on past the entrance to the Palazzo Vecchio (note: a copy of Michelangelo's *David* now stands where the original was) and through the courtyard of the **Uffizi** (Piazzale degli Uffizi). Even more statues— mostly of great Italian statesmen—are here to greet you. At the end of the courtyard, you'll see the banks of the Arno unfold in front of you. Turn right and continue along Lungarno degli Archibusieri toward the **Ponte Vecchio.** As you approach the Ponte Vecchio, resist the temptation to walk across—you can do that later. Instead, make a right up Via Por Santa Maria, then a left on Borgo Sant'Apostoli. This street, along with Via del Proconsolo, Via dei' Cerretani, and Via Tornabuoni, formed a section of Florence's first city walls, built in the 11th century. As you stroll along this street, glance down the alleys that radiate from here. On the left, an alley opens up to Piazza del Limbo, an eerily quiet square, named because it was once the site of a cemetery for unbaptized infants. Exit left from the piazza to the **Lungarno degli Acciaiuoli.** This is a good place to get out your camera and snap a few shots of the Ponte Vecchio. Walk in the opposite direction of the Ponte Vecchio toward the **Ponte Santa Trinità,** built to commemorate Florence's defeat of Siena and considered to be the most noble and elegant bridge in the city. Turn right to face the Piazza Santa Trinità, a busy square lined with *palazzi* and high-end boutiques. This square is the gateway to Via Tornabuoni, Florence's ritziest shopping street, full of expensive boutiques and even more Renaissance mansions. Make a right at the **Palazzo Strozzi,** the largest of the city's noble palaces, onto Via degli Strozzi, where you'll be able to spot the grand archway of the Piazza della Repubblica. This square occupies the site of an ancient Roman forum that was destroyed to make way for the city's food market. Later, in 1895, when Florence enjoyed a brief stint as the capital of Italy, the market here was torn down to build a triumphal arch. The tour ends at Piazza della Repubblica, where you can enjoy an aperitif or a cappuccino at one of the square's outdoor cafes.

Tour 2: A Walk to San Miniato and the Hills above Florence

Duration   2 hours

Difficulty   Moderate to hard (includes an uphill climb)

This tour starts at the **Ponte Vecchio** and goes south to the Oltrarno. Follow Via Guicciardini for approximately two blocks and turn left at the Piazza di Santa Felicità. Facing the church of the same name, take the steep road that forks to the right. As you hike up the street of Costa di San Giorgio, you'll leave behind the bustle of the city and enter into a real Florentine neighborhood. Galileo once lived in this neighborhood, and you can see the outside of his house at #19 (a plaque commemorates his residency). Crowning the lane is the **Porta San Giorgio,** Florence's oldest city gate. Already, from this vantage point, you can see the hills around Florence and the glint of olive groves. To the right of the gate is the **Forte di Belvedere** (currently closed for renovations), which has views over the Boboli Gardens and across to San Miniato. From the fortress, make a left down the hill of Via di Belvedere. Travel down the quiet country road for about half a mile, watching out for the occasional vehicle (cars will usually blow their horns before approaching a curve).

The second part of the ascent to San Miniato begins at Via del Monte alle Croci, a right turn off of Via di Belvedere. Once you've mounted this hill, make a right at Viale Galileo Galilei until you come face to face with the grand staircase of **San Miniato.** You'll have to cross the street here, so proceed at the crosswalk and watch out for cars. Climb the steps of San Miniato and turn around—a postcard view of Florence is your treat. The grounds around San Miniato are some of the most tranquil environs you'll find and, if you decide to take a look at the church, you may even be in time to hear monks doing traditional chants. Take a breather here. Once you've had time to take in the sights and (lack of) sounds, head west toward the church of **San Salvatore al Monte.** From here, you can return to Viale Galileo Galilei and follow the signs to Piazzale Michelangelo, again heading west. Here, you can get another eyeful of the city, then take the bus back into town. Tickets can be purchased from a vendor in the piazza.

Exploring Points of Interest

Where to Get the Best Views

Florence lies in a valley surrounded by lush green hills. It takes only minutes by bus and less than an hour by foot to hike to **Fiesole,** a town with such sweeping views of Florence that the Medici built their country home there. From just outside the gates of the Villa Medici (the home is not open to the public), you'll have no trouble spotting the city center, punctuated by the Palazzo Vecchio and the colossal dome of Santa Maria del Fiore, the Duomo. Equally beautiful panoramas of the city exist from the steps of the church of **San Miniato al Monte** and, just below, from **Piazzale Michelangelo,** and you can reach these perches by bus or by foot (see walking itineraries). Closer to home, the **Duomo** and the **Campanile** (belltower) on the Piazza del Duomo offer a chance to exercise your legs, for you must climb an exhausting number of stairs (463 for the Duomo and 414 for the Campanile) to reach viewing stations on top. Sorry, no elevators here. Finally, if you're lucky, you will have reserved a spot on a guided tour of the **Vasari Corridor.** This walkway, built so that the Medici didn't have to mingle with the commoners, extends from the family's home, the Pitti Palace, across the Ponte Vecchio, and further through the Uffizi and the Palazzo Vecchio. You'll find no finer views of the Arno and the swarming crowds below.

On the Trail of the Medici

Travel almost anywhere in central Italy, and you'll likely see churches, public buildings, and monuments adorned with a crest of six balls arranged in a circular pattern. This ubiquitous emblem is the Medici family's crest and is most evident in Florence, a city that experienced the height of its power during the Medici reign. From the time of Cosimo the Elder to Anna Maria Luisa, the last of the clan, the Medici stamp appeared on almost every municipal structure. The Medici coat-of-arms was even represented in the artworks that the family commissioned, usually in the branches of orange trees. For fun, meander about Florence and see how often you spot the Medici crest. Or check out these key sites (also see profiles below):

San Lorenzo   Parish church of the Medici

Medici Chapels   Tombs of the Medici family

Palazzo Pitti   Palatial Medici home on the Arno

Giardino Boboli   Miles of manicured gardens through which the Medici once strolled

Uffizi Gallery   The Medici art collection

Palazzo Vecchio   Palace of Grand Duke Cosimo I and Florentine seat of power

Piazza della Signoria   Main square of Florence and an outdoor gallery of statues commissioned by Cosimo I, including Michelangelo's *David*

Taking Classes in Florence

Since the days of the Grand Tour, Florence has been a magnet for hordes of English-speaking travelers wishing to learn more about Italy's culture and language. Even Mark Twain, who ceaselessly complained about the inconsistencies of Italian in his travel guide *The Innocents Abroad,* felt the need to try out some Italian vocabulary in a speech he gave to Florentines in 1904.

There are several dozen schools in Florence that offer language, culture, and history courses to foreigners. Classes usually last from two weeks to one month and can be quite expensive, starting from €200 up to as much as €600, not including accommodations. Cooking and art courses range from one-day sessions to semester-long intensive study. These classes are very popular in Florence and, therefore, tend to cost a pretty penny. Expect to pay approximately €150 per person for a one-day course, and up to €1,000 for a semester spent learning cooking or art techniques.

Language Classes

Centro Lorenzo de' Medici   Via Faenza, 43; 50122 Florence; phone 055 287 360, fax 055 239 8920; **www.lorenzodemedici.it**

Centro Linguistico Italiano   Dante Alighieri Piazza della Repubblica, 5; 50123 Florence; phone 055 210 808, fax 055 287 828; **www.clidante.com**

Scuola Leonardo da Vinci   Via Bufalini, 3; 50122 Florence; phone 055 294 420, fax 055 294 820; **www.scuolaleonardo.com**

Art Classes

Charles H. Cecil Studios   Borgo San Frediano, 68; 50121 Florence, phone/fax 055 285 102; **www.ritratto.com.** Techniques of classical drawing and painting, plus life-drawing classes.

L'Istituto per L'Arte e Il Restauro   (Palazzo Spinelli), Borgo Santa Croce, 10; 50125 Florence; phone 055 246 001, 055 246 0094; **www.spinelli.it.** Classes in drawing, gilding, restoration, and more.

Oro e Colore   Via della Chiesa, 25; 50121 Florence; phone/fax 055 229 040; **www.oroecolore.com.** Extended study course on art and restoration, taught in Italian only.

Cooking and Wine

Divina Cucina   Via Taddea, 31; 50122 Florence; phone 055 292 578; **www.divinacucina.com.** Food-lover's walking tour and time in the kitchen with Florence-based American chef Judy Witts.

Enoteca de' Giraldi   Via de' Giraldi, 4; 50125 Florence; phone 055 216 518; **www.vinaio.com.** Wine tastings and cooking classes.

La Cucina del Garga   Via del Moro, 48r; 50123 Florence; phone 055 211 396; **www.garga.it.** One-day cooking classes and instruction on wine selection.

Getting Tickets and Passes

As far as tourist destinations go, Florence *is* the beaten track. So don't wait until the day of to purchase your tickets to the Uffizi Gallery, one of the most famous collections in the world. On any given day, the line to get tickets to the museum snakes out the door, through the courtyard, and, often, all the way out along the Arno. If you're traveling during high season, you could likely spend your entire day waiting in line, only to walk away empty-handed. **If you'd prefer not to play it by ear, call 055 294 883.** The English-speaking operators at this special booking service will reserve timed tickets for you for an extra €2 on top of the admission price. You can also use this service for tickets to the Accademia, the Medici Chapels, and the Bargello. Only telephone bookings are accepted.

Florence Attraction Profiles

Within Florence's compact city center is an overwhelming array of museums, churches, monuments, and piazzas. Below we profile some of the city's best, as well as some of our favorites.

FLORENCE ATTRACTIONS		
Attraction	Author's Rating	Comments
Accademia (The Academy)	★★★★	Home of Michelangelo's *David*
Badia Fiorentina	★★	Medieval monastery and church
Baptistry	★★★★★	"Gates of Paradise" and medieval mosaics
Bargello	★★★★	Premier sculpture museum
Campanile	★★★★★	Giotto-designed belltower
Casa Buonarroti	★★★	Michelangelo home
Casa di Dante	★	Dante home
Cimitero degli Inglesi (English Cemetery)	★★	Graves of expat Brits and Protestants
Duomo (Santa Maria del Fiore)	★★★★★	Florence's main cathedral
Giardino Boboli	★★★★	Medici Gardens at Palazzo Pitti
Giardino dei Semplici	★★	Botanical gardens
Medici Chapels	★★★½	Tombs of the Medici family
Museo Archeologica	★★	Ancient art and artifacts
Museo dell'Opera del Duomo	★★★★	Art from Duomo and Battistero
Museo di Storia della Scienza	★★★	Early science exhibits
Museo di Firenze Com'era	★★★	Pictorial timeline of Florence's development
Museo Mario Marini	★★½	Marini abstract art
Museo Salvatore Ferragamo	★★★	Fashionable art
Museo di San Marco	★★★★★	Fra Angelico frescoes
Museo Stibbert	★★½	Antique armor and weapons
Ognissanti	★★★	Ghirlandaio fresco

FLORENCE ATTRACTIONS (continued)

Attraction	Author's Rating	Comments
Opificio delle Pietre Dure	★★½	Premier art conservation institute
Orsanmichele	★★★	Gothic church
Palazzo Pitti	★★★½	Medici palace and galleries
Palazzo Strozzi	★★	Largest palace in Florence
Palazzo Vecchio	★★★½	Town hall and belltower
Parco delle Cascine	★★★	Florence's largest park
Piazza della Repubblica	★★★½	Café-lined square
Piazza della Signoria	★★★★★	Italy's most attractive square
Piazzale Michelangelo	★★★★	Excellent city views
Ponte Vecchio	★★★★½	Popular tourist stop and jewelry market
San Lorenzo	★★	Medici church
San Miniato al Monte	★★★★	Tranquil Romanesque church
Santa Maria del Carmine	★★★★★	Early Renaissance frescoes
Santa Maria Novella	★★★★	Gothic church with frescoes
Santo Spirito	★★	Church with ornate chapels
Uffizi Gallery	★★★★★	Huge Renaissance art collection
Vasari Corridor	★★★★★	Private walkway of the Medici

Accademia (The Academy)

Type of Attraction Home of Michelangelo's *David*

Location Via Ricasoli, 58-60 (San Giovanni)

Admission €8.50

Hours Tuesday–Sunday, 8:15 a.m.–6:50 p.m.; extended hours on Easter (10 p.m.) and May 1 (8 p.m.)

Phone 055 238 8609

When to Go Late-evening visits mean fewer tourists, especially around dinner

Overall Appeal by Age Group

Pre-school ★		Teens ★★★★		Over 30 ★★★★
Grade school ★★★		Young Adults ★★★★		Seniors ★★★★

Author's Rating ★★★★

How Much Time to Allow 30 minutes

Description and Comments What you're paying for when you visit the Accademia is a chance to gawk at one of Michelangelo's pre-eminent works, *David*. Carved from one giant slab of marble, this famous statue once stood in the Piazza della Signoria, a symbol of confrontation to Medici detractors. In 1873, the city decided to move the statue here to prevent it from suffering further water damage and pollution; but *David* hadn't been washed since he arrived. However, in late 2002, conservators at the Accademia began the arduous and delicate task of cleaning the landmark. (Luckily, the restoration, which should last several years, will take place after hours.) In addition to *David,* the Accademia houses Michelangelo's four unfinished Prisoners *(Prigioni)* or Slaves, which were to decorate the tomb of Pope Julius II, as well as works by Andrea Orcagna, Giambologna, and Andrea del Sarto. Upstairs in the Accademia is a collection of art from the 13th and 14th centuries.

Other Things to Do Nearby Visit the beautifully frescoed Museo di San Marco.

Badia Fiorentina

Type of Attraction Medieval monastery and church

Location Via del Proconsolo and Via Dante Alighieri (San Giovanni)

Admission Donation expected

Hours Monday–Friday, 4:30–6:30 p.m., Sunday, 10:30–11:30 a.m.

Phone 055 234 4545

When to Go Sunday mornings are the most crowded, but offer the best light

Overall Appeal by Age Group

Pre-school —		Teens ★		Over 30 ★★
Grade school ★		Young Adults ★★		Seniors ★★

Author's Rating ★★

How Much Time to Allow 15 to 30 minutes

Description and Comments Founded in 978, this Benedictine abbey is one of the oldest houses of worship in Florence. It was here that Dante purportedly set eyes on the love of his life, Beatrice Portinari, in 1274, and where, years later, Boccaccio staged the first reading of Alighieri's *Divine Comedy.* Take note of Vasari's altarpiece, painted in 1568 to replace one by Giotto (which was moved to the Uffizi) and Filippino Lippi's *Madonna Appearing to St. Bernard,* to the right of the exit.

Other Things to Do Nearby The Bargello is directly across the street.

Baptistry

Type of Attraction Octagonal baptistry famous for its doors

Location Piazza San Giovanni (San Giovanni)

Admission €2

Hours Monday–Saturday, noon–7 p.m., Sunday, 8:30 a.m.–2 p.m.

Phone 055 230 2885

When to Go For best light, go in morning; for lighter crowds, try the late afternoon

Overall Appeal by Age Group

Pre-school ★★★		Teens ★★★★★		Over 30 ★★★★★
Grade school ★★★★★		Young Adults ★★★★★		Seniors ★★★★★

Author's Rating ★★★★★
How Much Time to Allow 30 minutes

Description and Comments Dating back to the fourth century, the Baptistry is in some ways more important than the Duomo, which dwarfs it. Florence's most famous poet, Dante, was baptized here; the building's ceiling impresses with a menacing 13th-century mosaic of the Last Judgment; and the floor is inlaid with signs of the zodiac. However, the Baptistry's doors garner the most attention. The original doors were of wood. But after Andrea Pisano crafted a new set of bronze doors consisting of scenes from the life of John the Baptist, the merchants' guild, known as the Calimala, decided to hold a design competition to replace the east doors, known as the Gates of Paradise because they faced the cathedral. In the final round, the Calimala chose Lorenzo Ghiberti, son of a goldsmith, and architect Filippo Brunelleschi as finalists. Some say that Brunelleschi bowed out of the competition after seeing Ghiberti's impressive entry, and others claim that the accomplished architect refused to work in tandem with Ghiberti. Nevertheless, Ghiberti won and, in 1403, was given the contract to create scenes of the life of Christ in 28 gilded relief panels. The elaborate east doors, considered by some as the first works of the Renaissance, were finally hung in 1424, prompting the Calimala to commission Ghiberti to design doors for the Baptistry's north entrance. Ghiberti completed the north doors, depicting scenes from the Old Testament, in about nine years. Immediately on seeing this new set of doors, the Calimala decided to place them at the east entrance, and move Ghiberti's first set to the north entrance. This was a monumental decision because it was a departure from the belief that only scenes from the New Testament could be displayed on the Gates of Paradise. Today, all of the Baptistry's original doors reside in the Museo dell'Opera del Duomo.

Touring Tips Visit the Museo dell'Opera del Duomo to see Ghiberti's original panels

Other Things to Do Nearby Climb to the top of the Campanile or visit the Duomo.

Bargello

Type of Attraction Premier museum of sculpture
Location Via del Proconsolo, 4 (Santa Croce)
Admission €4
Hours Daily, 8:15 a.m.–1:50 p.m. Closed every 2nd and 4th Monday, the 1st, 3rd and 5th Sunday of each month, and public holidays
Phone 055 238 8606
When to Go Afternoon
Overall Appeal by Age Group

Pre-school —	Teens ★★	Over 30 ★★★★
Grade school ★★	Young Adults ★★★	Seniors ★★★★

Author's Rating ★★★★
How Much Time to Allow 2 hours

Description and Comments Easily one of the world's top sculpture museums, the Bargello houses a stunning collection of Renaissance statues by Michelangelo, Donatello, Cellini, and Leonardo mentor Verrocchio, among others. Built around 1250, the Bargello was the city's original town hall, or the Palazzo del Popolo. Later, it became a prison and its courtyard was used as a site of multiple executions, mostly of Medici enemies. In the 16th century, the Medici chose the heavily fortified palazzo as the headquarters of the chief of police, or the "Bargello." In 1865, the building was transformed into one of Italy's first museums. Works of note in the Bargello include Michelangelo's tipsy *Bacchus,* Giambologna's *Mercury* (you may recognize it if you've ever ordered flowers), Verrocchio's *Lady with a Posy* bust, and Donatello's *David,* one of the first nude sculptures of the Renaissance. Near Donatello's works on the second floor are the original panels submitted by Filippo Brunelleschi and Lorenzo Ghiberti for the 1401 Baptistry doors competition.

Other Things to Do Nearby Check out Florence's oldest church, the Badia Fiorentina, or the Casa di Dante, a museum dedicated to the life of the poet Dante Alighieri.

Campanile (Giotto's Belltower)

Type of Attraction Belltower designed by Giotto
Location Piazza del Duomo (San Giovanni)
Admission €6
Hours Daily, 8:30 a.m.–7:30 p.m.
Phone 055 230 2885
When to Go Early morning or late afternoon
Overall Appeal by Age Group

Pre-school ★★		Teens ★★★★★		Over 30 ★★★★★
Grade school ★★★★★		Young Adults ★★★★★		Seniors ★★★

Author's Rating ★★★★★
How Much Time to Allow 1 hour

Description and Comments Resembling an elegant Roman candle, Giotto's 276-foot campanile (belltower) features a facade of white, green, and pink marble from Carrara, Prato, and Siena, respectively. Though Giotto designed the belltower, he only worked on it for three years, from 1334 until his death in 1337. Taking over the reigns was Andrea Pisano, whose octagonal terra cotta reliefs decorate the lower stories. Pisano also added a series of niches on the second story, which display statues of various prophets and sybils, including Abacuc, affectionately known as *lo zuccone* (pumpkinhead) because of his bald dome. Following Pisano was Francesco Talenti, who accepted the belltower project in 1348, eventually adding the last three stories, including the tower's Gothic windows and the terrace. The belltower was completed in 1359. Climb the Campanile's 412 steps to the terrace to enjoy a bird's-eye view of the cathedral.

Touring Tips The terra cotta reliefs and niche statues are copies. The originals are in the Museo dell'Opera del Duomo.

Other Things to Do Nearby Inspect the Baptistry doors.

Casa Buonarroti

Type of Attraction Former home of Michelangelo
Location Via Ghibellina, 70 (Santa Croce)
Admission €6.50
Hours Wednesday–Monday, 9:30 a.m.–4 p.m.
Phone 055 241 752
When to Go Anytime
Overall Appeal by Age Group

Pre-school —		Teens ★★		Over 30 ★★★
Grade school ★★		Young Adults ★★		Seniors ★★★

Author's Rating ★★★
How Much Time to Allow 30 minutes

Description and Comments The Uffizi Gallery, Accademia, Medici Chapels, and St. Peter's Basilica have the lion's share of Michelangelo's sculpture and paintings. But this small group of three houses where Buonarroti once lived houses a few visit-worthy works. The Madonna della Scala is one standout–it is so subtly crafted it appears to be wrought of creamy white chocolate. There are also a number of sketches, personal effects, and unfinished works.

Other Things to Do Nearby See Michelangelo's tomb in Santa Croce.

Casa di Dante

Type of Attraction Poet's childhood home
Location Via Santa Margherita, 1
Admission €6.50
Hours Summer: Wednesday–Saturday and Monday, 10 a.m.–6 p.m.; Sunday, 10 a.m.–2 p.m.; Winter: Wednesday–Saturday and Monday, 10 a.m.–4 p.m., Sunday, 10 a.m.–2 p.m.
Phone 055 219 416
When to Go When it's not crowded
Overall Appeal by Age Group

Pre-school —		Teens ★		Over 30 ★
Grade school ★		Young Adults ★		Seniors ★★

Author's Rating ★
How Much Time to Allow 30 minutes

Description and Comments This is most probably not the childhood residence of Dante, but scholars are certain that the Florentine poet lived in this neighborhood. Instead, this foreboding-looking house was originally a 13th-century tower that was restored at the beginning of the 20th century. A museum devoted to Dante's life and works takes up the second floor of the building, and the downstairs features temporary modern art exhibits and a small museum gift shop. Only serious fans of Dante will get a kick out of seeing vintage printings of his *Divine Comedy.* But even then, they'll be disappointed with the fact that this museum is a mere novelty.

Other Things to Do Nearby Around the corner from Dante's "house" is the small church of Santa Margherita de' Cerchi (in Via Santa Margherita), the actual church where Dante first laid eyes on Beatrice.

Cimitero degli Inglesi (English Cemetery)

Type of Attraction Resting place of expat Brits and Protestants

Location Piazzale Donatello, 38 (Santa Croce)

Admission Donation expected

Hours Monday, 8 a.m.–noon; Tuesday–Friday, noon–sunset

Phone 055 582 608

When to Go Anytime

Overall Appeal by Age Group

Pre-school —		Teens ★★		Over 30 ★★
Grade school —		Young Adults ★★		Seniors ★★

Author's Rating ★★

How Much Time to Allow I hour

Description and Comments Only ardent fans of Elizabeth Barrett Browning take the pilgrimage to this pretty, leafy cemetery. This writer was interred here, as well as many Britons who called Florence home. You'll find a fairly tranquil oasis here at Porta a Pinti (the other name for this cemetery), but good luck crossing the traffic circle that envelops it.

Duomo

Type of Attraction The icon of Florence

Location Piazza del Duomo (San Giovanni)

Admission Church: free; Dome: €5; Crypt of Santa Reparata: €2.50

Hours Church: Monday–Friday, 10 a.m.–5 p.m.; Saturday, 10 a.m.–4:45 p.m.; Sunday, 1:30 p.m.–4:45 p.m.; Dome: Monday–Friday, 8:30 a.m.–7 p.m.; Saturday, 8:30 a.m.–5:40 p.m.; Crypt of Santa Reparata: Monday–Friday, 10 a.m.–5 p.m.

Phone 055 230 2885

When to Go Early morning or after lunch

Overall Appeal by Age Group

Pre-school ★★★		Teens ★★★		Over 30 ★★★★★
Grade school ★★★		Young Adults ★★★★		Seniors ★★★★★

Author's Rating ★★★★★

How Much Time to Allow 1 hour

Description and Comments Florence's main cathedral, Santa Maria del Fiore, known as the Duomo, is the fourth-largest church in Europe. Work on the cathedral began in 1296 with the demolition of the fourth-century Santa Reparata church, ruins of which can still be seen in the basement. Arnolfo di Cambio drew up the blueprints for the Duomo but did not see the church finished, as it took some 150 years to build. Filippo Brunelleschi designed the church's massive cupola, which was one of the greatest engineering feats ever accomplished—as well as the largest dome in the world—at the time. The exterior of Santa Maria del Fiore repeats the same ornate design as Giotto's belltower, with bands of white, pink, and green marble, but, truth be told, the church's neo-Gothic façade was added only in the late 1800s. Inside, the Duomo is an enormous, empty shell, with a sparse number of artworks. However, there are frescoes by Vasari and Zuccari, and gorgeous stained-glass windows by Lorenzo Ghiberti, Paolo Uccello, and Andrea del Castagno. Brunelleschi is entombed in the basement near the ruins of Santa Reparata and the church gift shop.

Touring Tips If you have a fear of heights, then a climb to the top of the dome is not recommended.

Other Things to Do Nearby Tour the Baptistry or the Campanile.

Giardino Boboli

Type of Attraction The Medici Gardens at Palazzo Pitti
Location Piazza Pitti (Oltrarno)
Admission €2
Hours June–August: daily, 9 a.m.–7:30 p.m.; April, May, September: daily, 9 a.m.–6:30 p.m.; March and October, daily 9 a.m.–5:30 p.m.; November–February, daily, 9 a.m.–4:30 p.m.; closed first and last Monday of the month
Phone 055 265 1816
When to Go Splendid anytime the sun is shining
Overall Appeal by Age Group

Pre-school ★★★★		Teens ★★★★		Over 30 ★★★★
Grade school ★★★★		Young Adults ★★★★		Seniors ★★★★

Author's Rating ★★★★
How Much Time to Allow 1 to 2 hours

Description and Comments The Boboli Gardens are the best thing about the Medici estate at Palazzo Pitti. The Renaissance-style landscaping here combines greenery with fountains, statues, and grottoes to a marvelous effect. As soon as you get past the entrance of the Boboli, which is separate from the main entrance of the Pitti museums, you'll find broad avenues of cypress trees interspersed with statues, an elegant stone amphitheater, and acres of lawns to laze on. There's even a little island (L'Isolotto) whose design includes a copy of a Giambologna's Mercury fountain (the original is in the Bargello), a wide porch, decorative columns, and a geometric grouping of shrubbery and lemon trees. There are even large goldfish in the pond. Picnics and lounging on the grass are frowned upon here—one of the reasons this author gave the gardens only four stars. But, the grounds are so extensive, you can likely steal a few restful moments anyhow.

Other Things to Do Nearby The other delights of the Palazzo Pitti.

Giardino dei Semplici

Type of Attraction Botanical gardens
Location Via Micheli, 3 (San Giovanni)
Admission Free
Hours Monday–Friday and Sunday, 9 a.m.–1 p.m.; closed public holidays, 1 week in August, and during Christmas holiday
Phone 055 275 7402
When to Go Not crowded
Overall Appeal by Age Group

Pre-school ★★		Teens ★★		Over 30 ★★
Grade school ★★		Young Adults ★★		Seniors ★★

Author's Rating ★★

Description and Comments This garden was set up for the Medici in 1545 to grow medicinal herbs. The name Semplici means "basics," or rather the raw ingredients that were necessary for preparing remedies. Medicinal herbs are still grown here, along with indigenous and tropical flora. The University of Florence is responsible for tending these gardens.

Other Things to Do Nearby Visit the cloisters of San Marco.

Medici Chapels (Cappelle Medicee)

Type of Attraction Tombs of the Medici family, a few designed by Michelangelo
Location Piazza di Madonna degli Aldobrandini (San Giovanni)
Admission €6
Hours Daily, 8:15 a.m.–5 p.m.; closed 2nd and 4th Sunday and 1st, 3rd, and 5th Monday of each month
Phone 055 238 8602
When to Go Late morning or after lunch
Overall Appeal by Age Group

Pre-school —		Teens ★★★		Over 30 ★★★★
Grade school ★★		Young Adults ★★★		Seniors ★★★★

Author's Rating ★★★½
How Much Time to Allow 30 minutes

Description and Comments In 1519, Michelangelo began designing this mausoleum for the Medici and would eventually create a few of the tombs found within it. The main room of the Medici Chapels is the Cappella dei Principi (Princes Chapel), where six of the Medici grand dukes rest, including Cosimo I and Giovanni delle Bande Nere. This round room was modeled after Florence's Baptistry and decorated with enormous slabs of polychrome marble. Work on the Princes Chapel lasted for more than three centuries, finally ending in 1962. Adjoining this chapel is the Sagrestia Nuova, where you'll find the tombs of Lorenzo the Magnificent, his brother Giuliano, and their cousins Lorenzo, duke of Urbino, and Giuliano, duke of Nemours. Lorenzo's tomb, which features the allegorical figures of Dawn, Dusk, Night, and Day, is considered to be among the best of Michelangelo's works.

Other Things to Do Nearby Browse the San Lorenzo market for bargains.

Museo Archeologica

Type of Attraction Ancient Etruscan, Egyptian, and Greek art and artifacts

Location Via della Colonna, 36 (San Giovanni)

Admission €4

Hours Monday, 2–7 p.m.; Tuesday and Thursday, 8:30 a.m.–7 p.m.; Wednesday, Friday–Sunday, and public holidays, 8:30 a.m.–2 p.m.

Phone 055 23 575

When to Go Anytime

Overall Appeal by Age Group

Pre-school ★★	Teens ★★★	Over 30 ★★
Grade school ★★★	Young Adults ★★	Seniors ★★

Author's Rating ★★

How Much Time to Allow I hour

Description and Comments One of the few museums in the city that strays from the Renaissance, the Archaeological Museum houses collections of Etruscan, Greek, and Egyptian art, relics, and crafts. The exhibit of Etruscan bronzes is worth a look, especially the fourth-century B.C. Chimera, a fierce-looking lion with a goat's head and a serpentine tail. The Egyptian collection contains decorative tombs, complete with mummies, and a bone and wood chariot dating from the 15th century B.C.

Other Things to Do Nearby Take a break in the peaceful Piazza della Santissima Annunziata.

Museo dell'Opera del Duomo

Type of Attraction Some masterpieces from Florence's Duomo and Baptistry

Location Piazza del Duomo, 9 (San Giovanni)

Admission €6

Hours Monday–Saturday, 9 a.m.–7:30 p.m.; Sunday, 9 a.m.–1:30 p.m.

Phone 055 230 2885

When to Go Early morning

Overall Appeal by Age Group

Pre-school ★★		Teens ★★★		Over 30 ★★★★
Grade school ★★		Young Adults ★★★★		Seniors ★★★★

Author's Rating ★★★★

How Much Time to Allow 30 minutes

Description and Comments Quite a few original pieces from Florence's Duomo complex (Santa Maria del Fiore, Campanile, and the Baptistry) were moved to this museum so that they could be in a controlled environment, free from everyday wear and tear. Among the artworks here are Ghiberti's Baptistry doors and a series of panels designed by Andrea Pisano and Luca della Robbia for the Campanile. You'll also see a number of statues that formerly occupied niches in the Duomo, including Donatello's *San Giovanni* and a *Pietà* by Michelangelo (this one features Nicodemus, probably modeled after the artist himself). The museum, which recently reopened after extensive renovations, also houses original plans of the Duomo and tools from Brunelleschi's studio.

Museo di Storia della Scienza

Type of Attraction Antique scientific devices used by early scientists, including Galileo

Location Piazza dei Giudici, I (Santa Croce)

Admission €6.50

Hours Monday and Wednesday–Saturday, 9:30 a.m.–5 p.m.; Tuesday, 9:30a.m.–I p.m.; closed Sunday

Phone 055 265 311

When to Go Anytime—this museum is rarely crowded

Overall Appeal by Age Group

Pre-school ★★		Teens ★★★		Over 30 ★★★
Grade school ★★★		Young Adults ★★★		Seniors ★★★

Author's Rating ★★★

How Much Time to Allow 30 minutes to an hour

Description and Comments The Renaissance was not just about painting and sculpture but also about advancements in science. Galileo, a scientist who benefited from the patronage of the Medici family, is well represented here, and you'll find two rooms devoted to his experiments and scientific devices, including his leather-bound telescope. A gruesome reliquary of Galileo's middle finger is also on display here, perhaps as a gesture to the detractors who persecuted him for refuting that the earth was the center of the universe. (By the way, the rest of his body is entombed in Santa Croce.) In the rest of the museum, you'll find globes and maps from the Renaissance era, nautical instruments, and early inventions.

Other Things to Do Nearby Visit Galileo's tomb in Santa Croce.

Museo di Firenze Com'era

Type of Attraction A pictorial timeline of Florence's development

Location Via dell'Oriuolo, 24 (San Giovanni)

Admission €2.60

Hours Friday–Wednesday, 9 a.m.–2 p.m.

Phone 055 261 6545

When to Go Sunday and Monday

Overall Appeal by Age Group

Pre-school —		Teens ★★		Over 30 ★★★
Grade school ★		Young Adults ★★★		Seniors ★★★

Author's Rating ★★★

How Much Time to Allow 1 hour

Description and Comments Through old maps, architectural plans, paintings, and small-scale models, the Museum of Florence "as it was" shows how the city grew from an outpost for Roman soldiers into a richly planned city of art and wealth. One engraved wood map called the Pianta della Catena, rimmed with a chain-like border, is a 19th-century copy of a map drawn up in 1470, when Florence was the hotbed of Renaissance activity. Lunettes of the Palazzo Pitti and other Medici villas painted by Giusto Utens in 1599 are among the most popular works on display.

Other Things to Do Nearby The museum is just down the block from the Duomo complex.

Museo Mario Marini

Type of Attraction Comprehensive collection of Marini's abstract art

Location Piazza San Pancrazio (Santa Maria Novella)

Admission €5

Hours Monday and Wednesday–Saturday, 10 a.m.–5 p.m.; Sunday, 10 a.m.–1 p.m.; June–September: open until 11 p.m. on Thursdays

Phone 055 219 432

When to Go An ideal choice for Mondays, when other museums are closed

Overall Appeal by Age Group

Pre-school ★★		Teens ★★		Over 30 ★★
Grade school ★★★		Young Adults ★★		Seniors ★

Author's Rating ★★½

How Much Time to Allow 1 to 1.5 hours

Description and Comments Young children may get more out of this museum than their parents, simply because Mario Marini's abstract art leaves much to the imagination. Marini is well known for his impressive bronze sculptures of horses and their riders, and the exhibit of multiple equine artworks will likely amaze grade schoolers and modern art buffs.

On another note, the museum is housed in the former church of San Pancrazio, one of Florence's oldest houses of worship. Visitors can see evidence of the ninth-century church and its Renaissance-era updates, including the Cappella di San Sepolcro, built in 1467 by Leon Battista Alberti to hold the tomb of Florentine merchant Giovanni Rucellai.

Other Things to Do Nearby Window shop on Via de' Tornabuoni.

Museo Salvatore Ferragamo

Type of Attraction Art for fashion fiends
Location Via Tornabuoni, 2 (Santa Maria Novella)
Admission Free
Hours Monday–Friday, 9 a.m.–1 p.m., 2–6 p.m.
Phone 055 336 0456
When to Go Anytime
Overall Appeal by Age Group

Pre-school ★		Teens ★★★★		Over 30 ★★★
Grade school ★★		Young Adults ★★★		Seniors ★★

Author's Rating ★★★
How Much Time to Allow 30 minutes

Description and Comments As if Florence didn't already have enough footwear temptation, the Museo Salvatore Ferragamo displays hundreds of shoes and boots—some practical, some definitely not—from the Ferragamo archive. Ferragamo got his start in Hollywood creating shoes for various films, including Cecil B. DeMille's *Cleopatra,* and later returned to Italy to set up shop in Florence. The designer died in 1960, leaving his business to his children. Today, Ferragamo is a favorite brand among the well-heeled, as well as one of the most desired Florentine souvenirs.

Other Things to Do Nearby After the museum, pop down to the Ferragamo store.

Museo di San Marco

Type of Attraction The former convent contains rich frescoes by Fra Angelico
Location Piazza San Marco, 1 (San Giovanni)
Admission €4
Hours Monday–Friday, 8:15 a.m.–1:50 p.m.; Saturday, 8:15 a.m.–6:50 p.m.; Sunday, 8:15 a.m.–7 p.m.; closed 2nd and 4th Monday and 1st, 3rd, and 5th Sunday of the month
Phone 055 238 8608
When to Go Weekdays and Sunday, early morning; Saturday, after lunch
Overall Appeal by Age Group

Pre-school ★★★		Teens ★★★		Over 30 ★★★★
Grade school ★★★		Young Adults ★★★		Seniors ★★★★★

Author's Rating ★★★★★

How Much Time to Allow I hour

Description and Comments Both the temperamental friar Savonarola and the saintly Fra Angelico lived in the dorm-like cells of the San Marco monastery, known today as the Museo di San Marco. In 1437, the Dominican order from Fiesole moved to this church at the invitation of Cosimo il Vecchio. Here on the walls and in the cells of the convent is where Fra Angelico created some of his most enlightened works. One of the friar/artist's most famous frescoes, the *Annunciation,* is the first you'll see on the first floor. To this day, this fresco remains humbly on the original spot where Angelico painted it. In cells 2 and 7 are his *Entombment* and *The Mocking of Christ,* featuring a blindfolded Christ surrounded by surreal images of a spitting face and bodiless hands. Rooms 12 through 14 contain the personal effects and a portrait of the religious tyrant Savonarola. As for the fate of the monastery's two most renowned residents? The pious Fra Angelico came to be known as *Beato* (beatific) Angelico to Italians and was buried in Rome. Savonarola, on the other hand, was burned at the stake in the Piazza della Signoria in 1498, a result of his unpopular fundamentalism.

Other Things to Do Nearby See more of Angelico's works in the adjacent San Marco church, or make a pilgrimage to Fiesole, specifically to the church of San Domenico.

Museo Stibbert

Type of Attraction Collection of antique armor, weaponry, sundry art and trinkets

Location Via Federico Stibbert, 26 (Outside the City Gates)

Admission €5

Hours Monday–Wednesday, 10 a.m.–2 p.m.; Friday–Sunday and public holidays, 10 a.m.–6 p.m.; closed Thursday and August 15

Phone 055 486 049

When to Go Anytime; the garden is nice on hot summer days

Overall Appeal by Age Group

Pre-school ★★		Teens ★★★		Over 30 ★★★
Grade school ★★★		Young Adults ★★★		Seniors ★★★

Author's Rating ★★½

How Much Time to Allow 1.5 to 2 hours

Description and Comments A Briton born in Florence in 1838, Frederick Stibbert was a military man who headed up campaigns to India and fought with the Garibaldini (soldiers loyal to Garibaldi) in 1866. In 1859, Stibbert inherited a large sum of money, with which he bought scores of art, antiques, and military effects from around the globe. One of the main features of the museum is Stibbert's collection of mounted soldiers, which he collected from Europe and the Islamic world. The Sala della Cavalcata (Room of the Cavalcade) has a number of life-sized armored cavalrymen atop well-dressed horses—a startling sight. Other military-inspired items include arms, armor, weapons, and costumes from Europe and as far abroad as Japan. The Museo Stibbert also boasts a lovely exhibit of tapestries from the 14th through the 19th centuries.

Touring Tips Guided tours in English and Italian are available every hour on the hour.

Ognissanti

Type of Attraction Site of a famous fresco cycle by Ghirlandaio
Location Piazza Ognissanti (Santa Maria Novella)
Admission Free; admission charge for Ghirlandaio's Cenacolo, €2
Hours Daily, 7 a.m.–noon, 3–6 p.m.
Phone 055 239 8700
When to Go Anytime
Overall Appeal by Age Group

Pre-school ★★	Teens ★★★	Over 30 ★★★
Grade school ★★★	Young Adults ★★★	Seniors ★★★★

Author's Rating ★★★
How Much Time to Allow 15–30 minutes

Description and Comments Recently restored to its 13th-century glory, All Saints church is known to art historians as the home of a *Last Supper* by Ghirlandaio and the site of Sandro Botticelli's tomb. Americans will also be intrigued to know that this church was also the parish of Amerigo Vespucci, the 15th-century explorer who lent his name to the New World. The Vespucci were wealthy merchants, and, as was the practice of entrepreneurs in the 1400s, the family was active in the church. Ghirlandaio's *Madonna della Misericordia* fresco in the second chapel on the right features a young Amerigo Vespucci kneeling before the Virgin Mary. He's the one clad in pink on Mary's left.

Other Things to Do Nearby Get a glimpse of more of Ghirlandaio's art in Santa Maria Novella.

Opificio delle Pietre Dure

Type of Attraction One of the world's greatest conservation institutions
Location Via Degli Alfani, 78 (San Giovanni)
Admission €2
Hours Monday–Wednesday, Friday, and Saturday, 8:15 a.m.–2 p.m.; Thursday, 8:15 a.m.–7 p.m.; closed Sunday and public holidays
Phone 055 265 11
Overall Appeal by Age Group

Pre-school —	Teens ★	Over 30 ★★
Grade school ★	Young Adults ★★	Seniors ★★

Author's Rating ★★½
How Much Time to Allow 30 minutes

Description and Comments The Opificio delle Pietre Dure (the workshop of hard stones) started life as a Medici-funded studio, where artists learned and honed the craft of inlaying precious and semi-precious stones into mosaics and furnishings. (The monumental apartments in Palazzo Pitti are rife with this stuff.) Here is a small museum with examples of the works produced at the Opificio. Today, the workshop is known for what goes on behind the scenes. In 1975, the Opificio joined forces with the Laboratori di Restauro and has since been the leading restoration institute in Italy.

Other Things to Do Nearby Visit the *David* in the Accademia.

Orsanmichele

Type of Attraction Grain-barn-turned-Gothic-church
Location Via Arte della Lana (San Giovanni)
Admission Free
Hours Monday–Friday, 9 a.m.–noon, 4–6 p.m.; Saturday, Sunday, and public holidays, 9 a.m.–1 p.m., 4–6 p.m.; closed first and last Monday of the month
Phone 055 284 944
When to Go Afternoons
Overall Appeal by Age Group

Pre-school —		Teens ★★		Over 30 ★★★
Grade school ★★		Young Adults ★★★		Seniors ★★★

Author's Rating ★★★
How Much Time to Allow 30 minutes

Description and Comments The most appealing part of Orsanmichele, a corrupted name for the Orto di San Michele (Garden of St. Michael), is the exterior, which features spindly, Gothic niches decorated with the patron saints of Florence's 14 traditional guilds. In an effort to outdo one another, the city's guilds had the most celebrated artists of the time design and cast their saint. The results were a bronze of St. John the Baptist (cloth importers' guild) by Ghiberti and a St. George (armor guild) by Donatello. All of the niche statues are now copies (most of the originals can be found in the Bargello). Inside Orsanmichele, the remnants of a grain market are less evident. Andrea Orcagna's altar, covered with cherubs *(putti)* and marble, is the highlight.

Other Things to Do Nearby Have a coffee in the Piazza della Repubblica.

Palazzo Pitti

Type of Attraction The palatial home and garden of the Medici
Location Piazza Pitti (Oltrarno)
Admission Palatine Gallery and Appartamenti Monumentali, €6.50; Museo degli Argenti and Galleria d'Arte, €4.50

Hours Palatine Gallery and Appartamenti Monumentali: Tuesday–Saturday, 8:30 a.m.–6:50 p.m.; Sunday, 8:30 a.m.–7 p.m.; Museo degli Argenti and Galleria d'Arte Moderna: daily, 8:30 a.m.–1:50 p.m.; the latter two museums are closed the 1st, 3rd, and 5th Monday and the 2nd and 4th Sunday of each month

Phone Palatine Gallery and the Appartamenti Monumentali, 055 210 323; Museo degli Argenti, 055 238 8710; Museo d'Arte Moderna, 055 238 8616

When to Go The Palatine Gallery and Appartamenti Monumentali, early morning; the other museums of the Pitti are rarely crowded

Overall Appeal by Age Group

Pre-school ★★		Teens ★★		Over 30 ★★★
Grade school ★★		Young Adults ★★★		Seniors ★★★

Author's Rating ★★½

How Much Time to Allow 30 minutes to 1 hour per museum

Description and Comments This massive, arrogant pile once belonged to Luca Pitti, a banker who went bankrupt trying to outdo the Medici. Ironically, Cosimo I ended up buying this palace from Pitti and made it the family home. Renovations to the original Pitti layout, which was designed by Brunelleschi, began immediately, but dragged on for nearly 300 years. All the while, the Medici decorated the mansion with the finest frescoes, sculpture, and furnishings. After the demise of the Medici, Palazzo Pitti was a residence for various rulers, including Napoleon and the Savoys. The latter bequeathed the estate to Italy in 1919.

Palazzo Pitti is home to five small museums and the extensive Giardino Boboli (see profile). The Palatine Gallery is the largest of the museums, with an impressive collection of works from Titian, Raphael, and Peter Paul Rubens, among others. The Medici grand dukes of the 17th and 18th centuries hand-picked the paintings in the Palatine, and the works still hang in the spots that the dukes chose for them. A ticket to the Palatine Gallery will also afford you a peek into the life of a royal. The Appartamenti Monumentali (monumental apartments) on the first floor of the south wing of the Pitti are lavishly decorated with gold, crystal, and rich, crimson fabric.

Lesser museums within Palazzo Pitti are the Museo degli Argenti and the Galleria d'Arte Moderna. The former is comprised of sumptuous furnishings and home accessories, including ebony furniture, marble vases, and fixtures of gold and semi-precious stones. The Galleria d'Arte Moderna contains paintings from the late 18th to the early 20th centuries, and the Galleria del Costume (entrance available with a ticket for the Giardino Boboli) shows the evolution of aristocratic fashion. The latter two collections are recommended for serious contemporary art or royal buffs; otherwise, check them off your list.

Other Things to Do Nearby Go antiques shopping in Santo Spirito.

Palazzo Strozzi

Type of Attraction The largest noble palace in Florence

Location Piazza degli Strozzi (Duomo)

Admission Courtyard, free; admission to exhibitions varies

Hours Monday–Friday, 9 a.m.–1 p.m., 3–6 p.m.; Saturday, 9 a.m.–1 p.m.

Phone 055 234 0742

When to Go Not crowded

Overall Appeal by Age Group

Pre-school ★★		Teens ★★		Over 30 ★★
Grade school ★★		Young Adults ★★		Seniors ★★

Author's Rating ★★

How Much Time to Allow 30 minutes; times for exhibitions vary

Description and Comments Many of Florence's Renaissance buildings tend to blend into one another from block to block, so at first you may not notice the Palazzo Strozzi. But, once you do, you'll recognize its massive size. Approximately 15 buildings were destroyed to build this palace, the home of banker Filippo Strozzi and his family. A longtime Medici rival, Filippo Strozzi fled Florence for a time, only to make a fortune as the banker to the king of Naples. When he returned, he commissioned three of the city's best architects to design and build the largest palace in all of Florence (later eclipsed, of course, by the Medici's Palazzo Pitti). Filippo Strozzi died in 1491, only three years after commissioning the grandiose project, but he left it to his heirs to see that the palace was completed. The building was finished in 1536, but, sadly, by this time, the Strozzi family was bankrupt. The Palazzo Strozzi today houses a library and various scholarly institutes. It also plays host to numerous exhibitions, including the Biennale dell'Antiquariato, an antiques fair held each September through October.

Other Things to Do Nearby Go bankrupt by shopping in the high-priced boutiques along Via Tornabuoni—or go window shopping.

Palazzo Vecchio

Type of Attraction Florence's old town hall and the "spike" in the city's skyline

Location Piazza della Signoria (Duomo)

Admission €5.70

Hours Monday, Tuesday, and Thursday–Sunday, 9 a.m.–7 p.m.; Wednesday, 9 a.m.–2 p.m.

Phone 055 276 8465

When to Go After lunch or early evening

Special Comments On the right edge of the Palazzo, nearest the Uffizi Gallery, is an etching of a man in profile, believed to be a self-portrait of Leonardo da Vinci.

Overall Appeal by Age Group

Pre-school ★★		Teens ★★		Over 30 ★★★
Grade school ★★		Young Adults ★★★		Seniors ★★★

Author's Rating ★★★½
How Much Time to Allow 1 hour

Description and Comments Florence's second-most recognizable building after the Duomo is the Palazzo Vecchio, an early 14th-century palace that has long served as the town hall. Its austere, stone facade with its slender, 308-foot belltower is immediately striking. Meanwhile, the upper register of the building features a frieze of various coats-of-arms. The interior of the *palazzo,* featuring rich frescoes by some of Florence's most gifted artists, is worth the price of admission. Vasari's paintings in the Salone del Cinquecento shouldn't be missed for their depictions of the history of Florence (as seen through the eyes of Cosimo I Medici). The overly glorified battle scenes between Florence and rivals Pisa and Siena are fawning at best and overdone at worst. Nevertheless, the illustrations of 16th-century Florence are of historic interest. Michelangelo' s statue, *Genius of Victory,* also located in this room, was not one of the artist's favorite works. It was only after Cosimo I Medici's victory over Siena, in 1565, that Buonarroti's nephew donated the sculpture to the duke.

Other Things to Do Nearby Browse the statues in the Loggia dei Lanzi (Piazza della Signoria) and in the courtyard of the Uffizi.

Parco delle Cascine

Type of Attraction Florence's largest park
Location Piazza Vittorio Veneto, beyond the Porta al Prato gate (outside the City Gates)
Hours Open daily, sunrise–sunset
Overall Appeal by Age Group

Pre-school ★★★		Teens ★★★		Over 30 ★★★
Grade school ★★★		Young Adults ★★★		Seniors ★★★

Author's Rating ★★★
When to Go Tuesday for the flea market, mornings or afternoons for exercise or a stroll

Description and Comments This two-mile expanse of green west of the city was originally a dairy farm for the Medici—cascine means "barns." Today, the park is a popular place for inline skating, jogging, biking, and family outings. There's a horse-racing track here (Ippodromo il Visarno) as well as tennis courts.

Touring Tips When the sun goes down, hustlers and transvestites move in.

Piazza della Repubblica

Type of Attraction Café-lined square

Location Piazza della Repubblica, at the intersection of Via Roma, Via Calimala, via degli Strozzi, and Vie de' Speziali (San Giovanni)

When to Go Fun day or night for people-watching

Overall Appeal by Age Group

Pre-school ★★	Teens ★★★	Over 30 ★★★★
Grade school ★★	Young Adults ★★★★	Seniors ★★★★

Author's Rating ★★★½

Description and Comments Lined with outdoor cafés and fancy hotels, the Piazza della Repubblica is a monumental square, flanked on one end by an enormous triumphal arch. The arch was built here in 1895 when Florence enjoyed a brief stint as the capital of Italy. Long before it was the Square of the Republic, this area was the site of the old market (Mercato Vecchio); before that, a Roman forum was here.

Other Things to Do Nearby Browse the wares at the Mercato Nuovo.

Piazza della Signoria

Type of Attraction Italy's most attractive square

Location At the south end of Via Calzaiuoli (Santa Croce)

When to Go Anytime

How Much Time to Allow At least 30 minutes

Overall Appeal by Age Group

Pre-school ★★★★	Teens ★★★★★	Over 30 ★★★★★
Grade school ★★★★	Young Adults ★★★★★	Seniors ★★★★★

Author's Rating ★★★★★

Description and Comments Sooner or later, you're going to wind up in the Piazza della Signoria, Florence's main square and, perhaps, the most important piazza in all the nation. It was here that Michelangelo's *David* first stood, and it is home to three more signature Florentine statues. Across from the copy of *David,* at the entrance of the Palazzo Vecchio, is the statue of *Hercules and Cacus,* by Bandinelli. The Loggia dei Lanzi, adjacent to the Palazzo Vecchio, is a covered outdoor sculpture garden featuring the famous bronze of *Perseus* (with the head of Medusa) by Cellini and the marble *Rape of the Sabine Women* by Giambologna. Another work by the latter, that being the equestrian statue of Cosimo de' Medici, sits in a prominent position in the center of the piazza.

Other Things to Do Nearby Grab a gelato and enjoy the square.

Piazzale Michelangelo

Type of Attraction The city with a view

Location Piazzale Michelangelo (Oltrarno); take bus 12 or 13 to reach it

When to Go On a clear day

How Much Time to Allow 30 minutes to 1 hour

Overall Appeal by Age Group

Pre-school ★★★★	Teens ★★★★★	Over 30 ★★★★★
Grade school ★★★★	Young Adults ★★★★★	Seniors ★★★★★

Author's Rating ★★★★

Description and Comments Piazzale Michelangelo is decorated with a number of bogus Buonarroti works, including a poor casting of *David*. But, that's not why you—and the hundreds of other people—are here. This wide piazza is perched on a hill just below the city center, with spectacular panoramas in all directions. Here is where you'll snap the picture that you take home and frame.

Other Things to Do Nearby Drop by the church of San Miniato al Monte for an undisturbed view.

Ponte Vecchio

Type of Attraction Florence's most storied bridge
Location Intersection of Lungarno Acciaiuoli and Via Por Santa Maria (Santa Croce)
When to Go Mornings, before the shops open
How Much Time to Allow 15 minutes
Overall Appeal by Age Group

Pre-school ★★	Teens ★★★	Over 30 ★★★★★
Grade school ★★	Young Adults ★★★★★	Seniors ★★★★★

Author's Rating ★★★★½

Description and Comments Jewelry vendors own this bridge. Before them, blacksmiths and butchers operated here, throwing waste from the bridge into the river and subsequently turning the Arno into a stinky fly-trap. In the late 16th century, Duke Ferdinando I evicted the smiths and butchers and invited the jewelers to set up shop on the Ponte Vecchio. As one of Florence's main tourist attractions, the bridge is consistently jammed with tourists—and pickpockets. If you're not into shopping for jewelry, perhaps your best course of action for enjoying the Ponte Vecchio is to take a quick stroll across, then follow along the Arno for a short distance. From afar, you can get a better view of the bridge's workshops, which always appear to be on the brink of falling off into the river. The view of the Ponte Vecchio at sunset, when the maize-colored shops are reflected in the water below, is not to be missed.

Other Things to Do Nearby The Borgo San Jacopo, past the bridge in the Oltrarno, is filled with high-end boutiques and good restaurants.

San Lorenzo

Type of Attraction Parish church of the Medici
Location Piazza San Lorenzo (San Lorenzo)
Admission Free
Hours Monday–Saturday, 8 a.m.–noon, 3:30–5:30 p.m.; Sunday, 3:30–5:30 p.m.

Phone 055 216 634

When to Go Anytime

Overall Appeal by Age Group

Pre-school ★		Teens ★★		Over 30 ★★★
Grade school ★★		Young Adults ★★		Seniors ★★★

Author's Rating ★★

How Much Time to Allow 30 minutes

Description and Comments Its exterior never decorated, San Lorenzo is a hulking, unattractive pile of bricks from the outside. But this parish church of the Medici has a relatively handsome interior, punctuated with vibrant, marble floors; the dramatic fresco of the *Martyrdom of St. Lawrence* by Bronzino; Filippo Lippi's *Annunciation;* bronze pulpits by Donatello; and the humble grave of Cosimo il Vecchio (in front of the altar).

Other Things to Do Nearby See other Medici tombs, including those designed by Michelangelo, in the adjacent Medici Chapels.

San Miniato al Monte

Type of Attraction Romanesque church is the most tranquil in Florence

Location Via delle Porte Sante, 34 (Outside the City Gates)

Admission Free

Hours Daily, 8 a.m.–noon, 2–7 p.m.

Phone 055 234 2731

When to Go Anytime, but especially at sunset

Overall Appeal by Age Group

Pre-school ★★★		Teens ★★★		Over 30 ★★★★
Grade school ★★★		Young Adults ★★★		Seniors ★★★★

Author's Rating ★★★★

How Much Time to Allow 30 minutes to 1 hour

Description and Comments From its peaceful perch on the mount to the south and east of Florence rests the church of San Miniato, built on this site in the first half of the 11th century. From a distance, the green and white marble façade of the church resembles that of Santa Maria Novella. Take a closer look, and you'll see that the upper register, designed in the 12th century, is decorated similar to Florence's Baptistry with unusual astrological symbols, a common practice during mystical medieval times. The very wealthy imported cloth guild, the Calimala, paid for the decoration of the exterior and also supervised the zodiac-inspired motif on the interior's marble floor. The inside of San Miniato is one of the most beautiful in Florence, comprised of a raised choir over the crypt and delicate artwork by Michelozzo, Rossellino, and Luca della Robbia. If you're lucky, you'll visit the church during the monks' daily chant, which usually takes place around 4:30 p.m.

Touring Tips See Tour 2 under "Suggested Walking Itineraries for Florence," above.

Other Things to Do Nearby Enjoy another stunning view of Florence from Piazzale Michelangelo.

Santa Maria del Carmine

Type of Attraction Site of one of the first gems of Renaissance painting
Location Piazza del Carmine (Oltrarno)
Admission Brancacci Chapel: €3
Hours Monday, Wednesday–Saturday, 10 a.m.–5 p.m., Sunday, 1–5 p.m.
Phone 055 238 2195
When to Go Early morning or after lunch
Special Comments There is a separate entrance for the Brancacci Chapel.
Overall Appeal by Age Group

Pre-school ★★		Teens ★★★		Over 30 ★★★★★
Grade school ★★		Young Adults ★★★★★		Seniors ★★★★★

Author's Rating ★★★★★
How Much Time to Allow 30 minutes (visits to the Brancacci Chapel are limited to 15 minutes)

Description and Comments Were it not for the Brancacci Chapel, this modest church in the Oltrarno would have few visitors. However, it is here that you'll find what would become one of the forebears of Renaissance art. In 1424, Florentine merchant Felice Brancacci commissioned the artist Masolino to decorate the chapel with frescoes. Masolino is responsible for painting the *Temptation of Adam and Eve* (top row, right wall), *St. Peter Healing the Cripple* (next to that), and *St. Peter Preaching* (top row, directly left of altar). Masolino's student Masaccio assisted his teacher and eventually revolutionized painting. All of his frescoes—*St. Peter Healing the Sick, St. Peter Baptizing the Converts, St. Peter and St. John Giving Alms* (all on the altar wall), *The Tribute Money* (top row, left wall), and *The Expulsion of Adam and Eve*—feature figures illuminated by a single source of light. At that time, such a concept had yet to be introduced into painting. Still, Masaccio was able to apply this idea to full effect, using light and shadow to evoke deep misery in the eyes of his subjects in *The Expulsion of Adam and Eve.* Masaccio also began painting the lower left wall before his sudden death at age 27. Here, *St. Peter Enthroned* features four cloaked men; the one in red staring out of the painting is said to be a self-portrait of the artist. Finishing up the fresco cycle 60 years after Masaccio's untimely death was Filippino Lippi, who contributed the lower panels, including *St. Peter Visited by St. Paul, Raising the Emperor's Son* (the continuation of Masaccio's *St. Peter Enthroned*), *Crucifixion, Before the Proconsul,* and *The Release of St. Peter.* The Brancacci Chapel recently received a much-needed facelift, and now the colors of the frescoes are as vibrant as they were centuries ago.

Other Things to Do Nearby Take a breather in the Giardino Boboli.

Santa Maria Novella

Type of Attraction Gothic church with dramatically frescoed chapels

Location Piazza Santa Maria Novella (Santa Maria Novella)

Admission Donation expected; Museo di Santa Maria Novella: €3

Hours Monday–Saturday, 7 a.m.–noon, 3–6 p.m., Sunday, 3–5 p.m.

Phone 055 210 113

When to Go Late morning or early afternoon (to avoid the rush-hour foot and vehicle traffic in the square)

Overall Appeal by Age Group

Pre-school ★★	Teens ★★★	Over 30 ★★★★
Grade school ★★★	Young Adults ★★★★	Seniors ★★★★

Author's Rating ★★★★

How Much Time to Allow 30–45 minutes

Description and Comments Its undesirable location (near the frenzy of the train station) should not deter you from visiting Santa Maria Novella, a treasure trove of Gothic architecture, Renaissance art, damning Dominican allegories, and the first of Florence's major basilicas. The Dominican order built this church in the late 13th to mid-14th centuries in typical Gothic fashion, but its attractive green and white marble façade, added in the mid-15th century, was the masterstroke of architect Alberti. As for the original interior designs, much of that was erased when Giorgio Vasari was hired in the 16th century to remodel the church; however, Masaccio's *Trinity*, on the left side of the aisle, was spared. Like other churches in the city during the 14th and 15th centuries, Santa Maria Novella enjoyed hefty donations from the Florentine elite eager to buy their way into heaven. Ghirlandaio frescoed the Tornabuoni Chapel behind the altar with scenes from the life of John the Baptist and the Virgin Mary, but the Tornabuoni family and their relatives are clearly the protagonists here, dressed in aristocratic garb. Filippo Strozzi (who, during his entire life, played a losing game of keeping up with the Medici) commissioned Filippino Lippi to decorate the chapel to the right of the altar with even more biblical scenes and his tomb. The beginning of Boccaccio's *Decameron* is set here. Another nod to Italian literature appears on the walls of an earlier Strozzi chapel, painted with scenes inspired by Dante's *Paradise* by Nardo di Cione and Andrea Orcagna. You'll have to pay to visit the museum and cloisters of Santa Maria Novella. (It has a separate entrance to the left of the main church door.) Here, scenes of hellfire and damnation peer out of the walls of the

Spanish Chapel, the private chapel of Eleonora of Toledo (the wife of Cosimo I Medici) and a former headquarters for the Inquisition. Gruesome devils and *domini canes* (hounds of the Lord, the phrase from which the name Dominican was derived) round up the evildoers. Another feature of the museum is the Green Cloister, named after the type of green pigment that Paolo Uccello used to paint fresco scenes of *Noah and the Great Flood*. Ironically, the flooding of the Arno in 1966 damaged these frescoes. The rest of the museum is a display of relics and vestments from the Dominican order.

Other Things to Do Nearby Hop a bus or train for a side trip to the Tuscan countryside.

Santo Spirito

Type of Attraction Early Oltrarno church
Location Piazza Santo Spirito (Oltrarno)
Admission Donation expected; Refectory: €2
Hours Monday, Tuesday, and Thursday–Saturday, 8:30 a.m.–noon, 3:45–6 p.m.; Wednesday, 8:30 a.m.–noon; Sunday, 9:30–10:25 a.m. , 3:45–5 p.m.
Phone 055 210 030
When to Go Anytime; never crowded
Overall Appeal by Age Group

Pre-school —		Teens ★		Over 30 ★★
Grade school ★		Young Adults ★★		Seniors ★★

Author's Rating ★★
How Much Time to Allow 15 minutes

Description and Comments Although Santo Spirito was one of Florence's first churches—having been founded in 1250 and lending its name to the quarter in which it sits—it is not the jaw-dropper that the rest of the city's churches are. In great contrast to its colorful, namesake piazza, Santo Spirito's 18th-century façade is wide, bland, and blank. The unadorned exterior also lends no hint to the interior's beauty. Brunelleschi drew up design plans for this church in the late 15th century, but he died long before its completion. Luckily, subsequent architects followed his blueprints, which included 38 side altars and a grand colonnaded aisle. Meanwhile, artists such as Ghirlandaio, Rosselli, and Filippino Lippi contributed their expertise to the decoration of the chapels; the latter's *Madonna and Child* is considered the highlight. Meanwhile, the controversial Baroque-style baldacchino, which clashes with the elegant, Renaissance aesthetic, was added in 1607.

Other Things to Do Nearby Grab lunch in the Piazza Santo Spirito or check out early frescoes in the Brancacci Chapel in Santa Maria del Carmine.

Uffizi Gallery

Type of Attraction One of the most dazzling Renaissance collections on earth

Location Piazzale degli Uffizi, 6 (Duomo)

Admission €8, last admission 45 minutes before closing

Hours Tuesday–Sunday, 8:30 a.m.–7 p.m.; in mid-April, the museum closes at 10 p.m.

Phone 055 23 885

When to Go Early morning or late afternoon

Special Comments No cameras allowed

Overall Appeal by Age Group

Pre-school ★★	Teens ★★★★★	Over 30 ★★★★★
Grade school ★★★	Young Adults ★★★★★	Seniors ★★★★★

Author's Rating ★★★★★

How Much Time to Allow At least 3 hours

Description and Comments If you can make it to only one museum in Italy, then go to the Uffizi Gallery. This assortment of painting and sculpture collected over the years by the Medici family is one of the most important and satisfying in the world and boasts some of the most recognizable masterpieces by the most well-known names. So, don't be surprised if the line to get in snakes around the block. In the late 16th century, the Medici collection was kept in a single, octagonal room on the top floor of the building housing the offices *(uffizi)* of the Florentine magistrate. Soon the room, known as the "Tribuna," proved too small for the family's art, and the offices gave way to a gallery. Anna Maria Luisa Medici, the last in the family line, bequeathed the entire collection to the city of Florence on her death in 1737. The collection is grouped in a series of 45 connected rooms on the second floor, bound by two long hallways packed with sculpture. In the first several rooms, you'll find altarpieces and other religious works by Giotto and his contemporaries. There are entire rooms devoted to Fra Filippo Lippi, Francesco Botticelli, Leonardo da Vinci, Raphael, Caravaggio, and other Italian masters. Foreign artists, such as Rubens and Rembrandt, are also represented here. Some of the most important works (if not the most lovely) are Botticelli's *Birth of Venus,* Michelangelo's "Holy Family" roundel known as the *Doni Tondo,* Leonardo's *Annunciation,* and Piero della Francesca's double-sided portraits of Battista Sforza and Federico da Montefeltro. The museum recently completed extensive renovations, but keep in mind that some rooms of the museum will be closed from time to time.

Vasari Corridor

Type of Attraction Private footpath of the Medici

Location Tours start at the Palazzo Vecchio

Admission €26.50

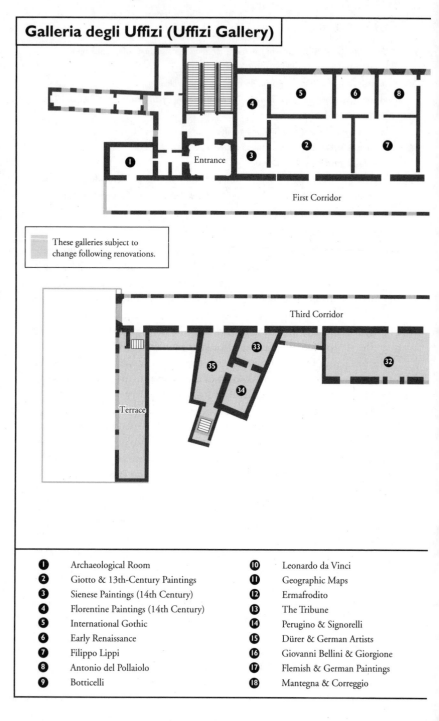

Galleria degli Uffizi (Uffizi Gallery)

These galleries subject to change following renovations.

Entrance

First Corridor

Third Corridor

Terrace

❶	Archaeological Room	❿	Leonardo da Vinci
❷	Giotto & 13th-Century Paintings	⓫	Geographic Maps
❸	Sienese Paintings (14th Century)	⓬	Ermafrodito
❹	Florentine Paintings (14th Century)	⓭	The Tribune
❺	International Gothic	⓮	Perugino & Signorelli
❻	Early Renaissance	⓯	Dürer & German Artists
❼	Filippo Lippi	⓰	Giovanni Bellini & Giorgione
❽	Antonio del Pollaiolo	⓱	Flemish & German Paintings
❾	Botticelli	⓲	Mantegna & Correggio

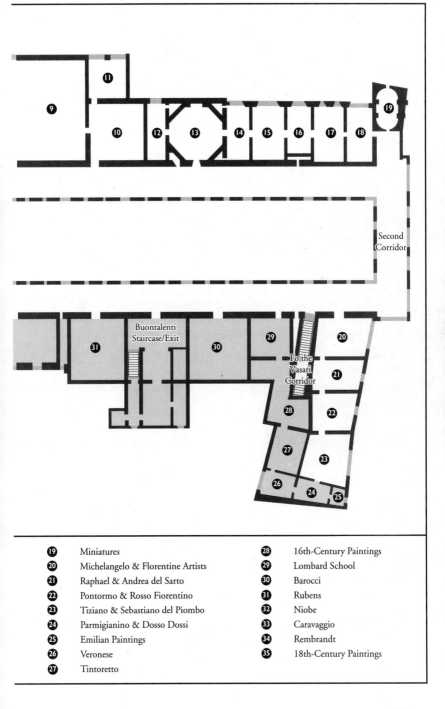

⑲	Miniatures	㉘	16th-Century Paintings
⑳	Michelangelo & Florentine Artists	㉙	Lombard School
㉑	Raphael & Andrea del Sarto	㉚	Barocci
㉒	Pontormo & Rosso Fiorentino	㉛	Rubens
㉓	Tiziano & Sebastiano del Piombo	㉜	Niobe
㉔	Parmigianino & Dosso Dossi	㉝	Caravaggio
㉕	Emilian Paintings	㉞	Rembrandt
㉖	Veronese	㉟	18th-Century Paintings
㉗	Tintoretto		

Hours Tuesday, Wednesday, Friday, and Saturday, 9 a.m.–2:30 p.m.; four tours per day: 9 a.m., 10:30 a.m., 1 p.m., and 2:30 p.m.

Phone 055 265 4321

When to Go Reservation required

Overall Appeal by Age Group

Pre-school ★		Teens ★★★★		Over 30 ★★★★★
Grade school ★★		Young Adults ★★★★★		Seniors ★★★★★

Author's Rating ★★★★★

How Much Time to Allow 1.5 hours

Description and Comments Known also as the "Prince's Passage," this covered walkway built by Giorgio Vasari in 1564 was dreamed up by Cosimo I (Medici) as a way to travel from his home at the Pitti Palace to his offices at the Uffizi without having to mingle with the public. The Vasari Corridor, opened to the public in 1973, cuts right through the heart of Florence, above rooftops, and over the Arno, affording visitors a unique view of the city below. On the tour, you are able to pass through a medieval tower, stop for mass in the balcony of the church of Santa Felicità, and peer down at the shoppers clogging the Ponte Vecchio. Inside the passageway, there are also a number of priceless artworks from the likes of Carracci, Rubens, Corot, and Andrea del Sarto. But, the paintings aren't half as interesting as being able to walk in the footsteps of the Medici.

Touring Tips Only 35 people are allowed per tour. Tours are in Italian and English. Call many months in advance to ensure your spot in line.

Other Things to Do Nearby Spend some time in the Uffizi, Palazzo Vecchio, or Pitti Palace.

Entertainment and Nightlife in Florence

Ask any Milanese or Roman, and they'll tell you that Florentine nightlife is about as exciting as a game of musical chairs. There's variety, all right, but very few options. If you stick around in Florence long enough, you're bound to end up at the same local pub, week after week.

That's not to say that you can't have a good time in Florence. This provincial town of about half a million people can paint itself red with the best of them. Florentine clubs are not short on style, nor do they lack energy. But in comparison to large clubs and pubs in bigger Italian cities, Florentine hangouts can be cliquish, due to the city's smaller size. On the other hand, you're more likely to find a handful of laid-back, more intimate bars, full of locals who feel no need to make a first impression. A bigger drawback to the Florentine scene is that most venues shut down by 1 a.m. Night owls will have to make do. Summer travelers may also be disappointed in the nightlife scene. From May through September, many large, un-air-conditioned clubs close their doors and move to the beach.

FLORENCE ENTERTAINMENT AND NIGHTLIFE

Name	Admission/ Cover	Comments
Nightclubs		
Cabiria	None	Café by day, hipster hangout by night
Club Blob	None	Friendly student dive bar
Jazz Club	€5	Smoky jazz and blues bar
JJ Cathedral Pub	None	Small, crowded Irish pub
Tenax	€10–€20	Major live-music and dance venue
Universale	None	Contemporary upscale club
The William	None	Faux-English pub
Classical Music, Opera, and Theater		
Teatro del Maggio Musicale Fiorentino (Teatro Comunale)	€15–€80+	Classic performance venue
Teatro della Pergola	€13–€26	Italy's oldest theater

Cabiria

CAFE BY DAY, HIPSTER HANGOUT BY NIGHT

Who Goes There Cool bohemian locals, students, tourists

Oltrarno/Santo Spirito; Piazza Santo Spirito, 4r; phone 055 215 732

Cover None. **Mixed Drinks** €5–€8. **Wine** €3–€5. **Beer** €3–€5. **Dress** By day, anything goes; by night, casual chic. **Food Available** Pizza, tapas, light fare.

Hours Sunday–Monday, 10 a.m.–2 a.m.; closed 1 week in August

What Goes On The sun sets on Piazza Santo Spirito, and the DJ begins to heat up the joint. You can occasionally enjoy live music, from samba to reggae to rock, which begins around 10 p.m. Outdoor seats are prime during the summer months, when live music is a fixture in the square.

Setting & Atmosphere The bossa nova– and jazz-inspired café with a zinc bar spills out onto the piazza to the tune of about a dozen tables. The scene is casual, but it does double duty as a pick-up haunt.

If You Go Snag an outdoor table early for nighttime schmoozing.

Club Blob

FRIENDLY NEIGHBORHOOD HANGOUT

Who Goes There Stylish art students

Santa Croce; Via Vinegia, 21r; phone 055 211 209

Cover None. **Mixed Drinks** €5. **Wine** €4–€8. **Beer** €3–€5. **Dress** Lots of black, jeans okay, no sneakers. **Food Available** Bar snacks.

Hours Daily, 6 p.m.–3 a.m.

What Goes On The locale of choice for the large student community, this semi-secret club is a no-frills place to grab a drink and decompress. Seating is ample, and the small dance floor heats up later in the evening when it becomes a popular after-hours spot.

Setting & Atmosphere A mezzanine allows for good people-watching.

If You Go The club's entrance is located behind an anonymous black door.

Jazz Club

GROWN-UP JAZZ AND BLUES

Who Goes There Mix of young and old beatniks

Santa Croce; Via Nuova de' Caccini, 3; phone 055 247 9700

Cover €5. **Mixed Drinks** €7. **Wine** €4. **Beer** €4. **Dress** Anything from work garb to hippie duds.

Hours Tuesday–Sunday, 9:30 p.m.–2 a.m.

What Goes On Sophisticated music lovers chat at the small tables, then coo when the performers arrive. All genres from blues to jazz fusion to gospel (occasionally) are treated with loving care.

Setting & Atmosphere This smoky basement bar has a stage just slightly big enough for a baby grand piano. Black-and-white photos of great jazz greats transport you to New Orleans.

If You Go Keep an open mind and enjoy whatever music is on.

JJ Cathedral Pub

TYPICAL IRISH DIVE

Who Goes There Tourists, young men

San Giovanni; Piazza San Giovanni, 44r; phone 055 280 260

Cover None. **Mixed Drinks** €6. **Wine** €4–€6. **Beer** €3–€5. **Dress** Whatever you want. **Food Available** Bar snacks.

Hours Daily, 11 a.m.–1 a.m.

What Goes On Depending on the time of day, the bar is populated with old saps nursing their pints or young backpackers having chugging contests.

Setting & Atmosphere The JJ has the location—on the same square as the Baptistry. It also has the view: Only two lucky souls at a time are able to fit on the pub's tiny balcony that overlooks the piazza.

If You Go Get there early and prepare to clamber for the best seat in the house.

Tenax

VENUE FOR MAJOR INTERNATIONAL ACTS

Who Goes There Live music lovers from all over Tuscany

Outside the City Gates; Via Pratese, 46; phone 055 308 160

Cover €10–€20. **Mixed Drinks** €8. **Wine** €4. **Beer** €3–€5. **Dress** Depends on the show; on DJ nights, your coolest duds. **Food Available** Snacks.

Hours Thursday–Saturday, 10:30 p.m.–4 a.m.; closed May–September

What Goes On Second-string bands of international acclaim—in other words, big-time bands without arena-size followings—usually make a stop here if Tuscany is on the itinerary. When there isn't a show, the DJ line-up helps make Tenax the area's most happening nightspot.

Setting & Atmosphere This is a warehouse-size club with deep caverns and dark niches for flirting. Decor is modern, but at press time, the club was undergoing an interior design overhaul.

If You Go Hop a bus at Piazza Indipendenza to the club. A free shuttle from Florence to the Tenax is available from until the club closes.

Universale

CATCHALL CLUB

Who Goes There Sybarites and chic types

Outside the City Gates; Via Pisana, 77r; phone 055 221 122

Cover None; minimum €6. **Mixed Drinks** €6. **Wine** €3–€4. **Beer** €3–€4. **Dress** Smart suits and designer labels. **Food Available** A restaurant and pizzeria are located on the premises.

Hours Tuesday–Sunday, 8:30 a.m.–2 p.m.; closed June–September

What Goes On If you're not careful, you'll feel like you're in Las Vegas. Universale has a couple of bars, places to dine, and a balcony for checking out the crowd. Florence's fickle in-crowd comes here and moves from room to room as if they were movie stars.

Setting & Atmosphere This enormous, multifunctional venue was a cinema in the 1950s. Now, it has been completely revamped with slick, modern furnishings and a fully stocked bar. This is the place to see and be seen.

If You Go Prepare for the cheese quotient—and bring lots of dough.

The William

FABRICATED ENGLISH PUB

Who Goes There Local beer connoisseurs, foreign students

Santa Croce; Via Magliabechi, 7/11r; phone 055 246 9800

Cover None. **Mixed Drinks** €7. **Wine** €3–€5, limited selection. **Beer** half pints, €2, pints, €5–€7. **Dress** Casual. **Food Available** English nibbles, bar snacks.

Hours Daily, 6 p.m. until late

What Goes On A young to middle-aged crowd settles in with pints on the weekdays and shows up for DJs on the weekends.

Setting & Atmosphere An elaborate, wooden bar and typical English pub accents, like Guinness ads and football paraphernalia, are key to the pub's look. The William's location far from the tourist attractions provides a welcome escape.

If You Go Stop by this pub on the weeknight. The crowds on Friday and Saturday can be intense.

Cultural Evenings

In the realm of theater and dance, Florence is by no means on the cutting edge. As the home of Italy's oldest theater, the **Teatro Pergola,** founded in 1656, Florence has enjoyed a long tradition of theatrical and operatic splendor. But some might say that the city is living in the past. Conservative operas and chamber concerts are well received here, but alternative fare is harder to find. One time when Florence really shines is during **Maggio Musicale Fiorentino,** a month-long extravaganza from late April through May of opera, ballet, modern dance, and orchestral concerts. You can find out more information about venues and performances online at **www.maggiofiorentino.com.**

While you're in Florence, check with the tourist office for information about upcoming classical events. They put out a bilingual monthly publication called *Florence Today* with a calendar of all of the goings on about town. You may also want to pick up a copy of *Firenze Spettacolo* or *La Nazione* at the newsstand. Both of these publications have extensive, up-to-date listings of plays, operas, and other events.

Classical Music, Opera, and Theater

The Teatro Comunale is now known by its snazzy new name, the **Teatro del Maggio Musicale Fiorentino** (Corso Italia, 16; Santa Maria Novella; phone 055 211 158, fax 055 277 9410; **www.maggiofiorentino.com**). For most of the year, you can catch concerts, ballets, and small opera performances in this 2,000-seat venue. October through December is the opera and ballet season, January to March is the concert season, and early spring (April through May) is the Maggio Musicale Fiorentino. Most of this music festival's performances are indoor affairs, but at least one major concert is held outdoors, typically in Piazza della Signoria. The occasional drama fills in the rest of the theater's calendar. Tickets for the opera range from €20 to €80, whereas symphony and ballet performances start at €15. Tickets can be purchased at the box office (AMEX, MC, V) or online for an additional fee.

The **Teatro della Pergola** (Via della Pergola, 12-32; San Giovanni; phone 055 226 4316) is Italy's oldest theater (founded 1656); it's a venue for intimate chamber concerts and small-scale opera productions. The Amici della Musica (phone 055 608 420), a group that helps secure big-name classical talent for the theater, hosts performances at Teatro della Pergola from September through late spring. Admission is typically €13–€26 for adults, €8.50–€16 for children, and €10–€20 for seniors. Tickets can be purchased at the box office (no credit cards accepted).

Ballet and Dance

For the most part, the **Teatro del Maggio Musicale Fiorentino** (Corso Italia, 16; Santa Maria Novella; phone 055 211 158, fax 055 277 9410; **www.maggiofiorentino.com**) is the place to go for ballet. Their dance troupe, MaggioDanza, stages lovely, traditional fare, such as *Swan Lake.* Their concerts are even easier on the eyes in the summer, when performances move to the Boboli Gardens.

Spectator Sports

As for Italian League soccer, **Fiorentina** is the only game in town. When the season is on, from August to May, crowds pile into the **Stadio Artemio Franchi** (at Campo di Marte). Going to a Fiorentina match while in Florence is a good chance to mingle with the locals. Just make sure you cheer for the right team.

Tickets for Fiorentina games go on sale approximately three hours before game time (usually noon) at the stadium box office. You can also purchase your tickets at the **Chiosco degli Sportivi** (Via Anselmi; phone 055 292 363), near Piazza della Repubblica.

Shopping in Florence

Leather, hand-made paper, fashionable footwear, gold jewelry, oodles of art . . . Florence may be a provincial town of only about 400,000 people, but it's known throughout the world for its fine wares. Touring through Florence without doing a bit of shopping is like going to a gourmet restaurant and not eating. Luckily, you don't have to max out your credit cards to take home a little piece of the city's unique charm.

Shopping Zones and Favorite Streets

The center of Florence is so jam-packed with leather vendors, stationery stores, perfumeries, designer boutiques, and accessory shops that it's difficult to pinpoint exactly where one shopping zone ends and another starts. To help get you on track, here is a brief outline of where to go and what to buy once you're there:

Via dei Tornabuoni and Environs

Florence's version of Fifth Avenue, Via Tornabuoni and its satellite streets have all the haute couture (rather, *alta moda*) boutiques, including:

Emilio Pucci   Via dei Tornabuoni, 20/22; phone 055 265 8082

Etro   Via della Vigna Nuova, 50; phone 055 267 0086

Giorgio Armani   Via dei Tornabuoni, 48; phone 055219 041

Gucci   Via dei Tornabuoni, 73r; phone 055 264 011

Miu Miu   Via Roma, 8; phone 055 260 8931

Salvatore Ferragamo   Via dei Tornabuoni, 14r; phone 055 292 123

Versace   Via dei Tornabuoni, 13/14r; phone 055 239 6167

Via Calzaiuoli and Environs

The "street of the stocking makers" is still the place to buy shoes and stockings, but it is also packed with mainstream retail shops, hotels, and a few restaurants. This is the main shopping drag of Florence, and the street is a pedestrian zone. Via Roma, which runs parallel to Via Calzaiuoli, also boasts a wide range of boutiques, men's wear stores, and accessory shops.

Mercato Nuovo

At the intersection of Via Calimala and Via Porta Rossa is the "New Market," built in 1547. Once a straw market, the Mercato Nuovo is largely an annex of the nearby Mercato San Lorenzo. Leather purses, wallets, belts, and jackets are the hot items, or you can pick up hand-woven baskets, art reproductions, and artisan jewelry. Open daily.

Mercato di San Lorenzo

Snaking for blocks and blocks on the streets near the church of San Lorenzo is an open-air market where hundreds of vendors are eager to sell you leather belts and jackets, ornately bound journals, silk scarves, knock-off designer handbags, souvenirs, and whole assortment of gizmos and gadgets. This can be one of the best places to find discounted leather accessories and various souvenirs, especially if you haggle.

Parco Le Cascine

The weekly market here is packed with Florentines rummaging for used clothing, designer knock-offs, and more. Open Tuesday mornings.

Piazza Santo Spirito

Traditionally Florence's bohemian neighborhood beyond the Arno, the artisan studios, antiques shops, and furniture restoration workshops lining the streets here are brimming with jewelry, pottery, and unique gifts. At Santo Spirito's daily clothing market, you'll find vintage duds by the kilo, silk scarves, and handmade candles. An arts and craft market sets up shop here every second Sunday of the month.

Ponte Vecchio

Gold jewelry is more plentiful than water when it comes to this landmark bridge. Prices for necklaces, bracelets, and rings are not always the most competitive, but, if you're shopping for jewelry, check out the Ponte Vecchio first.

Department Stores

Two of Italy's premier department stores, COIN and Rinascente, are located in the center near the Duomo.

COIN   Via de' Calzaiuoli, 56r; phone 055 280 531; **www.coin.it**

Rinascente   Piazza della Repubblica, 1; phone 055 219 113; **www.rinascente.it**

Produce Markets

Mercato Centrale

Just a block or so from the San Lorenzo market is the Central Market, where many Florentines purchase meat, cheese, fresh fruits, and vegetables. You can't bring most of the stuff sold in this immense 19th-century building overseas, but you can put together a movable feast to nosh during your stay here. Open daily.

Piazza Santo Spirito

Here you'll find a daily offering of seasonal produce, oil-cured olives, cheese, meats, and a tripe stand. Closed Sundays.

Great Gifts from Florence and Where to Find Them

Wines and Spirits

Pitti Gola e Cantina   Piazza Pitti, 16. A variety of wines, as well as Tuscan and Florentine cookbooks in English.

Enoteca de' Giraldi   Via de' Giraldi. The widest assortment of Tuscan vintages available. You can also take wine-tasting classes here (see "Taking Classes").

Linens and Fabric

Casa dei Tessuti   Via de' Pecori, 20/24r (Santa Maria Novella); phone 055 215 961. The finest linens, wools, and fabrics.

Leather

The best selection of leather in Florence can be found on Via della Vigna Nuova and on Via del Parione. On these two central streets, you'll find trendy styles for every budget.

Santa Croce Leather Workshop   Piazza Santa Croce, 16 (Santa Croce). This leather school occupies part of the cloister of the church of Santa Croce. The finely crafted goods are for more conservative tastes.

Perfume and Cosmetics

Spezieria-Erboristeria Palazzo Vecchio   Via Vaccherreccia, 9r; Piazza della Signoria (Santa Croce); phone 055 239 6055. In operation since the height of Medici rule, this old apothecary still makes herbal remedies and perfumes according to old recipes. Some fragrances here are the same ones that were made especially for Caterina Medici.

Stationery and Art Supplies

Il Papiro   Piazza del Duomo, 24r (San Giovanni); phone 055 281 628. Makers of stationery, journals, and gifts using the traditional, marble paper technique.

Zecchi   Via dello Studio, 19r (San Giovanni); phone 055 211 470. One of the most renowned art stores in the world, selling oils, acrylics, canvases, brushes—the works.

The Best of Tuscany

It's no surprise that travelers often talk about Tuscany as if it were another country. With slices of alpine peaks, ribbons of sun-drenched beaches, pockets of towns in the rolling hills, and lush valleys filled with perfectly geometric rows of grapevines, olive groves, and a rich patchwork of black and umber soil, Tuscany is Italy in miniature. Its diverse geography says much about Tuscany as a mirror for the peninsula's cultural and social history. Italy's past can be traced from all reaches of Tuscany, one of the nation's largest regions. Scant traces of the Etruscans and Romans can be found from **Volterra** to **Arezzo.** A better picture of medieval Italy cannot be found outside of regional gems like **Siena** and **San Gimignano.** Meanwhile, the spirit of the Renaissance hangs heavy in the air around the lovely walled city of **Lucca.** In Tuscany, you can see architectural movements and advancements in painting and sculpting techniques literally unfold before your eyes. Almost every town here is a proud owner of at least one priceless fresco, statue, or altarpiece.

In the following sections, we highlight the best of Tuscany's ten provinces—**Firenze, Siena, Arezzo, Prato, Pistoia, Lucca, Massa e Carrara, Pisa, Livorno,** and **Grossetto.**

Tuscany Tourism Board

You can pick up information about the entire region of Tuscany at the main APT office in Florence. Provincial and municipal tourism offices are listed with their respective sections.

Tuscany Regional Tourist Board   Via A. Manzoni, 16; 50121 Florence; phone 055 23320, fax 055 23462; turismo@apt.toscana.it, **www.turismo.toscana.it**

Getting around Tuscany

Rent a set of wheels if you plan to see the Tuscan countryside *(campagna)*. The region's winding roads are ideal for long, scenic drives by car or by motorbike. However, some of these roads are a little slow-going. If you're in a hurry (hopefully, you're not in too much of a rush to enjoy the journey), then follow the *autostrada.* The toll-roads **A1** (Florence–Rome), **A11** (Florence–Lucca–Tuscan coast), and **A12** (Livorno–Versilian coast) are the most useful.

Your second-best option for getting around hard-to-reach areas of Tuscany is by bus. The region's bus network is extensive, with a number of private and subsidized bus companies covering the bulk of the region. The four most useful lines, which depart from Florence and/or Siena, are **CAP, Lazzi, SITA,** and **Tra-In.**

The train covers less ground, but it can be a convenient and inexpensive travel option if you're traveling to larger cities. There is regular service between Florence and towns north and west of Florence, including Prato, Lucca, and Pisa. Service to Siena and points south is spotty. For more information on train schedules, see the **Ferrovie dello Stato's** website at **www.trenitalia.com.**

CAP Via Nazionale, 13, Florence; phone 055 214 627

Lazzi Piazza della Stazione, 4, Florence; phone 055 351 061; **www.lazzi.it**

SITA Via Santa Caterina da Siena, Florence; phone 055 483 651

Tra-In Piazza San Domenico, Siena; phone 0577 204 111; **www.trainspa.it**

Quick Glance at the Towns of Tuscany

Following is a listing of cities and touring areas in Tuscany by province. For each city or area, we provide an overall rating to describe how rewarding that place is to visit. We also include a short comment about the place. Use this as a reference for day trips or extended holidays.

City/Area	Overall Rating	Comment
Province of Florence		
Chianti	★★★★★	Textbook Tuscany
Fiesole	★★★★★	Perfect panorama of Florence
Galluzzo	★★★	Pontormos housed in Certosa
Vinci	★★★	Home of Leonardo
Province of Siena		
Montalcino	★★★	Well-known fortress and wine
Montepulciano	★★★★	Sangallo's San Biagio is a study in symmetry
San Gimignano	★★★★★	Medieval metropolis
Siena	★★★★★	Few towns are finer
Province of Arezzo		
Arezzo	★★★½	Piero della Francesca's frescoes
Cortona	★★★	Pastoral Tuscany on the Umbrian border
Sansepolcro	★★½	On the Piero della Francesca trail
Province of Prato		
Prato	★★★½	Florence's rarely-visited neighbor
Province of Pistoia		
Collodi	★★★½	Inspired *Pinocchio*
Pistoia	★★½	Noteworthy blues festival
Province of Lucca		
Bagni di Lucca	★★★	Curative baths favored by Brits
Lucca	★★★★	Hill town gave birth to Puccini

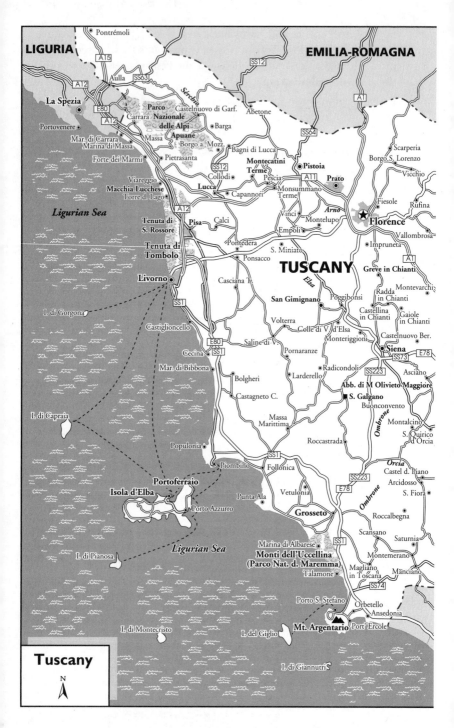

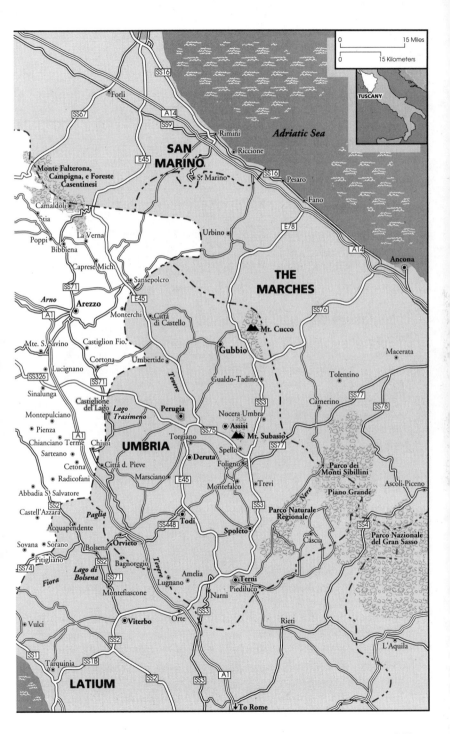

Quick Glance at the Towns of Tuscany *(continued)*

City/Area	Overall Rating	Comment
The Garfagnana	★★★	Tuscan mountains
Riviera Versilia	★★★★	Home to ritzy resorts and a grand Carnevale
Province of Massa e Carrara		
Massa e Carrara	★★	Michelangelo shopped here for marble
Province of Pisa		
Pisa	★★★★★	The Leaning Tower and other architectural beauties
Volterra	★★★	Once a major Etruscan stronghold
Province of Livorno		
Livorno	★★½	Bustling Tuscan port
Tuscan Archipelago	★★★	Includes Napoleon's isle of exile and natural landscapes
Province of Grosseto		
Ansedonia	★★★	Surfing, sunbathing, and Roman ruins
Grosseto	★	Archeological museum houses Etruscan and Roman finds
The Maremma	★★★½	Wildlife preserve dotted with crenellations
Massa Marittima	★★	Mining town with medieval core
Monte Argentario and the Isola del Giglio	★★★½	Summery spots away from the crowds
Pitigliano	★★★	Tuscany's "Little Jerusalem"

The Province of Florence

Province of Florence Tourist Office   Via Cavour, 1r (near San Lorenzo); 50120 Florence; phone 055 290 832; **www.provincia.firenze.it**

Fiesole

Today, the modest hilltop village of Fiesole is practically an outgrowth of Florence, and is certainly the best-known of the villages in the Florentine hills. However, during Etruscan times, Faesulae (Fiesole's Etruscan moniker) was powerful enough to hold off the Romans who set up camp in the valley below (which would later become Florence). By the 12th century, after countless sieges and battles, Fiesole finally fell under Florentine control, essentially becoming a perch from which the wealthy could watch the town blossom into a powerful city-state.

By comparison, Fiesole has always been the humble cousin to Florence's wealth and excess, and this quality is reflected in many of the town's attractions, including the 11th-century **Duomo.** Furthermore, Fiesole was once the home of one of Italy's most respected artists, Fra Angelico. Giovanni da Fiesole, later Fra Angelico, was a monk at the church of **San Domenico** (in the hamlet of San Domenico, just below Fiesole) before he and his fellow friars moved to the Florence's church of San Marco. It was there, in San Marco's cloister (now the Museo di San Marco), where he painted some of the most important religious frescoes of the Renaissance.

To get to Fiesole, take the number 7 bus from Piazza San Marco (originating at Santa Maria Novella). The ride takes about 20 minutes and loop-de-loops the hillside, with magnificent views of Florence.

APT Fiesole   Via Portigiani, 3; 50014 Fiesole; phone 055 598 720, fax 055 598 822

Galluzzo

In Florence's southern suburban hills is the town of Galluzzo, famous for its dramatic **Certosa** (Località Galluzzo; phone 055 204 9226; open for guided visits Tuesday–Sunday, 9 a.m.–noon, 3–6 p.m.; admission free). Still home to several dozen monks, who oversee the upkeep of the monastery's grounds and gardens, the Certosa is the area's most somber getaway. Built in the mid-14th century, the imposing Carthusian monastery was commissioned by Niccolò Acciaiuoli, a Florentine banker who hoped the investment would earn him a place in Heaven. The Certosa is comprised of the **Palazzo Acciaiuoli,** the church of **San Lorenzo,** two cloisters, and a *pinacoteca,* all connected by a wide courtyard and arcaded walkways. Many local artists visited the Certosa during its heyday, including Fra Angelico, who painted a triptych (now in the Museo di San Marco) while on retreat here. In addition, Andrea and Giovanni della Robbia contributed a number of terra cottas, still on view in the church. The works of art that most visitors come to see are the five fresco lunettes by Jacopo Pontormo, who lived here from 1522 to 1525 in order to escape the plague in Florence. The richly colored panels, *Christ's Passion,* are housed in the *pinacoteca* along with other religious paintings dating from the 14th to the 18th centuries.

For more information about Galluzzo, contact the provincial tourist office in Florence (phone 055 290 832; **www.provincia.firenze.it**).

Vinci

Leonardo da Vinci, the Renaissance man who put this small village on the map, lived in Vinci until the age of 15, when his father sent him to Florence to study art with Andrea del Verrocchio. During Leonardo's time, Vinci was renowned for the Castello Conti-Guidi, an imposing fortress built in the 11th and 12th centuries. Today, the castle houses the **Museo Leonardiano** (Via la Torre, 2; phone 0571 56 055; open daily,

9:30 a.m.–6 p.m.; admission €4). Founded in 1953, this small museum dedicated to Vinci's most famous son is the main tourist draw in town. The three-story museum is dedicated to displaying the master's scientific inventions, including working models of a worm screw, a ladder, a loom, a bicycle, a parachute, and more than a dozen other innovative machines. To complete the Leonardo da Vinci itinerary, visit **Casa di Leonardo** (Località Anchiano; phone 0571 56519; open March–October, daily, 9:30 a.m.–7 p.m., winter hours until 6 p.m.; admission free), the supposed birthplace of the artist, located roughly two miles outside of Vinci in the town of Anchiano.

Associazione Pro Vinci   Via delle Torri, 11; 55020 Vinci; phone 0571 568 012

Chianti

This verdant ribbon of rolling hills and country roads between Florence, Arezzo, and Siena is what Tuscan dreams are made of. Around every bend you'll find surprises, like silvery olive groves and lone cypresses, an almond and green patchwork of tilled land and rows of grapevines, and the occasional medieval castle that seems to materialize in the mist. Chianti is a region within a region, where grapes soften into wine and people take off their watches. The dozen or so small villages of the Chianti share a landscape, a similar heritage, and a stake in the production of fine Chianti Classico wine. A sense of history hangs heavy in the air here, yet towns here flirt with your senses rather than overwhelm you with obligatory itineraries.

You'll need a car to get from town to town in Chianti. The best route to follow is the SS222, also known as the Via Chiantigiana, which cuts a well-worn, scenic path from Florence to Siena. If you're driving from Florence, the first and largest Chianti town is **Greve in Chianti,** notable for being the birthplace of Giovanni da Verrazzano, discoverer of the New York harbor. In the middle of Greve's Piazza Matteotti is a statue of the explorer, and lining the square are arts and craft shops, small restaurants, and wine sellers. The piazza also plays host to a market on Saturdays. Further south, smaller towns fan out along the SS222, the SS429, and the SS408 highways. The valley below **Castellina in Chianti** was the site of fierce fighting between Florence and Siena. Its well-kept fortifications, including a central tower, give this hill town a decidedly cool, medieval feel. Giving off similar vibes with its narrow streets and stone turrets is **Radda in Chianti,** the former capital of the Lega del Chianti, a medieval military alliance of Florentine principalities. The coat-of-arms of the Lega, the black rooster or *gallo nero,* was born in Radda, and today the symbol lives on as the trademark of the Chianti Classico Consortium. The town even has a small museum devoted to decanting at the **Piccolo**

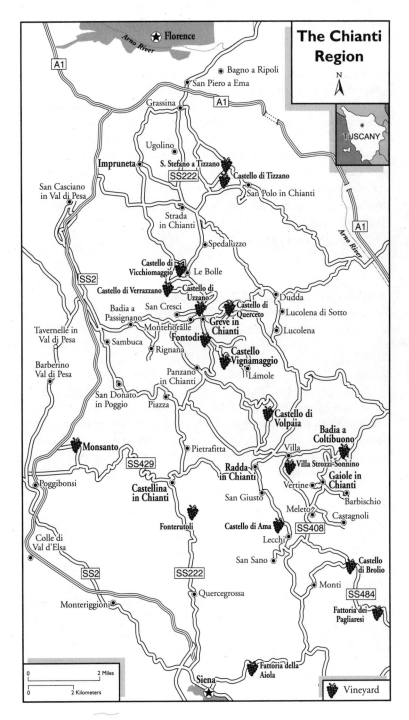

The Chianti Region

N

TUSCANY

Arno River

★ Florence

Ⓐ A1

● Bagno a Ripoli
● San Piero a Ema

Grassina

A1

● Ugolino

Impruneta ● **S. Stefano a Tizzano**
SS222
● Castello di Tizzano

San Casciano
in Val di Pesa ●
● San Polo in Chianti

Strada
in Chianti

● Spedaluzzo

Castello di
Vicchiomaggio ● Le Bolle

SS2

Castello di Verrazzano ●
Castello di
Uzzano
● Dudda

Badia a ● San Cresci
Passignano
Castello di
Querceto
● Lucolena di Sotto

Montefioralle ● **Greve in
Chianti**
● Lucolena

Tavernelle in
Val di Pesa
● Sambuca
Fontodi

Barberino
Val di Pesa ● Rignana
**Castello
Vignamaggio**

Panzano
in Chianti
● Lámole

San Donato
in Poggio ● Piazza

**Castello di
Volpaia**

Monsanto
● Villa
**Badia a
Coltibuono**

● Poggibonsi
SS429
● Pietrafitta
● Villa Strozzi-Sonnino

**Radda-
in Chianti**
**Gaiole in
Chianti**

Vertine ●

**Castellina
in Chianti**
● San Giusto
● Barbischio

Fonterutoli
Castello di Ama
Meleto ● Castagnoli

Colle di
Val d'Elsa
● Lecchi
SS408

● San Sano
**Castello
di Brolio**

● Monti

SS2
SS222
● Quercegrossa
SS484

Monteriggioni ●
**Fattoria dei
Pagliaresi**

0   2 Miles
0   2 Kilometers

**Fattoria della
Aiola**

Siena
★

🍇 Vineyard

249

Museo del Chianti (Fattoria di Montevertine; phone 0577 738 009; open Monday–Saturday, 9 a.m.–noon, 2–5 p.m.; admission free, flights of wine for a small fee).

Of course, no trip to Chianti would be complete without sampling the local wine. You need to make an appointment to visit most vineyards of Chianti. Check with the **Consorzio Chianti Classico (www.chianti-classico.com)** for details and itineraries. A couple other wineries you might want to visit, **Tenuta di Castello Vicchiomaggio** and **Badia a Coltibuono,** are outlined in Part Five, Dining in Central Italy.

APT Greve in Chianti   Viale Giovanni da Verrazzano, 59; 50022 Greve in Chianti (Provincia Firenze); phone 055 854 6287

APT Castellina in Chianti   Via Rocca; 53011 Castellina in Chianti (Provincia Siena); phone 0577 740 620

APT Radda in Chianti   Piazza Ferrucci, 1; 53017 Radda in Chianti (Provincia Siena); phone 0577 738 494

The Province of Siena

Province of Siena Tourist Office   Via di Città, 43; 53100 Siena; phone 0577 280 551, fax 0577 281 041, **www.terresiena.it**

Siena

Standing tall and shoulder-to-shoulder, the 13th- and 14th-century buildings of Siena cast a perpetual shadow over the gray cobbled streets and squares below. Despite imposing first impressions, Siena is a cheerful city with an equally ebullient citizenry. What keeps the populace abuzz throughout the year is the anticipation of the **Palio,** a twice-annual horse race that features medieval pageantry and breakneck racing antics. This sporting tradition dates back to the Middle Ages, and each year pits 10 of Siena's 17 districts *(contrade)* against one another in a startling bareback horse race around a dirt-filled Piazza del Campo.

Every citizen in Siena belongs to a contrada, and each one of these is represented by a mascot. Siena's *contrade* are giraffe *(giraffa)*, turtle *(tartuca)*, goose *(oca)*, unicorn *(leocorno)*, shell *(nicchio)*, porcupine *(istrice)*, dragon *(drago)*, owl *(civetta)*, she-wolf *(lupa)*, wave *(onda)*, forest *(selva)*, tower *(torre)*, eagle *(aquila)*, caterpillar *(bruco)*, snail *(chiocciola)*, panther *(pantera)*, and ram *(montone)*. If you're in Siena around Palio time (July 2 and August 16), you should decide right away for whom you want to cheer, or else remain neutral. The Senesi are a fiercely loyal bunch and will try their very best to sway you one way or the other.

Given Siena's utterly intriguing traditions, it isn't hard to see why this central Tuscan town has blossomed as a favorite destination for tourists from around the world. Many come first for the Palio, then serendipitously discover an austere medieval town virtually unchanged since succumbing to Florentine rule in the mid-16th century. At the center of Siena's marvelous stone cityscape is the enormous, shell-shaped Piazza del Campo and the sky-scraping **Torre del Mangia.** Beyond the tourist hubbub and months after the initial excitement of a Palio victory has faded, Siena's calm, hushed allure is undeniable.

City of Siena Tourist Office Piazza del Campo, 56; 53100 Siena; phone 0577 280 551, fax 0577 270 676; **www.siena.turismo.toscana.it**

Duomo

Type of Attraction Siena's Romanesque/Gothic cathedral
Location Piazza del Duomo
Admission Free
Hours Daily, 7:30 a.m.–1 p.m., 2:30–5:30 p.m.
Phone 0577 47 321250
When to Go Mass is at 9 and 10 a.m. daily
Overall Appeal by Age Group

Pre-school ★★	Teens ★★★	Over 30 ★★★★★
Grade school ★★★	Young Adults ★★★★	Seniors ★★★★★

Author's Rating ★★★★★
How Much Time to Allow 1 hour

Description and Comments One of the most splendid Gothic churches in all of Italy, Siena's Duomo is noted for its ornately carved façade, spectacular mosaic floor, and overwhelming use of black-and-white striping. The front exterior of the church, built in two parts between 1284–1297 and 1382–1390, is overloaded with relief statues of saints, mythological animals, and angels. The giant sun symbol above the central door was the idea of San Bernardino, who thought that the sun could be a unifying symbol for a citizenry more concerned with their individual *contrade*. A rose window high above the sun symbol sheds light on the interior, which is characterized by its zebra-striped marble columns and polychrome patterned floor.

The pavement *(pavimento)* depicts a variety of scenes from the Bible and from civic life. The 56 pavements are meant to be viewed in a certain order. Start with the *Delphic Sybil* on the far right at the entrance, continue along the right side of the nave to behind the altar and back around to the far left entrance. From there, you are to walk down the central aisle to the area underneath the dome. Here, you'll find a hexagon filled with 13 scenes from the *Sacrifice of Elias* and the *Execution of False Prophets*. The pavements continue along until the altar, where you'll find the *Sacrifice of Abraham*. Some of Siena's most talented artists are said to have worked on some of the pavements in the church from 1369 until the early

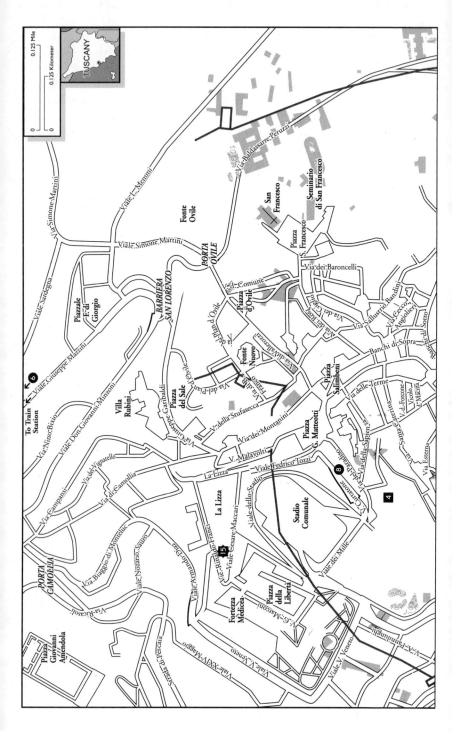

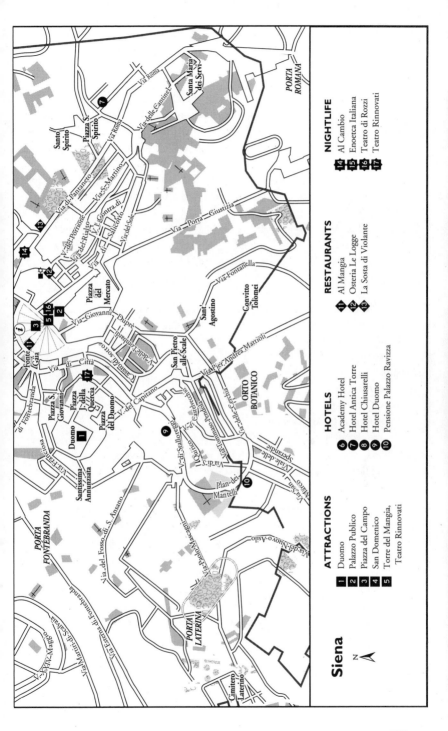

Siena

N

ATTRACTIONS
1 Duomo
2 Palazzo Publico
3 Piazza del Campo
4 San Domenico
5 Torre del Mangia,
Teatro Rinnovati

HOTELS
6 Academy Hotel
7 Hotel Antica Torre
8 Hotel Chiusarelli
9 Hotel Duomo
10 Pensione Palazzo Ravizza

RESTAURANTS
11 Al Mangia
12 Osteria Le Logge
13 La Sosta di Violante

NIGHTLIFE
14 Al Cambio
15 Enoeca Italiana
16 Teatro di Rozzi
17 Teatro Rinnovati

17th century, among them possibly Duccio di Buoninsegna. Elsewhere in the church you'll find works from other masters, such as Nicola Pisano, who carved the *Life of Christ* scenes on the pulpit, and Pinturicchio, who frescoed the walls of the Piccolomini Library (on the left side of the nave).

A few other stops to make while inside the Duomo: Follow the pathway to the right of the dome through the unfinished nave. Started in 1339, the new nave would have reconfigured the layout of the church and would have made it the largest in Christendom. Sadly, the plague hit Siena before the nave could be completed. Today, part of it has been covered over to house the Museo del Opera del Duomo, where you'll find many original sculptures from the façade. You can also climb the stairs to a narrow lookout point where the new façade would have been.

Touring Tips Many of the *pavimenti* in the Duomo are covered over throughout the year until September. A map of the *pavimenti*, and a notice of which ones are on view, is usually available at the church entrance.

Palazzo Pubblico

Type of Attraction Medieval town hall, includes the Museo Civico
Location Piazza del Campo
Admission €7
Hours Daily, 10 a.m.–7 p.m.
Phone 0577 292 263
When to Go Early
Overall Appeal by Age Group

Pre-school ★★		Teens ★★★		Over 30 ★★★★
Grade school ★★★		Young Adults ★★★★		Seniors ★★★★

Author's Rating ★★★★
How Much Time to Allow 1 hour

Description and Comments Siena's superlative town hall, built between 1288 and 1342, opens up into a dark, stony courtyard that still seems to resonate with the sounds of medieval skirmishes. Siena prospered when humanism was at its peak, and, as such, the "palace of the people" was decorated in fine style. The upper floors of the Palazzo Pubblico now make up the Museo Civico, where you'll find some of the finest works from the Siena school. Chief among these is the *Maestà,* by Simone Martini, completed in 1315. Located in the Sala del Mappamondo, the badly faded work features the Madonna as the Queen of Heaven. The Sienese tend to prefer Martini's other work here, which is located on the opposite wall from the *Maestà.* The fresco of *Guidoriccio da Fogliano,* an early study in perspective depicting the legendary knight, is a favorite postcard subject here. Adjacent to the Sala del Mappamondo is the Sala della Pace, which contains a pair of damaged but amusing frescoes by Ambrogio Lorenzetti. The *Allegory of Good Government* depicts the ideal society, where crops are tended, government rules with benevolence, and people dance in the streets. The tongue-in-cheek *Allegory of Bad Government* features a devilish tyrant, who takes bribes, ignores public works, and lets the city fall to ruin. We imagine the latter image dogged crooked Sienese governors with guilt.

Piazza del Campo

Type of Attraction Famed shell-shaped piazza
Location Piazza del Campo
Admission Free
Hours ·Always open
Phone None
When to Go Anytime
Overall Appeal by Age Group

Pre-school ★★★★★	Teens ★★★★★	Over 30 ★★★★★
Grade school ★★★★★	Young Adults ★★★★★	Seniors ★★★★★

Author's Rating ★★★★ .
How Much Time to Allow As long as you like

Description and Comments The first thing you'll notice about the Piazza del Campo is that it is unexpectedly large and light-filled, given the tight warren of dark streets that surround it. The shell-shaped piazza sits on a slant, with a clutter of medieval *palazzi* to its back and the awesome Palazzo Pubblico and Torre del Mangia at its front. During the Palio, Siena's famous, twice-yearly horse race, the Campo is filled with dirt and teeming with people. If you're in Siena any other time of the year, you can make out the nine sectors that the shell is divided in. These represent the Council of Nine, the group that ruled the city during medieval times. A small, ornate fountain opposite the town hall is a copy of an original carved by Jacopo della Quercia.

San Domenico

Type of Attraction Holds relic of St. Catherine
Location Piazza San Domenico
Admission Free
Hours Daily, 8 a.m.–noon, 2–6:30 p.m.
Phone None
When to Go Anytime
Overall Appeal by Age Group

Pre-school —	Teens ★★	Over 30 ★★
Grade school ★★	Young Adults ★★	Seniors ★★

Author's Rating ★★
How Much Time to Allow 15–30 minutes

Description and Comments Siena's second-largest church is in stark contrast to the magnificently Gothic Duomo. San Domenico is boxy, almost barn-shaped, and definitely not a dazzler. However, followers of St. Catherine, one of the patron saints of Italy who was born here in the early 1300s, will want to take a detour here. Legend has it that Catherine experienced the stigmata in the church in the Cappella delle Volte. Some years after that miracle, and after Catherine's death, a chapel of the church was set aside in her honor. Oddly enough, the chapel was built to hold a rather gruesome reliquary—that of Catherine's preserved head. Her head is now kept in a gilded marble case below San Domenico's altar. (The rest of her body, by the way, is in the church of Santa Maria Sopra Minerva in Rome.)

Torre del Mangia

Type of Attraction Symbol of Siena
Location Palazzo Pubblico
Admission €5.50
Hours Daily, 10 a.m.–7 p.m.
Phone 0577 226 822
When to Go On the hour
Special Comments The stairwell is narrow, and may be difficult for persons suffering from claustrophobia.

Overall Appeal by Age Group

Pre-school ★★★★	Teens ★★★★★	Over 30 ★★★★★
Grade school ★★★★	Young Adults ★★★★★	Seniors ★★★

Author's Rating ★★★★
How Much Time to Allow 1 hour

Description and Comments When it was built between the early 14th and 15th centuries, the bell tower of the Palazzo Pubblico was the highest in Italy, at some 330 feet. After more than 550 years, the Torre del Mangia holds steady as the second-highest *campanile* in the land. The tower was named after its first bell ringer, who, despite his daily climb of more than 505 steps, was considered quite lazy. He earned the nickname "Mangiaguadagni," which means, roughly, "eater of profits." You can follow Mangiaguadagni's path up the extremely narrow, winding staircase to the top for great views over the city.

Entertainment and Nightlife in Siena

This is a rather quiet town when it comes to nightlife. The residents seem to conserve their rabble-rousing energy for the festivities that center around the Palio. The days leading up to and between the two horse races—namely, the summer months—are packed with events, including the **Settimana Musicale Senese** (Via di Città, 89; phone 0577 46152) and the **Siena Jazz Fest** (Fortezza Medicea, 10; phone 0577 271 401; **www.sienajazz.it**). Concerts are held in churches and squares throughout Siena, and some classical events are held in either **Teatro di Rozzi** (Via di Città, 36; phone 0577 280 122; **www.accademiarozzi.it**) or **Teatro Rinnovati** (Piazza del Campo, Palazzo Comunale; phone 0577 292 266). When it's off-season in Siena, these theaters' seasons really begin, with offerings of orchestral symphonies, opera, drama, and ballet. Expect to pay €10–€50 per ticket.

A more casual evening in Siena is best spent at a sidewalk café, watching crowds wax and wane in the Piazza del Campo. For more excitement, head to **Enoteca Italiana** (Fortezza Medicea, Viale Maccari; phone 0577 288 497). Here, you can choose from more than 400 vintages and mingle with the locals past midnight. The Enoteca becomes a piano bar on the weekends. A wider range of music is available at **Al Cambio** (Via Pantaneto, 48; phone 0577 43183). On nights when there isn't live music, you can usually hear the latest dance tracks and Top 40 hits.

Montalcino

Montalcino, with its medieval **Fortezza** (Piazzale della Fortezza; phone 0577 849 211; open March–October: daily, 9 a.m.–8 p.m.; winter hours: Tuesday–Sunday, 9 a.m.–6 p.m.; admission €3) and its pretty countryside, holds the recipe for an ideal Tuscan hilltop village. Built on the orders of Siena in 1361, the Fortezza is the highest point in town and offers sweeping views of central Tuscany. The Fortezza is renowned in Tuscany as a safehouse for a group of Sienese republicans who fled to Montalcino in 1555 after their city fell to Florence. Siena remembers the loyalty of the Montalcini each year by letting representatives from the town lead the Palio parade.

For those outside of Tuscany, however, Montalcino's name is more closely associated with its DOCG Brunello vintage, one of the finest in Italy. There are about 30 vineyards in the Montalcino area that produce the bold Brunello, and countless *enoteche* that sell the stuff. If you want to sample the DOCG wine, head to the source, **Biondi Santi** (Tenuta il Greppo, 183; phone 0577 848 087; open Monday–Friday, 8 a.m.–noon, 2–4 p.m.; closed August), where Ferruccio Biondi-Santi first produced the famous *rosso*. For more information, contact the **Consorzio del Vino Brunello di Montalcino** (Costa del Municipio, 1; 53024 Montalcino; phone 0577 848 246; **www.consorziobrunellodimontalcino.it**).

APT Montalcino   Costa del Municipio, 8; 53024 Montalcino; phone 0577 849 331

Montepulciano

A city that reaches to the clouds, Montepulciano is one of Tuscany's steepest hill towns, towering at an elevation of almost 2,000 feet. Like Florence, its ally during more than four centuries of regional conflict, Montepulciano grew up to be a lovely Renaissance city, with a harmonious assortment of edifices designed by the likes of Michelozzo and Vignola. Antonio da Sangallo the Elder designed the city walls, which separate the core of town from the scores of vineyards that surround it. From these vineyards, the Vino Nobile di Montepulciano, another one of Tuscany's great red wines, is manufactured. Further afield, Sangallo's **San Biagio** (Via San Biagio, 14; no phone; open daily, 8 a.m.–1 p.m., 3–7 p.m.; admission free) is worth a visit. This perfectly proportioned 16th-century church is considered architect Antonio da Sangallo the Elder's masterpiece. Commonly called the temple of San Biagio, the plans of the classical, Greek cross–style church strictly follow the Renaissance design aesthetic that called for a symmetrical building in an uncluttered setting, à la the classical temples of ancient Greece and Rome. To get to San Biagio, follow the signs from the city center downhill to the Porta al Prato. From there, you can follow the Via di San Biagio.

Like Montalcino, Montepulciano has a reputation for fine wine. Several vineyards offer tastings of the Vino Nobile and tours; we like **Poliziano** (Via Fontago, 11; phone 0578 738 171; open Monday–Friday, 8:30 a.m.–12:30 p.m., 2:15–6 p.m.; closed August and December). Montepulciano also has a consortium to answer any question you may have about the local DOCG wine. For more information, contact **Consorzio del Vino Nobile di Montepulciano** (Piazza Grande, 7; 53045 Montepulciano; phone 0578 757 812).

APT Montepulciano Via Gracciano del Corso, 59a; 53045 Montepulciano; phone 0578 757 341

San Gimignano

Tall, windowless, stone towers characterize San Gimignano, the medieval version of a modern metropolis, often referred to by tourist office brochures as a medieval Manhattan. During the 13th and 14th centuries, when San Gimignano was at its economic peak, the city's skyline bristled with more than 76 towers, each of which were built by rival families to assert their wealth and power. The 13 towers that remain today give San Gimignano one of the most unusual cityscapes in all of Italy, transforming this town from a peaceful getaway to a tourist haunt. During high season, the foot traffic can be stifling. Nevertheless, a trip here can be rewarding, especially for the chance to climb to the top of one of the antique skyscrapers for a look around the Tuscan countryside. If you decide to visit, it makes sense to purchase a combined museum ticket *(biglietto cumulativo)*, which grants admission to the **Collegiata,** the **Museo Civico,** the **Torre Grossa,** and other, smaller museums. Combined tickets costs approximately €11 per person, or €9 per person within a group or family.

The bus is your only public transportation option to San Gimignano. From Florence, SITA buses take about two hours. Tra-In buses from Siena connect the two towns in about an hour. Transportation is spotty on Sundays. If you're driving, follow the Siena–Florence (Si-Fi) *autostrada* to the Poggibonsi exit, then follow the signs to San Gimignano. Cars are mostly prohibited within the city, so you will have to park in the lot at Porta San Giovanni.

Associazione Pro Loco San Gimignano   Piazza del Duomo, 1; 53037 San Gimignano; phone 0577 940 008; **www.sangimignano.com**

Collegiata

Type of Attraction San Gimignano's so-called Duomo

Location Piazza del Duomo

Admission €3 for the dome and the Cappella di Santa Fina, or visit using combined ticket

Hours Monday–Friday, 9:30 a.m.–7:30 p.m.; Saturday, 9:30 a.m.–5 p.m.; Sunday, 1–5 p.m.; closed January–March

Phone 0577 940 316

When to Go Early morning

Overall Appeal by Age Group

Pre-school ★★★	Teens ★★★	Over 30 ★★★★
Grade school ★★★	Young Adults ★★★★	Seniors ★★★★

Author's Rating ★★★★★

How Much Time to Allow 30 minutes

Description and Comments Not exactly a cathedral but a collegiate church, the Collegiata is a diamond in the rough. Nothing on the church's exterior is enticing enough to make you want to go inside, which is exactly what makes the brilliantly frescoed interior so magnificent. The work of pre-Renaissance artists decorates much of the church. Lippo Memmi, a student of Sienese master Simone Martini, painted a series of frescoes based on the New Testament; Bartolo di Fredi designed the Old Testament fresco cycle. Furthermore, on the back wall of the church, there is a strikingly gruesome *Last Judgment* by Taddeo di Bartolo. Equally creepy is the preserved body of San Gimignano's patron saint, Santa Fina, which is encased at the foot of the Collegiata's altar. It is said that Santa Fina earned her sainthood by placing herself in a self-imposed prayer detention, in which she repented day and night for five years after having accepted, against her mother's wishes, an apple from a young suitor. The Santa Fina Chapel, on the right side of the church, contains a dazzling set of frescoes by Ghirlandaio. Note the jumbled San Gimignano skyline in the fresco depicting Santa Fina's funeral.

Museo Civico and Torre Grossa

Type of Attraction Home of historical frescoes and the city's tallest tower

Location Palazzo del Popolo, Piazza del Duomo

Admission €6, or visit using combined ticket

Hours Summer: daily, 9:30 a.m.–7 p.m.; winter: Tuesday–Sunday, 10:30 a.m.–4:20 p.m.

Phone 0577 940 008

When to Go Before lunch

Overall Appeal by Age Group

Pre-school —	Teens ★★	Over 30 ★★★
Grade school ★★★	Young Adults ★★★	Seniors ★★★

Author's Rating ★★★★½

How Much Time to Allow 30 minutes to 1 hour

Description and Comments The paintings housed in San Gimignano's municipal museum are significant links to the city's medieval life. The highlights are *Wedding Scene* by Memmo di Filipucci, which depicts a newlywed couple sharing a bath and a bed, and *San Gimignano and His Miracles,* a painting by Taddeo di Bartolo, which shows the saint holding a miniature version of the "City of Towers" in his hand. After you've had a gander at the art here, you can climb to the top of the Torre Grossa (the big tower), which stands at attention at approximately 175 feet. Several hundred stone steps lead to the top, where there's a small lookout point. Plan accordingly—the arduous climb is not ideal on a very empty stomach.

The Province of Arezzo

Province of Arezzo Tourist Office Piazza Risorgimento, 116; 52100 Arezzo; phone 0575 23952; fax 0575 28042; **www.apt.arezzo.it**

Arezzo

This provincial capital to the east of Florence is largely ignored by the touring masses. Its Etruscan and Roman ruins, viewable at the **Anfiteatro Romano** and adjacent **Museo Archeologico,** are much less spectacular than comparable sites in central Italy. Only die-hard art history buffs seem to make the pilgrimage here to view the stupendous Piero della Francesca fresco cycle in the church of **San Francesco.** The masterpiece recently came out of restorative hiding and hundreds of years of dirt were wiped away to reveal vivid hues and subtle lines. Vasari once lived in Arezzo, and you can visit the home he decorated for himself at the **Casa di Vasari.**

Arezzo

N

ATTRACTIONS

1 Anfiteatro Romano e
    Museo Archeologico
2 Casa di Vasari
3 San Francesco

HOTEL

4 Hotel Continentale

RESTAURANTS

5 Il Saraceno
6 Le Logge Vasari
7 Le Tastevin

Arezzo itself is only half the beauty that its artwork is, and its stony buildings and wide *piazze* appear bleak, saddened by the fact that centuries of tourists have paid it no mind. World War II damage also laid waste to some of the city's quaint medieval alleyways and edifices. Nevertheless, the Aretini have much to smile about. The economy is thriving, thanks in no small part to the gold industry. Many of Italy's premier goldsmiths keep workshops here while distributing their wares to merchants in Florence, Venice, Rome, and abroad. Furthermore, the region's oldest and largest antiques fair can be found in Arezzo on the first Saturday and Sunday of each month.

Arezzo is reachable by train from Florence, and Lazzi and SITA buses also service the region. However, the easiest way to get to town is by driving. Arezzo lies just off the A1, approximately one hour from Florence and two to two and a half hours from Rome.

City of Arezzo Tourist Office Piazza della Repubblica, 28; 52100 Arezzo; phone 0575 377 678; **www.comune.arezzo.it**

Anfiteatro Romano e Museo Archeologico

Type of Attraction Roman amphitheater and archaeological museum

Location Via Margaritone, 10

Admission Amphitheater grounds, free; Museo Archeologico, €4

Hours Amphitheater, daily, 7 a.m.–8 p.m.; Museo Archeologico, Monday–Saturday, 9 a.m.–2 p.m., Sunday, 9 a.m.–1 p.m.

Phone 0575 20 882

When to Go Anytime

Special Comments The amphitheater is accessible from Via Margaritone or Via Crispi

Overall Appeal by Age Group

Pre-school ★		Teens ★		Over 30 ★★
Grade school ★★		Young Adults ★★		Seniors ★★

Author's Rating ★★★

How Much Time to Allow 1 hour

Description and Comments Whatever notable ruins were left over from the Etruscan-then-Roman city of Arretium that haven't been carted off to other museums can be found here. The archaeological museum holds a collection of Etruscan votives, coins, and funerary urns as well as a handsome but small set of Roman-era ceramics. Many of the Roman finds were discovered at excavations near the museum and the adjacent amphitheater, which, in its heyday, could hold about 10,000 spectators. Today, the amphitheater is practically a shell, having been plundered for its travertine blocks during the Middle Ages.

Casa di Vasari

Type of Attraction Former home of famed Renaissance painter and architect

Location Via XX Settembre, 55

Admission Free

Hours Monday and Wednesday–Saturday, 9 a.m.–7:30 p.m.; Sunday, 9 a.m.–1 p.m.

Phone 0575 409 040

When to Go Anytime

Overall Appeal by Age Group

Pre-school —		Teens ★		Over 30 ★★½
Grade school ★		Young Adults ★★		Seniors ★★½

Author's Rating ★

How Much Time to Allow 15–30 minutes

Description and Comments Nothing of this 16th-century building hints of the exquisite works that Giorgio Vasari went on to create in Florence. The overly confident Medici architect decorated his home with bold frescoes and even laid out for himself a Sala del Trionfo della Virtù (Room of the Triumph of Virtue). Today, the Casa di Vasari holds the Archivio Vasariano, which contains scores of the artist's personal documents, including letters from contemporaries, such as Michelangelo.

San Francesco

Type of Attraction Site of a Piero della Francesca masterpiece
Location Piazza San Francesco
Admission €5
Hours Monday–Friday, 9 a.m.–6 p.m.; Saturday, 9 a.m.–5:45 p.m.; Sunday, 1–5:45 p.m.
Phone Information, 0575 900 404; reservations, 06 32 810; fax, 06 326 51 329 **Web** www.pierodellafrancesca.it
When to Go Early, before the day trippers arrive
Special Comments Only 25 persons at a time are allowed entry. Reservations are required and can be made by phone, by fax, or online.

Overall Appeal by Age Group

Pre-school ★★	Teens ★★½	Over 30 ★★★★
Grade school ★★	Young Adults ★★★★	Seniors ★★★★

Author's Rating ★★★★★
How Much Time to Allow 30 minutes

Description and Comments To locals, this church is known as the Chiesa di San Francesco, but to art lovers, it might as well be known as the Chiesa della Francesca. Piero della Francesca, one of the *quattrocento's* most important perspective painters, left his mark here with a fresco cycle called *The Legend of the True Cross.* Begun shortly after Constantinople fell to the Turks—a fearful time for Christians—the fresco cycle recalls the story of the wood that was used to crucify Christ, following it from seedling to its humble return to Jerusalem. Considered Francesca's masterpiece, more than 15 years of conservation work has gone into returning *The Legend of the True Cross* to its original glory. Put this landmark on your itinerary.

Cortona

Ironically, this idyllic, unspoiled town in eastern Tuscany, romanticized in Frances Mayes's bestseller *Under the Tuscan Sun,* has become a sort of tourist trap, attracting hordes of visitors and an equally large number of entrepreneurial souvenir vendors. Even a new festival—the **Tuscan Sun Festival,** which celebrates the art of living well—has taken root. Cortona has come to be known as quintessentially Tuscan, when in reality, this border town has split personalities, with one foot planted in sophisticated

Tuscany, the other one in pastoral Umbria. Teetering on a 1,900-foot promontory with views over Lake Trasimeno, the town is crowded with medieval dwellings, dotted with crenellated towers, and has a charming web of narrow—and steep—streets in which to get lost. Cortona gave birth to Luca Signorelli and Pietro da Cortona—the former, whose works are displayed in the **Museo Diocesano** (Piazza del Duomo; phone 0575 62830; open Tuesday–Sunday, 9:30 a.m.–1 p.m., 3:30–7 p.m.; admission €4), is considered one of the giants of Umbrian painting, while the latter is known for his decoration of the Pitti Palace in Florence. Historically, Cortona, once a city in the Etruscan Dodecapolis, became a source of contention between Perugia and Arezzo. But by the 15th century, Florence gained ownership of Cortona. Since then, this hill town has been a jewel in the Tuscan crown.

APT Cortona   Via Nazionale, 42; 52044 Cortona; phone 0575 630 352

Sansepolcro

Situated in the Tiber valley at the crossroads between easternmost Tuscany, westernmost Marches, and northern Umbria, Sansepolcro can be an ideal day trip, especially for those following the Piero della Francesca trail. This compact, walled town is famous for being the birthplace of the Renaissance artist and has two of his works in its **Museo Civico** (Via Aggiunti, 65; phone 0575 732 218; open daily, 9:30 a.m.–1 p.m., 2:30–7:30 p.m.; admission €5). The triangular *Resurrection,* featuring an expressionless Christ emerging from his tomb with sleeping soldiers at his feet, is one of the artist's most recognizable works outside of Arezzo and Florence. An early della Francesca work, the *Madonna della Misericordia,* and works by Luca Signorelli and Pontormo are also on display here.

If you're traveling to the town in September, a highlight is the **Palio della Balestra,** an annual crossbow tournament against medieval rival Gubbio (in Umbria). Set on the second Sunday of that month, Sansepolcro's Palio sees the whole town gather in the main square of Piazza della Torre di Berta for a day of pageantry, drinking, and merriment.

Sansepolcro is easily reached by car on the SS73. As for public transport, hourly SITA buses connect Sansepolcro with Arezzo. In addition, the Perugia–Terni train line makes a stop in Sansepolcro.

Associazione Pro Loco Sansepolcro   Piazza Garibaldi, 2; 52037 Sansepolcro; phone 0575 740 536

The Province of Prato

The small province of Prato, just 20 minutes outside of the city of Florence, was carved out only in 1992, a result of its namesake provincial capital becoming the third-largest city in Tuscany. The towns in the Province of Prato make for an easy day trip from Florence.

Province of Prato Tourist Office   Via Luigi Muzzi, 38; phone 0574 35 141, fax 0574 607 925; **www.prato.turismo.toscana.it**

Prato

A mere 20 minutes away from the suburbs of Florence, sophisticated Prato should be swarming with day trippers—but it isn't. Today a land of conference centers and convention hotels, Prato has always been to commerce what its sister city has been to art. Since the 1100s, the textile industry has fueled the local economy, first with the production of worsted wool, and today with the manufacture of a variety of fabrics, from cashmere to cotton. One of Prato's most famous sons, the 14th-century businessman Francesco di Marco Datini, is widely recognized (in Italy, anyway) as the founder of modern accounting and is perhaps one of the most accessible figures from the late Middle Ages. As accountants are wont to do, Datini saved almost every scrap of paper he had ever written on, resulting in a collection of more than 15,000 letters, notations, and business documents, now housed in Prato's archives. In her 1957 novel, Iris Origo immortalized the bean counter in *The Merchant of Prato.*

Prato, the third-largest city in Tuscany, is a city full of workaholics and the nouveau riche, where the modern often overshadows the historic. The **Centro per L'Arte Contemporanea L. Pecci,** the city's contemporary art museum, is one of the most comprehensive in Italy. Furthermore, sculptures from 20th-century notables, including Henry Moore and Vittorio Tavernari, are sprinkled throughout town as a reminder that Prato is a city on the move. As for medieval and Renaissance art in Prato, it can be found in the **Duomo** and adjacent museum.

City of Prato Tourist Office   Via Luigi Muzzi, 38; phone 0574 35 141; fax 0574 607 925; **www.prato.turismo.toscana.it**

Centro per L'Arte Contemporanea L. Pecci

Type of Attraction Modern art museum
Location Viale della Repubblica, 277
Admission Permanent collection, free; special exhibitions, €6.50
Hours Wednesday–Monday, 10:30 a.m.–1 p.m., 3–7:30 p.m.
Phone 0574 5317 **Web** www.centropecci.it (in Italian)
Overall Appeal by Age Group

Pre-school ★	Teens ★★	Over 30 ★★
Grade school ★★	Young Adults ★★★	Seniors ★

Author's Rating ★★★
How Much Time to Allow 1 hour

Description and Comments One of Italy's premier centers for 20th-century art, the museum's permanent collection is comprised of a diverse display of works from the likes of Burri, Schnabel, and LeWitt, and the sculpture garden creates a postmodern escape from Renaissance overload. The museum hosts temporary installations each season.

Duomo

Type of Attraction Prato's Duomo

Location Piazza del Duomo

Admission Free

Hours Daily, 8 a.m.–noon, 3–7 p.m.

Phone 0574 29 339

When to Go On the days when the Sacra Cintola (Holy Girdle) is shown: Easter, May 1, August 15, September 8, Christmas

Overall Appeal by Age Group

Pre-school ★★		Teens ★★		Over 30 ★★★
Grade school ★★		Young Adults ★★★		Seniors ★★★

Author's Rating ★★★

How Much Time to Allow 30 minutes

Description and Comments The unusual design of Prato's Duomo di Santo Stefano can be attributed to the fact that funds ran out before it was completed. About three-quarters of the Romanesque/Gothic facade is striped with alternating green and white marble, a clock peers out from the circle where a rose window should have been, and a questionable design decision left one corner of the Duomo with an umbrella-shaped canopy. Nevertheless, devout Catholics flock to Santo Stefano to see its relic. Inside the church, behind a Donatello-designed pulpit, lies the relic of the Sacra Cintola, or the sacred girdle, worn by the Virgin prior to the Assumption. Apparently, Mary gave this article to St. Thomas the Apostle, who then passed it along to a Palestinian woman, who later brought it with her to Prato when she married a local merchant. Agnolo Gaddi records the story of the girdle in a fresco cycle. Elsewhere in the church is a fresco by Fra Filippo Lippi of the *Life of St. John the Baptist.* The Pratese celebrate the holy girdle in a ceremony each year at Easter and Christmas, as well as on May 1, August 15, and September 8. At five times per year, this very intimate of relics sees the light of day probably more than it did when it was in Mary's possession.

Shopping in Prato

There are several factory outlets in and around Prato that sell fabric and fashions at wholesale prices. Note that the outlets are closed during the month of August.

Creazioni Smak   Piazza del Mercato Nuovo, 4; phone 0574 604 333, fax 0574 605 761; c.smak@flashnet.it. Open Monday–Friday, 9 a.m.–12:30 p.m., 2:30–7 p.m., by appointment only; AMEX, MC, V.

Maglificio Denny   Via Zarini, 261 (Prato Est exit); phone 0574 592 191, fax 0574 572 481; denny@denny.it, **www.denny.it.** Open Monday–Friday, 9 a.m.–1 p.m., 3–7:30 p.m., Saturday, 9:30 a.m.–1 p.m., by appointment only. MC, V.

The Province of Pistoia

Province of Pistoia Tourist Office   Piazza San Leone, 1; phone 0573 3741, fax 0573 374 307; **www.provincia.pistoia.it** (in Italian)

Pistoia

Outside of Italy, Pistoia is known for having given its name to the pistol and as the headquarters of Breda, a railway vehicle manufacturer who built cars for the Washington, D.C., and Atlanta subway systems, among others. Despite its industrial reputation, Pistoia has a handsome city center sprinkled with Pisan-Romanesque buildings, and beyond the town's medieval walls lies a lush countryside where a number of tree and plant nurseries flourish. Pistoia's **Duomo** (Piazza del Duomo; phone 0573 369 272; open daily. 8 a.m.–noon, 3–7 p.m.; admission free, Chapel of St. James €2), the Cattedrale di San Zeno, was built around a 12th-century defensive tower, which later became its bell tower *(campanile)*. Inside the church is a surfeit of medieval and Renaissance art. Especially striking is the Chapel of St. James, containing a sparkling silver altar laden with more than 600 statues. Brunelleschi and other Florentine artists contributed to the decoration of the altar, which is thought to weigh almost a ton.

July is the right time to visit Pistoia. Two very different festivals—the **Pistoia Blues Festival** (phone 0573 358 195; **www.pistoiablues.com**) and **La Giostra dell'Orso** (Bear Joust)—command the attention of Pistoiese and (mostly Italian) tourists.

Pistoia lies about halfway between Florence and Pisa. By car, it takes about a 30-minute drive along the A11 from Florence. Trains from Florence to Pistoia take 45 minutes to an hour. If you're traveling from Pisa, driving is best. You'll have to transfer in either Florence or Lucca should you take the train between Pisa and Pistoia, taking you up to an hour out of your way. Lazzi buses offer service between Pistoia and most other towns in Tuscany.

City of Pistoia Tourist Office   Piazza Duomo, 4; phone 0573 21622, fax 0573 34327; **www.comune.pistoia.it**

Collodi

Though Walt Disney would have you believe otherwise, the author of the popular children's tale *Pinocchio* was actually Carlo Collodi (born Carlo Lorenzini), a native son who gained inspiration from Collodi's steep, cobbled paths, terra cotta thatched cottages, and the geometric gardens of the 17th-century **Villa Garzoni** (Giardino di Villa Garzoni; phone 0572 429 592; guided tours only, available daily, 9 a.m.–dusk; admission €5.50). Today, Collodi, a municipality of the town of Pescia, has capitalized on its claim to fame with the **Parco di Pinocchio** (Via San Gennaro, 3; phone 0572 429 342; open Tuesday–Sunday, 9 a.m.–6 p.m.; winter: Saturday and Sunday, 10 a.m.–4 p.m.; admission €7.50 adults, €3.50 children under age 14 and seniors over age 65). Built in 1956, the park has loads of whimsical sculptures based on characters from the story, spurting fountains, and acres to romp around in. The best sight here is that of a bulbous shark head, mouth agape, in the middle of a pond. A puppet show (performed in Italian, but nonetheless enjoyable) caps off the day. Vendors throughout town sell wooden marionettes, books, T-shirts, and anything *Pinocchio*-related—great gifts for young nieces and nephews.

The Province of Lucca

Province of Lucca Tourist Office   Cortile Carrara,12; phone 0583 417 486, fax 0583 417 735; www.provincia.lucca.it

Lucca

Already a town by the second century B.C., Lucca was of strategic importance to the Romans because the trade routes Via Cassia, Via Aurelia, and Via Clodia intersected nearby. Because it was such a major crossroads, Lucca was responsible for minting money. It is no surprise, then, that the Lombards, who invaded northern and central Italy in the sixth century, chose Lucca as their capital. Lucca remained the capital of the Lombard duchy of Tuscia (later, Tuscany) until the ninth century. Then, in 1162, the city became a free municipality *(comune)*. Lucca prospered as a banking and mercantile center during the 13th and 14th centuries, thanks in no small part from its long trading history and coin production expertise. And, it was during this time that the **Duomo** and **San Michele in Foro**—two very unusual churches—began to take shape. Over the next few centuries, Lucca vied with Florence and Pisa for control of Tuscany's trade routes. During this time, Lucca built the massive, fortified brick walls that today still frame this lovely hill town. Modern Lucca is noteworthy as the birthplace of the great composer Giacomo Puccini. The small house (**Casa di Puccini**) in Lucca in which he was born is now

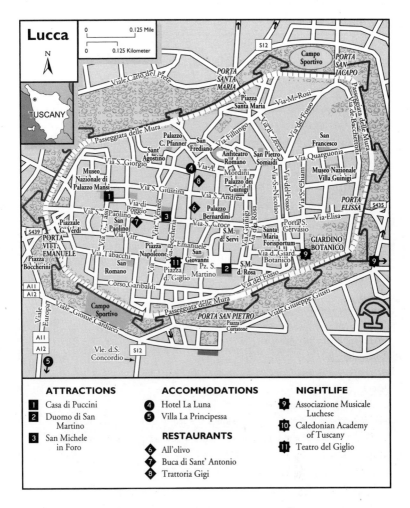

ATTRACTIONS

1 Casa di Puccini
2 Duomo di San
   Martino
3 San Michele
   in Foro

ACCOMMODATIONS

4 Hotel La Luna
5 Villa La Principessa

RESTAURANTS

6 All'olivo
7 Buca di Sant' Antonio
8 Trattoria Gigi

NIGHTLIFE

9 Associazione Musicale
   Luchese
10 Caledonian Academy
   of Tuscany
11 Teatro del Giglio

a shrine and museum, and the annual opera extravaganza, the **Festival Puccini,** is one of the most coveted tickets around.

Lucca is about an hour-and-a-half train ride and a two-hour bus ride from Florence. **Lazzi** buses (phone 055 363 041; **www.lazzi.it**) connect the two cities with about one bus per hour from 6 a.m. until 8 p.m. CLAP (phone 0583 587 897) buses connect Lucca with other towns in its province. If you're arriving by car, there are exits from the A11 and the A12. Once in town, consider renting a bicycle, the preferred mode of transport of the Lucchesi. **Cicli Bizarri** (Piazza Santa Maria; 32, phone 0583 496 031) has a big selection of bikes and reasonable rates.

City of Lucca Tourist Office   Via Guidiccioni, 2; phone 0583 91991, fax 0583 490 766; **www.luccatourist.it**

Casa di Puccini

Type of Attraction Childhood home of Lucca's most famous son
Location Corte San Lorenzo, 9 (Via di Poggio)
Admission €3
Hours June–September: daily, 10 a.m.–6 p.m.; March–May and October–December: Tuesday–Sunday, 10 a.m.–1 p.m., 3–6 p.m.; closed January and February
Phone 0583 584 028
Overall Appeal by Age Group

Pre-school —	Teens ★	Over 30 ★★
Grade school ★	Young Adults ★★	Seniors ★★

Author's Rating ★★
How Much Time to Allow 30 minutes
Description and Comments This small house where Giacomo Puccini grew up has been turned into a museum. On display are the composer's private letters, early librettos, and personal effects, including the piano on which he composed *Turandot.*

Duomo

Type of Attraction Lucca's Romanesque cathedral
Location Piazza San Martino
Admission €2
Hours Summer, daily, 7 a.m.–7 p.m., winter, daily, 7 a.m.–5 p.m.
Phone 0583 957 068
Overall Appeal by Age Group

Pre-school ★★★	Teens ★★★	Over 30 ★★★
Grade school ★★★	Young Adults ★★★	Seniors ★★★★

Author's Rating ★★★
How Much Time to Allow 30 minutes
Description and Comments Lucca's Duomo di San Martino is by far one of Tuscany's most interesting cathedrals. The Romanesque church's asymmetrical plan developed around the 11th-century tower, thus explaining why the arches and tiers of the exterior are cut short on one end. At the entrance, you'll find a three-tiered gabled façade with elaborately carved columns, each of them different, and sculptures of wild animals and other beasts. Underneath, on the porch, are three doorways decorated with relief sculptures and inlaid marble patterns. Two biblical scenes carved by Nicola Pisano in the second half of the 13th century decorate the space above and around the left door. The central doorway features *The Labors of the Month,* a medieval depiction of the chores most appropriate for each season. Surrounding the right door are scenes of daily life and intricate maze patterns, done in dark green and ivory marble. The

interior is much less spectacular, but it's worth a look around. The most notable works here are a 15th-century marble funerary sculpture of a young woman by Jacopo della Quercia, a 13th-century wooden cross, and an altar painting by Ghirlandaio.

San Michele in Foro

Type of Attraction Lucca's most photographed church
Location Piazza San Michele
Admission Free
Hours Daily, 7:30 a.m.–12:30 p.m., 3–6 p.m.
Phone None
Overall Appeal by Age Group

Pre-school ★★	Teens ★★	Over 30 ★★★
Grade school ★★	Young Adults ★★★	Seniors ★★★

Author's Rating ★★★
How Much Time to Allow 15 minutes

Description and Comments Built over the site of a Roman forum (hence, "in Foro"), this church has a most unusual façade. The upper three registers are semidetached from the rest of the church, giving the impression that a second tier was planned but only one wall was raised. As on Lucca's Romanesque-style Duomo, each of the columns on the upper tiers of San Michele in Foro are uniquely decorated with spirals, inlaid marble, and detailed carvings. Inside the church, you'll find a painting of *Saints Jerome, Sebastian, Rocco, and Helena* by Filippino Lippi.

Entertainment and Nightlife in Lucca

If you're looking for wild bars and music clubs, get out of town and head to the coastal resorts along the Versilian Riviera. Opera, classical music, and theater are in abundance in Lucca—what else would you expect from the town that spawned Puccini?

The symphonic season kicks off in January, with productions by the **Associazione Musicale Lucchese** (Via San Micheletto, 3; phone 0583 469 960; **aml.interfree.it**). Promoting the music of the Anglo-Saxon world, including Austria, the Netherlands, Great Britain, and the United States, the **Caledonian Academy of Tuscany** (Via Orzali, 76; phone 0583 955 657; **www.musick.it**) puts on a spring concert series, "Lucca in Orchestra," and sponsors events throughout the summer. The academy also sponsors a program called "English World," which offers English language and literature classes. To hear Puccini and other opera composers of note, visit the **Teatro del Giglio** (Piazza del Giglio, 13/15; phone 0583 46531; **www.teatrodelgiglio.it**), one of Tuscany's finest musical venues.

The Garfagnana

Hemmed in by the stark white marble ridges of the Apuane Alps and the Serchio River valley, the wild Garfagnana region lies in the temperate northern finger of Tuscany. Home to cozy villages and two nature preserves, **Parco dell'Orechiella** (phone 0583 955 525) and the **Parco Naturale delle Alpi Apuane** (phone 0583 644 354), the valley is far off the usual tourist track, though a must for bird-watchers, wildlife lovers, hikers, and outdoor enthusiasts.

The town of **Barga** serves as the best base for vacationing in this area. Barga is a medieval village, whose 11th-century **Duomo** contains a nativity scene by Andrea della Robbia. A more popular attraction just outside of Barga is the **Grotta del Vento** (Fornovolasco; no phone; open April–September: daily, 10 a.m.—5 p.m.; winter hours: weekends only; admission €6–€15 depending on tour length). Millions of years of water and earth went into creating the "Cave of the Wind," through which a torrent of wind is sucked in or blown out, depending on the season. Locals have known about the mysterious cave since the 17th century, and even built a small hut over its cooling blowhole *(buco soffiante),* using it as a refrigerator until World War II. About two miles of tunnels have been explored since 1964, when Lucchese spelunkers began doing formal research on this natural wonder. Visitors to the Cave of the Wind can take one-, two-, or three-hour tours, which feature stalactites and stalagmites, underground streams, and "bottomless pits."

All of the villages in the Garfagnana and the Apuane Alps are generally less than 40 miles away from Lucca and no more than a two-hour drive from Florence. Take the S12, which becomes the S445 at Barga, and follow the signs to your desired destination. There is no train service to the region, however both the **Lazzi** (phone 0583 584 877) and **CLAP** (phone 0583 587 897) bus lines service the larger towns.

Associazione Pro Loco Barga   Piazza Angelio, 3; 55051 Barga; phone 0583 723 499

Bagni di Lucca

Bagni di Lucca, about 17 miles north of Lucca, is famous for its curative thermal baths and was once the stomping grounds of British expats such as Percy Bysshe Shelley, Elizabeth Barrett, and Robert Browning. Most recently, the spa town has embraced the holistic healing trend and is making a comeback. Two spas make good use of the area's thermal springs. The **Terme Jean Varraud** (Piazza San Martino, 11; phone 0583 87221) has two steam grottoes, ancient baths from Roman times, and a modern spa with fitness facilities, massage, and treatment rooms. The **Antico Albergo Terme** (Via del Paretaio, 1; phone 0583 86034, fax

0583 808 700) has similar amenities, and attached is a hotel and restaurant. For more information, visit **www.termebagnidilucca.it.**

Associazione Pro Loco Bagni di Lucca   Piazza Circolo dei Forestieri; 55022 Bagni di Lucca; phone 0583 805 813

Riviera Versilia

Rich Italians, sun-worshipers, and Florence's nightlife scene populate the seaside towns along the northern Tuscan coast, commonly called the Versilian Riviera. The resort towns of **Viareggio** and **Forte dei Marmi** are the hubs of activity here. The healthy and wealthy holiday in Forte dei Marmi, appropriately distant from the snarl and squalor of spring-break excess in Viareggio. Expensive hotels and pricey boutiques line the promenades of Forte dei Marmi, and beachside cabanas are passed down from generation to generation. Viareggio's claim to fame is its raucous **Carnevale** (phone 0584 963 501; **www.viareggio.ilcarnevale.com**), or Carnival, second only to Venice in the number of floats, fantastical costumes, and parades. In the summer, Viareggio is jammed with tourists sunning on the beach or strolling under the shade of rows of palm trees. When Florence's clubs shut down for the summer, many of them move here. At any rate, many Florentine clubgoers relocate here, and the gay scene is especially vibrant. Popular hangouts for both gay and straight clubgoers include **Area Disco** (location varies, Viareggio; phone 0335 538 2929; **www.discoarea.com**) and **Voice Music Bar** (Viale Margherita, 61, Viareggio; phone 0584 45814). Those looking for more traditional entertainment along the Versilian coast should visit the village of **Torre del Lago Puccini,** where the **Puccini Opera Festival** (phone 0584 350 567, fax 0584 341 657; **www.puccinifestival.it**) is held each August.

The A11 (via Lucca) and A12 (via coastal Tuscany) are the fastest and easiest ways to get to Versilia. The SS1 is also convenient, though it can be a traffic nightmare in the summer and during Carnevale. If you need public transport to get you there, there is a train that runs from Florence to Viareggio that takes about two hours. Viareggio is about a 20-minute ride from Lucca and Pisa. Lazzi buses connect Florence and Viareggio, and CLAP buses run between Lucca and the coast. Be prepared to wait for local buses that connect Viareggio with the rest of the coast.

APT Versilia   Piazza Mazzini 22; 55049 Viareggio; phone 0584 48881, fax 0584 47406; **www.versilia.turismo.toscana.it**

Forte dei Marmi Tourist Office   Via Franceschi, 8/b; phone 0584 80091, fax 0584 83214; forte@versilia.turismo.toscana.it

Viareggio Tourist Office   Viale Carducci, 10; phone 0584 962 233, fax 0584 47336; viareggio@versilia.turismo.toscana.it

The Province of Massa e Carrara

APT Massa e Carrara   Viale Vespucci, 24; 54037 Marina di Massa; phone 0585 240 046, fax 0585 869 015; **www.aptmassacarrara.it**

Massa e Carrara

Famous for gleaming white marble and little else, the industrial twin towns of Massa and Cararra, which head up this northern Tuscan province, are of little interest to tourists. Only devoted fans of Michelangelo tend to make the trek to this slice of land between the Apuane Alps and the sea. Michelangelo preferred to work with pure Carrara marble and would spend months in these parts hand-picking the slabs of stone he would eventually use for such works as the *Pietà* in Rome and many sculptures in Florence. A further testament to the quality—and limitless quantity—of Carrara marble came in the early 1970s when Italy chose to donate 3,700 tons of marble to the United States for the construction of the Kennedy Center for the Performing Arts in Washington, D.C.

If you're headed to Massa e Carrara, driving is recommended. Both the A12 coastal autostrada (from Viareggio) and the SS1 (Via Aurelia) will lead you to exits for the towns. You can take a tour around the quarries *(le cave)* of Massa e Carrara by heading to the town of **Colonnata.** Furthermore, the **Museo Civico del Marmo** (Viale XX Settembre, 85, Località Stadio; phone 0585 845 746) has an exhibit on the history of Carrara marble from mountain to museum.

APT Massa e Carrara   Viale Vespucci, 24; 54037 Marina di Massa; phone 0585 240 046, fax 0585 869 015; **www.aptmassacarrara.it**

The Province of Pisa

Province of Pisa Tourist Office   Piazza Vittorio Emanuele II, 14; phone 050 929 111; **www.provincia.pisa.it**

Pisa

A powerful maritime center rivaling Venice and Genoa from the 11th through the 13th centuries, Pisa's fate was sealed when the Arno River, its outlet to the sea, began to silt up. In fact, this natural event also gave rise—or rather, a slant—to Pisa's current claim to fame, the Leaning Tower. Pisa is a frequent day trip for travelers to Florence, though it certainly warrants a longer visit. Away from the touristy **Campo dei Miracoli,** Pisa is a tranquil town. Streets are wider, meals are more relaxed, and the Arno looks mightier than it does in Florence. Furthermore, Pisa has been a university town since 1343, and the large student population puts a youthful face on an old city.

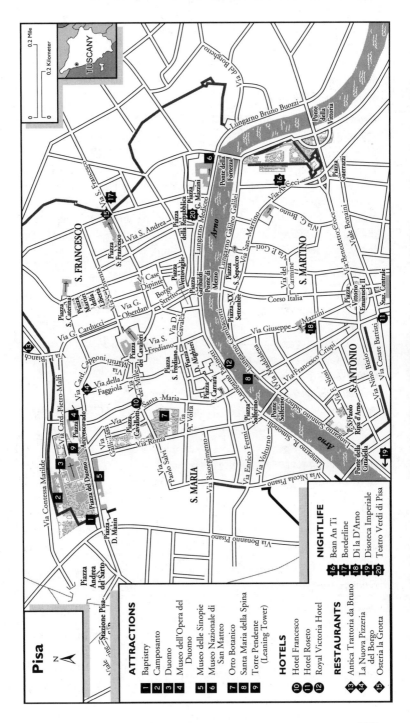

Pisa

N

ATTRACTIONS
1. Baptistry
2. Camposanto
3. Duomo
4. Museo dell'Opera del Duomo
5. Museo delle Sinopie
6. Museo Nazionale di San Matteo
7. Orto Botanico
8. Santa Maria della Spina
9. Torre Pendente (Leaning Tower)

HOTELS
10. Hotel Francesco
11. Hotel Roseto
12. Royal Victoria Hotel

RESTAURANTS
13. Antica Trattoria da Bruno
14. La Nuova Pizzeria del Borgo
15. Osteria la Grotta

NIGHTLIFE
16. Bean An Ti
17. Borderline
18. Di la D'Arno
19. Disoteca Imperiale
20. Teatro Verdi di Pisa

TUSCANY

0   0.2 Mile
0   0.2 Kilometer

275

Getting to Pisa is as easy as taking the train. Approximately two trains each hour travel between Florence's Santa Maria Novella station and Pisa Centrale, with the duration of the trip lasting about an hour.

APT Pisa   Via Cammeo; 56100 Pisa; phone 050 560 464; **www.pisa. turismo.toscana.it**

Campo dei Miracoli Attractions

Situated on a carpet of the greenest grass, the "Field of Miracles" complex, northwest of the city center, consists of the **Baptistry, Duomo, Leaning Tower, Museo dell'Opera del Duomo,** and **Museo delle Sinopie.** Also on-site is the **Camposanto** cemetery. There is a confusing ticketing system for the attractions on the Campo, so we suggest that you buy the complete ticket *(visita completa),* which includes admission to the Baptistry, Camposanto, Duomo, Museo dell'Opera del Duomo, and the Museo delle Sinopie for €10. The Leaning Tower is priced separately.

Baptistry

Type of Attraction   Romanesque/Gothic Baptistry
Location   Campo dei Miracoli
Admission   €3, €10 with combined ticket
Hours   Daily, 8 a.m.–7:40 p.m.; November–March: daily, 9 a.m.–4:40 p.m.
Phone   050 560 547 **Web**   www.duomo.pisa.it
When to Go   Early morning or late afternoon
Overall Appeal by Age Group

Pre-school —		Teens ★★		Over 30 ★★
Grade school ★★		Young Adults ★★		Seniors ★★

Author's Rating ★★
How Much Time to Allow   15–30 minutes

Description and Comments   Started in 1153 but not completed until 1395, Pisa's Baptistry represents a transition from Romanesque to Gothic architecture. The lower register of the cylindrical building features blind arcades, and the upper registers have pointed arches. Of note here is the ornate marble pulpit designed by Nicola Pisano, father and mentor of Giovanni Pisano.

Camposanto

Type of Attraction   Cemetery for Pisa's Duomo complex
Location   Campo dei Miracoli
Admission   €2, €10 with combined ticket
Hours   Daily, 8 a.m.–7:40 p.m.; November–March: daily, 9 a.m.–4:40 p.m.
Phone   050 560 547 **Web**   www.duomo.pisa.it
When to Go   Late afternoon

Overall Appeal by Age Group

Pre-school —		Teens ★★		Over 30 ★★★
Grade school ★		Young Adults ★★★		Seniors ★★★

Author's Rating ★★★

How Much Time to Allow 30 minutes to 1 hour

Description and Comments This long, rectangular cloister building to the left of the Duomo and Baptistry has been a cemetery for Pisan VIPs since 1278. Said to be built on a foundation of Holy Land soil imported by Crusaders, the "Sacred Field" once boasted walls painted with more than 6,500 feet of frescoes. Sadly, Allied bombing during World War II destroyed most of the cloistered cemetery's art. One fresco that did survive— *Triumph of Death* by Francesco Traini—is worth a look because of its rich colors and sobering depictions of mortality.

Duomo

Type of Attraction Pisa's main cathedral

Location Campo dei Miracoli

Admission €4.50, €10 with combined ticket

Hours Monday–Saturday, 10 a.m.–7:40 p.m.; Sunday, 1.–7:40 p.m.

Phone 050 560 547 **Web** www.duomo.pisa.it

When to Go Early morning or late afternoon

Overall Appeal by Age Group

Pre-school ★★		Teens ★★		Over 30 ★★★★
Grade school ★★		Young Adults ★★★		Seniors ★★★★

Author's Rating ★★★

How Much Time to Allow 30–45 minutes

Description and Comments The dark green and cream marble striping that is the signature of many churches throughout Tuscany was first used on Pisa's Duomo. Work on Italy's largest Romanesque church began in 1064 under the supervision of Buscheto and included many design elements borrowed from classical, Byzantine, and Moorish architecture. Rainaldo, Buscheto's successor, completed the cathedral's four-tiered façade, adding decorative moldings to windows, blind arcades, intricate mosaics incorporating flower and animal patterns, and an inlaid wall tomb for Buscheto to the far left of the main entrance. The interior consists of five naves lined with a total of 68 Corinthian columns; a wooden, coffered ceiling; and a soaring dome. Featured above the altar is a mosaic of St. John by Cimabue. A raging fire swept through the Duomo in 1595, destroying much of the church, including its entrance doors. New brass doors, designed by the school of Giambologna, replaced the originals in 1602. Giovanni Pisano's Gothic-style pulpit of Carrara marble also suffered serious damage in the fire and sat in pieces in storage until 1926. One thing that did survive the 1595 fire was the Portale di San Ranieri, the Duomo's entrance facing the Leaning Tower. Bonnano Pisano, the same architect that designed the tower, designed these bronze doors in 1180.

The Leaning Tower (Torre Pendente)

Type of Attraction Icon of Pisa

Location Campo dei Miracoli

Admission €15

Hours Daily, 9 a.m.–5 p.m., guided tours every 40 minutes

Phone 050 560 547 **Web** www.torre.duomo.pisa.it

When to Go Reservations required; online reservations can be made by e-mailing primaziale@sirius.pisa.it

Special Comments Local superstition has it that seeing the Leaning Tower before an exam will guarantee a bad grade.

Overall Appeal by Age Group

Pre-school ★★★★★	Teens ★★★★★	Over 30 ★★★★★
Grade school ★★★★★	Young Adults ★★★★★	Seniors ★★★★★

Author's Rating ★★★★★

How Much Time to Allow 30 minutes

Description and Comments Pisa's main attraction reopened in December 2001 after more than a decade of renovations to stabilize the tower's slant. Intended as the bell tower *(campanile)* of Pisa's new Duomo complex, construction of the tower began on August 9, 1173, the plan of which is carved into a frieze on the first level. Local architect Bonanno Pisano took into account the shallow soil below the Leaning Tower by including a sort of flexible raft framework into the foundation. However, the weight of the structure's bricks and marble was too much, and the tower started to tip in 1274, shortly after the third floor was completed. Despite all of this, builders continued work on the Leaning Tower, finishing it in 1350. For more than 600 years, the Leaning Tower inched further and further to the right, eventually tilting about 16 feet from the perpendicular. In 1990, the tower closed to the public so that the city could save its cash cow before it collapsed. Visitors to the Leaning Tower can again climb the 294 steps to the top, though only 30 visitors or less are allowed in the tower at one time, making it difficult to secure tickets.

Touring Tip Make reservations far in advance.

Museo dell'Opera del Duomo

Type of Attraction Collection of original artworks from the Campo dei Miracoli

Location Piazza del Duomo

Admission €3, €10 with combined ticket

Hours April–September: daily, 8 a.m.–7:20 p.m.; March and October: daily, 9 a.m.–5:20 p.m.; November–February: daily, 9 a.m.–4:20 p.m.

Phone 050 560 547 **Web** duomo.pisa.it

When to Go Anytime

Special Comments There's a spectacular view of the Leaning Tower from the museum's cloister.

Overall Appeal by Age Group

Pre-school —	Teens ★★	Over 30 ★★★
Grade school ★★	Young Adults ★★	Seniors ★★★

Author's Rating ★★

How Much Time to Allow 30 minutes

Description and Comments Original works from the Duomo, Leaning Tower, and Baptistry are on display here, including Giovanni Pisano's *Virgin and Child,* carved for the high altar of the Duomo, and a towering bronze hippogriff (half horse, half griffin) carved in the 10th century. The museum, located in the former chapter house of the Duomo, also has many exhibits that show up-close the dual influences—Islamic and Roman—that led to Pisan-Romanesque architecture, including original arabesque panels, columns with inlaid tiles, and Corinthian capitals.

Museo delle Sinopie

Type of Attraction Small museum of original 14th-century sketches

Location Piazza del Duomo

Admission €2.50, €10 with combined ticket

Hours June–August: daily, 8 a.m.–7:40 p.m.; March–May and September–November: daily, 9 a.m.–5:40 p.m.; December–February: daily, 9 a.m.–4 p.m.

Phone 050 560 547 **Web** duomo.pisa.it

Overall Appeal by Age Group

Pre-school —	Teens ★	Over 30 ★★
Grade school ★	Young Adults ★	Seniors ★★

Author's Rating ★★

How Much Time to Allow 30 minutes

Description and Comments This museum of sketches *(sinopie)* is a collection of works that was found behind the walls in the Camposanto just after all the bombing in World War II. The drawings are early drafts of the Camposanto frescoes, done by the likes of Benozzo Gozzoli and Piero di Puccio in the 14th century.

Museo Nazionale di San Matteo

Type of Attraction National museum of art

Location Piazzetta San Matteo in Soarta

Admission €4.50

Hours Tuesday–Saturday, 9 a.m.–7 p.m.; Sunday, 9 a.m.–2 p.m.
Phone 050 541 865
Overall Appeal by Age Group

Pre-school —	Teens ★★	Over 30 ★★★
Grade school ★	Young Adults ★★	Seniors ★★★

Author's Rating ★★★
How Much Time to Allow 1 to 2 hours

Description and Comments In charge of a collection of religious works from around the city, the National Museum houses approximately 200 works from the Tuscan school. Many of the artists featured here, including Masaccio, Gentile da Fabriano, and Simone Martini, are precursors to the great Renaissance masters. Martini's seven-panel polyptych is a masterpiece of shimmering gold and vibrant colors with depictions of no fewer than 43 apostles, bishops, prophets, and martyrs.

Orto Botanico

Type of Attraction Pisa's Botanical Garden
Location Via Luca Ghini, 5
Admission Free
Hours Monday–Friday, 8 a.m.–1 p.m.,–5:30 p.m., Saturday, 8 a.m.–1 p.m.
Phone 050 560 045
When to Go Make it a rest stop after a visit to the Leaning Tower.
Overall Appeal by Age Group

Pre-school ★★★	Teens ★★★★	Over 30 ★★★★
Grade school ★★★★	Young Adults ★★★★	Seniors ★★★★

Author's Rating ★★★★
How Much Time to Allow As little or as long as you like

Description and Comments Not too many tourists to Pisa stop to smell the roses in the Botanical Gardens, but they should. The oldest botanical garden in Europe, founded in 1595, is now managed by students from the University of Pisa. The grounds are just down the block from the Campo dei Miracoli, but worlds away from the tourist drag.

Santa Maria della Spina

Type of Attraction Petite Gothic church
Location Lungano Gambacorti
Admission €2
Hours June–August: Tuesday–Friday, 11 a.m.–1:30 p.m., 2:30–6 p.m.; Saturday and Sunday, 11 a.m.–1:30 p.m., 2:30–8 p.m.; April, May, and September: Tuesday–Friday, 10 a.m.–1 p.m., 2:30–5 p.m.; Saturday and Sunday, 10 a.m.–1:30 p.m., 2:30–7 p.m.; October–March: Tuesday–Sunday, 10 a.m.–2 p.m.
Phone 050 321 8017

Overall Appeal by Age Group

Pre-school ★★		Teens ★★★		Over 30 ★★★
Grade school ★★★		Young Adults ★★★		Seniors ★★★

Author's Rating ★★★

How Much Time to Allow 15–30 minutes

Description and Comments This tiny, unusual church on the banks of the Arno appears out of nowhere, looking like a crown of thorns. That's exactly how its early-14th-century architects would have you think of it. Santa Maria della Spina—St. Mary of the Thorn—once contained a reliquary of a thorn from Christ's crown, and its exterior Gothic spires, added around 1323, echo the sharpness of the spike. In fact, the outside of the church is an eye-popping assortment of niches sheltering sculptures of saints and steely-faced statues. Santa Maria's proximity to the river was always a concern, and, so, in 1871, the city elected to dismantle the church and rebuild it on a site one yard higher. Consequently, all of the statues you see today are copies—the originals are in the Museo Nazionale di San Matteo.

Entertainment and Nightlife in Pisa

The student population in Pisa contributes to the nightlife vibe. In town, there are many pub options. The requisite Irish pub, **Bean An Ti** (Via Ceci, 56, at Via San Martino; phone 050 23062; closed Sunday), is the place to go for a Irish pint, an English chat, and pub fare. Another good bet not far from the university is **Di La D'Arno** (Via Mazzini, 70; phone 050 49449), which serves bite-size appetizers and cocktails.

Discoteques are scarce in the city, as most dance clubs are located about seven miles from town in **Tirrenia** and **Marina di Pisa.** One of the more popular discos on the water is **Discoteca Imperiale** (Piazzale Belvedere, Tirrenia; phone 0587 736 048), which blasts techno and house music until the wee hours. Closer to town and less chaotic is **Borderline** (Via Vernaccini, 7; phone 050 580 577), whose DJs play funk, acid jazz, reggae, electronica, and world music.

For a well-heeled night out on the town, consider the **Teatro Verdi di Pisa** (Via Palestro, 40; phone 050 941 111; **www.teatrodipisa.pi.it**), the city's center for drama, opera, ballet, and concerts. Classical offerings are the norm, but jazz and modern dance show up now and again. Tickets range from €18–€45, depending on the production—there's almost always something on stage.

Volterra

For years touted as Tuscany's "next big thing" as far as hill towns go, Volterra is still considered off the beaten track for most tourists. Staring down from a rocky, 1,750-foot peak, this stern-looking town was a member of the Etruscan Dodecapolis and the last Etruscan city to fall to the Romans in 260 B.C. The **Museo Etrusco Guarnacci** (Via Don Minzoni, 15; phone 0588 86347; open March–October: daily, 9 a.m.–7 p.m.; November–February: daily, 9 a.m.–2 p.m.; admission €3) contains one of the most complete records of Volterra's Etruscan heritage, and includes a collection of approximately 600 funerary urns. The most famous piece of the museum is the bronze *Ombra della Sera (Shadow of the Night)* statue, a super-elongated figure of a man that dates back to about the third century B.C. Dug up by a local farmer in 1879, the bronze was used as a fireplace poker until it was discovered that this piece was actually an Etruscan artifact.

Much of Volterra's Etruscan origins were erased during a building boom in medieval times. Poet Gabriele D'Annunzio called Volterra a "town of wind and rock," referring to its imposing ramparts, stone squares, and watchtowers, all built during the 12th and 13th centuries when the city was at war with Florence. Volterra is also known for its alabaster, which has been local craftsmen's material of choice for centuries.

Associazione Pro Volterra   Via Giusto Turazza, 2; phone 0588 86 150, fax 0588 90 350; **www.comune.volterra.pi.it**

The Province of Livorno

Province of Livorno Tourist Board   Piazza Cavour, 6; 57100 Livorno; phone 0586 898 111; **www.provincia.livorno.it**

Livorno

Livorno began to gain prominence shortly after Pisa's access to the sea silted up. Cosimo I (Medici) chose the fishing village to become Tuscany's main port in 1571, and he hired architect and engineer Buontalenti to construct its harbor. Following Cosimo I as the grand duke of Tuscany was Ferdinand I Medici, whose forward-thinking policies and desire to turn Livorno into a booming commercial port led to the signing of the Livornina, a constitution that ensured freedom of thought, religion, and trade. In turn, Jews, Moors, Greeks, Turks, English Catholics, and other groups fleeing persecution sought asylum in Livorno, and helped shape the city into an eclectic mixture of cultures, colors, and ethnicities. Even today, Livornese like to compare themselves to the seaside town's traditional dish *cacciucco,* a perfectly blended stew consisting of a variety of fish and spices.

Livorno is still one of Italy's most significant ports (after Genoa and Naples) and sees its share of commercial and cruise ship traffic. During the heyday of the British Empire, Livorno, also known as Leghorn, was one of the most important ports for British ships, and it was one of the stops along the slave trade, importing and exporting Moors. The **Monumento dei Quattro Mori** by the port at Piazza Micheli is a stark reminder of the port city's role as a thriving European slave center. The upper portion of the statue, created in 1595, features a proud Duke Ferdinand I, whereas the lower portion, added in 1626, features two half-naked Moorish slaves, shackled and struggling to break free. Further down the port, fronting the Viale Italia, is the recently restored **Terrazza Masacagni.** Named for native son Pietro Mascagni, the broad checkerboard promenade is popular with children, bicyclists, and anyone looking to take in the invigorating salty air.

Sadly, much of Livorno was destroyed by bombing during World War II, and a number of postwar public-works projects led to the demolition or restructuring of many of the town's 16th-century monuments.

If you're traveling to Livorno by rail from Florence, you will have to switch trains at Pisa. Livorno is approximately 20 minutes away from Pisa. Otherwise, Livorno lies on the main line between Rome and Pisa. Lazzi buses connect Livorno with Pisa, Florence, Lucca, and towns along the coast. Take the SS1 or the A12 autostrada if you're driving.

APT Livorno Piazza Cavour, 6; phone 0586 898 111; **www.livorno. turismo.toscana.it**

The Tuscan Archipelago

Part of the province of Livorno, the Tuscan archipelago includes the notorious exile isle, **Elba,** and the island of **Capraia.** Were Napoleon to be exiled to Elba today, he would have found a sun-drenched playground plagued by traffic jams and beach umbrellas. In the summer, Elba becomes a sort of mini–United Nations, as vacationers from Italy, France, Germany, England, and elsewhere set up camp here. Those with modest incomes schlep by ferry from Piombino, while the well-to-do approach Elba by yacht, docking in **Portoferraio,** the island's chic port city and capital. After Sicily and Sardegna, partially mountainous Elba is Italy's third largest island, but its size does little to disperse the tourist hordes. If you can, avoid visiting Elba in July or August, as the population swells more than tenfold. From Elba, you can take a ferry to Capraia. At only seven square miles, the tiny island, which once was a refuge for Christian monks, remains a haven for nature lovers, and it's a tranquil alternative to bustling Elba.

During the summer, ferries and hydrofoils to the islands run frequently from Piombino and less frequently from Livorno. The trip from Piombino to Portoferraio takes about an hour, whereas you can expect to travel up to five hours from Livorno to Elba's main town. Boats to Capraia depart from Elba about once a day during the summer, and about once a week during the winter. The main ferry companies are **TOREMAR** (Via Calafati, 6; Livorno; phone 0586 896 113) and **NAVARMA** (Piazzale Premuda, 13; Piombino; phone 0565 221 212).

APT Elba   Calata Italia, 26; 57037 Portoferraio, Isola d'Elba; phone 0565 914 671, fax 0565 916 350; **www.arcipelago.turismo.toscana.it**

Associazione Pro Loco Capraia   Via Assunzione; 57032 Capraia Isola; phone 0586 905 138

The Province of Grosseto

Province of Grosseto Tourist Office   Via Monterosa, 206; 58100 Grosseto; phone 0564 462 611; **www.grosseto.turismo.toscana.it**

Grosseto

Still suffering from bombing damage from World War II, Grosseto is southern Tuscany's largest, if, perhaps, least attractive town. The best thing to do in Grosseto is pass it by. However, if you feel like sticking around, then we suggest a stop at the small **Museo Archeologico** (Piazza Baccarini, 3; phone 0564 488 750) for a gander at some of the Etruscan and Roman artifacts found nearby.

City of Grosseto Tourist Office   Via Monterosa, 206; 58100 Grosseto; phone 0564 462 611; **www.grosseto.turismo.toscana.it**

Ansedonia

Would-be surfers and Italian yuppies escape to Ansedonia during the summer, where there is a chic mixture of villa-crowned hills and lively beach life. Ruins from the ancient Roman town of Cosa have been found here. Most of these artifacts, such as cooking utensils and stone slabs, have been collected in the **Museo di Cosa** (Via delle Ginestre; phone 0564 881 421; open daily, 9 a.m.–7 p.m.; admission €2). Romans settled the town of Cosa (formerly the Etruscan town of Cusi) in about the third century B.C., creating a fortified port to fend off Hannibal and the Carthaginians. During the Republican period, Cosa became an important Tyrhennian center of trade, and many Romans chose to build homes here. But an economic crisis hit as the Roman Empire faded, and Cosa was abandoned by the third century A.D. For more information about Ansedonia, contac Grosseto's provincial tourism office.

Massa Marittima

The mining town of Massa Marittima isn't far from the shores of the Tyrrhenian Sea, but it hardly deserves the "maritime" moniker. The town enjoys a prime spot in the Colle Metallifere, or iron-rich hills, a fact that made the town attractive to the resource-seeking Sienese. Nevertheless, this is not a typical, blue-collar town. Massa Marittima has a pretty, if unspectacular **Duomo** and a city center that has hardly strayed from its original 13th-century blueprint.

APT Massa Marittima   Via Norma Parenti, 22; 58024 Massa Marittima; phone 0566 902 756

Monte Argentario and the Isola del Giglio

Today, three narrow isthmuses connect the rocky outcrop of Monte Argentario to the rest of Tuscany, but the area was an island until the 18th century. **Monte Argentario** is made up of two port cities, **Porto Santo Stefano** and **Porto Ercole,** which are packed in the warmer months with sunbathers, yachters, and vacationers on their way to the islands. Located on the middle isthmus that links Monte Argentario, **Orbetello** is a crowded resort town in the summer, where Italians, mostly from Tuscany and northern Latium, come to relax. The town's history is rather interesting, having been the capital of a Spanish enclave called Presidio for almost 300 years from 1557 to 1808. The Spanish coat of arms decorates the town's main gate, the **Porta del Soccorso.**

The **Isola del Giglio,** the second-largest Tuscan island, seems to have split off from the Alps. The road here is treacherous, cutting a jag from **Giglio Porto,** the port and largest town, to the apex of **Giglio Castello,** and back down to **Campese.** About 1,600 people live on "lily island" during the off-season. Summer attracts nature lovers, windsurfers, and the wealthy set. Ferries to the island leave from Porto Santo Stefano.

APT Monte Argentario   Corso Umberto, 55a; 58019 Porto Santo Stefano; phone 0564 814 208

Pro Loco Orbetello   Piazza della Repubblica; 58015 Orbetello; phone 0564 861 226

Pro Loco Isola del Giglio   Via Umberto, 1; 58012 Giglio Porto; phone 0564 809 400

The Maremma

The unspoiled southern swath of the Grosseto province is known as the Maremma and encompasses the land from the coast, including the **Parco della Naturale della Maremma** (Visitors Center, Via del Fante, Località Alberese; phone 0564 407 098), and inland to the towns of **Saturnia** and **Pitigliano.** Surrounded by the Monti dell'Uccelina, the Parco della Maremma (sometimes called the Parco dell'Uccellina) is the wild heart of southern Tuscany. A wildlife preserve since 1975, the park covers approximately 25,000 acres between the Tyrrhenian coast and the Aurelian Road and attracts nature lovers from Tuscany and Latium, especially in the spring and fall, when the change of the seasons brightens the ancient landscape. An abundance of wild fowl, including falcons and herons, inhabit these parts, and animals such as wild boar, deer, and fox have been able to proliferate here thanks to increasingly strict antihunting legislation. For centuries, would-be rulers contested this bountiful area, erecting random watchtowers and tollhouses along the trails. The combination of the wild countryside dotted with crumbling fortifications is most striking.

The easiest way to get to the park is via SS1(Via Aurelia) to the exit at Alberese. There, you must park your car and take a bus or walk to the entrance of the park (approximately 2.5 miles). The **RAMA** bus company (phone 0564 404 169) services this route. The bus is also available from Grosseto. Note that the bus only runs Monday through Saturday. The park is closed May 1 and December 25.

Pitigliano

Known for years as "Little Jerusalem" or "Piccola Gerusalemme," Pitigliano had a thriving Jewish community from the 16th century until the 20th century. During these centuries, the town was both a safe haven and ghetto for the Jews of Pitigliano. The tolerance of the Medici brought the first Jews here after they had been forced out of the papal territories. However, in the early 17th century, when the Jewish community was threatened by anti-Semitic sentiments within the grand duchy of Tuscany, a ghetto was built here so that the Jews did not have to relocate to Florence or Siena. At its height, the Jewish population in the small town numbered approximately 420. However, by the time World War II engulfed Europe, Pitigliano's Jewish population was less than 70. Today, only remnants of Little Jerusalem remain, including the synagogue (rebuilt several times), a narrow warren of ghetto streets, a traditional Jewish bakery, and only three Jewish residents. Nevertheless, this cliffside *comune* is a site of pilgrimage for Jews from throughout Italy and around the world.

Driving is the best way to get to Pitigliano, as buses (from Grosseto) are very infrequent. The town lies just off of S74, the highway that runs from the coast until north of Lake Bolsena. You can access the S74 from the S2, or Via Cassia.

IAT Pitigliano   Via Roma, 6; 58017 Pitigliano; phone 0564 614 433

Part Seven

Rome and the Best of Latium

A Brief History of Rome

Mark Twain once remarked, "What is there in Rome for me to see that others have not seen before me?" In fact, little new can be said about Rome (Roma), arguably the most documented place on Earth. But romanticized history of the Eternal City—which has seen the buildup and demise of empires, the construction of monumental temples, and the comings and goings of great legends in arts, engineering, science, politics, literature, and religion—continues to mesmerize even the most passive of tourists. Well before the **Colosseum** was built, Roman historian Livy concluded that Rome was "overwhelmed by its own greatness." Little did he know what was in store.

Rome has existed for more than 2,000 years, and, if you believe the legend, it was founded on the Palatine Hill in 753 B.C. by Romulus. Subsequently, Romulus and his men abducted and raped the women from the nearby Sabine tribe, and thus the seeds of population sprouted. A long line of Etruscan kings followed until the sixth century B.C., when Rome became a republic. By the time German King Odoacer conquered Rome in the second half of the fifth century A.D., Rome had moved from republic to empire and had seen the reign of more than 250 rulers.

Christianity had also taken root in Rome by the first century A.D., and Christian cults were forced to practice in secret until 313 A.D., when Emperor Constantine granted Christians the freedom of worship. From that point on, Christianity became the be-all and end-all of the Roman experience. The papacy soon took the helm of the Church and carried out massive conquests in the name of Rome and Christianity. The Crusades and expeditions to the New World brought massive wealth and new converts to the church, and Rome grew rich and handsome with lavish architectural projects and thousands of artistic commissions.

Michelangelo, Raphael, and dozens of other Renaissance masters left their mark on Rome. Even after 1527, when Charles V sacked Rome,

CALENDAR OF EVENTS IN ROME AND LATIUM

March

Settimana Santa (Holy Week)   The week leading up to Easter (March or April).

Settimana dei Beni Culturali (Cultural Week)   One week in March or April. During cultural week, all state-owned museums and archaeological sites are open free of charge. For more information, phone 06 589 9359.

Rome City Marathon, Rome   Third Sunday of the month.

April

Natale di Roma, Rome   Rome's birthday. Sunday before April 21. A festival takes place on the Campidoglio.

May

Primo Maggio (Labor Day), throughout Italy   May 1. Labor demonstrations and street festivals take place in *piazze* throughout the country and especially in the capital.

The Italian Open, Rome   Two weeks during the month. This tournament, which takes place at the Foro Italico, is the biggest tournament on the tennis circuit before the summer grand slams get under way. For tickets and information, phone 06 321 9021.

June

Genzano Infiorata, Genzano (Castelli Romani)   Sunday after Corpus Domini. Carpets of flowers are laid out in dazzling displays.

Festa di San Giovanni, Rome   June 23. A feast of snails *(lumache)* and suckling pig in the Piazza San Giovanni in Laterano.

Festa di San Pietro e San Paolo, Rome   June 29. This feast day celebrates Rome's two patron saints, Peter and Paul.

the city overflowed with treasures, as Baroque artists such as Bernini and Borromini worked tirelessly to create luxurious new churches, fountains, and chapels that would awe the uninspired and glorify the Holy See. Rome was the site of revolution during the late 19th century under freedom-fighter Garibaldi and served as the nation's capital under the reign of Vittorio Emanuele II, Italy's first king. Later, Benito Mussolini, who ruled from 1922 to 1943, and the Nazis, who occupied the city from 1943 to 1944, almost laid waste to Rome until it was retaken by Italian partisans and Allied troops.

July

Expo Tevere, Rome   First two weeks of July. Arts and crafts fair along the Tiber River.

Festa de Noantri, Rome   Last two weeks of July. Traditional street fair of arts, crafts, and food in Rome's Trastevere quarter.

Le Donne Sotte Le Stelle (a.k.a., Roma Alta Moda), Rome   Late July. This glamorous fashion show sees famous designers and models show off their goods at the Spanish Steps.

August

Fiera del Vino Est! Est! Est!, Montefiascone   August 1–15. A two-week festival celebrating one of Latium's best-loved wines.

Festa della Madonna della Neve, Rome   August 5. On this date, the church of Santa Maria Maggiore celebrates the miracle of snow, during which thousands of white flower petals are released from the church's ceiling.

October

Festa del Vino, Marino (Castelli Romani)   First Sunday in October. Wine tastings and street fairs in the Castelli Romani.

December

Day of the Immaculate Conception, Rome   December 8. The pope makes one of his rare public appearances outside of the Vatican and celebrates mass at the church of Trinità dei Monti.

Piazza Navona Christmas Market, Rome   All month.

Christmas Creche Displays, Rome   Elaborate nativity scenes decorate churches throughout the city. Best displays are at St. Peter's (life-size display), Santa Maria Maggiore, San Giovanni in Laterano, and Santa Maria in Aracoeli.

Postwar Rome has experienced numerous troughs and crests. In the 1950s and 1960s, as the Roman economy rebounded, the city exported its art and style through films such as Fellini's *La Dolce Vita* and the Audrey Hepburn vehicle *Roman Holiday*. International sporting events, such as the Olympics in 1960 and the World Cup soccer tournament in 1990, acted as catalysts for major renovations and public works projects. No doubt, the Millennium Jubilee, which marked the 2,000th anniversary of the birth of Christ and the holiest of holy years for Catholics, resulted in the greatest city cleanup ever staged.

Truth be told, terrorism, both by the left-wing Red Brigade and by the mafia, marred the city's reputation during the 1970s and 1980s. By some accounts, terrorist activity continues to seethe beneath the surface. For now, though, Rome's biggest challenges lie in solving a dreadful traffic problem; tackling mounting immigration; curtailing government corruption; and learning the live in harmony with its European neighbors. The more things change . . .

Rome and Latium Tourist Board

Your best source for information about Rome and nearby towns is from tourist information kiosks, which are located throughout the city. Some of the most useful ones are at the following locations:

- Piazza San Giovanni in Laterano, phone 06 772 035 35
- Piazza del Cinquecento, Termini Station, phone 06 478 251 94
- Piazza del Tempio della Pace, Via dei Fori Imperiali, phone 06 699 243 07
- Piazza Sonnino, Trastevere, phone 06 583 334 57

If you need more information, you can contact the following tourist offices. We have also listed tourist office addresses after each city profile in the Latium section where applicable.

City of Rome Tourist Office   Via Parigi, 11; 00185 Rome; phone 06 488 991, fax 06 481 9316; **www.romaturismo.com**

Vatican Tourist Office (Ufficio Informazioni Pellegrini e Turisti)   Piazza San Pietro; Città del Vaticano; phone 06 698 844 66, fax 06 698 851 00

Province of Rome Tourist Office Via XX Settembre, 26; 00187 Rome; phone 06 421 381, fax 06 421 382 21; **www.oltreroma.it**

Latium Regional Tourist Board   Via Rosa Raimondi Garibaldi, 7; 00145 Rome; phone 06 516 881 66, fax 06 516 881 72; **www.regione. lazio.it**

Understanding Rome

Think of Rome as an egg turned on its side, with the narrow end pointing northwest. Better yet, imagine the city as a priceless bejeweled Fabergé egg, with the **Vatican** at its northwest end; major attractions like the **Spanish Steps,** the **Pantheon,** and the **Trevi Fountain** as the yolk; and the ruins of ancient Rome rounding out the bottom.

The ancient Tiber (Tevere) River separates Rome's left and right banks, with most attractions lying to the east of the river. On the left side of the Tiber is the Borgo, the gateway to the world's smallest city-state, **Vatican City.** Within the gates of the Vatican, we are reminded of Catholicism's centuries-old wealth and power with such landmarks as **St. Peter's Basilica** and such priceless artworks as Michelangelo's paintings in the **Sistine Chapel.** The mostly residential **Gianicolo** (Janiculum) hill separates the staunchly conservative Vatican from laid-back **Trastevere,** an area teeming with authentic *trattorie,* hipster artists, and enduring bohemian flair.

Rome's right bank accounts for two-thirds of the egg in our visual metaphor and will be where you will likely spend most of your time in the Eternal City. In the southern quadrant, you can visit the **Ancient City,** hemmed in by the **Aurelian Walls** and littered with ruins dating back more than 2,000 years, including the **Colosseum** and the **Forum.** North of the here lies the **Centro Storico** (CHENT-ro STOR-ee-ko), or historic center, an area whose boundaries are ambiguous because it is packed with sights to see. Let yourself get lost in the maze of medieval streets while taking in the majesty of the **Pantheon** and the persistent buzz in **Campo de' Fiori** or **Piazza Navona.** A few paces away from the Centro Storico is the area defined as the **Tridente,** which is, for the most part, a shopper's paradise. The Tridente consists of three streets—**Via di Ripetta, Via del Corso,** and **Via Babuino**—that radiate from the wide **Piazza del Popolo.** Overlooking the Piazza del Popolo and merging with the southwestern edge of the **Villa Borghese** are the **Pincio Gardens,** a wide expanse of parkland dotted with replica Greek temples, recreational areas, and art museums.

From the Villa Borghese, head south again to fill out the remaining third of the egg. The eastern reaches of Rome consist of four distinct areas. The **Via Veneto** (a.k.a., the *La Dolce Vita* street) snakes down from the Villa Borghese park with high-class hotels, designer shops, and outrageously-priced abodes. The **Quirinale** hill is the site of the **Presidential Palace** and the **Trevi Fountain.** Next is the **Esquiline** hill, where you'll find **Stazione Termini,** the main train station, and the church of **Santa Maria Maggiore.** Finally, the **Laterano** neighborhood, home to the monumental **San Giovanni in Laterano** cathedral, is the last section of Rome proper before the suburbs unfold past the city gates.

This is just a rough sketch to help you understand how the city is laid out. Of course, you'll find a wide range of attractions and neighborhoods both inside and outside of each of these neighborhoods. If you happen to get lost—a possibility, given the city's tight warren of streets and alleys—you can rely on this loose idea of Rome's landscape to help orient you in the right direction.

Touring Rome's Neighborhoods

Rome is a sprawling city of more than a dozen diverse neighborhoods, each defined by geography, geometry, or a famous landmark. Here, we have outlined 13 zones in Rome and two additional quarters that lie outside the city gates.

Ancient City

Though remnants of ancient days are scattered throughout Rome, the city's ancient quarter is defined clearly by the **Colosseum,** the **Roman**

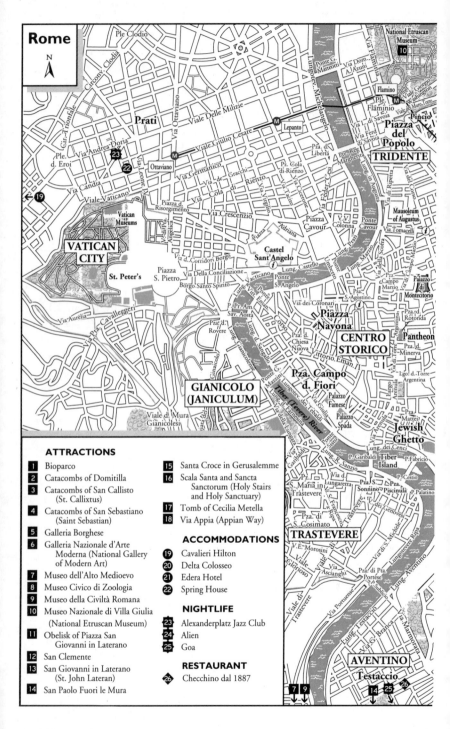

Rome

N

ATTRACTIONS

1. Bioparco
2. Catacombs of Domitilla
3. Catacombs of San Callisto (St. Callixtus)
4. Catacombs of San Sebastiano (Saint Sebastian)
5. Galleria Borghese
6. Galleria Nazionale d'Arte Moderna (National Gallery of Modern Art)
7. Museo dell'Alto Medioevo
8. Museo Civico di Zoologia
9. Museo della Civiltà Romana
10. Museo Nazionale di Villa Giulia (National Etruscan Museum)
11. Obelisk of Piazza San Giovanni in Laterano
12. San Clemente
13. San Giovanni in Laterano (St. John Lateran)
14. San Paolo Fuori le Mura
15. Santa Croce in Gerusalemme
16. Scala Santa and Sancta Sanctorum (Holy Stairs and Holy Sanctuary)
17. Tomb of Cecilia Metella
18. Via Appia (Appian Way)

ACCOMMODATIONS

19. Cavalieri Hilton
20. Delta Colosseo
21. Edera Hotel
22. Spring House

NIGHTLIFE

23. Alexanderplatz Jazz Club
24. Alien
25. Goa

RESTAURANT

26. Checchino dal 1887

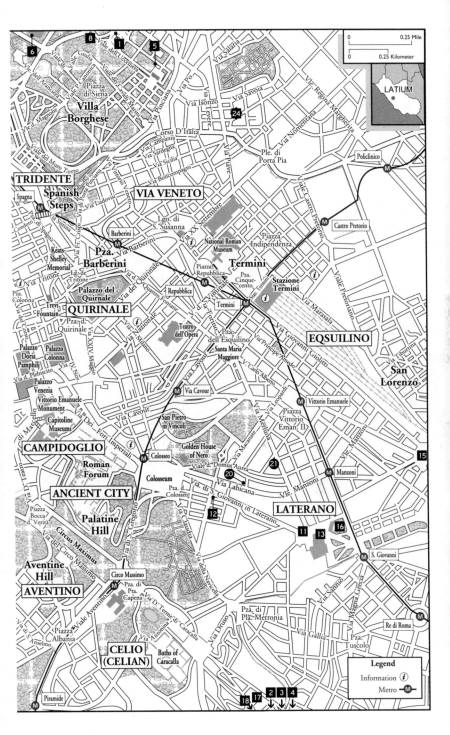

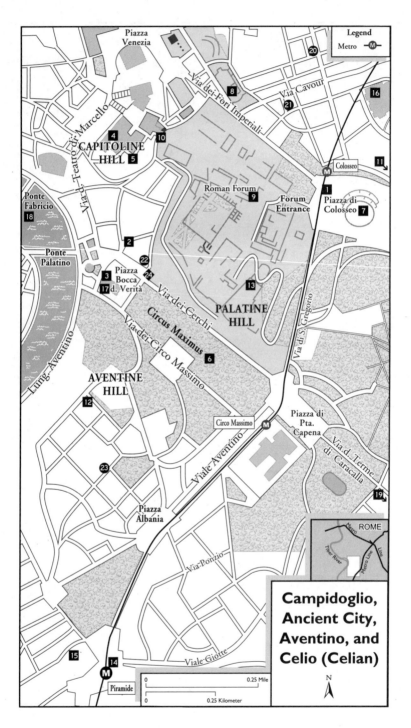

Piazza
Venezia

20

Via dei Fori Imperiali

8

21

Via Cavour

16

Via d. Teatro di Marcello

CAPITOLINE
HILL

4

10

5

Ponte
Fabricio

18

Roman Forum

9

Forum
Entrance

Colosseo

Ⓜ

1

11

Piazza di
Colosseo

7

Ponte
Palatino

2

22

24

3

Piazza
Bocca
d. Verità

17

Via dei Cerchi

13

PALATINE
HILL

Circus Maximus

Via dei Circo Massimo

6

Via di S. Gregorio

AVENTINE
HILL

12

Lung. Aventino

Circo Massimo

Ⓜ

Piazza di
Pta.
Capena

23

Viale Aventino

Via d. Terme
di Caracalla

19

Piazza
Albania

ROME

Metro Line

Tiber River

Metro Line

Via Ponzio

15

14

Ⓜ

Piramide

Viale Giotte

0   0.25 Mile

0   0.25 Kilometer

Campidoglio, Ancient City, Aventino, and Celio (Celian)

N

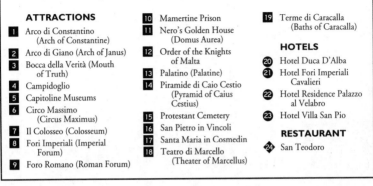

Forum, the **Imperial Forum,** and the **Palatine** hill. Within roughly a two-square-mile valley lies impressive visual evidence of Rome's illustrious past, including imperial palaces, mammoth archways, toppled columns, sporting fields, and deserted markets. Because it is a major tourist hub, the Ancient City is well served by public transportation, including a Metro stop—Colosseo—on Line B. The main artery here is Via dei Fori Imperiali, a wide boulevard constantly abuzz with traffic. On weekends, this road sometimes becomes a pedestrian thoroughfare. There has long been talk in the city government to eliminate the Via dei Fori Imperiali altogether to make way for more excavations and/or a pedestrian boulevard.

Campidoglio

Consisting of the **Capitoline** hill and the enormous **Vittoriano** monument, the area that we define as the Campidoglio juts up from the middle of Rome like a mountain range, capping off the ancient city from the beginnings of the historic center. Campidoglio means "capitol," so it's no surprise to find the city's local government buildings here. Michelangelo designed the unique, black-and-white, geometric-patterned **Piazza del Campidoglio,** and a copy of an equestrian statue of Marcus Aurelius stands guard in the square. The original of this famous statue is in the **Capitoline Museums,** a vast store of classical art and sculpture that occupies the **Palazzo Nuovo** and the **Palazzo dei Conservatori,** respectively, on the left and right of the Piazza del Campidoglio. Around the corner is **Santa Maria in Aracoeli,** a church renowned as much for the 123 intimidating stairs that lead up to it as for the religious icon housed

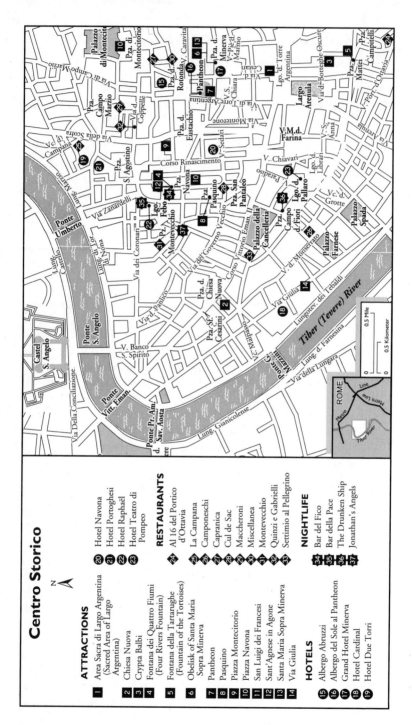

Centro Storico

N

ATTRACTIONS

1 Area Sacra di Largo Argentina (Sacred Area of Largo Argentina)

2 Chiesa Nuova

3 Crypta Balbi

4 Fontana dei Quattro Fiumi (Four Rivers Fountain)

5 Fontana della Tartarughe (Fountain of the Tortoises)

6 Obelisk of Santa Maria Sopra Minerva

7 Pantheon

8 Pasquino

9 Piazza Montecitorio

10 Piazza Navona

11 San Luigi dei Francesi

12 Sant'Agnese in Agone

13 Santa Maria Sopra Minerva

14 Via Giulia

HOTELS

15 Albergo Abruzzi

16 Albergo del Sole al Pantheon

17 Grand Hotel Minerva

18 Hotel Cardinal

19 Hotel Due Torri

20 Hotel Navona

21 Hotel Portoghesi

22 Hotel Raphaël

23 Hotel Teatro di Pompeo

RESTAURANTS

24 Al 16 del Portico d'Ottavia

25 La Campana

26 Camponeschi

27 Capranica

28 Cul de Sac

29 Maccheroni

30 Miscellanea

31 Montevecchio

32 Quinzi e Gabrielli

33 Settimio al Pellegrino

NIGHTLIFE

34 Bar del Fico

35 Bar della Pace

36 The Drunken Ship

37 Jonathan's Angels

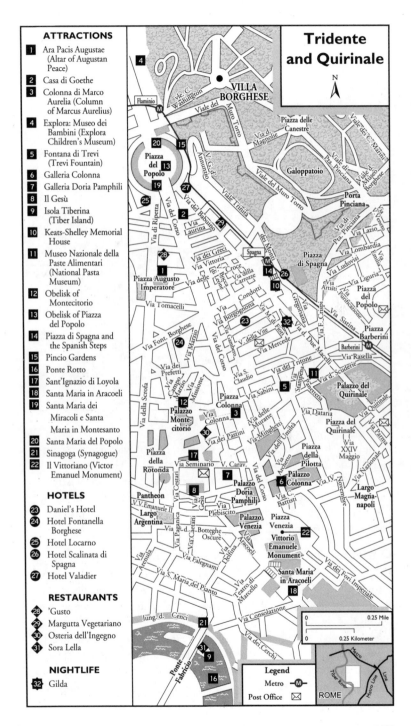

ATTRACTIONS

1 Ara Pacis Augustae (Altar of Augustan Peace)
2 Casa di Goethe
3 Colonna di Marco Aurelia (Column of Marcus Aurelius)
4 Explora: Museo dei Bambini (Explora Children's Museum)
5 Fontana di Trevi (Trevi Fountain)
6 Galleria Colonna
7 Galleria Doria Pamphili
8 Il Gesù
9 Isola Tiberina (Tiber Island)
10 Keats-Shelley Memorial House
11 Museo Nazionale della Paste Alimentari (National Pasta Museum)
12 Obelisk of Montecitorio
13 Obelisk of Piazza del Popolo
14 Piazza di Spagna and the Spanish Steps
15 Pincio Gardens
16 Ponte Rotto
17 Sant'Ignazio di Loyola
18 Santa Maria in Aracoeli
19 Santa Maria dei Miracoli e Santa Maria in Montesanto
20 Santa Maria del Popolo
21 Sinagoga (Synagogue)
22 Il Vittoriano (Victor Emanuel Monument)

HOTELS

23 Daniel's Hotel
24 Hotel Fontanella Borghese
25 Hotel Locarno
26 Hotel Scalinata di Spagna
27 Hotel Valadier

RESTAURANTS

28 'Gusto
29 Margutta Vegetariano
30 Osteria dell'Ingegno
31 Sora Lella

NIGHTLIFE

32 Gilda

Tridente and Quirinale

N

VILLA BORGHESE

Flaminio

vle. C. Washington
Viale del Muro Torto

Piazza delle Canestre

Viale dei C. Marini

Galoppatoio

Viale del Muro Torto

Porta Pinciana

Piazza del Popolo

V.G.d'Annunzio

Viale Trinità

Via di Ripetta

Via del Corso

Via del Babuino

V. Laurina

Via dei Greci
Via Vittoria

Spagna

Piazza di Spagna

Via Lazio
Via Lombardia
Via Ludovisi
Via Liguria
Via Artisti
Piazza del Popolo

Piazza Augusto Imperatore

Via delle Croce
Via della Carrozze
Condotti

Via Sistina
Piazza Barberini

Via Tomacelli

Via Font. Borghese

Via Borgognona
Via della Vite

Barberini

Via Rasella

Via del Corso

Via Mercede
Via del Tritone

Palazzo del Quirinale

Via della Scrofa

Via dei Prefetti

Via S. Claudio
Via Sabini

Via della Dataria

Piazza del Quirinale

Piazza Colonna

Via delle Muratte
Via Minghetti
Via dell'Umiltà

Piazza della Pilotta

Via XXIV Maggio

Palazzo Montecitorio

Via Colonna
Via dei Pastini

Piazza della Rotonda

Via Seminario   V. Carav.

Palazzo Doria Pamphilj

Palazzo Colonna

Largo Magnanapoli

Pantheon
V.V.Emanuele II
Largo Argentina

Via Gesù
Via Plebiscito

Palazzo Venezia

Piazza Venezia

Via IV Novembre

Via C. Battisti

Via del Plebiscito
Via Paganica
d. Botteghe Oscure

Vittorio Emanuele Monument

Santa Maria in Aracoeli

Via dei Fori Imperiali

Via S. Maria del Pianto

Via del Teatro di Marcello

lung. d. Cenci

Via Consolazione

Via dei Cerchi

Ponte Fabricio

| | 0 | 0.25 Mile |
| 0 | 0.25 Kilometer | |

Legend
Metro — M
Post Office — ✉

ROME

Tiber River
Metro Line

297

Vatican Area

N

ATTRACTIONS

1 Castel Sant' Angelo
2 Musei Vaticani
   (Vatican Museums)
3 Il Passetto
   (Vatican Corridor)
4 St. Peter's Basilica
5 Via Giulia

HOTELS

6 Hotel Amalia
7 Hotel Columbus

Legend

Metro ─M─

0   0.25 Mile
0   0.25 Kilometer

ROME

within. Finally, gleaming white as a glacier is the easily recognizable Vittoriano monument, Rome's tribute to its first king. Three main thoroughfares—Via dei Fori Imperiali, Via del Corso, and Via del Teatro di Marcello—converge at **Piazza Venezia,** the intersection in front of the Vittoriano, so you should have no problem making your way here with public transportation.

Centro Storico

Because all corners in Rome are historic, the title Centro Storico may seem a bit of a misnomer for the city's central wedge of medieval and Renaissance alleyways and edifices. You will spend most of your time within this chunk of central Rome, because a large number of the city's hotels, restaurants, pubs, and shops are located here. For the most part, the Centro Storico is defined as the area between the Tiber and Via del Corso, including the **Piazza della Rotonda** (the Pantheon), **Campo de' Fiori,** and **Piazza Navona.**

Trastevere and Gianicolo (Janiculum)

N

ATTRACTIONS
1. Orto Botanico (Botanical Gardens)
2. San Francesco a Ripa
3. Santa Maria in Trastevere

HOTELS
4. Hotel Santa Maria
5. Ripa All Suites Hotel
6. Villa Farnesina

RESTAURANTS
7. Asinocotto
8. Da Augusto
9. Dar Poeta
10. Ripa 12

NIGHTLIFE
11. Big Mama
12. RipArte Café

Tridente

Called the trident, or *tridente,* because of the three roads that radiate from the **Piazza del Popolo,** this is one of the liveliest and haughtiest sections of town. Down Via Ripetta, the site of Rome's old port, you'll find refined restaurants and bars and usually fewer tourists than natives. The central avenue of the Tridente is Via del Corso, Rome's extra-long shopping concourse. Finally, Via del Babuino, or Baboon Street, is cluttered with antiques stores, high-end boutiques, and chic hotels, and it leads to one of the city's most famous attractions, the **Spanish Steps.** The southern reaches of the Tridente are Via Tomacelli and Via Condotti in the west and Via del Tritone in the east.

Vatican Area

The smallest city-state in the world, **Vatican City** is its own entity, yet simultaneously it symbolizes Rome. From every rooftop and vantage point, the dome of **St. Peter's Basilica** looms large in the distance, and traces of former Vatican rule over Rome can be found in everything from city works projects to governmental policies to works of art. For all intents and purposes, our Vatican zone consists of the Vatican City, including the basilica and Vatican museums, the shops and residences lining the Borgo area around Via della Conciliazione, and beyond **Castel Sant'Angelo** to the monied Prati neighborhood.

Trastevere

Considered the home of "true" Romans, Trastevere is a largely residential neighborhood that is literally across *(tras-)* the Tiber (Tevere), extending from the river to the foot of the Gianicolo hill. Made up of fiercely independent locals—among them students, artisans, greengrocers, masons, and chefs—Trastevere echoes Rome's past while representing its future. In this zone, medieval churches abut stylish cafes and hip boutiques front quaint cobbled squares. Appropriately lording over the entrance of the neighborhood at the **Ponte Garibaldi** is a statue of Giuseppe Giacchino Belli, the working man's poet and the embodiment of Trastevere. This native son followed a long line of Roman poets, yet became famous for his use of Roman dialect in his verse.

Gianicolo (Janiculum)

The Gianicolo hill starts above the Trastevere neighborhood at the **Botanical Gardens** and extends high above the city. The area has remained largely residential thanks mostly to its lack of attractions and public transportation. For stunning views of the city, take the 870 bus to the top of the hill. Here you'll also find a monument to freedom fighter Garibaldi and his wife, Anita.

Via Veneto

Wealthy travelers may want to stay in a hotel on the Via Veneto, a street renowned for celebrity sightings and high style since the release of the 1960 Fellini film *La Dolce Vita*. Within the Via Veneto neighborhood, we have included the attractions around the **Villa Borghese** (at the top of the street) and the **Piazza Barberini** (at the base of the hill).

Quirinale

Defined by the major boulevards of Via del Tritone and Via Nazionale, the Quirinale hill includes landmarks as diverse as the **Trevi Fountain,** the **Palazzo delle Esposizioni,** and the **Baths of Diocletian.** The traditional summit of the Quirinale is the **Presidential Palace** and the **Piazza del Quirinale,** which is remarkable for its gargantuan statues of Castor and Pollux with their horses. This section of the Quirinale is sometimes referred to as Monte Cavallo, or Horse Mountain.

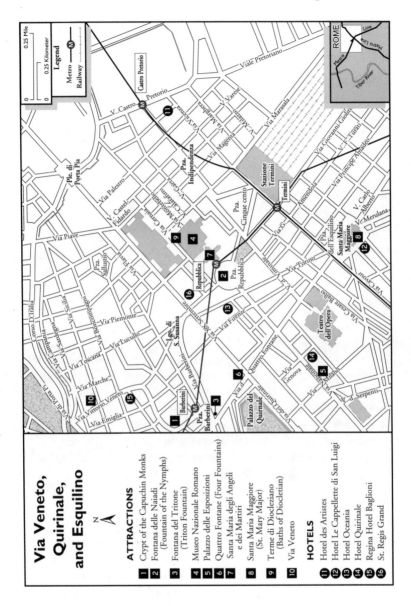

Via Veneto, Quirinale, and Esquilino

N

ATTRACTIONS

1 Crypt of the Capuchin Monks
2 Fontana delle Naiadi (Fountain of the Nymphs)
3 Fontana del Tritone (Triton Fountain)
4 Museo Nazionale Romano
5 Palazzo delle Esposizioni
6 Quattro Fontane (Four Fountains)
7 Santa Maria degli Angeli e dei Martiri
8 Santa Maria Maggiore (St. Mary Major)
9 Terme di Diocleziano (Baths of Diocletian)
10 Via Veneto

HOTELS

11 Hotel des Artistes
12 Hotel Le Cappellette di San Luigi
13 Hotel Oceania
14 Hotel Quirinale
15 Regina Hotel Baglioni
16 St. Regis Grand

Esquilino

The Esquiline hill, though not the prettiest section of town, has the advantage of being close to public transportation and the attractions of the Ancient City. Here you'll find **Termini Station,** the city's major train and bus hub, and two stellar churches, **Santa Maria Maggiore** and **San**

Pietro in Vincoli. This being a largely immigrant neighborhood, the Esquiline is also home to one of the most vibrant meat and produce markets in Rome at **Piazza Vittorio.**

Laterano

Perhaps the holiest section of Rome outside the Vatican, the Laterano neighborhood encompasses three major churches and two holy sites. **San Giovanni in Laterano** is the second-largest church within the city gates and is the diocese of Rome. **Santa Croce in Gerusalemme** is equally mammoth and full of holy relics. The **Basilica of San Clemente** has sections that date back to the first century A.D. Across from the broad **Piazza San Giovanni,** you'll find the **Scala Santa** and the **Sancta Sanctorum.** The **Colosseum** is easily accessible from the Laterano neighborhood.

Celio (Celian)

The Celian hill is the gateway to many sites of ancient Rome, including the **Baths of Caracalla.** From here, you can also access the Via Appia Antica, or the old Appian Way. The Celian hill's other attraction is the **Villa Celimontana,** a lovely park often used for picnics and summer concerts.

Aventino

The Aventino proper is a hill shaped by elegant homes, attractive churches, and quiet side streets. From atop the hill, you can gaze down on the cityscape or visit the **Order of the Knights of Malta,** which offers an unforgettable view of St. Peter's Basilica. Sandwiched between the Aventine and the Tiber River is the Testaccio neighborhood, a working-class quarter that has evolved into one of Rome's favorite spots for nightclubbing and dining. Meanwhile, the eastern slope of the Aventine extends down to the **Circus Maximus** and the sites surrounding the **Piazza della Bocca della Verità.**

Farther Afield

Appia Antica

Beyond the **Porta San Sebastiano,** where the ancient Appian Way starts, so do clusters of tombs and catacombs. Three major networks of catacombs, including those of **San Callisto, San Sebastiano,** and **Domitilla,** can be found here, as well as the **Tomb of Cecilia Metella,** often depicted in Romantic-era paintings. A more recent gravesite in the area, the **Fosse Ardeatine,** dates from World War II. Many Romans still spend Sundays walking along the tree-lined Via Appia, paying homage to their ancestors.

EUR

What was to be Mussolini's utopia, Esposizone Universale di Roma, the EUR, is a suburb to Rome's south. With its wide boulevards and stark, stone buildings, EUR is a model of fascist architecture, where you'll find the **Square Colosseum.** Almost all of Mussolini's ideal buildings have been converted into office space, but a few now house museums. EUR is near the airport and reachable via the Metro.

Public Transportation

Smart travelers learn to use Rome's public transportation to their benefit, and you can, too. Not only are Rome's trains, buses, and trams efficient ways to get from point A to point B, they are also intriguing glimpses into the soul of the city. At one time, you may be sharing a seat with a nun, a trend-setting schoolkid, an East African nanny, a government worker, or a young army officer. Of course, public transport has its drawbacks, including panhandlers, gropers, and pickpockets. But if you mind your belongings, you may come to enjoy watching Rome file in and out of sliding doors.

Rome's public transportation is run by **ATAC** (Azienda Tramvie Autobus Communali), which includes the **Metropolitana** (the Metro), **Metrobus,** and **Tram** systems. You can purchase ATAC's Rome Metrobus map at any newsstand in Rome for approximately €4. Tourist offices usually hand out bus/tram/Metro maps of central Rome on request.

Overland bus service throughout Latium is operated by **COTRAL** (Consortile Trasporti nel Lazio). More information about COTRAL and its routes is listed in the Latium section in this chapter.

ATAC	800 555 666 (toll-free in Italy)	www.atac.roma.it
COTRAL	800 150 008 (toll-free in Italy)	www.cotralspa.it

Buying and Using Tickets for Public Transportation

Before you board a bus, tram, or the Metro, you must first buy a ticket. Tickets *(biglietti)* are available at tobacconists *(tabacchi),* at some newspaper kiosks (usually those close to Metro stops), and from machines located in every Metro station.

A single-use ticket *(biglietto integrate a tempo,* or BIT) costs €0.75 and is valid for 75 minutes on any bus, tram, or Metro train. You can also purchase a daily ticket *(biglietto integrate giornaliero,* or BIG) for €3 or a weekly ticket *(carta integrate settimanale,* or CIS) for €12.

Having spent a lot of time in Rome, we have found that it is essential to stock up on bus tickets on arrival, so we don't have to keep running to the *tabacchi.* Tobacconists tend to run out of bus tickets quickly and rarely sell daily or weekly tickets. We often rely on the pale green ticket machines, found in all of the Metro stations. The ticket kiosks vend all three types of tickets, and they accept most bills (watch out, though: change is given in coins). Simply touch the kiosk screens, choose your language (English is denoted by the British Union Jack flag), and follow the instructions.

Rome Metropolitana

Remember: You must validate *(convalidare)* your ticket on entry to the bus. For more information, see Part Three, Arriving, Getting Oriented, and Departing.

Trains

Rome's underground subway system, known as the Metropolitana, or simply the Metro, may not be the prettiest or the most comfortable in the world—rail cars are layered with graffiti, platforms are dingy, and trains are consistently packed to the gills with commuters and tourists. But the Metro is fairly reliable and an efficient way to zip around the city. The Metro consists of two lines—A and B—that intersect at Termini Station, Rome's main rail station for the Ferrovia dello Stato, Italy's national train network. (A plan for a third line, C, is still in the works.) Meanwhile, the Piazza del Cinquecento outside of Termini is the depot for most city buses.

Useful stops on Line A include **Spagna** for accessing the Spanish Steps; **Flaminio** for Piazza del Popolo and the Tridente; and **Ottaviano** for St. Peter's Basilica and Vatican City. Useful Line B stops include **Colosseo,** for the Colosseum and Forum; and **Circo Massimo,** for the Circus Maximus and the Aventine hill. Other useful train stations in Rome include **Ostiense** and **Tiburtina.** Ostiense Station is connected to the Metro via the **Piramide** stop, and it is the station you will want to use should you take a day trip to Ostia Antica or nearby beaches. If you're heading to Tivoli, another favorite day trip for visitors to Rome, you can take the train from Tiburtina station, or you can ride the Metro to the **Rebibbia** stop, the northern end point of Line B, and catch a COTRAL bus. Two other convenient stations in Rome are **Trastevere** and **Tuscolana.** Local trains to and from Fiumicino Airport make stops at these stations.

Buses

Riding the bus in Rome is quite simple, as there are signs at each stop that list which buses stop there and what the route of each bus is. Even if you are not sure exactly which bus you need to ride, you can always check the signs to determine which bus will get you closest to your destination. The current stop is indicated with a red rectangle, with both previous stops and future stops listed on each sign. Major bus hubs are located at Termini Station, Piazza San Silvestro, Largo Argentina, and Piazza Venezia.

You should board the bus at either the front doors or the back doors, and exit through the middle doors. Although it may seem strange at first, you'll come to realize that this system accommodates as many riders as possible. Most buses in Rome are standing-room only, especially during rush hour. Don't forget to stamp your ticket, hold onto a pole or strap, and pay attention to your belongings.

You'll also encounter small, environmentally friendly, electric-powered buses, which scoot through the streets of Rome with nary a sound. The mini-buses connect such high-traffic areas as Piazza della Rotonda (site of the Pantheon) and Piazza di Spagna. True, these buses can't hold too many passengers—10 to 15 at the max—but they're useful if you no longer can bear the feeling of cobblestone under your feet. The electric bus numbers are 115, 116, 116T, 117, and 119.

Buses generally run from 6:30 a.m. until midnight. Night buses (indicated by an owl on bus-stop signage) run about every 30 minutes to an hour from midnight until 6:30 a.m. Night buses can be useful in a pinch, but they are fairly unreliable and tend to attract unsavory types. If you opt for a night bus instead of a taxi, you'll find at least one night-bus stop near main tourist attractions, like the Colosseum. Most night buses make stops at Termini Station. It's worth noting that line 40N takes the same route as Metro Line B, and 55N follows the Line A route.

If you can stand to put up with a little discomfort, you can turn your bus ride into a sightseeing adventure. Some useful and picturesque bus routes are:

Bus #64 Termini to the Vatican

Bus #81 San Giovanni in Laterano, Campidoglio, along Tiber River

Bus #85 Past the Colosseum and Forum

Trams

Of all of Rome's public transportation options, we find the tram the most enjoyable. On the whole, the city's trams are less crowded and many are new. Also, because the tram runs on a fixed rail line, it usually runs on time. Tram tracks usually run in the middle lanes of a street, which means that you have to cross at least one lane of traffic to get to the tram platform. Once you've figured out how to get to the tram stop, the rest is easy. The tram works much the same way as the bus does, in that you use the same *biglietto,* which you must stamp on boarding. The most useful tram lines are:

Tram #8 Largo Argentina to Trastevere

Tram #19 St. Peter's Basilica, Villa Borghese, Santa Croce in Gerusalemme

Tram #30b Villa Borghese, Colosseum, Circus Maximus, Trastevere

Taxis

At this point in your trip, you may have already ridden in a cab from the airport. Though taxis provide you with a quick getaway from Fiumicino, they are not always the best mode of in-town transportation. For one, they are often hard to find. Romans don't hail taxis. Instead, they head to taxi stands, which are located at *termini* and near major *piazze,* or they call a radio taxi. Second, cabs in Rome are expensive. Base fares start at approximately €2.25, but cab drivers tack on other surcharges for luggage (€1 extra per bag), night rides (€2.50 extra), Sundays (€1 extra), and for whatever else they think they can get away with. Another "hidden" charge that really irks us is that the meter will begin running at the time you phone the cab, not when you are picked up! In short, your fare will rarely ever be what you think it should be. To be safe, read the cab's pricing list, located in the seatback pocket, which is printed in Italian and English, and/or ask the driver what the fare will be before you ever get in the car. Travelers should also watch out for rogue taxi drivers in Rome. Some pretenders will wait at taxi stands and pounce on unsuspecting tourists. Ride only in authorized yellow or white taxis, and make sure your cab has a meter. If you're staying in a hotel, have your concierge phone the radio taxi.

Driving and Parking in Rome

Driving in Rome is best left to those with nerves of steel. Lanes are unmarked, traffic lights are rarely obeyed, and Roman drivers, especially the ones on motor scooters, are erratic. When not plagued with swift traffic, Rome's streets still tend to be clogged, particularly near pedestrian zones in the Centro Storico. Alas, driving in Rome is not for the faint of heart, but renting a car can be your ticket to far-flung attractions in the rest of the region.

Worse than driving in Rome is parking, as you will witness from the dozens of creative parking jobs on sidewalks and street corners. If you choose to drive, you should park in one of the city's designated parking garages to save yourself frustration and potential fines. The most convenient parking garage is located at Villa Borghese, where you can park for approximately €1 per hour for the first four hours, or pay up to €15 for a full day. The Villa Borghese parking lot is open 24 hours. If you are staying at a hotel, ask the concierge if parking is available or if a garage is nearby. Many garages in the city are open to visitors only through agreements with hotels.

Sight-seeing and Tours in Rome

Planning Visits of Three, Five, and Seven Days

Well-laid plans call for at least a one-week stay in the Eternal City, but some ambitious travelers try to see it all in just a few days. We don't recommend rushing through Rome, but if you must, these are the attractions you just can't miss while you're here.

Appian Way   See at least one catacomb. 1 to 2 hours.

Bocca della Verità (Mouth of Truth)   Stick your hand in its mouth and snap a picture. 15 minutes or less.

Campidoglio   Parade to the top of the wide stairs *(cordonata)* and visit the Michelangelo-designed square. 30 minutes. Pay a visit to the Capitoline Museums. 2 to 3 hours.

Campo de' Fiori   Get there early for market or hang out by night. Half an hour or longer.

Colosseum   Walk around the perimeter, and explore the cavernous interior. 1 to 2 hours.

Isola Tiberina   Cross the bridge (Ponte Cestio or Ponte Fabricio) to Rome's boat-shaped island. Walk around the base. 15 to 30 minutes.

Pantheon   Admire this feat of ancient Roman architecture. 30 minutes.

Piazza Navona   Take your evening *passeggiata* here. 30 minutes to an hour.

Piazza del Popolo   Sit by the fountain and get your bearings. 15 to 30 minutes.

Pincio Gardens   Gaze out from Rome's most perfect perch. 15 minutes.

Roman Forum   Start at the Colosseum end or the Capitoline end and lose yourself in the ruins. 1 to 2 hours.

San Giovanni in Laterano   Stand before the awesome façade and tour the cloisters. 30 minutes to 1 hour.

Santa Maria Maggiore   Highlights include the gilded and coffered ceiling, fifth-century mosaics, and Bernini's grave. 30 minutes.

St. Peter's Basilica and St. Peter's Square   Check out the statues in the piazza, step back and examine the size of St. Peter's dome, then go inside. St. Peter's merits at least an hour-long gander, and Piazza San Pietro is doable in an hour. Expect to spend about an hour and a half if you go up to the dome.

Spanish Steps   Sit a spell and watch the crowds go by. Half an hour or longer.

Trastevere   Window-shop, have lunch or dinner. 1 hour or longer.

Trevi Fountain   Grab a gelato and chill out. 15 to 30 minutes.

Vatican Museums   Meander through the Etruscan and Egyptian collections, the Raphael rooms, and finish up at the Sistine Chapel. At least 3 hours; if you bee-line it to the Sistine Chapel, 1 hour.

Vittoriano   If you miss this monster, you've missed Rome. Climb the stairs for a nice view. 30 minutes.

Touring Rome in Three Days

Day 1

Begin your tour with a visit to ancient Rome, starting at the **Colosseum** and working your way through the **Forum.** The afternoon can be spent visiting the **Pantheon** and lingering outside store windows on and around Via del Corso. Have dinner in or near **Campo de' Fiori,** and walk it all off with an evening stroll around **Piazza Navona.**

Day 2

Line up early for entry to the **Vatican Museums.** You can expect to spend at least three hours here, the majority of your day. See **St. Peter's** next. When evening beckons, make your way to Trastevere. Check out the mosaics in **Santa Maria in Trastevere** before having dinner at an authentic Roman *trattoria.*

Day 3

Learn the truth at the **Bocca della Verità** (at Santa Maria in Cosmedin), then make your way to the **Campidoglio** or the **Vittoriano** monument, where you can enjoy fine views of surrounding Rome. Make your way to the **Trevi Fountain.** Window-shop with the rest of the world on the Via Condotti. Then watch the sun go down from the **Spanish Steps.**

Touring Rome in Five Days

Follow the first three days above, then:

Day 4

Rome's amazing churches deserve their own itinerary. Start in the south with visits to **San Giovanni in Laterano, San Clemente, San Pietro in Vincoli** (where Michelangelo's *Moses* is housed), and **Santa Maria Maggiore.** Have a restful afternoon on the leafy Via Veneto, ending with quiet time in the **Villa Borghese.**

Day 5

Get out of the city and head to **Tivoli, Ostia Antica,** or the **Appian Way.** Say goodbye to Rome with dinner and a stroll in **Piazza Navona.**

Touring Rome in Seven Days

Follow the first five days above, then:

Day 6

History buffs can choose between visits to the **Domus Aurea** (Nero's Golden House), the **Museo Nazionale Romano,** or **Museo Nazionale di Villa Giulia** (the National Etruscan Museum at Villa Giulia). Art lovers will do well to check out the **Borghese Gallery** or **Capitoline Museums.**

Day 7

Follow your interests by shopping, visiting churches, or seeing one last museum. Or return to your favorite landmarks—Rome's attractions deserve more than one look. Laze away the evening with a glass of wine in Campo de' Fiori.

City Tours

To maximize your sight-seeing time and minimize your fatigue, you may want to hop aboard a tour bus. There are many full-day and half-day coach tours available in Rome, and most tours are quite reasonably priced, starting at around US$15 per person. Motor-coach tours are also practical if you are a senior and/or if you are traveling with kids. **Green Line Tours** has an extensive network throughout Italy and English-speaking guides. Its Rome city tours include Classical Rome, Imperial Rome, and Christian Rome, among many others. Offering the stop-and-go option for tourists is **Stop & Go City Tours,** which allows tourists to get off at any of 14 sights and reboard later. Half-day excursions by Stop

& Go include visits to Tivoli, Ostia Antica, Castelli Romani, and to the Etruscan towns of Cerveteri and Tarquinia.

Appian Line specializes in tours of the Roman countryside, including the sights beyond the Appian Way. Meanwhile, the most cost-effective tour going is one hosted by **ATAC,** the city's public transportation company. Its #110 bus tours departs five times daily during the spring and summer, making 20-minute stops at the Vatican, the Forum, and other attractions. This no-frills, three-hour tour costs €7.50. (Note that ATAC's guides speak a bit of English.) Look for the gray bus. More information about ATAC is listed under "Public Transportation" above.

If you're the type of traveler who'd rather stretch your legs than be stuck on a tour bus, consider taking a walking tour. **Scala Reale** and **Through Eternity** offer walking itineraries that are hardly run of the mill. For instance, the former has an evening tour of Baroque Rome, while the latter's three-hour dinner and tour of Trastevere allows participants the chance to dine and mingle among the locals. Both companies also operate tours to the Roman countryside.

Finally, after centuries of neglect, Rome has begun to pay attention to the Tiber river. Riverboat tours with **Battelli di Roma** snake past the Castel Sant'Angelo and duck under ancient bridges, affording tourists the chance to see St. Peter's Basilica and other landmarks in a new light. A simple day pass costs €2.30 and dinner cruises are also available. There is also a 75-minute guided tour; however, English is limited.

Appian Line	phone 06 487 866 01	www.appianline.it
Battelli di Roma	phone 06 692 941 47	www.battellidiroma.it
Green Line Tours	phone 06 483 787	www.greenlinetours.com
Scala Reale	phone 06 474 5673	www.scalareale.org
Stop & Go City Tours	phone 06 489 057 29	www.romecitytours.com
Through Eternity	phone 06 700 9336	www.througheternity.com

Exploring Points of Interest

Where to Get the Best Views

Rome is a city of seven major hills—Aventino, Celio, Esquilino, Viminale, Quirinale, Capitolino, and Palatino—and many minor ones, so it's no wonder that there are a host of places from which to survey the valley of ancient ruins, church steeples, and ochre-toned buildings. One of the most popular perches is from the **Pincio Gardens.** From a landing high above Piazza del Popolo, you can see Rome's landscape punctuated by the dome of **St. Peter's** (straight ahead) and the bright, white marble of the **Vittoriano monument** (far to the left). The Pincio perch is a tourist favorite at dusk. Cross the Tiber River and walk the dark, winding ramp inside the **Castel Sant'Angelo** to arrive at the citadel's terrace. Included in the panorama is a close-up of St. Peter's and the riverside skyline. If you're so inclined—and have the energy—you may want to climb the 575 steps that lead up to the dome of **St. Peter's Basilica**.

Papal Audiences and Religious Services

You don't have to be Catholic to get a kick out of seeing the pope *(il Papa)*. After all, the man is one of the most recognizable and revered figures in the world. Luckily, it's not too difficult to get a glimpse of the head of the Catholic Church if you plan ahead. Every Wednesday, usually at 10 a.m., the pope addresses groups of approximately 2,000 to 3,000 people. To attend this free papal audience, you should call the **Prefettura della Casa Pontificia** to secure tickets. This can be done when you arrive, or you can arrange it from home shortly before you leave for your trip. However, because seating is limited, we advise that you secure your tickets as far in advance as possible, so that you can plan the rest of your itinerary around your Vatican visit. Write to the Prefettura and specify the date you would like to attend and the number of people in your party. If you get to Rome without having made any plans to attend a papal audience, you still may be able to get tickets at the last minute. The Prefettura's office is located beyond the bronze doors to the right of the basilica as you're looking at it.

Being the benevolent man that he is, the pope also gives those tourists who can't attend a papal audience the opportunity to see and hear him. On the last Sunday of each month, usually at 9 a.m., he speaks to the rapt throngs from the window of his apartment high above St. Peter's Square. Bring binoculars for a better view. Furthermore, if you happen to be in Rome during the second week of December, you can get a glimpse of the papal motorcade. December 8 marks the Day of the Immaculate Conception, when the pope travels down Via Condotti to Santa Trinità dei Monti to celebrate a special mass.

For listings of Catholic masses in English, see our suggestions at the end of Part Three, Arriving, Getting Oriented, and Departing.

Prefettura della Casa Pontificia   00120 Città del Vaticano; phone 06 698 832 73

Getting Tickets and Passes

Museum tickets can get a bit pricey in Rome, as most of the major sites charge an admission of €4–€5. Almost all state-owned sites offer discounts for children, students, and seniors, and if you're a citizen of the European Union, you may qualify for a discount as well. Inquire before purchasing tickets. A number of sites also offer joint tickets for related attractions. For example, for approximately €10, you can get a pass to the Colosseum, the Palatine, and the Museo Nazionale Romano that's good for three days. If you're lucky, you'll visit Rome during **Cultural Heritage Week** (Settimana dei Beni Culturali), when admission to all state-owned museums is free. Cultural Heritage Week is usually scheduled for early spring. Travelers should also be aware that to visit some sites, they must make reservations or get permission in advance. You can purchase tickets and make reservations for timed visits at the **Centro Servizi per l'Archeologia** for attractions like Nero's Golden House. Other archaeological sites, such as the Area Sacra, require that you get permission from the agency **Ripartizione X** months in advance. See the attraction profiles below for details. If the attraction expects a donation, feel free to give whatever you can afford. A minimum of €1 is usually appropriate.

Centro Servizi per l'Archeologia　Via O. Amendola, 2; phone 06 481 5576. Open Monday–Saturday, 9 a.m.–1 p.m., 2–5 p.m.

Il Ministero per i Beni e le Attività Culturali　Via del Collegio Romano, 27; phone 06 672 31

Ripartizione X　Via del Portico di Ottavia, 29; phone 06 671 038 19, fax 06 689 2115

Rome Attraction Profiles

Rome has an overwhelming number of attractions, so we simply cannot profile them all here. However, we have compiled a list of the city's most significant attractions as well as some of our personal favorites.

ROME ATTRACTIONS		
Attraction	Author's Rating	Comments
Ara Pacis Augustae	★★★★	Imperial monument, friezes
Arch of Constantine	★★	Triumphal arch
Arch of Janus	★★★	Triumphal arch
Area Sacra di Largo Argentina	★★★	Caesarean ruins
Baths of Caracalla	★★★	Ancient Roman baths
Baths of Diocletian	★★	Huge bath complex
Bioparco	★	Rome city zoo
Campidoglio	★★★	Rome's Capitol Hill
Capitoline Museums	★★★★	Sculpture and art museums
Casa di Goethe	★★★	Small Goethe museum
Castel Sant' Angelo	★★★	Mediaval fortress
Catacombs of Domitilla	★★★	Largest network of catacombs
Catacombs of San Callisto	★★★	Burial site of early Christians
Catacombs of San Sebastiano	★★	Once housed Sts. Peter and Paul's remains

ROME ATTRACTIONS *(continued)*

Attraction	Author's Rating	Comments
Chiesa Nuova	★★	Church with Rubens art
Circus Maximus	★★	Site of ancient chariot races
Column of Marcus Aurelius	★★★	Triumphal column
Colosseum	★★★★	One of Italy's most famous monuments
Crypta Balbi	★★	Museum of Roman city history
Crypt of the Capuchin Monks	★★★★★	Burial ground decorated with bones
Explora Children's Museum	★★★	Hands-on kids' museum
Fontana delle Naiadi	★★★★★	Fountain with cavorting nudes
Fontana della Tartarughe	★★★★	Charming fountain
Fontana del Tritone	★★★★	Berinini-sculpted fountain
Fontana dei Quattro Fiumi	★★★	Bernini-sculpted fountain
The Forum	★★★★★	Ancient city center
Galleria Borghese	★★★★★	Renaissance and Baroque sculpture
Galleria Colonna	★★★	Private collection of Italian art
Galleria Doria Pamphilj	★★★★	Museum of Renaissance art
Galleria Nazionale d'Arte Moderna	★★	Huge collection of 18th- & 19th-century Italian art
Il Gesù	★★★	Beautiful Jesuit church
Imperial Forum	★★	Annex of the Roman Forum
Isola Tiberina (Tiber Island)	★★★	Small island in Tiber River
Keats-Shelley Memorial House	★★	Shrine to the English poets
Mamertine Prison	★★★	Ancient prison
Museo Civico di Zoologia	★★	Small natural history museum
Museo dell'Alto Medioevo	★★	Museum of Middle Ages Rome
Museo della Civiltà Romana	★★★	Scale models of ancient Rome
Museo Nazionale della Paste Alimentari (National Pasta Museum)	★★	History and production of Italy's national dish
Museo Nazionale Romano	★★	Italy's main museum for ancient art
Museo Nazionale di Villa Giulia	★★★½	Replete with Etruscan relics
Nero's Golden House (Domus Aurea)	★★★★	Mansion of the mad emperor
Obelisk of Piazza San Giovanni in Laterano	★★★	Largest Egyptian obelisk in Rome
Obelisk of Santa Maria Sopra Minerva	★★★★	Cute obelisk on elephant's back
Order of the Knights of Malta	★★★★	Perfect view of St. Peter's
Orto Botanico (Botanical Gardens)	★★★★	Beautiful city gardens

ROME ATTRACTIONS *(continued)*

Attraction	Author's Rating	Comments
Palatino (Palatine)	★★★	Ruin-covered hill
Palazzo delle Esposizioni	★★★	Exhibition space
Pantheon	★★★★★	Oldest building in Rome
Pasquino	★★★	"Talking" statue
Piazza del Popolo	★★★★★	City square of stunning scale
Piazza di Spagna and the Spanish Steps	★★★★★	Famous place for lounging and people-watching
Piazza Montecitorio	★★½	Home of the Italian Parliament
Piazza Navona	★★★★★	Site of ancient races, Baroque churches, and modern cafés
Pincio Gardens	★★★★★	Rome's best overlook
Ponte Rotto	★★	Ancient broken bridge
Protestant Cemetery	★★★★★	Final resting place of poets Keats and Shelley
Pyramid of Caius Cestius	★★	Elaborate tomb
Quattro Fontane (Four Fountains)	★★	Baroque fountains on four street corners
San Clemente	★★★★★	Church built on ancient temple
San Francesco a Ripa	★★	Relics of St. Francis of Assisi
San Giovanni in Laterano	★★★	The cathedral of Rome
San Luigi dei Francesi	★★★★	Major artworks of Caravaggio
San Paolo Fuori le Mura	★★★★	One of Rome's four patriarcha basilicas
San Pietro in Vincoli	★★★★	Modest church with major artwork
Sant'Agnese in Agone	★★	Main church on Piazza Navona
Sant'Ignazio di Loyola	★★★	Jesuit church with
Santa Croce in Gerusalemme	★★	Relics of True Cross, St. Thomas
Santa Maria degli Angeli e dei Martiri	★★	Michelangelo-designed church
Santa Maria dei Miracoli e Santa Maria in Montesanto	★★	Twin churches
Santa Maria del Popolo	★★★★	Renaissance, Baroque art
Santa Maria in Aracoeli	★★	Church with long staircase
Santa Maria in Cosmedin	★★½	Greek national church
Santa Maria in Trastevere	★★★★★	Church rich in mosaics
Santa Maria Maggiore	★★★	One of Rome's four patriarchal basilicas
Santa Maria Sopra Minerva	★★★★★	Gothic church, art, tombs
Scala Santa and Sancta Sanctorum	★	Pope's private chapel

ROME ATTRACTIONS *(continued)*

Attraction	Author's Rating	Comments
St. Peter's Basilica	★★★★★	Largest and most important church in Christendom
Sinagoga (Synagogue)	★★★	Jewish temple, museum
Teatro di Marcello	N/A	Concert venue
Tomb of Cecilia Metella	★★	Patrician tomb
Trevi Fountain	★★★★	Rome's largest and most famous fountain
Vatican Corridor	N/A	Fortified papal hallway
Vatican Museums	★★★★★	Sistine Chapel, huge art collection
Via Appia (Appian Way)	★★★★	Ancient road, catacombs, monuments
Via Giulia	★★★★	Ivy-covered Renaissance street
Via Veneto	★★★	Street from movie *La Dolce Vita*
Villa Borghese	★★★★★	Where Romans go for greenery
Villa Farnesina	★★★½	Fresco by Raphael
Il Vittoriano	★★★★	Huge monument with views

Ara Pacis Augustae (Altar of Augustan Peace)

Type of Attraction Imperial monument and significant artistic treasure

Location Via di Ripetta (Tridente) **Bus** 70, 81, 115, 186

Admission Not available at press time

Hours Tuesday–Saturday 9 a.m.–5 p.m., Sunday 9 a.m.–1 p.m.

Phone 06 671 1035

When to Go The Ara Pacis remains closed for renovations.

Special Comments At press time, the Ara Pacis was still undergoing restorations. Admission and times may change when the monument reopens, a date which is, as yet, unknown.

Overall Appeal by Age Group

Pre-school —	Teens ★★	Over 30 ★★
Grade school ★★	Young Adults ★★	Seniors ★★

Authors' Rating ★★★★

How Much Time to Allow 30 minutes

Description and Comments The Roman Senate commissioned this grandiose marble monument in 13 B.C. to celebrate peace *(pacis)* throughout the Mediterranean after successful military campaigns by Emperor Augustus in Gaul and Spain. One of the most important works of the Imperial Age, the altar's north frieze depicts a number of senators; the south frieze depicts members of Augustus's family, making it one of the first artworks to feature the likenesses of real people rather than gods. Some family members featured on the altar include the emperor's son-in-law and heir apparent, Marcus Agrippa, stepson Tiberius, third wife Livia, and even his grandson Lucius. Carved out of Carrara marble, every inch of the square altar is covered with allegorical scenes of peace.

The Ara Pacis was dedicated on January 30, 9 B.C. (according to Ovid). Ironically, the Altar of Peace contained a sacrificial altar, on which animals were sacrificed each year on the anniversary of the inauguration of the monument. The Ara Pacis was essentially "lost" until the 16th century, when parts of it were unearthed. It was not until 1938, at the behest of Mussolini, that scientists began to piece together the Ara Pacis—indeed, as a way to restore the mystical legend of the Roman empire and add to Mussolini's cult of personality. The Ara Pacis was relocated during the 1940s to its present location near the Mausoleum of Augustus.

Other Things to Do Nearby Stroll along the banks of the Tiber, or shop on the Via del Corso.

Arch of Constantine

Type of Attraction Triumphal arch

Location Piazza del Colosseo (Ancient City) **Bus/Metro** Buses 11, 27, 81, 85, 87, 186, 673; Metro Colosseo (Line B)

Admission Free

Hours Always open

Phone None

When to Go Anytime

Overall Appeal by Age Group

Pre-school —		Teens ★★		Over 30 ★★
Grade school ★★		Young Adults ★★		Seniors ★★

Authors' Rating ★★

How Much Time to Allow Less than 15 minutes

Description and Comments Strikingly similar to the Arch of Septimus Severus in the Roman Forum, the Arch of Constantine was one of the last major monuments built in Rome. Erected in A.D. 315, the arch was meant to commemorate Emperor Constantine's victory over Maxentius at the Battle of the Milvian Bridge, a triumph that Constantine, who proclaimed Christianity the sole religion of Rome in A.D. 312, attributed to God. However, Constantine did not pay heed to the Seventh Commandment—thou shalt not steal—when building the arch. Many sections of the monument were decorated with statues and medallions pilfered from Trajan's Forum.

Other Things to Do Nearby See the Roman Forum and the Colosseum.

Arch of Janus

Type of Attraction Triumphal arch

Location Via del Velabro (Aventino) **Bus** 81, 95, 160, 175, 204, 628

Admission Free

Hours Always open

Phone None

When to Go Anytime

Overall Appeal by Age Group

Pre-school —	Teens ★★	Over 30 ★★
Grade school ★★	Young Adults ★★	Seniors ★★

Authors' Rating ★★★

How Much Time to Allow Less than 15 minutes

Description and Comments This four-sided arch was built in the fourth century A.D. as a covered cattle market near the former docks of the Tiber. Although it was built during a time when Christianity was flourishing, the Arch of Janus was named after the god of doors, Janus, and was adorned with statues of the Roman goddesses Ceres (earth), Minerva (wisdom), Juno (queen of gods), and Roma (patron goddess of Rome). Admittedly, the Arch of Janus is squat and plain (most decorative elements are missing), but its four-faced construction is unusual and therefore a point of interest.

Other Things to Do Nearby Lounge on the Circus Maximus or have your fortune told by the Mouth of Truth (Bocca della Verità).

Area Sacra di Largo Argentina (Sacred Area of Largo Argentina)

Type of Attraction Ruins from the time of Julius Caesar

Location Largo di Torre Argentina (Centro Storico) **Bus** 44, 46, 56, 60, 62, 64, 70, 81, 492

Admission Free

Hours By appointment only; get permission from Ripartizione X (phone 06 671 03 819)

Phone None

When to Go Early morning

Special Comments This is a very busy intersection. Watch out for speeding cars and buses when crossing over to view the site.

Overall Appeal by Age Group

Pre-school ★★	Teens ★★★	Over 30 ★★★
Grade school ★★★	Young Adults ★★★	Seniors ★★★

Authors' Rating ★★★

How Much Time to Allow 30 minutes

Description and Comments At one time or another, you may be waiting for a bus or tram at Largo Argentina, a transportation hub east of Campo de' Fiori. If so, take a moment to check out the big hole in the ground while you're there. Four Republican-era temples were discovered here in the 1920s while the city was undergoing major restructuring under Mussolini. Temples A, B, C, and D, as they are labeled on a crude map located above the pit, are among the oldest ruins ever found in Rome. Temples A, B, and D date back to the third century B.C., and Temple C dates back to the fourth century B.C. Archaeologists have also identified a large platform of *tufa* stones behind Temples B and C as part of the Curia of Pompey, the site where Julius Caesar was assassinated on the Ides of March in 44 B.C.

Touring Tips The Largo Argentina Cat Sanctuary (**www.romancats.com**), an organization that tends to the neighborhood's stray cats, sits at the south end of the Area Sacra. You can watch the cats play and sleep among the ruins. If you're so inclined, you can also stop by the shelter to make a donation.

Other Things to Do Nearby Pick up some fresh fruit or flowers from a vendor in Campo de' Fiori, or sit for a glass of wine in one of the square's outdoor restaurants.

Baths of Caracalla

Type of Attraction Best-preserved baths in Rome

Location Viale delle Terme di Caracalla, 52 (Celio) **Bus** 160, 628, 760

Admission €4

Hours Tuesday–Saturday, 9 a.m.–sunset; Sunday–Monday, 9 a.m.–1 p.m.; closed January 1, May 1, and December 25

Phone 06 575 8626

When to Go The baths are less crowded on weekdays and are best when the weather is pleasant

Special Comments Handicap-accessible

Overall Appeal by Age Group

Pre-school ★★		Teens ★★★		Over 30 ★★★
Grade school ★★		Young Adults ★★★		Seniors ★★★

Authors' Rating ★★★

How Much Time to Allow 1–1.5 hours

Description and Comments Built by Caracalla, this large complex consisted of a cold bath *(frigidarium)*, a lukewarm bath *(tepidarium)*, a hot bath *(caldarium)*, an open-air pool, and a gym. Caracalla was known as a tyrant (he carried out a coup d'état on his father, Severus, and murdered his brother Geta), but this construction project was a boon to his citizens. Men, women, and slaves were all permitted to bathe and socialize here (albeit in shifts), and the baths could handle a capacity of approximately 1,500 bathers at a time. Romans used the Baths of Caracalla for some 300 years after their inauguration in A.D. 217 until invading Goths cut off the water supply. The baths are today only a shell; however, many walls of the complex are still as tall as they were some 1,500 years ago. In fact, the monumental size of the ruins is said to have inspired expat resident Percy Bysshe Shelley, who penned *Prometheus Unbound* in 1819 while gazing at the baths. Even more impressive are the remaining mosaics, which range from simple, black-and-white patterns to colorful depictions of muscular athletes. (Most of the other mosaics from this site were removed by the Farnese family and installed in their palace.) Up until a few years ago, open-air opera performances were a regular summer event, but archaeologists have called a halt to such dramatic spectacles, as the orchestra's instruments and singers' voices were inflicting heavy damage on the structures.

Other Things to Do Nearby The baths are practically equidistant from the Circus Maximus and the beginning of the Appian Way.

Baths of Diocletian

Type of Attraction Once the largest bath complex in Rome

Location Piazza della Repubblica (Quirinale) **Bus/Metro** Buses 57, 64, 65, 75, 170, 492, 910; Metro Repubblica (Line A), Termini (Line A, B)

Admission €6, or €10 included in the Museo Nazionale Romano combined ticket with the Colosseum and the Palatine

Hours See profiles for Santa Maria degli Angeli e dei Martiri and Museo Nazaionale Romano

Phone See profiles for Santa Maria degli Angeli e dei Martiri and Museo Nazaionale Romano

When to Go Anytime

Overall Appeal by Age Group

Pre-school ★		Teens ★★★		Over 30 ★★★
Grade school ★★		Young Adults ★★★		Seniors ★★

Authors' Rating ★★

How Much Time to Allow 30 minutes to 1 hour

Description and Comments Not content with Caracalla's impressive bath complex in the south of town, the malevolent Emperor Diocletian, persecutor of thousands of Christians, set out in the late third century to build even larger baths. Completed in 306, the *terme* covered more than 2.5 acres between what is today the Piazza della Repubblica and the Piazza dei Cinquecento and could hold as many as 3,000 bathers at a time. The complex also included a gymnasium, a heated lavatory, a library, art galleries, concert halls, and brothels. Like the Baths of Caracalla, the Baths of Diocletian ceased operation after the Goths destroyed the aqueducts that supplied the water to the baths. Today, the complex is a multiuse facility, housing a church and cloister designed by Michelangelo (Santa Maria degli Angeli e dei Martiri, see profile) and the Museo Nazionale Romano (National Roman Museum, see profile).

Other Things to Do Nearby Examine the vast store of classical art in the National Roman Museum, see how Diocletian's Baths were converted into a church in Santa Maria degli Angeli e dei Martiri, or have a peek at Rome's most provocative fountain, the Fountain of the Nymphs.

Bioparco

Type of Attraction The city zoo
Location Via del Giardino Zoologico, 1 (Via Veneto) Tram 30
Admission €5
Hours Daily, 9:30 a.m.–6 p.m.
Phone 06 360 8211
When to Go When the kids need a break
Overall Appeal by Age Group

Pre-school ★★★	Teens ★	Over 30 ★
Grade school ★★★	Young Adults ★	Seniors ★

Authors' Rating ★
How Much Time to Allow 1 hour

Description and Comments For the most part, Rome's zoo is far from an animal paradise. Many animals still pace about in cramped cages and behind bars. Efforts are being made to improve the situation, the first being a name change to the more earth-friendly moniker Bioparco. Children will be captivated, nevertheless.

Other Things to Do Nearby Have a picnic in the Villa Borghese.

Campidoglio

Type of Attraction Rome's Capitol Hill
Location Piazza del Campidoglio (Campidoglio) **Bus** 44, 46, 64, 70, 81, 110 and other routes to Piazza Venezia
Admission Free; see profile for Capitoline Museums for further information
When to Go Early; the Capitoline Museums are closed on Monday, making it a good day for general touring
Overall Appeal by Age Group

Pre-school —	Teens ★★★	Over 30 ★★★
Grade school ★★	Young Adults ★★★	Seniors ★★★

Authors' Rating ★★★
How Much Time to Allow 30 minutes

Description and Comments Featuring a black-and-white cobbled piazza with an unmistakable geometric pattern, the Campidoglio is the location of some of the city's municipal government buildings and the Capitoline Museums. Michelangelo drafted the design for the Campidoglio and the *cordonata* ramp of stairs in the 1530s. It took approximately 100 years for architects to complete the project, but for the most part, Michelangelo's original design remains. The giant central statue of Marcus Aurelius, once the largest equestrian statue in world, is a copy; the original is in the Palazzo dei Conservatori of the Capitoline Museums.

Other Things to Do Nearby Spend a morning or afternoon in the Capitoline Museums, or visit the Vittoriano monument.

Capitoline Museums

Type of Attraction Impressive collection of ancient sculpture, late Renaissance art
Location Piazza del Campidoglio (Campidoglio) **Bus** 44, 46, 64, 70, 81, 110 and other routes to Piazza Venezia
Admission €6; free last Sunday of month
Hours Tuesday–Sunday, 9 a.m.–7 p.m.; holidays, 9 a.m.–1:45 p.m.; closed January 1, May 1, and December 25
Phone 06 671 020 71
When to Go Weekday mornings
Overall Appeal by Age Group

Pre-school —	Teens ★★★★	Over 30 ★★★★
Grade school ★★★	Young Adults ★★★★	Seniors ★★★★

Authors' Rating ★★★★★
How Much Time to Allow 2–3 hours

Description and Comments Closed for years for renovations, the Capitoline Museums reopened in 2000 having undergone a much-needed reorganization and extensive renovations. The museum is housed in two parts in the Palazzo dei Conservatori and the Palazzo Nuovo and contains artworks that are indelibly linked with the Eternal City's history and character. Most notably, in the Palazzo dei Conservatori, you'll find the venerated fifth-century B.C. She-Wolf bronze *(La Lupa),* which continues to be the most recognizable symbol of Rome. Also in this wing of the museum is *Il Spinario,* an oft-copied second-century B.C. bronze of a boy removing a thorn from his foot. We find in the yard of the Palazzo dei Conservatori the remnants from a giant statue of Constantine; on the third floor of the building is a collection of Renaissance and Baroque paintings from the likes of Caravaggio and Guercino. The Palazzo Nuovo houses the original equestrian statue of Marcus Aurelius (a copy now sits in the Campidoglio Square) and renowned Roman copies of classical Greek statues, including the *Discobolus* and the *Dying Gaul.* The Capitoline Museums were opened to the public in 1734 at the behest of Pope Clement XII, establishing them as the first open museums in the world.

Touring Tips Enjoy spectacular views of the Forum from the Tabularium, an ancient Roman archive now featured on the underground passage between the Palazzo Nuovo and the Palazzo dei Conservatori. The museum's café, on the roof of the Palazzo dei Conservatori, also should not be missed for its sweeping views of the city.

Other Things to Do Nearby Climb the Aracoeli Staircase or mount the Vittoriano monument for excellent panoramas, or visit the Mamertine Prison and the Forum.

Casa di Goethe

Type of Attraction Small gallery looks at the life of famous German writer during his residency in Rome

Location Via del Corso, 18–20 (Tridente) **Bus** 81, 115, 117, 204

Admission €3

Hours Wednesday–Monday, 11 a.m.–6 p.m.

Phone 06 326 504 12

When to Go When you need to escape the chaos of Via del Corso

Special Comments Ring the doorbell for entry

Overall Appeal by Age Group

Pre-school —		Teens ★★		Over 30 ★★
Grade school —		Young Adults ★★		Seniors ★★

Authors' Rating ★★★

How Much Time to Allow 30 minutes

Description and Comments This apartment, which overlooks the Via del Corso, was the home of Johann Wolfgang von Goethe for two years, from 1786 until 1788. During this time, Goethe came to enjoy the climate and landscape of Rome and the quirkiness of Romans. He transcribed his thoughts on the city in *The Italian Journey,* one of the most influential texts ever written about Italy. Today, Goethe's former apartment serves as an exhibition space, displaying his personal effects, original printings of his book, and several portraits of the author, including the famous landscape portrait of him by Tischbein.

Touring Tips There is no elevator.

Other Things to Do Nearby Window shop on Via del Corso and Via Condotti, rest on the Spanish Steps, or visit another literary museum, the Keats-Shelley Memorial House.

Castel Sant'Angelo

Type of Attraction Medieval fortress

Location Lungotevere Castello (Vatican) **Bus/Metro** 23, 34, 64, 70, 186, 280; Metro Lepanto (Line A)

Admission €5

Hours Tuesday–Sunday, 9 a.m.–6 p.m. (last admission 1 hour before closing); closed holidays and 2nd and 4th Tuesday of month

Phone 06 687 5036

When to Go Before or after a visit to the Vatican

Special Comments Handicap accessible

Overall Appeal by Age Group

Pre-school ★★	Teens ★★★★	Over 30 ★★★
Grade school ★★★★	Young Adults ★★★	Seniors ★★★

Authors' Rating ★★★

How Much Time to Allow 1–2 hours

Description and Comments This rotund medieval fortress seems out of place with Rome's classical structures, yet it is very much a significant element of Rome's cityscape and history. Built atop Hadrian's mausoleum, Castel Sant'Angelo served as part of the Aurelian wall, then took shape as a prison and fortress in medieval times. In 1277, the Vatican constructed a walkway between the Vatican Palace and Castel Sant'Angelo to provide a convenient escape route for popes during times of political unrest. The Vatican Corridor still exists today and is best seen from the outer ramparts of the castle. Castel Sant'Angelo derives its name from the Archangel Gabriel, who, legend has it, appeared to Gregory the Great over the fortress during the plague in 590. Soon after, the plague abated, and the mausoleum was renamed. A statue of Castel Sant'Angelo's namesake sits atop the citadel.

Touring Tips A must for opera fans; visit the castle's terrace, where the last act of Puccini's *Tosca* took place. The terrace offers spectacular views across the Tiber.

Other Things to Do Nearby Follow the path of the Vatican Corridor to Vatican City.

Catacombs of Domitilla

Type of Attraction Largest network of catacombs

Location Via delle Sette Chiese, 282 (Appia Antica) **Bus** 218, 660

Admission €3.50

Hours Wednesday–Monday, 8:30 a.m.–noon, 2:30–5:30 p.m. (October–March: until 5 p.m.); closed January

Phone 06 511 0342 **Web** www.catacombe.domitilla.it

When to Go On hot summer days

Overall Appeal by Age Group

Pre-school ★★	Teens ★★★★	Over 30 ★★★★
Grade school ★★★★	Young Adults ★★★★	Seniors ★★

Authors' Rating ★★★

How Much Time to Allow 1–2 hours

Description and Comments The art in the *columbaria* at Domitilla, the largest network of catacombs near Rome, includes one of the earliest depictions of Christ as the good shepherd. Most of the private tombs located in Domitilla date from the first and second centuries.

Other Things to Do Nearby See more catacombs at San Callisto and San Sebastiano.

Catacombs of San Callisto

Type of Attraction Burial site of many Christians, including early popes

Location Via Appia Antica, 110 (Appia Antica) **Bus** 218, 660

Admission €3.50

Hours Thursday–Tuesday, 8:30 a.m.–noon, 2:30–5:30 p.m. (October–March: until 5 p.m.); closed January 1, February, Easter Sunday, and December 25

Phone 06 513 01 580

When to Go On hot summer days

Overall Appeal by Age Group

Pre-school —		Teens ★★★		Over 30 ★★★
Grade school ★★		Young Adults ★★★		Seniors ★★★

Authors' Rating ★★★
How Much Time to Allow 1 hour

Description and Comments The cemetery for the Church of Rome, the Catacombs of St. Callixtus were the first major find for archaeologist Giovanni Battista de Rossi in the mid-19th century. These catacombs are notable for the Chapel of the Popes, where nine Holy Fathers, including Sts. Sixtus II and Cornelius, are interred. A total of 14 papal crypts are located in these catacombs, and St. Cecilia was buried here before her remains were moved to her eponymous church in Trastevere. Coincidentally, St. Callixtus was not buried here, but in a cemetery along the Aurelian Road. His remains are now kept in Santa Maria in Trastevere.

Other Things to Do Nearby Visit the other tombs and catacombs along the Via Appia Antica.

Catacombs of San Sebastiano

Type of Attraction The bodies of Sts. Peter and Paul once laid here

Location Via Appia Antica, 136 (Appia Antica) **Bus** 218, 660

Admission €3.50

Hours Monday–Saturday 9 a.m.–noon, 2:30–5:30 p.m. (May–September: until 6:30 p.m.); closed November

Phone 06 788 7035

When to Go On hot summer days

Overall Appeal by Age Group

Pre-school —		Teens ★★★		Over 30 ★★★
Grade school ★★		Young Adults ★★★		Seniors ★★★

Authors' Rating ★★
How Much Time to Allow 1 hour

Description and Comments The Catacombs of St. Sebastian owe their fame to the fact that the remains of Sts. Peter and Paul were housed here temporarily to avoid destruction at the hands of anti-Christian Emperor Valerian. Also buried here was Sebastian, the saint who failed to die after being pierced with dozens of arrows. (He was eventually clubbed to death.) There is a modern shrine to St. Sebastian in the catacombs, and the church of St. Sebastian rises over the site.

Other Things to Do Nearby Visit the other tombs and catacombs along the Via Appia Antica.

Chiesa Nuova

Type of Attraction Church famous for artworks by Rubens
Location Piazza della Chiesa Nuova (Centro Storico) **Bus** 46, 62, 64
Admission Free
Hours Daily, 7:30 a.m.–noon, 4:30–7 p.m.
Phone 06 687 5289
When to Go Anytime
Overall Appeal by Age Group

Pre-school —		Teens ★★		Over 30 ★★
Grade school ★★		Young Adults ★★		Seniors ★★

Authors' Rating ★★
How Much Time to Allow 15–30 minutes

Description and Comments Unless you're an art buff, you can probably skip this unpleasantly dark church. The "New Church" was originally built as a headquarters for the Oration Order, a Counter-Reformation group, lead by Filippo Neri. The new church was to be a simple, unadorned sanctuary, but when Neri died, elders went against his wishes and allowed Pietro da Cortona to fresco the apse, dome, and nave. Though Pietro's work is splendid, it is overshadowed by three paintings by Peter Paul Rubens, who studied in Rome in the early 17th century. From left to right, Rubens paintings are *Saints Gregory, Maurus, and Papias; Madonna and Angels* (the altarpiece); and *Saints Domitilla, Nereus, and Achilleus.* St. Filippo is buried in his own chapel to the left of the altar.

Other Things to Do Nearby Check out the action in Piazza Navona or Campo de' Fiori.

Circus Maximus

Type of Attraction Stadium formerly used for chariot racing
Location Via del Circo Massimo (Aventino) **Bus/Tram/Metro** Buses 81, 10, 175, 628; tram 30; Metro Circo Massimo (Line B)
Admission Free
Hours All day

Phone None

When to Go Anytime, but especially on warm afternoons

Overall Appeal by Age Group

Pre-school ★★★		Teens ★★		Over 30 ★★
Grade school ★★★		Young Adults ★★		Seniors ★★

Authors' Rating ★★

How Much Time to Allow 30 minutes

Description and Comments Today it's nothing more than a enormous, overgrown football field, but the oblong Circus Maximus was once the site of heated chariot races, grueling athletic contests, and animal fights—a precursor to the Colosseum. Built in the fourth century B.C. and expanded and improved up until the sixth century A.D., the Circus once held as many as 250,000 spectators. The layout of the Circus Maximus included a central dividing barrier, or mound *(spina),* on top of which were planted seven large egg-shaped markers, used for counting the laps of the chariot races. Later, bronze dolphins were added. Emperor Augustus was reputedly a huge fan of the races and built an imperial box below the Palatine that looked out over the Circus Maximus. He also "imported" an obelisk from Egypt to decorate the end of the *spina* (this now stands in the Piazza del Popolo). Constantine II (ruled A.D. 337–340) was responsible for adding a second obelisk, which now stands in the Piazza di San Giovanni in Laterano.

Touring Tips Pack a lunch and enjoy a picnic on the Circus grounds. The Circus Maximus is also a favorite with joggers and dog walkers.

Other Things to Do Nearby Hike up the Palatine or Aventine hills for views over the Circus Maximus; have your fortune told by the Bocca della Verità (Mouth of Truth) at the church of Santa Maria in Cosmedin.

Column of Marcus Aurelius

Type of Attraction Triumphal column

Location Piazza Colonna (Centro Storico) **Bus** 56, 60, 85, 116, 492

Admission Free

Hours Always open

Phone None

When to Go Anytime

Overall Appeal by Age Group

Pre-school ★		Teens ★★		Over 30 ★★★
Grade school ★★		Young Adults ★★★		Seniors ★★★

Authors' Rating ★★★

How Much Time to Allow Less than 15 minutes

Description and Comments Clearly an imitation of Trajan's Column, this column was erected in 180 after the death of Marcus Aurelius. The reliefs on the structure chronicle the emperor's victories over the barbarians during the German war of 171–173 and the Sarmatic war of 174–175. The column stands approximately 100 feet high and has at its summit a statue of St. Paul. The statue of Marcus Aurelius, which had previously perched on top of the column, was ordered removed by Pope Sixtus V in 1588.

Touring Tips To get a better view of the Column of Marcus Aurelius, head to the Museo della Civiltà Romana at EUR, where you can study casts of the original.

Other Things to Do Nearby Shop on Via del Corso.

Colosseum

Type of Attraction The most recognized symbol of Rome and Italy

Location Piazza del Colosseo (Ancient City) **Bus/Metro** Buses 27, 81, 85, 87; Metro Colosseo (Line B)

Admission €6; consider purchasing a combined pass (also good for the Palatine and Museo Nazionale Romano) for €10

Hours Monday–Saturday, 9 a.m.–1 hour before sunset; Sunday 9 a.m.–2 p.m.; closed January 1, May 1, and December 25

Phone 06 700 4261 **Web** www.colosseumweb.org

When to Go Lines for the Colosseum are always long; consider a morning visit

Special Comments The Colosseum is now equipped with an elevator.

Overall Appeal by Age Group

Pre-school ★★★★	Teens ★★★★★	Over 30 ★★★★★
Grade school ★★★★★	Young Adults ★★★★★	Seniors ★★★★★

Authors' Rating ★★★★

How Much Time to Allow 1–1.5 hours

Description and Comments The lore of the Colosseum, one of Italy's most famous monuments, should be enough to lure you here. Known the world over for symbolizing the excesses of the Roman empire, this mammoth stadium was the scene of countless deadly battles between gladiators and animals. Commissioned by Emperor Vespasian, ruler of the Flavian dynasty, in A.D. 72, the Colosseum, sometimes called the Flavian Amphitheater, was inaugurated by Vespasian's son Titus and completed during the reign of Domitian.

During the first 100 days of games after its inauguration, the Colosseum saw some 5,000 wild beasts, including lions, tigers, elephants, and zebras, slaughtered within its walls. Meanwhile, gladiators were culled from Rome's many slaves and prisoners of war and were expected to battle to the death. Only the emperor could spare the life of a gladiator. Games continued in the Colosseum until 523, when animal fights were banned. Gladitorial combats had been banned some 100 years before.

The architecture of the Colosseum is no less significant than its history. The original exterior gleamed with travertine and marble and featured four stories of Doric, Ionic, and Corinthian columns. Eighty numbered archways allowed for up to 50,000 spectators to easily access their seats. (If you look closely, you can still see the Roman numerals above the entranceways.) Inside the stadium were wide corridors, again easing the movement of thousands of Romans. Each section of the Colosseum also included a *vomitorium*, or simply, an exit, so that spectators could come and go without much hassle.

The design of the amphitheater was also quite innovative. When rains threatened, workers could unfurl the *velarium*, a huge awning, which was anchored to bollards outside of the stadium. Underneath the Colosseum was a labyrinth of trap doors and cages connected to a series of pulleys and cables, allowing for animals, men, and scenery to suddenly appear from below the ground. Excavations of the Colosseum's basement (viewable from the upper tiers but not open to the public) give visitors an idea of how complex the underground maze was.

Although the Colosseum is still one of the most impressive sights in the world, it suffered through earthquakes and vandalism before it was consecrated as a holy site in the 1700s. During the Renaissance, many popes had the travertine and marble from the Colosseum quarried to build churches and religious monuments. Parts of St. Peter's Basilica even include marble from the Colosseum. All of the pockmarks that you see today on the structure's exterior are a result of the removal of tons of decorative stone.

Touring Tips One of the best ways to admire the Colosseum is from a distance. Climb the steps to the Oppian Hill (Colle Oppio), across the Via dei Fori Imperiali, for a bird's-eye view.

Other Things to Do Nearby Meander through the Forum and/or the Palatine, visit Nero's Golden House (Domus Aurea), or explore the multilayered Basilica of San Clemente.

Crypta Balbi

Type of Attraction A look at Rome's urban development

Location Via delle Botteghe Oscure, 31 (Centro Storico) **Bus** 44, 46, 56, 60, 62, 64, 65, 70, 75, 81, 492, and many other routes to Largo Argentina

Admission €4; though, as part of the Museo Nazionale Romano, admission to the Crypta Balbi is included in a combined ticket with the Colosseum and Palatine

Hours Tuesday–Sunday, 9 a.m.–7:45 p.m.

Phone 06 397 499 07

When to Go Anytime—the museum is rarely crowded

Overall Appeal by Age Group

Pre-school —		Teens ★		Over 30 ★★
Grade school ★		Young Adults ★★		Seniors ★★

Authors' Rating ★★★

How Much Time to Allow 1 hour

Description and Comments This relatively new museum space gives tourists the chance to see a cross-section of Rome from antiquity through the modern age. Laid out in two buildings, the exhibit of the Crypta Balbi starts with a look at early Rome and a Mithraeum that was discovered on the site during excavations. Further along, you can see evidence of a medieval street and a seventh-century workshop and the foundations of Renaissance-era buildings. If you visit the Crypta Balbi, we highly recommend taking a guided tour, as the docents can point out the significance of each part of the exhibit.

Other Things to Do Nearby Have lunch in the Jewish quarter (the Ghetto), or hop the tram at Largo Argentina to Trastevere, where you can explore more of medieval Rome.

Crypt of the Capuchin Monks

Type of Attraction Eerily artistic burial ground

Location Via Veneto, 27 (Via Veneto) (in the basement of Santa Maria della Concezione) **Bus/Metro** Buses 52, 53, 56, 58, 58B, 490, 495; Metro Barberini (Line A)

Admission Donation expected

Hours Friday–Wednesday, 9 a.m.–noon, 3–6 p.m.

Phone 06 488 2748

When to Go Early morning or late afternoon

Special Comments No photographs are permitted inside the crypt

Overall Appeal by Age Group

Pre-school —	Teens ★★★★★	Over 30 ★★★★★
Grade school —	Young Adults ★★★★★	Seniors ★★★★

Authors' Rating ★★★★★

How Much Time to Allow 15–30 minutes, or as crowds will allow

Description and Comments A gorgeous (if creepy) chapel lovingly decorated with chandeliers, starbursts, and crucifixes, the Crypt of the Capuchin Monks is entirely decorated with the bones of more than 4,000 monks. This above-ground cemetery also features stacks of skulls and several complete skeletons, including that of an infant, most likely a member of the Barberini family. Be on the lookout for arm bones forming the shape of the cross, a hooded skeleton with scythe in hand, and the placard at the end of the exhibit that reads: "What you are now, we once were, and what we are now, you will be."

Touring Tips This is a pretty gruesome exhibit and can be frightening for young children. Exercise your judgment on whether you want to take the little ones or not.

Other Things to Do Nearby The massive U.S. embassy is a few blocks away from here, as are exclusive Via Veneto hotels and dining venues.

Explora: Museo dei Bambini (Explora Children's Museum)

Type of Attraction Hands-on, kid-friendly attraction

Location Via Flaminia, 80 (Tridente) **Bus/Metro** Buses 490, 495; Metro Flaminio (Line A)

Admission Children, €6, Adults, €5, children under age 3, free

Hours Tuesday–Friday, 9:30 a.m.–5 p.m.; Saturday and Sunday, 10 a.m.–5 p.m.

Phone 06 360 054 88 **Web** www.mdbr.it (in Italian)

When to Go When the kids need a break

Special Comments Play visits last 1 hour and 45 minutes; reservations are required for groups, on holidays, and on the weekends.

Overall Appeal by Age Group

Pre-school ★★★★★	Teens ★	Over 30 ★★
Grade school ★★★★★	Young Adults ★★	Seniors ★★

Authors' Rating ★★★

How Much Time to Allow Visits last 1 hour, 45 minutes

Description and Comments Modeled after children's museums in the United States, this new play space is the first of its kind in Rome. Nick-named Explora, the museum gives kids the option of learning about the world through art, science, and hands-on projects, such as T-shirt making and TV reporting.

Other Things to Do Nearby Kick around in the Piazza del Popolo.

Fontana delle Naiadi (Fountain of the Nymphs)

Type of Attraction Once-controversial fountain

Location Piazza della Repubblica (Quirinale) **Metro** Repubblica (Line A)

When to Go Gorgeous day and night

Special Comments The fountain is located in the middle of a busy traffic circle. Use caution when crossing the street to view it!

Overall Appeal by Age Group

Pre-school ★★★★	Teens ★★★★★	Over 30 ★★★★★
Grade school ★★★★	Young Adults ★★★★★	Seniors ★★★★

Authors' Rating ★★★★★

How Much Time to Allow Less than 15 minutes

Description and Comments A playful creation of bronze and water, the Fountain of the Nymphs by artist Mario Rutelli was controversial when it debuted in 1901. Featured are four naked nymphs, each reclining on an aquatic creature meant to represent four different types of waterways. The seahorse symbolizes the ocean; the water snake, rivers; a swan, lakes; and a lizard, freshwater streams. What made the fountain so controversial at the turn of the century was its peep-show quality—the unclothed nymphs appear to be having a lot of fun under the shower of water. The central figure of the fountain, the god Glaucus, victor over nature, was added some ten years later, perhaps to lend the fountain a mythological (rather than salacious) feel.

Other Things to Do Nearby A fountain tour. From here, head down Via Nazionale and make a detour to see the Quattro Fontane (Four Fountains). Or walk down Via Vittorio Emanuele Orlando to view the Fontana del Mosè (Moses Fountain), then down Via Barberini to the Fontana del Tritone (Triton Fountain). The Trevi Fountain is not far beyond here.

Fontana della Tartarughe (Fountain of the Tortoises)

Type of Attraction One of Rome's most playful fountains
Location Piazza Mattei (Centro Storico) **Bus** 44, 56, 60, 65, 75, 170
When to Go Anytime during the day
Overall Appeal by Age Group

Pre-school ★★★	Teens ★★★	Over 30 ★★★★
Grade school ★★★★	Young Adults ★★★★	Seniors ★★★★

Authors' Rating ★★★★
How Much Time to Allow Less than 15 minutes

Description and Comments This whimsical fountain is not so easily found. Located in the Ghetto area, the fountain was commissioned by the powerful Mattei family in the late 16th century to decorate "their" square, Piazza Mattei. The original design, dreamed up by Giacomo della Porta, did not include the fountain's signature turtles. It did feature two bronze youths astride dolphins with arms upraised to the lip of the fountain's basin. Only later did an unknown artist add two struggling turtles between the youths' hands and the basin, improving on an already charming composition.

Other Things to Do Nearby Munch on *filetti di baccalà* and other Roman Jewish delights in the Ghetto (see Part Five, Dining in Central Italy).

Fontana del Tritone (Triton Fountain)

Type of Attraction Another Bernini fountain
Location Piazza Barberini (Via Veneto) Metro Barberini (Line A)
When to Go Anytime
Overall Appeal by Age Group

Pre-school ★★★	Teens ★★★★	Over 30 ★★★★
Grade school ★★★★	Young Adults ★★★★	Seniors ★★★★

Authors' Rating ★★★★
How Much Time to Allow Less than 15 minutes

Description and Comments This font is the singular decoration of the wide Piazza Barberini. Here, a muscular triton saddles a bed of scallops held erect by four fish while tooting into a conch shell that spews water.

Pope Urban VIII Barberini was the patron for the Fontana del Tritone, and his family's crest with three bees and the pontifical keys are displayed prominently on the work.

Other Things to Do Nearby Tour the Crypt of the Capuchin Monks.

Fontana dei Quattro Fiumi (Four Rivers Fountain)

Type of Attraction Bernini creation

Location Piazza Navona (Centro Storico) **Bus** 46, 62, 64, 70, 81, 87, 186, 492

When to Go Anytime, but especially at night when the fountain is illuminated

Overall Appeal by Age Group

Pre-school ★★		Teens ★★★		Over 30 ★★★
Grade school ★★★		Young Adults ★★★		Seniors ★★★

Authors' Rating ★★★

How Much Time to Allow Less than 15 minutes

Description and Comments Considered Bernini's greatest fountain, the Fontana dei Quattro Fiumi depicts the personification of four great rivers: the Nile, Danube, Ganges, and Rio de la Plata. These four rivers were chosen because they symbolized the continents that were (at that time) under papal rule. Surrounding the giant statues are various flora and fauna indigenous to the areas that the rivers represent, including lions, dragons, and fronds from a palm tree, and a giant obelisk taken from Egypt rises from the middle of the fountain. Bernini began working on the Four Rivers Fountain in 1647, some ten years before his rival, Borromini, began working on the façade of Sant'Agnese in Agone. For years, art historians have tried to create a controversy between the two artists, claiming that Bernini's statue of the Nile is in the action of shielding his eyes from the ugliness of the church; the start dates of each project lay this legend to rest.

Other Things to Do Nearby Window-shop and people-watch in the piazza.

The Forum (a.k.a. The Roman Forum)

Type of Attraction Ruins from the ancient city

Location Via dei Fori Imperiali (Ancient City); entrances at Largo Romolo e Remo and by the Arch of Titus **Bus/Metro** Buses 11, 27, 81, 85, 87, 186; Metro Colosseo (Line B)

Admission Free

Hours March–October: Monday–Saturday, 9 a.m.–dusk; Sunday, 9 a.m.–1 p.m.; November–February: Monday–Saturday, 9 a.m.–3 p.m.; Sunday, 9 a.m.–1 p.m.; closed January 1, May 1, and December 25

Phone 06 699 0110

When to Go The Forum is least crowded on Sunday and Monday mornings; shadow-play on the columns and arches is dramatic in the late afternoon

Special Comments The Forum is best viewed from the approach from the rear of the Capitoline hill.

Overall Appeal by Age Group

Pre-school ★★★★★	Teens ★★★★★	Over 30 ★★★★★
Grade school ★★★★★	Young Adults ★★★★★	Seniors ★★★★★

Authors' Rating ★★★★★

How Much Time to Allow 1–2 hours

Description and Comments Looking out over this vast graveyard of marble, granite, and travertine, it's hard to believe that these monumental ruins from ancient Rome were once buried under hundreds of feet of dirt. Excavations begun in the 18th century uncovered the Arch of Septimius Severus and the columns of the Temple of Saturn, still two of the most important finds within the Forum. Subsequent digs turned up hundreds of fragments from temples, columns, platforms, churches, and statues. In its heyday, the Roman Forum was the epicenter of legal, political, and judicial life and the site of rousing speeches and religious and military processions. As republican Rome transitioned to the Roman empire, the area of the Forum proved too small, and a number of imperial fora were erected nearby (see profile for Imperial Forum). Starting from the Campidoglio, some of the major excavations in the Forum include:

The Arch of Septimius Severus dates from A.D. 203 and is one of the best-preserved constructions in the Forum.

The Curia, a large barn-like structure, was built over the main chamber hall of the Roman Senate.

The Column of Phocas stands solo to the left of the Arch of Septimius Severus and is part of one of the last buildings erected in the Forum, dating from 608.

The House of the Vestal Virgins, about midway through the Forum, was erected to priestesses who worshiped the goddess Vesta. Here you'll find a row of statuettes and ruins lining a rectangular pool.

The Arch of Titus was built after the emperor's death in A.D. 82 to commemorate his victory in capturing Jerusalem.

Touring Tips The area can be very muddy after a hard rain.

Other Things to Do Nearby Check out the Colosseum, or explore the Campidoglio.

Galleria Borghese

Type of Attraction Prized sculpture collection from the Renaissance and Baroque periods

Location Villa Borghese, Piazzale Scipione Borghese, 5 (Via Veneto) **Bus/Tram** Buses 52, 53, 116, 910 to Via Pinciana, 3, 4, 57 to Via Po; trams 19, 30B to Viale delle Belle Arti

Admission €4.50

Hours Tuesday–Saturday, 9 a.m.–5 p.m.; Sunday, 9 a.m.–1 p.m.; closed holidays

Phone 06 842 416 07

When to Go Early afternoon

Special Comments Visitors are encouraged to pre-order tickets for Saturday and Sunday.

Overall Appeal by Age Group

Pre-school —		Teens ★★★★		Over 30 ★★★★★
Grade school ★★★		Young Adults ★★★★★		Seniors ★★★★★

Authors' Rating ★★★★★

How Much Time to Allow 1–2 hours

Description and Comments The Borghese Gallery is one of Rome's best-kept secrets. Tucked away in the park of the same name (the Villa Borghese), the gallery houses the Borghese family's personal collection of paintings and sculpture, including three superb works by Gianlorenzo Bernini. *Apollo and Daphne,* considered one of Bernini's finest sculptures, depicts Daphne fleeing Apollo at the moment of her transformation into a tree. You can also get close enough to the artist's *Pluto and Persephone* and *David* to inspect each sculpture's remarkably life-like renderings of the human form cast in marble.

Other Things to Do Nearby Discover contemporary Italian art at the Galleria Nazionale d'Arte Moderna (National Gallery of Modern Art), or enjoy the overlook at the Pincio Gardens.

Galleria Colonna

Type of Attraction Private art collection

Location Via della Pilotta, 17 (Quirinale) **Bus** 64, 65, 70, 75, 170

Admission €5

Hours Saturday, 9 a.m.–1 p.m. (last admission at noon); closed August and holidays

Phone 06 679 4362

When to Go Get there early

Overall Appeal by Age Group

Pre-school —		Teens ★★		Over 30 ★★★
Grade school ★★		Young Adults ★★★		Seniors ★★★

Authors' Rating ★★★

How Much Time to Allow 1 hour

Description and Comments The lavish art gallery of the Palazzo Colonna, still used as a residence for the wealthy family, was built between 1654 and 1665. Included among the artworks in the galleries are paintings by such masters as Bronzino, Ghirlandaio, Guercino, Guido Reni, Tintoretto, and Veronese. However, the prized possession is Annibale Carracci's humble *Bean Eater,* one of the earliest depictions in Italian art of everyday life.

Other Things to Do Nearby Hold court with the crowds at the Trevi Fountain.

Galleria Doria Pamphilj

Type of Attraction Museum of Renaissance art
Location Piazza del Collegio Romana, 2 (Centro Storico) **Bus** 44, 46, 94, 710, 718, 719, and other buses to Piazza Venezia
Admission €7.50
Hours Monday–Wednesday and Friday–Sunday, 10 a.m.–5 p.m.
Phone 06 679 7323
When to Go This museum is rarely crowded on weekdays
Overall Appeal by Age Group

Pre-school —		Teens ★★		Over 30 ★★★
Grade school —		Young Adults ★★★		Seniors ★★★

Authors' Rating ★★★★
How Much Time to Allow 1–2 hours

Description and Comments The works on display at the Galleria Doria Pamphilj (pronounced PAM-fee-lee) would be right at home on the walls of the Uffizi in Florence. Here, the fabulously rich family amassed more than 400 paintings and sculptures from Renaissance greats, including Raphael, Correggio, Caravaggio, and Titian. The Doria Pamphilj also had an eye for non-Italian art, collecting paintings from Flemish master Brueghel, tapestries from Gobelin, and art by Spanish court painter Velásquez. The latter's portrait of Pope Innocent X Pamphilj is the highlight of the gallery.

Other Things to Do Nearby Meander over to the Pantheon or check out the treasures of Santa Maria Sopra Minerva.

Galleria Nazionale d'Arte Moderna

Type of Attraction Largest collection of Italian art from 19th and 20th centuries
Location Viale delle Belle Arti, 131 (Via Veneto) **Tram** 19, 30
Admission €4
Hours Tuesday–Saturday, 9 a.m.–7 p.m.; Sunday, 9 a.m.–1 p.m.
Phone 06 322 4152
When to Go Best saved for a rainy day
Overall Appeal by Age Group

Pre-school —		Teens ★★		Over 30 ★★
Grade school ★★		Young Adults ★★		Seniors ★★

Authors' Rating ★★
How Much Time to Allow 1–2 hours

Description and Comments Shifting gears to admire modern art in a city full of antiquities is difficult, and most tourists rarely take the time to peruse the National Gallery's collection. Frankly, unless you're familiar with contemporary Italian artists, such as Giorgio de Chirico and Giorgio Morandi, you may find this collection a bit uninspiring. Occasional admirers of modern art will be happy to know that works by more familiar artists—such as Pollock, Twombly, Klimt, Miró, and Kandinsky—are also on display here.

Touring Tips   The museum's Café delle Belle Arti is one of Rome's most sophisticated places to grab a bite or a beverage.

Other Things to Do Nearby   Stroll through Villa Borghese, check out Baroque gems at the Museo e Galleria Borghese (Borghese Museum and Gallery).

Il Gesù

Type of Attraction   Splendidly decorated Jesuit church
Location   Piazza del Gesù (Centro Storico) **Bus** 44, 46, 56, 60, 62, 64, 65, 70, 81, and other routes to Piazza Venezia or Largo Argentina
Admission   Free
Hours   Daily, 7 a.m.–12:30 p.m., 4–7:15 p.m.
Phone   06 678 6341
When to Go   Anytime
Overall Appeal by Age Group

Pre-school —	Teens ★★	Over 30 ★★★
Grade school ★★	Young Adults ★★	Seniors ★★★

Authors' Rating ★★★
How Much Time to Allow   30 minutes

Description and Comments   Located on a busy intersection between Piazza Venezia and Largo Argentina, the façade of Rome's first Jesuit church, Il Gesù (Jesus), is a bit worse for wear. However, step inside and you're transported to richly decorated world of gold and marble. Built between 1568 and 1584, Il Gesù is perhaps the example of Counter-Reformation Baroque design, and its style has been copied throughout the Catholic world. Special features here include illusionistic artwork on the nave ceiling and in the dome, painted by Il Baciccia, and a chapel dedicated to St. Ignatius, the founder of the Jesuit order. The severely ornate Cappella di Sant'Ignazio was built by Andrea Pozzo between 1690 and 1700.

Other Things to Do Nearby   Walk a few blocks to Sant'Ignazio di Loyola, Rome's other Jesuit church.

Imperial Forum

Type of Attraction   The Forum, part II
Location   Via dei Fori Imperiali (Ancient City) **Bus/Metro** Buses 27, 81, 85, 87, 186; Metro Colosseo (Line B); the entrance to Trajan's Markets is on Via IV Novembre
Admission   €4

Hours Tuesday–Saturday, 9 a.m.–7 p.m.; Sunday, 9 a.m.–1 p.m. (last admission 1 hour before closing)

Phone 06 679 0048

When to Go Most impressive by night when the ruins are floodlit

Overall Appeal by Age Group

Pre-school —	Teens ★★	Over 30 ★★★
Grade school ★★	Young Adults ★★★	Seniors ★★★

Authors' Rating ★★

How Much Time to Allow 30 minutes to 1 hour

Description and Comments When the Forum became too small for the population and the egos of Rome's rulers, later Roman emperors began constructing their own fora on a site near the main Forum. Julius Caesar was the first to build a forum here in 51 B.C., and Augustus followed suit in 31 B.C. Vespasian's "Temple of Peace," built in A.D. 71 commemorated victories in Jerusalem (as had the Arch of Titus, across the way), and Nerva dedicated his forum temple to Minerva in A.D. 98. Because his was the last of the fora to be built, Trajan's Forum was the grandest. Trajan's Forum and the intricately carved Column of Trajan memorialized the emperor's victories in Dacia. Meanwhile, his vast network of shops and warehouses, called Trajan's Markets, formed a semicircle around his massive temple, thereby allowing the citizens to admire the emperor's successes.

Touring Tips If you want a closer look of Trajan's Column, visit the Museo della Civiltà Romana in EUR.

Other Things to Do Nearby Visit the Roman Forum.

Isola Tiberina (Tiber Island)

Type of Attraction Small island in the middle of the Tiber River

Location Wedged between the Ghetto area and Trastevere (Centro Storico) **Bus** 23, 44, 56, 60, 65, 75, 170, 710, 774, 780

When to Go After lunch for a siesta

Author's Rating ★★★

Description and Comments Tiber Island was formed when part of the river silted up, and it has been in use since ancient times. It owes its ship-like shape to early Romans, who laid huge slabs of travertine around the island to resemble a stern and bow. Today, the Isola Tiberina is home to a hospital, a church, a couple of shops, and a restaurant (Sora Lella; see profile in Part Five, Dining in Central Italy). Pedestrians can still use two ancient bridges to get to the island. The Ponte Fabricio was built in 62 B.C. and is the oldest original bridge across the Tiber still in use. Also a relic, the Ponte Cestio was constructed around 46 B.C. to connect Trastevere with the main part of Rome. Byzantine emperors restored the Ponte Cestio in 370, and their names are inscribed thereon.

Keats-Shelley Memorial House

Type of Attraction Shrine to English Romantic poet and author

Location Piazza di Spagna 26 (Tridente) **Bus/Metro** Bus 117; Metro Spagna (Line A)

Admission €3.50

Hours Monday–Friday, 9 a.m.–1 p.m., 3–6 p.m. (October–March afternoon hours are 2:30–5:30 p.m.), closed holidays and 10 days in August

Phone 06 678 4235 **Web** www.keats-shelley-house.org

When to Go Early morning is best

Overall Appeal by Age Group

Pre-school —	Teens ★★	Over 30 ★★★
Grade school —	Young Adults ★★★	Seniors ★★★

Authors' Rating ★★

How Much Time to Allow 30 minutes

Description and Comments John Keats, Joseph Severn, and Percy Bysshe Shelley all once lived here in this pink house on the Spanish Steps. Today, the Keats-Shelley House is a shrine to these and other Romantic literary figures and contains the writers' personal effects as well as one of the most extensive libraries of Romantic literature in the world.

Touring Tips Fans of Keats and Shelley should visit the writers' graves in the Protestant Cemetery.

Other Things to Do Nearby People-watch on the Spanish Steps.

Mamertine Prison

Type of Attraction Early prison

Location Clivo Argentino, 1 (Ancient City) **Bus** 81, 85, 87, 186.

Admission Donation expected

Hours April–September: daily, 9 a.m.–noon, 2:30–6 p.m.; October–March: daily, 9 a.m.–noon, 2–5 p.m.

Phone 06 679 2902

When to Go As a side trip after visiting the Forum or Campidoglio

Special Comments Difficult entry for disabled travelers; also claustrophobic

Overall Appeal by Age Group

Pre-school —	Teens ★★★	Over 30 ★★★
Grade school ★★	Young Adults ★★★	Seniors ★★

Authors' Rating ★★★

How Much Time to Allow Less than 15 minutes

Description and Comments This odd and eerie prison sandwiched between the Campidoglio and the Forum is where St. Peter was imprisoned. Legend has it that Peter was able to summon a small spring in the cell, which he used to baptize the other prisoners. The well is still visible, as is a small hole at the top of the cell, an opening that served as a passageway for prison guards and probably the only source of light for Peter and his cellmates. Take note of the two stone lists flanking the entry of the prison, which name some of Mamertine's most famous prisoners and their method of execution (e.g., *decapitato* = decapitated).

Touring Tips Visit the church of San Pietro in Vincoli (St. Peter in Chains), where you'll find the shackles to which St. Peter was chained while in the Mamertine Prison.

Other Things to Do Nearby Visit the Roman Forum or Palatine Hill, or explore the treasures of the Capitoline Museums (on the Campidoglio).

Museo Civico di Zoologia

Type of Attraction Small natural history museum
Location Via Aldrovandi, 18 (Via Veneto) **Tram** 30
Admission €3, children under age 18 free
Hours Tuesday–Sunday, 9 a.m.–5 p.m.
Phone 06 321 6586
When to Go Avoid weekends; this museum sees mostly local traffic
Overall Appeal by Age Group

Pre-school ★★★	Teens ★★	Over 30 ★★
Grade school ★★★	Young Adults ★★	Seniors ★★

Authors' Rating ★★
How Much Time to Allow 1 hour

Description and Comments The natural history section of Rome's "Bioparco" zoo complex contains the taxidermied bodies of hundreds of animal species. The coolest thing on display is the 50-foot whale skeleton, which is sure to keep the young ones enthralled long enough for the rain to stop.

Other Things to Do Nearby Rent bikes in the Villa Borghese.

Museo dell'Alto Medioevo

Type of Attraction Rome during the Middle Ages
Location Viale Lincoln, 3 (EUR) Metro Marconi (Line B)
Admission €3
Hours Tuesday–Saturday, 9 a.m.–2 p.m.; Sunday, 9 a.m.–1 p.m.
Phone 06 542 281 99
When to Go When your schedule allows it
Overall Appeal by Age Group

Pre-school —	Teens ★★★	Over 30 ★★★
Grade school —	Young Adults ★★★	Seniors ★★★

Authors' Rating ★★
How Much Time to Allow 1–2 hours, plus commuting time to EUR

Description and Comments The art and everyday objects created between the fall of the empire and the Renaissance are documented at this museum. The most interesting finds from the Dark and Middle Ages include suits of armor, decorative swords, horseshoes, pottery, and sundry metal works. Also check out the set of embroidered robes worn by clergy during the eighth and ninth centuries.

Other Things to Do Nearby See the Museo della Civiltà Romana.

Museo della Civiltà Romana

Type of Attraction An up-close look at the glory of ancient Rome

Location Piazza Giovanni Agnelli 10 (EUR) Metro EUR Palasport (Line B)

Admission €3

Hours Tuesday– Saturday, 9 a.m.–7 p.m.; Sunday, 9 a.m.–1 p.m.

Phone 06 592 6041

When to Go When your schedule allows

Overall Appeal by Age Group

Pre-school —		Teens ★★		Over 30 ★★★
Grade school ★★		Young Adults ★★★		Seniors ★★★

Authors' Rating ★★★

How Much Time to Allow 1–2 hours, plus commuting time to EUR

Description and Comments Ancient history buffs would do well to visit this EUR museum, which displays scale models of Rome's grandest buildings and monuments, including imperial palaces and elaborate temples. A model of the Forum, as it stood in the fourth century, is helpful in understanding how all of the fragments once fit. Meanwhile, the full-scale cast of Trajan's column allows a closer view of the elaborate carving.

Other Things to Do Nearby Visit the Museo dell'Alto Medioevo.

Museo Nazionale della Paste Alimentari (National Pasta Museum)

Type of Attraction An in-depth look into the history and production of Italy's national dish

Location Piazza Scanderberg (Quirinale) **Bus** 52, 53, 58, 60, 61, 62, 71, 95, 492

Admission €6

Hours Tuesday– Saturday, 9 a.m.–7 p.m.; Sunday, 9 a.m.–2 p.m.

Phone 06 699 1119

When to Go When rain dampens your trip to the Trevi Fountain

Special Comments Audio guides in Italian and English are included in the price of admission

Overall Appeal by Age Group

Pre-school —		Teens ★		Over 30 ★★
Grade school —		Young Adults ★★		Seniors ★★

Authors' Rating ★★

How Much Time to Allow The audio tour lasts approximately 45 minutes

Description and Comments Ever wonder how pasta got from the factory to your plate? At the National Pasta Museum, you'll learn everything you ever wanted to know about how wheat is processed into semolina, how grinding mills work, and how pasta can "feed the world." The exhibit is extremely well organized—almost to the point of tedium—but rightly fascinating. The highlight of the museum has to be the room full of posters and photographs of Italian celebrities, such as Sophia Loren, enjoying pasta. In fact, you may want to stop by the museum just to purchase prints and postcards. Sorry—there are no free pasta samples at the end of the tour.

Other Things to Do Nearby Marvel at the Trevi Fountain, or climb the stairs to the Quirinale hill.

Museo Nazionale Etrusco di Villa Giulia

Type of Attraction Italy's foremost Etruscan museum
Location Piazzale di Villa Giulia, 9 (Via Veneto) Tram 19, 30
Admission €4
Hours Tuesday–Sunday, 8:30 a.m.–7:30 p.m.
Phone 06 322 6571
When to Go Anytime
Overall Appeal by Age Group

Pre-school ★★	Teens ★★★	Over 30 ★★★
Grade school ★★	Young Adults ★★★	Seniors ★★★

Author's Rating ★★★½
How Much Time to Allow 1 to 2 hours

Description and Comments The former summer home of Pope Julius III, the 16th-century palace designed by Vignola and Ammannati holds the treasures of the Etruscan era. The founding of Italy's national Etruscan museum, in 1889, followed on the heels of an archaeological boom experienced around Central Italy in the mid- to late-19th century. Some of the most impressive finds unearthed from the areas around Veio, Tarquinia, Cerveteri, and Tuscania include fifth-century B.C. red-figure vases; larger-than-life statues of deities; bronze funerary ornaments; and sarcophagi hewn of marble. More than 30 rooms on two stories are dedicated to Etruscan artifacts. Outdoors in the courtyard, you'll find a reproduction of an Etruscan temple and the Nympheum, a sunken courtyard featuring classical mosaics. Anyone with a passing interest in Rome's ancient history should not pass this museum up. What's more, it's rarely crowded.

Other Things to Do Nearby Switch gears and marvel at modern art at the Galleria Nazionale d'Arte Moderna.

Museo Nazionale Romano

Type of Attraction Italy's main museum for ancient art

Location Baths of Diocletian, Via de Nicola, 79; Palazzo Massimo alle Terme, Large di Villa Peretti, 1; Palazzo Altemps, Piazza Sant'Apollinare, 44 **Bus/Metro** Buses 70, 81, 87, 116, 492; Metro Repubblica (Line A)

Admission €6 per museum, or €10 included in combined ticket with Colosseum and Palatine

Hours Tuesday–Saturday, 9 a.m.–7 p.m.; Sunday, 9 a.m.–2 p.m.

Phone Baths of Diocletian, 06 488 0530; Palazzo Massimo alle Terme, 06 481 5576; Palazzo Altemps, 06 689 7091

When to Go Anytime

Overall Appeal by Age Group

Pre-school —	Teens ★★	Over 30 ★★★
Grade school ★	Young Adults ★★	Seniors ★★★

Authors' Rating ★★

How Much Time to Allow At least 1 hour per museum

Description and Comments Housing one of the largest collections of ancient Italian art in the world isn't easy, which is why the exhibits of the Museo Nazionale Romano are spread out in three different museums. At the Baths of Diocletian, hundreds of pieces of everyday pottery, jewelry, and coins are on view. Across Piazza della Repubblica is the Palazzo Massimo, which until recently housed the bulk of the antiquities collection. Among the treasures still here are coins from the age of Augustus, elaborate sarcophagi, and detached frescoes from various imperial and republican villas. The Ludovisi sculpture collection, which was once a highlight of the latter museum, was recently moved to a larger space across town in the Palazzo Altemps.

Nero's Golden House (Domus Aurea)

Type of Attraction Cavernous palace of one of Rome's most notorious rulers

Location Via Labicana, 136 (Ancient City) **Bus/Tram/Metro** Buses 85, 87, 117, 186; tram 30; Metro Colosseo (Line B)

Admission €6, reserve tickets with the Centro Servizi per l'Archeologia (phone 06 481 5576)

Hours Daily, 9 a.m.–5 p.m.

Phone 06 699 0110

When to Go Mornings (before visiting the Colosseum)

Special Comments The *Laocoön*, featured in the Vatican Museums, and the *Dying Gaul*, in the Capitoline Museums, once decorated Nero's Golden House

Overall Appeal by Age Group

Pre-school ★	Teens ★★★	Over 30 ★★★★
Grade school ★★	Young Adults ★★★★	Seniors ★★★

Authors' Rating ★★★★

How Much Time to Allow 1.5–2 hours

Description and Comments The extensive excavations that make up the Domus Aurea are only a small portion of Nero's former palace. In fact, much of Nero's Golden House went undiscovered for years, as succeeding emperors did their best to erase all traces of the crazy dictator. Nero, the son of Emperor Claudius and Agrippina, built his elaborate home shortly after A.D. 64, after having allegedly set fire to Rome (thus clearing the way for his mansion). Fancying himself a god, Nero commissioned his builders to construct an enormous, outlandish estate that covered part of the Palatine hill and most all of the Celian and Esquiline hills, roughly a third the size of Rome at the time. On the grounds was an artificial lake and private gardens, and the interior was adorned with gold, mother-of-pearl, and ornate frescoes. With such an impressive palace, it's no wonder that Nero threw lavish parties, which consisted of lakeside brothels, orgies, and gluttonous feasts.

Nero committed suicide in 68 A.D., so he didn't get to spend a very long time in his palace. Not surprisingly, Vespasian, the emperor who followed Nero, wanted nothing to do with his predecessor. So he had Nero's artificial lake drained to make way for the Colosseum. Later, both Titus and Trajan erected baths over the site of Nero's estate, virtually filling in the rooms with dirt. Interestingly, however, not all of the rooms were covered up. Sections of the Domus Aurea were rediscovered during the Renaissance. It has long been documented that Raphael and his contemporaries would lower themselves down by ropes into the "grottoes" that once were rooms of Nero's palace to study the frescoed walls and ceilings. They dubbed the colorful, flowery style of painting that they saw "grotesque," short for "grotto-esque." The style was highly mimicked in Renaissance art.

Touring Tips Bring a sweater. The palace is underground and can be drafty.

Other Things to Do Nearby Marvel at the Colosseum.

Obelisk of Piazza San Giovanni in Laterano

Type of Attraction The largest Egyptian obelisk in Rome

Location Piazza San Giovanni in Laterano (Laterano) **Bus/Metro** Buses 16, 85, 87, 117; Metro San Giovanni (Line A)

When to Go Anytime

Author's Rating ★★★

How Much Time to Allow Less than 15 minutes

Description and Comments This Egyptian obelisk dates back to around 1500 B.C. Constantine's son, Constantius, took it from Egypt to Rome, where it served the purpose of a mile marker for races at the Circus Maximus. Years later, in 1588, Pope Sixtus V rediscovered the obelisk and had it placed in the Piazza San Giovanni in Laterano, where it has stood ever since.

Obelisk of Santa Maria Sopra Minerva

Type of Attraction An obelisk the kids will adore
Location Piazza della Minerva (Centro Storico) **Bus** 56, 64, 70, 81, 116
When to Go Anytime
Overall Appeal by Age Group

Pre-school ★★★	Teens ★★★	Over 30 ★★★★
Grade school ★★★★	Young Adults ★★★★	Seniors ★★★★

Authors' Rating ★★★★
How Much Time to Allow Less than 15 minutes

Description and Comments The obelisk of Santa Maria Sopra Minerva wins the prize for Rome's most endearing landmark. This tiny obelisk rises from the back of a Bernini-designed elephant. The animal was chosen case to symbolize the piety, strength, and wisdom of the Catholic Church during the years when the religion's popularity was flagging.

Order of the Knights of Malta

Type of Attraction A perfect view of St. Peter's Basilica
Location Piazza dei Cavalieri di Malta (Aventino) **Bus/Metro** Buses 23, 95, 175, 715; Metro Circo Massimo (Line B)
Admission Free
Hours Always open
Phone None
When to Go Anytime, though night views are special
Overall Appeal by Age Group

Pre-school ★★★	Teens ★★★★	Over 30 ★★★★
Grade school ★★★	Young Adults ★★★★	Seniors ★★★★

Authors' Rating ★★★★
How Much Time to Allow Less than 15 minutes

Description and Comments Far off the tourist track on the leafy Aventine hill rests the headquarters of the Order of the Knights of Malta. The view of St. Peter's Basilica through the front door's keyhole has become a cult favorite. Peer through the large hole and you'll see a perfectly centered, postcard view of St. Peter's.

Touring Tips *Carbinieri* are always on guard just outside of the building. Ask for permission before barreling up to the door.

Other Things to Do Nearby Rest in the Circus Maximus.

Orto Botanico (Botanical Gardens)

Type of Attraction Thousands of flowers and an arboretum
Location Via Corsini (Gianicolo) **Bus/Tram** Buses 44, 56, 60, 75; tram 8

Admission €2.50

Hours Monday–Saturday, 9 a.m.–5:30 p.m.

Phone 06 499 17 106

When to Go When you need some quiet time

Special Comments A cannon on the Gianicolo above the gardens booms daily at the stroke of noon; if you aren't prepared, the sound will scare the living daylights out of you.

Overall Appeal by Age Group

Pre-school ★★★★★	Teens ★★★★	Over 30 ★★★★
Grade school ★★★★★	Young Adults ★★★★	Seniors ★★★★

Authors' Rating ★★★★

How Much Time to Allow 30 minutes to 1 hour

Description and Comments Tended by the students of the University of Rome, the Botanical Gardens were established in 1883 to document the world's various flora. Here you'll find beautifully landscaped gardens of hundreds of rose varieties, a bamboo forest, and a grove of dozens of different types of trees. The signs say "Stay Off the Grass," but you can usually spot many a kid traipsing about in the thick of the green. Local nannies and *nonne* love this place.

Other Things to Do Nearby See Raphael frescoes in the Villa Farnesina.

Palatino (Palatine)

Type of Attraction Hill of palace ruins and respite from the crowds

Location Entrance on Via di San Gregorio or via the Forum (Ancient City)
Bus/Metro Buses 27, 81, 85, 87, 186; Metro Colosseo (Line B)

Admission €6, or €10 with combined ticket to the Colosseum and Museo Nazionale Romano

Hours Monday–Saturday, 9 a.m.–dusk; Sunday, 9 a.m.–2 p.m.; October–March: Monday–Saturday, 9 a.m.–3 p.m.; Sunday, 9 a.m.–2 p.m.

Phone 06 699 0110

When to Go On a clear day

Special Comments From the Palatine, you'll find great picture-snapping opportunities of the Forum and the Circus Maximus.

Overall Appeal by Age Group

Pre-school ★★	Teens ★★★	Over 30 ★★★
Grade school ★★★	Young Adults ★★★★	Seniors ★★★

Authors' Rating ★★★★

How Much Time to Allow 1.5–2 hours

Description and Comments The shady Palatine hill served as the site on which wealthy emperors and patricians built their villas, laid out gardens, and basically whiled away their days far from the poor masses. Augustus and his second wife, Livia, most probably lived in the house now called the House of Livia, while Nero constructed the Cryptoporticus, a network of underground corridors that linked his Domus Aurea to the other imperial homes on the hill. Domitian was the first to really exploit the Palatine's enviable position, and he built an enormous palace and stadium here. His mansion, separated into public (Domus Flavia) and private (Domus Augustana), served as the imperial residence for the next 300 years. The long stadium was most probably used for exercise and private chariot races. However, when the stadium was empty, the emperor could take in a spectacle at the Circus Maximus, as the palace included boxed seats overlooking the oblong stadium—the best in the house, of course.

The Palatine is home to pre-Roman ruins, as well, including the Temple of Cybele (a cult that practiced ritualized castration) and the ninth-century huts of Romulus and Remus. The date on the latter checks out, although the attribution is most likely dubious. The Farnese Gardens, landscaped in the mid-16th century with orange trees, roses, and lavender bushes, add a bit of color and fragrance to the Palatine.

Other Things to Do Nearby Stretch your legs in the Forum or the Circus Maximus.

Palazzo delle Esposizioni

Type of Attraction Exhibition space for temporary installations

Location Via Nazionale, 194 (Quirinale) **Bus/Metro** Buses 64, 65, 70, 71, 75, 117, 170; Metro Repubblica (Line A)

Admission Varies by exhibit

Hours Wednesday–Monday, 10 a.m.–9 p.m. (last admission at 8:30 p.m.); closed January 1, May 1, and December 25

Phone 06 474 5903

When to Go Weekday afternoons are ideal

Overall Appeal by Age Group

Pre-school —	Teens ★★★	Over 30 ★★★
Grade school ★★	Young Adults ★★★	Seniors ★★★

Authors' Rating ★★★

How Much Time to Allow 1 hour

Description and Comments This mammoth building on Via Nazionale bridges the gap between old and new Rome and houses one of the city's newer exhibition halls, with space for films, conferences, multimedia installations, and art displays. Every spring, the PalaExpo hosts a multicultural film festival, and there are typically at least three temporary art exhibits ongoing at any time. A recent well-curated show focused on the many faces of Christ in art, examining works from ancient times to the modern age.

Touring Tips Grab a bite to eat at the museum's self-serve cafeterias—an inexpensive, nontouristy meal option.

Other Things to Do Nearby Enjoy wide vistas of the city from Piazza del Quirinale.

Pantheon

Type of Attraction Oldest building in Rome and an architectural wonder

Location Piazza della Rotonda (Centro Storico) **Bus** 64, 70, 75, 116

Admission Free

Hours Open Monday–Saturday, 9 a.m.–6:30 p.m.; Sunday and public holidays, 9 a.m.–1 p.m.; closed January 1, May 1, and December 25

Phone 06 683 002 30

When to Go Anytime

Special Comments Mass is celebrated here on some Sundays and holidays.

Overall Appeal by Age Group

Pre-school ★★	Teens ★★★★	Over 30 ★★★★★
Grade school ★★★	Young Adults ★★★★★	Seniors ★★★★★

Authors' Rating ★★★★★

How Much Time to Allow 30 minutes

Description and Comments Built by Hadrian in A.D. 120, the Pantheon is the oldest, best-preserved building of imperial Rome. The "temple of all the gods" that we see today was actually built on top of another pantheon erected by Emperor Augustus's son-in-law Marcus Agrippa, and the latter's name is inscribed on the frieze above the entrance as a nod to his original idea. Hadrian's Pantheon was the first example of a building to consist of an unsupported dome, made possible by the fact that the building's height and the dome diameter are of exactly equal measure (140 feet).

From the outside, the Pantheon is a spectacular sight of thick, granite columns and a soaring, spacious portico, but the monument's interior elicits true awe. Polychrome marble makes for a stunning floor, while the dramatic, coffered ceiling and oculus—the building's only source of light—give the Pantheon depth. Although the temple was originally built for the planetary gods, it was given over to the Church in 608. Unfortunately, its consecration didn't stop the Vatican from vandalizing it. Pope Urban VIII had the bronze ceiling on the portico removed and melted down to create the *baldacchino* in St. Peter's Basilica as well as some 80 cannon for Castel Sant'Angelo. Today, the Pantheon contains the tombs of Italy's two kings—Vittorio Emanuele II and Umberto I—and Renaissance artist Raphael.

Other Things to Do Nearby People-watch in Piazza Navona, or pay a visit to the gorgeous Gothic church of Santa Maria Sopra Minerva.

Pasquino

Type of Attraction The "talking" statue

Location Piazza di Pasquino (Centro Storico) **Bus** 46, 62, 64, 70, 81, 87, 492

When to Go Anytime

Overall Appeal by Age Group

Pre-school —		Teens ★★★		Over 30 ★★
Grade school ★★		Young Adults ★★★		Seniors ★

Authors' Rating ★★★

How Much Time to Allow Less than 15 minutes

Description and Comments This unfinished block of carved marble known as Pasquino began "talking" in 1501 when a local cobbler decided to post handwritten diatribes on the statue. During this time, Romans were forbidden to speak out against such things as living conditions, for it was seen as an affront to the rule of the Church. Early bulletin boards such as Pasquino allowed the people to post their gripes anonymously. Consequently, Pasquino became a useful tool for satire and revolt. Soon other statues began to "talk." For instance, Marforio (now in the Capitoline Museums) had an ongoing dialogue with Pasquino. Today, Pasquino dons the occasional complaint letter; for the most part, he remains mute.

Other Things to Do Nearby Have a snack at Cul de Sac, one of the friendliest wine bars in town (see profile in Part Five, Dining in Central Italy).

Piazza del Popolo

Type of Attraction City square with quite an entrance

Location Tridente **Bus/Metro** Buses 81, 95, 115, 117, 204; Metro Flaminio (Line A)

When to Go People-watching here is always fun

Overall Appeal by Age Group

Pre-school ★★★		Teens ★★★★		Over 30 ★★★★
Grade school ★★★★		Young Adults ★★★★		Seniors ★★★

Author's Rating ★★★★★

Description and Comments Modeled to impress pilgrims as they entered Rome from the northern consular road Via Flaminia, the Piazza del Popolo is still one of the grandest entrances to any city in the world. Ringed with monumental walls and decorated with statues and fountains, the square is great emptying point for foot traffic from the Via del Corso. Punctuating the square is an Egyptian obelisk, the second to sit on the *spina* at the Circus Maximus, which was placed here in 1589. For years, the piazza was the site of numerous public executions—by hanging and, during Napoleonic times, by guillotine; that gruesome practice ended in 1870. Today, you may be privy to other spectacles in the Piazza del Popolo, including workers' strikes, food fairs, and teenage roughnecking.

Touring Tips While the piazza is a pedestrian zone, watch out for cars that zoom around the outside loop and through the gates.

Other Things to Do Nearby Climb the stairs to the Pincio Gardens, from the terrace of which you can steal a jawdropping view of Castel Sant-Angelo and St. Peter's.

Piazza di Spagna and the Spanish Steps

Type of Attraction A place for lounging and people-watching

Location Situated below the Trinità dei Monti church at the north end of Via Condotti Metro Spagna (Line A)

When to Go In the early evening to watch Romans during their nightly stroll through town *(passeggiata)*

Author's Rating ★★★★

Description and Comments The Piazza di Spagna and its famous stairs were named for the Spanish ambassador to the Holy See, who had his headquarters here. In the beginning, the steps served as a direct way to get to the Trinità dei Monti church from the piazza. Today, the Spanish Steps are a destination unto themselves. All tourists and Romans end up lounging here at least once, taking in the sights and sounds of flirting, camera clicking, and teenage chatter. A straight-away view down the wealthy shopping street of Via Condotti makes for hours of vicarious entertainment.

Touring Tips This is a big tourist area. Watch out for scam artists.

Piazza Montecitorio

Type of Attraction Government hub with noteworthy architecture

Location Centro Storico **Bus** 56, 60, 85, 116, 492

When to Go Weekdays, when Parliament is in session

Overall Appeal by Age Group

Pre-school ★★	Teens ★★	Over 30 ★★
Grade school ★★	Young Adults ★★	Seniors ★★

Author's Rating ★★

How Much Time to Allow 15 to 30 minutes

Description and Comments Bernini designed the curving Palazzo Montecitorio, the home of Italy's parliament building and just one of the landmarks on the piazza of the same name. The obelisk of Montecitorio, brought to Rome from Egypt by Augustus in 10 B.C., originally stood near the Ara Pacis but was moved here when renovation plans for the square took shape. It is interesting to note that the current site of Parliament sits atop ruins of ancient funeral pyres, where various Roman emperors were cremated. Today, burning issues tend to stay within the walls of the *palazzo,* though you'll often see heated conversations and media swarms out front following debate sessions.

Piazza Navona

Type of Attraction A grand square

Location Centro Storico **Bus** 56, 60, 85, 116, 492

When to Go Playful by day, romantic by night

Overall Appeal by Age Group

Pre-school ★★★★★	Teens ★★★★★	Over 30 ★★★★★
Grade school ★★★★★	Young Adults ★★★★★	Seniors ★★★★★

Author's Rating ★★★★★

How Much Time to Allow At least an hour

Description and Comments One of the largest and liveliest squares in Rome is the Piazza Navona, which fills the expanse between churches, former palaces, and the sky. The shape of the Circus Maximus, the oblong square was also once used for horse races, animal fights, and gladiatorial combats. In fact, remnants of ancient stadium seating are visible on the piazza's outer curve. Today's Navona is largely a product of a renovation project commissioned by Pope Innocent X and undertaken by artists Bernini and Borromini. The latter redesigned the façade of Sant'-Agnese in Agone, while Bernini erected the large, Baroque Four Rivers Fountain in front of it.

Pincio Gardens

Type of Attraction Rome's best sunset spot

Location Il Pincio **Bus/Metro** Buses 81, 95, 115, 117, 204; Metro Flaminio or Spagna (Line A)

When to Go Dusk

Overall Appeal by Age Group

Pre-school ★★★★★	Teens ★★★★★	Over 30 ★★★★★
Grade school ★★★★★	Young Adults ★★★★★	Seniors ★★★★★

Author's Rating ★★★

How Much Time to Allow Long enough for the sun to set

Description and Comments The overlook above the Piazza del Popolo, better known as the Pincio, was terraced and landscaped by Giuseppe Valadier in the early 19th century. At sunset, the Pincio is hopping with tourists, eager to get a glimpse of Rome's rooftops bathed in the fading light of the sun.

Ponte Rotto

Type of Attraction Ancient bridge

Location Below Ponte Palatino (Centro Storico) **Bus** 23, 44, 56, 60, 65, 75, 170, 710, 774, 780

When to Go Best viewed during the day from the banks of the Isola Tiberina

Overall Appeal by Age Group

Pre-school —	Teens ★	Over 30 ★★
Grade school —	Young Adults ★★	Seniors ★★

Authors' Rating ★★

How Much Time to Allow Less than 15 minutes

Description and Comments Built in 179 B.C., the Pons Aemilius was the first all-stone bridge across the Tiber. Centuries of wear and tear did a number on the bridge, and it was eventually abandoned in 1598. Today, the Ponte Rotto ("broken bridge") is merely a ruin in the midst of the Tiber.

Protestant Cemetery

Type of Attraction Cemetery; Keats and Shelley are buried here

Location Via Caio Cestio, 6 (Aventino) **Bus/Tram/Metro** Buses 23, 27, 95, 716; trams 13, 30B; Metro Piramide (Line B)

Admission Donation expected

Hours Tuesday–Sunday, 9 a.m.–6 p.m. (October–March: until 5 p.m.); last admission 30 minutes before closing

Phone 06 574 1900

When to Go Anytime

Overall Appeal by Age Group

Pre-school ★★★	Teens ★★★	Over 30 ★★★
Grade school ★★★	Young Adults ★★★	Seniors ★★★

Authors' Rating ★★★★★

How Much Time to Allow 30 minutes to 1 hour

Description and Comments A cemetery probably won't be at the top of your itinerary, but Rome's Protestant Cemetery, also called the Non-Catholic Cemetery, is actually one of the most tranquil places to while away an afternoon. Percy Bysshe Shelley said of the cemetery that it was "an open space among the ruins, covered in winter with violets and daisies. It might make one in love with death, to think that one should be buried in so sweet a place." Subsequently, Shelley was buried here, as was his contemporary John Keats. The grave of the founder of the Italian Communist Party, Antonio Gramsci, is also located on the grounds.

Other Things to Do Nearby Enjoy more quiet hours on the Aventino with a walk to the headquarters of the Order of the Knights of Malta.

Pyramid of Caius Cestius

Type of Attraction Elaborate tomb

Location Piazzale Ostiense (Aventino) **Bus/Tram/Metro** Buses 123, 27, 95, 716; trams 13, 30B; Metro Piramide (Line B)

Hours Not open to the public

Phone None

Overall Appeal by Age Group

Pre-school ★★	Teens ★★	Over 30 ★★
Grade school ★★	Young Adults ★★	Seniors ★★

Authors' Rating ★★

How Much Time to Allow 10 minutes (just to view from outside)

Description and Comments Prior to his death in 12 B.C., Caius Cestius (Caio Cestio, in Italian), a wealthy Roman magistrate, left instructions that his burial tomb be a pyramid. Set in the Aurelian Wall, the giant marble pyramid stands roughly 89 feet high and, according to an inscription on its face, took 330 days to build. Without a doubt, the pyramid looked as out of place then as it does now. Perhaps Cestius thought it would fit in with the Egyptian obelisk in the Circus Maximus, not far from here.

Other Things to Do Nearby Meander through the peaceful Protestant Cemetery.

Quattro Fontane (Four Fountains)

Type of Attraction Fountains on four street corners

Location At the intersection of Via delle Quattro Fontane and Via XX Settembre (Quirinale) **Metro** Barberini, Repubblica (Line A)

When to Go Anytime during the day

Overall Appeal by Age Group

Pre-school —	Teens ★★★	Over 30 ★★★
Grade school ★★	Young Adults ★★★	Seniors ★★★

Authors' Rating ★★

How Much Time to Allow Less than 15 minutes

Description and Comments Making lively a niche of town that is otherwise quite dreary is the Quattro Fontane, four fountains that were built into the corners of the streets at the intersection of Via XX Settembre and Via delle Quattro Fontane. These Baroque-era fountains were completed in 1593 and represent two river gods, the Tiber and the Nile, and the goddesses Juno and Diana. The four fountains also serve as important mile markers, in that one can see the obelisks of Santa Maria Maggiore, Trinità dei Monti, and Piazza del Quirinale from the crossroads.

Other Things to Do Nearby Check out art installations in the Palazzo delle Esposizioni.

San Clemente

Type of Attraction Church with multiple personalities

Location Via di San Giovanni in Laterano (Laterano) **Bus/Metro** Buses 16, 81, 85, 87, 810; Metro Colosseo (Line B)

Admission €2.50 for the lower basilica and Mithraeum

Hours Monday–Saturday, 9 a.m.–12:30 p.m., 3:30–6:30 p.m. (October–March: until 6 p.m.), Sunday, 10 a.m.–12:30 p.m., 3:30–6:30 p.m.

Phone 06 704 51 018

When to Go Mornings, promptly after visiting the Colosseum, or early afternoon

Overall Appeal by Age Group

Pre-school ★★	Teens ★★★★	Over 30 ★★★★
Grade school ★★★	Young Adults ★★★★	Seniors ★★★★

Authors' Rating ★★★★★
How Much Time to Allow I hour

Description and Comments A hidden treasure near the beaten path of the Colosseum, the Basilica of San Clemente is three churches in one. Visitors enter the more "modern" 12th-century church, which contains a skillfully detailed apse mosaic *(The Triumph of the Cross)* and recently restored frescoes by Florentine artist Masolino in the Santa Caterina Chapel. Below the upper church lies the remains of a fourth-century church, much of which was destroyed during Norman invasions in the 11th century. Farther down is a temple dedicated to Mithras (a Mithraeum), which dates back to the first century. Mithraism was imported from Persia and was an all-male fertility cult that rivaled Christianity during Roman imperial times. Among the finds in the Mithraeum is an altar with a relief of Mithras slaying a bull. Since the 17th century, the order of Irish Dominicans have occupied this church, and it is because of their dedication to the history of this site that we are able to visit its fascinating excavations.

Other Things to Do Nearby Walk a few block northwest to get to the Colosseum or a few blocks southeast to San Giovanni in Laterano.

San Francesco a Ripa

Type of Attraction Church containing relics from St. Francis of Assisi
Location Piazza San Francesco d'Assisi, 88 (Trastevere) **Bus** 23, 44, 100, 175
Admission Free
Hours Daily, 7:30 a.m.–noon, 4–7 p.m.
Phone 06 581 9020
When to Go Anytime
Overall Appeal by Age Group

Pre-school —		Teens ★		Over 30 ★★
Grade school —		Young Adults ★★		Seniors ★★

Authors' Rating ★★
How Much Time to Allow 15–30 minutes

Description and Comments On view here are St. Francis's personal effects from when he visited this church in 1219, including his crucifix and stone pillow. There's also a Bernini work, the spectacular *Ecstasy of Beata Ludovica Albertoni.*

Touring Tips Check out Bernini's other Ecstasy sculpture at Santa Maria Vittoria.

Other Things to Do Nearby Peruse the wares in Trastevere.

San Giovanni in Laterano (St. John Lateran)

Type of Attraction The cathedral of Rome
Location Piazza di San Giovanni in Laterano, 4 (Laterano) **Bus/Tram/Metro** Buses 4, 16, 85, 87; trams 13, 30B; Metro San Giovanni (Line A)

Admission Free

Hours Daily, 7 a.m.–7 p.m. (October–March: until 6 p.m.)

Phone 06 772 079 91

When to Go Anytime

Special Comments The pope addresses the masses from the balcony on Maunday Thursday.

Overall Appeal by Age Group

Pre-school ★★		Teens ★★		Over 30 ★★★★
Grade school ★★		Young Adults ★★★		Seniors ★★★★

Authors' Rating ★★★

How Much Time to Allow 30–45 minutes

Description and Comments This basilica, the second largest after St. Peter's, has undergone major renovations over the years, due to extensive damage by an earthquake (in 896) and two fires (in 1308 and 1360). The main façade, designed by Alessandro Galilei between 1730 and 1740, features giant statues of Christ and the apostles. Inside you'll find the work of Borromini, who was responsible for renovating the basilica for the 1650 Holy Year. The highlight of the interior is the fresco of Boniface VII, attributed to Giotto.

Other Things to Do Nearby See the Holy Stairs and the pope's personal chapel at the Sancta Sanctorum.

San Luigi dei Francesi

Type of Attraction Houses three major works by Caravaggio

Location Via Santa Giovanna d'Arco (Centro Storico) **Bus** 70, 81, 87, 116, 492

Admission Free

Hours Daily, 8 a.m.–12:30 p.m., 3:30–7 p.m.; closed Thursday p.m.

Phone 06 688 271

When to Go Anytime

Special Comments Bring change to illuminate the paintings

Overall Appeal by Age Group

Pre-school —		Teens ★★		Over 30 ★★★★
Grade school ★★		Young Adults ★★★		Seniors ★★★★

Authors' Rating ★★★★

How Much Time to Allow 15–30 minutes

Description and Comments The French National Church of Rome owes its fame to three major works by Caravaggio, which hide in darkness in a chapel on the left of the aisle. These three paintings— *The Calling of St. Matthew, The Martyrdom of St. Matthew,* and *St. Matthew and the Angel,* are some of the artist's earliest works, drafted between 1597 and 1602. San Luigi dei Francesi is also home to the tomb of French painter Claude Lorrain, who gained prominence for his canvases depicting the Roman *campagna.*

Touring Tips More works by Caravaggio can be viewed free of charge in the church of Santa Maria del Popolo, off of Piazza del Popolo.

Other Things to Do Nearby Check out the comings and goings in Piazza Navona.

San Paolo Fuori le Mura

Type of Attraction One of the four patriarchal basilicas of Rome

Location Via Ostiense, 186 (Outside city gates, near EUR) **Bus/Metro** Buses 23, 170, 673; Metro San Paolo (Line B)

Admission Free

Hours Daily, 7:30 p.m.–6:40 p.m. (last admission 15 minutes before closing)

Phone 06 541 0341

When to Go Anytime

Overall Appeal by Age Group

Pre-school ★	Teens ★★	Over 30 ★★★★
Grade school ★★	Young Adults ★★★	Seniors ★★★★★

Authors' Rating ★★★★

How Much Time to Allow 30 minutes

Description and Comments One of the four main churches of Rome, San Paolo was built over the grave of St. Paul. By the fourth century, the original church was replaced by a monumental basilica at the behest of Emperor Theodosius (the ruler who declared Christianity the official religion of the empire), becoming the largest church in Christendom until the construction of St. Peter's in the 1600s. Fires destroyed much of the original church, and earthquakes did their part to jostle free many of the decorative mosaics that once decorated San Paolo. However, the fifth-century mosaics in the triumphal arch remain, depicting scenes of the apocalypse in brightly gilded tiles. The rest of the interior was refurbished after 1823 when a fire swept through the basilica.

Today, no fewer than 80 granite pillars line the nave, and 265 painted medallions of every pope in Christendom, from St. Peter to Pope John Paul II, decorate the upper walls. Catholic lore has it that once all the space on the wall is filled, then the apocalypse is nigh. The exterior of San Paolo remains mostly a creation of the 19th century; however, the cloister, built between 1205 and 1241, is worth a look for its unusual twisting columns.

Other Things to Do Nearby The church is located approximately two miles outside of town, near the attractions of EUR.

San Pietro in Vincoli

Type of Attraction Modest church with major artwork

Location Piazza di San Pietro in Vincoli, 4A (Esquilino) **Bus** 27, 115, 117, 204

Admission Free

Hours Daily, 7 a.m.–12:30 p.m., 3:30–7 p.m. (October–March: until 6 p.m.)

Phone 06 488 2865 **Web** www.progettomose.it

When to Go Avoid crowds by getting there in the early morning

Overall Appeal by Age Group

Pre-school —		Teens ★★★		Over 30 ★★★★
Grade school ★★★		Young Adults ★★★★		Seniors ★★★★

Authors' Rating ★★★★

How Much Time to Allow 15 to 30 minutes

Description and Comments St. Peter in Chains gets its name from the relic of shackles that St. Peter supposedly wore while incarcerated in the Mamertine Prison. However, the church's claim to fame is the statue *Moses,* designed by Michelangelo. At press time, a team of conservators was still hard at work trying to clean *Moses.* The larger-than-life carving of Moses and sibyls was designed in 1505 by Michelangelo for the tomb of Pope Julius II. However, bigger projects, such as the reconstruction of St. Peter's, beckoned, so he was unable to finish the tomb. Once belonging to this set of carvings were the *Quattro Prigioni,* now on display in Florence's Accademia and in Paris's Louvre. Stairs have been added on to the scaffolding, allowing visitors to view the upper reaches of the statues. You can also watch the conservation process online at **www.progetto mose.it.**

Other Things to Do Nearby Nero's Golden House.

Sant'Agnese in Agone

Type of Attraction Main church on Piazza Navona

Location Piazza Navona (Centro Storico) **Bus** 70, 81, 87, 116, 492

Admission Free

Hours Tuesday–Saturday, 4:30–7 p.m.; Sunday, 10 a.m.–1 p.m.

Phone 06 679 4435

When to Go Anytime

Overall Appeal by Age Group

Pre-school —		Teens ★		Over 30 ★★
Grade school —		Young Adults ★★		Seniors ★★★

Authors' Rating ★★

How Much Time to Allow 15 minutes

Description and Comments The largest building on the Piazza Navona was realized by Borromini from 1653 to 1657 after he took over the work from the quarreling Rainaldi brothers. The concave façade of Sant'-Agnese in Agone is considered one of Borromini's best achievements and a leading example in Baroque architecture. The church is dedicated to St. Agnes, who has a most curious story of martyrdom. Legend has it that pagan persecutors stripped Agnes when she refused to renounce Christ, but her hair then miraculously grew long and covered her body, saving her embarrassment. The pagans then tried to burn her at the stake, but that effort also failed. Finally, the mob decapitated her, supposedly on the spot where the church was later built. Her head is venerated in a reliquary in the church. You'll also find the tomb of Pope Innocent X here.

Other Things to Do Nearby Check out Bernini's Four Rivers Fountain in front of the church.

Sant'Ignazio di Loyola

Type of Attraction Jesuit church with a curious dome
Location Piazza di Sant'Ignazio (Centro Storico) **Bus** 56, 60, 81, 85, 492
Admission Free
Hours Daily, 7:30 a.m.–12:30 p.m., 4–7:15 p.m.
Phone 06 679 4406
When to Go Natural light floods into the church in the late morning, making it easier to view the dome
Overall Appeal by Age Group

Pre-school —	Teens ★★★	Over 30 ★★★
Grade school ★★	Young Adults ★★★	Seniors ★★★

Authors' Rating ★★★
How Much Time to Allow 15–30 minutes

Description and Comments Fronting a tranquil square just steps from the Pantheon, Sant'Ignazio is located in surroundings exactly opposite of those of its Jesuit sister church in Rome, Il Gesù. However, the similarities begin indoors. The interior of the church is dramatic, with ornaments of gold, precious stones, marble, and stucco and features ceiling frescoes by none other than the Jesuit artist Andrea Pozzo. But, it's Sant'Ignazio's "dome" that elicits the most admiration. For some reason or another, the architects of the church never followed through with a plan to build a dome, so they faked one. The space where the dome would have been was covered with a trompe-l'oeil painting, that, when standing in the right spot on the nave, appears as a coffered dome with a skylight.

Other Things to Do Nearby See Rome's other Jesuit church, Il Gesù, or window-shop on the way to the Pantheon.

Santa Croce in Gerusalemme

Type of Attraction Some holy relics are housed here
Location Piazza di Santa Croce in Gerusalemme, 12 (Laterano) **Bus/Tram** Bus 9; tram 13, 30B
Admission Free
Hours Daily, 6 a.m.–12:30 p.m., 3:30–7 p.m.
Phone 06 701 4769

When to Go Anytime; this church is wanting for visitors

Overall Appeal by Age Group

Pre-school —		Teens ★★★		Over 30 ★★
Grade school ★		Young Adults ★★★		Seniors ★★

Authors' Rating ★★

How Much Time to Allow 15–30 minutes

Description and Comments Geography hasn't been very kind to Santa Croce in Gerusalemme. In any other city, this large church would be a landmark, but here it's an afterthought, relegated to a far corner of the Lateran neighborhood. Nothing is particularly noteworthy about Santa Croce's façade, which was last tinkered with in the early 18th century. However, several important relics are housed here. Most important are pieces of the True Cross, which Emperor Constantine's mother, Helena, pilfered on a visit to the Holy Land, and the doubting finger of St. Thomas. These and other sacred objects are kept behind panels of glass in a chapel behind the altar.

Other Things to Do Nearby Visit San Giovanni in Laterano.

Santa Maria degli Angeli e dei Martiri

Type of Attraction Michelangelo-designed church

Location Piazza della Repubblica (Quirinale) **Bus/Metro** Buses 57, 65, 75, 170, 492, 910; Metro Repubblica (Line A), Termini (Lines A, B)

Admission Free

Hours Daily, 8 a.m.–12:30 p.m., 4–7 p.m. (winter: until 6:30 p.m.)

Phone 06 488 0812

When to Go Anytime

Overall Appeal by Age Group

Pre-school —		Teens ★★		Over 30 ★★★
Grade school ★★		Young Adults ★★		Seniors ★★★

Authors' Rating ★★

How Much Time to Allow 15–30 minutes

Description and Comments Occupying part of the Baths of Diocletian, this church was realized by Michelangelo in 1563, although many of his plans were later ignored. Luigi Vanvitelli, architect to the Vatican under Clement XII, altered much of the church's original character, moving the entrance and changing the nave into a transept. An exhibit in the church's sacristy details Michelangelo's blueprints.

Other Things to Do Nearby Take a tour of the rest of the Baths of Diocletian, and check out the displays in the Museo Nazionale Romano.

Santa Maria dei Miracoli e Santa Maria in Montesanto

Type of Attraction Look-alike churches

Location Piazza del Popolo (Tridente) **Bus/Metro** Buses 81, 115, 117, 204; Metro Flaminio (Line A)

Admission Free

Hours Santa Maria dei Miracoli: Monday–Saturday, 6 a.m.–1 p.m., 4:30–7:45 p.m.; Sunday, 4:30–7:45 p.m.; Santa Maria in Montesanto: daily, 4–7 p.m.; closed August

Phone 06 361 0250 (Miracoli); 06 361 0594 (Montesanto)

When to Go Anytime

Overall Appeal by Age Group

Pre-school —	Teens ★★	Over 30 ★★
Grade school ★★	Young Adults ★★	Seniors ★★

Authors' Rating ★★

How Much Time to Allow Less than 15 minutes

Description and Comments These twin churches flanking the Via del Corso (on the south end of Piazza del Popolo) aren't twins at all but were designed to look symmetrical. Carlo Rainaldi designed both Santa Maria in Montesanto (on the left) and Santa Maria dei Miracoli (on the right) so that they would look balanced, even though he had dissimilar spaces to work with. To solve the problem, Rainaldi gave Montesanto an oval-shaped dome, while giving Miracoli a traditional round dome.

Other Things to Do Nearby Check out the Caravaggio paintings in Santa Maria del Popolo.

Santa Maria del Popolo

Type of Attraction Full of Renaissance and Baroque art

Location Piazza del Popolo, 12 (Tridente) **Bus/Metro** Buses 81, 95, 115, 117, 204; Metro Flaminio (Line A)

Admission Free

Hours Monday–Saturday, 7 a.m.–noon, 4–7 p.m.; Sunday 8 a.m.–2 p.m., 4:30–7:30 p.m.

Phone 06 361 0836

When to Go Anytime

Overall Appeal by Age Group

Pre-school —	Teens ★★★	Over 30 ★★★★
Grade school ★★★	Young Adults ★★★★	Seniors ★★★★

Authors' Rating ★★★★

How Much Time to Allow 30 minutes

Description and Comments Housed behind an inconspicuous stone façade is one of Rome's great churches in which to see art. Perhaps Santa Maria del Popolo is best known for two works by Caravaggio—the *Conversion of St. Paul* and the *Crucifixion of St. Peter*—in the Cerasi Chapel. The wealthy Chigi and Della Rovere families also commissioned lavish chapels in the church. Raphael designed the Chigi chapel (to the left of the entrance); Bernini, Lorenzetto, and Piombino later decorated it with frescoes and sculptures. But the highlight here is a creepy mosaic of a kneeling skeleton, added to the chapel floor in the 17th century. The Della Rovere chapel, to the right of the entrance, glimmers with lunette fresco and an altarpiece by Pinturicchio. This artist also painted the scenes on the apse ceiling. Rounding out the collection in Santa Maria del Popolo is the church's main altarpiece, *The Assumption,* painted by Annibale Carracci.

Other Things to Do Nearby Take the stairs to the Pincio Gardens, where you can look down over the Piazza del Popolo and enjoy a panorama of the city.

Santa Maria in Aracoeli

Type of Attraction Church noteworthy for its long staircase

Location Piazza d'Aracoeli (Campidoglio) **Bus** 64, 65, 70, 75, 170 from Termini; or, 56, 60, 492 from Piazza Barberini; also, 44, 46, 57, 90, and 90B

Admission Free

Hours Daily, 7 a.m.–noon, 4–5:30 p.m. (June–September: until 6:30 p.m.)

Phone 06 679 8155

When to Go Early morning, when your energy level is up

Special Comments Legend has it that a person who climbs all 124 of the church's stairs on his or her knees will win the lottery.

Overall Appeal by Age Group

Pre-school —	Teens ★★	Over 30 ★★★
Grade school ★★	Young Adults ★★★	Seniors ★★

Authors' Rating ★★

How Much Time to Allow 30 minutes

Description and Comments One-hundred twenty-four steps lead to the barn-like church of Santa Maria in Aracoeli. The people of Rome dedicated this church to Mary at the Heavenly Altar in 1348 to express their gratitude to her for delivering them from the plague. Inside the vast church—perhaps the emptiest in all of Rome, thanks to the steep climb—is a store of ancient granite and marble columns, taken from the Forum and the Palatine Hill; a polychrome tiled floor; and a gilded coffered ceiling. Aside from the Aracoeli steps, Santa Maria in Aracoeli is known for being the home of the Santo Bambino. Believers claim that this idol of Christ was rendered from the wood of an olive tree grown in the Garden of Gethsemane. The Santo Bambino is on view during Christmas season.

Other Things to Do Nearby See the treasures of the Capitoline Museums.

Santa Maria in Cosmedin

Type of Attraction The Greek National Church and home of the Bocca della Verità

Location Piazza della Bocca della Verità, 18 (Aventino) **Bus** 23, 81, 160, 204

Admission Free

Hours Daily, 9 a.m.–1 p.m., 2:30–6 p.m. (until 5 p.m. in winter)

Phone 06 678 1419

When to Go Anytime

Overall Appeal by Age Group

Pre-school ★★★		Teens ★★★★		Over 30 ★★★★
Grade school ★★★★		Young Adults ★★★★		Seniors ★★★★

Authors' Rating ★★★½

How Much Time to Allow 30 minutes

Description and Comments Were it not for the Bocca della Verità, which sits in the portico of Santa Maria in Cosmedin, very few people would visit this church. A tourist favorite since well before the release of *Roman Holiday*, the "mouth of truth" is actually an ancient sewer cover, dating from around the fourth century B.C. The old wives' tale that portends that the sewer cover's "jaws" will snap down on the hand of liars comes from a medieval trick used to test a spouse's mettle.

Santa Maria in Cosmedin, Rome's Greek National Church, dates from the sixth century, and its early origins are evident in the interior frescoes, which have virtually faded away over time. The church's most prized piece of art, an eighth-century mosaic of the *Adoration of the Magi*, hangs in the sacristy (now the gift shop). This is the only church in Rome to celebrate under the Greek Orthodox tradition, and masses here are celebrated in Italian, Greek, and Arabic.

Santa Maria in Trastevere

Type of Attraction Church rich in mosaics

Location Piazza Santa Maria in Trastevere (Trastevere) **Bus/Tram** Buses 44, 56, 60, 75; tram 8

Admission Free

Hours Daily, 7 a.m.–1:30 p.m., 3:30–7 p.m.

Phone 06 581 4302

When to Go Anytime

Overall Appeal by Age Group

Pre-school ★★		Teens ★★★		Over 30 ★★★★★
Grade school ★★★		Young Adults ★★★★		Seniors ★★★★★

Authors' Rating ★★★★★

How Much Time to Allow 30–45 minutes

Description and Comments The parish church of Trastevere is beautiful both inside and out. The façade, recognizable by its bell tower and arcaded porch, features a broad band of glittering mosaics depicting Mary, Jesus, ten other women (probably virgins), and church patrons (in miniature at the foot of Mary). Inside, the mosaics overwhelm, covering almost every inch of the ceiling in the apse. Santa Maria in Trastevere was the first church in Rome to be dedicated to the Virgin Mary, and here she is portrayed in bold tiles of gold and blue as the bride of Christ. Below the allegory of Christ and Mary on the throne, a brilliant ribbon of royal blue contrasts with mosaics of 13 white lambs, symbolizing Christ (in the center) and the apostles. The life of Mary is illustrated below here in mosaics designed in the 13th century by Pietro Cavallini. The triumphal arch is decorated with images of Matthew, Mark, Luke, and John as the four beasts of the apocalypse.

Other Things to Do Nearby   Window-shop or grab a bite to eat in the Trastevere neighborhood.

Santa Maria Maggiore

Type of Attraction   One of the four patriarchal basilicas of Rome

Location   Piazza di Santa Maria Maggiore (Esquilino)   **Bus/Metro**   Buses 16, 27, 70, 71; Metro Termini (Lines A, B), Cavour (Line B)

Admission   Free

Hours   Daily, 7 a.m.–7 p.m. (last admission 15 minutes before closing)

Phone   06 483 195

When to Go   Early afternoon, when traffic near the church is lightest; August 5 marks the church's founding

Overall Appeal by Age Group

Pre-school ★★	Teens ★★★	Over 30 ★★★★
Grade school ★★	Young Adults ★★★	Seniors ★★★★

Authors' Rating   ★★★

How Much Time to Allow   30 minutes

Description and Comments   Built on the spot where a miraculous August snow fell, the Basilica of Santa Maria Maggiore, one of the four major basilicas of Rome, is a blend of architectural styles. Its nave was part of the original church, built during the fifth century, and its bell tower and marble floor were added during medieval times. Santa Maria Maggiore's gilded, coffered ceiling is a product of the Renaissance, and the gold used here was most probably taken from the spoils plundered in the Americas. The façade you see today, including the twin domes flanking the north face and the wide staircase, came about during reconstruction projects during the Baroque period. Notable highlights of the interior are the 12th-century mosaics above the apse and the tomb of Gianlorenzo Bernini. This is the largest church in Rome dedicated to the Virgin Mary and therefore is one of the most important stops on the pilgrimage trail.

Other Things to Do Nearby   Take a short walk to the small church of Santa Maria della Vittoria (Via XX Settembre, 17), where you can view Bernini's most excellent sculpture, *Ecstasy of St. Teresa.*

Santa Maria Sopra Minerva

Type of Attraction   Gothic-style church with important art and tombs

Location   Piazza della Minerva, 42 (Centro Storico)   **Bus** 56, 64, 70, 81, 116

Admission Free

Hours Daily, 7 a.m.–noon, 4–7 p.m.; cloister open Monday–Saturday, 8:30 a.m.–1 p.m., 4–7 p.m.

Phone 06 679 3926 **Web** www.basilicaminerva.it (in Italian)

When to Go The light during the early morning hours is best

Overall Appeal by Age Group

Pre-school —	Teens ★★★	Over 30 ★★★★★
Grade school ★★	Young Adults ★★★★★	Seniors ★★★★★

Authors' Rating ★★★★★

How Much Time to Allow 30 minutes

Description and Comments One of our favorite attractions in all of Rome, Santa Maria Sopra Minerva stands out as the city's only purely Gothic church. The interior dances with light, from its richly hued groin-vaulted ceiling to its stained-glass windows and wide marble floor. Artistic treasures abound, too: Fra Filippo Lippi contributed the frescoes in the Carafa Chapel (to the right of the altar). Standing by the altar is Michelangelo's statue *Risen Christ* (the golden loincloth was added later). Many other artists contributed to the church's grandeur, including Mino da Fiesole (tomb of Francesco Tornabuoni), Perugino (fresco in the Grazioli Chapel), and Carlo Maderno (Chapel of the Annunciation, Lante Della Rovere Chapel, and the Aldobrandini Chapel). You can also find several important tombs here, including those of Popes Leo X and Clement VII, St. Catherine of Siena, and Fra Angelico. The latter's only work in Rome can also be found in the church in the Capranica Chapel.

Touring Tips A guard and/or docent is almost always on duty here and will be happy to give you a map of the church. You can also view the layout of the church at **www.basilicaminerva.it,** though information is in Italian only.

Other Things to Do Nearby Have lunch in the shadow of the Pantheon.

Scala Santa and Sancta Sanctorum

Type of Attraction Pope's private chapel

Location Piazza di San Giovanni in Laterano, 14 (Laterano) **Bus/Tram/Metro** Buses 4, 16, 85, 87; trams 13, 30B; Metro San Giovanni (Line A)

Admission Free

Hours Daily, 6:30–11:50 a.m., 3:30–6:45 p.m. (October–March: evening hours are 3–6:45 p.m.).

Phone 06 704 944 89

When to Go Anytime; not crowded

Overall Appeal by Age Group

Pre-school —	Teens ★	Over 30 ★★
Grade school —	Young Adults ★★	Seniors ★★★

Authors' Rating ★

How Much Time to Allow 15–30 minutes

Description and Comments Domenico Fontana designed the building that houses the Holy Staircase and the Sancta Sanctorum (the pope's private chapel), two sections of the Lateran Palace that were saved from fire in the 1300s. On Good Friday, pilgrims line up to climb the stairs of the Scala Santa on their knees as part of their Easter penance. The rest of the year, you are obliged to walk up the stairs that flank the central staircase.

Other Things to Do Nearby The Basilica of San Giovanni in Laterano is across the street.

St. Peter's Basilica

Type of Attraction The largest and most important church in Christendom

Location Piazza San Pietro (Vatican) **Bus/Tram/Metro** Buses 64, 23, 81, 492, 991; tram 19; Metro Ottaviano (Line A)

Admission Free

Hours Daily, 7 a.m.–7 p.m. (October–March: until 6 p.m.); Treasury: daily, 9 a.m.–6:30 p.m. (October–March: until 5:30 p.m.); Vatican Grottoes: daily, 7 a.m.–6 p.m. (October–March: until 5 p.m.); Dome: daily, 8 a.m.–6 p.m. (October–March: until 5 p.m.)

Phone 06 698 844 66, 06 698 848 66

When to Go Sunday mass is particularly moving, but the crowds are thick. Weekdays (except for Wednesday, when the pope has his weekly audience) are best for going at your own pace.

Special Comments Bring a sweater to cover your shoulders, and refrain from wearing shorts to St. Peter's; you will be turned away if not properly attired.

Overall Appeal by Age Group

Pre-school ★★★	Teens ★★★★★	Over 30 ★★★★★
Grade school ★★★★	Young Adults ★★★★★	Seniors ★★★★★

Authors' Rating ★★★★★

How Much Time to Allow 1 hour, minimum

Description and Comments St. Peter's is a relatively new building by Roman standards, having been completed only in 1626. But at a size larger than two football fields, it is by far the largest church in Christendom. Brass markers on the floor of the basilica show the actual sizes of other large cathedrals from around the world.

Michelangelo drew up the plans for St. Peter's magnificent dome, a landmark that can be seen from miles around, but the great artist did not live to see the finished product. The interior of St. Peter's is largely styled in the Baroque, as evidenced by the bronze canopy *(baldacchino)* and gilded sunburst altarpiece (both by Bernini), and many larger-than-life statues of cherubs, angels, and men.

Almost all of the niches and chapels in St. Peter's have been filled with the elaborate tombs of various popes, or with art such as Michelangelo's superb *Pietà* (now behind protective Plexiglas). Other papal tombs are located beneath St. Peter's in the crypt, including the tomb of the church's first pope, St. Peter. Sitting about midway down the main aisle is a bronze statue of St. Peter, whose foot has been rubbed smooth by millions of visitors.

Other Things to Do Nearby Save time for a visit to the Vatican Museums. Otherwise, make your way to Castel Sant'Angelo by following the Vatican Corridor.

Sinagoga

Type of Attraction Jewish temple and museum
Location Lungotevere dei Cenci (Centro Storico) **Bus** 23, 44, 56, 60, 65, 75, 170, 710, 774, 780
Admission €3
Hours Monday–Thursday, 9 a.m.–5 p.m.; Friday, 9 a.m.–2 p.m.; Sunday, 9:30 a.m.–12:30 p.m.; closed Saturday and holidays
Phone 06 684 006 61
When to Go Anytime
Overall Appeal by Age Group

Pre-school —		Teens ★★		Over 30 ★★★
Grade school ★★		Young Adults ★★★		Seniors ★★★

Authors' Rating ★★★
How Much Time to Allow 30 minutes to 1 hour

Description and Comments Even though Jews have called Rome home since the second century B.C., they haven't always had the easiest time getting by in this overwhelmingly Christian city. Numerous purges and the consequences of World War II reduced the Jewish population to some 16,000 souls, who continue to keep Giudeo-Romano traditions alive. Admission to the synagogue and the adjacent Jewish museum gives you a window into the Roman Jewish experience through relics, photographs, and personal letters. For a peek inside the lovely, rainbow-hued temple, completed in 1904, you must go on a guided tour. Tours in English are given approximately every half-hour.

Touring Tips Security around the Sinagoga is tight. Be prepared to present your passport upon entry.

Other Things to Do Nearby Walk across the Ponte Fabricio to the Isola Tiberina, or have a kosher lunch in the Ghetto.

Teatro di Marcello

Type of Attraction Roman theater
Location Via del Teatro di Marcello (Campidoglio) **Bus** 23, 81, 95, 160, 204, 717, 744, 780
Admission Closed to the public except during summer concerts
Hours Closed to the public except during summer concerts
Phone 06 481 4800

When to Go For a show

How Much Time to Allow Less than 15 minutes

Description and Comments Looking much like a missing wall of the Colosseum from the outside, the Theater of Marcellus was built by Emperor Augustus in 23 B.C. Like the Colosseum, the theater was ritually looted for its marble and travertine, but by the 13th century, aristocratic families began incorporating the structure into various architectural projects. The Theater of Marcellus found new life as a fortress under the Savelli family, and then was converted into a palace in the 16th century by Baldassare Peruzzi. Today, the exterior of the theater forms the outer wall of some unique apartments. The gardens outlying the theater make for a favorite summer concert venue.

Other Things to Do Nearby Get a better look at the theater from the Capitoline hill.

Tomb of Cecilia Metella

Type of Attraction Patrician tomb

Location Via Appia Antica (Appia Antica) **Bus** 660

Admission €3

Hours Tuesday–Saturday, 9 a.m.–1 hour before sunset; Sunday and Monday, 9 a.m.– 1 p.m.; closed holidays

Phone 06 780 2465

When to Go Weekdays

Overall Appeal by Age Group

Pre-school —		Teens ★★		Over 30 ★★
Grade school ★★		Young Adults ★★		Seniors ★★

Authors' Rating ★★

How Much Time to Allow 30 minutes to 1 hour

Description and Comments The drum-shaped tomb of Cecilia Metella is one of the main landmarks along the Appian Way and is perhaps best known as a feature in Romantic landscape painting, which was popular during the late 1800s. (See Tischbein's portrait of Goethe in the Roman *campagna* in the Casa di Goethe.) Not much is known about Cecilia, except that she married well. The Metella family erected this unusually extravagant tomb for her shortly after the young woman's sudden death in the third decade B.C. During the Middle Ages, the structure was fortified with crenellations and served as a sort of toll-collecting booth, where the wealthy Caetani family became even wealthier by charging a toll for passing on the Via Appia. A bit of lavish marble work is still visible on the tomb; however, Pope Sixtus V made off with most of the mausoleum's marble at the end of the 16th century for use in his own city beautification projects.

Other Things to Do Nearby Picnic among the ruins of the Appia Antica.

Trevi Fountain

Type of Attraction Rome's largest and most famous fountain

Location Piazza di Trevi (Quirinale) **Bus** 52, 53, 58, 60, 61, 62, 71, 95, 492

When to Go Anytime, but nighttime can be especially romantic

Special Comments Beware of pickpockets and scam artists

Overall Appeal by Age Group

Pre-school ★★★★	Teens ★★★★★	Over 30 ★★★★★
Grade school ★★★★★	Young Adults ★★★★★	Seniors ★★★★★

Authors' Rating ★★★★

How Much Time to Allow 15–30 minutes

Description and Comments Because of its size and popularity, most tourists assume that the Trevi Fountain has always been a fixture in Rome. In fact, the fountain is relatively new by Roman standards, though the aqueduct for which it was built was constructed in 19 B.C. Designed by Nicolò Salvi for Pope Clement XII, the dramatic Trevi Fountain was completed in 1762. The pope had Salvi build this enormous fountain to commemorate the terminus of the Acqua Vergine aqueduct, which feeds the fountain to this day. The Trevi is one of Rome's must-see sights, but we find it largely unappealing due to the overwhelming crowds that congregate around it daily.

Touring Tips Throw a couple coins in the fountain to ensure your return to Rome.

Other Things to Do Nearby Hike up the stairs to the Piazza del Quirinale or make your way over to Piazza Barberini, where you can admire one of Rome's least-appreciated fountains, Bernini's Fontana del Tritone (Triton Fountain; see profile).

Vatican Corridor

Type of Attraction Fortified papal pathway

Location Connects Castel Sant'Angelo with the Vatican (Vatican)

Hours Not open to the public

Description and Comments Only a few popes have had to utilize the Vatican Corridor (in Italian, il Passetto) to escape invading troops. Pope Nicholas III had the Passetto built in 1277 as a fortified link between the Vatican and the impregnable Castel Sant'Angelo. While the pontiff ran nervously to the fortress, soldiers were able to shoot bows and arrows through niches that were built into the fortifications. Popes Alexander VI Borgia and Clement VII de' Medici both had to use the corridor to escape from their enemies. The former was running from the troops of Charles VIII of France, and the latter had to flee the Bourbons and the impending sack of Rome.

Vatican Museums

Type of Attraction Overwhelming collection of artifacts and artworks culled from four centuries of faith-based funding; home of the Sistine Chapel

Location Viale Vaticano, Città del Vaticano (Vatican) Metro Ottaviano, Cipro (Line A)

Admission €10, free on the last Sunday of every month

Hours Mid-March–mid-June and September–October: Monday–Friday, 8:45 a.m.–4:45 p.m.; Saturday, 8:45 a.m.–1:45 p.m.; rest of the year: Monday–Saturday, 8:45 a.m.–1:45 p.m.; last Sunday of the month, 8:45 a.m.–1:45 p.m.; closed for all religious holidays

Phone 06 69 883 333

When to Go Monday, Tuesday, or Thursday morning

Overall Appeal by Age Group

Pre-school ★★★	Teens ★★★★★	Over 30 ★★★★★
Grade school ★★★★	Young Adults ★★★★★	Seniors ★★★★★

Authors' Rating ★★★★★

How Much Time to Allow 3–4 hours

Description and Comments Thankfully, the Vatican Museums underwent extensive renovations prior to the 2000 Jubilee, resulting in better signage and speedier entrances. Assembled over several centuries to the tune of billions of collection plate dollars, the six museums that make up the Vatican Museums are filled with art from ancient Egypt to the modern age. The highlights of the Vatican Museums include the following.

The Egyptian Museum This collection of artifacts consists of sarcophagi, personal effects, pottery, and other items brought to Rome during imperial times and found in excavations during the 16th and 20th centuries. Many of the original Roman copies of classical Egyptian statues were taken from Hadrian's Villa in Tivoli.

The Museum of Etruscan and Pre-Roman Art Relics from the excavations at Cerveteri and other Etruscan cities compose the bulk of this somewhat small collection.

Greek and Roman Art A large percentage of the Vatican Museums as a whole is taken over by the collection of statues and mosaics. There are so many busts of philosophers and statesmen here that few are labeled (however, all are numbered). Perhaps the most important piece of this group is the *Laocoön,* a magnificent first-century marble work that clearly inspired Michelangelo to greatness.

The Gallery of Maps These frescoes cover the walls of a long hall that connects the Egyptian collection with Renaissance art treasures. The maps depicted here show the territories that were under papal control during the 16th century.

The Raphael Rooms These richly painted rooms were once the papal apartments of Julius II. Many of the Vatican Museums' most prized possessions can be found here, including Raphael's *School of Athens* and *Fire in the Borgo.* Other rooms in this series include the Stanza della Segnatura .

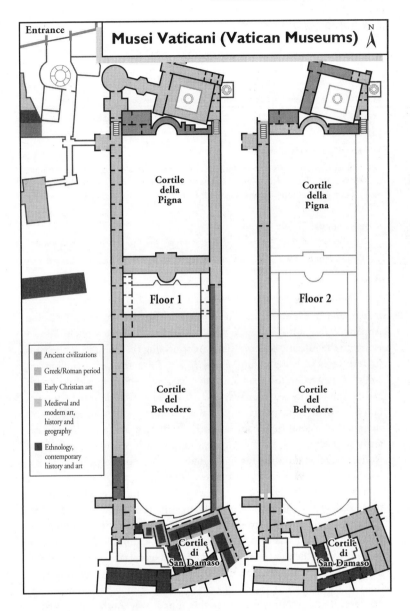

and the Stanza d'Eliodoro. The diminutive Cappella Nicolina, with frescoes by Fra Angelico and Bennozzo Gozzoli, is located nearby.

The Sistine Chapel Michelangelo painted the ceiling and the *Last Judgment* altarpiece, and masters Botticelli, Ghirlandaio, and Perugino (among others) contributed to the wall frescoes.

Other Things to Do Nearby Take a tour of St. Peter's Basilica.

Via Appia (Appian Way)

Type of Attraction This ancient Roman road of legend is the address of many catacombs and funerary monuments

Location Via Appia Antica (Appia Antica) **Bus** 218, 660

Admission Free; specific sites on the road charge admission

Hours Always open; closed to traffic on Sunday and holidays, 9:30 a.m.–7 p.m.

Phone None

When to Go Sundays are best

Special Comments Visitors to the Appian Way can now take the Archeobus (phone 06 469 546 95), a city-run tour bus that travels from Piazza Venezia to the Appia Antica every hour on the hour from 9 a.m. until 5 p.m. Tickets are available on board for €7.50.

Overall Appeal by Age Group

Pre-school ★★★	Teens ★★★★	Over 30 ★★★★
Grade school ★★★	Young Adults ★★★★	Seniors ★★★★

Authors' Rating ★★★★

How Much Time to Allow 2–3 hours

Description and Comments The Queen of Roads since 312 B.C., the Appian Way, known today as Via Appia Antica, once stretched from Rome to the Adriatic port of Brindisi, connecting the Roman empire with its territories in eastern Europe and Africa. Over the years, millions of souls have traversed this road, including St. Peter, who entered Rome with his disciples on the Appian Way in A.D. 42. However, despite its importance as a main route of the empire, the Via Appia is most associated with the afterlife. Along this road, hundreds from Spartacus's rebellious slave army were crucified in 71 B.C., creating a ghastly string of death from Rome to Capua (now the town of Santa Maria Capua Vetere).

During Roman times, no citizen could be buried within the city walls, so wealthier families erected extravagant tombs along the road. One of the more famous of these burial sites being the Tomb of Cecilia Metella. Christians also built an extensive network of catacombs, including the Catacombs of St. Callistus, St. Sebastian, and Domitilla just off of the Appian Way, which served as secret and sacred burial places for their dead. During the Middle Ages, a number of watchtowers and fortifications were built on top of ancient tombs to keep out the invading barbarian armies. Modern times also brought death to the Appian Way. At the caves of Fosse Ardeatine, 335 prisoners of war were executed by the occupying Nazi force in retribution for an Italian partisan attack on German soldiers.

Touring Tips Today, the road is still utilized for traffic, if only as a shortcut to the wider *autostrade*. There is little in the way of a shoulder or sidewalk, so exercise caution when touring here. Beyond the Tomb of Cecilia Metella, you can walk on the road's original paving stones.

Other Things to Do Nearby Visit the Tomb of Cecilia Metella or the Catacombs of Domitilla, St. Callistus, or St. Sebastian.

Via Giulia

Type of Attraction Ivy-covered Renaissance street

Location Parallel to the Tiber between Lungotevere streets Tebaldi and Sangallo and the Corso Vittorio Emanuele (Centro Storico) **Bus** 23, 41, 65, 280

When to Go Anytime

Author's Rating ★★★★

Description and Comments One of the few streets built during the Renaissance, the Via Giulia was the idea of Pope Julius II, who gave it his name. Spanning the road is the ivy-draped Farnese Arch, which was built to the designs of Michelangelo. The Fontana del Mascherone (Fountain of the Big Mask) and intermittent Renaissance-era carvings add to the long street's charm. Today, the Via Giulia is lined with tony antiques shops and restaurants with pretty courtyards.

Via Veneto

Type of Attraction The *La Dolce Vita* street

Location The street extends from the Piazza Barberini and weaves uphill to the Villa Borghese (Via Veneto) Metro Barberini (Line A)

When to Go Anytime

Author's Rating ★★★

Description and Comments The reality of the Via Veneto must follow the hype, which is still very much alive even many decades after the film *La Dolce Vita* was shot. Today, rather than celebrity-packed sidewalk cafés, you're more likely to see high-priced outdoor restaurants filled with German and American tourists. Even the Hard Rock Café is here. Alas, some of the finest buildings in Rome are located on the Via Veneto. The American embassy is located about halfway up. Ritzy hotels account for the rest of the street's real estate. You may very well see a celebrity sighting at one of these hotels, but it will be guaranteed to be fast and fleeting.

Villa Borghese

Type of Attraction Rome's not-so-central park

Location Villa Borghese (between Spagna, Tridente, and Via Veneto neighborhoods) Metro Spagna, Flaminio (Line A) Tram 19, 30

Admission Free; admission charged for museums and activities

Hours Sunrise to sunset

Overall Appeal by Age Group

Pre-school ★★★★★	Teens ★★★★★	Over 30 ★★★★★
Grade school ★★★★★	Young Adults ★★★★★	Seniors ★★★★★

Author's Rating ★★★★★

How Much Time to Allow Time enough to smell the roses

Description and Comments Formerly the estate of the Borghese family, this vast parkland was gifted to the Italian state in 1902. Small temples, massive museums, and rows of pines and palms define the park, and it is a favorite destination for children and parents, tourists and locals. Besides being home to the Galleria Borghese, Galleria Nazionale d'Arte Moderna, the Villa Giulia, and the zoo, the park also has a man-made lake, a horseback riding school, miles of bike and running paths, and lots of open green space for picnics, sunbathing, and afternoon naps. Watch out for crowds on the weekends.

Villa Farnesina

Type of Attraction Contains a brilliant Raphael fresco
Location Via della Lungara, 230 (Trastevere) **Bus** 44, 56, 60, 75 Tram 8
Admission €3.50
Hours Tuesday—Saturday, 9 a.m.—7 p.m., Sunday 9 a.m.—1 p.m.
Phone 06 322 6571
Overall Appeal by Age Group

Pre-school —		Teens ★★★		Over 30 ★★★★
Grade school ★★★		Young Adults ★★★★		Seniors ★★★★

Author's Rating ★★★★
How Much Time to Allow 30 minutes to 1 hour

Description and Comments A charming little building on the left bank of the Tiber, the Villa Farnesina was a vacation home for Roman banker Agostino Chigi. Designed in grand style by the top painters of the day, the holiday hideaway contains a loggia painted by Raphael and his apprentices, and the lovely Sala di Galatea. The latter room's *Triumph of Galatea*, which features the sea nymph cloaked in a vibrant shade of red, is one of Raphael's most recognized frescoes outside of the Vatican. What's more, the fresco is typically viewable *sans* crowds. Other artists contributed to the villa, including Sebastiano del Piombo and Sodoma. Villa Farnesina's architect, Baldassare Peruzzi, painted the impressive *trompe l'oeil* depicting a balcony of polychrome marble columns overlooking a Roman garden. Consequently, the villa earned its name from Alessandro Farnese, who bought the property in 1577.

Il Vittoriano (Victor Emanuel Monument)

Type of Attraction Gargantuan monument with sweeping views over city
Location Piazza Venezia (Campidoglio) **Bus** 44, 46, 94, 710, 718, 719, and other buses to Piazza Venezia
Admission Free
Hours Tuesday–Sunday, 10 a.m.–4 p.m.
Phone 06 360 043 99

When to Go By day, you can climb to the top of the monument, by night, the monument is stunningly floodlit

Special Comments There is no elevator access.

Overall Appeal by Age Group

Pre-school ★★★	Teens ★★★★	Over 30 ★★★★
Grade school ★★★★	Young Adults ★★★★	Seniors ★★★

Authors' Rating ★★★★

How Much Time to Allow 30 minutes to 1 hour

Description and Comments Romans love to hate the Vittoriano monument, the stark, white colossus that sits on the Piazza Venezia. Some despise it for what it stands for. Built in honor of Italy's first king, King Vittorio Emanuele II, the Vittoriano symbolizes a unified Italy while simultaneously representing the monarchy, hardly the preferred form of government for such an independent populace. Others take issue with the Vittoriano because of its architecture. The enormous, Teutonic-looking structure is an excessive heap of marble and travertine that completely overpowers the uniform look of ochre-toned Rome. At any rate, most Romans call the Vittoriano by one of several nicknames, either the "wedding cake," the "dentures," or the "typewriter," because of its pompous-looking, multitiered façade.

Like it or not, the Victor Emanuel Monument houses the Tomb of the Unknown Soldier, which is marked by an eternal flame and two guards who stand watch over it day and night. The upper levels of the monument offer spectacular views.

Touring Tips The Complesso del Vittoriano, which regularly features art exhibits, is located in the southeast wing of the monument. It's open Tuesday–Sunday, 9 a.m.–8 p.m.; and Friday and Saturday until 11 p.m. Call 06 678 0664 for further info. Admission charges vary.

Other Things to Do Nearby Climb the stairs to Santa Maria in Aracoeli or make your way up the wide *cordonata* to the Piazza del Campidoglio.

Entertainment and Nightlife in Rome

Rome is big enough and diverse enough to satisfy your nightlife desires, no matter if you want to savor a glass of wine under the stars or dance the night away under the strobe lights. The key is knowing where to go and when. Rome has no shortage of sidewalk cafés and leafy courtyards where you can sit and chat while watching the sun mellow into the night sky. Restaurants and wine bars that line the Piazza Navona and Campo de' Fiori rely on tourists to seek out such romantic spots. But if you want real action, you will have to wait. Romans get a late start, with most activity beginning around 11 p.m. As a tourist, you may find it difficult to balance your daytime touring with nighttime rabble-rousing.

Below is a list of just some of our favorite nightspots in Rome. New venues are popping up all the time, so check the English listings in *Roma C'è* for additional ideas. You can buy the weekly at any newsstand.

Mixed drinks are expensive at clubs, so if you're trying to save your money, go for beer or wine. Note, too, that many clubs are not obliged to serve food. Those that do usually only have pizza or prepackaged snacks. Consult Part Five, Dining in Central Italy, for information on Rome's restaurants and wine bars.

	ROME ENTERTAINMENT AND NIGHTLIFE	
Name	**Admission/ Cover**	**Comments**
Nightclubs		
Alexanderplatz Jazz Club	€5–€7.50	International jazz club
Alien	€15–€20	Meat-market dance club
Bar del Fico	None	Upscale cocktail bar
Bar della Pace	None	See-and-be-seen cocktail bar
Big Mama	€5–€10	Premier blues venue
The Drunken Ship	None	American-style bar
Gilda	€20	Upscale lounge with dance floor
Goa	€7.50–€15	Exotic dance club
Jonathan's Angels	None	Trendy bar with eclectic decor
RipArte Cafe	€15	Ultra-hip DJ and sushi bar
Classical Music, Opera, and Theater		
Accademia Nazionale di Santa Cecilia	€7.50–€40	Rome's premier symphony
Teatro Argentina	€15.50+	Classic venue for opera and drama
Teatro dell'Opera	€10.50–€90	Main opera venue

Alexanderplatz Jazz Club

JAZZ PERFORMED BY INTERNATIONAL AND LOCAL TALENT

Who Goes There Cool cats age 30 and over

Vatican Area; Via Ostia, 9; Metro Ottaviano; phone 06 397 42 171

Cover €5–€7.50. **Dress** Casual but sophisticated. **Food available** Reservations are recommended for dinner.

Hours Monday–Saturday, 10 p.m.–2 a.m.

What Goes On Established and up-and-coming stars have been known to tickle the ivories, blow the sax, and sing scat at Rome's most famous jazz club. As such, Alexanderplatz attracts a crowd of regulars and tourists.

Setting & Atmosphere Patrons play it cool over dinner and drinks. Late-night jam sessions have music lovers be-bopping in their seats.

If You Go Bring your own fumigator—the bar tends to get smoky.

Alien

A MEAT MARKET SET TO MODERN BEATS

Who Goes There Rome's young and trendy, visiting frat boys

Outside the City Gates; Via Velletri, 13/19; bus 63; phone 06 841 2212

Cover €15–€20. **Drinks** €7.50. **Dress** Club duds. **Food available** None.
Hours Tuesday–Sunday, 10:30 p.m.–4 a.m.

What Goes On Hip-hop, house, and Top 40 tunes blare from two dance floors, inspiring club kids to dance their socks off. The pick-up scene is hot and heavy.

Setting & Atmosphere The owners of the Alien have pulled out all the stops by hiring known DJs and professional dancers to keep the party moving. Strobe lights and smoke machines provide the desired seductive atmosphere.

If You Go Bring a friend or two.

Bar del Fico

UPSCALE COCKTAIL BAR

Who Goes There Wealthy yet laid-back Romans and head-turners

Centro Storico (Piazza Navona); Piazza del Fico, 26–28; phone 06 686 5205

Cover None. **Drinks** €4–€7. **Dress** European chic. **Food available** Light snacks.
Hours Daily, 9 a.m.–2 a.m.

What Goes On The café/bar's name is a play on words, meaning simultaneously the "bar under the fig tree" and "the cool bar." Both statements are true. You can hang out here for a chat and drinks, or stick around until late when live music heats up the joint.

Setting & Atmosphere Romans and an increasing number of out-of-towners show up here for drinks and snacks. The best seats in the house are on the sidewalk beneath the fig tree.

If You Go Bring your Italian-English dictionary—you may feel like networking with the locals.

Bar della Pace

SEE-AND-BE-SEEN BAR

Who Goes There Designers, musicians, out-of-towners

Centro Storico (Piazza Navona); Via della Pace, 3–7; buses 46, 64, 70, 81, 492; phone 06 686 1216

Cover None. **Drinks** €7.50–€10. **Dress** Smart evening wear; something in black will do. **Food available** Light snacks.

Hours Daily, until late.

What Goes On Definitely not the most economical of bars, but a good place to people-watch, around the corner from Piazza Navona.

Setting & Atmosphere The atmosphere is similar to that of Bar del Fico, also with outdoor seating fronting the street. Conversely, regular customers tend to be more aloof.

If You Go Brace yourself for the high price of a small cocktail.

Big Mama

ROME'S PREMIER BLUES VENUE

Who Goes There   Mixed-age, mostly local, crowd and starving artists

Trastevere; Via San Francesco a Ripa, 18; phone 06 581 2551

Cover Monthly membership card, €5; yearly membership, €10. **Drinks** €3–€7. **Dress** Casual.

Hours Daily, 9 p.m.–1:30 a.m.; closed July–October

What Goes On   The girth of this basement venue is found in its talent roster. International performers, such as the Blues Brothers, Maceo Parker, and Chet Baker, have held court here. There's ample room for rock acts, too.

Setting & Atmosphere   Leave all your pains behind you. This place is laid-back.

If You Go   Consider a stroll around Trastevere after midnight.

The Drunken Ship

AMERICAN-STYLE BAR

Who Goes There   Students, Americans, tourists

Centro Storico; Campo de' Fiori, 20–21; phone 06 683 005 35

Cover None. **Drinks** Beer, €3–€4, mixed drinks, €5–€8. **Dress** Casual. **Food available** Bar snacks.

Hours Daily, 5 p.m.–2 a.m.

What Goes On   Local and foreign students compete in chugging contests and meat-market maneuvers.

Setting & Atmosphere   The Drunken Ship is a no-frills kind of place where you'll get a good measure of beer, poured with a good measure of English.

If You Go   Hang out near the bar's entrance on Campo de' Fiori to remind yourself that you're actually in Rome.

Gilda

NIGHTCLUB FOR OLD AND NEW MONEY

Who Goes There   Celebs and sycophants

Tridente; Via Mario de' Fiori, 97; Metro Spagna (Line A); phone 06 678 4838

Cover €20. **Drinks** Starting at €8 for mixed drinks. **Dress** To the hilt. **Food available** None.

Hours Daily, 10 p.m.–4 a.m.

What Goes On   When the club isn't playing the latest Top 40 dance hits, it plays host to fashion shows and private parties. The piano bar is popular on weeknights.

Setting & Atmosphere   Stars and wannabes cozy up to each other—or their cell phones—in one of the club's many private nooks.

If You Go   Be sure to wear a conspicuous designer label—it will increase your cool quotient.

Goa

AMBIENT TRANCE AND DISCO SOUNDS

Who Goes There Professional dancers, Roman college students

Aventino (Testaccio);Via Libetta, 13; Metro Garbatella (Line B); phone 06 574 8277

Cover €7.50–€15. **Dress** Think exotic. **Food available** Light snacks.

Hours Tuesday, Thursday–Saturday, 11 p.m.–3 a.m.

What Goes On Two dance floors mean twice the opportunity to shake your groove thang. When you're ready for a break, retreat to the mezzanine, where onlookers loll and smooch on couches.

Setting & Atmosphere Goa's backdrop changes periodically. Past styles have been inspired by such themes as a Ranee's Boudoir and a Desert Disco.

If You Go Arrange your transportation home before going out. Taxis can be scarce late at night.

Jonathan's Angels

ROME'S MOST DECORATIVE BAR

Who Goes There Artists, eccentrics, tourists

Centro Storico;Via della Fossa, 16; buses 46, 64, 70, 81, 492; phone 06 689 3426

Cover None. **Dress** Trendy. **Food available** Light snacks.

Hours Daily, 4 p.m.–2 a.m.

What Goes On Nino (a.k.a. Jonathan), the eccentric owner, serves up drinks and bravado. Those not within earshot can sit back and enjoy the bizarre decorations.

Setting & Atmosphere The owner certainly went to the flea market several times to pick out this bar's furnishings. A variety of contrasting elements, including a fresco of a Harley Davidson, plaster busts of Victorian ladies, and sundry news clippings and photographs framed on the walls, are fodder for conversation starters.

If You Go Be sure to check out the bathroom, which has the most decorative seat in the house!

RipArte Cafe

SUSHI, COCKTAILS, AND DJS

Who Goes There Rome's trendsetters

Trastevere;Via Orti di Trastevere, 7; bus 63, 75; tram 8; phone 06 586 1852; www.riparte.com

Cover €15. **Dress** Smart. **Food available** Sushi and sashimi rolls, light Asian fare.

Hours Daily, 8 p.m.–3 a.m.

What Goes On Beautiful people and beatniks come together here to enjoy designer cocktails, highbrow conversation, and some of the coolest DJs in town.

Setting & Atmosphere Sushi is only one part of RipArte's appeal. This is one of the slickest venues in town, where you can lounge on leather and critique modern art installations.

If You Go Get yourself a copy of *ArtNews* before going. Learn how to use chopsticks.

Cultural Evenings

Roma C'è and *Time Out Roma* have extensive listings in Italian for film, theater, and musical performances. The tourist office also puts out the monthly *L'Evento,* which highlights up-and-coming performances in Italian and English (for some listings). There's really no central source for reserving tickets, so you'll have to go to the individual cinema, theater, or music hall to secure your seats. To add to the hassle, credit cards are not always accepted. Make sure you have cash.

Classical Music, Opera, and Theater

The **Accademia Nazionale di Santa Cecilia** (Via Vittoria, 6; phone: info 06 328 171; tickets 06 808 8352; **www.santacecilia.it**), Rome's premier symphony orchestra, has been drawing rave reviews since its inception in the 16th century. The academy divides its symphonic, choral, and chamber music schedules among various venues, including the **Auditorio Pio** (Via della Conciliazione, 3; phone 06 688 01 044), the grounds of the **Villa Giulia,** and the new Renzo Piano–designed **Parco della Musica** (Viale Pietro de Coubertin, 30; phone 06 806 92 492; **www.musicaperroma.it**). Symphony tickets range from €13 to €40; under age 26, tickets cost €10.50 to €18. Chamber music concert tickets range from €10.50 to €24; under age 26, tickets cost €7.75 to €10.50. Tickets are available at the box office or online at the Accademia's web site.

The main stage for the Teatro di Roma is at the landmark building **Teatro Argentina** (Largo Argentina, 52; phone 06 688 04 601; **www.teatrodiroma.net**), where Rossini's *Barber of Seville* debuted. Today, the theater's repertoire includes opera, as well as dance and a heavy dose of dramatic theater. Most seats at Teatro Argentina are available for season ticket holders only. Prices for all performances start at approximately €15.50. The box office accepts cash only.

Though it has been the setting for several groundbreaking operas (*Tosca,* anyone?), Rome lacks the kind of world-class opera scene found in such other Italian cities as Venice and Milan. Still, Rome occasionally hosts a number of big names and the big productions at its **Teatro dell'Opera** (Via Firenze, 72; phone 06 481 601). The theater season runs from October through March, and the summer season is held at the Stadio Olimpico. Also check listings in *Roma C'è* and *Il Messagero*'s "Trova Roma" section for smaller lyrical dramas. Some churches put on operas during the fall to raise money. These spectacles are typically inexpensive, but no less engaging. Prices range from €15.50 to €90 for opera performances and from €10.50 to €45 for ballets and concerts. All credit cards are accepted at the box office.

Spectator Sports

As the capital and the largest city in Italy, Rome is blessed (or is it cursed?) with two soccer teams, the **A.S. Roma** (gold and crimson, or *giallorosso*) and **S.S. Lazio** (baby blue and white). Both teams share home turf at the Stadio Olimpico, and you can bet that their rivalry is fierce when they meet one another in the annual Derby. Both squads play their regular-season games from September through April; In recent years, both have been good enough to host other teams from Europe in the Champions League. Tickets can be purchased on game day at the Stadio Olimpico or at the teams' respective stores in town. Official tickets cost from between €15 and €75; scalped tickets cost much more.

Stadio Olimpico   Viale dello Stadio Olimpico; phone 06 323 7333

A.S. Roma Store   Via Colonna, 360; phone 06 678 6514

Lazio Point   Via Farini, 34; phone 06 482 6768

Shopping in Rome

If you want it, Rome's got it. From halter-tops to altar tops, the Italian capital is a veritable clearinghouse for the latest Italian styles in fashion, technology, and accessories for the home and church. The Metropolis is also a breeding ground for starving artists, who scrape together a living by creating unique pieces of jewelry or by selling their paintings of Roman cityscapes. Don't expect to get a bargain here—but don't be afraid to haggle for something you really want.

Shopping Zones and Favorite Streets

Nifty shops tend to turn up just about everywhere in Rome, but most are concentrated in a few key areas. Here is a thumbnail sketch of the best places to browse and buy.

Via del Corso

Rome's main thoroughfare cuts a straight path from Piaza Venezia to Piazza del Popolo. Along the way, it is lined with name-brand retail shops, department stores, funky boutiques, and tourist dives. A small portion of Via del Corso, from approximately Via Condotti north, is closed to traffic, allowing for lazy games of window-shopping. Below here, pedestrians are relegated to too-narrow sidewalks. The strolling crowds are especially thick in the early evening, when all of Rome shows up for a *passeggiata*.

Via Condotti

New York may have its Fifth Avenue, but Rome has Via Condotti, a street flanked by designer shops, such as Gucci and Prada. Crowning the end of this prêt-à-porter paradise is the Spanish Steps, a perfect rest stop after a day of browsing.

Though most of Italy's top ateliers are headquartered in Milan, a few homegrown talents, including Valentino and Fendi, have remained in the Eternal City. You'll find most of Rome's high-fashion boutiques on and around Via Condotti.

Alberta Ferretti   Via Condotti, 34; phone 06 699 1160

Brioni   Via Barberini, 79; phone 06 484 517

Dolce & Gabbana   Via Borgognona, 7d; phone 06 678 2990

Etro   Via del Babuino, 102; phone 06 678 8257

Fendi   Via Borgognona, 36a/39; phone 06 679 7641

Giorgio Armani   Via Condotti, 77; phone 06 699 1460

Gucci   Via Condotti, 8; phone 06 678 9340

Prada   Via Condotti, 92–95; phone 06 679 0897

Roberto Cavalli   Via Borgognona, 7a; phone 06 693 801 30

Valentino Uomo/Donna   Via Condotti, 13; phone 06 678 3656

Versace   Via Bocca di Leone, 26; phone 06 678 0521

Via del Babuino

One of the streets of the Tridente, the Via del Babuino, or "Baboon Street," is renowned for its high-priced antiques shops. It also enjoys Piazza di Spagna's spillover of haute couture shops.

Via dei Coronari

Better deals on antiques can be found on the Via dei Coronari, which is lined with antique restoration workshops and furniture refurbishment businesses. In medieval times, the street was renowned for its rosary *(coronari)* shops, as this was a preferred pilgrimage route.

Campo de' Fiori

Many hip boutiques catering to the young and beautiful are situated near Campo de' Fiori, especially along Via dei Giubbonari. More antiques dealers can be found on Via del Pellegrino.

Via dei Cestari

This narrow street running behind the Pantheon is the holy equivalent of New York's Fifth Avenue, where the city's thousands of priests, cardinals, and seminary students buy their garb. Also on sale here are liturgical accessories, including candelabra, chalices, and ornate crucifixes.

Trastevere

Not surprisingly this neighborhood of artists and bohemians has Rome's most original boutiques, especially when it comes to jewelry and accessories. Trastevere is also the place to head to look for vintage clothing and consignment shops.

Department and "Dime" Stores

Arrived in Rome without a warm scarf? Need to buy a pair of undies, pantyhose, or a tie? Head to one of the city's department stores for a one-stop shopping trip. **COIN** and **Rinascente** have quality clothing for men and women, and they also carry unique accessories. COIN also has a shoe department. If you just need a quick fix while you're waiting for your lost luggage to be found, try a dime store. The chains **UPIM** and **Oviesse** (a.k.a., Standa), sell "disposable" clothing, accessories, cosmetics, housewares, books, and more.

COIN　Piazzale Appio, 7; phone 06 708 0020; and Via Cola di Rienzo, 173, phone 06 360 042 98

Rinascente　Largo Chigi, 20; phone 06 679 7691

Oviesse　Viale Trastevere, 62/64; phone 06 589 5342

UPIM　Piazza di Santa Maria Maggiore; phone 06 446 5579

Outdoor and Flea Markets

Porta Portese

Between Via Portuense and Via Ippolito Nievo in Testaccio, the market at Porta Portese is a regular Sunday affair. Vendors selling everything from antique postcards to CDs to bicycle parts set up shop around 6 a.m. and pack it all in at 2 p.m. Get their early to get the best deals and avoid the crowds. The throngs can be maddening after 10 a.m.

Via Sannio

Located just outside the city gates beyond the church of San Giovanni in Laterano, the market at Via Sannio is open Monday through Saturday and sells a good deal of new and used clothing. Look out for deals on leather jackets, scarves, and clothes by the pound.

Produce Markets

Campo de' Fiori

Rome's most picturesque market sets up shop daily in the Campo de' Fiori. The fruits, vegetables, and herbs here are of the utmost quality, but they also tend to be pricey, given their glamorous market surroundings. Go for the atmosphere.

Piazza delle Coppelle

A smaller market off of Piazza Navona, this is a tranquil alternative to the bustling Campo. You might occasionally catch a visiting celeb eyeing the tomatoes here. Prices are competitive.

Piazza Vittorio

Rome has become a sort of melting pot for people from Africa, Asia, and the Caribbean in recent years, and the market at Piazza Vittorio reflects this diversity. This one-of-a-kind market has one of Rome's largest selections of meat and produce, and you can purchase a variety of zesty spices in bulk.

Testaccio

Chefs and locals shop the daily meat and produce market in Testaccio. Fewer tourists here mean that prices are kept low and that the atmosphere remains authentically Roman.

Great Gifts from Rome and Where to Find Them

Wines and Spirits

If Rome is your only destination in Italy, look for unique brands and vintages. Reds like Barolo and Barbaresco are available in the United States, but sell for much less in Italy. You can throw down a chunk of change for a Brunello, an expensive wine made a bit cheaper if you import it yourself. White wines are a specialty of the Latium region, with Frascati and Est! Est! Est! leading the pack.

Buccone   Via di Ripetta, 19–20; phone 06 361 2154. The Buccone sons speak fluent English and are ever so helpful when it comes to choosing the perfect wine. Oh yeah—they also ship anywhere in the world.

Chocolate

La Bottega del Cioccolato   Via Leonina, 82; phone 06 482 1473. Fresh dark, milk, and white chocolate concoctions shaped like local landmarks. A Colosseum or St. Peter's bon bon is the ultimate indulgence.

Kitchenware and Dining Accessories

C.U.C.I.N.A   Via Mario de' Fiori 65; phone 06 679 1275. Funky kitchen accessories at bargain prices.

LeoneLimentani   Via Portico d'Ottavia; phone 06 688 066 86. Equipped with china patterns from major designers. Worldwide shipping available.

Modigliani   Via Condotti, 24; phone 06 678 5653. Unique ceramics and gifts.

Leather and Leather Accessories

Sermoneta Gloves   Piazza di Spagna, 61; phone 06 679 1960. Giorgio Sermoneta's name is synonymous with quality leather products, and his gloves are the tops.

Skin   Via Capo la Case, 41; phone 06 678 5531. The finest assortment of leather jackets for men and women. Belts and bags are unique.

Religious Items

Shop the Via dei Cestari for bona fide robes and vestments. You can also find a good assortment of religious jewelry here, including rosaries and charms. If you're looking for kitsch, peruse the schlock shops near the entrance to the Vatican City.

Slabbinck   Via dei Cestari, 35/37; phone 06 686 5809. As the pope's tailor, Belgian-born Slabbinck has the competition beat. The family's large store on the Via dei Cestari has everything under the heavens.

Children's Toys

Berte   Piazza Navona, 107; phone 06 687 5011. This shop is packed with handmade wooden toys and plenty of gift ideas for tiny tots.

Art and Antiques

We don't suggest that you lug home a full-size replica of the *Pietà*. But if you're an art connoisseur or antiques freak, you may just want to check out Rome's many antique boutiques. Just think what a great conversation piece that Baroque-style candelabra could be! Via dei Coronari and Via Babuino are renowned for their selection of authentic and unique antique items. You'll also find a number of art galleries on and just off these streets. Watch out, though—prices in the big city can be staggering. You may be better off scouring the Porta Portese flea market.

Marmi Line   Via de' Coronari 113–141/145; phone 06 689 3795

W Apolloni   Via del Babuino 132; phone 06 679 2429

Jewelry

Roman women are not shy when it comes to jewelry, preferring chunky baubles and gold to anything subtle. The exclusive **Bulgari** is the Tiffany of Rome, and has its headquarters on Via Condotti. Another great area to search for unique jewels is in the Ghetto, the traditional neighborhood of the city's gold- and silversmiths. Here, artisan jewelers will make custom individual pieces to suit the customer's taste. **Oddi e Seghetti** is a particularly reliable shop for such commissions. For costume jewelry or anything with a bit of panache (and a matching price tag), check out the side streets around Piazza di Spagna. Modern, earthy jewelry can be found around Trastevere.

Bulgari   Via Condotti, 10; phone 06 679 3876

Bozart   Via Bocca di Leone, 4; phone 06 678 1026

Massoni   Largo Carlo Goldoni, 48; phone 06 678 2679

Oddi e Seghetti   Via del Cancello, 20; phone 06 686 1384

The Best of Latium

The power and size of Rome cast a long shadow over the rest of Latium, so much so that few travelers ever take—or ever have—the time to explore the region. But there is much to be seen in this "crossroads" region. Within the province of Rome, you'll find ruins of ancient settlements in **Tivoli, Ostia Antica,** and **Cerveteri,** and relaxing getaways—either in the hills of the **Castelli Romani** or on the banks of Lake Bracciano. The provinces of **Frosinone** and **Rieti** harbor noteworthy monasteries in **Cassino** and **Farfa,** respectively. **Viterbo's** province was once the domain of Etruscans and popes, and it has the palaces, parks, and archeological sites to prove it. Finally, the province of **Latina,** on the Tyrrhenian Sea, boasts a string of seaside resorts, including **Gaeta, Terracina, Sperlonga,** and the **Pontine Islands.**

Latium Tourism Board

You can pick up information about the entire region of Latium at the tourist office in Rome or from city kiosks. Provincial and municipal tourism offices are listed with their respective sections.

Latium Regional Tourist Board   Via Rosa Raimondi Garibaldi, 7; 00145 Rome; phone 06 516 881 66, fax 06 516 881 72; **www.regione.lazio.it**

Getting around Latium

Driving is the best way to get around Latium, but if you must take public transportation, then the bus is the way to go. Almost all towns in the region are serviced by **COTRAL** (Consortile Trasporti nel Lazio, phone 06 591 5551). For destinations northwest of Rome, catch the bus at Lepanto Metro station (Line A). For points north and northeast, bus depots are located at Saxa Rubra (via train from Piazzale Flaminio) and at Tiburtina Station. Bus stops at Ponte Mammolo (Metro Line B), EUR Fermi (Metro Line B), and Anagnina (Metro Line A) service destinations east, southwest, and southeast of Rome. COTRAL also runs a regular schedule of buses from Viterbo. Most train service from Rome to other towns in Latium is available from Ostiense and Tiburtina stations.

Quick Glance at the Towns of Latium

Following is a listing of cities and touring areas in Latium by province. For each city or area, we provide an overall rating to describe how rewarding that place is to visit. We also include a short comment about the place. Use this as a reference for day trips or extended holidays.

Quick Glance at the Towns of Latium *(continued)*

City/Area	Overall Rating	Comment
Province of Rome		
Castelli Romani	★★★★★	Quiet hill towns are preferred getaway for Romans, including the Pope
Cerveteri	★★★½	Remnants from Etruscan times
Civitavecchia	★★	Port city with a few sites of religious interest
Lake Bracciano	★★★	Clean air and a castle
Ostia	★★★★★	Ancient ruins at Ostia Antica
Tivoli	★★★★★	Garden estates at Villa d'Este and Hadrian's Villa
Province of Frosinone		
Cassino	★★★	Known for its Benedictine monastery
Province of Rieti		
Castelnuovo di Farfa	★★★	Home to yet another Benedictine monastery
Province of Viterbo		
Bagnaia	★★★½	Home of the Villa Lante
Bomarzo	★★★★	Surreal Sacro Bosco will leave you speechless
Civita di Bagnoregio	★★★★	Fairy-tale village set high on a hill
Lake Bolsena	★★★½	Site of miracles and celebrated white wine
Lake Vico	★★★	Big draw is the Farnese Palace
Norchia	★★★	Noteworthy for Etruscan Necropolis
Tarquinia	★★★½	Etruscan finds are among the best
Tuscania	★★★	Etruscan and medieval heritage
Viterbo	★★★★	Impressive medieval cityscape
Province of Latina		
Isole Pontine	★★★★	Islands far off the tourist beat
Ninfa	★★★★	Otherworldly gardens
Riviera d'Ulisse	★★★★	Pristine beaches enjoyed by Aeneas, Tiberius, and modern Romans

The Province of Rome

Province of Rome Tourist Office   Via XX Settembre, 26; 00187 Rome; phone 06 421 381, fax 06 421 382 21; **www.oltreroma.it**

Tivoli

Set in the hills some 25 minutes east of Rome, Tivoli was founded by an Italic tribe and was eventually conquered by the Romans in 338 B.C. Just

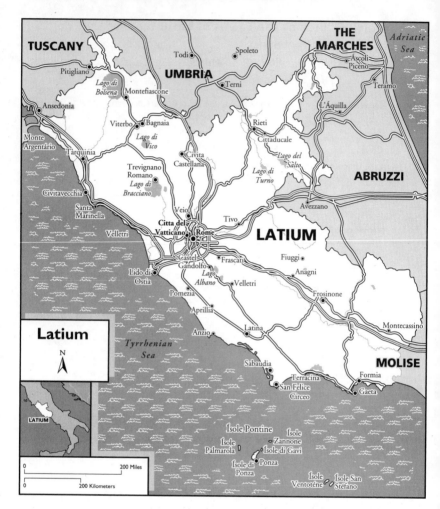

far enough away from the stress of the big city, Tivoli has long served as a summer escape. In fact, many rich Romans have built villas or estates here. One such Roman was Emperor Hadrian, who constructed a vast complex of baths, dining halls, courtyards, art spaces, and studios on a plot of roughly 300 acres. **Hadrian's Villa** (Villa Adriana; phone 0774 530 203; open daily, April–September, 9 a.m.–6:30 p.m.; October–March: 9 a.m.–4 p.m.; admission €6.50) was one of the largest imperial palaces and certainly merits a day trip in itself. Tivoli's other must-see site is the **Villa d'Este** (Piazza Trento; phone 0774 312 070; open Tuesday–Sunday, 9 a.m.–6:30 p.m. or 1 hour before sunset; admission €6.50), an estate developed by the son of Lucrezia Borgia, Cardinal

Ippolito d'Este, on the site of an old Benedictine convent. The gardens—with their dramatic grottoes, intricate landscaping, and avenue of a 100 fountains—make for a delightful diversion.

To get to Tivoli, you can take the Metro to Rebibbia (Line B), and then take a blue COTRAL bus (about 20 minutes) into town. Buses run to and from Tivoli about every 20 minutes on weekdays, about every 30 minutes on weekends. Buy tickets for the bus at the newsstand by the bus stop. You can also take an FS train from Termini or Tiburtina station. The ride takes approximately 20 to 25 minutes.

IAT Tivoli   Largo Garibaldi; 00019 Tivoli; phone 0774 311 249, fax 0774 331 294

Ostia

Ostia was the main commercial port of Rome until the fourth century, when trade declined and the harbor was gradually overwhelmed by silt. Shortly thereafter, malaria threatened the citizens of Ostia, and they fled, leaving behind a massive city of homes, taverns, shops, brothels, temples, a theater, and burial grounds. After the exodus, silt further consumed the town, and it lay buried for centuries. Excavations turned up an ancient city larger than Pompeii. However, because Ostia died a gradual death, the excavations at **Ostia Antica** (Scavi Ostia Antica; phone 06 563 58 099; open Tuesday–Sunday, 9 a.m.–7 p.m., last admission at 6 p.m.; admission €5) are not quite as eerie as those found in the charred ruins of Pompeii.

Ostia Antica is easily reached by train from the Roma-Lido station, which is connected by a passageway with the Metro at Piramide (Line B). For more information, contact the provincial tourist office in Rome (Via Rosa Raimondi Garibaldi, 7; 00145 Rome; phone 06 516 881 66, fax 06 516 881 72; **www.regione.lazio.it**).

Castelli Romani

Nestled among the dormant volcanic hills south of Rome, the Castelli Romani get their name from the numerous castles and villas that were erected here by bishops and aristocrats. From imperial times until the Renaissance, the Roman status quo called for a summer home here. These days, Romans, both rich and poor, like to escape the chaos of the city with a weekend or a day trip to the countryside. Thirteen towns—**Castel Gandolfo, Frascati, Monte Porzio Catone, Montecompatri, Rocca Priora, Colonna, Rocca di Papa, Grottaferrata, Marino, Albano Laziale, Ariccia, Genzano,** and **Nemi**—make up the Castelli circuit, but only a few are worth a visit if you're short on time. The most notable town here is Castel Gandolfo, the attractive and tidy town where the pope summers. Romans seem to prefer picturesque Nemi, a small town perched over a tree-lined crater. Meanwhile, the towns of Frascati, Genzano, Grottaferrata, and Montecompatri have a long history with viticulture, making them pleasant destinations for Sunday lunch.

Trains to Albano and Frascati depart from the Ferrovie Laziale (Latium Railway) platform of Rome's Termini Station almost hourly from 5 a.m. until 10 p.m. The trip to Albano takes about 50 minutes, whereas the trip to Frascati lasts about 30 minutes. COTRAL bus service to the Castelli Romani is available from Anagnina Station at the end of Rome's Metro Line A. The best way to get to Latium's hill towns is to drive and take in the splendor of the countryside. Driving also allows you the opportunity to explore several towns in one day. Take the A2 and follow the signs to Frascati, Genzano, Grottaferrata, or Nemi. The SS5 also passes through the Castelli Romani.

IAT Laghi e Castelli Romani Viale Risorgimento, 1; 00041 Albano Laziale; phone 06 932 4081, fax 06 932 0040

Cerveteri

Estimated to be at least 20 times larger than its current size, the Etruscan city of Caere (today's Cerveteri) was founded in the eighth century B.C. and became a bustling Mediterranean trading hub between the seventh and fifth centuries B.C. During this time of prosperity, Cerveteri became a major crafts center, developing the black glaze *bucchero* pottery that became the main characteristic of Etruscan art. The Etruscans in Cerveteri also used their artistic skills to revolutionize funeral rites, shifting from cremating their dead to burying them in elaborate tomb dwellings. Ruins from these cities of the dead can be found in the **Banditaccia Necropolis** (Via della Necropoli; no phone; open Tuesday–Sunday, 9 a.m.–7 p.m.; winter: 10 a.m.–4 p.m.; admission €5), a series of cone-shaped burial chambers built into the Cerveteri hillside. Relics found here include *bucchero* vases, funerary statues, chalices, and all manner of other objects that would have made the dead more comfortable during the afterlife. Additional Etruscan artifacts from the tombs are on exhibit in the town's **Museo Nazionale di Caerite** (Castello Ruspoli, phone 06 995 0003; open Tuesday–Sunday, 9 a.m.–7 p.m.; winter: 10 a.m.–4 p.m.; admission free).

Cerveteri is approximately 40 minutes northwest of Rome. By car, take the A12 *autostrada* via Civitavecchia or the Via Aurelia (S1). You can also reach Cerveteri by COTRAL bus from the Lepanto Metro station (Line A) in Rome.

Pro Loco Cerveteri Piazza Risorgimento, 19; 00052 Cerveteri; phone 06 995 51 971; **www.caere.it**

Civitavecchia

Founded by Emperor Trajan as a port city in A.D. 108, Civitavecchia is still the main port for Rome. If you are taking a cruise around Italy or if you plan to take the ferry to Sardinia, then you will surely set foot here. Sadly, there isn't much to see, as industry from the shipping business has sullied the air and the water, and heavy bombing during World War II left the city in shambles. Civitavecchia's few cultural attractions include the **Fort of Michelangelo,** commissioned by "warrior pope" Julius II, designed by Bramante and Andrea da Sangallo, and finalized by Buonarroti, and the monumental, travertine **Vanvitelli Fountain** commissioned by Pope Urban VIII in 1635. Religious highlights include the **Chiesa dei Santis-simi Martiri Giapponesi** (Church of Holy Japanese Saints, Largo San Francesco di Assisi; phone 0766 23 649; open daily, 7 a.m.–1 p.m., 3:30–7 p.m.; admission free) and the **"Madonnina."** The former was built in 1864 to memorialize the first Japanese Christian martyrs in Nagasaki and is the only church in Italy to be decorated with frescoes by a Japanese artist. The Madonnina (Pantano; phone 0766 560 185; open daily, 7 a.m.–1 p.m., 3:30–7 p.m.; admission free), a statue who reportedly cried tears of blood on February 2, 1995, is located in the Pantano parish of Civitavec-chia, and has become a place of pilgrimage since scientists deemed that the blood was real. (The Vatican, however, has yet to authenticate the miracle.)

IAT Civitavecchia Viale Garibaldi, 42; 00053 Civitavecchia; phone 0766 25 348, fax 0766 21 834

Lake Bracciano

Romans love the clean air and idyllic views around Lake Bracciano, the volcanic crater-lake northwest of Rome. The most popular villages in the area are the aptly named **Bracciano** and **Trevignano Romano.** In Brac-ciano, the **Castello Orsini-Odescalchi** (Via del Castello, 1; phone 06 998 043 48; open Tuesday–Sunday, 10 a.m.–noon, 3–6:30 p.m.; admis-sion €5.50) dominates the skyline. The 15th-century castle, commis-sioned by the Orsini family, is admired for its sumptuous apartments, decorated by the Zuccari brothers and Antonizzo Romano, and secret garden. Trevignano Romano, once a stronghold of the Orsini, Colonna, and Borgia families because of its enviable position on the lake, is today a peaceful village with a pretty medieval center. On sunny days, you can find many leisure cyclists along the town's tree-lined promenade.

Trains from Rome's Ostiense Station leave hourly from 4:30 a.m. until 10 p.m. The ride takes about an hour. You can also take a COTRAL bus from Lepanto Station. If you're driving to Bracciano, follow the SS493 northwest from Rome about 25 miles (40 km).

Ufficio Turistico   Bracciano Piazza IV Novembre, 5; 00062 Bracciano; phone 06 998 40 062, fax 06 233 246 404; info@lakebracciano.com

The Province of Frosinone

Province of Frosinone Tourist Office   Via Aldo Moro, 465; 03100 Frosinone; phone 0775 833 81; **www.apt.frosinone.it**

Cassino

Cassino was little more than a sleepy provincial town until World War II, when it was virtually destroyed in a clash between Allied and Axis forces. Back then and today, the main tourist draw in Cassino was the abbey of **Montecassino** (Piazza del Montecassino; phone 0776 311 529; open daily, 9 a.m.–1 p.m., 4–6 p.m.; admission €3). Situated high above town at the end of a steep road of switchbacks and undulating curves, this Benedictine abbey was founded in 529. The abbey you see today was completely rebuilt after the original was destroyed by Allied bombs in World War II. There is a vast cemetery on the same hill that contains the graves of hundreds of Canadian, American, and Italian soldiers. Note that the cemetery grounds are open all day, from 9 a.m.–6 p.m. Cassino is reachable via train from Rome.

IAT Cassino   Piazza De Gasperi, 6; 03043 Cassino; phone 0776 212 92, fax 0776 256 92

The Province of Rieti

Province of Rieti Tourist Office Via Cinthia, 87; 02100 Rieti; phone 0746 201 146; **www.apt.rieti.it**

Castelnuovo di Farfa

The **Abbey of Farfa** (Abbazia di Farfa; phone 0765 277065; **www. abbaziadifarfa.it;** open daily, 9:30 a.m.–1 p.m., 3:30–6:30 p.m.) is not especially far away from Rome—about 25 miles—but the landscape of the surrounding Sabine hills evokes a feeling of peace and solitude not easily acquired in the Eternal City. However, the atmosphere wasn't always tranquil. Founded in the sixth century by San Lorenzo Siro, the abbey was destroyed by invading Longobards, Saracens, and warring families; even the French felt the need to ransack the well-positioned abbey in the late 18th century. In fact, the monumental monastery we see today has been at peace only since 1921. The Abbey of Farfa was of major importance during the Middle Ages, having taken up sides with the Holy Roman Empire rather than the Papacy. Its loyalty and strategic location resulted in a grant of autonomy from Charlemagne as well as a measure of protection against papal invasions. A visit to the abbey today rewards you with an opportunity to view some of the ruins of the destroyed monasteries; the cathedral, which contains the ancient Madonna of Farfa; and the green, undulating valley below.

To reach Farfa by train from Rome, alight at Fara Sabina and take a bus from the station to the abbey. By car, take the A1 autostrada and exit at Roma Nord Fiano Romano.

Pro Loco Castelnuovo di Farfa   Via Roma, 42; phone 0765 36217

The Province of Viterbo

Province of Viterbo Tourist Office   Piazza San Carluccio, 5; 01100 Viterbo; phone 0761 304 795, fax 0761 220 957

Viterbo

Like other Etruscan settlements, Viterbo eventually fell under Roman control, where it remained an unimportant outpost in the empire. However, it was not until the 13th century, when Viterbo became home to popes and anti-popes, that the town began to gain prominence. A number of pontiffs fled to Viterbo during the 1200s when the papacy and the Holy Roman Empire were vying for control of Rome, and the town soon became the site of several papal elections. The early Gothic **Palazzo Papale** (Piazza San Lorenzo; phone 0761 341 124; open Tuesday–Sunday, 9 a.m.–6 p.m.; admission €4) was built to house the popes, and its *loggia* was the place from which newly elected popes would bless the awaiting Viterbesi. Despite heavy bombing during World War II, much of Viterbo has retained its medieval charm, including its turreted walls and its medieval quarter defined by the Via San Pellegrino. The **Quartiere San Pellegrino,** though tiny, is considered to have one of the finest groupings of medieval buildings in Latium. A stroll in the neighborhood, through tight, dark streets and beneath lofty arcades, is one of the city's most pleasurable—and cheapest—activities.

Though old man-made Viterbo is impressive, its natural hot springs are the big draw today. About two miles south of the city, you'll find the sulfur baths of **Terme di Papi** (Strada Bagni, 12; phone 0761 3501, fax 0761 352 451; open year-round). A soak will cost you about €22, but it's the perfect way to relax after a stressful trip. Don't forget to pack your own towel and bathing suit.

Driving to Viterbo will take about one and a half hours on the S2 (Via Cassia). If you're taking public transportation, opt for the COTRAL bus, which leaves the Saxa Rubra bus terminal every half hour. To get to Saxa Rubra, take the train from Roma-Nord Station (at Piazza del Popolo). The journey by bus also takes about one and a half hours. Trains to Viterbo are irregular. Check the schedules at Termini or Ostiense stations for details.

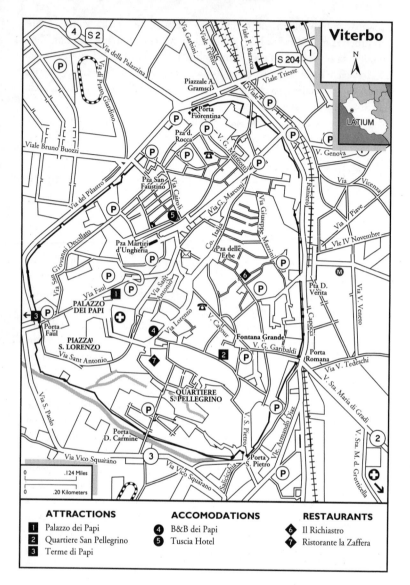

ATTRACTIONS

1 Palazzo dei Papi
2 Quartiere San Pellegrino
3 Terme di Papi

ACCOMODATIONS

4 B&B dei Papi
5 Tuscia Hotel

RESTAURANTS

6 Il Richiastro
7 Ristorante la Zaffera

APT Viterbo   Piazza dell'Oratorio, 2, Palazzo Doria Pamphilj; 01030 San Martino al Cimino (VT); phone 0761 3571, fax 0761 379 233; **www.apt.viterbo.it**

Bagnaia

Known for the **Villa Lante** (Piazza della Villa Lante; phone 0761 288 008; open daily, 9 a.m.–5:30 p.m.; May–August: until 7:30 p.m.;

November–February: until 4 p.m.; guided tours €4), Bagnaia was to Viterbo what Tivoli was to Rome—that is, a retreat for the city's religious nobility. Designed by Vignola in the mid-16th century, the villa is made up of two palaces, the **Palazzo Gambara** and the **Palazzo Montalto,** named for two bishops who lived here, and sprawling, highly manicured gardens, complete with fountains, grottoes, mazes, and pools. Highlights include the **Fountain of the Cardinal's Table,** the **Water Organ,** and the massive **Moorish Fountain,** which joins the villa's two buildings.

Bagnaia is a short trip from Viterbo on Route 205. You can also take bus #6 from Piazza Caduti in Viterbo. For more information on Bagnaia, contact the provincial tourist office in Viterbo (Piazza dell'Oratorio, 2, Palazzo Doria Pamphilj; 01030 San Martino al Cimino (VT); phone 0761 3571, fax 0761 379 233; **www.apt.viterbo.it**).

Bomarzo

The town of Bomarzo was the hereditary home of the powerful Orsini family, who sided with the Guelphs (papal proponents) in their rift with the Ghibellines (Holy Roman Empire supporters). Most of Bomarzo's attractions are due to this wealthy clan's investments. Dominating the town is the **Palazzo Orsini;** however, the star attraction is the Orsini-commissioned **Sacro Bosco** (Via del Parco; phone 0761 924 029; open daily from dawn to dusk; admission €7.50), better known as the "Parco dei Mostri." Drafted by Duke Vicino Orsini in the 16th century after the death of his wife, this macabre park contains grotesques and enormous monsters carved from boulders among the vegetation. Until the beginning of the 20th century, the park had been virtually abandoned and overgrown. After it was rediscovered, the Parco dei Mostri and its "residents," such as the ogre *(orco),* giant mask *(mascherone),* and the crooked house, became hits among the surrealist set, including Salvador Dalí and Jean Cocteau.

To get to Bomarzo, take the COTRAL bus from Viterbo's Viale Trento. By car, take the A29 east from Viterbo, then follow the signs to Bomarzo. Get off at Attigliano-Bomarzo if you are taking the train.

Pro Loco Bomarzo Via Borghese, 10; 01020 Bomarzo; phone/fax 0761 924 021

Civita di Bagnoregio

An easy day trip from Viterbo and Orvieto (see Part Eight, The Best of Umbria), Civita di Bagnoregio, located uphill from the burg of Bagnoregio, has a fairy tale–like quality. The tiny medieval village of approximately 30 inhabitants is perched high on a hill whose sides have eroded over time. The result is unusually dramatic and offers fantastic views of the rolling landscape of Latium. However, years of erosion also meant the collapse of many buildings and the eventual evacuation of most of Civita di Bagnoregio's residents. Today, many of the village's original citizens live in the town of Bagnoregio. Wealthy foreigners and artists occupy most of Civita's remaining buildings.

COTRAL buses from Viterbo and ASP buses from Orvieto make regular trips to Bagnoregio, at least three times daily. Once in Bagnoregio, follow the signs to the passageway *(passaggio)* to Civita. More information is available in the province of Viterbo's tourist office (Piazza dell'Oratorio, 2, Palazzo Doria Pamphilj; 01030 San Martino al Cimino (VT); phone 0761 3571, fax 0761 379 233; **www.apt.viterbo.it**).

Lake Bolsena

Wine has played a starring role in history of this area north of Viterbo, near the Umbria border. In 1263, in the town of **Bolsena,** wine turned to blood in the hands of a doubting priest celebrating mass at the church of **Santa Cristina** (Piazza del Miracolo, 1; phone 0761 799 067; open daily, 7 a.m.–12:30 p.m., 4–8 p.m.; admission free). Immediately upon hearing of this miracle of transubstantiation, Pope Clement IV inaugurated the Feast of Corpus Domini, still celebrated today throughout the Catholic world. Within the 11th-century church of Santa Cristina, you can visit the Altar of the Miracle, the Chapel of the Miracle, and a network of catacombs where some tombs remain sealed.

Located approximately halfway between Viterbo and Bolsena, **Montefiascone** is known by wine lovers as the town that produces one of Latium's most famous whites, Est! Est! Est! As the story goes, before 12th-century bishop Johann Fugger set off on a journey to Rome, he had his charge Martin go ahead of him and mark with chalk the inns that served the best wine. When Martin reached Montefiascone, he wrote "Est! Est! Est!" to proclaim that the wine here was particularly excellent. Bishop Fugger was eventually interred here at the church of **San Flaviano.** The Fiera del Vino Est! Est! Est!, a festival dedicated to the wine, takes place during the first half of August.

The towns around Lake Bolsena merit a day trip from Viterbo, but they are a bit far if coming from Rome. The area is most easily reached via the S2 highway northwest through Viterbo. Or, take the A1 *autostrada,* exit at Orvieto (Umbria), and follow the signs to Bolsena. You can also take the COTRAL bus to Bolsena from the Saxa Rubra station (take the train from Roma-Nord to get there). However, Montefiascone is most easily reached by car.

Pro Loco Bolsena   Piazza Matteotti, 25; 01023 Bolsena; phone 0761 7951, fax 0761 795 555; comunebolsena@pelagus.it

IAT Montefiascone   Largo Plebiscito, 1; 01027 Montefiascone; phone 0761 824 567, fax 0761 824 745; **www.cittadimontefiascone.it**

Lake Vico

Caprarola

Like the town of Bagnaia, Caprarola has as its star attraction an aristo-cratic residence designed by Vignola. Originally conceived as a fortress, the reconstruction of the **Palazzo Farnese** (Piazza del Farnese; phone 0761 646 052; open Monday–Saturday, 9 a.m.–5 p.m.; summer: until 7 p.m.; admission €4) was commissioned by Cardinal Alessandro II Far-nese (nephew of Pope Paul III) in 1559 to be used as the Farnese family's country estate. The pentagon-shaped building crowns the hill above the austere town of Caprarola and is considered one of the most notable examples of Mannerist architecture. You can view richly decorated fres-coes by such artists as Vignola and Taddeo Zuccaro (guided tours only) or stroll through the estate's formal gardens. In summer, there are Renais-sance music concerts in the *palazzo's* courtyard.

Caprarola is located approximately ten miles southeast from Viterbo. Take the A1 to the Attigliano exit, and follow the signs. You can catch one of seven daily buses to Caprarola from Viterbo at the Riello station just outside the city.

Pro Loco Caprarola   Via F. Nocolai, 2; 01032 Caprarola; phone 0761 646 157

Norchia

Not to be confused with Norcia (see Part Eight, The Best of Umbria), Norchia was a powerful Etruscan settlement in Latium, reaching its peak between the fourth and third centuries B.C. As in all other Etruscan cities, the only remnants of the Norchian civilization are the tombs. However, Norchia's **Etruscan Necropolis** (Via delle Necropoli; no phone; open daily; admission free) is considered to be one of the most impressive finds. It consists of Archaic period (sixth–fifth centuries B.C.) tombs and Hel-lenistic period (fourth–second centuries B.C.) tombs, built high on rocky cliffs using a terracing method. The highest tombs are the most elaborate and are decorated with moldings, high façades, and a *finta porta* (fake door). Lower tombs contain less decorative sarcophagi. According to Etr-uscologist George Dennis, who traveled throughout Italy in the 1840s, a traveler visiting Norchia "must admit, that though nameless and unchron-icled, there are few sites in Etruria so interesting as this."

You will need a car to get to Norchia. Take the S2 north from Rome or south from Viterbo to Vetralla and follow the signs to Norchia. More information about Norchia is available from the tourist office in Tar-quinia (Piazza Cavour, 1; 01016 Tarquinia; phone 0766 856 384, fax 0766 840 479; **www.tarquinia.net**).

Tarquinia

One of the most important cities of Etruria, Tarquinia was already a major agricultural and industrial center in the seventh century B.C. The city enjoyed a powerful position in the region until the mid-fourth century B.C., when it went to war with Rome. By 281 B.C., Tarquinia was under Roman control, and its population and wealth began to decline. Luckily, one of the most extensive collections of Etruscan artifacts was left behind. The **Museo Nazionale di Tarquinia** (Piazza Cavour, 1; phone 0766 856 036; open Tuesday–Sunday, 8:30 a.m.–7:30 p.m.; admission €5, €8 with necropolis), housed in the Renaissance-era Palazzo Vitelleschi, chronicles the Etruscan way of life in Tarquinia with ceramics, coins, sculptures, and jewels, and features a pair of terra cotta winged horses, the erstwhile symbol of Tarquinia. On the Monterozzi hill, the **Necropolis of Monterozzi** (Via delle Necropoli; phone 0766 856 308; open Tuesday–Sunday, 8:30 a.m.–1 hour before sunset; admission €5, €8 with museum) contains a spectacular variety of stone tombs, many of which are painted. The tombs of the Panthers, Bulls, Jugglers, Lionesses, Leopards, and Shields, to name a few, are some of the earliest examples of Italic art.

Tarquinia can be reached by COTRAL bus. From Rome, take the bus from Lepanto station to Civitavecchia and change. COTRAL bus service to Tarquinia is also available from Viterbo. Tarquinia is about an hour away by car via the A12 or SS1. Train service to Tarquinia is irregular.

IAT Tarquinia Piazza Cavour, 1; 01016 Tarquinia; phone 0766 856 384, fax 0766 840 479; **www.tarquinia.net**

Tuscania

Deriving its name from the Tuscia (a.k.a., southern Etruria) region, the quaint, walled city of Tuscania was a major city under the jurisdiction of Tarquinia. Like Tarquinia, Tuscania also contained a number of richly decorated tombs. Many of the sarcophagi from these tombs can be found at the **Museo Nazionale Archeologico ex Convento di Santa Maria del Reposo** (Piazza del Reposo, 36; phone 0761 436 209; open Tuesday–Sunday, 8:30 a.m.–7:30 p.m.; admission free). Also worth a look are the 11th-century churches of **San Pietro** and **Santa Maria Maggiore,** both located in the town's medieval quarter.

You need a car to reach Tuscania. Follow the Via Cassia north, then east, from Tarquinia. It is approximately 20 miles from Tarquinia.

Ufficio Turistico Tuscania Piazza Basile, 4; 01017 Tuscania; phone 0761 436 371, fax 0761 443 664

The Province of Latina

Province of Latina Tourist Office Via Duca Del Mare, 19; 04100 Latina; phone 0773 695 404; **www.aptlatinaturismo.it**

Riviera d'Ulisse

This string of beach resorts on the Tyrrhenian Sea, the biggest tourist draw in the province of Latina, derives its name (the "Riviera of Ulysses") from Homer's *Odyssey*. In the epic tale, the hero, Aeneas, flees from Troy and lands in on these shores. The lore of the entire area from Gaeta to the rocky outcroppings along Monte Circeo is tied up with Greek mythology, and, to the ancient eye, the natural landscape could very well have been mistaken for a rugged Greek isle ringed with white sand.

Gaeta is historically significant because it was the last stronghold of the Bourbons before falling to Garibaldi's red shirts in 1861. But few people travel to Gaeta looking for the past. As one of Latium's main beach towns—it boasts seven gorgeous, if cluttered, strands—Gaeta fills up in the summer with fishing boats, Italian and German tourists, and Italy-based American soldiers on leave. The town is divided into two sections. The medieval core is built above the more modern town, and it consists of a cluster of churches and a towering medieval castle, which was built over the course of the three centuries. Modern Gaeta juts out into the Gulf of Gaeta, creating a horn-shaped stretch of beaches, low-rise hotels, and cliffside hideaways.

Situated on a promontory with a bleached white fortress at cliff's edge, **Sperlonga** is a stunning fishing village where more Romans than tourists summer. Other than its crystalline beaches (some of the cleanest of the Tyrrhenian) and tranquil mien, Sperlonga is most known for the **Grotto and Villa of Tiberius,** located at the far left end of the beach *(spiaggia)*. Emperor Tiberius had this villa built along the seaside after the death of his son. The adjacent grotto, which served as a banquet hall, was decorated with statues depicting gods from the *Odyssey*. Not much of the villa is left. However, many magnificent, allegorical statues from the grotto, including the *Blinding of Polyphemus* and *Scylla's Attack on Ulysses*), have been reconstructed and placed in the **National Archaeological Museum of Sperlonga** (Via Flacca; phone 0771 54 028; open Tuesday–Sunday, 9 a.m.–1 hour before sunset; admission €4).

Further along the coast is **Terracina,** a city of possibly Etruscan origin with a direct link to Rome along the Via Appia. Terracina's Roman heritage is evident among its ruins, most dramatic of which is the **Temple of Jupiter,** which sits atop an Acropolis, also known as Monte Sant'Angelo. Terracina's 11th century **Duomo** (Piazza Municipio; phone 0773 701 100; open daily, 8 a.m.–6:30 p.m.), San Cesario, is built on the ruins of the Roman Forum Emiliano and contains beautiful mosaics.

Finally, **San Felice Circeo,** named for the sorceress Circe, is known for its natural beauty. Dozens of grottoes, spectacular rock faces along the sea, and the **Parco del Circeo** (information office at Via Carlo Alberto, 107; 04016 Sabaudia; phone 0773 511 386) draw kayakers, windsurfers, hikers, bird-watchers, and sybarites to its shores.

The best way to reach the cities of the Ulysses Riviera is to follow the coastal highway Via Flacca. Trains are available from Rome to Terracina and Sperlonga (at Fondi-Sperlonga). Other destinations along the coast can be reached by bus; but, note that the buses are infrequent, even in the high season.

Pro Loco Gaeta   Buonomo Vico IV, 24; 04024 Gaeta; phone 0771 450 317, fax 0771 465 040; **www.prolocogaeta.it**

Pro Loco Sperlonga   Piazza della Rimembranza; 04029 Sperlonga; phone 0771 54 796, fax 0771 549 798

Pro Loco Terracina   Via Leopardi; 04019 Terracina; phone 0773 727 759

Pro Loco San Felice Circeo   Piazza Lanzuisi, 1; 04017 San Felice Circeo; phone 0773 547 770; **www.circeomare.com**

Isole Pontine

The closest cluster of islands to Rome has long been a favorite vacation spot for Italians, but foreign tourists are only now discovering the Pontines. Only two of the Pontine Islands—**Ponza** and **Ventotene**—are inhabited; only Ponza has adequate accommodations and dining. Wildlife preserves on both islands should be teeming with interesting migratory fowl; however, these areas are threatened by the many visitors who come here for sport shooting and bird-hunting. Likewise, the beaches in Ponza and Ventotene are charming, but they are suffering from erosion and poor zoning laws. But don't strike the Pontine Islands from your list too quickly; they can be an ideal, relaxing weekend getaway should you be staying in Rome for an extended period.

The Pontine Islands can only be reached by ferry in about 1½ to 2 hours; you'll want to drive to the ferry so you have transportation once you arrive. Ferries leave from ports at Anzio and Formia, and the schedules vary by season. In the summer, check the "Cronaca di Roma" section of the newspaper *Il Messaggero* for times, or visit **www.gruppotirrenia.it** (in Italian only).

Pro Loco Isole Pontine   Via Piazzetta, 11; 04020 Ventotene; phone 0771 85257

Ninfa

The ghost town of Ninfa has all the makings of a medieval fairy tale. As legend has it, a nymph's tears formed the stream that hems in the gardens and abandoned medieval buildings here. Scant records show that Ninfa prospered from the 8th through the 14th centuries, but countless turf wars and then malaria virtually wiped out all of the residents here. Only in the 1920s was Ninfa rediscovered by a member of the Caetani family (the family who last laid claim to the town). Don Gelasio Caetani decided that Ninfa was the perfect place for planting botanical gardens. Today, travelers can visit the gardens and explore Ninfa's mysterious environs. There is also a World Wildlife Fund (WWF) bird sanctuary on the land here. You can purchase tickets for the **Gardens of Ninfa** from the WWF in Rome (Viale Giulio Cesare, 128; phone 06 372 3646; open April–October on the first Saturday and Sunday of the month, 9 a.m.–noon, 3–6:30 p.m.; admission €7.50). Ninfa is reachable by car on the SS7.

Additional information about Ninfa is available from the WWF or the provincial tourist office in Latina (Via Duca Del Mare, 19; 04100 Latina; phone 0773 695 404; **www.aptlatinaturismo.it**).

Part Eight

The Best of Umbria

Italy's Green Heart

Umbria, an agricultural region of unspoiled hill towns, has earned many nicknames. Bordered by Tuscany, Latium, and the Marches, this verdant, landlocked swath of olive groves, sunflower crops, ilex bushes, and emerald pastures is often referred to as the Green Heart of Italy. National and regional parks and nature preserves make up about a third of Umbria, and the region is a favorite getaway for city dwellers from Tuscany and Latium. Yet even in the more trafficked areas around **Perugia** and **Assisi,** the landscape is largely uninterrupted by sprawl.

Rife with Renaissance art and noteworthy churches, tourism has slowly but surely crept into Umbria. Some have even ventured to call Umbria "the new Tuscany." Travelers who have opted to forego the predictable pleasures of the region to Umbria's west have found here uncrowded museums; *piazze* populated with locals; and an overall slower pace of life.

That there's room for reflection in Umbria is no surprise. Also called the "Land of the Saints," the region gave birth to many of Christianity's most pious followers, including Saints Benedict, Scholastica, Clare, and Francis. Assisi, native home of St. Francis and the site of the one of the most significant churches in Christendom, is second only to Rome in religious tourism. But, even when Assisi becomes overrun with pilgrims and tour buses, its idyllic charms are not entirely lost.

Umbria is made up of only two provinces—**Perugia** and **Terni.** The former takes up about three-quarters of Umbria's land mass, and includes the cities of Perugia and Assisi, among many others. In contrast, the province of Terni is quite sparse. But don't overlook it. **Orvieto,** one of the gems of Central Italy, can be found here.

APT Umbria   Via Mazzini, 21; 06100 Perugia; phone 075 575 951, fax 075 573 6828; **www.umbria2000.it**

CALENDAR OF EVENTS IN UMBRIA

February

Bruschetta Festival, Spello   February 5. Toasted bread slathered with garlic, tomatoes, and other spreads takes center stage.

Festa di San Valentino, Terni   February 14. The hometown of the patron saint for lovers throws a party in his honor.

March

Settimana dei Beni Culturali (Cultural Week)   One week in March or April. During cultural week, all state-owned museums and archaeological sites are open free of charge. For more information, phone 075 574 111.

April

Antiques Fair, Todi   First three weeks of the month.

Settimana Santa (Holy Week)   Throughout the region. Special Holy Week processions are held in Assisi.

May

Coloriamo I Cieli (Let's Color the Skies), Castiglione del Lago   May 1. A kite-flying and hot-air balloon event.

Corsa dei Ceri, Gubbio   May 15. Townspeople race to the top of Mt. Ingino carrying three enormous candles.

Palio della Balestra, Gubbio   Last Sunday in May. Traditional crossbow tournament pits teams from Gubbio against rivals from nearby Sansepolcro (Tuscany). Sansepolcro hosts the same event on the second Sunday in September.

June

Corpus Christi, Orvieto   Early to mid-June. Though this procession takes place all over the Catholic world, Orvieto is where a cathedral was built to commemorate the miracle of transubstantiation.

Spello Infiorate, Spello   Same date as Corpus Christi. Spello's historic center is carpeted with flowers to commemorate the religious holiday.

Mercato delle Gaite, Bevagna   Last ten days of June. Food and crafts in the old tradition.

Visiting the Region

Getting around Umbria

The countryside of Umbria is best explored by car, but most areas are accessible via bus and some via rail. Because the region is off the beaten track, there is no guarantee that towns are directly linked to one another.

Festival of Two Worlds, Spoleto   June–July. Contemporary festival of music, theater, and dance, one of the largest and best known in Italy.

July

Giostra della Quintana, Foligno   First Sunday of the month (also in September). Medieval jousting tournament between the town's ten wards.

Umbria Jazz Festival, Perugia and Terni   Throughout the month. Italy's premier jazz festival features performances by international legends in jazz and blues.

August

Agosto Corcianese, Corciano   Throughout the month. Traditional fair highlighting medieval craft-making traditions.

Torneo dei Quartieri, Gubbio   August 14. Gubbio's three districts compete against one another in archery and flag-tossing.

Chamber Music Festival, Città di Castello   August–September.

September

Giostra della Quintana, Foligno   Second Sunday of the month. Medieval jousting tournament between the town's ten wards. Also held in July.

Sagra Musicale Umbra (Sacred Music Festival), Perugia   Last week in September.

October

Festa di San Francesco, Assisi   October 3–4. Festival and ceremony in honor of St. Francis.

Eurochocolate Festival, Perugia   Mid–late October.

November

All Souls' Fair, Perugia   First week in November.

December

Umbria Jazz Winter, Orvieto   December 29–early January.

For instance, if you are riding the rails from Orvieto to Perugia, you will have to transfer along the way. Umbria's main train transfer stations are at Foligno and Terni.

Bus service between cities is most efficient on weekdays, when Umbrians depend on the bus to commute. **APM** (Azienda Perugia della Mobilità) is the largest bus company in Umbria, offering frequent service

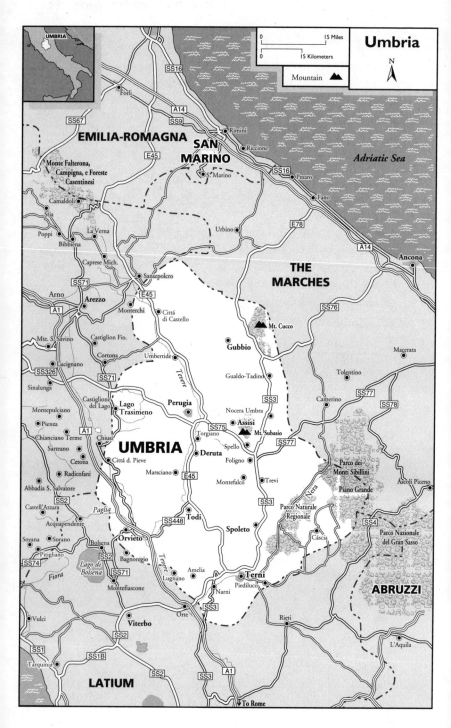

between Perugia and northern Umbrian towns and, less frequently, to towns in southern Umbria. **ATC** (Azienda Trasporti Consorziale Terni) serves the southern corridor, with regularly scheduled weekday service. **SSIT** (Società Spoletina di Imprese Trasporti) has a number of weekday and Saturday itineraries between Spoleto, Foligno, and points south, and also makes scheduled trips to Assisi, Perugia, and Rome.

Ironically, though a car is necessary to traverse the undulating terrain of the region, most of Umbria's well-preserved hill towns do not allow cars in their city centers. Orvieto, Perugia, and Assisi all have laws limiting vehicles other than taxis during certain times of the day. In these towns, it is best to park outside the city walls in designated parking lots (near the train station, in most cases). You will usually find bus service into the city.

APM	phone 075 506 781	www.apmperugia.it
ATC	phone 0744 492 711	www.atcterni.it
SSIT	phone 0743 212 208	www.spoletina.com

When to Visit

Umbria blossoms in the spring, and its hill towns are refreshingly cool in the summer. Musical fans of all stripes head to Umbria in June and July, when Spoleto hosts the **Festival of Two Worlds** and Perugia hosts the **Umbria Jazz Festival**—the crowds can be intense. Fall and winter are perhaps the best time to visit this region. In the late fall, the valleys of Umbria are awash in autumnal shades of red, burnished orange, and yellow; virgin olives are going to press; and vineyard grapes are harvested. The region's culinary fare reaches its pinnacle in winter, when robust flavors from truffles to *porchetta* are brought to the table. Winter can be bitter here, but it's the best time to get to know the real Umbria and its people.

Quick Glance at the Towns of Umbria

Following is a listing of cities and touring areas in Umbria by province. For each city or area, we provide an overall rating to describe how rewarding that place is to visit. We also include a short comment about the place. Use this as a reference for day trips or extended holidays.

City/Area	Overall Rating	Comment
Province of Perugia		
Assisi	★★★★★	The Basilica of St. Francis should not be missed
Bettona	★★½	The Etruscans' only outpost on the Tiber's left bank
Bevagna	★★★	Ancient Roman outpost with a noteworthy theater
Città di Castello	★★★★	One of the most important modern art collections in Italy resides here
Corciano	★★½	Medieval roots are highlighted during traditional August festival

Quick Glance at the Towns of Umbria *(continued)*

City/Area	Overall Rating	Comment
Province of Perugia *(continued)*		
Deruta	★★★½	Hand-made ceramics have put the town on the map
Foligno	★★★	The Giostro della Quintana rivals Siena's Palio in authenticity and drama
Gubbio	★★★★★	Stern, medieval Italy on glorious display
Lake Trasimeno	★★★★	Idyllic, lakeside views and priceless Peruginos
Montefalco	★★★★	The "Balcony of Umbria"
Norcia	★★★½	Birthplace of salami and St. Benedict
Perugia	★★★★★	Umbria's liveliest city
Spello	★★★½	Historically Roman, with a "beautiful" chapel
Spoleto	★★★★½	Picturesque home of famous music festival
Todi	★★★★	"The most livable small town in the world"
Torgiano	★★★	Visit its wine museum
Province of Terni		
Orvieto	★★★★★	Gorgeous melding of Etruscan, medieval, and Gothic eras
Terni	★★½	Waterfalls and St. Valentine

The Province of Perugia

Province of Perugia Tourist Office   Piazza Italia, 11, 06100 Perugia; phone 075 36811; **www.provincia.perugia.it**

Perugia

Americans may know Perugia as the home of Perugina, the chocolate factory that produces the ubiquitous, silver-wrapped hazelnut and chocolate "kisses" called Baci. Perugina has been a modern moneymaker for the capital of Umbria, as has Buitoni, Italy's largest manufacturer of pasta. Perugia's transformation from its agrarian roots to an industrial hub has meant a rise in the population, and a lower town of urban housing and business hotels has sprung up around the base of the old town. Meanwhile, the State University and the School for Foreigners (Università per Stranieri) draws about 30,000 students and academics to Perugia each year, helping the city maintain its coffers and its role as a cultural center. Today's Perugia is best witnessed along the Corso Vannucci, the main drag in the historical center, and in **Piazza Italia,** Perugia's lovely, landscaped perch high above the countryside, both of which are constantly abuzz with locals, students, and tourists.

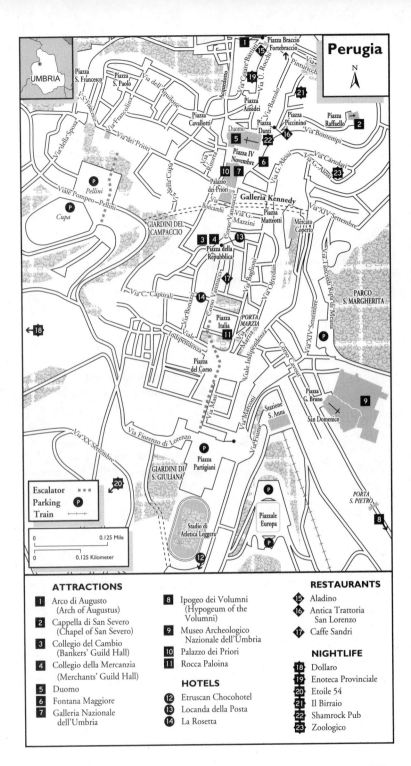

Perugia

N

UMBRIA

ATTRACTIONS

1. Arco di Augusto (Arch of Augustus)
2. Cappella di San Severo (Chapel of San Severo)
3. Collegio del Cambio (Bankers' Guild Hall)
4. Collegio della Mercanzia (Merchants' Guild Hall)
5. Duomo
6. Fontana Maggiore
7. Galleria Nazionale dell'Umbria
8. Ipogeo dei Volumni (Hypogeum of the Volumni)
9. Museo Archeologico Nazionale dell'Umbria
10. Palazzo dei Priori
11. Rocca Paloina

HOTELS

12. Etruscan Chocohotel
13. Locanda della Posta
14. La Rosetta

RESTAURANTS

15. Aladino
16. Antica Trattoria San Lorenzo
17. Caffe Sandri

NIGHTLIFE

18. Dollaro
19. Enoteca Provinciale
20. Etoile 54
21. Il Birraio
22. Shamrock Pub
23. Zoologico

Given such lively scenes, it is hard to believe that this town has a dark past. Founded in the fifth century B.C., the town of Peiresa was one of the last cities of the Etruscan League to suffer conquest at the hands of the Romans. Revolts were common during the Republican period, and a power struggle in 140 B.C. led to the complete destruction of the city. From this, Emperor Augustus took his cue and rebuilt over the rubble, naming the new city Augusta Perusia. The Middle Ages were particularly turbulent and saw the patrician Oddi and Baglioni families wage war against one another for control of the *comune*. In one battle, in which the Baglioni family used the **Duomo** as a fortress, so much blood was spilled that the church had to be scoured clean and reconsecrated. Various mercenaries, including Braccio Fortebraccio ("Strong Arm") and small-time rulers of provincial kingdoms, captured—and lost—power of the city during the 14th and 15th centuries, none being able to stay out of trouble, nor win over the rambunctious Perugians.

Since its days as an Etruscan city, Perugia prided itself on being self-sufficient; No one—not even the pope, to whom Perugia was mostly loyal—was fully able to quell the citizens' independent streak. Pope Paul III didn't take too kindly to the Perugian attitude and levied a heavy tax on salt in 1538. As expected, the Perugians revolted, giving the pope a reason to send in troops to squash the rebellion. Shortly thereafter, the pope seized Baglioni property and erected the **Rocca Paolina,** a fortress on the edge of town that was inscribed with the words "Ad Repellandam Perusinorum Audaciam" ("to curb the audacity of the Perugian people"). Today, an escalator and walkway from the modern town to the historical center cuts through the shadowy medieval halls and galleries of the Rocca—you can just imagine the gory scenes that must have played out here.

Perugia lies at the junction of several highways, including the S220, S75, S3b-E45, off of the A1 *autostrada*. Parking is available outside the city center in the Piazza Vittorio Veneto, outside the main rail station, Stazione Fontivegge, and in Piazza dei Partigiani. The car parks are open from around 6 a.m. until midnight, and charge approximately €1.50 per hour. Piazza dei Partigiani is the main bus hub, where you'll find APT buses that connect to the rest of Umbria and SULGA (phone 075 500 9641) buses, which run between Perugia and Rome and Perugia and Florence. Travel to Perugia by rail is relatively frequent but not always easy, especially if you are carrying a lot of luggage. If coming from Rome, you will need to transfer at Foligno, from Florence at Terontola. Direct trains from these cities are rare.

APT Perugia   Palazzo dei Priori, Corso Vannucci, 19; 06100 Perugia; phone 075 5771, fax 075 572 4276; **portal.comune.perugia.it**

Arch of Augustus

Type of Attraction Ancient Roman archway

Location Piazza Fortebraccio

Admission Free

Hours Always open

Phone None

When to Go Anytime

Overall Appeal by Age Group

Pre-school —		Teens ★★		Over 30 ★★
Grade school ★★★		Young Adults ★★		Seniors ★★

Authors' Rating ★★

How Much Time to Allow Less than 15 minutes

Description and Comments After the Roman conquest of the Etruscan stronghold of Peiresa in 310 B.C., Emperor Augustus reclaimed the town and renamed it Augusta Perusia. The city's "new" name is inscribed on this arch, one of the best-preserved in Italy. Today, the Arco di Augusto shares the same piazza as the Università per Stranieri.

Cappella di San Severo

Type of Attraction Home of Perugia's largest Raphael fresco

Location Piazza Raffaello

Admission €2

Hours April–September: daily, 10 a.m.–1:30 p.m., 2:30–6:30 p.m.; October–March: daily, 10:30 a.m.–1:30 p.m., 2:30–4:30 p.m.

Phone 075 573 3864

When to Go Mornings

Special Comments The chapel is out of the way and small, with only enough room for a handful of people. Hours are occasionally left up to the attendant on duty.

Overall Appeal by Age Group

Pre-school —		Teens ★★		Over 30 ★★★
Grade school ★★		Young Adults ★★★		Seniors ★★★★

Authors' Rating ★★★

How Much Time to Allow 15–30 minutes

Description and Comments At the top of a hill in a sleepy corner of town, you'll find the small church of San Severo which houses one of Raphael's first frescoes, the *Holy Trinity and Saints*. His teacher, Perugino, painted the lower register of saints some years after Raphael's untimely death.

Collegio del Cambio

Type of Attraction A showcase of Perugino's art

Location Corso Vannucci, 25

Admission €3, includes the Collegio della Mercanzia

Hours March–October and December 20–January 6: Monday–Saturday, 9 a.m.–12:30 p.m., 2:30–5:30 p.m.; Sunday, 9 a.m.–12:30 p.m.; November–December 19 and January 7–February: Tuesday–Saturday, 8 a.m.–2 p.m.; Sunday, 9 a.m.–12:30 p.m.

Phone 075 572 8599

When to Go Early morning or late afternoon

Overall Appeal by Age Group

Pre-school —		Teens ★★		Over 30 ★★★
Grade school ★★		Young Adults ★★★		Seniors ★★★

Authors' Rating ★★★

How Much Time to Allow 30 minutes

Description and Comments A little over a decade after painting one of the Sistine Chapel's most recognized frescoes—the *Giving of the Keys to St. Peter*—Umbria's greatest Renaissance artist, Perugino (born Pietro Vannucci), returned to his home province to decorate the bankers' and money-changers' guild hall. On the hall's four walls, Perugino, who was a self-proclaimed nonbeliever, painted typical biblical themes, such as the Transfiguration, but he also included the mythological figures of Fortitude, Temperance, Prudence, and Justice. What's fascinating about these scenes is that the artist clothed all of his subjects in the finest Renaissance garb, most likely the same type of clothing that the wealthy bankers wore when they met in this hall. Art historians are almost certain that Perugino's pupil, Raphael, painted all or part of the figure of Fortitude, because the style is considered much more advanced than that of the then-aging Perugino. The latter's curmudgeonly self-portrait can be seen on the left wall.

Collegio della Mercanzia

Type of Attraction Luxurious 14th-century meeting room

Location Corso Vannucci, 15

Admission €3, includes the Collegio del Cambio

Hours March–October: Monday–Saturday, 9 a.m.–1 p.m., 2:30–5:30 p.m.; Sunday, 9 a.m.–1 p.m.; November–February: Tuesday–Sunday, 8 a.m.–2 p.m.

Phone 075 573 0366

When to Go Mornings

Overall Appeal by Age Group

Pre-school —		Teens ★★		Over 30 ★★
Grade school ★★		Young Adults ★★		Seniors ★★

Authors' Rating ★★

How Much Time to Allow 15 minutes

Description and Comments Another guild hall in the Palazzo dei Priori, this one for Perugia's merchants, is richly decorated with carved wooden paneling from floor to vaulted ceiling. The 14th-century hall is notable because its woodwork—designed with repetitive motifs of clovers, diamonds, and other angular shapes—shows evidence of Islamic influence.

Duomo

Type of Attraction Perugia's Gothic cathedral
Location Piazza IV Novembre
Admission Free
Hours Daily, 8 a.m.–7 p.m.
Phone 075 572 3832
When to Go Anytime
Overall Appeal by Age Group

Pre-school ★★	Teens ★★★	Over 30 ★★★★★
Grade school ★★★	Young Adults ★★★★	Seniors ★★★★★

Authors' Rating ★★★★★
How Much Time to Allow 30 minutes to 1 hour

Description and Comments A modest building in comparison to the city's town hall, the Palazzo dei Priori, the Cathedral of San Lorenzo, or Duomo, has a largely unadorned façade, except for the hundreds of pigeons that take shelter in the church's outer niches. Perugia's Duomo is significant because it holds the so-called wedding ring of Mary, which the Perugians stole from the nearby town of Chiusi in 1488. The ring is kept locked inside 15 nested boxes that are hidden behind a red velvet curtain high above the Cappella del Santo Anello. Each year on July 30 (the day the ring was brought to Perugia) and on the penultimate Sunday in January (said to be Mary and Joseph's wedding anniversary), the golden band is brought out of hiding during a lavish ceremony. In addition to this important relic, the Duomo houses an altarpiece of Madonna and saints by Luca Signorelli, decorative choir stalls by Giovanni Battista Bastone, and a collection of amulets and trinkets left by believers who experienced miracles after having prayed at the cathedral.

Fontana Maggiore

Type of Attraction Perugia's main fountain
Location Piazza IV Novembre
Admission Free
Hours Always open
Phone None
When to Go Anytime
Overall Appeal by Age Group

Pre-school —	Teens ★★	Over 30 ★★
Grade school ★★	Young Adults ★★	Seniors ★★

Authors' Rating ★★

How Much Time to Allow Less than 15 minutes

Description and Comments If you've seen the elaborate municipal fountains that grace *piazze* in Florence or Rome, your first impression of the medieval Fontana Maggiore will surely be disappointing. But you have to move closer (as close as the menacing iron fence will allow) to appreciate the fountain's artistic subtleties. Fra Bevignate designed the polygonal fountain around 1278, and Niccola Pisano—and, to a greater extent, his son Andrea—is credited with creating the intricately carved panels and figures that line the fountain's two basins. Note the 12 signs of the zodiac, a favorite theme in the Middle Ages, and the depictions of the sciences and arts.

Galleria Nazionale dell'Umbria

Type of Attraction Italy's largest collection of Umbrian art
Location Corso Vannucci, 19, 3rd floor (2nd *piano*)
Admission €4
Hours Monday–Saturday, 9 a.m.–7 p.m.; Sunday, 9 a.m.–8 p.m.; closed 1st Monday of each month
Phone 075 574 1247
When to Go Mornings or late afternoon—the museum is not typically crowded
Overall Appeal by Age Group

Pre-school —	Teens ★★★	Over 30 ★★★★
Grade school ★★	Young Adults ★★★	Seniors ★★★★

Authors' Rating ★★★★
How Much Time to Allow 1 hour

Description and Comments At press time, the lower floors of the Palazzo dei Priori, which houses the National Gallery of Umbria, were being renovated so that the large collection of Umbrian masterpieces could be spread out. For the time being, the exhibit is an intimate maze of altarpieces, polyptychs, sculptures, and paintings from some of Italy's most notable artists. Spanning the 13th through the 19th centuries, the museum's collection features treasures from the Umbrian and Tuscan schools, including works by Perugino, Pinturicchio, Duccio di Buoninsegna, and Piero della Francesca. Marchigiano artist Gentile da Fabriano is also represented with a somber *Madonna and Child with Angels,* as is Florentine painter Fra Angelico, whose gilded *San Domenico Polyptych* is one of the finest Renaissance pieces this side of Florence.

Museo Archeologico Nazionale dell'Umbria

Type of Attraction Remnants of ancient Umbrian civilizations on display
Location Piazza Giordano Bruno, 10
Admission €2.50

Hours Monday–Saturday, 9 a.m.–7 p.m.; Sunday, 9 a.m.–1 p.m.

Phone 075 572 7141

When to Go Anytime

Overall Appeal by Age Group

Pre-school ★★		Teens ★★★		Over 30 ★★★
Grade school ★★		Young Adults ★★★		Seniors ★★★

Authors' Rating ★★★

How Much Time to Allow 1–2 hours

Description and Comments A thoroughly modern museum despite its subject, Perugia's archaeological museum features multimedia displays, well-written English descriptions of relics, and good lighting. The museum is divided into two time periods—the Prehistoric and the Etrusco-Roman eras—the former occupying the ground floor of the former Dominican cloister of San Domenico, the latter occupying the upper floor. The Prehistoric collection is further divided into the Stone Age, the Metal Age, and the Bellucci Collection, which includes a fascinating store of some 1,700 amulets and folkloric trinkets dug up in central and southern Italy. The Etrusco-Roman collection includes ancient funerary monuments, reconstructed chariots, artworks of bronze and black *bucchero* ceramic, and various household tools. The prize of the entire museum is also located here. The third-century B.C. "Cippo" di Perugia is a large stone on which the longest surviving piece of Etruscan text has survived. The Cippo is believed to have been a real estate contract between two families.

Palazzo dei Priori

Type of Attraction Perugia's town hall

Location Piazza IV Novembre

Admission Free

Hours March–October: Tuesday–Sunday, 9 a.m.–1 p.m., 3–7 p.m.; October–March: Tuesday–Saturday, 10 a.m.–1 p.m., 3:30–6 p.m.; Sunday, 1–4 p.m. (see also times for Collegio del Cambio, Collegio della Mercanzia, and Galleria Nazionale dell'Umbria)

Phone 075 574 1247

When to Go Anytime

Overall Appeal by Age Group

Pre-school ★		Teens ★★		Over 30 ★★★
Grade school ★★		Young Adults ★★★		Seniors ★★★

Authors' Rating ★★★

How Much Time to Allow 30 minutes

Description and Comments The vessel of Perugia's civic life, the Priors' Palace was built in phases between the 13th and 15th centuries, which explains its asymmetrical façade. Sitting in the heart of the city at the intersection of the Corso Vannucci and Piazza IV Novembre, the *palazzo* houses three of the most significant rooms in Perugia—the Collegio del Cambio, the Collegio della Mercanzia, and the Galleria Nazionale dell'Umbria—all three of which have differing hours and admission prices. The Portale Maggiore, the original door of the heavily Gothic structure, is now the entrance to the National Gallery, and above the door is a lunette depicting Perugia's three patron saints, Lorenzo, Ercolano, and Costanzo. The building's exterior is also decorated with reproductions of a griffin and a Guelph lion, both of which are symbols of the city (the originals casts are located inside). The grand 13th-century Sala dei Notari was the original meeting place for local merchants; today it is the only room of the palazzo that is open free to the public. The room is richly frescoed with coats-of-arms, scenes from Aesop's fables and other allegorical themes, and is sometimes the site of classical concerts.

Rocca Paolina

Type of Attraction Erstwhile fortress, now the "guts" of Perugia

Location Piazza Italia

Admission Free

Hours Always open

Phone None

When to Go Daytime

Overall Appeal by Age Group

Pre-school —	Teens ★★★★★	Over 30 ★★★★
Grade school ★★★	Young Adults ★★★★★	Seniors ★★★★

Authors' Rating ★★★★

How Much Time to Allow 30 minutes

Description and Comments The massive Rocca Paolina was built as a result of Perugia's rebellion during the Salt War, when the city refused to pay the pope's tax on salt. (In fact, even today, defiant Umbrians refuse to add salt to their bread dough.) Pope Paul III ordered the Rocca Paolina built after papal troops finally recaptured the rogue city. Its construction meant the demise of the Baglioni palace; the destruction of many homes, churches, and buildings; and the broken will of many Perugians.

What is interesting about Perugia's erstwhile fortress is that it was built to keep the townspeople in, more than to keep invaders out, and was used for years as a prison. Paul III even had his architect, Antonio da Sangallo the Younger inscribe on the Rocca *Ad repellandam Perusinorum audaciam* ("to curb the audacity of the Perugian people"). The Rocca stood for some 300 years until 1860, when the city was liberated from the rule of the papacy. At that point, the townspeople set about demolishing the fortress and erected the lovely Piazza Italia and Carducci Gardens in its stead. However, not all of the Rocca Paolina was destroyed. Perugians rediscovered the fortress's uninviting chambers when they started construction on a connecting escalator between Piazza dei Partigiani and the historic center. Today, you can wander through the Rocca's labyrinth of stony, medieval halls as part of your commute.

Entertainment and Nightlife in Perugia

Perugia is best known as the site of the annual **Umbria Jazz Festival** (Piazza Danti, 28; phone 075 573 2432; **www.umbriajazz.com**), which has hosted acts such as Gilberto Gil, Paolo Conte, Wayne Shorter, David Sanborn, and Bobby McFerrin, to name just a few. You'll be hard-pressed to find accommodations if you come to Perugia in July, when the festival is in full swing. To sample a bit of jazz in the off-season, try the club **Contrappunto** (Via Scortici, 4a; phone 075 573 3667), which regularly books a range of emerging and well-known jazz acts.

As for the classical music scene, there is another festival. During the **Sagra Musicale Umbra** (Piazza Danti, 28; 06122 Perugia; phone 075 572 1374; **www.sagramusicaleumbra.com**), held August through mid-September, orchestras and choirs from throughout Europe descend on Perugia and nearby towns. Most concerts take place in local churches.

Perugia's large student population keeps the club scene fresh, and there are dozens of pubs, wine bars, and discos in the compact historic center alone. Near the university are several good spots. **Enoteca Provinciale** (Via U. Rocchi, 16; phone 075 572 4824) though not open late (till 10 p.m.), has a good selection of wines and Umbrian-style hors d'oeuvres. Beer drinkers can try **Il Birraio** (Via delle Prome, 18; phone 075 572 3920), which brews its own beer. Piazza Danti, just beyond the Duomo, is an excellent place to go if you want to mingle with Americans and other English speakers; here, we like Irish-owned **Shamrock Pub** (Piazza Danti, 18; phone 075 573 6625), which is good for a pint of Guinness any day of the week. If you're in a dancing mood, head to **Zoologico** (Via Alessi, 66; phone 075 572 1308; open September–June) or **Etoile 54** (Madonna del Piano, 109; phone 075 38710); both discos are frequented by students and locals. Cocktail bar **Dollaro** (Via Piccolpasso, 24; phone 075 505 7857) is currently the place to see and be seen.

The best place to find out about nightlife goings-on is in *Viva Perugia,* a monthly with a small section in English (available at newsstands). Also look for signs in the university area for impromptu rock concerts, dance parties, and so on.

Assisi

From the farming valley below, it seems that the town of Assisi radiates a pale, pink light, a sort of hazy halo between the clouds and the Earth.

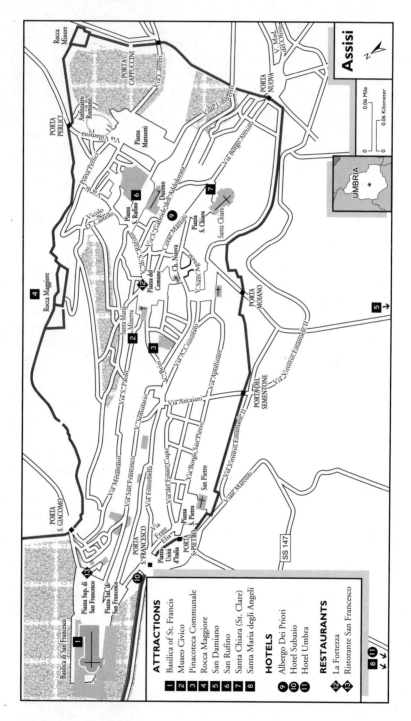

Assisi

UMBRIA

0   0.06 Mile
0   0.06 Kilometer

ATTRACTIONS
1 Basilica of St. Francis
2 Museo Civico
3 Pinacoteca Communale
4 Rocca Maggiore
5 San Damiano
6 San Rufino
7 Santa Chiara (St. Clare)
8 Santa Maria degli Angeli

HOTELS
9 Albergo Dei Priori
10 Hotel Subasio
11 Hotel Umbra

RESTAURANTS
12 La Fortezza
13 Ristorante San Francesco

Flanked by the enormous **St. Francis Basilica,** whose façade is, in fact, of rose- and ivory-colored marble, the modest hill town of Assisi awakens a sense of awe in all of those who lay eyes on it. The birthplace of St. Francis, founder of the brown-cloaked Franciscan order, and his follower, St. Clare (Santa Chiara), founder of the all-female Franciscan Order of the Poor Clares, Assisi has been a mecca for Christian pilgrims since the 12th century. It was the town's basilica—dedicated to its native son—that became a beacon to pilgrims, art lovers, and tourists alike. Sadly, in 1997, an earthquake rocked Umbria, killing four people and virtually destroying many of the 13th- and 14th-century frescoes housed within it. From that point onward, conservators pieced together thousands of fragments from the priceless paintings, and engineers worked to stabilize the basilica against further seismic shocks. St. Francis opened again in 1999, just in time for the Jubilee celebrations.

Assisi is a small town of approximately 10,000 souls, but its population swells into the tens of thousands during the Easter and Christmas seasons and during the first week of October, when the death of St. Francis is commemorated with numerous religious ceremonies.

A magnet for tourists, Assisi is well connected via bus and rail. You will find major and minor cities with bus services to Assisi. The town is about a 30-minute train ride from Perugia on the Foligno-Terontola line; from the station, catch a bus to Piazza Unità d'Italia. By car, take the S75 and follow the signs.

IAT Assisi   Piazza del Comune, 12; 06081 Assisi; phone 075 812 534; info@iat.assisi.pg.it

Basilica of St. Francis

Type of Attraction   One of Christianity's most important churches

Location   Piazza di San Francesco

Admission   Free

Hours   Easter–October: daily, 7 a.m.–7 p.m.; November–Easter: daily, 7 a.m.–12:30 p.m., 2–6 p.m.

Phone   075 819 0084

When to Go   Earlier is better

Overall Appeal by Age Group

Pre-school ★★★		Teens ★★★★		Over 30 ★★★★★
Grade school ★★★★		Young Adults ★★★★★		Seniors ★★★★★

Authors' Rating   ★★★★★

How Much Time to Allow   1 hour or longer

Description and Comments   Maintained by the Vatican and visited by tens of thousands each year, St. Francis's Basilica is one of the most revered houses of worship in the world. Francesco Bernardone (a.k.a. St.

Francis) led such a pious life and was so instrumental in personalizing the Catholic faith that his followers were certain that he would one day be beatified. Work on his church began in 1228, just two years after his death, and was justified one month later by Pope Gregory IX, who canonized Francis during a special mass in Perugia.

The Basilica of St. Francis is divided into two sections—the Lower Church (Chiesa Inferiore) and the Upper Church (Chiesa Superiore). The former was completed around 1230 and is where you'll find the crypts of St. Francis and four of his most loyal followers. Francis's sepulcher was discovered only in 1818 after a search lasting more than two months. The saint's brother Elias had secretly transferred Francis's coffin to a hiding place under the high altar of the church, where it rested unharmed for almost 600 years.

The shadowy lower section of the basilica is a somber, Romanesque church, with a low, barrel-vaulted ceiling; it houses some of St. Francis's lesser-known but equally astounding pre-Renaissance frescoes. Above the altar are frescoes of the four Franciscan virtues (Le Quattro Vele) of poverty, chastity, obedience, and the glory of St. Francis, painted by assistants of Giotto. To the right of the altar are a set of rich frescoes by Cimabue, Giotto, Simone Martini, and Pietro Lorenzetti. Lorenzetti is also credited with painting frescoes of the Passion on the wall to the left of the altar. Look to the Chapel of St. Martin (the first chapel on the left side of the nave) for Martini's depiction of the life of France's most venerated saint. St. Steven's Chapel is directly across from here and contains late Renaissance frescoes by Dono Doni. Giotto is said to have supervised the design and painting of the Chapel of Mary Magdalene, located in the last niche on the right of the nave before the transept.

The Gothic-style Upper Church of St. Francis suffered the most damage during the 1997 earthquake, though its large rose window withstood the tremors. Here you'll find the cathedral's most celebrated fresco cycle, the *Life of St. Francis* by Giotto. The cycle tells the story of the church's namesake, starting from the right wall of the intersection of the nave and transept with *St. Francis Honored by the Simple Man* and wrapping around the church to the opposite side with the *Liberation of a Prisoner Accused of Heresy.* There are 28 frescoes in Giotto's groundbreaking work, including the *Sermon to the Birds* immediately to the left of the entrance, which recalls one of the more touching episodes from the nature-loving friar's journey to sainthood. Above Giotto's work are 34 frescoes attributed to Cimabue that detail scenes from the Old Testament (on the right) and New Testament (on the left). Giotto's teacher also painted the heavily faded *Crucifixion* to the right of the apse. Some of the Upper Church is still pockmarked with blank plaster, especially where Cimabue's paintings of Sts. Jerome and Matthew used to be, a result of the earthquake; conservation efforts continue. Lest you forget that Assisi is the City of Peace, groomed hedges outside the basilica spell out the word "pax."

Museo Civico

Type of Attraction Assisi's archaeological museum

Location Via Portica, 2

Admission €2

Hours March–October: daily, 10 a.m.–1 p.m., 3–7 p.m.; October–March: daily, 10 a.m.–1 p.m., 2–5 p.m.

Phone 075 813 053

When to Go Anytime; not crowded

Overall Appeal by Age Group

Pre-school ★★		Teens ★★		Over 30 ★★★
Grade school ★★		Young Adults ★★★		Seniors ★★★

Authors' Rating ★★

How Much Time to Allow 30 minutes

Description and Comments Those tired of the art and religion trail can take a much-needed break at the Museo Civico. Housing displays of Etruscan and Roman art found around Assisi, the museum starts in the crypt of San Niccolò, an 11th-century church demolished in the early 20th century, and leads to the archaeological area believed to be the Temple of Minerva (called the Roman Forum). Here you'll find visible remains of an ancient city, including two statues of Castor and Pollux, dating back to second decade A.D.

Pinacoteca Comunale

Type of Attraction Assisi's municipal art gallery

Location Via San Francesco, 12

Admission €2

Hours March–October: daily, 10 a.m.–1 p.m., 3–7 p.m.; October–March: daily, 10 a.m.–1 p.m., 2–5 p.m.

Phone 075 813 053

When to Go Anytime; not crowded

Overall Appeal by Age Group

Pre-school —		Teens ★★		Over 30 ★★
Grade school ★★		Young Adults ★★		Seniors ★★★

Authors' Rating ★★½

How Much Time to Allow 30 minutes

Description and Comments This small museum, which recently reopened after undergoing years of renovations, is on the ground floor of the Palazzo dei Priori and came into being in 1912 as a way to collect and protect local art. The modest collection consists of works by the Umbrian school, and date from the 13th to the 17th centuries. Among the paintings is a *Madonna in Maestà* from the workshop of Giotto and an *Annunciation* and *Stigmata of St. Francis,* both attributed to Dono Doni.

Rocca Maggiore

Type of Attraction Has the best views over Assisi
Location Via della Rocca
Admission €3
Hours Daily, dawn–dusk
Phone 075 815 292
When to Go Early morning
Overall Appeal by Age Group

Pre-school ★★		Teens ★★★★		Over 30 ★★★★
Grade school ★★★		Young Adults ★★★★		Seniors ★★★

Authors' Rating ★★★★
How Much Time to Allow 1–2 hours (including walking time to the top)

Description and Comments This massive citadel crowning the ridge opposite the Basilica of St. Francis existed as far back as the 12th century, but was refortified in the 14th century. Visually, it is one of the most striking features of the town and affords spectacular views down to the basilica and the valley.

San Damiano

Type of Attraction Place of pilgrimage for St. Francis
Location San Damiano, 1 mile south of Assisi
Admission Free
Hours Daily, 10 a.m.–noon, 2–6 p.m.
Phone 075 812 273
When to Go Anytime
Overall Appeal by Age Group

Pre-school —		Teens ★★★		Over 30 ★★★
Grade school ★★		Young Adults ★★★		Seniors ★★★

Authors' Rating ★★★
How Much Time to Allow 30 minutes; up to 2 hours if walking to the site

Description and Comments Christians familiar with the story of St. Francis of Assisi flock to the church of San Damiano. It was here that the Crucifix of San Damiano spoke to St. Francis, telling him, "rebuild my church." Taking the vision literally, St. Francis promptly sold all of his possessions and set about rebuilding the church of San Damiano with his own hands. St. Francis had also sold fabric from his father's shop to raise money to repair the church. Angered, his father disowned Francis, forcing him into a life of dire poverty. By 1212, the restoration was complete, and

St. Francis brought his friend Clare to see the new house of worship. Clare later founded the Order of the Poor Clares here. In the garden at San Damiano is where St. Francis wrote his poignant *Canticle of Creatures,* a scene that is lovingly frescoed on the walls of the Basilica of St. Francis.

San Rufino

Type of Attraction The original Duomo of Assisi
Location Piazza San Rufino
Admission Free; crypt and Museo Capitolare, €2.50
Hours Daily, 10 a.m.–noon, 3–8 p.m.
Phone 075 81228
When to Go Anytime—rarely crowded
Overall Appeal by Age Group

Pre-school —		Teens ★★		Over 30 ★★★
Grade school ★★		Young Adults ★★		Seniors ★★★

Authors' Rating ★★★
How Much Time to Allow 30 minutes

Description and Comments Sts. Francis, Clare, and Agnes and Emperor Francis II of Swabia were all baptized here in Assisi's original cathedral. Dedicated to St. Rufinus, the man who brought Christianity to the town after the fall of the Roman empire, the church houses the martyr's crypt and a handful of Umbrian paintings. Actually built over several centuries, the Duomo has a magnificent, three-register façade and an adjacent bell tower. Although San Rufino is grossly overshadowed by the Basilica of St. Francis, it still plays a part in liturgical celebrations, especially on Holy Thursday, when a wooden image of Christ is carried from San Rufino to St. Francis and back again in a nocturnal procession.

Santa Chiara

Type of Attraction 13th-century church founded by St. Clare
Location Piazza Santa Chiara
Admission Free
Hours Daily, 8 a.m.–1 p.m., 3–6 p.m.
Phone 075 812 282
When to Go Anytime
Overall Appeal by Age Group

Pre-school —		Teens ★★		Over 30 ★★★
Grade school ★★		Young Adults ★★		Seniors ★★★

Authors' Rating ★★
How Much Time to Allow 30 minutes

Description and Comments A somewhat smaller version of the Upper Church of St. Francis, the 13th-century Basilica of Santa Chiara is made of pink and white limestone, has a lovely rose window, and features giant, flying buttresses which were added a century later. Built over the ancient church of San Giorgio, the Basilica of Santa Chiara houses two relics important to the Order of the Poor Clares. First, the remains of its namesake saint, St. Clare, lie in a crystal coffin in the crypt below the altar. Second, this church is home to the Crucifix of San Damiano. When the Poor Clares moved from the church of San Damiano to San Giorgio, they took the wooden altarpiece with them. The crucifix now hangs in Santa Chiara's San Giorgio Chapel. At press time, renovations were still ongoing to repair parts of the basilica badly damaged during the 1997 earthquake.

Santa Maria degli Angeli

Type of Attraction Modern basilica built over Franciscan shrine
Location Santa Maria degli Angeli, 5 miles south of Assisi
Admission Free
Hours Daily, 6 a.m.–8 p.m.
Phone 075 80511
When to Go On your way into or out of town
Overall Appeal by Age Group

Pre-school —		Teens ★★		Over 30 ★★★
Grade school ★★		Young Adults ★★★		Seniors ★★★

Authors' Rating ★★★
How Much Time to Allow 30 minutes

Description and Comments The Basilica of Santa Maria Angeli was built over the ancient Porziuncola where both Francis and Clare took vows of poverty. The original church dates back to the sixth century, around the time of St. Benedict, and the chapel here was already in disrepair when St. Francis began to pray here. St. Clare ran away to the Porziuncola in 1212, where she met up with St. Francis, who assisted her with her transition from patrician's daughter to pious pauper. Its location, set in the woods far from the main town of Assisi, made the Porziuncola a favorite retreat for St. Francis, St. Clare, and their followers. Eventually, St. Francis died here in the Cappella del Transito 1226. Today, a number of modern buildings surround the pilgrimage church of Santa Maria degli Angeli. The train station is also nearby.

Bettona

Founded around the seventh century B.C., Bettona was the only Etruscan settlement on the left bank of the Tiber. Its enviable position near the river made the town susceptible to invaders, prompting the construction of the **Mura Etrusche,** or Etruscan walls, the feature for which this Umbrian hamlet is best known. Bettona's history is most tied with Assisi, with whom it united after a barbarian invasion. Like Assisi, the town saw a flurry of activity in the 13th and 14th centuries, when the papacy sought to fortify this territory. Today, Bettona and Assisi are aligned against another invader—tourists. The hotels and inns of Bettona handle the overflow from the City of Peace during high season. If you go there, have a peek at the **Pinacoteca Civica** (Piazza Cavour, 3; phone 075 987 306; open November–February: daily, 10:30 a.m.–1 p.m., 2:30–5 p.m.; March–May and September–October: daily, 10:30 a.m.–1 p.m., 2–6 p.m.; June–August: daily, 10:30 a.m.–1 p.m., 3–7 p.m.; admission €3). Perugino is represented with the frescoes of *Madonna with Saints Jerome and Mauro* and *Gonfalone*. Also on display are works from Dono Doni, Taddeo Gaddi, Niccolò Alunno, and, Luca della Robbia.

IAT Bettona   Piazza Matteotti; 06080 Bettona; phone 075 986 9482

Bevagna

Bevagna owes its walled-in good looks to the Romans, who founded this city (known back then as Mevania) as an outpost on the Flaminian Way in the second century B.C. Here, weary Romans traveling from the capital to points north could go for a soak in the baths and partake in this lush area's agricultural bounty. Many features of the ancient town are still extant, including sections of the original Roman walls and mosaics in the baths. The consular road of Via Flaminia lives on as the town's main street. Bevagna is also one of the finer medieval towns in Umbria, with the wide cobblestone **Piazza Silvestri** serving as the site of four churches (all of which are still undergoing earthquake repairs), and the 13th-century **Palazzo dei Consoli,** which has housed, since 1886, the **Teatro Francesco Torti** (Piazza Silvestri; phone 0742 361 667; tickets €7–€12), a handsome 250-seat venue that puts on classic and modern plays. The theater is especially active each year during the **Mercato delle Gaite.** During the last ten days of June, Bevagna's medieval past is resurrected with traditional performances and concerts and a fair featuring local foods and crafts.

Pro Loco Bevagna   Piazza Silvestri; 06031 Bevagna; phone 0742 361 667

Città di Castello

Even today, the people of Città di Castello call themselves Tifernati, after the ancient Roman town of Tifernum Tiberinum that once existed here. During the first and second centuries A.D., this Roman city was one of the most important of the Upper Tiber Valley, and wealthy Romans, such as Pliny the Younger, built lavish country villas here. Only a trace of Pliny's villa can be found today, and hardly anything from this early Roman settlement made it past Totila. He and his tribe of Goths laid waste to Tifernum Tiberinum in 550 A.D. The devastation was so thorough, in fact, that the town lay virtually abandoned for 200 years. By the eighth century, the now papal-controlled city had been rebuilt around a fortified castle named Castrum Felicitatis (Happy Castle). Città di Castello (City of the Castle) was born. The Renaissance left its mark on Città di Castello, thanks in no small part to the patronage of the Vitelli family. Niccolo Vitelli hired many artists, including Raphael, to decorate the city. You can find his work, and the works of other Renaissance artists at the **Pinacoteca Comunale** (Via della Cannoniera, 22/a; phone 075 852 0656; open April–October: daily, 10 a.m.–1 p.m., 2:30–6:30 p.m.; November–March: daily, 10 a.m.–12:30 p.m., 3–5:30 p.m.; admission €4). Housed in the Palazzo Vitelli alla Cannoniera, the museum has a stunning collection of paintings by Umbrian and Tuscan school artists, such as Luca Signorelli, Domenico Ghirlandaio, and Maestro di Città di Castello, and an array of altarpieces and reliquaries from the workshops of Ghiberti and Luca della Robbia.

Despite its Renaissance credentials, Città di Castello may be better known today as the birthplace of Alberto Burri, one of Italy's groundbreaking modern artists. Born in Città di Castello, Alberto Burri's life as an artist began in Texas, where he was a POW during the war. There, he worked with found objects and materials, namely burlap, jute, and recycled metals. At the end of the war, Burri moved to Rome, where his abstract creations were hailed as innovative. Throughout his career, Burri produced hundreds of canvases and sculptures that combined multimedia surfaces with tweaked proportions and textures. Though Burri's art has appeared in the Guggenheim Museum, the Musée Nationale d'Art Moderne in Paris, and at Sotheby's, the bulk of his collection is here, spread out in two locations. The **Collezione Burri** (Palazzo Albizzini, Via Albizzini, 1 and Via Pierucci; phone 0758 554 649; open Tuesday–Saturday, 9 a.m.–noon, 2:30–6 p.m.; Sunday, 9 a.m.–1 p.m.; admission €3.50) is one of Italy's most celebrated contemporary art museums.

IAT Città di Castello   Via Sant'Antonio, 1; 06012 Città di Castello; phone 0758 554 817, fax: 0758 552 100

Corciano

On the road from Perugia toward Lake Trasimeno is the castle town of Corciano, which boasts a well-preserved medieval center and a perimeter of turreted walls. Though expanding industry has swallowed up the outlying area around Corciano, the town safeguards its past with a museum dedicated to farm life, the **Museo della Civiltà Contadina** (Via Tarragone, 12; phone 075 518 8253, fax 075 518 8237; open on request, call or fax in advance; admission €2). Here is a reproduction of a traditional home—reminiscent of a pioneer home in the American West—complete with period furnishings, looms, wine jugs, and personal effects. Further-more, **Agosto Corcianese,** an annual fair held each August, celebrates local arts and crafts, including rope making, and medieval traditions.

IAT Corciano Via della Corgna, 6; 06073 Corciano; phone 075 697 9109

Deruta

Renowned for its brightly colored pottery, Deruta has become somewhat of a shopping haven for anyone looking for unique, authentic Umbrian gifts. The City of Ceramics has a museum dedicated to majolica, a church covered with hundreds of hand-painted tiles, and plenty of workshops where you can watch artisans hone their craft. First, the **Museo Regionale della Ceramica** (Ex Convento di San Francesco, Largo di San Francesco; phone 075 971 1000; open Tuesday–Sunday, 10 a.m.–1 p.m., 3–6 p.m.; admission €2) highlights ceramics from the Middle Ages to the early 20th century. Fans of Deruta's highly stylized, colorful majolica work will delight in seeing more than 6,000 pieces of art, including decorative plates, jars, jugs, cups, pepper mills, and other dressed-up household items. Located approximately two miles south of the town center you'll find the **Santuario della Madonna dei Bagni** (Località Casalina, Via Tiberina; no phone; open daily, 8 a.m.–noon, 3–7 p.m; donation requested), which is decorated with more than 600 votive ceramic tiles offered by church patrons since the 17th century to the present. As for taking home a little piece of Deruta, you'll find plenty of shops and ven-dors that sell local artisan majolica. Two outlets that we recommend visit-ing are **Puntoceramica** (Via Tiberina, 283; phone 075 972 282, fax 075 971 1365) or **Sberna Ceramiche** (Via Tiberina, 146; phone 075 971 0206, fax 075 971 0428; **www.sberna.com**).

Associazione Pro Deruta Piazza dei Consoli, 4; 06053 Deruta; phone 075 971 1559

Foligno

Since its inception as a Roman city in 295 B.C., Umbria's third-largest city has been destroyed countless times. In the sixth century, the Lom-bards attacked Foligno and claimed it for the duchy of Spoleto. In the ninth and tenth centuries came the Saracens and the Hungarians, led by Frederick I Barbarossa. The papacy also staked its claim to this ancient town, and, after a long battle with the local Ghibellines, Rinaldo Trinci was installed as leader of Foligno in 1310. For the next century, the power-hungry Trinci dynasty ruled the dominion, until the church called for the family's ouster in 1439. Under the Trinci family, Foligno became a prosperous commercial center, especially of iron; under the papacy, the city became one of Italy's main printing hubs, producing the first editions of Dante's *Divine Comedy*. Because of Foligno's strong industrial background, it was chosen for bombing by Allied troops during World War II. However, despite all of the damage done by humans, earthquakes are responsible for wreaking the most havoc here. Most recently, the aftershocks of the 1997 quake caused the 14th-century bell tower of the **Palazzo Comunale** to crumble to the ground.

Tourism to this industrial town is understandably weak. However, if you're passing through, a few sites are worth adding to your itinerary. Within the halls of the **Palazzo Trinci** (Piazza della Repubblica; phone 0742 357 989; open Tuesday–Sunday, 10 a.m.–7 p.m.; admission €5) you'll find Foligno's greatest storehouse of treasures. Located here are the **Pinacoteca Civica** and the **Museo Archeologico,** which display, respectively, paintings from the 14th through 16th centuries and ancient Roman sculpture. Also here is the **Museo Multimediale dei Tornei delle Giostre e dei Giochi** (phone 0742 357 697; open 10 a.m.–1 p.m., 4–8 p.m.; admission free), which chronicles the city's biggest tourist draw, the **Giostra della Quintana** (**www.quintana.it**). This tournament, with origins from the 17th century, takes place in July and September, and sees knights from each of the city's ten districts take part in a mock joust. The spectacle includes riders, horses, and spectators in period dress, a cooking competition, a parade, and plays performed in the Umbrian dialect.

Foligno is one of the main train transfer points in Umbria, so you can easily stop here for a day of sight-seeing. If you're driving, Foligno lies just off the S75, halfway between Perugia and Spoleto—but be warned that traffic is heavy at this crossroads. Bus service to Foligno is fairly frequent from these cities, too.

IAT Foligno Piazza Garibaldi, 12; 06034 Foligno; phone 0742 350 493; **www.comune.foligno.pg.it**

Gubbio

Unspoiled (so far) by tourism or modern industry, Gubbio is a medieval city of steep, winding walkways; stern, stone buildings; and deep Umbrian roots. The **Palazzo dei Consoli,** the majestic, crenellated, 14th-century town hall that dominates the skyline, holds the seven bronze Eugubine Tablets, which document, in the ancient Umbrian language, the existence of Ikuvium, Gubbio's original name. Situated on the slopes of Mount Ingino, Gubbio was also an early Roman settlement, evidence of which is visible in the lower town where stand remains of a first-century amphitheater. Gubbio's importance stretches back more than 65 million years. Scientists believe that the Camignano valley may have been the place where "the Great Dying" occurred, signaling the end of the Cretaceous period (i.e., the end of the dinosaurs) and the beginning of the Tertiary period.

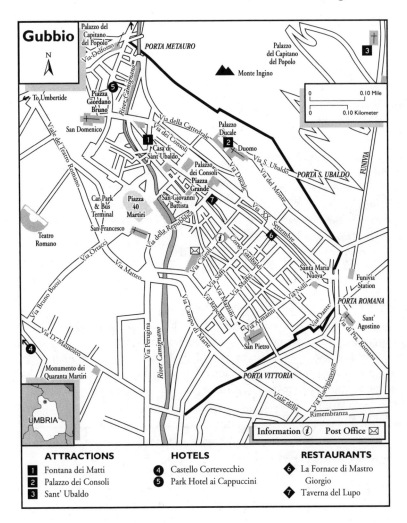

ATTRACTIONS
1. Fontana dei Matti
2. Palazzo dei Consoli
3. Sant' Ubaldo

HOTELS
4. Castello Cortevecchio
5. Park Hotel ai Cappuccini

RESTAURANTS
6. La Fornace di Mastro Giorgio
7. Taverna del Lupo

Much of Gubbio's lore and traditions are tied up with the memory of **St. Ubaldo,** who, as a bishop in the mid-12th century, helped the city repel the advances of Perugia. The saint's sepulcher can be found in his eponymous church on the peak of Mount Ingino, as can the enormous candles *(ceri)* that are hauled to this site each year in an exciting medieval foot race. The **Corsa dei Ceri,** one of Umbria's best-known medieval traditions, sees candle-bearers *(ceraioli)* from each of Gubbio's three parishes dash uphill from the Palazzo dei Consoli to the church of St. Ubaldo—approximately 2.5 miles—in less than ten minutes. Each can- dle is topped with an effigy of the parish patron saints—Ubaldo,

George, and Anthony—and it is in this order that the race always ends, with Ubaldo winning. The event, which happens each May 15, is fueled with plenty of music and local San Giovese–Trebbiano wine.

APT Gubbio   Piazza Oderisi; 06024 Gubbio; phone 075 922 0693, fax 075 927 3409

Fontana dei Matti

Type of Attraction Fountain with a funny legend
Location Largo del Bargello
Admission Free
Hours Always open
Phone None
When to Go Anytime
Overall Appeal by Age Group

Pre-school ★★★		Teens ★★★		Over 30 ★★
Grade school ★★★		Young Adults ★★		Seniors ★★

Authors' Rating ★★★
How Much Time to Allow Less than 15 minutes

Description and Comments Legend has it that circling this 16th-century fountain three times will earn you a diploma in craziness. The Fontana dei Matti, also known as the Fountain of Fools or the Fountain of Lunatics, is a popular attraction in Gubbio; you'll often see tourists running around the font, and, in turn, making the locals crazy.

Palazzo dei Consoli

Type of Attraction Gubbio's town hall and site of its municipal museum
Location Piazza Grande
Admission €3
Hours April–July and September: daily, 10 a.m.–1:30 p.m., 3–6 p.m.; August: daily, 10 a.m.–1:30 p.m., 3–7 p.m.; October–March: daily, 10 a.m.–1 p.m., 2–5 p.m.
Phone 075 927 4298
When to Go Mornings
Overall Appeal by Age Group

Pre-school ★★★		Teens ★★★		Over 30 ★★★★
Grade school ★★★		Young Adults ★★★★		Seniors ★★★★

Authors' Rating ★★★★
How Much Time to Allow 1 hour

Description and Comments The "Hall of Consuls," set on the wide, windswept Piazza della Signoria, is one of Gubbio's most recognizable landmarks and one of the best examples of medieval civic architecture. Built in the first half of the 14th century by Gattapone (born Matteo di Giovanello) and Angelo da Orvieto, the Palazzo dei Consoli is supported by an arched foundation, which was necessary to even out the hilly terrain. Furthermore, the palazzo features a graceful *loggia,* a slender *campanile,* rooftop crenellations, and a broad fan-shaped staircase that appears semi-detached from the austere structure. The inside has been turned into the Museo Civico, which now houses the city's prized Eugubine Tablets. Elsewhere in the museum, you'll find scads of items, including crossbows, sarcophagi, and Roman coins, from eras gone by.

Sant'Ubaldo

Type of Attraction   Church of Gubbio's patron saint

Location   Piazza Sant'Ubaldo

Admission   Free

Hours   Daily, 9 a.m.–noon, 4–7 p.m.

Phone   075 927 3872

When to Go   Mornings are ideal, but sunsets from here can't be beat

Overall Appeal by Age Group

Pre-school ★★		Teens ★★		Over 30 ★★★
Grade school ★★		Young Adults ★★★		Seniors ★★★

Authors' Rating   ★★★

How Much Time to Allow   30 minutes to 1 hour

Description and Comments   The destination for candle-bearers during Gubbio's Corsa dei Ceri celebrations is the church of Sant'Ubaldo, located on the summit of Mt. Ingino. The interior of the medieval church is rather unimpressive. Most tourists visit Sant'Ubaldo to venerate the saint, whose remains are kept in a Renaissance-era urn on the altar, and to view the three 450-pound *ceri* that are kept here throughout the year. St. Ubaldo is the patron saint of migraine headaches (among other things), so to avoid getting one, you may want to take the funicular to the top of Mount Ingino. One way costs €2.50; round trip, €4. Otherwise, it's a long and arduous—but picturesque—climb up the winding Corso delle Candele.

Lake Trasimeno

Approaching Perugia from Tuscany, you will bypass Lake Trasimeno, Italy's fourth largest lake. At almost 30 miles around, the lake supports a small fishing industry and sustains a wetland climate replete with waterfowl. The Lake Trasimeno district consists of more than a half-dozen towns and lesser villages that border the lake's endless shore. Of these, **Castiglione del Lago** and **Città della Pieve** are most ideal for a holiday.

With a landscape befitting that of an oceanside resort, Castiglione del Lago is understandably one of the favorite tourist haunts for Italians, who escape here for *primo* views, clean air, and rural recreation. Perched on the shores of the lake, Castiglione del Lago was a fishing village turned military stronghold, and it remained important through the 16th century. The most striking features of the town are the 13th-century **Rocca del Leone** (Piazza Antonio Gramsci, 1; phone 075 96581; open April–October: daily, 10 a.m.–1 p.m., 3–7 p.m.; November–March: Saturday and Sunday, 10 a.m.–4 p.m.; admission €4, includes Palazzo della Corgna), whose crenellations lend the village its name. Frederick II of Swabia had this intimidating landmark built in 1247 so that he and his troops could have a military lookout post on the lake. The ramparts of the "Lion's Fortress" form a pentagon with four corner towers and a triangular keep *(mastio),* and Ascanio della Corgna added a covered walkway from his palace to the castle when he built the latter in the 16th century. His **Palazzo della Corgna** (see details for Rocca) looks more like a country home than a mansion, but it contains a number of rich frescoes. Niccolò Circignani ("Il Pomarancio"), Giovanni Antonio Pandolfi, and other Mannerist artists frescoed approximately eight rooms of the palace with scenes glorifying Ascanio della Corgna's mercenary skills, including the *Battle of Trasimeno,* the *Battle of Lepanto,* and the *Duel with Giannetto Taddei.* The walkway from the palazzo to the Rocca del Leone provided safe passage for the Della Corgna family when under threat. Today, visitors to either attraction can walk in the family's footsteps.

Pietro Vannucci (a.k.a., Perugino), the skilled Renaissance painter who died an unabsolved atheist, was born in Città della Pieve, a handsome parish *(pieve)* town several miles southwest of Trasimeno's shores. Though the town isn't swimming with works from its native son, it does possess some significant pieces, including the *Deposition from the Cross* at the church of Santa Maria dei Servi, a few panels in the **Duomo,** and, more famously, the *Adoration of the Magi* in **Santa Maria dei Bianchi** (Via Vannucci, 25; phone 075 829 9696; open Monday–Saturday, 10:30 a.m.–12:30 p.m., 3:30–6 p.m.; Sunday, 10 a.m.–1 p.m., 3–6 p.m.; admission free). Perugino's take on this common Renaissance theme is probably one of the most recognizable of the lot. Here, the Virgin Mary cradles baby Jesus under a wooden canopy, as dozens of townspeople in colorful Renaissance finery look on. In the background, you can make out the Città delle Pieve's view of Lake Trasimeno and the rolling Valdichiana valley. A well-preserved hill town enveloped in terra cotta brick—a local specialty—Città della Pieve has an authentic medieval center complete with an imposing, turreted fortress and a slither of a street, Vicolo Bacciadonne (Kiss-the-Women Lane), one of the narrowest in Italy.

If you'd like to continue on the Perugino trail, you can take a bus—or drive a short distance—from Città della Pieve to the village of **Panicale,** where the artist's famous *Martyrdom of St. Sebastian* resides in the church **San Sebastiano** (Piazza Umberto I; no phone; open daily, 9 a.m.–1 p.m., 3 p.m.–6 p.m.; donation requested).

APT Parco del Trasimeno Viale Europa; 06065 Passignano sul Trasimeno; phone 075 828 059

IAT Castiglione del Lago Piazza Mazzini, 10; 06061 Castiglione del Lago; phone 075 965 2484

IAT Città della Pieve Piazza del Plebiscito, 1; 06062 Città della Pieve; phone 0578 299 375

Pro Loco Panicale Piazza Umberto I, 19; 06064 Panicale; phone 075 837 183

Montefalco

Few towns in central Italy are more pleasing to the senses than Montefalco. This pristine hill town of approximately 5,500 crowns the top of a hill high above the Umbrian plain. Because of Montefalco's fortunate position it has been called the Ringhiera dell'Umbria, or the Balcony of Umbria, and views from the village's medieval Piazza del Comune are the kind that make the soul sing. In addition to the landscape, Montefalco's **Museo Civico di San Francesco** (Via Ringhiera Umbra, 5; phone 0742 379 598; open March–May and September–October: daily, 10:30 a.m.–1 p.m., 2–6 p.m.; June–August: daily, 10:30 a.m.–1 p.m., 3–7 p.m.; November–February: daily, 10:30 a.m.–1 p.m., 2:30–5 p.m.; admission €2) is worth a look. Here, from 1450 to 1452, Benozzo Gozzoli painted the fresco cycle, perhaps the most important illustrations of the life of St. Francis outside of Assisi. Gozzoli's light-hearted paintings were some of his first commissions, but he nevertheless displayed a mastery of perspective and color. Meanwhile, his frescoes are poignant in that they depict St. Francis before 15th-century cityscapes, including those of Montefalco and Arezzo.

While its scenery and art awe, Montefalco is better known the world over for its Sagrantino di Montefalco wine. Produced since the Middle Ages, the celebrated red is of DOCG status. The finest place in the area to sample the premium vintage is at **Rocca di Fabbri** (Località Torre di Montefalco; phone 0742 378 802; open by appointment Monday–Friday, 8:30 a.m.–12:30 p.m., 2–6 p.m.; Saturday, 9 a.m.–noon). You may also want to check out the **Strada del Sagrantino** (**www.stradadelsagrantino.com**), an association of local growers.

APT Montefalco Museo Civico di San Francesco; Via Ringhiera Umbra; 06036 Montefalco; phone 0742 379 598

Norcia

Although few Italians have ever set foot in Norcia, all can tell you what its chief export is—prosciutto. This southern Umbrian town has long been the mecca for pork *(maiale)*, the center for cured meats *(salumi)*, and the hub for ham. In fact, throughout Italy, you need only to venture into your local *norcineria* for thickly sliced pork cutlets and sausage links. Fine butchering skills led the Nursini (the ancient name of the people of Vetusta Nursia) to their profession; during the Middle Ages, this expertise took another turn. By the 17th century, tens of thousands of parents interested in furthering their sons' singing careers had brought their spawn to Norcia, where these very same pork butchers routinely performed castrations. Gruesome history aside, Norcia merits a visit because of its stunning location, set in the shadow of the Sibillini Mountains. The town also produced two saints: St. Benedict, Christianity's first monk, and his twin sister, St. Scholastica. The Gothic-style **Basilica San Benedetto** (Piazza San Benedetto; no phone; open daily, 8 a.m.–noon, 3–6 p.m.; admission free) is built over the twins' birthplace on a foundation that dates back to the second century B.C. Contained within is a vivid Baroque work by Filippo Napoletano depicting *St. Benedict and Totila*. Located on the same broad square is the Duomo, dedicated to Santa Maria Argentea, and the squat, 16th-century Castellina, today the seat of Norcia's municipal government.

IAT Norcia   Piazza San Benedetto; 06046 Norcia; phone 0743 828 044

Spello

A smaller, less-crowded version of Assisi, the hill town of Spello is located approximately 10 minutes by rail from St. Francis's home and boasts a tranquil setting filled with dainty churches and deserted, medieval side streets. Starting out as Splendidissima Colonia Julia Hispellum, Spello was a sort of laid-back retirement community for Roman veterans of the Perugian wars under Augustus. Spello was always of strategic importance, lying so close to contested Perugia, and fell under the domain of the Lombards of the Duchy of Spoleto in the sixth century. During the early Middle Ages, Spello struggled for independence from nearby Assisi and Perugia, and by the beginning of the 13th century, the town had gained *comune* status. Spello was self-governed for about a century before the Baglioni family of Perugia added the town to its dominion. During their reign, from the end of the 13th century until the end of the 16th century, the Baglioni family commissioned numerous artworks in town, including the Pinturicchio frescoes in the church of **Santa Maria Maggiore** (Piazza Mateotti, 18; phone 0742 301 792; open daily, 8 a.m.–12:30 p.m., 2:30–7 p.m.; admission free). Commissioned in 1500 by Troilo Baglioni, the frescoes depict the *Annunciation, Nativity,* and *Dispute in the Temple.* Some art critics consider these three panels to be among the artist's best works, the result being that the Cappella Baglioni was nicknamed Cappella Bella (Beautiful Chapel).

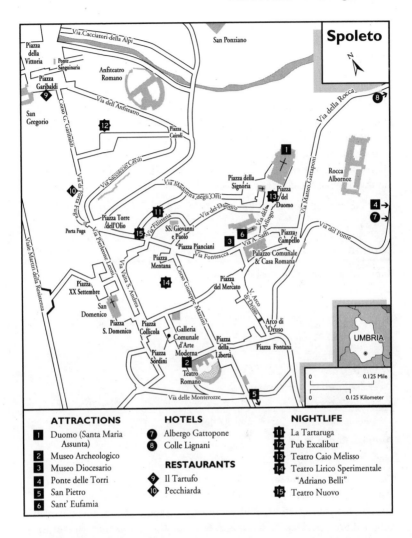

ATTRACTIONS

1. Duomo (Santa Maria Assunta)
2. Museo Archeologico
3. Museo Diocesario
4. Ponte delle Torri
5. San Pietro
6. Sant' Eufamia

HOTELS

7. Albergo Gattopone
8. Colle Lignani

RESTAURANTS

9. Il Tartufo
10. Pecchiarda

NIGHTLIFE

11. La Tartaruga
12. Pub Excalibur
13. Teatro Caio Melisso
14. Teatro Lirico Sperimentale "Adriano Belli"
15. Teatro Nuovo

IAT Spello   Piazza Matteotti, 3; 06038 Spello; phone 0742 301 009

Spoleto

Known today for the cultural extravaganza that is the **Two Worlds Festival** (Festival dei Due Mondi), Spoleto has grown from a dot on the map in 1958 into a city of the arts. Fancy hotels, posh boutiques, and wealthy residents have all moved in, hoping to live the magic of the Two Worlds Festival the whole year round. Nevertheless, Spoleto has maintained a sort of provincial charm, which is in full bloom in the spring and fall when the festival crowds are home.

Of course, Spoleto's history stretches back much further than the 20th century. Significant Roman ruins, such as the **Roman Theater,** have been found here, which date the city to before the third century B.C. Records also show that the Spoletini were integral at beating back Hannibal's troops in 217 B.C. Because Spoleto was an important Roman settlement, the Lombards singled it out as a central base during invasions in the sixth century. For some 500 years thereafter, Spoleto became the seat of one of the most important Lombard duchies. The duchy of Spoleto lasted until 1155, when it was defeated by one of its own—Frederick I Barbarossa. Many of the buildings that exist today in Spoleto were built on the ruins of the city that Frederick destroyed.

IAT Spoleto Piazza della Libertà, 7; 06049 Spoleto; phone 0743 220 311

Duomo

Type of Attraction Contains frescoes by Fra Filippo Lippi

Location Piazza del Duomo

Admission Free

Hours March–October: daily, 8 a.m.–1 p.m., 3–6:30 p.m.; November–February: 8 a.m.–1 p.m., 3–5:30 p.m.

Phone 0743 44307

When to Go Anytime

Overall Appeal by Age Group

Pre-school —		Teens ★★		Over 30 ★★★
Grade school ★★		Young Adults ★★★		Seniors ★★★

Authors' Rating ★★★★

How Much Time to Allow 30 minutes

Description and Comments Spoleto's odd-looking Duomo, Santa Maria Assunta, rebuilt after Frederick I Barbarossa destroyed the original church, is a mishmash of architectural styles ranging from the medieval to the Baroque. Details such as a Romanesque *campanile,* Byzantine mosaics, Gothic rose windows, a Renaissance *loggia,* and various Baroque additions together form a composite reminiscent of many other churches throughout central Italy. But few tourists take the time to examine Santa Maria Assunta's façade; they come to see the frescoes. Fra Filippo Lippi, one of the foremost Renaissance painters, decorated the apse with scenes from the life of the Virgin. His colorful—almost psychedelic—*Coronation of the Virgin* should not be missed, nor should the artist's tomb, located in the right transept. The body of Florence-born Filippo Lippi should have been sent to his hometown after he died in 1469, but the Spoletini—perhaps seeing the potential tourist draw—refused to send the corpse home.

Museo Archeologico

Type of Attraction Archaeology museum with remnants of ancient Rome

Location Via Santa Agata

Admission €3.50

Hours Monday–Saturday, 9 a.m.–1:30 p.m., 2:30–7 p.m.; Sunday, 9 a.m.–1 p.m.

Phone 0743 223 277

When to Go Anytime

Overall Appeal by Age Group

Pre-school —	Teens ★★	Over 30 ★★
Grade school ★★	Young Adults ★★	Seniors ★★

Authors' Rating ★★★

How Much Time to Allow 1 hour

Description and Comments Housed in a former Benedictine convent, Spoleto's archaeological museum contains a sizable collection of artifacts unearthed from nearby Roman settlements. Included in the treasures are busts of the Caesars and sundry architectural fragments from Republican and Imperial Rome. Admission to the museum also includes a look at the Roman Theater, once completely concealed by medieval building projects, now back in use as a venue for ballet performances during the Festa dei Due Mondi. Be sure to take a look at the theater's tiled floor, one of the best-preserved Roman orchestra platforms to be found anywhere.

Museo Diocesano

Type of Attraction Art from the 13th through the 18th centuries

Location Palazzo Vescovile, Via A. Saffi, 13

Admission €2

Hours Daily, 10 a.m.–12:30 p.m., 3:30–7 p.m.

Phone 0743 231 021

When to Go Anytime

Overall Appeal by Age Group

Pre-school —	Teens ★=	Over 30 ★★
Grade school ★†	Young Adults ★†	Seniors ★★

Authors' Rating ★

How Much Time to Allow 30 minutes

Description and Comments A collection culled from the Diocese of Spoleto's stockpile, this museum has a number of second-tier paintings from Umbrian school artists. Among the best works here are an *Adoration of the Child* by Beccafumi, a *Madonna delle Neve* by Neri di Bicci, and a dossal (ornamental cloth displayed behind an altar) by Maestro di Cesi. An exhibit of medieval sculpture, including carved wooden crucifixes and stone vases, mixes things up.

Ponte delle Torri

Type of Attraction Breathtaking bridge
Location Via del Ponte
Admission None
Hours Always open
Phone None
When to Go By day
Overall Appeal by Age Group

Pre-school ★★		Teens ★★★		Over 30 ★★★
Grade school ★★★		Young Adults ★★★		Seniors ★★★

Authors' Rating ★★★
How Much Time to Allow 30 minutes

Description and Comments Appearing like a string of connected sky-scrapers across the valley, the Ponte delle Torri, or Bridge of Towers, does nothing less than awe. Built around the 13th or 14th centuries to carry water to the upper town of Spoleto, the bridge consists of nine 250-foot towers joined by a walkway. Views from the bridge are superb, but the curves along the streets of Via del Ponte and Via della Rocca provide better photo opportunities of the old viaduct.

San Pietro

Type of Attraction Lombard church with outrageous façade
Location Strada di Monteluco (approximately 0.5 mile from the city center)
Admission Free
Hours Hours vary according to guard on duty; call ahead
Phone 0743 44882
When to Go The light is best in the late afternoon
Overall Appeal by Age Group

Pre-school —		Teens ★★★		Over 30 ★★★
Grade school ★★★		Young Adults ★★★		Seniors ★★★

Authors' Rating ★★★
How Much Time to Allow 30 minutes

Description and Comments Cross the Ponte delle Torri to get to the hamlet of Monteluco, where you'll find one of the finest examples of Umbrian Romanesque architecture. Rebuilt in the 13th century by the Lombard dukes, San Pietro has a façade filled with carvings of real and imaginary animals, including lions, peacocks, oxen, griffins, and bulls. If you happen upon the church when it is open, step inside to see its Baroque interior.

Sant'Eufemia

Type of Attraction Medieval church unique in Umbria
Location Via Saffi, 13

Admission Free

Hours Daily, 10 a.m.–12:30 p.m., 3:30–7 p.m.

Phone 0743 223 245

When to Go Anytime

Overall Appeal by Age Group

Pre-school —		Teens ★★		Over 30 ★★
Grade school ★★		Young Adults ★★		Seniors ★★

Authors' Rating ★★

How Much Time to Allow 15 minutes

Description and Comments This church, a few paces from the Duomo, was completed around 1140 and is unique for its Byzantine-style details. Particularly interesting here is the Matroneum, a second-floor gallery intended to separate the women from men during mass and the Cosmatesque altar, once a part of Spoleto's Duomo.

Entertainment and Nightlife in Spoleto

In late June and early July, Spoleto becomes one of the world's chief cultural centers as the **Festival dei Due Mondi** (Via del Teatro; phone 0743 44325; **www.spoletofestival.it**) gets underway. A tour-de-force for almost half a century, the Festival of Two Worlds celebrates the performing arts with a full schedule of opera, drama, and ballet productions. The festival is far from being an amateur event, attracting such VIPs as the Three Tenors, the Martha Graham Dance Company, and Lina Wertmüller. Since its founding in 1958 by composer Gian Carlo Menotti, the festival has expanded to include jazz, prose readings, film, and the visual arts. The landmarks of Spoleto, including the Piazza del Duomo and the Roman Theater, provide an unforgettable backdrop to the performances. Tickets for events are available from the box office and online.

Two main festival venues, the **Teatro Nuovo** (Via Filetteria, 1; phone 0743 223 419) and the **Teatro Caio Melisso** (Piazza Duomo, 1; phone 0743 222 209), also figure prominently in Spoleto's post-festival nightlife. With 550 and 300 seats, respectively, these theaters regularly feature large dramatic and musical productions. These two also put on classic and experimental opera productions by the **Teatro Lirico Sperimentale "Adriano Belli"** (Piazza Bovio, 1; phone 0743 221 645; **www.tls-belli.it**) early in the fall.

On- or off-season, Spoleto plays to a very sophisticated crowd. But, like any good midsize Italian town, it has a smattering of pubs and wine bars. Young and old tend to like **Pub Excalibur** (Via Maurizio Quadrio, 9; phone 0743 48536), which is, despite its hokey, medieval theme, a good place to go for wine, beer, and late-night snacks. Go with a group to **La Tartaruga** (Via Filetteria, 12; phone 0743 223 282), the only disco in the city center, and one of the trendier spots for students and under-30s.

Todi

Hugging a ridge high over the Tiber, Todi is approximately equidistant from Umbria's two provincial capitals—Perugia and Terni—and has probably been in existence since 1955 B.C. Once you have had a chance to walk back in time through Todi's medieval, Roman, and Etruscan bastions, it is easy to see how Todi earned the title "the most livable small town in the world." Its well-kept historic center of majestic medieval buildings could easily serve as inspiration for any film set in small-town central Italy. Most of Todi's attractions front the wide cobbled **Piazza del Popolo.** The **Palazzi Pubblici,** consisting of the Gothic-style **Palazzo del Popolo** and **Palazzo del Capitano,** house the town hall and Todi's small **Museo Pinacoteca** (Palazzi Pubblici, Piazza del Popolo; phone 075 894 4148; open Tuesday–Sunday, 10:30 a.m.–1 p.m., 2–5 p.m.; admission €3). The *pinacoteca* contains a prized leather saddle of Anita Garibaldi, a *Coronation of the Virgin* by Lo Spagna, and an assortment of relics from Todi's past, including Etruscan pottery, Roman coins, medieval vestments, Deruta ceramics, and articles from the Risorgimento. Todi's **Duomo** (Piazza del Popolo; no phone; open daily, 8 a.m.–1 p.m., 3:30–7 p.m.; admission free) is situated at the north end of the square. It features an intricate rose window; a handsome wooden *portone;* a 13th-century crucifix altarpiece; and a fantastical Baroque fresco by Ferraù Fenzone that was clearly inspired by Michelangelo's *Last Judgment.* Scholars from Cambridge to Kentucky have heaped praise on Todi because of its clean air, dreamy streetscapes, and slow pace of life. In fact, its "slow city" *(città lente)* status is exactly what draws vacationers and pensioners from far and wide. So, watch out—Todi's population can quintuple in the summer.

IAT Todi   Piazza Umberto I, 6; 06059 Todi; phone 075 894 2686; **www.comune.todi.pg.it**

Torgiano

No fewer than 973 acres of grape vines attest to Torgiano's long-standing involvement with viticulture. One of Umbria's hubs for the production of red wine, this small town outside of Perugia has been for generations the home of the Lungarotti family, purveyors of one of two DOCG wines in the region (the other is in Montefalco). Fittingly, in 1974, they opened the **Museo del Vino** (Palazzo Graziani-Baglioni, Corso Vittorio Emanuele II; phone 075 988 0200; **www.lungarotti.it**; open October–April: daily, 9 a.m.–1 p.m., 3–6 p.m.; May–October: daily, 9 a.m.–1 p.m., 3–7 p.m.; admission €4). Housed in the 17th-century **Graziani Baglioni Palace,** the museum has an extensive collection of winemaking items dating from the Etruscan age to the present, including barrels, decanters, flasks, and grape presses. The guided tour will also inform you about how wine travels from the vine to the table. The reward for such a dry tour? A flight of *vino* from the Lungarotti estate.

The Province of Terni

Province of Terni Tourist Office   Viale Cesare Battisti, 7; 05100 Terni; phone 0744 483 575; **www.provincia.terni.it**

Terni

Had fate worked out differently, Terni might have become the capital of Italy. In 1867, when Rome was still under French control, the centrally located town was considered a potential candidate for the capital. Of course, that proposal didn't sit too well with many members of the newly unified government. Instead, by the early 1900s, Terni had become an industrial center, and Umbrians flocked to the town to work at its steel mill, calcium carbide facility, munitions factory, and hydroelectric plant. The latter is powered by the nearby **Màrmore Falls** (SS Valnerina; phone 0744 484 239; open on an irregular schedule, usually March–October: Monday–Friday at noon and 4–5 p.m.; and Saturday and Sunday, 10 a.m.–1 p.m., 3–10 p.m.; November–mid-March: open weekends, 3–4 p.m.), the highest waterfall in Europe. Because of these industries, Terni was a prime target for bombing during World War II. As a result, the town is far from being a picturesque hill town like its regional sisters. But don't think that Terni is lacking in the romance department. Valentino, the patron saint of lovers, was born here, and a big festival is held in his honor each February 14.

IAT Terni   Viale Cesare Battisti, 7; 05100 Terni; phone 0744 423 047

Orvieto

A citadel crowning a mountain of tufaceous rock, Orvieto's earliest incarnation was as the city of Velzna (Volsinium in Latin), a wealthy member of the Etruscan Dodecapolis and an enemy of nearby Rome. After Rome eventually sacked the town some time in the third century B.C., the remaining Etruscans retreated, and Orvieto—the Italian slurring of the Latin *urbs vetus* (old city)—was born. As time went by, Romans, Goths, and Lombards ruled the city, until 1201, when it became an independent *comune*. Meanwhile, the papacy realized the importance of Orvieto's strategic position on a volcanic mesa some 1,066 feet (325 meters) high. Pope Adrian IV had the town fortified around 1155, and various popes who followed scurried off to Orvieto when the going got tough in Rome. Thanks to papal involvement, Orvieto's **Duomo** is one of the most attractive Gothic cathedrals in Italy, its ornamental façade and the Cappella San Brizio by Luca Signorelli being the highlights. Though Pliny the Elder reported that Romans carted off more than 2,000 statues after

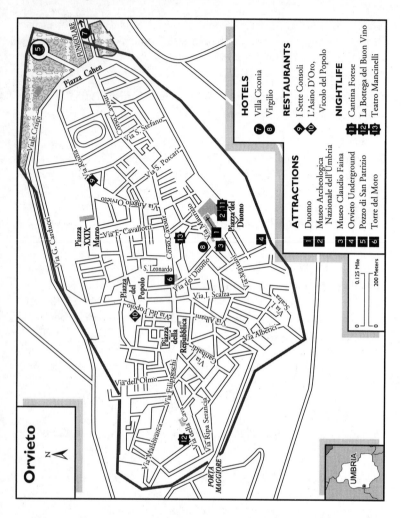

Orvieto

N

HOTELS

7 Villa Ciconia
8 Virgilio

RESTAURANTS

9 I Sette Consoli
10 L'Asino D'Oro,
     Vicolo del Popolo

NIGHTLIFE

11 Cantina Forese
12 La Bottega del Buon Vino
13 Teatro Mancinelli

ATTRACTIONS

1 Duomo
2 Museo Archeologica
   Nazionale dell'Umbria
3 Museo Claudio Faina
4 Orvieto Underground
5 Pozzo di San Patrizio
6 Torre del Moro

0   0.125 Mile

0   200 Meters

UMBRIA

conquering Orvieto, many relics from the Etruscan town remain, including a vast system of underground caves and tunnels and coins, tools, and vases in the **Claudio Faina** and **Archaeological Museums.** Orvieto Classico, the white wine that put the city on the map, was also a byproduct of Etruscan innovation.

Close to the border with Latium, and approximately one hour by rail from Rome, Orvieto is a popular day trip from Italy's capital. You'll only need about a day to traverse this small town and see its main sights, but a longer stopover of two to three days will be well worth it. If you're driving, you can park near the Orvieto Scalo train station and take bus #1 or the funicular (cable car) up to the main town. By purchasing a ticket on the funicular, you can get a discount to the **Museo Claudio Faina.** Consider purchasing a single ticket *(biglietto unico)* for €10.50, which entitles you to free parking, unlimited funicular rides, and one-time admission to the **San Brizio Chapel,** the Claudio Faina Museum, the **Torre del Moro,** and the **Orvieto Underground.**

Orvieto IAT   Piazza Duomo, 24; 05018 Orvieto; phone 0763 341 772; info@iat.orvieto.tr.it

Duomo

Type of Attraction One of Italy's most beautiful Gothic cathedrals
Location Piazza del Duomo
Admission Free; San Brizio chapel, €2
Hours Daily, 7 a.m.–1 p.m., 2:30 p.m.–dusk
Phone 0763 342 477
When to Go Weekdays
Overall Appeal by Age Group

Pre-school ★★★	Teens ★★★★	Over 30 ★★★★★
Grade school ★★★	Young Adults ★★★★★	Seniors ★★★★★

Authors' Rating ★★★★★
How Much Time to Allow 30 minutes to 1 hour

Description and Comments Arnolfo di Cambio, the architect of Florence's Santa Maria del Fiore cathedral, is also responsible for Orvieto's Duomo, a Gothic jewel. The exterior reveals a highly ornamental façade, from which familiar events from the Old and New Testaments come alive in inlaid mosaics done in hues of blue, pink, and shimmering gold. Surrounding the church's rose window, which was designed by Andrea Orcagna, are dozens of niches in which small carvings of saints stand guard. Three arched doorways, sculpted by Lorenzo Maitani, feature scenes from the Creation (on the left) and the Last Judgment (on the right) in high relief. The latter, now under protective Plexiglas, was sculpted with such detail that you can almost hear the screams of those condemned to an eternity in hell.

For Gothic standards, the interior of the Duomo is relatively plain, punctuated only by the Dominican black-and-white striping and an elegant nave arcade. However, down the aisle and to the right, you'll find the San Brizio chapel, a veritable showcase of art from Luca Signorelli. In 1447, Fra Angelico and Benozzo Gozzoli began frescoing the vault of the San Brizio chapel, but they never finished. Signorelli, who had gained a reputation in Siena, was then contracted to finish the ceiling, and asked that a portion of his payment be in Orvieto Classico wine. Signorelli finished the ceiling in just over a year and promptly began work on one of

Umbria's most important fresco cycles, second only to Giotto's *Life of St. Francis* in Assisi. The fresco cycle is said to have inspired Michelangelo, and was based on the story of the Last Judgment, a favorite theme in the late 15th century to early 16th century. Starting from the left is the *Sermon of the Antichrist,* followed by the *End of the World* (over the archway). Continuing on the right wall is the *Resurrection of the Body,* a masterful (if creepy) depiction of the rising of the dead. Here, muscular men and skeletons crawl from their graves in preparation to meet their maker. Next to this is *Casting Out of the Damned,* followed by the altar fresco *Angels Drive the Sinners to Hell* and *Guide the Elect to Paradise.* Curiously, on the lower registers below the fresco cycle, Signorelli painted medallions of notable classical figures, including Dante, Homer, and Virgil.

The history of Orvieto's Duomo dates back to 1263, when a priest at nearby Lake Bolsena is said to have witnessed the miracle of transubstantiation. After blessing a wafer at mass, the host began to drip blood, staining the linen covering the altar. When the pope learned of this event, he proclaimed a holy day, thus beginning the feast of Corpus Christi. At that time, Orvieto was the largest city near Lake Bolsena and was in need of a new, more dazzling cathedral. The miracle was an impetus to build a glorious temple, and—30 years later—construction began on the church that would hold the cloth stained with the blood of Christ. Each year, on Easter and on the Feast of Corpus Christi, the cloth is removed for viewing.

Touring Tips The best views of the façade of the Duomo are from across the piazza on the second floor of the Museo Claudio Faina, which houses a well-organized collection of Etruscan relics.

Museo Archeologico Nazionale dell'Umbria

Type of Attraction Umbria's primary archaeological museum
Location Piazza del Duomo
Admission €2
Hours Monday–Saturday, 9 a.m.–7 p.m.; Sunday, 9 a.m.–I p.m.
Phone 0763 341 039
When to Go Anytime
Overall Appeal by Age Group

Pre-school —		Teens ★★		Over 30 ★★★
Grade school ★★		Young Adults ★★★		Seniors ★★★

Authors' Rating ★★½

How Much Time to Allow I hour

Description and Comments Quite a number of Etruscan artifacts have been unearthed from the countryside in and around Orvieto. Those relics that haven't ended up in bigger museums throughout Italy have been set aside in Umbria's National Archaeological Museum. Some of the highlights of the museum include vases (Greek and Etruscan *bucchero* style), a full suit of bronze armor, and two reconstructed fourth-century B.C. tombs, complete with original Etruscan frescoes.

Museo Claudio Faina

Type of Attraction Private collection with extensive archaeological finds

Location Piazza del Duomo, 29

Admission €4; €5 combined with round-trip bus or funicular ticket

Hours April–September: daily, 9:30 a.m.–6 p.m.; October–March: Tuesday–Sunday, 10 a.m.–1 p.m., 2:30–5 p.m.

Phone 0763 341 511

When to Go Crowds are light on weekday afternoons

Overall Appeal by Age Group

Pre-school —		Teens ★★★		Over 30 ★★★
Grade school ★★★		Young Adults ★★★		Seniors ★★★

Authors' Rating ★★★

How Much Time to Allow 1–1.5 hours

Description and Comments Worth the price of admission for its full frontal view of the Duomo, the Museo Claudio Faina is one of the finest formerly private archaeological museums in all of Italy. Given over to the city in 1954, the collection features an ample display of red and black Attic vases, *bucchero* ware, and some 3,000 ancient Etruscan coins found in various nearby necropolises. The museum also has an exhibit of painted sarcophagi and a sixth-century B.C. nude sculpture called the *Venus of Cannicella*. High marks are given the Claudio Faina for its children's program. Kids are given a brochure at the entrance, and signposts throughout the museum encourage children to learn about Etruscan history, culture, and art. At the end, kids can take a quiz to see how much they've learned.

Orvieto Underground

Type of Attraction Subterranean caverns in existence since Etruscan times

Location Via della Cava, 28

Admission €4.50, or €10.50 if you purchase a *biglietto unico*

Hours Guided visits daily at 9:45 a.m., 11:15 a.m., 3:45 p.m., and 5:15 p.m.

Phone Call the tourist office for info, phone 0763 341 772

When to Go Anytime, but especially on a hot summer day

Special Comments The Orvieto Underground is not ideal for very young children

Overall Appeal by Age Group

Pre-school —		Teens ★★★		Over 30 ★★★
Grade school ★★		Young Adults ★★★		Seniors ★★★

Authors' Rating ★★★

How Much Time to Allow 1 hour

Description and Comments Almost all of Orvieto's buildings were constructed of tufa and *pozzulana* (volcanic sand used for concrete) unearthed from the dense mount on which the city stands. The Etruscans were the first to dig into the mass of stone below; in the process, they created a series of tunnels, grottoes, natural wine cellars, and dovecotes. The tunneling was so extensive that many homes and businesses in Orvieto have underground access. This tour introduces you to the history of the Etruscans in Orvieto and the known techniques they used in creating these underground systems—some methods of digging by these early settlers are still a mystery. Spelunkers have found endless perfectly rounded wells that could have only been formed by highly sophisticated drills. The Etruscans also dug out holes in which to store their trash, and researchers have yet to reach the bottom of these heaps. The tour of Orvieto's underground is a must for anyone with a passing interest in Etruscan culture. For others, the tour is a worthwhile escape from medieval and Renaissance Italy.

Touring Tips Bring a sweater and wear sensible shoes.

Pozzo di San Patrizio

Type of Attraction 16th-century well
Location Via Sangallo, Piazza Cahen
Admission €3; €5 combined with the Museo Emilio Greco
Hours April–September: daily, 9:30 a.m.–6:45 p.m.; October–March: daily, 10 a.m.–5:45 p.m.
Phone 0763 343 768
When to Go Anytime
Overall Appeal by Age Group

Pre-school —		Teens ★★		Over 30 ★★
Grade school ★★		Young Adults ★★		Seniors ★

Authors' Rating ★★
How Much Time to Allow 30 minutes

Description and Comments After Rome was sacked in 1527, Pope Clement VII took refuge in Orvieto. While here, he worried that Orvieto would also come under siege and that its water supply would be threatened. Subsequently, he commissioned Antonio Sangallo the Younger to construct a well under the fortress in which he hid. The well, finished some years after the pope's death, was quite an architectural accomplishment for the time and featured a double-helix stairway wide enough to accommodate mule-drawn carts to descend down one staircase and ascend up another. As for the name of the well, the story goes that the *pozzo* resembled a well in Ireland, and so was named for the country's patron saint.

Torre del Moro

Type of Attraction Belltower with lovely views
Location Intersection of Corso Cavour and Via del Duomo
Admission €3
Hours May–August: daily, 10 a.m.–8 p.m.; March–April and September–October: daily, 10 a.m.–7 p.m.; November–February: daily, 10 a.m.–1 p.m., 2:30–5 p.m.
Phone 0763 344 567
When to Go Early afternoon
Overall Appeal by Age Group

Pre-school —		Teens ★★★		Over 30 ★★★
Grade school ★★		Young Adults ★★★		Seniors ★★★

Authors' Rating ★★★★
How Much Time to Allow 30 minutes

Description and Comments Few tourists would think to visit the rather plain Torre del Moro, but it is one attraction that shouldn't be missed. A modern stairwell leads to the top of the tower, from which you'll be able to survey the layout of the town of Orvieto as well as the countryside of Umbria and Latium. The tower's bell, decorated with icons representing Orvieto's 24 traditional arts and crafts guilds, dates from the 14th century and is still in working condition. We suggest that you venture to the top of the tower shortly after lunch (when its tolling of the hour will be shorter). Otherwise, the repetitive clanging of the bell at noon will leave you shaken for some time.

Entertainment and Nightlife in Orvieto

Orvieto is a rather sleepy town, with few overnight tourists to fuel its nightlife scene. However, the popularity of Perugia's **Umbria Jazz Festival** spawned a winter edition in Orvieto. During the colder months, the jazz programs head indoors to social clubs, restaurants, and to the **Teatro Mancinelli** (Corso Cavour; phone 0763 340 493). When not playing host to modern music concerts, the theater is the centerpiece of Orvieto cultural life, putting on mostly plays and operas.

However, we find that the best way to spend the evening in Orvieto is at an *enoteca,* where dozens of bottles of local Classico and other vintages are available by the glass or bottle. **Cantina Forese** (Piazza del Duomo, 2; phone 0763 341 611) and **La Bottega del Buon Vino** (Via della Cava 26; phone 0763 342 373) are located near the Duomo, and offer small plates of olives, cheese, and local specialties.

Part Nine

The Best of the Marches

"Italy in One Region"

The Marches region (Le Marche) is a tangle of contradictions. Its wild landscape of craggy hills and dramatic mountains gives way to lush forests and pristine beaches. The tidy, sleepy hill towns and farming villages that dot the sage- and wheat-colored patchwork countryside give no hint that this region is commercially successful, with a bustling port in **Ancona** and dozens of family-owned businesses from **Pésaro** to **Áscoli Piceno.** The Marchigiani, as the region's denizens are called, have a less-than-glowing reputation among their compatriots. *"Meglio un morto in casa che un marchigiano fuori della porta"* (better to have a corpse in the house than a Marchigiano at the door) is a saying that dates back to the days when men from the Marches collected taxes for the pope. On the other hand, some of Italy's most revered figures—most notably Raphael and composer Giacchino Rossini—have hailed from here. Ironically, the region that routinely resisted the authority of the papacy, characterized as the Infidelitas Marchianorum, is home to one of Europe's major pilgrimage sites. **Loreto's Santa Casa** (Holy House), said to be the home where the Holy Family lived when they returned from Egypt, is one of the biggest draws in the Marches.

Separated into four, parallel provinces—**Pésaro-Urbino, Ancona, Macerata,** and **Áscoli Piceno,** each consisting of mountains, plains, and the sea—the Marches reflect a recent tourist board catchphrase, "Italy in One Region." Tourists from North America seeking the refinement of Tuscany and the tranquility of Umbria's hill towns will find a prize in the Marches, a region whose secrets are quickly coming to light.

The Marches Regional Board of Tourism   Via Gentile da Fabriano, 9; 60125 Ancona; phone 071 806 2284, fax 071 806 2154; **www.turismo. marche.it**

March

Settimana dei Beni Culturali (Cultural Week)   One week in March or April. During cultural week, all state-owned museums and archaeological sites are open free of charge. For more information, phone 071 202 790.

April

Palio della Rana, Fermignano (Pésaro-Urbino)   First Sunday after Easter. A hotly contested race in the main square that features frogs in wheelbarrows rather than riders on horses.

May

Palio di San Floriano, Jesi   May 4. A Jesi tradition since the 12th century, this medieval pageant features a crossbow tournament and banner-waving procession fueled by plenty of singing, dancing, and eating.

Urbino Città Fiorita (Urbino in Bloom), Urbino   Mid-May. This flower festival includes garden tours, special floral exhibitions, and markets.

June

Palio di San Giovanni and the Sfida del Maglio (Challenge of the Hammer), Fabriano   June 24. Residents representing this blacksmithing town's four gates—Borgo, Cervara, Piano, Pisana—compete in races, games of rings, and hammer handling.

July

La Contesa del Pozzo della Polenta (Festival of the Well of Polenta), Corinaldo   Third week of July. Archery and jousting contests commemorate the 1517 victory over Francesco Maria I della Rovere.

Visiting the Region

Getting around the Marches

Unless you're traveling to Ancona, which lies at the end of the intersection of the Rome-Ancona and Adriatic train lines, or to Urbino, which is easily reached by bus, train, and car from Umbria and Tuscany, getting around the Marches can be difficult. The Adriatic Route A14 is the main *autostrada* in the region, bypassing major port cities like Pésaro and Ancona. Naturally, this highway won't help you much if you intend to spend your time inland. Other major roads in the Marches include the S73B, which connects Urbino with the E78, which leads into Tuscany; the S76, which bisects the region from Ancona to Jesi to Fabriano; and

July (continued)

Macerata Opera Festival, Macerata   July–August. Held in Macerata's Sferisterio. For information, phone 0733 230 735.

Festival Internazionale di Musica Antica (Early Music Festival), Urbino   Last week of July. A festival of sacred, classical, and folk music from around the world. For information, phone 0722 309 601.

August

La Giostra della Quintana, Áscoli Piceno   First Sunday of August. A medieval jousting festival in the city's main piazza.

Festa del Duca, Urbino   Third Sunday in August. This festival celebrates the memory of Urbino's most famous former resident, Duke Federico da Montefeltro.

The Rossini Opera Festival, Pésaro   Mid-August. Information, phone 0721 34473, fax 0721 30979.

September

Festa dell'Aquilone (Kite Festival), Urbino   First weekend of the month. A high-flying affair in nearby Cèsane.

October

Fiera Nazionale del Tartufo (National Truffle Fair), Acqualagna (Pésaro-Urbino)   Last weekend in October and first three weekends in November.

November

Ancona Jazz Festival, Ancona   Early November. For information, phone 071 217 4239.

---

the S4, the old Via Salaria, which connects the Marches with Rome. In the winter, the steep, winding country roads in the Marches, of which there are many, can be icy and slick.

Train routes basically follow the same path as the A14, making stops in Ancona, Pésaro, and further south to San Benedetto del Tronto. Private companies, such as the ones listed below, provide much of the bus service in the region.

A.P.M. (Macerata)   phone 0733 29351

Bucci (Pésaro-Urbino)   phone 0721 32401

Conerobus (Ancona)   phone 071 280 2092

CO.TR.AN (Ancona)   phone 071 202 766

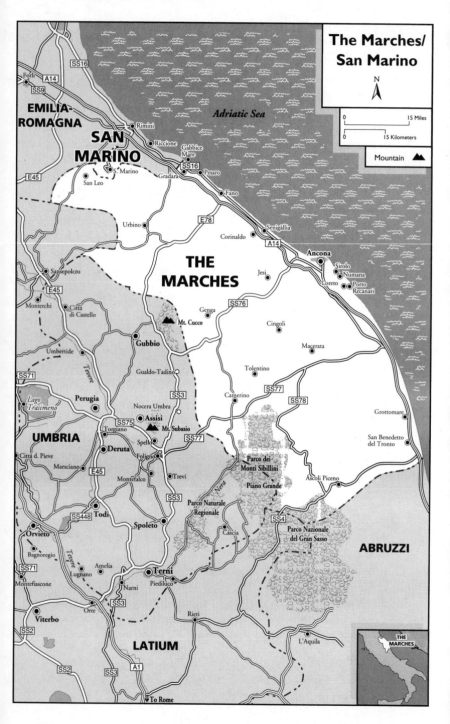

Reni (Ancona)   phone 071 804 6504

SAPUM (Pésaro-Urbino)   phone 0721 371 318

START (Áscoli-Piceno)   phone 0736 263 053

When to Visit

Summer finds the region's beach resorts, like **Gabicce Mare** and **San Benedetto del Tronto,** hopping with Italian and European tourists. Meanwhile, the Marches' rather mountainous interior provides a much-needed break from heat and holidaymakers. Spring is a popular time to visit, both for the mild weather and the numerous local festivals that help end the long, winter slumber. Gastronomes will want to visit the Marches in the fall, when truffles are celebrated in food fairs throughout the region, especially in the otherwise quiet towns of **Acqualagna** and **Sant'Angelo in Vado,** where the tubers are harvested. Winter travel in the Marches can be trying, as the steep, narrow paths make driving treacherous, and a number of the region's farmhouse inns and family-owned hotels close for the season. On the other hand, skiers will find adequate slopes in the **Monti Sibillini.**

Quick Glance at the Towns of the Marches

Following is a listing of cities and touring areas in the Marches by province. For each city or area, we provide an overall rating to describe how rewarding that place is to visit. We also include a short comment about the place. Use this as a reference for day trips or extended holidays.

City/Area	Overall Rating	Comment
Province of Pésaro-Urbino		
Fano	★★★★	Roman ruins and Renaissance palaces steps from the beach
Gradara	★★★	Model medieval walled city
Pesaro	★★★	Birthplace of Rossini
San Leo	★★★	Papal stronghold
Republic of San Marino	★★★½	The tiniest republic on earth
Urbino	★★★★★	One of Italy's finest Renaissance burgs
Province of Ancona		
Ancona	★★★½	Handsome harbor town, largest in Marches
Corinaldo	★★★	Off-the-beaten-track medieval town
Genga	★★½	Contains the Frassasi Caverns
Jesi	★★★	Features Lotto masterpieces
Loreto	★★★★	Madonna's house is enshrined here
Riviera Conero	★★★★★	Spellbinding shores

Quick Glance at the Towns of the Marches *(continued)*

Province of Macerata

Cingoli	★★★½	The "Balcony of the Marches"
Macerata	★★★	Grand Sferisterio is the highlight
Tolentino	★★★½	Home to Saint Nicholas

Province of Áscoli Piceno

Áscoli Piceno	★★★★	Ancient village
Parco Nazionale dei Monti Sibillini	★★★	Peaceful and rugged
Riviera delle Palme	★★★★	All of Europe flocks to its beaches

The Province of Pésaro-Urbino

Province of Pésaro-Urbino Tourist Office   Via Mazzolari 4; 61100 Pésaro; phone 0721 30258.

Urbino

If ever there were a person who could be so closely identified with a city, it would be Federico da Montefeltro, the duke who remade this jewel of a town into a center of art and culture. The crook-nosed, toad-faced ruler, whose likeness is featured on a celebrated double-sided panel by Piero della Francesca (now at the Uffizi in Florence), virtually laid waste to the old town of Urbino during his reign from 1442–1482, completely rebuilding it into a model of Renaissance city. The centerpiece of the town, the refined **Palazzo Ducale,** was built on the duke's watch, and today houses the **Galleria Nazionale delle Marche,** a treasure trove of *quattrocento* painting.

Following in Federico's footsteps was his son Guidobaldo, who established a university here in 1506. While the university flourished—today it is one of the oldest and most respected colleges in the country—local boys Raphael and Bramante were busy with the renewal and decoration of the Vatican complex under the commission of Pope Julius II. Only a couple works from Raphael are on display in Urbino—most are in Florence and Rome—and none of Bramante's designs can be found here.

Nevertheless, the Renaissance lives on in Urbino. After Guidobaldo da Montefeltro passed away without any heirs, his nephew Francesco Maria I della Rovere moved his court to Pèsaro, signaling the end of the city's cultural revolution and unwittingly saving it from a Baroque assault. In 1998, UNESCO named Urbino a World Heritage Site, and it is one of the best-preserved Renaissance cities in Italy.

Daily buses to Urbino depart Florence and Arezzo in the west and Perugia and Gubbio from the south. The bus depot in Urbino is located just

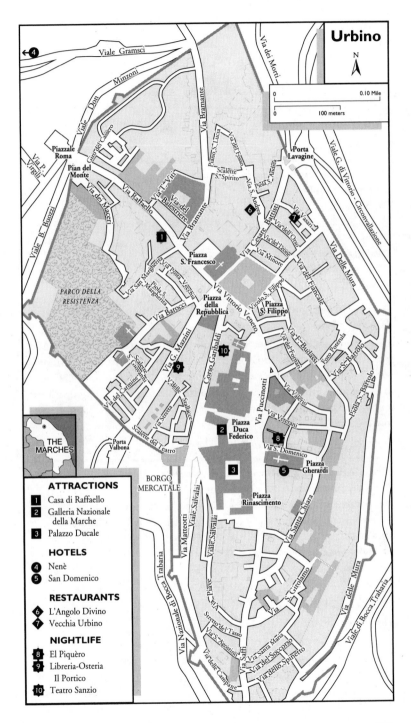

Urbino

N

| 0 | | 0.10 Mile |
| 0 | 100 meters | |

ATTRACTIONS

1. Casa di Raffaello
2. Galleria Nazionale della Marche
3. Palazzo Ducale

HOTELS

4. Nenè
5. San Domenico

RESTAURANTS

6. L'Angolo Divino
7. Vecchia Urbino

NIGHTLIFE

8. El Piquèro
9. Libreria-Osteria Il Portico
10. Teatro Sanzio

THE MARCHES

below the city center at Piazzale Mercatale, where you'll find buses for other destinations in the Pésaro-Urbino province. The closest train station is in Pésaro. Highways S423 and S73B bypass Urbino. If you're driving, parking is available near Piazzale Mercatale, which is a short walk uphill to the center of town, and in Piazzale Roma, on the city's northern edge.

IAT Urbino   Piazza Rinascimento, 1; 61029 Urbino; phone 0722 2613; **www.comune.urbino.ps.it**

Casa di Raffaello

Type of Attraction   Childhood home of Raphael
Location   Via Raffaello, 57
Admission   €3
Hours   Tuesday–Saturday, 9 a.m.–1 p.m., 3–7 p.m.; Sunday, 10 a.m.–1 p.m.
Phone   0722 320 105
Overall Appeal by Age Group

Pre-school —		Teens ★★		Over 30 ★★
Grade school ★★		Young Adults ★★		Seniors ★★

Authors' Rating   ★★
How Much Time to Allow   30 minutes

Description and Comments   In a small home centered around a court-yard, Raffaello Sanzio, or Raphael, was born in 1483. In the very room where Raphael was born, you'll find an early *Madonna and Child* fresco by the young painter; otherwise, the museum is filled with reproductions of his works. Raphael's father and first art teacher, Giovanni Santi, is also represented.

Galleria Nazionale delle Marche

Type of Attraction   The Marches' most important art museum
Location   Palazzo Ducale, Piazza Duca Federico
Admission   €5, ticket includes Palazzo Ducale and the Museo Archeologico
Hours   Tuesday–Saturday, 9 a.m.–7 p.m.; Sunday, 9 a.m.–8 p.m.
Phone   0722 322 625
Overall Appeal by Age Group

Pre-school ★★		Teens ★★		Over 30 ★★★★
Grade school ★★		Young Adults ★★★★		Seniors ★★★★

Authors' Rating   ★★★★
How Much Time to Allow   1–2 hours

Description and Comments   This collection, which contains one of the best representations of Renaissance art outside of Florence, was culled from the holdings of the Montefeltro and Della Rovere families as well as from local churches and monasteries. Opened in 1912, the National Gallery of the Marches features *The Flagellation* by Piero della Francesca and *Ideal City*, designed by Luciano Laurana and painted by Piero della Francesca; both are considered to represent the best of *quattrocento* perspective painting. Piero's *Madonna of Senigállia* is also here. Paolo Uccello's altarpiece pedestal *(predella)* paintings of the *Miracle of the Desecration of the Host*, which were recently restored, depict a harrowing anti-Semitic tale in almost comic strip–like form. Other standouts in the collection include a *Madonna and Child* by Gentileschi, a *Pentecost and Crucifixion* by Luca Signorelli, and a *Last Supper and Resurrection* by Titian. The only Raphael in the museum, *La Muta (The Mute)*, is as complex a portrait as Leonardo's *Mona Lisa*. Indeed, one of the most popular works here, *Portrait of Duke Federico* by Spanish artist Pedro Berruguete, shows the old duke, ever in profile, cloaked in armor and a rich red wrap, with his young heir, Guidobaldo, at this knee.

Palazzo Ducale

Type of Attraction Federico da Montefeltro's elaborate Renaissance estate

Location Piazza Duca Federico

Admission €5, ticket includes Galleria Nazionale delle Marche and the Museo Archeologico

Hours Tuesday–Saturday, 9 a.m.–7 p.m.; Sunday and Monday, 9 a.m.–2 p.m.

Phone 0722 2760

Overall Appeal by Age Group

Pre-school ★★★		Teens ★★★		Over 30 ★★★★★
Grade school ★★★		Young Adults ★★★★		Seniors ★★★★★

Authors' Rating ★★★★★

How Much Time to Allow 2–3 hours, including Galleria Nazionale

Description and Comments Begun in 1465, the Ducal Palace, with its elegant, arcaded courtyards and twin turrets, is right out of a fairy tale—and that's how Duke Federico da Montefeltro would have wanted it. This mansion was to be his contribution to the world of art and architecture and an oasis to guests. What set the palace apart from other castles in the region was that it was at once impregnable and pleasing to the eye, imposing but genteel. Luciano Laurana, whom the duke hired in 1465, drew up plans for the noble courtyard and designed the castle's pair of turrets, which are today the very symbol of Urbino. Francesco di Giorgio Martini, one of the duke's favorite architects, took over in 1472 and built the façade; Ambrogio Barocci decorated the Courtyard of Honor (Cortile d'Onore) with Latin inscriptions honoring Montefeltro. The duke didn't skimp on the interior details, either, enlisting local and national artists to fresco rooms and chisel out handsome reliefs. The elaborate, wooden trompe l'oeil inlay work in the duke's study includes renderings of everyday objects (books, an hourglass, even a squirrel at the window) and have to be seen to be believed. The Galleria Nazionale delle Marche, located on the noble floor *(piano nobile)* of the palace, contains a number of works that were originally commissioned by the duke for the palace. Within the palace walls, you'll also find a small archaeological museum that boasts a relatively modest display of ancient tombstones and column remnants.

Entertainment and Nightlife in Urbino

A university located in the center of town does much to provide a youthful, if small, nightlife scene in Urbino. A town favorite, located on the main thoroughfare of Via Mazzini, is the **Libreria-Osteria Il Portico** (Via Mazzini, 7; phone 0722 2722), which has rooms for dining, drinking, listening to live music, and checking your e-mail. Note that the Osteria area of the bar is more upscale and you'll need a reservation. Behind the Palazzo Ducale, on Via San Domenico, try **El Piquèro** (Via San Domenico, 1; phone 0722 327 463) sometimes called Pub Cagliostro, where you'll find plenty of beer and wine, and a friendly mix of students and tourists.

Meanwhile the **Teatro Sanzio** (Corso Garibaldi; phone 0722 2281) is the cultural meeting point in town. Its season (autumn and spring) features experimental dance programs and modern dramas. Even English-language musicals ramble in on occasion. Single tickets cost between €8 and €20.

Pésaro

Like many towns in central Italy, Pésaro's importance on the political and cultural stage has ebbed and flowed. Its origins date back to the fourth century B.C., when it was a mere fishing village on the Adriatic. Some centuries later, after the city had been sacked and overrun by the Goths, Pésaro became a member of the Maritime Pentapolis of the Exarchate of Ravenna, the center of Byzantine rule in Italy. The Holy Roman Empire and the popes argued over the port city for years, and in 1285, Pésaro came under the rule of the Malatesta family of Rimini (in nearby Emilia-Romagna). By the early 16th century, several noble families had used Pésaro as a bargaining chip, until it finally fell into the hands of Francesco Maria I della Rovere, nephew of both Guidobaldo da Montefeltro and Pope Julius II. Francesco Maria moved his court here from Urbino.

The modern history of this provincial capital can be summed up in one word: Rossini. The great composer of *The Barber of Seville* and *William Tell* left Pésaro a music school, the **Giacchino Rossini Conservatory,** while his legacy led to the establishment of the **Teatro Rossini** and the **Rossini Opera Festival,** one of the biggest events in the region.

Pésaro was one of the main ports on the Adriatic during World War II, and therefore suffered under the advance of Allied troops in 1944. Luckily, much of the old center remains intact, including its lovely **Piazza del Popolo.** The city has become a beach destination in recent years, and in summer, the strand becomes a sea of striped umbrellas. If you want to see

Pésaro at its most vibrant, head here in August when Rossini-lovers and sun-worshipers converge.

APT Pésaro   Viale Trieste, 164; 61100 Pésaro; phone 0721 69341, fax 071 30462; **www.comune.pesaro.ps.it**

Casa di Rossini

Type of Attraction The composer's childhood home
Location Via Rossini
Admission €2
Hours Tuesday–Saturday, 9 a.m.–7 p.m.; Sunday, 9 a.m.–1 p.m.
Phone 0721 387 357
Overall Appeal by Age Group

Pre-school —		Teens ★★		Over 30 ★★
Grade school —		Young Adults ★★		Seniors ★★

Authors' Rating ★
How Much Time to Allow 30 minutes

Description and Comments Rossini's birthplace contains memorabilia from the composer, including original scores, letters, and other personal effects. This small museum on the second floor also contains the original furnishings from Rossini's time.

Museo Archeologico Oliveriano

Type of Attraction Archaeology museum
Location Via Mazza, 97
Admission Free
Hours Monday–Saturday, 9:30 a.m.–noon, or by appointment
Phone 0721 33344
Overall Appeal by Age Group

Pre-school —		Teens ★★		Over 30 ★★
Grade school ★★		Young Adults ★★		Seniors ★★

Authors' Rating ★
How Much Time to Allow 30 minutes

Description and Comments This collection of antiquities, donated by local scholar Annibale degli Abbati Olivieri Giordani, documents finds from the Novilara necropolis, a lost Roman settlement not far from Pésaro. Included in the gallery are boundary stones, sarcophagi, ancient furnishings, and a large marble tablet inscribed with both Latin and Etruscan characters.

Musei Civici

Type of Attraction Local museums with works from the Tuscan, Bolognese, and Venetian schools
Location Piazza Toschi Mosca, 29

Admission €2

Hours May–September: Tuesday–Saturday, 9 a.m.–7 p.m.; Sunday, 9 a.m.–1 p.m.; October–April: Tuesday–Saturday, 8:30 a.m.–1:30 p.m., Sunday, 9 a.m.–1 p.m.

Phone 0721 67815

Overall Appeal by Age Group

Pre-school —		Teens ★★		Over 30 ★★
Grade school ★		Young Adults ★★		Seniors ★★

Authors' Rating ★★

How Much Time to Allow 30 minutes to 1 hour

Description and Comments Pésaro's municipal museums house a collection of Marchigian and Umbrian ceramics and a small art gallery. Of particular note here is Giovanni Bellini's *Coronation of the Virgin,* also called the Pésaro Altarpiece. This exceptional work includes a central panel of the Virgin Mary and saints in front of a backdrop of Pésaro and a fanciful frame decorated with nine saints and seven religious scenes. It is considered Bellini's masterpiece.

Fano

Save for the **Arco di Augusto,** which guards the entrance into town, only a few remnants from Fano's Roman past are still evident. But, during its heyday, the city of Fanum Fortunae was the first of several stops on the Adriatic extension of the Flaminian Way. A port city, and today, the Marches' third largest in terms of population, Fano's fortunes have largely depended on the fishing and trade industries. As a result, the town has seen many incarnations, the most lasting being that of a stronghold for the patrician Malatesta family. Throughout the city, they built palaces and forts to protect their interests from marauding pirates and—more importantly—the land-grabbing Borgia and Montefeltro clans. In the center of the old city on the lively Piazza Maggiore (now **Piazza XX Settembre**), the Malatesta commissioned the **Palazzo Malatesta,** which now houses the **Museo Civico and Pinacoteca** (Palazzo Malatesta; phone 0721 828 362; open Tuesday–Saturday, 8:30 a.m.–12:30 p.m.; Sunday, 8:30 a.m.–1 p.m.; admission €2.50). Exceptional, as far as civic museums are concerned, Fano's contains works by Guido Reni, Guercino, and Domenichino, and has an extensive collection of medallions emblazoned with the crests and countenances of the Malatesta family members. Another major Malatesta contribution to the Fano cityscape is the **Rocca Malatestiana,** a towering 15th-century fortress and former prison. From the Rocca, the Malatesta would have been able to keep an eye on ships entering the port. But, today, from the same perch, the view would be of the modern hotels and shops that have cropped up around Fano's two lovely beaches, Lido and Sassonia.

IAT Fano   Via Battisti, 10; 61032 Fano; phone 0721 887 401

Gradara

Just inland from the resort town of Gabicce Mare and a short distance from Pésaro on the A14 is the impressively compact walled city of Gradara. The Malatesta clan, who saw the strategic importance of this area, had the outer walls and **Porta dell'Orologio** (the Orologio Gate, the village's only entrance), built in the 14th century. Within the ramparts is yet another set of walls, which separate the Malatesta castle from the main town. Students of Dante may be familiar with this castle, as it was the site of a clandestine kiss between Paolo Malatesta and his brother's lover, Francesca da Rimini, as related in the fifth canto of the poet's *Inferno*.

Pro Loco Gradara   Via Borgo Mancini; 61012 Gradara; phone 0541 964 115

San Leo

Guelph conquerors memorialized the impenetrable fortress town of San Leo with the battle cry: "There is but one pope, there is but one God, and there is but one San Leo." In fact, this town on the Montefeltro hill was so difficult to enter or escape from that its imposing castle eventually became a prison, a role it played until the 20th century. San Leo's history is neatly tied up with that of the nearby Republic of San Marino, whose patron saint, St. Marinus, was pals with St. Leo of Dalmatia, the man who brought Christianity to these parts in the fourth century. Like modern San Marino, San Leo today enjoys a healthy heaping of curious tourists.

Pro Loco San Leo   Piazza Dante, 14; 61018 San Leo; phone 0541 916 231

The Republic of San Marino

Nestled on a peak between the province of Pésaro-Urbino and the region of Emilia-Romagna, the Republic of San Marino is worth a visit if you're in these parts simply because it is, at 37 square miles, the smallest republic in the whole world. Founded in the fourth century by St. Marino, who at the time was a simple Christian craftsman fleeing persecution from Diocletian, this community on Mount Titano was essentially overlooked for centuries. In the 11th century, San Marino gained its independence, and by 1243, the republic had a constitution (by which it still abides today).

Medieval structures are abundant in San Marino, and the most recognizable of these is the **Guaita** (Via Salita alla Rocca; phone 0549 991 369), or the First Tower, which is surrounded by a complex containing a church, a belltower, a pentagonal donjon and a prison. A steep, panoramic path to the peak of Mount Titano leads to the **Second Tower,** which served as a commanding lookout post between the mid-13th and 17th centuries. The atmosphere around the austere tower makes the thought of heavily-armored knights very realistic, which is why its appropriate that San

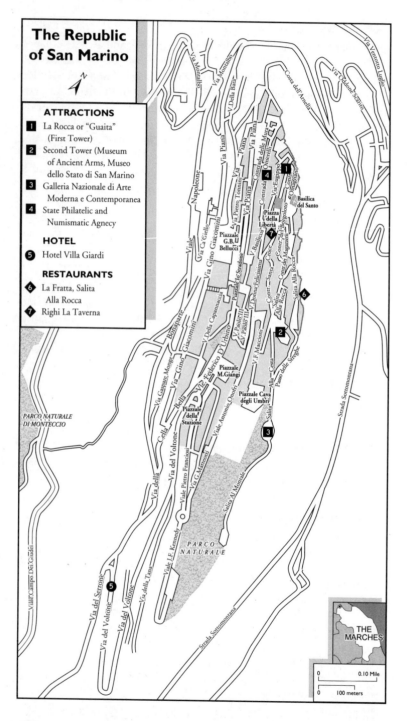

The Republic of San Marino

ATTRACTIONS

1 La Rocca or "Guaita" (First Tower)

2 Second Tower (Museum of Ancient Arms, Museo dello Stato di San Marino

3 Galleria Nazionale di Arte Moderna e Contemporanea

4 State Philatelic and Numismatic Agnecy

HOTEL

5 Hotel Villa Giardi

RESTAURANTS

6 La Fratta, Salita Alla Rocca

7 Righi La Taverna

PARCO NATURALE DI MONTECCIO

PARCO NATURALE

THE MARCHES

0   0.10 Mile

0   100 meters

Marino's **Museum of Ancient Arms** (Via Salita all Cesta; phone 0549 991 295) is located here. Occupying two floors, the museum has a slew of metal breastplates, spears, and swords, and a wing devoted to the development of modern firearms. Additional fragments from San Marino's history are on display at the **Museo dello Stato di San Marino** (Palazzo Pergami Belluzzi, Piazzetta del Titano, 1; phone 0549 883 835). A wide array of stone tools, bronze statuettes, Roman pottery, and Ostrogothic jewelry makes up the bulk of the museum's archeological collection. But, you may also enjoy the picture gallery, which contains works by artists such as Reni, Guercino, and Alberoni. There is also an entire room devoted to paintings depicting the republic's patron saints, Marino and Agata. Conversely, San Marino's **Galleria Nazionale di Arte Moderna e Contemporanea** (Via Eugippo; phone 0549 883 002) is a surprise, with more than 750 works by emerging artists from San Marino, Italy, and Europe. Note that these and other state-run museums are open in the summer from 8 a.m.–8 p.m., and in winter hours from 8 a.m.–5 p.m. The price of admission is €3; however, €4.50 will buy you a pass to two museums of your choice. And, if you visit, don't forget to pick up some of San Marino's rare stamps and coins, which can be purchased from the **State Philatelic and Numismatic Agency** (Piazza Garibaldi, 5; phone 0549 882 365, fax 0549 882 363).

The tiny republic is most easily approached from Rimini (region Emilia-Romagna), where a bus departs hourly from the main train station. If you're traveling by car, San Marino is approximately 18 miles southwest of Rimini on highway S72. You must follow the Adriatic coastal route A14 to reach the exit for San Marino, else you can depend on a web of small country roads to get you there.

San Marino Tourist Board   Contrada Omagnano, 20; 47890 Città San Marino; Republic of San Marino; phone 0549 378 549, fax 0549 882 575; **www.visitsanmarino.com**

The Province of Ancona

Province of Ancona Tourist Office   Corso Stamira, 60; 60100 Ancona; phone 071 58941; **www.provincia.ancona.it**

Ancona

Hardly the typical tourist haunt, Ancona is the mid-Adriatic's largest port, handling hundreds of container vessels, fishing fleets, and cruise ships daily. In fact, most of the travelers who wind up in Ancona are here to catch a ferry *(traghetto)* to Turkey, Albania, Croatia, or Greece. Similarly, travelers coming from the east tend to stop in Ancona only long enough to transfer from the boat to a direct train to Rome. Ancona is a bit rough around the edges, having survived bombings in World War II and at least two severe earthquakes, but its major sites are worth a look.

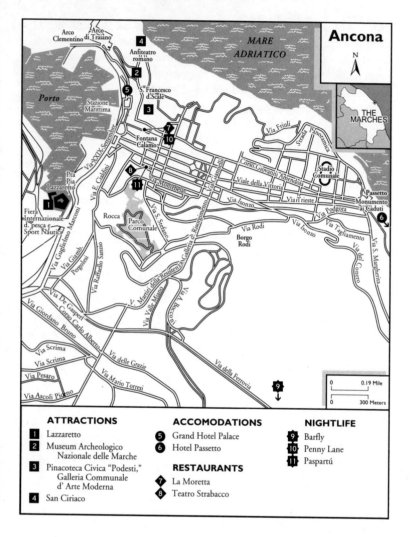

ATTRACTIONS
1. Lazzaretto
2. Museum Archeologico Nazionale delle Marche
3. Pinacoteca Civica "Podesti," Galleria Communale d' Arte Moderna
4. San Ciriaco

ACCOMODATIONS
5. Grand Hotel Palace
6. Hotel Passetto

RESTAURANTS
7. La Moretta
8. Teatro Strabacco

NIGHTLIFE
9. Barfly
10. Penny Lane
11. Paspartú

Ancona was first settled by Greeks from Siracusa who named it Ankon (elbow) because of its elbow-shaped bay. Under Trajan's rule, the walls of the harbor were fortified; consequently, the triumphal arch, which still dominates the northernmost edge of the port, was erected in memory of the emperor's achievement. Another feature of Ancona's port is Vanvitelli's pentagonal **Lazzaretto,** which once served as a quarantine for visitors from the east.

Though much of Ancona is highly industrial, the natural area around the city is nothing less than stunning. High above Trajan's Arch is Guasco Hill (Colle Guasco), a steep, rocky mount crowned by the church of **San Ciriaco.** Here on the hill is the old center of town and where you'll find the bulk of the city's museums and churches, plus a spectacular view out to sea from the steps of San Ciriaco.

Ancona lies on one end of the Rome–Ancona rail line and is a stop on the Milan–Bari line. Trains arrive and depart from the main train station in Piazza Rosselli hourly, while a few arriving trains continue on to Ancona's Stazione Marittima, which has connections to the ferries.

If you're driving, you must take the A14 motorway and exit at Ancona-Nord. You'll find a 24-hour parking garage in Piazza Stamira, in the center. Parking costs approximately €1 per every two hours, and up to €10 for the day. The Ancona Falconara airport, also known as Aeroporto Raffaello Sanzio, is just outside of the city, but it probably won't be worth your time to fly here. Only small flights from London's Stansted Airport and from Milan arrive here. However, if you do fly, you can catch a CO.TR.AN bus for about €1 one way, which will bring you to Piazza Stamira.

APT Ancona   Via Thaon de Revel, 4; 60100 Ancona; phone 071 33249; **www.comune.ancona.it**

Lazzaretto

Type of Attraction 18th-century quarantine turned exhibition space
Location Porto Sud
Admission Depends on event
Hours Depends on event
Phone Contact the APT for information, phone 071 33249
Author's Rating ★★

Description and Comments Luigi Vanvitelli designed this pentagon-shaped hospital, commonly referred to in Italian as the Mole Vanvitelliana, or "Vanvitelli Hulk," to handle the masses of visitors who carried contagious diseases from across the Adriatic Sea. During World War II, the Lazzaretto became military barracks. Today, the distinct structure is regularly put to use as a temporary exhibition hall.

Museo Archeologico Nazionale delle Marche

Type of Attraction Premier archaeological museum of the Marches
Location Via Ferretti, 1
Admission €4
Hours Tuesday–Saturday, 8:30 a.m.–1:30 p.m.
Phone 071 202 602
Overall Appeal by Age Group

Pre-school —		Teens ★★		Over 30 ★★
Grade school ★		Young Adults ★★		Seniors ★★

Authors' Rating ★★

How Much Time to Allow 30 minutes to 1 hour

Description and Comments Located inside the 16th-century Palazzo Ferretti, which features frescoes by Federico and Taddeo Zuccari, is the National Archaeological Museum of the Marches. Here you'll find the history of the Marches and its early settlers told through the fragments of Picene, Senonian-Gallic, Roman, and Etruscan civilizations. Included is Attic pottery from Picene and Gallica, gold jewelry from Greece, Bronze Age daggers, and Etruscan burial objects.

Pinacoteca Civica "Podesti" and the Galleria Comunale d'Arte Moderna

Type of Attraction Ancona's main art gallery
Location Via Pizzecolli, 17
Admission €2
Hours Tuesday–Saturday, 10 a.m.–7 p.m.; Sunday and Monday, 9 a.m.–1 p.m.
Phone 071 222 5046
Overall Appeal by Age Group

Pre-school —	Teens ★	Over 30 ★★★
Grade school ★	Young Adults ★★	Seniors ★★★

Authors' Rating ★★★
How Much Time to Allow 1 hour

Description and Comments The city's art gallery is not the best in the region, but it does have its share of masterpieces. Of particular importance is a *Madonna and Child* by Carlo Crivelli, a *Sacra Conversazione* by Lotto, and the *Apparition of the Virgin,* Titian's first signed work, painted in 1520. A few other 15th- and 16th-century masters are here, too, including Guercino, Gentileschi, and Sebastiano del Piombo. When you've had your fill of religious subjects, venture over to the contemporary wing for an introduction to 20th-century Italian art.

San Ciriaco

Type of Attraction Ancona's Duomo
Location Piazzale del Duomo
Admission Free
Hours Daily, 7 a.m.–noon, 3–6 p.m.
Phone 071 52688
Overall Appeal by Age Group

Pre-school ★	Teens ★★	Over 30 ★★★
Grade school ★★	Young Adults ★★★	Seniors ★★★

Authors' Rating ★★★
How Much Time to Allow 15–30 minutes

Description and Comments The view from San Ciriaco over the natural port of Ancona is reason enough to visit. Outside is the cathedral porch, which features columns supported by lions and a decorative portal with carvings of animals and saints. The Romanesque church sits at the summit of Colle Guasco, where once stood a fourth-century B.C. temple, then a sixth-century place of worship for early Christians. At the end of the 11th century, San Ciriaco was promoted to cathedral status when the remains of Ancona's patron saint, St. Cyriacus, were buried in the church's crypt alongside the remains of Sts. Marcellinus and Liberius. Of artistic importance here is the Chapel of the Madonna, which has an altar designed by Vanvitelli.

Entertainment and Nightlife in Ancona

The longest-running jazz festival in the Marches, **Ancona Jazz** (phone 071 207 4239; **www.anconajazz.com**), comes to the capital city each November, with an encore in the spring. When there's no festival in town, the best place to catch live music and go dancing is at **Barfly** (Via Grandi Achille, 3; phone 071 290 0623), which hosts everything from swing bands to reggae and rock acts to DJs, Wednesday through Sunday. In the summer, the best discos can be found close to Ancona's seaside resorts, especially in Numana.

Should you be waiting for a ferry, why not belly up for a few pints near the port? You can't go wrong at **Penny Lane** (Piazza del Plebiscito, 52; phone 071 207 2226), which has Guinness on tap, or at **Paspartú** (Via O. Guglielmo, 7; phone 071 200 889), which offers and assortment of single-malt whiskeys, draft beers, cocktails, and light snacks.

Riviera Conero

Approximately seven miles south of Ancona, where limestone outcroppings of the Apennines plunge into the sea, is the Cònero Riviera, one of the more stunning seaside environments on the Adriatic. Established only in 1987, the **Parco Regionale del Cònero** encompasses the 1,876-foot Mount Conero, and includes dense forests, jagged cliffs, and a protected territory that is ideal for hiking, birdwatching, and communing with nature. Like Ancona, this area traces its history back to the Greeks and Romans, who set up temples, markets, and ports on these shores; however, many of the ancient artifacts found here are located in Ancona's archeological museum.

Portonovo, on the north slope of Monte Conero is notable for its bay and beaches, which are scattered with monuments, including the 11th-century Romanesque church of **Santa Maria di Portonovo,** the 18th-century **Torre Clementina,** and a **Napoleonic Fortress** built by French general's troops in 1808; all three require requests before visiting. For more information, contact the tourist office in Ancona (Corso Stamira, 60; 60100 Ancona; phone 071 58941; **www.provincia.ancona.it**).

On the south side of the park are perhaps the best-known towns of the Conero. From the beaches of **Sirolo** and **Numana** you can gaze upon the "Due Sorelle," two rocky spurs that jut out of the sea. Several sea vessels have succumbed to the unpredictable rockiness near the Conero coastline, making these waters ideal for scuba diving. The area also provides fantastic opportunities for snorkeling, sunbathing, and windsurfing. At night, the resorts' discos are packed to the gills with sun-bronzed bodies. Come to Numana's **Taunus** (Via della Querce, 1; phone 071 933 0381) or **Aqua Disco** (Via Marina Marcelli, 33; phone 071 739 0942) dressed to impress.

Parco Regionale del Monte Cònero   Via Vivaldi 1/3; 60020 Sirolo; phone 071 933 1161, fax 071 933 0376

Pro Loco Sirolo   Piazza V. Veneto; 60020 Sirolo; phone 071 933 0611

Pro Loco Numana   Piazza del Santuario; 60026 Numana; phone 071 970 020

Loreto

Though Umbria has its Assisi and France its Lourdes, the Marches has Loreto, a major pilgrimage site for believers of the Cult of Mary. Tradition holds that on December 9, 1294, angels transported Mary's house in Nazareth to a spot in the laurel *(loreto)* woods near Ancona. The tale may or may not be true, but the legend has inspired thousands to make the journey. Nevertheless, it is hardly a coincidence that this religious event occurred at a time when Muslims had taken control of Nazareth and the pope was trying to drum up support for another crusade to the Holy Land. The second half of the 15th century saw a proper shrine erected to commemorate the miracle at Loreto, and today the dome of the **Santuario della Santa Casa** (Piazza della Madonna; phone 071 970 291; open daily, 6 a.m.–7 p.m.; admission free) is the crowning glory of these hills. Inside the church and directly below its massive dome is the shrine to the Holy House, the former home of the Virgin Mary. Legend holds that angels airlifted the home out of Palestine and resituated it on a Loreto hill, so as to put it out of harm's way from conquering Muslims in the Holy Land. Bramante designed the marble screen that confines the Holy House, and the artists Antonio da Sangallo the Younger, Andrea Sansovino, Raniero Nerucci, and Giovanni Cristoforo Romano decorated it with scenes from the *Early Life of the Virgin.* The highly ornamental carvings of sibyls and prophets and a detailed *Annunciation* by Sansovino contrast with the rather stark interior walls of the modest house. Elsewhere in the church, you'll find works by Luca Signorelli in the St. John Sacristy (behind the shrine, to the right of the altar), and a gorgeous set of 15th-century frescoes by Melozzo da Forlì in the St. Mark Sacristy (on the right side of the aisle, before the shrine). The treasury, to the right in the north transept, was decorated in the early 1600s and features a fresco cycle of the life of St. Mary. The Sanctuary of the Holy House was first conceived in 1468 and was subsequently expanded and adorned into a vast holy complex to handle—and further impress—the pilgrims who flocked here. Giuliano da Sangallo oversaw the construction of the Brunelleschi-style dome in 1500; 250 years later, Luigi Vanvitelli designed the sanctuary's belltower.

IAT Loreto   Via Solari, 3; 60025 Loreto; phone 071 977 139

Corinaldo

Approximately 12 miles west of Senigállia, Corinaldo is arguably one of the best-preserved—and least known—walled towns in the Marches (and in Central Italy). Completed in 1490 under the rule of Pope Sixtus IV, the fantastically dramatic walls are punctuated with crenellations, watchtowers, and oversized, unwelcoming gates. The **Piaggia,** or "One Hundred Steps," lead from the base of the walled town to the historic center. On the hike upward, take note of a huge well to the left. It is here that each year the Corinaldese celebrate the **Festival of the Well of Polenta** (La Contesa del Pozzo della Polenta), which recalls the tale of a thief who stole a sack of corn meal, and, fearing that he would be caught, disposed of the evidence in the town well.

Corinaldo is reachable by bus from Senigállia or by rail on the Bologna-Senigállia line, though times are irregular. Your best bet is to follow the A14 highway to Senigállia, then follow the route to Corinaldo.

Pro Loco Corinaldo   Via del Velluto, 20; 60013 Corinaldo; phone/fax 071 679 047; **www.procorinaldo.it**

Genga

For touring purposes, the small hill town of Genga is a jumping-off point for a visit to the **Frasassi Caves** (Largo Leone XII; phone 0732 97211, fax 0732 972 001; tours daily every 1.5 hours, 9:30 a.m.–6:30 p.m.; admission €10). Italy's largest complex of limestone caverns, discovered only in 1971, include the Hall of Candles, a paradise of stalactites and stalagmites, and the Grotta Grande del Vento, which could, according to local tourist board literature, "comfortably fit Milan's Duomo inside of it." Elsewhere in the caves are crystalline lakes and evidence of prehistoric settlements.

To get to Genga, take the Ancona-Nord exit from the A14 and follow the road toward Rome until the Genga/Sassoferrato exit. Signs to the Frasassi Gorge (Gola di Frasassi) are well marked.

Pro Loco Genga   Via Roma, 4; 60040 Genga; phone 0732 973 014

Jesi

Travelers who make a stop in Jesi, a workaday city of roughly 40,000 inhabitants down the *autostrada* from Ancona, will be surprised to find a center of art and culture within its 15th-century walls. Here, the **Teatro Pergolesi** (Piazza della Repubblica, 9; phone 0731 538 350, fax 0731 538 356; **www.teatropergolesi.org**), named after locally born composer Giovanni Battista Pergolesi, produces one of the finest opera seasons around and consistently plays host to some of the best lyrical talent in the world. In Jesi, discover one of the most comprehensive collections of works by Titian contemporary Lorenzo Lotto in the city's **Pinacoteca Civica** (Palazzo Pianetti, Via XV Settembre; phone 0731 538 342; open Tuesday–Sunday, 9:30 a.m.–12:30 p.m., 5–8 p.m.; from July–August: Tuesday–Saturday, 9:30 a.m.–12:30 p.m., 5 p.m.–midnight; Sunday, 9:30 a.m.–5 p.m.; admission €2.50). Lotto admirers can see his polyptych of the *Life of St. Lucy*, thought to be one of his greatest works. Four other paintings in the gallery can be attributed to him as well. A number of other Renaissance artists are featured at the Pinacoteca, including Pomarancio and Agabiti. A wide portion of the museum is now devoted to modern art, with works by Guttuso, Paolucci, and Pistoletto, among others. When the sight-seeing is over, settle down with a chilled glass of Verdicchio wine, a local white vintage.

Ufficio Turistico Jesi   Piazza della Repubblica; 60035 Jesi; phone 0731 59788

The Province of Macerata

Province of Macerata Tourist Office   Via Garibaldi, 87; 62100 Macerata; phone 0733 234 807; **www.provincia.mc.it**

Macerata

Macerata is best known for its **Sferisterio** (Piazza Nazario Sauro; phone 0733 230 735; open Monday–Saturday, 10:30 a.m.–1 p.m., 5–8 p.m.; admission depends on event), an oblong, neoclassical stadium built in the early 1800s as a venue for playing *pallone al bracciale,* the most popular local sport at the time. Over the years, the arena has remained a sporting site—it now hosts soccer matches—but, in the summer, it takes on the more refined role of opera house. Because of its impeccable acoustics, the Sferisterio is also the site of the annual **Macerata Opera Festival** (phone 0733 230 735, fax 0733 261 499; **www.macerata-opera.org**), which has been going strong since 1921. One of central Italy's best musical celebrations of the summer, it has featured such dignified performers as José Carreras. Although it is one of the newer structures in town, the Sferisterio is, without a doubt, the symbol of this central Marches town.

Macerata is just a short distance inland from Adriatic route A14. Several trains pass through here each day, stopping at Piazza della Libertà in the new town. From here, you can take buses 2 or 6 into the city.

IAT Macerata   Piazza della Libertà, 12; 62100 Macerata; phone 0733 234 807; **www.comune.macerata.it**

Cingoli

Known as the "Balcony of the Marches" because of its enviable position on Mount Cingoli, the city is located right in the middle of the southern half of the region, with views toward the Monti Sibillini in the west and Monte Conero in the east. For an equally breathtaking view, step into Cingoli's **Pinacoteca Comunale "Donatello Stefanucci"** (Via Mazzini, 10; phone 0733 602 877; open Monday–Saturday, 10:30 a.m.–12:30 p.m. or by appointment; admission €3) for a peek at a stunning altarpiece by Lorenzo Lotto. The complex *Madonna of the Rosary with Saints,* which features an enthroned Mary and Jesus below 15 *tondi* from the life of Christ, is the highlight. The works of the museum's namesake, Cingolese artist Donatello Stefanucci, who died in 1987, are also well represented here.

Pro Loco Cingoli   Via Ferri, 17; 62011 Cingoli; phone 0733 602 769

Tolentino

Perhaps no other town in the Marches, other than Loreto, is holier than Tolentino, home to Sts. Catervo and Nicola. Like St. Francis, Nicola (Nicholas) of Tolentino was well on his way to becoming a saint before his death in 1305. A pious hermit, Nicola preached in Tolentino for the last 30 years of his life. Today, his remains are enshrined in the **Basilica of San Nicola** (Piazza San Nicola; phone 0733 976 311; open daily, 9 a.m.–noon, 3–6 p.m.), a pretty church with a façade containing elements from the Gothic and Baroque periods. Similar to the basilica at Assisi, San Nicola is home to an exquisite fresco cycle. These Giottoesque-style paintings are arranged on two registers—the upper one depicts the *Scenes from the Life of Christ,* the lower one has *Scenes from the Life and Miracles of the Saint.* Elsewhere in the church are works by Reni, Lucatelli, and artists from the Rimini school. Though Nicola is highly revered, his church is not the town's cathedral. Just a few paces from San Nicola is the **Duomo** (Piazza del Duomo; no phone; open daily, 9 a.m.–noon, 3–6 p.m.), which houses the remains and the Paleo-Christian sarcophagus of San Catervo, the patron saint of the Tolentino. And, just beyond the city limits, in the valley between Tolentino and Macerata, is the **Abbey of**

Chiaravalle di Fiastra (Località Urbisaglia; phone 0733 202 190; open Monday, 3:30–6:30 p.m.; Tuesday–Sunday, 9:30 a.m.–12:30 p.m., 3:30–6:30 p.m.; donation requested), a lovely 12th-century Cistercian monastery set among acres of woodland. Its best to visit this serene place of worship during the spring or fall, when the changing of seasons illuminate the natural beauty of the surroundings.

IAT Tolentino   Piazza della Libertà; 62029 Tolentino; 0733 972 937

The Province of Áscoli-Piceno

Province of Áscoli-Piceno Tourist Office   Piazza del Popolo; 63100 Áscoli Piceno; phone 0736 244 975; **www.provincia.ap.it**

Áscoli-Piceno

The ancient Piceni tribe dwelled here at the confluence of the Tronto and Castellano Rivers and, by the first half of the third century B.C., the Romans, recognizing the strategic importance of this area, took over. Asculum Picenum became a main stop on the Via Salaria, the famous "Salt Road" that radiated from Rome. Today, traces of the Roman city remain, including bleachers from a first-century amphitheater (located off of Via Ricci); the **Porta Gemina,** the gateway to Áscoli from the Salt Road; and a Roman-style grid of streets and long avenues. Most of the original Republican structures, however, were covered over during a flurry of construction in the 11th through 14th centuries. One example is the city's **Piazza Arringo,** a site of haranguing *(arringo)* speeches during medieval times, which was once the site of a Roman forum.

The city's slender bell towers, of which there were at least 200 at one time, were built by competing nobility during the Middle Ages, and they must have made the city look like a metropolis back in those days. Besides having one of the most inviting medieval cityscapes in Central Italy, Áscoli-Piceno is also the site of the annual **Giostro della Quintana** tournament, which pits riders from each of the city's six districts in an authentic medieval jousting contest. The festival, which takes place the first Sunday in August and includes plenty of local food and drink, garners only a handful of tourists, perhaps making it the answer to the overcrowded Palio in Siena.

Áscoli-Piceno is a bit out of the way, but it's most easily reached by car on the old Via Salaria (now the S4). The rail station in Viale Marconi sees only a few trains per day, and buses to and from other towns in the region are infrequent.

APT Áscoli-Piceno   Piazza Arringo, 7; phone 736 298 204, fax 736 298 232; **www.comune.ascoli-piceno.it**

Galleria d'Arte Contemporanea

Type of Attraction Modern art gallery
Location Corso Mazzini, 224
Admission €3
Hours June 15–September: Sunday and Tuesday–Friday, 9 a.m.–1 p.m., 4–7 p.m.; Saturday, 9 a.m.–1 p.m.; closed Monday and in winter
Phone 0736 250 760
Overall Appeal by Age Group

Pre-school ★		Teens ★★		Over 30 ★★★
Grade school ★		Young Adults ★★★		Seniors ★

Authors' Rating ★★
How Much Time to Allow 30 minutes to 1 hour

Description and Comments This museum is considered to be one of the finest modern art museums in the regions, with etchings and paintings from 20th-century Italian artists like Giorgio Bompadre, Carmelo Cappello, Gino Severini, and Enrico Ricci.

Pinacoteca Comunale

Type of Attraction Municipal art gallery with 15th- and 16th-century works
Location Piazza dell'Arringo
Admission €3.50
Hours June–September: Tuesday–Sunday, 9 a.m.–1 p.m., 4–7:30 p.m.: October–May, Tuesday–Sunday, 9 a.m.–1 p.m.
Phone 0736 298 213
Overall Appeal by Age Group

Pre-school —		Teens ★		Over 30 ★★
Grade school ★		Young Adults ★★		Seniors ★★★

Authors' Rating ★★½
How Much Time to Allow 30 minutes to 1 hour

Description and Comments The holdings in Áscoli's city gallery come from various monasteries and churches in the region. Featured are paintings by Carlo Crivelli, Guido Reni, and Titian; sketches from Guercino and Cortona; and various ceramic pieces and ornamental furniture. Most dear to the Áscolani is a cope (embroidered tapestry) given to the city by Pope Nicholas IV, a native, in 1288.

Parco Nazionale dei Monti Sibillini

Spanning the provinces of Macerata and Áscoli Piceno and reaching into eastern Umbria is the **Sibillini Mountain Range,** a massive extension of the Apennines, with some peaks reaching elevations as high as 6,400 feet. Early on, these rugged bluffs were the stuff of myth, and travelers on the

Grand Tour in the 17th and 18th centuries would come here to investigate Mount Sibilla and its cave, a former place of worship for a pagan cult. **Lake Pilato** is a place of intense interest for geologists, as it is the only Apennine lake of glacial origins. More than 1,800 types of flowers and dozens of different animal species are indigenous to these mountains, prompting the Italian Parks Authority to finally declare this area a nature preserve in 1993.

There are many villages clustered around the Sibillini Mountains that are ideal for a stopover. Nestled beneath the clouds at more than 3,200 feet is tiny **Montemonaco,** one of the highest spots in the area where you can get a spectacular view of Mount Sibilla. The largest town, **Amàndola,** is dotted with small churches and a couple of museums to appease the summer tourists. **Arquata del Tronto,** defined by its 13th-century **Rocca** (Piazza della Rocca; phone 0736 809 122; open summer: daily, 10:30 a.m.–12:30 p.m., 4–6 p.m.; winter: daily, 3–5 p.m.; admission €2), was once an outpost on the Via Salaria consular road. Serious hikers may want to consider **Acquasanta Terme,** a town near the convergence of two mountain parks—Monti Sibillini and Gran Sasso—which has been renowned since Roman times for its therapeutic hot springs and mud pools.

Pro Loco Acquasanta Terme   Piazza XX Settembre, 12; 63041 Acquasanta Terme; phone/fax 0736 801 291

Casa del Parco Arquata del Tronto   Via del Mattatoio, 2; 63043 Arquata del Tronto; phone/fax 0736 809 600

Pro Loco Amàndola   Piazza Risorgimento; 63021 Amàndola; phone 0736 847 439

Pro Loco Montemonaco   Piazza Risorgimento, 8; 63048 Montemonaco; phone 0736 856 141

Riviera delle Palme

Further down the Adriatic coastal highway lies the **Riviera delle Palme,** so dubbed because of the hundreds of palm trees that dot the landscape and line the promenades of its two most famous resorts—**Grottammare** and, more importantly, **San Benedetto del Tronto.** Both are favored—and heavily frequented—by German and English tourists, so you're sure to find adequate lodging and dining facilities here. But, besides San Benedetto's **Museo delle Anfore** (Viale de Gasperi; phone 0735 86855; open Monday–Saturday, 9 a.m.–noon, 3:30–6:30 p.m.), which contains a handful of relics, including vases and amphorae, from Greek, Roman, and Picene civilizations, this coastal area is not rife with tourist attractions, leaving you to laze in the sun, dine on fresh seafood, and splash around in the sea without feelings of guilt.

Note that the tourist offices of these resort towns, listed below, are open only from April through September.

IAT San Benedetto del Tronto   Via delle Tamerici, 5; 63039 San Benedetto del Tronto; phone 0735 582 542

IAT Grottammare   Piazza Pericle Fazzini; 63013 Grottammare; phone 0735 631 087

Accommodations Index

Restaurant Index

Page numbers in **bold** type indicate restaurant profiles.

Subject Index

Abbey of Chiaravalle di Fiastra, Tolentino, 469–70
Abbey of Farfa, 390–91
Accademia (The Academy), Florence, 192–94, 207–8
Accademia Nazionale di Santa Cecilia (music venue), Rome, 378
Acqualagna, 451
Acquasanta Terme, Parco Nazionale dei Monti Sibillini, 472
Admission. *See* Tickets
Aeroport Amerigo Vespucci (Peretola), Florence, 43, 73
Aeroport Galileo Galilei (Pisa International Airport), 42–43, 73
Agosto Corcianese, 425
Agriturismo (farm holiday), 70–71
Air conditioning, in lodging, 75
Air travel. *See also* Airports
   departing, 44–46
   flight confirmation, 45
   information for, 27–33
      airlines, 29–30, 45
      government tourist office, 31–32
      newspaper, 28
      tour operators, 30–31
      travel agent, 27–28
      web, 28–29
   jet lag in, 39
   security in, 34–35
Airports
   Ancona Falconara, 73
   bus service at, 42–44
   car rental at, 42, 44, 46
   Ciampino, Rome, 42
   contact information for, 45
   departing from, 44–46

Leonardo da Vinci (Fiumicino), Rome, 40–41, 73
   lodging at, 73
   money changing at, 44
   phone numbers of, 45
   Pisa International Airport (Aeroport Galileo), 42–43, 73
   taxis at, 41–44
   train service at, 40–41, 43
   transportation from, 40–44
   Umbria International (San Egidio), 43–44
Albano Laziale, 387
Alpi Apuane, 272
Amàndola, 472
American Express, services of, 56
Amphitheaters
   Colosseum (Il Colosseo), 294–95, 327–28
   Roman, Arezzo, 261, 262
   Roman Theater, Spoleto, 434
   Sferisterio, Macerata, 468–69
Ancient City, Rome, 291, 294–95
Ancona, 461–65
   history of, 461–62
   lodging in, 128, 131–32
      airport, 73
   map of, 462
   places of worship in, 64
   restaurants in, 180, 183–84
   transportation in, 463
Ancona Falconara, 73
Anfiteatro Romano e Museo Archeologico, Arezzo, 261, 262
Ansedonia, 284
A.N.T.H.A.I., for disabled visitors, 73
Antico Albergo Terme, Lucca, 272–73
Antiques, shopping for, 383